AMERICAN DEMOCRACY DEBATED
An Introduction
to American
Government

CRITICAL READERS

Irving Berg
Western Illinois University

Larry Berkson
American Judicature Society

Robert Friedman
The Pennsylvania State University

Harlan Hahn
University of Southern California

Sam Hawkins
San Jacinto College

Ivan Martinez
Eastfield College, Dallas Community College District

Robert O'Connor
The Pennsylvania State University

Leroy Rieselbach
Indiana University

Richard Scher
University of Florida

C. Frederick Stoerker
City University of New York, Kingsborough Community College

Roy Young
San Jose State University

AMERICAN DEMOCRACY DEBATED
An Introduction to American Government

Charles W. Dunn
Clemson University

GENERAL LEARNING PRESS
SCOTT, FORESMAN AND COMPANY

For my mother, Teresa Dunn, and in memory of my father, Charles G. Dunn (1855–1959)

Manufactured in the United States of America

Published simultaneously in Canada

Library of Congress Catalog Card Number 77–92125

ISBN 0–382–18274–X

For information write to GENERAL LEARNING PRESS, 250 James St., Morristown, N.J. 07960.

Preface

He who decides a case without hearing the other side ... though he decide justly, cannot be considered just.–Seneca

Communication is a two-way dialogue. It demands a willingness to listen as well as to teach, and to appreciate the sensitivities and convictions of others as well as our own. ... Only by dialogue can issues be exposed and goals defined—free of passion and intolerance which hinder rational and constructive decisions.–Plato

"Everybody loves an argument," according to one saying. Another holds that "if you want to draw a crowd, start an argument." There are exceptions, of course, but it is generally true that an argument arouses strong mental and emotional reactions. Arguments stimulate and provoke the human psyche.

One day when I was walking to class, prepared to teach using the traditional lecture-discussion method, I thought, "Why not have a debate today?" When I got to class, I wrote a debate topic on the board, divided the class into two groups, and gave them fifteen minutes to prepare. Then I called on one student from each side to present the group's arguments. The response was immediately and overwhelmingly favorable. My students wanted more debate and more time to prepare for them outside of class.

Since then, relying on my collegiate debate experience, I have refined the debate method without diluting the content of an introductory course in American government. This text is the result.

FORMAT OF THE BOOK

What is a debate? It is a formal argument wherein opposite sides of an issue are presented. Therefore the most important stylistic feature of *American Democracy Debated* is its organization into debate topics—each a separate chapter—and the subdivision of each of these topics into affirmative and negative cases. Every element of the book is designed to enhance this unique approach.

American Democracy Debated is divided into three parts, each containing four chapters. (There is, in addition, an epilogue on the general subject of policy making.) Chapters are organized as follows:

The *chapter title* is a debate topic. Each one is a provocative but realistic proposition that also allows for the presentation of information on the basic structure, concepts, and theoretical models of American government.

A *chapter outline* appears at the beginning of each chapter. This is a sort of road map for readers, orienting them in the direction they will be traveling so that they can better understand the relationships among points along the route.

A *chapter introduction* exposes students to the scope of the debate topic and provides important background information, often of a historical nature.

Analytical questions at the end of the introduction help readers focus on what to look for in analyzing the debate.

The *affirmative case* opens with a brief introductory discussion, lists the major points to be covered, and then argues each one in detail. The *negative case* follows, with its major points paralleling those in the affirmative case.

Margin quotations either support or refute arguments or amplify background information. They come from such diverse sources as Presidents, well-known political figures, and writers from different periods of American history.

The chapter ends with a *glossary* summarizing every term defined in the chapter. It is followed by *notes* and a *bibliography*, Recommended Rebuttal Reading, directing readers to additional books that will help them develop arguments in greater depth.

COMBINING TRADITION AND INNOVATION

Every introductory course in American government must deal with a certain body of knowledge: our Constitution, the branches of government, the operation of political parties and interest groups, and so on. The advantage of the debate technique is that it allows for the presentation of this traditional information through an innovative method that sparks student interest and increases teaching options for the instructor. How does it work? Let us take a look.

Chapter 11, on Congress, begins with a comprehensive introduction on the history, functions, and organization of this branch of the federal government. Charts show how the legislative process works and summarize congressional committees. In addition, however, students benefit from a focus on which to concentrate—Is Congress archaic?—and four issues around which debate is organized: (1) Congress as a representative body; (2) the nature of the complex legislative process; (3) the role of politics; and (4) abuses and reforms.

The issues debated make use of information contained in the introduction, and add new data as well. For example, the affirmative case notes that the chart showing the bill-to-law process is essentially simplified; in practice, roadblocks and detours—among them pigeonholing and the filibuster—make the legislative procedure unnecessarily clumsy and time-consuming.

The gain is obvious: All the "nuts and bolts" are present. But they are not simply arranged in neat display compartments. They are used to build something—an argument, a case, a point for or against. Thus they are easier to study and more rewarding to assimilate.

DEBATE AS A FORCE IN AMERICAN POLITICS

Examples of debate as a force in American politics are legion. President Ford summed it up when he wrote: "Throughout our nation's life, debate has been a basic ingredient in our decision-making process. We have always felt that the best and wisest decisions are made when ideas are tested and challenged by constructive argument." *

The adversary process prevails in American courtrooms, with one side prosecuting and the other defending. The premise is that truth will emerge from the crucible of conflict. Under John Marshall, the great Chief Justice of the United States, cases were often debated before the Court for several days to allow a full airing of opposing views.

Out of debates over political issues have emerged new ideas and new leaders. The famous Lincoln-Douglas debates of 1858 spotlighted Abraham Lincoln on the stage of national prominence as an opponent of slavery. To many observers, the Nixon-Kennedy television debates of 1960 were the turning point in Kennedy's successful drive for the White House.

The United States Senate, considered the domain of great debate

* Letter of August 6, 1975, as published in Bicentennial Youth Debates, *Participant and Administrative Guide* (Washington, D.C.: Bicentennial Youth Debates, 1975), p. 1.

for much of American history, in 1957 designated five senators as "Senate Immortals." All had significantly shaped American politics by their skill in setting forth new ideas in debate. John F. Kennedy, then a freshman senator, said of three of those five—Henry Clay, Daniel Webster, and John C. Calhoun: "For over thirty years they dominated the Congress and the country, providing leadership and articulation on all the great issues of the growing nation." * The other two senators were powerful figures in the twentieth century—progressive Robert La Follette and conservative Robert A. Taft.

American government and politics cannot be adequately understood without examining debates over such great issues as ratification of the Constitution itself, the creation of a national bank, the right of a state to secede from the Union, reconstruction of the South after the Civil War, regulation of business, the New Deal, civil rights, Vietnam, and Watergate.

Without doubt, the field of American politics is illuminated by a knowledge of the great debaters and their debates. With this tradition in mind, *American Democracy Debated* seeks to reexamine the fundamentals of American government itself.

Acknowledgments No textbook can be developed without the cooperation of a number of dedicated people. For their efforts and help, I would like to thank the following people from General Learning Press: Judy Green and Walter Kossmann for their conviction that a new and innovative text was needed, Paula Franklin for her incisive and intelligent editing, Jane Schrader for research on margin quotations, and Edith Vann for her patience with the labyrinth of copy editing. I would also like to thank the reviewers who are listed opposite the title page. Their criticisms and suggestions were invaluable to us in the preparation of the final manuscript. They are not, however, responsible for any errors of fact or interpretation that may remain. Once again, Martha Morris demonstrated the highest standards of typing excellence in preparing the manuscript. My colleagues in the Department of Political Science at Clemson University provided numerous suggestions. And my wife, Carol, patiently and thoughtfully encouraged me. Without all of these people, this book would not be.

Charles W. Dunn

* John F. Kennedy, Speech in the Senate, May 1, 1957, from a press release.

Contents

Monday July 10, 1978

PART TWO   WHAT ARE AMERICAN POLITICS REALLY LIKE?

Tuesday, July 11

3a

Monday, July 17

Tuesday July 18

48

ONE

IS
THE
UNITED STATES
REALLY
A
DEMOCRACY?

AT ISSUE: DEMOCRACY

1

RESOLVED THAT:
The United States Is Undemocratic

At Issue: Democracy

Is the United States really a democracy? If so, how much of a democracy? Did the Founders intend us to have a democracy? Has the American idea of democracy changed since the founding of our country? If so, for better or worse?

Democracy, a popular word, is used even by dictators to describe their nations and governments. For example, several communist countries—East Germany, North Korea, and Vietnam—refer to themselves as democracies: the German Democratic Republic, the Democratic People's Republic of Korea, and the Democratic Republic of Vietnam. Are these countries as well as the United States democracies?

The word *democracy* comes from two Greek words—*demos*, meaning "people," and *kratos*, meaning "rule." Thus the term indicates that governmental authority in a democracy resides in the people; it is a form of government in which power is exercised by the people. There are two major types of democracy. In a *pure*, or *direct*, *democracy*, all citizens participate equally in decision making; this occurs in a New England town meeting. In an *indirect*, or *representative*, *democracy*, which is sometimes called a *republic*, people elect representatives to make their decisions; this is the form considered by many to be the American system. Common to both types is *majority rule* wherein the people make their decisions based on the wishes of the majority or plurality.

If democracy means anything, it means that sooner or later the majority gets its way.—*Morris K. Udall*

I believe that there is no defect of democracy which more democracy can't cure.—*Henry S. Reuss*

Democracy is like a raft: It won't sink, but you will always have your feet wet.—*Russel B. Long*

1

The first principle of American democracy is that, given the basic freedoms, majority rule is right even when it's wrong (as often happens), because it encourages free men to struggle as adversaries, using established legal means, to keep government working at the business of justice for all. The theory was and is that if the majority causes the minority too much pain, the minority will scream (with the help of a free press and the right of assembly) until the majority is badgered or shamed into changing its mind.—*John Gardner*

Also generally considered of absolute importance to democracy are *minority rights*. For example, even though a minority loses to the majority in the selection of representatives, the minority still retains the right to exist, to express its point of view, and to challenge the majority when the people next decide who their leaders will be. In general, the principle of majority rule necessitates that (1) public officials should be chosen by majority vote; and that (2) every citizen should have the right to influence government policy. With respect to the principle of minority rights, the minority should be free to criticize majority decisions, and people in the minority should be free to try to win majority support for their opinions.

Representative democracy depends on two primary ingredients, democratic procedures and democratic principles. Democratic procedures provide for competitive elections between and among candidates, through which people choose their leaders. There is freedom of speech and the press so that voters can make knowledgeable decisions. Democratic principles form the substance behind the procedures. Although Adolf Hitler was elected to office in Germany, one could hardly look upon his government as democratic since basic human freedoms and rights were grossly abused. In a democracy, democratic procedures should reflect democratic principles. The procedure of an election should allow the majority or plurality to elect their representatives while protecting the rights of the minority. Hitler was elected but did not respect the rights of Jews.

Whether a nation is a democracy may be measured against certain abstract ideas, such as liberty and equality. The Declaration of Independence embodies American ideals about liberty, stating that "all men are created equal, that they are endowed by their Creator with certain unalienable Rights, that among these are Life, Liberty and the pursuit of Happiness." In other words, the individual is more important than the state. He or she has rights on which government procedures should not trample. As noted by Carl Becker, democracy's fundamental "assumption is the worth and dignity of the individual." [1] Procedures should be the means of achieving democratic principles.

For the purpose of the following debate, a nation may be considered a democracy only if there are both democratic procedures and democratic principles. Basic procedures such as competitive elections and voting and freedom of speech and press must exist as well as fundamental principles such as majority rule and minority rights. The meaning of these and other democratic procedures and principles will be developed more fully in the debate.

Americans are deeply divided in their perceptions of American democracy. Some contend that democracy was never intended by the

Founders; others think that despite the Founders' intentions, the United States has become a democracy; still others believe that the United States has always been a democracy. This issue continues to be heatedly debated.

- Do you think the United States is a democratic nation? Why or why not?
- List five procedures or principles that you associate with democracy (such as freedom of speech and voting). Do you think they exist in the American system of government?
- Are vast differences in wealth acceptable in a democracy?

The Affirmative Case

Yes, the United States is undemocratic.

Finally and most importantly the United States . . . experienced two presidencies in succession whose arbitrary, illegal, and unconstitutional rule tended to reduce democratic choice to exercises in futility.[2]–Hans J. Morgenthau

One of the first things many school children learn about government is that the United States is a democracy. We are taught, in Lincoln's words, that ours is a "government of the people, by the people, and for the people." Is this true? Actually, a very strong case can be made that our country is *not* a democracy for the following reasons:

- The Founders never intended a democracy for the United States;
- Democratic procedures have frequently been disregarded in the United States; and
- Democratic principles, particularly liberty and equality, have been grossly violated many times in American history.

THE FOUNDERS' VIEWS

Far from believing in the principle of government by the people, many of those who wrote our Constitution disliked the principle of majority rule. Some of them, notably Alexander Hamilton, even equated democracy with mobocracy—rule by the mob. As a result, the Constitution of the United States was designed to restrain the majority of the people or even to prevent them from acting. Ironically, the Founders believed in

The fundamental article of my political creed is that despotism, or unlimited sovereignty, or absolute power is the same in a majority of a popular assembly, an aristocratical council, an oligarchical junto, and a single emperor. Equally arbitrary, cruel, bloody, and in every respect diabolical.—*John Adams*

the ultimate authority of the people, but they feared an unrestrained majority. The idea of a pure democracy was hardly represented at the Convention.

At best, then, the Founders had in mind a republic, or a representative democracy, with a complicated set of restraints on the majority. Among these restraints are (1) the division of governmental power between the national and state governments, and (2) the separation of power among the three branches of the national government—legislative, executive, and judicial. The people, of course, only had direct influence in the selection of members of the House of Representatives. Members of the Senate were chosen by state legislatures; the president, by the electoral college; and judges, by presidential nomination and senatorial confirmation. Could a government be called democratic when the people had direct influence on only one of the four major units of the national government?

What these restraints on popular participation in government indicate is the Founders' basic distrust of popular majorities, a conclusion for which there is substantial support as indicated by James Madison in No. 10 of *The Federalist:** "Complaints are everywhere heard from our most considerate and virtuous citizens . . . that our governments are too unstable, that the public good is disregarded in the conflicts of rival parties, and *that measures are too often decided,* not according to the rules of justice and the rights of the minor party, but *by the superior force of an interested and overbearing majority* (emphasis supplied)." [3]

The Founders reflected a belief in the Judeo-Christian assessment of human nature that people are capable of both good and evil. They viewed restraints and restrictions as necessary to prevent the abuse of governmental power by a majority that might trample on the rights of others.

The real irony of American democracy is that democracy was never intended. One might argue that we have *become* a democracy, but one cannot say that the purpose of our government was to be democratic in the sense of *demos* and *kratos*—rule by a majority of the people. The American government was established as a republic that restrained the ability of the majority to govern.

DISREGARD FOR DEMOCRATIC PROCEDURES

How could a nation be called democratic when large numbers of its people could not exercise the most basic democratic right, the right to

*The Federalist is a collection of eighty-five essays written by Alexander Hamilton, James Madison, and John Jay in support of the Constitution; they were influential in securing adoption of the document and in shaping later interpretations of it.

vote? Consider these groups, which at various times in American history were not allowed to vote: (1) nonproperty owners; (2) women; (3) blacks; and (4) other minority groups, such as Puerto Ricans. Even today, as evidenced by the 1975 debate on extending the Voting Rights Act of 1965, substantial numbers of Americans, especially Mexican Americans, are not allowed to register and vote (see Chapter 8 for a full discussion of voting).

How could a nation be called democratic when urban and suburban residents, far outnumbering rural residents, did not have a fair and proportionate share of representation in the U.S. House of Representatives or in state legislatures until the late 1960s? As a result of malapportioned legislatures, these bodies were dominated by rural representatives who denied urban and suburban populations their rightful majority of representatives. In Florida, for example, fewer than 30 percent of the people elected a majority of members to the state house of representatives, and fewer than 15 percent elected a majority of the state senate. In Texas, Sam Rayburn, long the Speaker of the U.S. House of Representatives, represented a district of some 200,000 people; his counterpart from Dallas represented a million.

How could a nation be called democratic when minority groups, such as blacks, have been denied the right to serve on juries during most of American history? Americans have been proud of their system of justice, which guarantees people the right to be tried by their peers. That is, ordinary citizens are to participate in the rendering of justice. Blacks, however, have until very recent years been denied this right throughout large parts of the nation, particularly in the South. A black accused of murder stood, not before a jury representing a cross section of the community, but before an all-white jury.

How could a nation be called democratic when its citizens do not have the right to elect their highest governmental official, the president? The American chief executive is elected, not by majority vote, but rather by the awkward and cumbersome electoral college. In this system voters in each state select delegates, who then vote for the president. On three occasions, this procedure has given us a president who actually came in second in the national popular vote.*

*In 1824 Democratic-Republican Andrew Jackson received more popular votes than Democratic-Republican John Quincy Adams. Since no candidate received an electoral-vote majority, the election was decided in the House of Representatives in favor of Adams. In 1876 Democrat Samuel Tilden received more popular votes than Republican Rutherford B. Hayes. Returns from several states were disputed, however, and the election was finally decided in Hayes' favor by a special electoral commission set up by Congress. Then in 1888, Democrat Grover Cleveland received 48.6 percent of the popular vote to 47.8 percent for Benjamin Harrison, but Harrison received a majority of electoral college votes.

How could a nation be called democratic when seniority, rather than democratic principles, has until recently determined who should head congressional committees? Throughout much of American history, an overwhelming proportion of congressional committee chairmen have been substantially older than the average member of Congress. Moreover, a disproportionate number came from the South, where the lack of a genuine two-party system insured the continual return of older members of the Democratic party. The result was to freeze out younger and more vigorous leadership and to stamp congressional leadership with a decidedly southern flavor (see Chapter 11 for a detailed discussion of Congress).

These—together with constitutional restraints previously discussed—are merely some examples of undemocratic procedures in what is commonly called a democratic nation. But we must look further at who actually governs America. Do these procedures cause the masses to be misrepresented? Who are our rulers? Do they really represent the whole of the American population? The fact is that the masses have little, if any, influence in making decisions. Two political scientists summed it up this way: "Government is always government by the few, whether in the name of the few, the one, or the many." [4]

Table 1. Social Characteristics of the General Public and Governmental Elites

	GENERAL PUBLIC	GOVERNMENTAL ELITES*
Average Age	28.7	58
Female Percentage	51.0	1.4
Schools		
Public	90.0	90.9
Private	10.0	9.1
Colleges		
Public	66.0	43.9
Private	34.0	56.0
Education		
College Educated	11.0	100.0

*President and vice-president; secretaries, undersecretaries, and assistant secretaries of all executive departments; White House presidential advisors; congressional leaders, committee chairmen, and ranking minority members; Supreme Court justices; Federal Reserve Board; Council of Economic Advisors; all four-star generals and admirals. N = 286.

Source: Data adapted from Thomas R. Dye and Harmon L. Ziegler, *The Irony of Democracy* (North Scituate, Mass.: Duxbury Press, a division of Wadsworth Publishing Co., 1975), p. 130; and the U.S. Bureau of the Census, *1976 Statistical Abstract*.

At best, American democracy can only be called a system of democratic *elitism*. The elites—the few who govern—are not like those who are governed. If the United States has a representative democracy, the representatives do not reflect the essential characteristics of the represented.

First, the representatives—the elites—have substantially greater resources. These include status, leadership skills, information, power, education, wealth, understanding of government and politics, and the skills of communication and organization.

Second, the representatives are much more likely to come from socially prominent and economically affluent groups than from the rank and file of society. Studies of the leaders in American government show that they are not typical of the American public in educational background, socioeconomic status, or other characteristics.[5] (See Table 1.)

Commenting on the key ingredients of "democratic elitism," the Italian political scientist Gaetano Mosca says: "In all societies . . . two classes of people appear—a class that rules and a class that is ruled. The first class, always the less numerous, performs all of the political functions, monopolizes power, and enjoys the advantages that power brings, whereas the second, the more numerous class, is directed and controlled by the first. . . ."[6]

Nor should we forget another powerful force: the bureaucracy and the technological-managerial elite who make decisions behind the scenes without adequate public influence. They operate procedurally in a way that raises serious questions about democracy. Dwight Eisenhower himself raised this issue when he left the presidency, noting that, although we should hold "scientific research and discovery in respect, . . . we must also be alert to the equal and opposite danger that public policy could itself become the captive of a scientific-technological elite." Eisenhower noted that the public can be denied the right (and history shows that it has been) to influence key public policy decisions made by elite groups. For instance, one of the critical problems with federal regulatory agencies, such as the Federal Trade Commission, is that those being regulated—such as big business and big labor—control the agency. (More will be said about this issue in Chapter 6.)

A major reason for Ralph Nader's existence as a government critic relates to elite control of public policy, especially in regulatory agencies. Louis M. Kohlmeier, a Pulitzer Prize winning reporter for the *Chicago Tribune*, points out that two Democratic presidents, John Kennedy and Lyndon Johnson, and two Republican presidents, Richard Nixon and Gerald Ford, have attempted to reduce the regulatory power of such agencies as the Interstate Commerce Commission. Both business and union interest groups, however, have combined to thwart these efforts,

The Teamsters Union, representing trucking employees, has written Ford that the union is "unalterably opposed" to deregulation. The Association of American Railroads says it is for "meaningful reform and is not for deregulating anything." The Air Transport Association of America is warning that the airlines "must not be placed in jeopardy" through deregulation.—*Louis M. Kohlmeier*

because they recognize that the regulations are in the interests of the regulated. Kohlmeier notes that "the impressive political power and the equally impressive political campaign contributions of regulated industries and their unions dissuaded Kennedy, Johnson, and Nixon from pursuit of deregulation." [7] Once President Gerald Ford attacked the Interstate Commerce Commission, Kohlmeier shows that the ICC in a 26-page white paper vigorously defended its regulatory policies. So did the American Trucking Association in its own white paper, which declared that "under regulation, America's surface transportation system has developed into the finest in the world." [8]

One of the principal objectives of regulation is reduced prices for the general public. However, many regulatory agencies and the regulated industries work so closely together that often an agency's first concern is the well-being of the industry rather than that of the public it was created to serve.

To call the United States a democracy in the sense of its having democratic procedures stretches the historic definition of democracy. First, undemocratic procedures have abounded. Second, our representatives differ in character and background from those represented. Third, key governmental decisions are often made by nonelected bureaucrats and technologists, influenced more by big business and big labor interests than by the public.

VIOLATION OF DEMOCRATIC PRINCIPLES

The philosopher Sidney Hook has said that democracy is simply a system of rules for playing the game, which allow some measure of mass participation and government accountability, and that the Constitution is a rule book for the game of democracy.[9] This definition of democracy is based on procedures; what of principles? Here we come up against a key fault in understanding American democracy: To say that a nation is democratic because it holds elections begs the question. The Soviet Union has elections, but is it a democracy? Democracy without certain principles is hollow. There are, therefore, what we might call "procedure democrats" and "principle democrats." So-called American democracy must be evaluated from both standpoints.

Concerning the principles of democracy, especially those of liberty and equality, we must ask searching questions. Can the United States be called a democracy when:

To this day I do not understand why I was made the subject of the wiretapping, the bugging, or the surveillance, or whether the purpose was really to entrap me or perhaps someone inside the government who might be speaking to me.

I am only sure that a monster has been allowed to grow up, and unless it is subject to regular control by impartial persons I think all of us will be the victims. . . .

We came a hell of a lot closer to a police state than I thought possible.—*Joseph Kraft*

- The intelligence agencies, such as the Central Intelligence Agency and the Federal Bureau of Investigation, abuse their power and illegally spy on Americans;

In a democracy, official amorality and lawbreaking take place in secret. The intelligence abuses have been able to flourish because of a pervasive system of official secrecy that has permitted the lawbreakers to conceal their illegal acts by stamping them "Top Secret." The government's classification system, which has existed for civilian agencies only since 1951, has thus provided a vital cocoon of secrecy to mask the illegalities from the public, the press, and the Congress. What has surfaced has been disclosed in spite of this system, partly through the accident of Watergate. How much is still going on today we do not know.—*David Wise*

"Why, you rat! You've been illegally opening the phony letters that I've been illegally writing."

- There are 25 million poor in a society that spends some $100 billion yearly on the military; and
- The court system prosecutes and penalizes poor and minority offenders more severely than it does the rich?

Each of these examples illustrates either an abuse of liberty or of equality. Citizens who are illegally spied on lose a basic human right to be free from an invasion of privacy, and the latter two examples show glaring inequalities between the rich and the poor. For a nation to be a democracy, there should be widespread respect for the liberty of all citizens and adequate provision for their equality.

The *Washington Post* and the Harvard University Center for International Affairs conducted a nationwide survey of elites in the United States. Leaders from nine areas of American life (business, farm, intellectuals, news media, Republican officials, Democratic officials, blacks, feminists, and youth) were asked to place ten goals in order of importance. Among these goals were "protecting freedom of speech," "curbing inflation," "fighting crime," "reducing unemployment," and "achieving equality for blacks." The study concludes that "of the ten goals presented, achieving equality for blacks was judged eighth in importance by business leaders, seventh by media leaders, ninth by Republican party workers, fifth by Democratic party workers, and fourth by feminists." Promoters of equality for blacks were most disappointed to find that those groups that have long been active supporters of the civil rights movement, intellectuals and youth in particular, now list other goals as having priority. The youth, as a group, ranked "developing energy sources" as most important and "equality for blacks" seventh. The intellectuals listed "equality for blacks" eighth with only "equality for women" and "reducing the role of government" ranking lower in importance.[10]

Table 2. Democratic and Non-Democratic Attitudes Among Leaders and the General Public (Percent Having Attitude)

	LEADERS	GENERAL PUBLIC	
		HIGH EDUCATION	LOW EDUCATION
	*(N = 3,020)	(N = 787)	(N = 697)
Democratic commitment	49%	36%	13%
Faith in democracy	40	24	13
Faith in direct action	26	32	53
Faith in freedom	63	53	43
Totalitarianism	10	22	47
Authoritarianism	15	21	48

*N refers to the number surveyed.

Source: Adapted from Herbert McClosky, "Personality and Attitude Correlates of Foreign Policy Orientation," in James N. Rosenau, ed., *Domestic Sources of Foreign Policy* (New York: The Free Press, 1967), pp. 87–89. Reprinted with permission of Macmillan Publishing Co., Inc. Copyright © 1967 by The Free Press, A Division of The Macmillan Company.

The *Washington Post*-Harvard study shows poignantly that America's leadership lacks a firm commitment to provide equality for that group which has suffered the greatest amount of discrimination.

Indeed, was there ever a time when the United States could have been called a democracy, considering the slavery of black people, the denial to labor of the right to organize, the incarceration of the entire Japanese-American population during World War II, and the slaughter of American Indians and plunder of their land?

Not only have basic democratic principles been violated, but they seem also to lack the support of the general public. As Table 2, based upon Herbert McClosky's study of democratic attitudes, shows, the public at large has only a very weak commitment to democratic principles and values. Note that less than a majority express faith in democracy, regardless of leadership status or level of education. No wonder that in another survey of democratic attitudes in Tallahassee, Florida, and Ann Arbor, Michigan, James W. Prothro and Charles M. Grigg conclude:

> The discovery that consensus on democratic principles is restricted to a few general and vague formulations might come as a surprise to a person whose only acquaintance with democracy was through the literature of political theory; it will hardly surprise those who have lived in a democracy. Every village cynic knows that the local church-goer who sings the creed with greatest fervor often abandons the same ideas when they are put in less lyrical form.[11]

Repression It is bad enough that American adherence to democratic principles is weak. A worse charge is that actual repression has been practiced in the United States. For years Americans have been taught that repression is practiced only in other countries, particularly in dictatorships like Hitler's Germany, Mussolini's Italy, and Stalin's Russia. A new breed of American scholars, however, contests this conclusion. "The U.S. government has hassled workers, Indians, blacks, women, left-wingers, right-wingers, immigrants. In this century alone there have been two Red scares, concentration camps, guilt by association, deportations, preventive detention, political espionage—all carried out by a government supposedly dedicated to freedom."[12]

A genuine paradox emerges from this analysis of democracy in the United States. While Table 2 shows that leaders (elites) are more committed to democratic principles than the masses, elites often engage in repression. Watergate, a phenomenon of the Vietnam era, demonstrates how the tools of repression can be used to silence critics. It suggests that in periods of mass unrest, such as occurred in reaction to the war in Vietnam, elites may convince themselves that repression is necessary to preserve the political system.

Conventional wisdom for years maintained that repression was alien to America; the country prided itself on being a refuge of freedom, of free thought, free expression, free communication, free worship. Other countries might see their governments harassing dissidents and trying to drive them out of existence, but America—it was said—tolerated diversity as much as possible. Since ideas like these were simply untrue, once the blinders were lifted, the structure fell. Suddenly, numbers of people discovered that, in many ways, the history of the United States is a history of repression.—*Alan Wolfe*

Watergate proved the conscience of America. That wrongs were committed in a world characterized by human propensity for evil seems less significant than that they demonstrated that Americans still have the moral sense and idealism associated with their past.—*Archibald Cox*

The Watergate affair involved the use of intimidation by the Internal Revenue Service, the Federal Bureau of Investigation, the Central Intelligence Agency, and the White House staff. Many political opponents of President Richard M. Nixon were subjected to special investigations by the Internal Revenue Service. A special investigatory group, "the Plumbers," was created in the White House and was responsible for the break-in at the office of Dr. Daniel Ellsberg's psychiatrist.

The antidemocratic attitude that set the stage for Watergate is revealed in a presidential staff meeting with Secretary of State Henry Kissinger and White House staffers H. R. Haldeman, John Ehrlichman, and Charles Colson, who were discussing how to respond to liberal Democratic criticisms of the Nixon administration. As described by Charles Colson, a White House aide:

> The President's finger circled the top of his wineglass slowly. "One day we will get them—we'll get them on the ground where we want them. And we'll stick our heels in, step on them hard and twist—right, Chuck, right?"
>
> Then his eyes darted to Kissinger. "Henry knows what I mean—just like you do it in the negotiations, Henry—get them on the floor and step on them, crush them, show no mercy."
>
> Kissinger smiled and nodded. Haldeman said not a word but the look on his face was one of hand-rubbing expectation. I spoke for all three of us: "You're right, sir, we'll get them." Only Ehrlichman, expressionless and often a lonely voice of moderation, jerked his head back and stared at the ceiling.
>
> And so on the *Sequoia* this balmy spring night, a Holy War was declared against the enemy—those who opposed the noble goals we sought of peace and stability in the world. They who differed with us, whatever their motives, must be vanquished. The seeds of destruction were by now already sown—not in them but in us.[13]

Economic Inequality   Most introductory textbooks in American government overlook the relationships between politics and economics. Such relationships, however, bring up very real questions about the application of democratic principles in America. There is an intense concentration of economic power in the United States, and the relationships between it and the political system are all too obvious. Some 1.6 percent of Americans own about 80 percent of all stock, 100 percent of all state and municipal bonds, and over 88 percent of corporate bonds. C. Wright Mills has pointed out the relationship in his now classic work, *The Power Elite:* "Not great fortunes, but great corporations are the important units of wealth, to which individuals of property are variously attached. The corporation is the source of, and the basis of, the continued power and privilege of wealth." [14]

Those who maintain that the United States is undemocratic often cite the unequal distribution of wealth evidenced by such problems as widespread unemployment. During the 1970s the number of out-of-work Americans soared into the millions. Unemployment offices such as this one in Detroit, Michigan, are frequently filled with people reporting to pick up their unemployment insurance checks and to look for work.

Cabinet members George Humphrey, David Packard, Charles Wilson, and Robert McNamara owned substantial amounts of stock when they accepted their appointments. McNamara, secretary of defense in the Johnson administration, held $1.6 million of Ford stock in addition to stock options totaling some $270,000, while Wilson, secretary of defense in the Eisenhower Administration, had General Motors stock valued at some $2.5 million. Little wonder that Wilson remarked, "What's good for General Motors is good for America."

The close relationships between the wealthy and the government are all too obvious. Glaring examples abound. Following the 1972 presidential election, officials of several leading corporations, such as Gulf Oil Company and American Airlines, were convicted of making illegal campaign contributions. In 1968, the C-5A aircraft program in the Department of Defense was cited for a two-billion-dollar cost overrun by a

I get a call at least once a week from people in government wanting to blow the whistle on practices they find wasteful or harmful. I tell them that before they do, they better have two things: a good lawyer and another job.—*Ernest Fitzgerald*

Pentagon official, A. Ernest Fitzgerald, who was later removed from his $32,000 per year position. In a 1973 Senate Watergate Committee hearing it was revealed that Fitzgerald had been removed because of a White House aide's memo which said, "Only a basic no-goodnik would take his official business grievances so far from normal channels." After the hearing he was returned to his position. When Chile's democratically elected president, Communist Salvador Allende, was overthrown in 1973, substantial evidence pointed to the International Telephone and Telegraph Company and the Central Intelligence Agency combining their efforts to assist in the overthrow. Following presidential elections, prestigious ambassadorial posts to countries like France and Great Britain seem to shift in a game of "musical money" in which major campaign contributors are rewarded with top diplomatic posts. (For additional discussion of these issues, see Chapter 6.)

Who Determines Our Values?   The distinguished American philosopher John Dewey once wrote that "the keynote of democracy as a way of life may be expressed as the necessity for the participation of every mature human being in formation of the values that regulate the living of men together." [15] In terms of this goal, the American scene shows a gross disparity between profession and performance. Not only governmental and corporate elites, which have already been discussed, but also other elites, such as intellectuals, pose substantial problems for democracy in the United States. Just as governmental and corporate elites can abuse democracy, so too can intellectuals. In a study of the power of intellectuals in the United States, Dale Vree notes: "Intellectuals, too, can abuse their considerable power and be a potential threat to democracy. They can set the tone, make or break reputations, lavish money and publicity on their allies, ignore their foes, and violate standards of fair play. . . ." [16]

Intellectuals are habitual moralizers—indeed, they have been perceived as 'moral experts.'' As such, they aspire to be the moral guardians of society, perhaps even its political guardians. But if the technological developments which are propelling us toward a "post-industrial" society enable them to become the guardians of society, small abuses may become enormous abuses, and the age-old question will again face us: Who will guard the guardians?—*Dale Vree*

    The enormous impact of intellectuals on American political life is illustrated by the shuttle of Harvard University professors between Cambridge, Massachusetts, and Washington, D. C. Former Secretary of State Henry Kissinger, former Secretary of Labor John Dunlop, and Senator Daniel Patrick Moynihan are among the many who have shuttled from the halls of ivy to the halls of marble. Prominent professors from other universities who have held high positions in the government are George Schultz (University of Chicago), former secretary of labor, director of the Office of Management and Budget, and secretary of the treasury; James Schlesinger (University of Virginia), former director of the Central Intelligence Agency and currently "energy chief"; and Paul McCracken (University of Michigan), former head of the Council of

Economic Advisers. Certainly we do not contend that these professors have abused their role in American democracy, but one does have to raise questions in some instances. For example, when University of Chicago sociologist James Coleman, the principal architect and proponent of school busing to achieve racial balance in the 1960s, apparently rejected his own proposal in the 1970s, a serious question had to be raised. For about a decade this nation agonized over school busing. Then its principal intellectual architect and proponent backed down on his own theory that had been imposed primarily by judicial decisions and administrative edicts, and not by the legislative branch of government.

Besides the power of the intellectual community to substantially influence the values and standards of society, one must also consider the enormous influence of television. Permeating seemingly every facet of American life, television has established itself in an enviable position to dominate American life and thought. Analyzing television in relationship to western civilization in which democracy has played a major role, the British intellectual Malcolm Muggeridge says:

> Let me boldly and plainly say that it has long seemed to me clear beyond any shadow of doubt that what is still called western civilization is in an advanced stage of decomposition, and that another dark age will soon be upon us, if, indeed, it has not already begun. With the media, especially television, governing all our lives as they indubitably do, it is easily imaginable that this might happen without our noticing. I was reading the other day about a distasteful but significant experiment conducted in some laboratory or other. A number of frogs were put into a bowl of water, and the water very gradually raised to the boiling point, with the result that they all expired without making any serious effort to jump out

... results indicate that compulsory two-way busing, or compulsory assignment of white children to schools in neighborhoods that are homogeneously black, have not worked in cities. They simply have not produced racially stable schools. Even when judges order racial balance, racial balance does not result. The previously black schools in black neighborhoods remain predominantly black.

Compulsory one-way busing ... is manifestly unfair to blacks. Consequently, the only form of desegregation that will assure equal rights and not exacerbate population instability in large cities is one in which busing is voluntary. Furthermore, population stability cannot occur so long as black children's rights to attend a school end at the city line, while their race or their income prevents them from moving to the suburbs.

Thus any policy of voluntary busing should, to bring population stability as well as equal rights, encompass the metropolitan area as a whole, removing the suburbs from their protected status—*James S. Coleman*

The busing of students in order to achieve racial balance in schools has been a controversial issue throughout the 1960s and 1970s. Forced busing was instituted by judicial decisions and administrative edicts rather than by legislative actions and has had mixed success. Parental opposition has been a problem. Buses are often less than full, and groups like this one in Boston, Massachusetts, in 1974 often actively protest forced busing to integrate schools.

of the bowl. The frogs are us, the water is our habitat, and the media, by accustoming us to the gradual deterioration of our values and our circumstances, insure that the boiling point comes upon us unawares. It is my own emphatic opinion that the boiling point is upon us now.[17]

The purpose here has not been to delineate fully and precisely all determinants of our American value system, but rather to demonstrate that rank-and-file citizens are having less and less influence in determining these values. To the extent that this is happening, democracy in the United States is being challenged.

The Paradox of Reform   Realistically, Americans must recognize not only the limitations of their so-called democracy, but also that there is little hope for change. If democracy does exist, it does so only as a system of democratic elitism, and, aside from revolution, there is little likelihood of any change to improve it.

Reforms designed to make the United States more democratic can actually have the reverse effect. Consider the 1974 Federal Election Campaign Act which, among other things, set limits on how much individuals and political committees could contribute to candidates. As noted by the *Washington Post's* Pulitzer Prize-winning journalist David Broder, this act had three adverse consequences on the 1976 campaign.

First, the campaign spending limitations forced the two presidential candidates, Gerald Ford and Jimmy Carter, to curtail "travel and personal appearances in favor of reaching voters wholesale through television ad campaigns—thus increasing the dependence on the mass-media manipulation which the reformers themselves abhor."[18]

Second, citizen participation in the campaign was curbed by financial limitations which forced cutbacks in literature distribution, bumper stickers, and buttons.

Third, since both campaign contributors and the recipients of those contributions had to comply with bureaucratic requirements in making and receiving contributions, private contributions to candidates, especially to challengers, were reduced. Of this, Broder said: "The result is that incumbents [had] a greater advantage than ever and the element of competition in political life has been reduced."[19]

Common to most reforms, including this one, is an increase in the size and power of government to inplement and administer the reforms.

Creeping Big-Brotherism   There is ample evidence that our government is becoming more and more powerful in relationship to the individual. Its pervasive power is illustrated by the increasing labyrinth of governmental regulations affecting virtually every area of life. Air, water, and land—all are subject to governmental controls vis-à-vis individual use.

James Buckley, former senator from New York, has noted:

> In recent years Congress has established a multitude of agencies to regulate everything from the environment to equal employment. . . . All too often, once the power to regulate has passed to the federal bureaucracy, the good intentions of Congress have been lost. Small businessmen are at the mercy of arbitrary federal regulations which drive up their costs. Local school-board members find themselves responsible not to those who elected them but to distant Washington bureaucrats. Union leaders assert that rigid racial quotas handed down under so-called affirmative-action programs make a mockery of fair play and equal opportunity. . . .
>
> The torrent of litigation unleashed by federal agencies affects us all. The taxpayer is stuck with the government's tab, and the consumer ultimately pays the other bills through higher prices for goods and services.[20]

Buckley's view, although written from a conservative perspective, is certainly not unique to conservatives. After listening to campaign speeches by men who wish to become president and after reflecting, Theodore H. White writes:

> It is harder now to think clearly about government in this year of the Bicentennial. It strikes me now that we are crossing some vast invisible ridge of the mind, that an era is ending. We are locked into a crush of big organizations that squeeze us all—Big Government, Big Business, Big Unions. From the candidates of the Right to the candidates of the Left, all are trying to pry open or keep open the opportunity which once lay only over the next ridge.[21]

Many others have come to share these views of Buckley and White, among them such liberals as California Governor Jerry Brown and Massachusetts Governor Michael Dukakis.

Even those who favor a greater role for the federal government acknowledge that the increasing emphasis on governmental action and regulation is contrary to the intentions of the Founders, who believed in a limited government. Rexford Guy Tugwell, himself an architect of increased federal regulation as an adviser to President Franklin D. Roosevelt, wrote of the Constitution:

> Above all, men were to be free to do as they liked, and since the government was likely to intervene, and because prosperity was to be found in the free management of their affairs, a constitution was needed to prevent such intervention. . . . The law would maintain order, but would not touch the individual who behaved reasonably. He must pay taxes to support a smallish government, and he must not interfere with commerce; but otherwise laws would do him neither good nor ill. The government of the Constitution was this kind of government.[22]

We have created two racial and ethnic classes in this country to replace the disgraceful pattern of the past in which some groups were subjected to an official and open discrimination. The two new classes are those groups that are entitled to statistical parity [affirmative action] in certain key areas on the basis of race, color, and national origin, and those groups that are not. The consequences of such a development can be foreseen . . . those groups that are not considered eligible for special benefits become resentful. This new course threatens the abandonment of our concern for individual claims to consideration on the basis of justice and equity, now to be replaced with a concern for rights for publicly determined and delimited racial and ethnic groups.—*Nathan Glazer*

According to Tugwell, changes that enhanced federal power, though designed to broaden democracy, were made "irregularly and according to doctrines the framers would have rejected." [23] Tugwell felt that the Constitution had been altered more through judicial interpretation of the Constitution than through such popular measures as constitutional amendments. The Supreme Court, of course, is an appointed, not a democratically elected, body.

Leaving aside the manner in which changes were made, there is little doubt that they increased the size and regulatory power of government. While this shift may have enhanced equality among citizens, it poses a threat to individual liberty.

For example, "affirmative action" guidelines, which are principally administered by the Department of Labor and the Department of Health, Education, and Welfare, have forced colleges and universities to set goals for minority group employment and enrollment. However, should a person with superior qualifications be denied a job or admission to an institution merely because the college or university needs to meet its "affirmative action" goals? Both the departments and the courts have evaded a clear answer to this question. In the meantime, the federal government has threatened to withhold all federal funds to some colleges and universities, such as the University of Michigan, which were deemed in violation of the federal government's "affirmative action" guidelines. Typically a college or university has to have at least one professional person (a full office staff in large institutions) to coordinate the paperwork necessary to establish compliance with these guidelines. Other administrators are also generally involved in filling out "affirmative action" forms. Private colleges with a marginal financial situation find themselves committing important educational resources merely to satisfy the federal bureaucracy's penchant for paperwork. While equality of opportunity in obtaining jobs and gaining admission to colleges and universities is a laudable objective, should the liberty of the institution to make its own choices as to the best qualified applicants be trampled upon? Should marginally secure institutions like some small, private colleges have their very existence threatened by bureaucratic guidelines?

Some argue that the American government has actually moved along the road toward totalitarianism, with governmental power more important than personal freedom. *Totalitarianism* is generally defined as a form of authoritarianism in which the government controls nearly every aspect of the individual's life. Indeed the American government has been establishing its regulatory power in more areas. In fact, it is difficult to think of any area of American life in which the federal government does not exercise at least some regulatory power. Although certainly not representative of mainstream American thought in the area of family planning, one writer has taken the position that "the right to unlimited breeding is not a constitutional guarantee. If education and propaganda failed, those who violated the birth control restrictions would have to pay for their act as for any other criminal offense. I suspect that, eventually, the whole idea of parenthood will vanish, when children are made impersonally by the laboratory insemination of ova."[24]

There are echoes here of the policies of Hitler, who declared that the government "has to declare unfit for propagation everybody who is physically ill and has inherited a disease, and it has to carry this out in practice."[25]

Clearly the American system has moved since its founding from a limited toward an unlimited government. This shift along the continuum decreases the liberty of American citizens. Although the United States may not now have a totalitarian government, it has shifted in that direction.

The Negative Case

No, the United States is not undemocratic.

In a democratic society like ours, relief must come through an aroused popular conscience that sears the conscience of the people's representatives.[26]–Felix Frankfurter

It is faddish today to criticize the government. Pointing out its pitfalls and shortcomings has become a favorite pastime. In some circles, defending the United States as a democracy may seem like an uphill battle, but there is a wealth of ammunition for the cause.

- The Declaration of Independence, the Constitution, and the Bill of Rights reveal that the Founders were both procedural and principle democrats.
- Democratic procedures in the United States have been broadened and extended.
- Democratic principles, such as liberty and equality, apply to a larger segment of American society today than ever before.

*"I want you to know, gentlemen, that at this moment I feel
I have realized my full potential as a woman."*

Examination of these arguments will lead us to the conclusion that American democracy is:

- participatory: most persons can participate if they choose to do so;
- representative: the needs and opinions of diverse groups in society influence governmental leadership; and
- responsible: the people can hold governmental leaders accountable for their actions through elections; these force leaders to be guided by the long-term interests and needs of the entire population.

WHAT THE FOUNDERS BELIEVED

The principles and procedures outlined in the Declaration of Independence, the Constitution, and the Bill of Rights represent an unprecedented advancement in the implementation of democratic ideas. No other nation had anything comparable at the time of their adoption in the late 1700s. The Founders extended the principles and procedures of democracy farther than any other nation had ever dared. With twentieth-century hindsight, we might be critical, but not if we fairly assess what the Founders did from an eighteenth-century perspective.

Fundamental to the concern of the Founders was the dignity of the individual—the right to be free to pursue one's own best interests on an equal footing with others. The individual was the central measure of value in their thinking. This concern reflected the writings of Locke, Montesquieu, and other theorists and philosophers of the Enlightenment, who condemned earlier political views upholding the state as the central measure of value. For example, John Locke, who greatly influenced the Founders, said:

> To understand political power aright, and derive it from its original, we must consider what state all men are naturally in, and that is a state of perfect freedom to order their actions and dispose of their possessions and persons as they think fit, within the bounds of the law of nature, without asking leave, or depending upon the will of any other man.
>
> A state also of equality, wherein all the power and jurisdiction is reciprocal, no one having more than another. . . .[27]

The Declaration of Independence, of course, exemplifies this emphasis on individual liberty and equality by stating that "all men are created equal; that they are endowed by their Creator with certain unalienable rights; that among these, are life, liberty, and the pursuit of happiness." A modern view of the interaction and relationship between liberty and equality is set forth by Carl Becker: "Means and ends are conjoined in the concept freedom: freedom of thought so that the truth may prevail; freedom of occupation, so that careers may be open to talent; freedom of self-government, so that none may be compelled against his will."[28]

The people reign in the American political world as the Deity does in the Universe. They are the cause and the aim of all things; everything comes from them, and everything is absorbed in them.—*Alexis de Tocqueville*

Central to liberty is the right to self-determination; central to equality is the right to have a fair chance, given one's abilities, to compete with everyone else. The Founders, recognizing the debilitating influence engendered when the state itself is supreme, felt that in a limited government, the liberty of the individual would be enhanced and the rights of each person to equal opportunity would be protected. The government, therefore, was not to be all powerful, but would have sufficient power to protect the individual's right to equal opportunity.

The Founders were both procedural and principle democrats. Their procedures were enunciated in the Constitution, their principles in the Declaration of Independence, and both principles and procedures in the Bill of Rights. They knew that democratic procedures without adequate guarantees of democratic principles would be a hollow shell, and vice versa.

That the Founders were democrats, especially advanced in political aims in their own time, is evident from the Declaration of Independence, wherein they state: "That, to secure these rights [life, liberty, etc.], governments are instituted among men, deriving their just powers from the consent of the governed; that, whenever any form of government becomes destructive of these ends, it is the right of the people to alter or to abolish it, and to institute a new government, laying its foundation on such principles, and organizing its powers in such form, as to them shall seem most likely to effect their safety and happiness." Clearly the people and their interests were at the heart of the Founders' concern in establishing the new government for the United States.

DEMOCRACY IN ACTION

Has not democracy been extended in the United States:

- by granting the right to vote to nonproperty owners, women, blacks, and other minority groups (see Chapter 8);
- by equalizing legislative representation among urban, suburban, and rural populations (see Chapter 4); and
- by allowing minority groups, such as blacks, the right to serve on juries (see Chapter 4)?

Moreover, it should be pointed out that the electoral college system provides for the people to select the electors who vote for president, and that since 1888, the system has always chosen the candidate with the highest popular vote.

With respect to the contention that the seniority system exemplifies the lack of democracy in the United States, two rebuttal points should be made. First, the seniority system could have been abolished if the majority in either the House or Senate had desired to abolish it in their respective bodies. The seniority system exists because the majority allows it to exist. Second, the seniority system has been substantially modified in the last few years to make the selection of congressional committee chairmen more democratic (see Chapter 11).

Critics suggest that legislative representation and governmental leadership should generally mirror characteristics of the population, such as age, sex, education, etc. Examples abound to refute this contention. A representative does not have to be of same sex or age or race to represent effectively those interests. To illustrate, the Nineteenth Amendment, granting suffrage to women, and the Twenty-sixth Amendment, granting suffrage to eighteen- through twenty-year-olds, were adopted primarily by men over twenty-one years of age.

Concerning two other charges, economic inequality and the determination of values by such groups as intellectuals, there never has been

Table 3. How Elites Would Redistribute Income

QUESTION: Leaders were asked what they thought people in certain occupations earned each year, and how much a "fair salary" would be. Figures shown are those for a "semi-skilled worker in an auto assembly plant" and "a president of one of the top 100 corporations."

LEADERSHIP GROUPS	HOW GROUPS THINK INCOMES ARE			HOW GROUPS THINK INCOMES OUGHT TO BE		
	AUTO WORKER	CORPORATE EXECUTIVE	EXECUTIVE/ WORKER PAY RATIO	AUTO WORKER	CORPORATE EXECUTIVE	EXECUTIVE/ WORKER PAY RATIO
Business	$14,200	$212,000	15 to 1	$16,000	$206,000	13 to 1
Farm	13,200	170,000	13 to 1	12,000	110,000	9 to 1
Intellectuals	18,000	224,000	12 to 1	17,000	119,000	7 to 1
News Media	16,300	212,000	13 to 1	16,000	131,000	8 to 1
G.O.P. Officials	15,000	184,000	12 to 1	13,000	146,000	11 to 1
Democratic Officials	15,000	223,000	15 to 1	16,000	128,000	8 to 1
Blacks	17,800	184,000	10 to 1	18,000	114,000	6 to 1
Feminists	12,500	215,000	17 to 1	15,000	88,000	6 to 1
Youth	12,500	200,000	16 to 1	13,000	105,000	8 to 1

Source: *Washington Post*, September 26, 1976, p. A8. © *Washington Post*. Reprinted by permission.

a society as large and as complex as American society with a relatively equal distribution of economic resources. What should be noted about American society is that despite its complexity, economic resources are better distributed than in most other societies today. The majority of the American population is in the middle class where resources are rather evenly distributed. Compared to many other societies, the upper and lower classes in the United States are relatively small by virtue of the large middle class.

In refuting these charges, it is important to distinguish between equality of opportunity and equality of results. The Founders never intended equality of results, and neither do today's leaders. In the *Washington Post*-Harvard study, "all the leadership groups overwhelmingly chose equality of opportunity." Indeed, when offered an opportunity to redistribute income to provide for equality of results, the groups conclude (see Table 3) that

the difference between emerging (i.e., those with fewer resources) and established (i.e., those with more resources) groups [of leaders] is not one of kind; they are both headed in the same direction. The establishment groups would, it seems, accept a modicum of income redistribution while the emerging groups want much more. But the emerging groups, again, don't seem to want to change the order of things.[29]

Certainly intellectuals have an important role in determining values for American society as well as in proposing and implementing public policies. Would we want it any other way? If anything, American society does not utilize its intellectual community enough. For example, American politics is sometimes described as void of intellectual content, particularly in our political campaigns. Regardless of the level of intellectual influence on American society, however, Americans may reject that influence.

Certain fundamental democratic procedures operating in the United States today offer ample reason to conclude that the nation is indeed a democracy.

First, voting power: Each citizen, with relatively few exceptions (and the government is acting to eliminate these), has the right to vote. Each vote is counted as one vote, and each person may cast only one vote. Through voting, the people can change their government's leadership.

Second, access to information: Individuals have access to facts and are free to criticize. With access to information, people can develop alternatives to government policies.

Third, political organization: Citizens are generally free to organize for political purposes, as long as their organizations do not abridge the constitutional rights of others. Political organizations, of course, help people to change governmental leadership if they so desire.

Fourth, majority rule: Elections are decided by a majority or plurality; the candidate with the most votes wins. The candidate or party with a majority or plurality assumes governmental leadership with a mandate from the people to govern.

Fifth, minority right: The minority has the right to compete to become the majority. The ability of the minority to challenge the majority is always a threat to the majority's leadership and policies.

Each of these procedures, of course, allows the people to limit governmental power by giving them the ability to change it.

Progress Against Racism   Let us consider one of the most crucial indictments of American democracy—namely, that it perpetrates bias and prejudice against racial minorities, particularly blacks. Consider these facts about blacks today. They

- can vote throughout the country;
- can be served in hotels, motels, and restaurants, and enjoy the facilities of all other public establishments;

- are being elected to high offices in rapidly increasing numbers;
- are entering colleges and universities in large numbers;
- are obtaining more and more lucrative jobs;
- appear regularly on television programs and in advertisements; and
- are the beneficiaries of "affirmative action" programs designed to provide greater opportunities in obtaining education and employment.

The courts have acquitted black militants of crimes for which there was insufficient evidence. De jure segregation of schools has ended. More schools are integrated than ever before. Little wonder that black leader Eldridge Cleaver has remarked:

> In the past, the question was raised as to whether or not blacks were going to be a part of America; whether we were going to be let into the political process. Now I think that question has been resolved, and we are here to stay. We are inside the system. And I feel that the No. 1 objective for Black Americans is to recognize that they have the same equal rights under the Constitution as Ford or Rockefeller. . . .
>
> I believe that this will call for a tremendous shift of energy—that black people need to focus their energies on improving the system, as opposed to banging on the door to get in, or to tearing it down because they are not let in.[30]

Improvements in Other Areas   There has been progress not only against racism, but in other fields as well. Consider the poor. In 1950, 30 percent of the population was considered poor; in 1960, 20 percent; in 1970, 13 percent. Moreover, the poor, through Medicare and Medicaid, now benefit from medical services that were hardly dreamed of two decades ago.

What of justice? Has not the Supreme Court broadly extended the rights of defendants in criminal cases? (See Chapter 4.)

What of the rural-dominated legislative bodies? Has not the Supreme Court mandated reapportionment in order to provide fair representation for the urban and suburban population? (See Chapter 4.)

What of discrimination against women? Has not the government established affirmative action programs, even going to the extent of denying federal funds if colleges and universities do not meet federal guidelines? (See discussion on p. 143.)

The Complexity of Decision Making   Critics contend that elites govern the United States and that American citizens do not participate directly in making decisions. Many, perhaps most, political scientists would refute this criticism with the idea of democratic *pluralism*, which is a governmental system based upon the interaction and competition of numerous (that is, plural) groups. Labor competes with man-

The government had tried less specific devices [than minority hiring quotas] for years, and these gentler approaches were largely unproductive. We had to have specific measures to determine what's happened. Most responses [of employers] had been ephemeral. We never got so many screams from people until we got a measure to lay alongside their rhetoric. . . . We are trying to achieve a social goal that's now fixed in the Constitution after a terrible, despicable period of American history. Some don't get anything out of it, true, that is a by-product of it—that some whites would lose. But there must be some kind of sharing to achieve the overall goal. It's not to do good to some and bad to others, but to achieve something the whole society wants.—*James Jones*

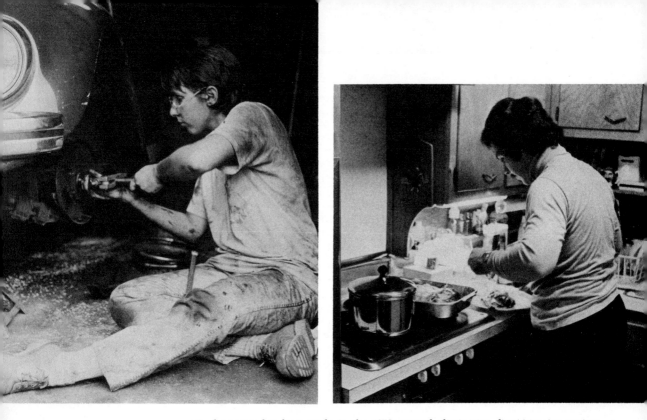

Real progress has been made in the 1970s toward eliminating discrimination against women. Affirmative action programs in businesses and educational institutions and equal opportunity laws barring job discrimination on the basis of sex have increased opportunities for women. As sex-role stereotypes diminish, such sights as women fixing cars and men fixing dinner are becoming commonplace.

agement; teachers with administrators; producers with consumers. All may compete with one another in influencing government policy. Pluralists argue that it is out of this competition that decisions are made and public policy emerges. In the words of one political scientist, public policy is made by "different small groups of interested and active citizens in different issue areas with some overlap, if any, by public officials, and occasional intervention by a larger number of people at the polls." [31] For example, automobile manufacturers resisted safety and antipollution measures until consumer pressure caused the government to adopt and enforce stiffer rules and regulations.

In the pluralist view, democracy is maintained by the equilibrium of group interaction. A center of power never becomes so powerful that it has no competition or allows for none. Elections provide people with a check on the groups and parties representing them. For example, overwhelming Republican losses in the 1974 congressional races probably indicated public dissatisfaction with the party after Watergate.

THE REALITY OF DEMOCRATIC PRINCIPLES

The very fact that American government can be criticized reveals its democratic character. Criticism is not only allowed, but protected. Critics, of course, provide the public at large with a diversity of viewpoints that enable us to make better judgments about the performance of our government. Both leaders and followers benefit. With more information and alternatives, better decisions can be made. And if the government makes a poor decision, critics can develop support for changing it.

From both the left and right of the political spectrum (and the center, too) have come volleys of attacks; some strong statements go so far as to advocate overthrow of the government. While the makers of such statements may not be universally admired, they are protected from harm by the government and its constitutional processes (see Chapter 4). (Indeed, some of them make substantial sums of money by "selling" their views through books and articles!) By contrast, consider a truly undemocratic society like that of the Soviet Union. The writer Alexander Solzhenitsyn was imprisoned and exiled after criticizing the Russian government. Thousands of other Russians remain in prison camps for similar "offenses."

Far from being repressive, the American government leans over backward to allow its antagonists and critics to speak out freely. (1) Angela Davis, an avowed Communist, travels freely and speaks widely on behalf of her cause. (2) Protesters against the Vietnam War demonstrated openly by the hundreds of thousands in Washington, D. C., and elsewhere. (3) Black Panthers and Vietnam protest leaders have campaigned for political office, some successfully. (4) When an administration did seek to repress the activities of the opposition, its leader—President Nixon—was forced out of office after legislative investigation and judicial action stimulated public pressure. (5) Highly vocal critics of American democracy, including Bobby Seale and Tom Hayden, have campaigned for public office.

Significantly and ironically, many of those who benefit most from their right to criticize are undemocratic in their own attitudes. For example, studies of violent antiwar protesters and demonstrators reveal a high degree of totalitarian sentiment and a low degree of regard for traditional democratic values.[32]

The Role of Government　What should the role of government be in insuring democratic principles? It should be pointed out that the men who wrote the Constitution saw the role of government as largely negative. That is, it was to remove constraints on the liberties of individuals, but it was generally not to act in a positive way to secure liberties except as provided for in the Bill of Rights. Liberalism in the late eighteenth

The American people may have low confidence in politics, politicians, government at all levels, the White House, the Congress, and the U. S. Senate, but they have not lost hope. They do not feel that we are a doomed giant of a nation in the last throes as other empires of the past, where corruption is rife. Where the disease of disintegration has reached an advanced stage and where desperation reigns. A solid 95 out of every 100 Americans believe in our system of pluralistic democracy. But, above all, they want it to work.—*Louis Harris*

A persuasive case can be made that if the American dream is dead, or dormant, it is because the dream of the fathers has been mostly realized, while the dream of the sons has not yet been successfully formulated.—*Thomas Griffith*

and nineteenth centuries meant allowing people to act free from governmental restraint insofar as possible. In the 1890s the distinguished English diplomat and scholar Lord Bryce wrote that "Jefferson would seem to have been not far from wrong when he said that the federal government was nothing more than the American department of foreign affairs." [33]

The concept of a purely negative role for the national government became less relevant in the twentieth century. Attacks were made on the principle that the government that governs least governs best. One such attack came from the pen of Charles Beard in 1931.

> The cold truth is that the individualist creed of everybody for himself and the devil take the hindmost is principally responsible for the distress in which Western civilization finds itself—with investment racketeering at one end and labor racketeering at the other. Whatever merits the creed may have had in days of primitive agriculture and industry, it is not applicable in an age of technology, science, and rationalized economy. Once useful, it has become a danger to society. [34]

Another critique, delivered by Arthur Schlesinger, Jr., thirty years later, noted the relationship between hands-off government and laissez-faire economics that illustrates the changing definition of liberalism between the nineteenth and twentieth centuries.

> American anti-statism was the function of a particular economic order. Jefferson had dreamed of a nation of small freeholders and virtuous artisans, united by a sturdy independence, mutual respect and the ownership of property. . . . But the industrial revolution changed all that. The corporation began to impersonalize the economic order. It removed the economy, in other words, from the control of a personal code and delivered it to agencies with neither bodies to be kicked nor souls to be damned. . . .
> The state consequently had to expand its authority in order to preserve the ties which hold society together. The history of governmental intervention has been the history of the growing ineffectiveness of the private conscience as a means of social control. The only alternative is the growth of the public conscience, whose natural expression is the democratic government. [35]

The dominant and controlling view changed from one favoring a negative government to one favoring a positive government that acted, for example, to enforce voting rights or provide for equal employment opportunity. The new idea was to strengthen government to compete more effectively with other centers of power, such as big business. Government's role became one of representing the public interest against competing private interests.

The principles of liberty and equality were once generally considered to be separate and distinct. At the same time it was felt that the more government, the less liberty, and vice versa. Many twentieth-century thinkers believe that absence of government does not guarantee liberty. When the government did not act to stop lynching, its inaction insured the liberty of the mob, not that of the individual at the other end of the rope.

In a theoretical sense, where there is total liberty, there is no equality, and where there is total equality, there is no liberty. If all people can act freely, disregarding the rights of others, then the armed assailant makes a mockery of his victim's equality of opportunity. But if all people must remain on an equal plane, with no one getting ahead of anyone else, then liberty to pursue one's own goals cannot be said to exist.

The twentieth century created a dynamic tension between liberty and equality. Equality came to be defined in rather specific ways—economic, political, legal, and social—through programs of the New Deal, Fair Deal, New Frontier, and Great Society. The government's role shifted to being the guarantor of equality of opportunity in all these areas, as evidenced by such measures as the Equal Employment Opportunity Act. Another example is the Voting Rights Act of 1965; by insuring that blacks could vote in the South, it allowed them to compete on a more equal plane with whites in political processes.

In sum, to achieve democratic principles, the role of government was expanded to insure that they were promoted by democratic procedures. In both areas, the goal was the enhancement of individual dignity.

Habit Versus Belief   Leading students of democracy have recognized that the existence of democracy does not depend on the public's belief in democratic principles. J. Roland Pennock has noted that democracy can tolerate disagreement on principles if people are willing to compromise and to follow established rules and procedures, and Carl J. Fredrich has concluded that democracy depends on habitual patterns of behavior rather than on conscious agreement on "democratic" principles.[36]

Thus, although survey data shows that the American public does not generally believe in democratic principles, the argument is meaningless so long as the public compromises its differences and adheres to accepted democratic procedures.

Comparisons with Other Nations   Several comparisons already made show American democracy in a favorable light. What about other nations that call themselves democratic? If we agree on the necessity for popular participation in the political process, it is not difficult to distinguish between the United States and the German Democratic Republic (Communist East Germany). Elections determine who shall rule in the American system. This is not the case in totalitarian countries.

American democracy has served as a model for other nations seeking to establish democratic governments. The North Vietnamese revolutionaries who were shaking off colonial rule used much of the thinking of Thomas Jefferson and the Declaration of Independence. The democratic spirit born in America in the eighteenth century has kindled similar aspirations elsewhere. It has been a beacon because of its emphasis on the dignity of the individual.

The strength of democracy is that it is subject to criticism, which can serve as a corrective to errant practices and policies. American democracy is dynamic, not static. Even today, during one of the greatest periods of criticism ever experienced by our government, the fact of that criticism illustrates the strength of the American democracy. What other government would tolerate the extent of criticism found in America?

Really what alternatives are there to American democracy? Even American democracy's most vocal critics do not offer any realistic alternative; indeed, sometimes they do not even bother to state an alternative. For example, political scientist Michael Parenti has written at the close of *Democracy for the Few:*

> There is no finished blueprint for the new society. The forms of challenge and change and the alternative community will arise from the actions of the people—as is already happening. With time and with struggle, as the possibility of a better social life grows stronger, people will become increasingly intolerant of the monumental abuses and injustices of the present socioeconomic system. The day will come, as it came in social orders of the past, when those who seem invincible will be shaken from their pinnacles and a new, humane and truly democratic society will begin to emerge.[37]

What do Parenti and other critics have in mind? Would a new "democracy" allow critics to speak and act as freely as they do now in criticizing American democracy? Until that question is answered, perhaps we should stick with American democracy lest we buy a pig in a poke.

Glossary

Democracy: a form of government in which power is exercised by the people.

Direct democracy: a form of government in which political decisions are made by the people directly rather than by their elected representatives; also known as *pure democracy*.

Elitism: a theory of government which holds that the control or making of political, economic, and social decisions is in the hands of those persons of greater wealth, higher social status, or intellectual superiority.

Indirect democracy: a form of government in which political decisions are made by the elected representatives of the people; also known as *republican government* or *representative democracy*.

Majority rule: a fundamental democratic principle which holds that the larger number of citizens should select officials and determine policies.

Minority rights: a fundamental democratic principle which holds that the minority, notwithstanding the majority's right to govern, has rights that the majority cannot abolish, such as the right to compete to win majority support.

Pluralism: a theory of government which holds that diverse groups and organizations compete to determine public policy on political, economic, and social issues.

Totalitarianism: a form of government in which the government controls almost all aspects of the individual's life.

Notes

1. Carl Becker, *Modern Democracy* (New Haven, Conn.: Yale University Press, 1941), p. 26.

2. Hans J. Morgenthau, "Power and Powerlessness: Decline of Democratic Government," *The New Republic* 171 (November 9, 1974):13.

3. Henry Cabot Lodge, ed., *The Federalist* (New York: G. P. Putnam's Sons, 1902), p. 52.

4. Harold Lasswell and Daniel Lerner, *The Comparative Study of Elites* (Stanford, Calif.: Stanford University Press, 1952), p. 7.

5. Donald R. Mathews, *The Social Background of Political Decision-makers* (New York: Doubleday, 1954); and David T. Stanley, Dean E. Mann, and Jameson W. Doig, *Men Who Govern* (Washington, D.C.: The Brookings Institution, 1967).

6. Gaetano Mosca, *The Ruling Class* (New York: McGraw-Hill, 1939), p. 50.

7. Louis M. Kohlmeier, "The Politics of Deregulation," *National Journal* 7 (April 10, 1975):10.

8. Ibid.

9. Sidney Hook, *Political Power and Personal Freedom* (New York: Criterion, 1959), pp. 19–28.

10. *Washington Post*, September 26, 1976, p. 8.

11. James W. Prothro and Charles M. Grigg, "Fundamental Principles of Democracy: Bases of Agreement and Disagreement," *The Journal of Politics* 22 (1960):281.

12. Alan Wolfe, *The Seamy Side of Democracy* (New York: David McKay, 1973), p. 4.

13. Charles W. Colson, *Born Again* (Old Tappan, N.J.: Chosen Books, 1976), p. 45.

14. C. Wright Mills, *The Power Elite* (New York: Oxford University Press, 1956), p. 116.

15. John Dewey, "Democracy and Educational Administration," *School and Society* 45 (April 3, 1937):457.

16. Dale Vree, "Intellectuals, Scholars and the Common People," *Freedom at Issue* 31 (May–June 1975):6.

17. Malcolm Muggeridge, "Living Through an Apocalypse," *Decision*, November 1974, pp. 8–9.

18. *Washington Post*, October 6, 1976, p. A15.

19. Ibid.

20. James L. Buckley, "Big Government vs. the Little Guy," *Reader's Digest*, August 1976, pp. 86, 88.

21. Theodore H. White, "What America Means to Me," *Reader's Digest*, August 1976, p. 60.

22. Rexford Guy Tugwell, "Rewriting the Constitution," *The Center Magazine*, March 1968, pp. 18–25.

23. Ibid.

24. Gore Vidal, quoted in M. Stanton Evans, "The Death of Liberalism," in Dorothy Buckton James, ed., *Outside, Looking In* (New York: Harper & Row, 1972), p. 27.

25. Adolf Hitler, *Mein Kampf* (West Caldwell, N.J.: Reynal and Hitchcock, 1939), p. 609.

26. *Baker* v. *Carr* (1962).

27. John Locke, "An Essay Concerning the True Original, Extent and End of Civil Government," *The English Philosophers from Bacon to Mill*, ed. Edwin A. Burtt (New York: The Modern Library, 1939), p. 404.

28. Becker, *Modern Democracy*, p. 27.

29. *Washington Post*, September 26, 1976, p. A8.

30. Laile E. Bartlett, "The Education of Eldridge Cleaver," *Reader's Digest*, September 1976, pp. 71–72.

31. Aaron Wildavsky, *Leadership in a Small Town* (Totowa, N.J.: Bedminster Press, 1964), p. 20.

32. Michael Lerner, "Anarchism and the American Counterculture," in James A. Gould and Willis H. Truitt, eds., *Political Ideologies* (New York: Macmillan, 1973), pp. 464–472.

33. James Bryce, *The American Commonwealth* (New York: Macmillan, 1891), I, 411–412.

34. Quoted in Howard Zinn, ed., *New Deal Thought* (Indianapolis, Ind.: Bobbs-Merrill, 1966), p. 10.

35. Arthur Schlesinger, Jr., *The Vital Center* (Boston: Houghton Mifflin, 1962), p. 176.

36. Prothro and Grigg, "Fundamental Principles of Democracy," p. 294.

37. Michael Parenti, *Democracy for the Few* (New York: St. Martin's Press, 1974), p. 298.

Recommended Rebuttal Reading*

On Democratic Theory

Cook, Terrence E., and Patrick M. Morgan, eds. *Participatory Democracy*. New York: Canfield Press, 1971.

Croly, Herbert. *The Promise of American Life*. New York: Macmillan, 1909.

Dahl, Robert A. *After the Revolution? Authority in a Good Society*. New Haven, Conn.: Yale University Press, 1970.

Handlin, Oscar, and Mary Handlin. *The Dimensions of Liberty*. Cambridge, Mass.: Harvard University Press, 1961.

Kariel, Henry S., ed. *Frontiers of Democratic Theory*. New York: Random House, 1970.

* These selected readings will help you to develop rebuttals to the affirmative and negative cases.

Pateman, Carole. *Participation and Democratic Theory.* New York: Cambridge University Press, 1970.

Purcell, Edward A., Jr. *The Crisis of Democratic Theory.* Lexington: The University Press of Kentucky, 1973.

Walzer, Michael. *Obligations: Essays on Disobedience, War and Citizenship.* Cambridge, Mass.: Harvard University Press, 1970.

On American Political Ideology

Hartz, Louis. *The Liberal Tradition.* New York: Harcourt Brace Jovanovich, 1955.

Lowi, Theodore J. *The End of Liberalism.* New York: Norton, 1970.

Rossiter, Clinton. *Conservatism in America.* New York: Alfred A. Knopf, 1962.

———. *Seedtime of the Republic.* New York: Harcourt Brace Jovanovich, 1955.

Wolff, Robert Paul. *The Poverty of Liberalism.* Boston: Beacon Press, 1968.

On Elitism Versus Pluralism

Bachrach, Peter. *The Theory of Democratic Elitism.* Boston: Little, Brown, 1967.

Dahl, Robert A. *A Preface to Democratic Theory.* Chicago: University of Chicago Press, 1956.

Kariel, Henry S. *The Decline of American Pluralism.* Stanford, Calif.: Stanford University Press, 1961.

Truman, David. *The Governmental Process.* New York: Alfred A. Knopf, 1951.

On American Political Thought Generally

Etzkowitz, Henry, and Peter Schwab, eds. *Is America Necessary? Conservative, Liberal and Socialist Perspectives of United States Political Institutions.* St. Paul, Minn.: West, 1976.

Hofstadter, Richard. *The American Political Tradition.* New York: Random House, 1948.

Mason, Alpheus T., and Richard H. Leach. *In Quest of Freedom.* Englewood Cliffs, N. J.: Prentice-Hall, 1959.

Parrington, Vernon L. *Main Currents in American Thought.* New York: Harcourt Brace Jovanovich, 1930.

AT ISSUE: THE CONSTITUTION

RESOLVED THAT: The Constitution Should Be Abandoned

2

At Issue: The Constitution

Some men look at constitutions with sanctimonious reverence and deem them . . . too sacred to be touched. They ascribe to the men of the preceding age a wisdom more than human and suppose what they did to be beyond amendment. . . . I am certainly not an advocate for frequent and untried changes in laws and constitutions. I think moderate imperfections had better be borne with, because, when once known, we accommodate ourselves to them and find practical means of correcting their ill effects. But I know also that laws and institutions must go hand in hand with the progress of the human mind. As that becomes more developed, more enlightened, as new discoveries are made, new truths disclosed, and manners and opinions change with the change of circumstances, institutions must advance also and keep pace with the times.[1]–Thomas Jefferson

The American Constitution is both revered and repudiated. Some people regard it as one of the greatest democratic documents in all history. They see it as a major milestone in the evolution of democracy. They rank it in importance with the Magna Carta, the English Bill of Rights of 1689, and the Declaration of Independence.

Other people, however, believe that the Constitution has outlived whatever usefulness it once had. To them, it is irrelevant to the needs and problems of the last quarter of the twentieth century. They contend that mass communications and advanced technology, together with the crisis atmosphere in which we live, necessitate a government that can

Thus I consent, Sir, to this Constitution because I expect no better, and because I am not sure that it is not the best.—*Benjamin Franklin*

37

act quickly. They claim that the structure set up by the American Constitution is slow and cumbersome. It divides power between the national and state governments and disperses national authority among the legislative, executive, and judicial branches.

A third view holds that, although the Constitution was a great document when drafted, its basic concepts have been corrupted. People who have this attitude are especially concerned by such developments as the centralization of power in the national government and extensive federal regulation of American society.

According to a fourth view, the American Constitution was not very democratic when drafted, but became more so with changes over the years. As evidence, people holding this view point to several constitutional amendments, among them those extending the rights of black Americans, those broadening the suffrage, and those providing for a graduated income tax, popular election of senators, and abolition of the poll tax.

A fifth view, held mostly by radical and revolutionary elements, contends that the Constitution was drafted and ratified to protect the interests of elite groups and that it has continued to do so. In other words, it was undemocratic when drafted and remains so today.

What is the correct view? Before examining some of these debatable issues, it will be helpful to see how the Constitution came into being, and to take a brief look at the document itself.

THE IMMEDIATE BACKGROUND

What prompted the drafting of the Constitution in the first place? Mainly it was dissatisfaction with the Articles of Confederation, under which the United States was governed from 1781 to 1789. The Articles went back to a proposal placed before the Continental Congress that a plan for "perpetual union" be created. Following the adoption of the Declaration of Independence in 1776, Congress appointed a committee to draw up a plan of confederation. After Congress approved the committee's work in 1777, four years passed before all the states finally ratified the Articles and they went into effect.

The United States achieved some successes under the Articles of Confederation. The Revolutionary War was won and a peace treaty ratified; important allies were established in the international community; a postal service was created; and a national bureaucracy was set up. But many American leaders were dissatisfied with the national government under the Articles of Confederation. Its drawbacks were several.

(1) It could not levy taxes. This inability threatened the financial investments of Americans who had lent money to the government dur-

ing the Revolutionary War but now had no way to regain their investments. Without taxing power, the government could not pay off its debts. (2) The national government could not regulate commerce between the states or with foreign governments. Commercial and shipping interests were at the mercy of the individual states, which set their own tariffs and thus impaired the flow of interstate and foreign commerce. (3) The government could not coin money. The states printed cheap paper bills with which debtors paid their creditors. The latter were therefore receiving payments in money worth substantially less than their original loans. (4) Because the government had to have unanimity among the states to raise taxes and to amend the articles, it lacked sufficient power to govern. The Congress, being very weak, often had second-rate delegates, because well-qualified persons frequently refused to serve.

Under the Articles of Confederation, the national government of the United States was more an alliance of thirteen independent states than a union of the people. And in this central government all power was in the hands of the Congress. There was neither an executive nor a judicial branch except insofar as the Congress created them. Governmental affairs were typically governed by committees of Congress. This strong legislative power, of course, reflected popular discontent with the centralized executive authority of the English Crown.

In addition to these structural deficiencies, national government under the Articles suffered from the inability to cope with some specific problems. (1) It seemed unable to handle domestic disturbances. In 1786 many Americans were disturbed by Shays' Rebellion, when farmers, artisans, and laborers—angry because of property seizures to satisfy their debts—joined to capture courthouses in several Massachusetts towns. Only a mercenary army paid for by propertied citizens quelled this uprising. (2) It could not oust the British from their forts in the Northwest Territory, posts that had been held since before the Revolution. Consequently, its ability to protect western settlers, and thus further the economic growth of inland America, seemed limited. (3) It had little prestige in foreign affairs. At a time when a strong sense of nationalism was developing, Americans felt frustrated by their poor showing on the international stage.

The Articles of Confederation did, it might be noted, contribute several features to the American Constitution. Under the Articles the national government had the power to declare war, send and receive ambassadors, make treaties, fix standards of weights and measures, regulate the value of coins, manage Indian affairs, establish post offices, borrow money, and build and equip an army and navy. These powers were retained. Under both systems each state was required to give "full faith and credit" to the records, acts, and judicial proceedings of every other state, and citizens of each state had the "privileges and immunities" of citizens in other states.

By 1785, there was a good deal of concern about economic problems. During a conference between Virginia and Maryland called to settle differences about commerce and navigation, delegates suggested calling a general economic conference of all the states. This meeting, held in Annapolis the following year, never did discuss economic problems, but rather focused on the weaknesses of the Articles of Confederation. Just after this convention met, Shays' Rebellion, and the government's difficulty in quelling it, dramatically reinforced the arguments of those opposed to the Articles.

In February 1787, Congress issued a call for a convention to meet in Philadelphia "for the sole and express purpose of revising the Articles of Confederation and reporting to Congress and the several legislatures such alterations and provisions therein as shall, when agreed to in Congress and confirmed by the states, render the federal Constitution adequate to the exigencies of government and the preservation of the union."

CONVENTION COMPROMISES

Should the states reject this excellent Constitution, the probability is that an opportunity will never again offer to make another in peace—the next will be drawn in blood.—*George Washington*

At the Constitutional Convention, differences among the thirteen states led to critical conflicts that frequently seemed insoluble. There was tension between the more populous and less populous states, between the nonslave and the slave states, between the somewhat commercial and the largely agricultural states. The Constitution embodies numerous compromises among these varying interests.

Large Versus Small Delegates spent a good deal of time debating two alternate ways of setting up the government—the Virginia Plan and the New Jersey Plan. Both had in common, however, separation of powers among legislative, executive, and judicial branches of the national government.

The Virginia Plan, introduced by Governor Edmund Randolph of Virginia, contained these provisions, among others: (1) A *bicameral* (two-house) legislature would have the lower house chosen by the people and the upper house chosen by the lower; representation in the lower house would be proportionate to population. (2) A "national executive" (its precise makeup not spelled out) would be elected by the legislature. (3) A national judiciary would be chosen by the legislature.

The New Jersey Plan, introduced by William Paterson of that state, was basically a continuation of the Articles of Confederation. It included these stipulations: (1) In a *unicameral* (one-house) legislature, each state would have one vote. (2) Congress was to choose an executive, to consist of more than one person. (3) The executive should appoint justices to a Supreme Court.

Clearly, the Virginia Plan favored the larger states, while the New Jersey Plan favored the smaller ones. The Convention finally adopted what came to be called the "Great Compromise" (sometimes called the "Connecticut Compromise" because it was proposed by Roger Sherman of Connecticut). It set up a bicameral legislature. The lower house—the House of Representatives—would be apportioned according to population. The upper house—the Senate—would consist of two members from each state, elected by the state legislatures. The large states obtained the advantage in the House of Representatives, where population determined the number of representatives. The small states had the advantage in the Senate, since each state had two senators regardless of population. The "Great Compromise" also resolved several other disputes.

Slavery and Taxation   The southern states wanted to count their slaves for the purpose of increasing their representation in the House of Representatives; the northern states held that they should be regarded solely as (taxable) property. To resolve this dispute, the Convention agreed on the "three-fifths compromise": three fifths of all slaves would be counted in apportioning members of the House of Representatives, and also for tax purposes.

As to the slavery issue itself, there was substantial antislavery sentiment among the delegates, but they agreed simply that the trade itself could be abolished after 1808. The conflicting feelings on this issue are well illustrated by statements of two delegates. Charles Pinckney of South Carolina declared that his state would not ratify the Constitution if the slave trade were abolished, while George Mason of Virginia said that slavery would "bring the judgment of heaven" on the nation.[2]

Another element of the compromise concerning slavery and taxation dealt with commerce. Since the South exported almost all of its agricultural products, it feared that export taxes would make its products noncompetitive in the international market. As a concession to the South, export taxes cannot, even today, be levied by the United States, one of the few nations not permitted this right.

Out of these compromises emerged a document which has now lasted almost two hundred years. Many of its provisions were then and remain today controversial.

I am persuaded no constitution was ever before as well calculated as ours for extensive empire and self-government.—*Thomas Jefferson*

THE RESULTING DOCUMENT

The American Constitution—approximately 7,500 words long—is brief in contrast to today's state constitutions, some of which contain well over 100,000 words. The Founders seemingly tried to write a document embodying general principles that could be adapted to succeeding generations, rather than draft a series of very specific and precise provisions. The seven articles and twenty-six amendments of the Constitution appear in the Appendix. The following is a brief summary.

Article I, in ten sections, concerns the legislative branch of the government. It vests all legislative powers "in a Congress of the United States, which shall consist of a Senate and House of Representatives," and outlines the qualifications and method of election of members of Congress. It provides for revenue legislation and outlines the procedure for overriding a presidential veto.

Section 8 of Article I explicitly lists such legislative powers as regulating commerce, coining money, establishing post offices, and declaring war. It also contains a clause—often referred to as the "elastic" clause—giving Congress the power "to make all Laws which shall be necessary and proper for carrying into Execution the foregoing Powers."

Section 9 of Article I provides several basic protections for citizens by prohibiting certain congressional actions. Congress cannot, under normal circumstances, suspend the *writ of habeas corpus.* This document directs an officer holding a suspect to show adequate grounds for holding that person, thus protecting the individual against illegal imprisonment. Nor can Congress pass *bills of attainder* (legislative acts punishing particular individuals without a trial) or *ex post facto laws* (those that impose punishment for acts that were legal when committed). This article also specifies that money can be drawn from the Treasury only "in Consequence of Appropriations made by Law." In other words, other branches of the government cannot spend money unless Congress has appropriated it.

Article II of the Constitution, in four sections, deals with the executive power. It provides for a president and vice-president and outlines their qualifications and manner of election. It also specifies numerous presidential powers—serving as commander in chief of the armed forces; making treaties (subject to the "Advice and Consent of the Senate"); and appointing ambassadors, judges, and other high officials.

Article III, in three sections, pertains to the judiciary. It places the judicial power in one Supreme Court and lesser courts to be established by Congress. It provides for trial by jury except in cases of impeachment. It also deals with the *jurisdiction* of the Supreme Court—that is, it specifies the types of cases over which it has authority.

The remainder of the Constitution proper contains four articles. Article IV governs relations among the states and between states and the federal government. Article V outlines the methods for amending the Constitution. Article VI specifies that the Constitution, plus laws and treaties made under its authority, "shall be the supreme Law of the Land." Article VII provides for ratification of the Constitution. Since its adoption, twenty-six amendments have been added (see the Appendix), including the Bill of Rights.

Now almost two hundred years old, the American Constitution poses many questions for a nation entering its third century. Many of these may be examined in discussing the issue under debate: Should the document itself be abandoned?

- Is the Constitution really relevant to government policies and problems in the 1970s?
- Are provisions of the Constitution that may have aided the upper classes in the eighteenth century still doing so, or are those same provisions now aiding the lower classes?
- Does separation of powers benefit the average citizen? If so, how?

The Affirmative Case

Yes, the Constitution should be abandoned.

This country, with its institutions, belongs to the people who inhabit it. Whenever they shall grow weary of the existing government, they can exercise their constitutional right of amending it, or their revolutionary right to dismember or overthrow it.[3]–Abraham Lincoln

In the minds of most Americans, it is probably little short of heresy to argue that the American Constitution should be abandoned. We have been taught that the United States is the world's greatest democracy and that the Constitution, which provides its structural framework, is a document of almost sacred inviolability. And yet several points can be raised demonstrating that it is undemocratic, has been distorted, and is no longer relevant to our times. To summarize:

- The Constitution was drafted in an undemocratic manner by an elite class of men, and embodies their attempts to dominate the government.

- The Constitution has been distorted and its original meaning in many cases corrupted.
- Because it is now outmoded, the Constitution has become an obstacle to change.

ELITIST ORIGINS

The movement for the Constitution of the United States was originated and carried through principally by four groups of personal interests which had been adversely affected under the Articles of Confederation: money, public securities, manufacturers, and trade and shipping.—*Charles Beard*

Who were the fifty-five men who drafted the American Constitution? Most of them were well-to-do, with interests in real estate, banking, manufacturing, shipping, and large-scale agriculture. They were men of extraordinary prestige and reputation. Many were personal friends. They had received excellent educations and typically had had some experience in governing. To be more specific:

- Over half the delegates held degrees from Princeton, Yale, Harvard, Columbia, Pennsylvania, William and Mary, or English universities.
- Occupations and interests included the following: twenty-four delegates were involved in moneylending and investments; fourteen speculated in land; fifteen owned plantations; and all fifty-five held public securities, such as bonds.
- At the time of the Convention, over forty delegates held important positions in state government, including three governorships; over forty had served in Congress.

The fifty-five delegates who first met at Philadelphia in May 1787 were hardly representative of the general population. There were some 4 million Americans at this time, most of them farmers, tradespeople, and servants or slaves. As noted by historian Charles A. Beard in his *Economic Interpretation of the Constitution*, the Constitution was "an economic document drawn with superb skill by men whose property interests were immediately at stake." [4]

At the time of the Constitutional Convention, there was only a minuscule middle class, composed primarily of shopkeepers, artisans, and successful farmers. A large proportion of the total population consisted of frontier settlers and debt-ridden farmers. Below them on the social scale were tenant farmers and indentured servants, both male and female, comprising perhaps 20 percent of the population. Below them were all slaves, comprising another 20 percent. Eight out of ten Americans eked out a marginal existence through farming; one in ten earned a living in fishing or lumbering; the rest were involved in commerce as merchants, lawyers, dockhands, or sailors. Interest and participation in political affairs was left mainly to the upper class. There was in addition a very modest level of participation among the middle class.

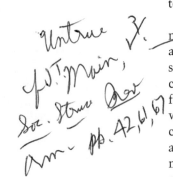

Undemocratic Provisions   It was fitting that the men who drafted the Constitution were from the upper classes. For it was they who stood to benefit most from it. It is clear that the deficiencies of the Articles of Confederation posed a threat to the propertied class. The national government's inability to levy taxes, regulate commerce, print money, and impose tariffs all harmed people of wealth more than they endangered citizens of ordinary means. And these same affluent Americans were the ones who worried most about debtor unrest, limitations to westward expansion, and international respectability.

The governmental structure and procedures embodied in the Constitution clearly reflected the interests of those serving as delegates to the Convention. They were aided by many of the powers granted to the national government. (a) The power to levy taxes and thus produce revenue would protect the investments of those who had helped to finance the government during the Revolution. The restriction against direct taxation was interpreted as a prohibition of a graduated income tax, further protecting the financial interests of the upper class. (b) The power to regulate interstate commerce would protect trading and commercial interests. (c) The power to protect money and property through the supervision of weights and measures, roads, copyrights, and patents also protected mercantile interests. (d) The sole power to mint money—previously enjoyed by the states as well—shut off a source of cheap currency that benefited the debtor classes. (e) The power to establish a military could be used to quell such disturbances as Shays' Rebellion, which threatened the upper classes.

These specific grants of power enhanced the interests of the elite groups, a small minority of Americans. So did the composition of the three branches of the national government. The Constitution provided that the people would have a direct voice in only one of them, the House of Representatives. Senators were to be elected by state legislatures; the president was to be protected from direct popular opinion by the device of the electoral college.

An additional historical, though not current, problem with the Constitution was the lack of a bill of rights, depriving the people of important guarantees and protections. Because states like New York insisted on a bill of rights before they would ratify the document, the Founders proposed the first ten amendments to the Constitution known collectively as the Bill of Rights.

In effect, the Constitution took power from the states, where the middle and lower classes had more influence, and shifted it to the national government, where the upper class was dominant. This basic shift was highlighted by Article VI, the so-called "supremacy" clause, which states:

All communities divide themselves into the few and the many. The first are the rich and well-born, the other the masses of people. The voice of the people has been said to be the voice of God; and however generally this maxim has been quoted and believed, it is not true in fact. The people are turbulent and changing; they seldom judge or determine right. Give therefore to the first class a distinct, permanent share in the government. They will check the unsteadiness of the second, and as they cannot receive any advantage by change, they therefore will ever maintain good government. Can a democratic assembly who annually revolves in the mass of the people, be supposed steadily to pursue the public good? Nothing but a permanent body can check the imprudence of democracy.—*Alexander Hamilton*

This Constitution, and the Laws of the United States which shall be made in Pursuance thereof; and all Treaties made, or which shall be made, under the Authority of the United States, shall be the supreme Law of the Land; and the Judges in every State shall be bound thereby, any Thing in the Constitution or Laws of any State to the Contrary notwithstanding.

"Whew! Can't We Find Some Other Route?"

from The Herblock Gallery (Simon & Schuster, 1968)

The Constitution as originally drafted probably would not be considered wholly democratic by today's standards. For example, women were not granted full rights of citizenship in the original document. Women like those pictured here campaigned vigorously throughout the late 1800s and early 1900s for the right to vote. National women's suffrage was finally achieved in 1920 when the Nineteenth Amendment was ratified in grateful recognition of women's contributions to the war effort during World War I.

There was nothing in the Constitution drafted at Philadelphia that might be construed as opposing the interests of the upper class. What the Constitution did was to consolidate the economic and social gains its members had achieved through the Revolutionary War. A strong national authority would protect and increase their position, which would be perpetuated by limited popular participation in the government.

The Constitution did nothing to abolish slavery. In fact, it guaranteed that the slave trade could continue until 1808. Nor did it grant women the full rights of citizenship. Democracy was neither the motif of the day nor the motive of the Founders.

The very purpose of the document as just described provides at least one historical reason for abandoning the Constitution, and the procedures used to draft and ratify the document provide another. In both instances elitist interests were served.

Arbitrary Procedures The Convention delegates acted arbitrarily from the very beginning. When they first met—in secret—they violated the stated purpose of the convention by not considering revisions of the Articles of Confederation, as they had been mandated to do. Rather, they focused on the Virginia Plan, which aimed to create a totally new governmental structure.

And, after they had created this new government, the delegates violated the ratification procedure they were supposed to follow. Instead of referring the new document to the state legislatures, they provided for special state constitutional conventions; approval by nine of these (out of thirteen) would establish the new government. It should be noted that the only state whose legislature was controlled by the debtor classes—Rhode Island—did not send delegates to the Constitutional Convention. It was also the last to ratify the new Constitution, and it did so by the narrowest margin (two votes) of any state.

Only an estimated 160,000 out of 4 million citizens voted on the new charter. This was no more than 5 percent of the population. Two leading speakers for the middle class, Richard Henry Lee and Patrick Henry, opposed ratification, because they felt that the Constitution disregarded middle- and lower-class interests. It could not be said that the American Constitution was adopted by what we would call democratic procedures in which the majority of citizens participated. Should we continue to be governed by a document that was undemocratically adopted?

THE CONSTITUTION DISTORTED

As to politics, we have no past, no future. After forty-four years of existence under the present Constitution, what single principle is fixed? . . . We are as much afloat at sea as the day when the Constitution went into operation.—*Henry Clay*

It is already evident that the Constitution was never intended to be a democratic document. It benefited the wealthy and allowed for little direct popular participation. And since its ratification, the Constitution has been warped in undemocratic ways, supposedly to make the document more democratic.

Especially in the twentieth century, conscious and determined efforts have been made to change the intent of the Founders without actually amending the Constitution. This alteration occurred in an effort to use the government as a planning agent for social welfare purposes. New Deal economist Rexford Guy Tugwell put it this way:

> The intention of the eighteenth and nineteenth century law was to install and protect the principle of conflict; this [principle], if we begin to plan, we shall be changing once for all, and it will require the laying of rough, unholy hands on many a sacred precedent, doubtless calling on an enlarged and nationalized police power for enforcement. We shall also have to give up a distinction of great consequence, and very dear to

a legalistic heart, but economically quite absurd, between private and public or quasi-public employments. There is no private business, if by that we mean one of no consequence to anyone but its proprietors; and so none exempt from compulsion to serve a planned public interest.[5]

Some years later, reflecting on delays in achieving this objective, Tugwell stated: "Organization for these purposes was very inefficient because they were not acknowledged intentions. Much of the lagging reluctance was owed to the constantly reiterated intention that what was being done was in pursuit of the aims embodied in the Constitution of 1787 when obviously it was in contravention of them."[6]

What Americans have done is to change the meaning of the Constitution's very words. Justice Felix Frankfurter, for example, said that words in the Constitution are "so restricted by their intrinsic meaning or by their history or by tradition or by prior decisions that they leave the individual justice free, if indeed they do not compel him, to gather meaning not from reading the Constitution but from reading life."[7] Justice Oliver Wendell Holmes made much the same point: "When we are dealing with words that also are a constituent act, like the Constitution of the United States, we must realize that they have called into life a being the development of which could not have been foreseen by the most gifted of its begetters."[8] This point of view has led to substantial changes in interpretation which substantially increased the power of the national government in relation to that of the states.

In 1936, the Supreme Court declared that the "general welfare" clause of Article I, Section 8, permitted Congress to appropriate funds for just about any purpose it chose. As the Court put it: "The power of Congress to authorize expenditure of public moneys for public purposes is not limited by the direct grants of legislative power found in the Constitution."[9]

In 1937, "interstate commerce" (Article I, Section 8) was defined as anything that substantially affects the flow of interstate business, whether or not it actually crosses state lines.[10]

In 1942 the Court held that the national government could regulate a product even if the producer did not intend to sell it, because the product could still affect interstate commerce. If a producer keeps what he or she produces, substitute products are not necessary, and interstate commerce is therefore affected.[11]

More recently, the clauses of the Fourteenth Amendment guaranteeing "equal protection of the laws" and "due process of law" have been used with increasing frequency to establish national regulation in matters dealing with education and criminal law. These subjects had for over 175 years been within the jurisdiction of the states.

Although the Founders wanted to strengthen the national government in relation to the states, they still envisioned a national government with limited powers. As James Madison observed in No. 45 of *The Federalist:*

> The powers delegated by the proposed Constitution to the federal government are few and defined. Those which are to remain in the state government are numerous and indefinite. The former will be exercised principally on external objects, as war, peace, negotiation, and foreign commerce; with which last the power of taxation will, for the most part, be connected. The powers reserved to the several states will extend to all the objects which, in the ordinary course of affairs, concern the lives, liberties, and properties of the people, and the internal order, improvement, and prosperity of the state.[12]

Ironically, we now have a Constitution which was (1) drafted and ratified in an undemocratic manner by upper-class persons to insure that the document satisfied their interests, and (2) changed in an undemocratic manner, i.e., by redefining the meaning of the Constitution's language without popular approval by constitutional amendment, thus increasing the power of the national government beyond the intentions of the Founders. Whether one likes the Constitution as it has now been interpreted and the national government's powers as expanded should not be the issue. Rather, the issue is that the basic document of government should, if the United States is a democracy, be the result of the people's action. The Constitution was not drafted by a cross section of the American public, and it has not been changed by a cross section. A Constitutional Convention should be called to allow the people to abandon the present Constitution and to propose a new one which is more ideally suited to the last quarter of the twentieth century.

AN IMPEDIMENT TO CHANGE

For the much slower and less sophisticated society of the eighteenth and nineteenth centuries, the American Constitution might have been excellent. But now, in a time of complex social and economic problems and international crises, the government it set up simply impedes progress. In 1790, the thirteen states had a population of 3,929,214, but in 1977, the population of the fifty states was approximately 215,000,000. There are more people today in New York City alone than there were in the entire United States in 1790. Population per square mile in 1790 was 4.5 while in 1977 it was about 60. From three small departments in 1790, the executive branch of the national government has increased to twelve departments and numerous agencies and commissions.

We have inherited from our forefathers a governmental structure which so divides power that effective dealing with economic problems is cumbersome. Local, state, and national governments each have their responsibility in housing and urban renewal, in the appropriate uses of water, in transportation, labor-management relations, and education. . . . At each level, the responsibility for appropriate action is divided between the executive and the legislature, and the judiciary is prepared to step in at a moment's notice to declare unconstitutional whatever notion the other two may decide upon.[13]

The separation of powers between the president and Congress is just one factor that slows down and often prevents implementation of necessary reforms. Public policy becomes the product of dispute and delay rather than the timely result of efficient planning. During the Nixon and Ford administrations, for example, the executive branch was controlled by the Republicans, the legislature by Democrats. Major proposals of these two presidents met strong resistance from Congress, and vice versa. Although an acute energy shortage confronted the nation, effective governmental policy could not be established for an extraordinarily long period of time due to partisan conflict. When Nixon proposed a major reform of government welfare programs and a far-reaching overhaul of the government bureaucracy, Congress resisted. Despite many major tax reform proposals made by several leading organizations, the tax structure remained basically the same.

Another difficulty is the existence of many units of government throughout the United States—state, county, and municipal. Developing a solution to a major national domestic problem typically requires coordination with many units of government, and this is frequently difficult to achieve.

Inefficient American government cannot take proper advantage of the planning potential afforded us by modern technology. Although the United States has had extraordinary success in the space program, the efficiency and technology of space exploration have not been applied to solving the problems of railroad transportation, the postal service, and inadequate public housing. Citizens suffer from train delays, inadequate mail service, and unfinished public housing projects. The national government finds it ever more difficult to act swiftly and efficiently to solve these and other more serious problems. The Constitution, therefore, should be abandoned in a manner befitting its inception.

What a truly glorious revolution our first constitutional one was . . . a peaceful, constitutional revolution of a fundamentally political nature! The theory was that a new political structure was necessary, one that would reorganize and strengthen the emerging economic structure, one that needed a pragmatically planned polity to succor and nourish it. The general theory worked for a time, but enough special parts have broken down that people feel frustrated about the effectiveness of political systems in general. Nonetheless, the theory is sound—what is needed is a new model with modern components.

So, I believe we once again need an "era" devoted to conceiving, discussing, and organizing for fundamental political change . . . nonviolent, discursive, and without nostalgia or reverence for institutions already existent in America or anywhere else. . . .[14]

The Negative Case

No, the Constitution should not be abandoned.

As you know, we hear frequent charges nowadays that the form of government provided by the Constitution is inappropriate to the needs of modern times. All of the three basic concepts embodied in that document— constitutionalism, federalism, and separation of powers—are thought by many to be outmoded means of carrying on affairs in the twentieth century when all governments must be "crisis governments" in order to survive. I, for one, emphatically do not believe that. I believe the deficiencies in our governmental structure result, not from adherence to the notion of federalism and separation of power, but rather from departure from them.[15]—Sam Ervin

Here was the document into which the Founding Fathers had poured their wisdom as into a vessel; the Fathers themselves grew ever larger in stature as they receded from view; the era in which they lived and fought became a Golden Age; in that age there had been a fresh dawn for the world, and its men were giants against the sky; what they had fought for was abstracted from its living context and became a set of "principles," eternally true and universally applicable.—*Max Lerner*

To say that the American Constitution should be jettisoned is to overlook the enormous gains in democracy that have occurred in American government and society in the two hundred years of its operation. In answer to the affirmative case, let us consider these points:

- The Constitution had republican, not elitist, foundations—thus providing the basis for representative democracy.
- By remaining silent on several issues, the Constitution has not burdened succeeding generations with principles that should not be in a nation's basic and fundamental charter of government.
- The Constitution demonstrated its relevance to each generation by the stability it affords through its flexibility.

FOUNDATIONS FOR DEMOCRACY

The motives of the Founders really are not relevant to the 1970s. Even if their motives were elitist and even if they acted to protect class interests, many of the Constitution's provisions have since been used to pro-

"There It Is, Just The Way It Came Off The Founding Fathers' Typewriter"

from Herblock Special Report (W. W. Norton & Co., Inc. 1974)

tect the interests of the middle and lower classes. For example, the very fact that the Constitution forbade the abolition of slavery until after 1808 was an implied invitation to abolish it and probably served to encourage the abolitionist forces after that date. Also the national supremacy clause contained in Article VI as well as the "necessary and proper" clause in Article I, Section 8, Clause 18, have helped the national government to act in preventing racial abuses, in providing financial aid to underprivileged school children, and in many other ways. Since the Constitution and the laws and treaties made pursuant to it are the supreme law of the land, actions of the national government have precedence over actions of state and local governments. Similarly, since Congress can "make all Laws which shall be necessary and proper for carrying into Execution" its enumerated powers in Article I, Section 8, the national government has very wide latitude in determining the issues and problems it can address. For example, in forbidding racial discrimination in interstate transportation, the national government has relied on the "necessary and proper" clause to execute its specific power of regulating interstate commerce.

But did the Founders represent only elite interests? Constitutional scholar Forrest McDonald states that, of the fifty-five delegates, no more than a dozen "clearly acted according to the dictates of their personal economic interests." McDonald concludes that Charles Beard's thesis is "impossible to justify." [16] Another constitutional scholar, Robert E. Brown, declares that "we would be doing a grave injustice to the political sagacity of the Founding Fathers if we assumed that property or personal gain was their only motive." [17] For example, George Mason—a wealthy Virginian who, in keeping with his economic interests, should have supported a strong central government—opposed it. On the other hand, Alexander Hamilton, who was far from wealthy, fervently supported powerful national authority.

Was the Constitution undemocratic because it was drafted in secrecy? Public meetings are not necessarily more democratic than secret ones. At any rate, the emphasis on open meetings, largely a product of the 1960s and 1970s, did not characterize the formative period of American government. Moreover, the Founders did debate at length and vote on what the new government should be like.

Did the Founders violate their expressed mandate to revise the Articles of Confederation? Yes, but certainly the result was preferable to the Articles.

Did the Founders violate the requirements of the Articles of Confederation by not submitting the proposed document to the state legislatures? Yes, but the state legislatures were more likely to have opposed the new document because it took power away from the states. State ratifying conventions gave the new Constitution greater legitimacy because the delegates were chosen expressly to consider the proposed document. The convention established a broad popular base of support for the Constitution.

Were the masses prevented from voting to choose delegates to these state ratifying conventions? Hardly! Of the adult white male population, Robert E. Brown shows that property qualifications kept barely more than 5 percent of them from voting. According to his analysis, most adult white males were farmers who owned land and were therefore eligible to vote. Though voter turnout was light, indicating that "the Constitution was adopted with a great show of indifference," [18] small farmers had the numerical strength to defeat the document if they had opposed it. Their failure to vote may be interpreted as passive support rather than active opposition. There is clearly no reason to abandon the Constitution because of the Founders' motives or actions.

Historic Significance   Standing out as a landmark in the growth and extension of democracy, the American Constitution embodies principles strikingly at variance with those animating most European governments in the late eighteenth century. As shown in Table 1, government and society in the United States had made significant advances.

These basic differences, of course, did not just happen; they evolved from the Americans' English heritage and colonial experiences. First, there was the political theory of John Locke, which emphasized man's natural rights. These rights, Locke argued, were more basic and fundamental than government itself, and indeed existed before government did. All people were free, equal, and independent, according to Locke, and could not be governed by others, unless they gave their consent.[19] Locke thus conceived of government as limited, an institution created by people who agreed through what he called a "social contract" (which the Constitution was).

Locke also advocated a separation or balancing of powers, with authority divided among different branches of government. This idea was also advanced by the French philosopher the Baron de Montesquieu, who had substantial influence among the men who drafted the American Constitution.

Power is always abused when unlimited and unbalanced. . . . Simple unchecked government is always despotic, whether it be government by a monarch, by aristocrats, or by the mass of people. All are equally intolerant, cruel, bloody, oppressive, tyrannical. The only sound and lasting government is one so balanced that ambition is made to counteract ambition, power to check power. . . . The executive and the legislative powers are natural rivals; and if each has not an effectual control over the other, the weaker will ever be the lamb in the paws of the wolf. The nation which will not adopt an equilibrium of power must adopt a despotism. There is no other alternative.—*John Adams*

Table 1. Government and Society in the Late Eighteenth Century

	UNITED STATES	CONTINENTAL EUROPE
Type of Government	Republic	Hereditary monarchy with a privileged nobility
Basis of Governmental Authority	Consent of the governed	Divine right of kings
Social Structure	Fluid: Belief in equality of citizens who possessed "certain inalienable rights"	Fixed: Rigid caste system

From their earliest days in America, the colonists gave ample indication of their belief in law and representative government. The Mayflower Compact (1620), drafted and signed by the Pilgrims before they landed at Plymouth, declared that "we ... do by Presents, solemnly and mutualy in the Presence of God and one another, covenant and combine ourselves together into a civil Body Politick." This document is important as a covenant establishing civil government by common consent. In 1619 settlers at Jamestown created the first representative assembly in America, the Virginia House of Burgesses. In 1639 New England Puritans drafted America's first written constitution, the Fundamental Orders of Connecticut. Another early document, the Massachusetts Body of Liberties (1641), guaranteed such rights as trial by jury and due process of law.

An additional factor in the democratic development of the Constitution was colonial government. Although the thirteen colonies were set up and ruled in various ways, they had certain elements in common. Each had a written charter, which established the form of government and the rights of the colonists. Each colonial government had executive, legislative, and judicial branches. Several of the legislatures were bicameral, and in two colonies the people elected members of the legislature.

There was a form of judicial appeal, in that decisions of colonial courts could generally be appealed to the Privy Council in London. Also, several colonies had bills of rights to protect their citizens. At least six characteristics of colonial government found their way into the United States Constitution: (1) the idea of a written document spelling out government functions and citizens' rights; (2) separation of powers; (3) a bicameral legislature; (4) elections; (5) judicial appeal; and (6) a bill of rights.

The paradox of the American Revolution is that the colonists generally rebelled because they felt that their rights as English subjects were being denied. To support their contention, they turned to such British legal landmarks as the Magna Carta, the Habeas Corpus Act of 1679, and the Bill of Rights of 1689. Numerous ideas in the American Declaration of Independence, the Constitution, and the Bill of Rights had their origin in English history. Of course, the whole English common law system—the cumulative body of law as expressed in judicial decisions and custom—influenced Americans, especially as it was conceived as a limitation on the power of the king.

Certainly, democracy as we know it today did not exist in colonial America. But, as compared with other governments of the eighteenth century, that established by the American Constitution was democratic.

Sharing Power Did the Founders allocate power through the Constitution only to benefit those of wealth and substance? Far from it. The Constitution utilizes both the concept of *federalism—division of power* between the national and state governments—and *separation of powers*—the checks and balances existing among the three branches of the national government. In reality, the term *shared powers* is more accurate. Power is neither completely divided nor completely separated. Both the national and state governments have some powers in common, such as taxation, road construction, and education. And within the national government, overlap exists among the executive, legislative, and judicial branches, even though they are independent of each other. For example, while the president can veto acts of Congress, the latter can refuse to confirm presidential nominations. Congress has the power to declare war, but the president is the commander in chief.

The average American benefits from these many centers of governmental power because they allow *multiple access points* to government. That is, a citizen may work to influence government or redress grievances through national, state, and local governments and through either the executive, legislative, or judicial branches. To illustrate, the National Association for the Advancement of Colored People (NAACP) has worked through the courts at local, state, and national levels as well as through the legislative and executive branches at all three levels of government. Its earliest successes were in the national judicial branch before the U.S. Supreme Court (see Chapter 4 for a discussion), but more recently it has been successful in influencing other "access points."

THE VIRTUES OF SILENCE

One of the singular virtues of the Constitution was its silence on several important issues. If provisions dealing with these had been written into the document, they might have damaged it irreparably, either in the process of obtaining ratification or in adapting to changes in later years. Some of these issues represented conscious decisions by the Founders. Others they simply did not consider.

A Bill of Rights The framers have been faulted for not including a bill of rights in the original Constitution. Their neglect, however, should not be interpreted simply as a conscious desire to strengthen government at the expense of individuals. For one thing, the issue of a bill of rights was not raised until near the end of the Convention, when the document had largely assumed its final form. Delegates were not inclined to launch into a new debate at that late stage, a debate that might

What promise this nation could realize if we all believed, without hint of doubt, that the words of the Constitution and the Bill of Rights mean precisely what they say and apply equally to every man of us, rich or poor, peasant or president, black or white, Northerner or Southerner—no matter how contemptible, untidy, or nonconformist either his thoughts or his appearance. This is the law of our land, and in its great fundamentals is the foundation of our past and our future.—*Walter Cronkite*

torpedo the successes already achieved during the Convention. In addition, to many of the delegates—well aware that eight of the thirteen states already had bills of rights with provisions like freedom of speech and press—it seemed superfluous to add another one to the national Constitution.

Parties, Conventions, and Primaries   The Constitution is totally silent on this whole matter, an oversight that might be considered rather serious in view of the important role played by political parties in our nation's political life. But this neglect allowed parties to develop and change without undue constitutional restrictions. Several of the framers were ill disposed toward what they called "factions." Given this attitude, constitutional regulation of parties might have made it exceedingly difficult for them to survive. It is difficult to imagine our nation without parties today. In many respects, they are the glue that holds the constitutional framework together.

The Cabinet   Another political institution not specifically established in the Constitution is the cabinet. Once again, silence reveals the virtue of keeping the document general rather than burdening it with precise and specific guidelines. The cabinet and the executive departments have grown as new problems emerged in American history. For example, no one in 1787 could have foreseen the need for a Department of Housing and Urban Development, a Department of Transportation, or a Department of Energy. During the last two decades, however, urban problems, traffic congestion, and the energy shortage became critical issues. And it made sense to incorporate these departments into the cabinet.

Slavery   Critics have leveled volleys of disapproval at the Founders for their failure to abolish slavery. All they did was to forbid Congress to abolish the slave trade until 1808. As a matter of human rights, their action was clearly wrong. In the interest of creating a nation and adopting a constitution, however, their action was clearly right. To have taken a position against slavery would have insured opposition to the proposed document in the six southern states—enough to defeat the Constitution. Although many delegates wanted to abolish slavery, they chose to be guided by political practicality.

Power of the National Government   The Constitution did not clearly define the scope of the national government's power. As a result, central authority has grown with changing circumstances, especially during times of national and international crises. During the Great Depression of the 1930s and also in wartime, presidential powers have been enlarged. President Franklin D. Roosevelt was given extraordinary powers by Congress to combat the depression and to conduct World War II. Other presidents like Harry Truman, John Kennedy, Lyndon Johnson, and Richard Nixon have either exercised or sought to expand these powers.

The national government received a major increase in power when the graduated income tax was approved by ratification of the Sixteenth Amendment in 1913. This amendment allowed the national government to have greater financial resources to accomplish projects on a national scale that the states were unable to do either individually or collectively. Most states, until the last ten to twenty years, have relied on taxes that do not respond as directly to economic growth as does the graduated income tax; hence, the national government has been able to assist state and local governments in solving some of their problems by providing them with needed programs and revenue. (See Chapter 3 for a discussion.)

The Supreme Court   As with the rest of the national government, so too with the Supreme Court—its precise limits were not defined, but left to history and circumstance to determine. As it turned out, John Marshall quickly extended the scope of the highest court's authority. As early as 1803, he exercised the concept of judicial review when he said: "It is emphatically the province and duty of the judicial department to say what the law is. . . . . A law repugnant to the Constitution is void." [20] (For additional discussion of judicial review, see Chapter 12.)

In all these six instances, what we might call inaudible signals show how valuable it is to be governed by a document of general principles. With the passage of time, the Constitution could adapt to a changing nation without severe problems. The Constitution provided a framework; time and circumstance have filled in the details.

When the states were powerless to regulate the railroads effectively in the late 1800s, Congress established the Interstate Commerce Commission to provide for uniform national regulation of an industry that affects all states. During the Great Depression of the 1930s when state and local governments were unable to cope with the enormous problems of relief administration, the national government acted to provide a unifying national approach to solving problems. Because it has allowed the national government to act effectively in critical situations, the Constitution's silence has been a good thing.

PROGRESS THROUGH FLEXIBILITY

The preeminent virtue of the Constitution is that it created the framework through which democracy could grow and mature. The Constitution did not straitjacket history by imposing the governmental and social forms of the late eighteenth century on the decades to come. Writing in 1819, Chief Justice John Marshall stated that the Constitution was "intended to endure for ages to come and, consequently, to be adapted to the various crises of human affairs." [21] Considering that the Constitution has withstood a civil war, two world wars, and a host of political, economic, and social changes, it has more than proved its worth as an effective instrument of government. The key is stability through flexibility—the ability to adapt to changing circumstances. Flexibility has been achieved partly through outright silence (as already discussed) and, even more importantly, through amendment and changed interpretation of the Constitution.

Recognizing that the Constitution would probably require some adaptation to changing circumstances, the framers devised an amendment process consisting of two ways of proposing and two ways of rati-

The amendment process allows the Constitution to adapt to changing needs and circumstances. Many people today are working for the passage of a twenty-seventh amendment, known as the Equal Rights Amendment (ERA), that would guarantee total equality for women under the law. However, the amendment cannot be ratified until it has been accepted by the legislatures of three quarters of the states.

fying an amendment. An amendment may be proposed by (a) a vote of two thirds of both houses of Congress or (b) a national convention called by Congress at the request of two thirds of the state legislatures. An amendment may be ratified by (a) legislatures in three fourths of the states or (b) ratifying conventions in three fourths of the states.

All existing amendments have been proposed by the first method. All but one—the Twenty-first—have been ratified by state legislatures.

There has been only one serious attempt to propose an amendment by a national convention. This was Senator Everett Dirksen's effort to overturn the Supreme Court's "one-man, one-vote" ruling for the redistricting of state legislative bodies. He encouraged states to petition Congress to call a constitutional convention. Between 1963 and 1970, thirty-three states (just one short of the two thirds necessary) did so. The Dirksen proposal died, however, mainly because six of the petitions contained procedural problems that made their legal status uncertain. In addition, some legal scholars and senators warned that a convention might open the entire Constitution to wholesale recommendations for change.

The fact that only twenty-six amendments have been added to the Constitution in close to two hundred years is a tribute to the basic document's versatility. These twenty-six amendments can be divided into three categories: early remedial amendments, Civil War amendments, and twentieth-century amendments.

Early Remedial Amendments It was evident soon after the Constitutional Convention ended that a bill of rights had to be added, or at least promised, in order to obtain the necessary support for ratification. The first ten amendments—the Bill of Rights—together with Amendments Eleven and Twelve are thus considered remedial; that is, they were designed to remedy deficiencies in the original document.

The Bill of Rights, ratified in 1791, was devised to protect American citizens against the power of the national government. It guaranteed, among other things, freedom of speech, religion, the press, and assembly; protection against "unreasonable searches and seizures"; and the right not to be deprived of life, liberty, or property "without due process of law." (For a full discussion of the Bill of Rights, see Chapter 4.)

Two other remedial amendments were ratified soon after the Bill of Rights. The Eleventh (1798) declared it illegal for a state to be sued in the federal courts by a citizen of another state or foreign nation. The Twelfth Amendment (1804) provided that presidential electors vote for president and vice-president separately; this resulted from the disputed election of 1800, when the House of Representatives had to choose between Thomas Jefferson and Aaron Burr, who had both received the same number of electoral votes for president.

Civil War Amendments   After the Civil War, three amendments protected the rights of the newly freed slaves. The Thirteenth Amendment (1865) forbade slavery in the United States and its territories. The Fourteenth Amendment (1868) made slaves citizens. It contained two clauses—relating to "due process" and "equal protection"—that were to have far-reaching effects in the field of civil liberties (see Chapter 4).

The Fifteenth Amendment (1870) precluded either the federal or state governments from denying the right to vote "on account of race, color, or previous condition of servitude."

Twentieth-Century Amendments   Three types of amendments have been ratified in the twentieth century: those relating to public policy, those extending democratic procedures, and those that refined and perfected the structure of the Constitution.

1. Public policy amendments consist of the Sixteenth (1913), allowing Congress to pass a graduated income tax; the Eighteenth (1919), enacting prohibition; and the Twenty-first (1933), repealing prohibition.
2. Democratic procedure amendments—the Seventeenth, Nineteenth, Twenty-third, Twenty-fourth, and Twenty-sixth—all have to do with voting. The Seventeenth (1913) provided for direct election of senators. The Nineteenth, Twenty-third, and Twenty-sixth extended suffrage to women (1920), to residents of the District of Columbia (1961), and to persons over eighteen (1971), and the Twenty-fourth abolished the poll tax as a requirement for voting in federal elections (1964).
3. Structural changes have been enacted in the Twentieth, Twenty-second, and Twenty-fifth Amendments. The Twentieth (1933) changed the terms of office for president and vice-president, while the Twenty-second (1951) limits presidents to two terms. The Twenty-fifth Amendment (1967) establishes the procedure to be followed in the event of presidential disability.

These amendments, relatively few in number, have generally broadened democracy. They have demonstrated the Constitution's adaptability to a changing society—from rural to urban, from agricultural to industrial, and from a government dominated by the legislature to one dominated by the executive.

The Constitution has demonstrated its relevance through adapting to economic and social changes. Before abandoning or replacing the Constitution, there should be clear indications that it inhibits or precludes meaningful changes, especially those that broaden democracy.

Since the Constitution is a flexible instrument, tailored to meet the needs of each generation, there is no need to replace it.

The legislative and executive branches may sometimes err, but elections and dependence will bring them to rights.—*Thomas Jefferson*

Glossary

Bicameral: a type of legislature consisting of two houses.

Bill of attainder: a legislative act punishing an individual without a trial.

Division of power: governmental power divided between national and state governments.

Ex post facto law: a law punishing an individual for an act that was not a crime when committed.

Federalism: division of power between the national and state governments.

Jurisdiction: the limits or the territory within the authority of a governmental agency or a court.

Multiple access points: availability to citizens of many levels of state and local government plus the three branches of the national government, allowing for redress of grievance or opportunity to influence government.

Separation of powers: the division of constitutional authority among the legislative, executive, and judicial branches of the national government.

Shared powers: constitutional provisions for interaction and sharing of functions among the three branches of the national government.

Unicameral: a type of legislature consisting of one house.

Writ of habeas corpus: a judicial document directing an officer holding a suspect to show adequate grounds for holding that person.

Notes

1. Edward Dumbauld, ed., *The Political Writings of Thomas Jefferson* (Indianapolis, Ind.: Bobbs-Merrill, 1955), pp. 123–124.

2. Carl Van Doren, *The Great Rehearsal* (New York: Viking Press, 1948), p. 153.

3. Abraham Lincoln, First Inaugural Address.

4. Charles A. Beard, *An Economic Interpretation of the Constitution of the United States* (New York: Macmillan, 1960), p. 188.

5. Rexford Guy Tugwell, quoted in Howard Zinn, ed., *New Deal Thought* (Indianapolis, Ind.: Bobbs-Merrill, 1966), p. 89.

6. Rexford Guy Tugwell, "Rewriting the Constitution," *The Center Magazine*, publication of the Center for the Study of Democratic Institutions, I, 3 (March 1968).

7. Felix Frankfurter quoted in Carl Brent Swisher, *The Growth of Constitutional Power in the United States* (Chicago: University of Chicago Press, 1963), p. 77.

8. Oliver Wendell Holmes, quoted in Alpheus T. Mason, *The Supreme Court from Taft to Warren* (New York: Norton, 1964), p. 15.

9. *United States* v. *Butler* (1936).

10. *National Labor Relations Board* v. *Jones and Laughlin Corp.* (1937).

11. *Wickard* v. *Filburn* (1942).

12. Henry Cabot Lodge, ed., *The Federalist* (New York: G. P. Putnam's Sons, 1902), p. 290.

13. Joseph S. Clark, *Challenges to Democracy* (New York: Praeger, 1964), pp. 104–105.

14. Theodore L. Becker, "An Invitation to Debate a Constitutional Revolution," *Intellect* 104 (February 1976):357.

15. Quoted in Bill M. Wise, *The Wisdom of Sam Ervin* (New York: Balantine Books, 1973), p. 45.

16. Forrest McDonald, *We the People* (Chicago: University of Chicago Press, 1958), pp. vii, 350, 415.

17. Robert E. Brown, *Charles Beard and the Constitution* (Princeton, N.J.: Princeton University Press, 1956), p. 198.

18. Ibid., pp. 170, 197.

19. Peter Laslett, ed., *Locke's Two Treatises of Government* (New York: Cambridge University Press, 1960), p. 348.

20. *Marbury* v. *Madison* (1803).

21. *McCulloch* v. *Maryland* (1819).

Recommended Rebuttal Reading

On the Constitution's History

Becker, Carl L. *The Declaration of Independence.* New York: Alfred A. Knopf, 1942.

Boorstin, Daniel J. *The Americans: The Colonial Experience.* New York: Random House, 1958.

Corwin, Edward S. *The Constitution and What It Means Today,* rev. by Harold W. Chase and Craig R. Ducat. Princeton, N. J.: Princeton University Press, 1973.

Farrand, Max. *The Framing of the Constitution.* New Haven, Conn.: Yale University Press, 1926.

Lipset, Martin. *The First Nation.* New York: Basic Books, 1963.

Rossiter, Clinton. *The Grand Convention.* New York: Macmillan, 1966.

Founders: Democrats or Elitists?

Beard, Charles A. *An Economic Interpretation of the Constitution of the United States.* New York: Macmillan, 1913.

Brown, Robert E. *Charles A. Beard and the Constitution: A Critical Analysis of AN ECONOMIC INTERPRETATION OF THE CONSTITUTION.* Princeton, N. J.: Princeton University Press, 1956.

Etzkowitz, Henry, and Peter Schwab, eds. *Is America Necessary? Conservative, Liberal and Socialist Perspectives of United States Political Institutions.* St. Paul, Minn.: West, 1976.

Roche, John P. "The Founding Fathers: A Reform Caucus in Action." *American Political Science Review* 61(December 1961):799–816.

What Is Constitutionalism?

Locke, John. *The Second Treatise of Civil Government,* ed. J. W. Gough. London: Oxford University Press, 1946.

Sartori, Giovanni. "Constitutionalism: A Preliminary Discussion." *American Political Science Review* 62(December 1962):853–864.

Vile, M. C. J. *Constitutionalism and the Separation of Powers.* New York: Oxford University Press, 1967.

AT ISSUE: FEDERALISM

THE AFFIRMATIVE CASE   THE NEGATIVE CASE

Harmful Conflicts   Harmony Through
  States' Rightists Versus   Flexibility
    Nationalists   Balancing Concurrent
  Interstate Confusion   Powers
  Business Versus Labor   Resolving Differences
  Conservatives Versus   Unity Amidst Diversity
    Liberals
  "Symmetry" Versus
    "Asymmetry"

State Weaknesses   State and Local Successes
  Regional Elites   Innovative Programs and
  Inadequacies and   Policies
    Inequities of National   Compacts
    Aid   Federal Aid

An Outdated Survival   A Valuable Tradition

RESOLVED THAT: Federalism Should Be Abolished

3

At Issue: Federalism

Is American federalism sacrosanct? Is there some special reason for the United States to retain it? Who gains, who loses power in our federal system? Does federalism advance or retard the welfare of the whole nation? Has contemporary federalism changed substantially from that envisioned by the framers of the Constitution? Does it enhance or impede democracy?

Before considering these questions, we must consider what federalism really is. Here we must distinguish among three forms of government.

1. A *federal* form of government divides governmental powers between a central (or national) government and constituent (or state) governments in a manner that provides each with substantial power and functions. The United States, Canada, Switzerland, India, Mexico, and Australia are among the nations with a federal form of government.
2. A *unitary* form of government places all governmental power in the central government. Subordinate units of government exist and have power only if the central government permits it. Among the nations with a unitary form of government are Great Britain, France, West Germany, Israel, and the Philippines.
3. A *confederation*, such as the American government under the Articles of Confederation, has a central government, but it exists only at

In the end, the Constitution emerged with no real clues as to what was in the framers' minds as they voted on the several resolutions before them or how they expected the federal system they had brought into being to work in practice. The reasons the framers avoided what now seems to be such a vital question are not hard to imagine. The very necessity for compromise in getting the Constitution drawn up and promulgated virtually ruled out an exhaustive excursion into theory. The framers were agreed on the need for a limited government; they saw the possibilities of federalism in this connection. But they also saw the dangers of going beyond that point of general agreement into the thicket of theoretical niceties which lay just on the other side. So they avoided theoretical considerations and advanced in their place the more utilitarian matter of preserving the union.— *Richard H. Leach*

the sufferance of the constituent governments. It is they who delegate certain limited authority to the national government.

The United States Constitution grants powers exclusively to the national government* in the first three articles. Many of these are *express powers*—those specifically enumerated. In addition there are *implied powers*—those inferred from the "elastic" clause of Article I, Section 8, which gives Congress the right "to make all Laws which shall be necessary and proper for carrying into Execution the foregoing Powers, and all other Powers vested . . . in the Government of the United States." A third category is composed of *inherent powers*—certain powers the national government may exercise in foreign affairs. Because the United States is a nation, it necessarily follows that the national government has powers inherent in guiding the country's foreign policy and international relations: declaring war, making treaties, and appointing and receiving ambassadors.

Some powers belong to both the national and state governments. These *concurrent powers* include the right to levy taxes and to borrow money. States may exercise these powers as long as there is no conflict with the national law.

To the states belong *reserved powers* that are theirs alone. These include the right to regulate local governments and to maintain the public health, welfare, safety, and morals. Such powers, however, cannot be used to frustrate or impede legitimate national government policies.

Constitutional safeguards of individual rights guaranteed in the Bill of Rights and by the Thirteenth, Fourteenth, Fifteenth, Nineteenth, and Twenty-sixth Amendments generally apply with some exceptions to both national and state governments. For example, the Fourteenth Amendment applies principally to the states, which are required to guarantee "due process of law" and "equal protection of the laws" to all citizens.

The national government has certain constitutional obligations to the states. (1) It must guarantee each of them a republican form of government; by this the framers probably meant a form distinguished from a monarchy on one hand and a pure democracy on the other. Although its meaning is unclear, Congress enforces this provision when it permits a state's representatives to take their seats in Congress. (2) It must protect the states against domestic violence. At various times Congress, upon the request of proper state authorities, has delegated to the President the power to send troops to quell violence in a state.

---

* It is common practice—in this book as elsewhere—to refer to our national government as the federal government. In a strictly technical sense, this term subsumes the entire system of national plus state governments.

As for the states, each has three obligations to the others. (1) Under the "full faith and credit" clause (Article IV, Section 1), each state shall enforce the civil judgments of other states and accept their records and acts as valid. (2) Article IV, Section 2, guarantees "all privileges and immunities" to citizens of one state who find themselves in another state. This clause means that a state shall not deny to a citizen of another state the full protection of its laws, the right to engage in a peaceful occupation, or access to its courts. Nor may it tax citizens of other states at a discriminatory rate or otherwise arbitrarily interfere with their property. (3) The third obligation is *extradition*. The Constitution provides that a state shall deliver anyone charged with a crime to the state making the accusation, when requested to do so by the latter's governor.

Besides these three obligations, states are restricted in not being permitted to settle their differences by force. Disputes are to be settled by the Supreme Court or through an *interstate compact*—an agreement through which two or more states with a common interest or problem establish a legally binding relationship aimed at a common solution. Before an interstate compact becomes effective, it must be approved by Congress, after which its terms are enforceable by the Supreme Court.

The complex and diffused system of government provided by the American federal system poses many provocative questions.

- Can two separate sets of governments rule over the same citizens without constant conflicts over jurisdiction?
- Does the federal system allow local private interests to frustrate efforts to solve national problems?
- Does federal aid to state and local governments accomplish its purpose?

The Affirmative Case

Yes, federalism should be abolished.

To continue with the old pattern, in the age of giant capitalism, is to strike into impotence that volume of governmental power which is necessary to deal with the issues giant capitalism has raised. Federalism ... is the appropriate governmental technique for an expanding capitalism. ... But a contracting capitalism cannot afford the luxury of federalism. It is insufficiently positive in character; it does not provide for sufficient rapidity of action; it inhibits the

—[To all shrimpers holding South Carolina commercial shrimping licenses June 20, 1977] As many of you are aware, the precise boundary between the States of South Carolina and Georgia from the Savannah River eastward to the limits of the territorial seas is currently being disputed between the two states. ... Georgia state boats may attempt to interfere with or arrest any shrimping boats in the area which both states claim as their territory. The shrimping season has not yet begun in Georgia, and any shrimping boats seized by Georgia may be confiscated and sold under Georgia state law. Furthermore, the captain of any boat seized risks being found guilty of a misdemeanor and being assessed a fine. Although it is hoped that the presence of South Carolina state boats will dissuade the Georgia state boats from taking any action against any of you shrimping in the disputed area, the Georgia boats may still attempt to act. Regardless of the fact that you have shrimped in this area in the past, *do not risk bloodshed*. If a Georgia state boat attempts to stop you, *do not fire upon it* and *do not risk it firing at you*. The South Carolina state boats will do what they can to protect you, but *do not participate in any act of violence against the Georgia boats*. The officers manning the South Carolina boats have been instructed to avoid bloodshed and violence at all costs. ... Please be aware that although South Carolina state boats will try to protect the sovereignty of South Carolina waters down to the North Jetty (*not* all the way to the middle of the channel), we can *not* guarantee your safety or protection in that area. We will keep you advised of any future developments in this controversy.—*South Carolina Department of Wildlife and Marine Resources*

... there are also some *a priori* reasons to be skeptical about the truth of the assertion that federalism encourages freedom. There are, for example, a number of societies that keep a high degree of freedom without the use of federalism and, on the other hand, a number of federalisms simultaneously have been dictatorships. Local self-government and personal freedom both coexist with a highly centralized unitary government in Great Britain and the Vargas dictatorship in Brazil managed to coexist with federalism.—*William H. Riker*

emergence of necessary standards of uniformity; it relies upon compacts and compromises which take insufficient account of the urgent category of time; it leaves the backward areas a restraint, at once parasitic and poisonous, on those which seek to move forward; not least, its psychological results, especially in an age of crisis, are depressing to a democracy that needs the drama of positive achievement to retain its faith.[1]–Harold Laski

Next to the Constitution itself, federalism is probably more revered than any other aspect of American government. One distinguished scholar has stated that it was the ideal system for "the great enterprise of appropriating the North American continent to western civilization."[2]

As with the Constitution, Americans have a deeply ingrained belief that federalism is next to godliness. But should it be? A substantial case can be made that many of our problems today, and our failure to resolve them, can be attributed to federalism.

- Federalism has fostered conflicts that impede progress.
- The states, even with federal aid, have shown themselves to be incompetent.
- Federalism is an outdated survival of a tradition.

HARMFUL CONFLICTS

Because of federalism, the American system exhibits numerous, damaging conflicts—between the national government and the state governments, between and among state governments, and among interest groups with special ties to one level of government or another. State and municipal tax structures may be used to compete for business and industry. Certainly southern states and municipalities have used tax incentives to lure business and industry from northern states. Perhaps the most dramatic example of business and industrial loss has occurred in New York City and the state of New York. By providing more services for their citizens, taxes had to be increased. This cycle has led to a loss of business and industry to other states with lower taxes and fewer services for their people.

Federal legislation may also be used as a weapon in this warfare between states. For example, one of the reasons for passage of the first federal minimum wage law in 1938 was the desire of some New England states to keep wages of textile workers in the South as high as those in New England so that industry would not relocate from the Northeast to the South.

States' Rightists Versus Nationalists Those advocating the *states' rights* position, including such American leaders as Thomas Jefferson

and John C. Calhoun, contend that the Constitution is like a treaty among the states whereby they have joined to give the national government specific and very limited authority. States' rightists believe that the powers of the national government—a government they view as heavy-handed and bureaucratic—should be narrowly construed in order to protect the federal system. In conflicts between the national and state government, doubts should be resolved in favor of the latter. In the twentieth century, the states' rights position has been espoused by such persons as U.S. Senator Barry Goldwater (Rep. Ariz.) and Ronald Reagan, former governor of California.

States' rights advocates advance two main arguments in their cause. One rests on the Tenth Amendment, which reserves to the states those powers not delegated to the national government. The other argument holds that, since state government is closer to the people, it can reflect their wishes and desires more accurately than can the national government.

The nationalists, who have been represented historically by such men as John Marshall, Abraham Lincoln, Theodore Roosevelt, and Franklin Roosevelt, reject the idea that the Constitution is a compact among states. They contend that it is a compact among *people,* who drew up the Constitution and established the national government as their agent. Nationalists hold that the people intended the national government's powers to be broadly construed and not to be denied unless specifically prohibited by the Constitution.

As to Amendment Ten, present-day nationalists argue that it was limited by the Supreme Court's decision in *United States* v. *Darby* (1941). Taking a broad view of the national government's commerce power, the Court declared that the Tenth Amendment merely states "a truism that all is retained which has not been surrendered." [3] Countering the states' rights claim that states are closer to the people, nationalists note that each state can speak for only a limited number of people, while the national government can speak for all. A government representing only some of the people, nationalists argue, should not be able to restrain a government representing everyone.

The nationalist cause has been aided by several Supreme Court decisions, one of the most important of which was Chief Justice John Marshall's in the case of *McCulloch* v. *Maryland* (1819). Maryland had levied a tax against a branch of the Bank of the United States, and the bank's cashier had refused to pay it. Two questions were to be resolved: (1) Did Congress have the right to incorporate a bank? (2) Did Maryland have the right to tax it?

The government of the United States, represented by Daniel Webster and others, based its argument on Article I, Section 8, of the Constitution, giving Congress the right to pass laws "which shall be necessary and proper" to carry out powers expressly delegated to it. A bank, said the government, is an appropriate, convenient, and useful way to exercise the express powers of collecting taxes, borrowing money, and caring for the property of the United States. Nor, according to Webster, could a state use its powers (in this case, taxation) to interfere with the operations of the national government.

Speaking for the Supreme Court, Marshall declared:

> The government of the *Union* ·... is emphatically and truly a *government of the people.* In form and in substance it emanates from them, its powers are granted by them, and are to be exercised directly on them. ... A government, intrusted with such ample powers, on the due execution of which the happiness and prosperity of the nation so vitally depends, must also be intrusted with ample means for their execution. The power being given, it is the interest of the nation to facilitate its execution (emphasis supplied).[4]

Therefore, the Court ruled, Congress did have the right to incorporate the Bank of the United States. As for Maryland's taxing of the bank, Marshall—stating that "the power to tax involves the power to destroy"—declared the state's action unconstitutional. By stating that the Congress had the *implied* powers to borrow money and to regulate commerce, the Supreme Court stretched the actual wording of the Constitution. The *McCulloch* v. *Maryland* case is regarded as one of the cornerstones for interpreting the Constitution broadly.

To give just one example from more recent times: For many years, coastal states tried to establish their rights to seabeds abutting their territories, in order to obtain control over offshore oil resources. Despite Supreme Court rulings against California in 1947 and Louisiana in 1950, Maine and twelve other states on the Atlantic coast claimed seabed ownership from beyond the three-mile limit (which states already control) to the outer edge of the continental shelf. In 1975 the Court held unanimously that this region belongs to the federal government. "Under our constitutional arrangement paramount rights to the lands underlying the marginal sea are an incident to national sovereignty and ... their control and disposition in the first instance are the business of the federal government."[5]

The first major setback in forty years to the nationalist position occurred in the 1976 case of *National League of Cities* v. *Usery, California,* in which the Supreme Court held that Congress cannot tell states and cities how much they must pay their employees. In this case, the Court struck down the 1974 extension by Congress of federal minimum wage and overtime provisions to cover state and local government employees. Justice William H. Rehnquist said in the majority opinion of the Court that "if Congress may withdraw from the states the authority to make those fundamental employment decisions upon which their systems for performance of these functions must rest, we think there would be little left of the states' 'separate and independent existence.' "[6]

The Port Authority [New York-New Jersey] does not have the right to overrule the federally authorized trials for the Concorde [supersonic jet] at Kennedy Airport. ... The ban is in irreconcilable conflict with federal supremacy and must give way under the supremacy clause in the Constitution. Nullification of the federal review of the noise problem at Kennedy is not a prerogative of the Port Authority. ... Congress made clear the federal government's exclusive statutory responsibility for noise abatement through regulations of flight operation and aircraft design.—*Judge Milton Pollack*

[Judge Pollack's ruling] would convey to the people who are impacted by this decision the clear impression that the Port Authority, which has the responsibility to maintain noise and other environmental standards, is left without power and due process to carry out its important functions.—*New York Governor Hugh Carey*

Under the system of *dual federalism*, which existed before the late 1930s, the Supreme Court served as the arbiter between two centers of power—the states and the federal government. The states and the national government were viewed as having definite areas of responsibility in which each was autonomous. After 1937, however, the Supreme Court began to uphold a variety of national government programs in social welfare and public works that were previously within the principal jurisdiction of the states. This shift led to what has been described as a system of *cooperative federalism*, in which national and state governments tend to cooperate and share functions more than under dual federalism, which allowed conflict and competition. Whether under dual or cooperative federalism, the courts still must arbitrate disputes between national and state governments.

In the struggles between states' rightists and nationalists, the former have consistently lost ground since the 1930s, as the power of the national government has increased. (The states' rights position continues to be advanced, however—theoretically, in the classroom and the writings of conservative scholars, and practically, in lawsuits and other efforts by the states.) The constitutional basis for the growth of central authority rests primarily on three provisions: the war power, the power to regulate interstate and foreign commerce, and the power to tax and spend for the general welfare.

The war power is very different today from what it was in 1787—which is only to be expected in a world where total war and total destruction are possible. All manner of things, from the study of chemistry to the building of highways, may have a fairly direct relationship to warfare. The national government has funded scholarships in colleges through the National Defense Education Act and has developed the interstate highway system through the National Defense Highway Act.

The regulation of interstate and foreign commerce is a power with enormous implications in conflicts between the national and state governments. It has been used by the Supreme Court as the basis for declaring constitutional a wide range of laws. For instance, it is legal to regulate farmers' corn or wheat crops, even though they grow it only to feed their own families, because growing and using such products affects the price of these commodities in interstate commerce.[7] In another case, the court upheld a law forbidding discrimination in hotel or motel accommodations, because such discrimination affects the flow of interstate commerce.[8]

The power to tax and spend for the public welfare has been used, especially since the New Deal era, to uphold a variety of national government programs. These have ranged from local airports, hospitals, and sewage disposal facilities, to employment services, slum control, and urban renewal projects. Each program contains controls or guidelines the states must follow if they wish to use federal revenues. The Supreme Court ruled such programs constitutional as long as states were free to accept or reject the accompanying controls. Realistically, of course, states were forced to accept the controls, because not to do so would deny them "free" federal funds. The national government has had superior taxing ability, such as the income tax, to finance these programs. Only in recent years have most states begun to improve their taxing ability by adopting the income tax.

Conflicts between the national and state governments have produced some bizarre manifestations. In his 1967 book *Storm Over the States*, former North Carolina Governor Terry Sanford gives these examples. In Florida, a public health nurse financed from a special heart fund is not supposed to render aid to cancer and tuberculosis patients, even when they are in a household she is visiting. State law in Georgia allows government officials reimbursement for meals if they travel more than three hours away from their home base. The federal government, however, will not reimburse Civil Defense workers unless they travel over ten hours away. In New Mexico, public schools must keep two sets of books, one for the state agency that supervises federal funds, the other for a different state agency that oversees *all* educational funds.[9]

National-state conflicts, with a concomitant growth of the power of the national government, have also served to protect immoral and inhumane practices. Racial discrimination is a case in point. Writing in 1964, William H. Riker assessed the relationship between federalsim and racial discrimination.

> Clearly the relationship, if any, between federalism and freedom is not immediately clear and deserves further investigation. . . . At the present time in the United States (*i.e.*, from roughly 1954 to that future time, if it ever comes, when most Negroes have full citizen rights) the chief question of public morals is whether or not the national decision [*Brown* v. *Board of Education* (1954)] will be enforced. To those who wish to enforce it, the plea for states' rights or for maintaining the guarantees of federalism is simply a hypocritical plea for the special privilege to disregard the national majority and, of course, to permit one minority, segregationist Southern whites, to tyrannize over another minority, the Southern Negroes. When freedom is defined as the right of self-direction for majorities, then the assertion that federalism promotes freedom is simply a hypocritical falsehood.[10]

Although the racial problem has been partially resolved since Riker's 1964 analysis, the problem of federalism and freedom remains. Children growing up in a northern industrial state generally have excel-

National–state conflicts were evident after the Supreme Court ordered racial integration of public schools in 1954. For several years, many of the southern states claimed that they had the right to maintain "separate but equal" schools. National Guardsmen were called out in 1957 in Little Rock, Arkansas, to ensure the safe passage of black students into formerly white schools. Since that time, however, many cities in the South have peacefully integrated their school systems.

lent opportunities to obtain quality public school education, beginning with kindergarten. In states like South Carolina, however, public school kindergartens were almost nonexistent until the mid-1970s. Students who lack a superior public school education are not as well equipped to compete in college or to obtain good positions after graduation from high school. Why should an American child be deprived of the freedom to obtain a quality education solely because he or she lives in a state which either cannot or will not provide quality public school education?

Interstate Confusion Although the Constitution clearly states that each state shall observe the obligations of full faith and credit, privileges and immunities, and extradition, each of these issues has led to substantial confusion. Concerning full faith and credit, for example: A state is not obliged to recognize a divorce granted in another state if one spouse has established residence in the latter in order to obtain the divorce and has then returned to the state where the couple had previously lived.

As to privileges and immunities, one example will serve: A state does not have to admit students from other states to its public colleges or universities at the same rate of tuition as its own students. And, regarding extradition: A state (*i.e.*, its governor) does not have to return an accused person to the state where the crime was allegedly committed even if the governor of the latter state has requested extradition. The word *shall* in Article IV, Sections 1 and 2, has been in practice interpreted to allow states discretion concerning their adherence to full faith and credit, privileges and immunities, and extradition.

To illustrate further the confusions among states resulting from federalism, a few questions will suffice.

Why not establish uniform national laws for such offenses as the possession and sale of drugs? In 1970, for example, the penalties for a first-offense sale of marijuana varied enormously: In Vermont, 0 to 5 years in jail; in Ohio, 20 to 40 years; in some states, life imprisonment.

Why not establish a single, uniform taxation system at the national level? At present, there are tax systems for all fifty states and for most units of local government, as well as for the national government.

Why not establish a national law governing the ownership and transmission of property? Citizens now confront different laws in each of the fifty states.

Confusion also arises because of outmoded state lines and overlapping jurisdictions within states, both of which impede the regional solution of problems. State boundaries are unnatural, the offspring of historical circumstance. They are also administratively inefficient, because many problems, being regional, do not stop at state boundary lines. The huge megalopolitan complexes stretching from Boston to Washington and from Pittsburgh to Chicago illustrate this problem. Air pollution and other regional problems do not regard state boundaries. A steel mill in Gary, Indiana, also produces air pollution in Chicago, Illinois.

While the large number of local governments in the United States may not be the result of federalism, certainly federalism does nothing to reduce their number. Indeed, many local governments benefit from and compete for federal government programs. By aiding these numerous local governments, the federal government may in effect be providing financial "props" for them. Without federal fiscal aid, these local governments might be more likely to consolidate and, therefore, to become more efficient and better able to solve regional problems.

The problem of local government proliferation and competition of these governmental units for federal financial assistance is obvious from an examination of the following data. Los Angeles County includes some 520 separate governmental units—77 cities, 100 school districts, and almost 350 special districts. The New York metropolitan area has some 1,500 distinct governmental units. Because of overlapping governmental boundaries, citizens face obvious difficulties, especially concerning taxes and voting. There are 228 major metropolitan areas in the United States. Averaged out, each has 91 different governments.

The problem is even worse when one considers the 38,000 counties, municipalities, and townships in the United States. Fewer than 1 percent of these have over 100,000 inhabitants; fewer than 10 percent have over 10,000 people; more than half have fewer than 1,000 inhabitants. Clearly, many city, county, and special district governments are too small to provide adequate and proper public services.

Why should local governments, which are created by state governments, be turning to Washington for financial assistance? By turning to Washington, local governments confuse the basic outline of federalism in the United States. Under our federal form of government, both the national and state governments are to have a certain degree of independence from one another based upon the division of powers between them. The relationship between state and local governments, however, is unitary, and the latter have only such powers as the states give them. Theoretically, states could abolish any or all local governments. This unitary relationship between the states and local governments has been damaged by the intrusion of federal financial assistance for local governments.

Business Versus Labor   Another type of conflict arising out of the federal system—especially since the advent of cooperative federalism—has been that between business and labor. Business has tended to ally itself with the states; labor, with the national government. Business recognized that it received greater protection from the states, since they were less likely to engage actively in business regulation. On the other hand, labor knew that the national government was more likely to pursue its interests.

It should be noted, however, that beginning in the late 1960s, some business organizations began to recognize that, on some issues at least, their interests would be better served at the national level. California, for example, has in some cases adopted more stringent pollution control laws than has the federal government.

Conservatives Versus Liberals   Particularly in this century, conservatives have identified with state governments; liberals, with the national government. Since *conservatives* are generally opposed to major and rapid changes in government, in the economy, and in society, they have naturally identified more with state and local governments, which have been less likely to change the status quo. *Liberals*, especially since the New Deal, have sought broad national programs for action in a wide variety of social welfare areas. At the same time they perceived states as being backward units of government that fought liberal objectives. During the congressional debate on Lyndon Johnson's "Great Society" program in 1965–1966, liberals generally fought to increase federal involvement, while conservatives either opposed the program or sought to have more state and local government involvement in its implementation. For example, on the issue of whether the governor of a state could stop a "Great Society" program from being administered in his or her state, conservatives supported the idea of a gubernatorial veto and liberals opposed it.

"Symmetry" Versus "Asymmetry"   To some extent this conflict could be titled the rich versus the poor, the large versus the small, or the populous versus the less populous states. Political scientist Charles Tarlton uses the terms *symmetrical* and *asymmetrical* to describe the relationships between the national government and the two types of states. The more a state is unlike the national norm, the more likely its policies are to conflict (or to be asymmetrical) with national government policies. A relatively poor or small or underpopulated state like Alabama or South Dakota is more likely to have policies conflicting with the national government than are Michigan, Illinois, or California, where the populations are more nearly representative of (or symmetrical to) the national population.[11]

STATE WEAKNESSES

And what of the states within the federal system? Simply speaking, they are unable to solve the problems within their boundaries. This can be demonstrated on at least five counts.

1. State decision-making machinery has been outmoded and inept for all too long. Unlike the national government, most states have lengthy and very specific constitutions that have curtailed their flexibility in solving problems. For example, states have historically relied on taxes that are not as responsive to economic growth, such as the sales tax. The national government, at least for most of this century, has profited from taxes that have grown as the economy grew, such as the income tax. State tax structures are generally more regressive than the federal tax structure in that they place a greater

burden on lower-income groups, while the federal tax structure is more progressive and places a greater tax burden on higher-income groups. As a result, the national government has been in a much better position to implement new programs and to distribute the results as well as to use its substantial revenues for public projects.

There are additional problems in making decisions. Divided power structures in states have prevented them from attacking problems on a unified, statewide basis. State legislatures and governors have lacked enough qualified professional staff members to provide the kind of ideas and administrative expertise necessary to make the states innovative contributors to problem solving in the federal system. Moreover, the corruption that has marred state governments has contributed to a lack of public confidence in their ability to make effective decisions. Illinois and Oklahoma—to name but two—have had massive political scandals involving high elected officials, including the governors.

2. States have been slow to use their fiscal and other resources innovatively in attacking modern problems. Proponents of federalism often argue that the states serve as laboratories for experimentation in developing new governmental programs, but this has happened only rarely. Experimentation usually requires new taxes, and these might adversely affect the location of industry. In this age of industrial mobility, businesses look for a favorable tax climate.

3. Closely related to fiscal timidity is the lack of political purpose in state government. For example, state governments have for decades been apathetic about urban problems, with state legislatures—first conservative-rural and now conservative-suburban—opposing innovative action. This opposition has caused city governments to turn increasingly to the more responsive federal government to obtain the financial assistance they need in order to solve transportation and other problems.

4. There is a serious gap between the rich and poor states. Rich states can, if they choose, provide more services for their citizens—higher teachers' salaries, better schools, and the like—while those in poor states suffer. Yet both rich and poor live in the same nation. Federalism is a natural breeding ground for such inequities.

5. State governments have the right to create interstate compacts, but they are slow to do so. Since the legislatures and governors in each state to be affected plus the Congress must consent to the creation of a compact, substantial time is generally required to create them. Moreover, each state affected has representation on the governing body for the compact, which tends to lead individual members to

look after state rather than regional interests. Also, a compact requires unanimous consent of all member states before it goes into effect and can begin work on a new problem.

Regional Elites   The fragmentation of authority in the federal system has allowed powerful pressure groups to gain tremendous influence in certain areas—the Dupont interests in Delaware, the textile industry in several southern states (such as South Carolina), oil concerns in Texas and Oklahoma, and the Anaconda Company in Montana. Under federalism public power is dispersed among many units of government, so concentrated private power can attain unwarranted influence in decision making. With federalism dividing power and therefore atomizing it, private interests can more easily gain authority: as the old adage has it, "divide and conquer."

In the textile manufacturing areas of the South, labor has had great difficulty in organizing unions because of the textile industry's firm grip on regional political machinery. For example, many of the states that have adopted section 14B of the Taft-Hartley Act are in the South. This "right-to-work" section of the Taft-Hartley Act prohibits making union membership a qualification for employment. The textile industry has vigorously encouraged adoption of "right-to-work laws," which in turn make union organization more difficult.

For a case involving the environment, take the battle over regulating disposable bottles by requiring a deposit on each bottle purchased. Presumably purchasers would return bottles to receive their deposits rather than throwing bottles along the roadside. Environmental groups, although successful on some national issues, have had substantial difficulty in winning environmental battles at the state and local levels of government. Other powerful elite groups are much better organized and financed to win these local skirmishes that result from our atomized federal structure. One example occurred in Dade County, Florida, where an alliance of big business and big labor defeated a bottle deposit referendum supported by local civic and environmental groups.

> The unusual alliance of Big Business and Big Labor has won all seven of the state and local referendums held since 1970 on proposed deposit legalization. . . .
>
> The U. S. Brewers Association, the National Soft Drink Association, and their member businesses are spending most of the money in the bottle and can battle. For example, in Dade County [Florida], the industry reported spending more than $180,000, of which $150,440 was raised in the name of the "Dade Consumer Information Committee."
>
> In contrast, [Dade County] referendum proponents, including more than 40 civic groups, reported raising a total of $1,741. According to an

analysis by Robert J. Brandt of Florida International University, only 23 percent of the opposition money came from Dade County, with 44 percent coming from out of state.[12]

Inadequacies and Inequities of National Aid   The national government, forced to respond to the weaknesses of state governments, has adopted several compensatory measures, particularly monetary grants to state and local governments. Before the New Deal, Congress provided only a limited amount of funding to the states to help underwrite programs of clearly national significance, such as the building of roads. The liberal Democratic presidencies of Franklin Roosevelt and Harry Truman gave impetus to many new federal aid programs so that by the beginning of the Kennedy administration, there were forty-four grant programs. Then, with the New Frontier and the Great Society, federal grants blossomed to the point where the national government had to publish a catalog of catalogs just to identify the federal programs available. (This document itself covered nine single-spaced pages).

In 1942 the amount of state and local government funds provided by the national government was 8.2 percent; today it is approximately 23 percent. Some 21 national departments and agencies now administer over 400 separate grant programs to the 50 states, 78,000 units of local government, and literally millions of individuals. In the 1960s alone, grant monies increased by 189 percent. The result is greater dependence by state and local government on the federal government.

In spite of all this aid, however, grants have occasionally been used for inefficient, duplicative, or allegedly corrupt purposes. They have helped pay for golf courses, and some local political organizations have benefited from them financially. Sometimes they have paid for projects for which local citizens were unwilling to tax themselves.

The duplication problem is illustrated by the Johnson administration's proposed agency to administer a new rat control program—when at least five departments or agencies already administered similar programs. The "Great Society" program did not propose to unify these several programs into one.

National grants have not abolished one of the major problems of state and local government—inefficient and outmoded governmental structures. On the contrary, federal aid has tended to prop up the existing authorities by not requiring them to adopt administrative and fiscal reforms as a precondition for receiving funds.

A new war between the states has resulted from federal aid programs, because southern and western states are benefiting more than the northern industrialized states. The six Great Lakes states in fiscal

1975 contributed $62.2 billion in federal taxes, but received only $43.6 billion in services, contracts, and salaries from the federal government. Their loss in the exchange of dollars with the federal government was $18.6 billion. U.S. Representative Michael Harrington (Dem. Mass.) says that "New England and its industrialized neighbors are taking a beating at the hands of a government that is promoting development of the sun belt at the expense of all other regions." [13] A regional and state breakdown of this inequitable transfer of federal tax dollars is shown in Table 1. The Northeast and Midwest show a combined loss of over $30 billion for fiscal year 1975, while the South and West show a combined gain of over $22 billion. Although such a regional war might be waged under another form of government, the federal system with its states' rights emphasis allows representatives and senators in the U.S. Congress to organize to represent state and regional needs.

AN OUTDATED SURVIVAL

Federalism, once considered by many scholars analogous to a layer cake where there were relatively clear lines of demarcation between the national and state governments, has become like a marble cake, with confusing and indistinct lines of authority between the two levels of government. Federalism has evolved into a form only faintly resembling what the Founders envisioned, even if they knew what they had in mind (and there is a very real question about that). The Founders were more concerned with creating a national government than they were with outlining a theory of federalism. What they did draft, however, has now become tradition.

It is quite possible to have federalism without truly effective decentralization. . . . It is also possible to have decentralization without federalism. Great Britain—a unitary government—gives great authority, both political and administrative, to its local units. Admittedly, federalism and decentralization are not synonymous.—*George C. S. Benson*

The test now is whether this tradition will collapse under the enormous pressures to make government more responsive, efficient, and economical in an era of scarce resources. Actually, we have gone a long way toward a unitary system of government in response to these pressures. History shows us moving from decentralization to centralization. But if it is decentralization we want, we can achieve it under a unitary system just as effectively. For example, local governments in Great Britain are allocated a great deal of authority by the national government. Certainly creating a unitary system would be less hypocritical than keeping our federal system. What if we could do it all over again? Should not a country that is essentially a national state by almost any measure—economic, cultural, educational, linguistic—have a unitary government? It is patently unrealistic to argue that federalism fits the national character of the United States today.

Table 1. Transfer of Tax Dollars Between States and the Federal Government

The table shows winners and losers in the battle for federal spending. The columns record: (1) federal spending per person in fiscal 1975, excluding interest payments; (2) the federal tax burden per person, with the federal deficit distributed as an added tax; (3) the amount of money received for each tax dollar sent to Washington; and (4) the total amount of money that flowed into or out of each state and region.

	SPENDING PER PERSON	TAXES PER PERSON	SPENDING-TAXES RATIO	DOLLAR FLOW (IN MILLIONS)
NORTHEAST	**$1,361**	**$1,579**	**$ .86**	**−$10,776**
New England	**1,470**	**1,533**	**.96**	**−762**
Maine	1,206	1,075	1.12	139
New Hampshire	1,399	1,399	1.00	1
Vermont	1,360	1,167	1.17	91
Massachusetts	1,456	1,535	.95	−462
Rhode Island	1,342	1,457	.92	−107
Connecticut	1,663	1,800	.92	−425
Mid-Atlantic	**1,325**	**1,594**	**.83**	**−10,013**
New York	1,449	1,636	.89	−3,392
New Jersey	1,154	1,760	.66	−4,436
Pennsylvania	1,241	1,426	.87	−2,185
MIDWEST	**1,128**	**1,477**	**.76**	**−20,074**
Great Lakes	**1,064**	**1,518**	**.70**	**−18,618**
Ohio	1,010	1,441	.70	−4,634
Indiana	1,027	1,411	.73	−2,036
Illinois	1,230	1,704	.72	−5,290
Michigan	996	1,539	.65	−4,971
Wisconsin	966	1,331	.73	−1,686
Great Plains	**1,287**	**1,374**	**.94**	**−1,456**
Minnesota	1,144	1,382	.83	−934
Iowa	970	1,405	.69	−1,249
Missouri	1,500	1,362	1.10	657
Kansas	1,398	1,432	.98	−78
Nebraska	1,193	1,420	.84	−351
South Dakota	1,395	1,081	1.29	215
North Dakota	1,734	1,288	1.35	283

Table 1. Transfer of Tax Dollars Between States and the Federal Government (continued)

	SPENDING PER PERSON	TAXES PER PERSON	SPENDING-TAXES RATIO	DOLLAR FLOW (IN MILLIONS)
SOUTH	**1,389**	**1,219**	**1.14**	**11,522**
South Atlantic	**1,454**	**1,303**	**1.12**	**4,986**
Delaware	1,145	1,743	.66	−347
Maryland	1,933	1,615	1.20	1,299
Virginia	1,809	1,355	1.34	2,257
West Virginia	1,318	1,091	1.21	410
North Carolina	1,124	1,145	.98	−115
South Carolina	1,240	1,041	1.19	561
Georgia	1,402	1,217	1.16	912
Florida	1,379	1,378	1.00	9
South Central	**1,327**	**1,137**	**1.17**	**6,536**
Kentucky	1,327	1,094	1.21	790
Tennessee	1,296	1,147	1.13	627
Alabama	1,374	1,026	1.34	1,255
Mississippi	1,599	908	1.76	1,621
Louisiana	1,236	1,064	1.16	652
Arkansas	1,202	970	1.37	492
Oklahoma	1,443	1,181	1.22	711
Texas	1,296	1,264	1.03	388
WEST	**1,712**	**1,431**	**1.20**	**10,639**
Mountain	**1,615**	**1,238**	**1.30**	**3,631**
Montana	1,512	1,183	1.28	246
Idaho	1,358	1,087	1.25	223
Wyoming	1,569	1,295	1.21	102
Colorado	1,646	1,368	1.20	704
Utah	1,449	1,072	1.35	455
Nevada	1,544	1,612	.96	−40
Arizona	1,639	1,256	1.41	853
New Mexico	1,974	1,024	1.93	1,090
Pacific	**1,745**	**1,497**	**1.17**	**7,008**
California	1,700	1,526	1.11	3,684
Oregon	1,282	1,371	.94	−202
Washington	1,968	1,402	1.40	2,008
Alaska	3,736	1,530	2.60	776
Hawaii	2,347	1,490	1.58	741
District of Columbia	**13,957**	**1,820**	**7.67**	**8,690**
UNITED STATES	**1,412**	**1,412**	**1.00**	**0**

Source: *National Journal*, June 26, 1976, p. 881. Reprinted with permission.

The Negative Case

No, federalism should not be abolished.

I am no believer in the literal inspiration of the Constitution or in its rigid interpretation. But those who do not see that liberty and progress in America both depend upon limiting the power of all government, upon preserving its federal nature, upon protecting local authority, are, I believe, tragically blind to the plainest lesson of the world they live in. For once a people lets all power become concentrated at one point, it is like an army trapped in a salient.[14]—Walter Lippmann

A nation of continental proportions, the United States has a wide variety of sections and groups that the abolition of federalism would not eliminate. There would remain North and South, East and West, rich and poor, integrationists and segregationists, executives and wage earners. The framers of the Constitution in their foresight provided a federal system of government well before the United States became either democratic or industrialized. This federal system has numerous assets.

- Its flexibility has helped harmonize diverse forces.
- States and localities have proved to be not only competent, but innovative as well.
- Federalism is a tradition of proven worth.

HARMONY THROUGH FLEXIBILITY

In sum the virtue of the federal system lies in its ability to develop and maintain mechanisms vital to the perpetuation of the unique combination of governmental strength, political flexibility, and individual liberty, which has been the central concern of American Politics.—*Daniel J. Elazar*

Federalism, by being adaptable to changing times and circumstances, has allowed us to alter our political system without enduring the trials of changing our basic governmental structure. For example, dual federalism prevailed in a much simpler era, whereas cooperative federalism characterizes our more complex and sophisticated age; yet each has existed within precisely the same constitutional structure.

One of the first American statesmen to argue in favor of the flexibility of the federal system was Alexander Hamilton, when seeking in 1787 to persuade the states to ratify the Constitution. It was his aim to obtain the support of both states' rightists and nationalists. In supporting federalism, he could argue for both decentralization and centralization.

At this time the states were dominant, and Hamilton had to convince them the national government would not usurp their powers. In No. 16 of *The Federalist*, he stated that the national government would have only limited powers; it would be foolish, he wrote, to imagine a time when the central authority could dominate the states. The only way the national government could attain this kind of power, Hamilton believed, was through recruiting and maintaining a national army, which he regarded as unlikely.

> Whoever considers the populousness and strength of these States singly at the present juncture, and looks forward to what they will become, even at the distance of half a century, will at once dismiss as idle and visionary any scheme which aims at regulating their movements by laws. . . . [15]

On the other hand, some Americans felt that there was not enough centralized authority in the proposed Constitution. Hamilton, recognizing this, pointed out that the central government could regulate the mutual concerns of the states. The central government, in his words, "must itself be empowered to employ the arm of the ordinary magistrate [law officer] to execute its own resolutions." From this premise, Hamilton argued that the states could not evade federal laws. What point would there be to a central government whose laws could be violated by state governments? Hamilton believed that nullification of federal law by individual states could not take place "without an open and violent exertion of an unconstitutional power." [16] Thus federalism allowed Hamilton to argue for both decentralization and centralization.

Balancing Concurrent Powers   The flexible framework of federalism has permitted the relative strengths of national and state governments to shift as time and circumstance indicated. One of the areas where shifts occur involves the concurrent powers of the two levels of government, where the controlling doctrine is *national preemption*. That is, when the national government has acted, it is presumed to have precluded state action. A relevant case is *Pennsylvania* v. *Nelson* (1956). At issue was the question of whether Steve Nelson, an acknowledged member of the Communist party, had violated a Pennsylvania statute by threatening to overthrow the federal government. The Supreme Court ruled:

> Congress has intended to occupy the field of sedition. Taken as a whole, they [the statutes] evince a congressional plan which makes it reasonable to determine that no room has been left for the States to supplement it. Therefore, a state sedition statute is superseded regardless of whether it purports to supplement the federal law. [17]

Recognizing that there are times when both national and state action should be valid under their concurrent powers, the Supreme Court

There is something noble and magnificent in the perspective of a great Federal Republic, closely linked in the pursuit of a common interest, tranquil and prosperous at home, respectable abroad; but there is something proportionably diminutive and contemptible in the prospect of a number of petty States, with the appearance only of union, jarring, jealous, and perverse, without any determined direction, fluctuating and unhappy at home, weak and insignificant by their dissensions in the eyes of other nations. Happy America, if those to whom thou hast intrusted the guardianship of thy infancy know how to provide for thy future repose, but miserable and undone, if their negligence or ignorance permits the spirit of discord to erect her banner on the ruins of thy tranquility!— *Alexander Hamilton*

has made exceptions to the preemption rule. In *Colorado Anti-Discrimination Commission* v. *Continental Airlines* (1963), the Court upheld a state antidiscrimination statute even though there were national laws on the subject. The Court reasoned that since the power of Congress is not always clearly defined, the judiciary must weigh each case on its merits before denying a state its traditional powers. In this case, the Court decided that commerce would not be adversely affected by upholding the state statute.

Another example also relates to commerce where both states and the national government have concurrent powers, the former over intrastate commerce and the latter over interstate commerce. For instance, states may set meat and poultry inspection standards for that which is raised and sold within the state, while the national government may do the same for meat and poultry shipped across state lines.

Resolving Differences Because of the flexibility of the federal systems, differences between the national and state governments have been resolved with relative ease. Three doctrines—nullification, interposition, and secession—have been advanced to settle nation-state differences in ways that would have harmed the interests of national unity. None of these prevailed.

Nullification occurs when a state disregards (declares null and void) a federal law within its boundaries. The Virginia and Kentucky Resolutions of 1798 and 1799, protesting the passage of the Alien and Sedition Acts, contended that such a course was the "rightful remedy" for states to follow when the national government overstepped its bounds. As it turned out, it is the judiciary, not the states, that determines whether this has happened.

Interposition—whereby a state might actually impede a federal law (by interposing its own authority)—was advocated by South Carolina's John C. Calhoun in opposing the national tariff of 1828. When his state tried to put the doctrine into practice in the 1830s, President Andrew Jackson forced it to back down. During the 1950s, southern states attempted to revive interposition in their battle against school desegregation following *Brown* v. *Board of Education* (1954).

Conflicts of this nature reached their climax with *secession*, when the Confederate states declared that they had left (seceded from) the Union. Northern victory in the Civil War determined that this doctrine could not be regarded as a valid solution to national-state conflicts.

Throughout most of American history, the flexibility of federalism has encouraged the national and state governments to find legal and peaceful solutions to their conflicts. And when the national government has had to act, it has been able to do so without being impeded by structural changes, such as constitutional amendments.

Unity Amidst Diversity   The flexible federal system provides for unity amidst diversity. Given the differences among the fifty states, it is obviously necessary to allow for diverse approaches in attacking state and regional problems. At the same time there is a need for unity, especially in foreign policy. In this area it is imperative that the entire country speak with one voice to the greatest extent possible.

The dominant role in education, health, and voting belongs to the states, which have the primary responsibility for financing and determining standards in each of these areas. States provide most of the funding for schools and set teacher certification standards, license doctors, and establish voting procedures. Each of these is an example of diversity among the states. It should be pointed out, however, that with improvements in communication and transportation, states have become less diverse in their policies for education, health, and voting. For example, national organizations have helped states develop similar approaches to common problems. The Council of State Governments in Lexington, Kentucky, provides states with model legislation on problem areas; the Citizens Conference on State Legislatures in Denver, Colorado, assists legislatures in becoming more efficient and effective; and the Education Compact of the States, also in Denver, Colorado, disseminates assistance to states in this area. By allowing the states to approach local problems in diverse ways, federalism permits states to tailor solutions to their own needs rather than forcing them to accept uniform national solutions, which might not adequately fit local situations.

Several Supreme Court decisions have helped clarify the role of the national government in foreign affairs. In *Missouri* v. *Holland* (1920), the Court declared that laws passed in accordance with the obligations of a national treaty take precedence over state law. Pursuant to a treaty with Canada negotiated in 1918, Congress had passed a law to enforce strict standards for the protection of birds migrating between the United States and Canada. Missouri contended that this law interfered with the reserved powers of the state inasmuch as it went beyond the express powers of Congress. The Court, noting that Article VI grants treaties the same status legally as the Constitution itself, ruled that the treaty was proper. It then concluded that any law passed in pursuance of a valid treaty would also be valid. With this decision, the Supreme Court ruled that in foreign affairs, the national government has precedence over state power.

Another case that dealt with national authority was *United States* v. *Curtiss-Wright Export Corporation* (1936). The corporation, a private concern, had been charged with conspiring to sell machine guns to Bolivia. The Court, in commenting on the need for unity in foreign affairs, ruled that only the president has the authority to be the representative of the nation.

In *United States* v. *Pink* (1942), the Supreme Court declared that national government action in the form of an executive agreement with another nation took precedence over state action.* After the United States recognized the Soviet Union in 1933 (through an executive agreement), the assets of a Russian insurance company's New York branch were assigned to the United States, whereupon the national government claimed the assets that had been deposited with the New York State superintendent of insurance. When the state of New York disputed this claim, the Supreme Court ruled that the national government is supreme over a state government even when the former has acted through an executive agreement.

STATE AND LOCAL SUCCESSES

Far from being incompetent, state and local governments have amply shown their ability to meet the challenges of modern society.

> Viewing the atrophy of state government in 1965, Sen. Everett McKinley Dirksen warned that the time was not far off when "the only people interested in state boundaries will be Rand-McNally."
> But a single decade has brought such a sweeping rejuvenation of state governments that no national politician would dare make that statement now.[18]

State governments, rather than being slow to modernize, have in recent years begun to update their constitutions, improve their judicial branches, and staff their legislatures adequately. Ethical and other reform issues are very much alive in the states today. Indeed, after the Watergate scandal, the public gained confidence in the states as it lost faith in the national government.

Although voter turnout is lower in state and local elections than in national contests, national elections attract much more attention from the news media. (It is possible, too, that low voter turnout may represent satisfaction with the job being done, rather than discontent.) By almost any measure, state and local government is nowhere near death. In the areas of employment, taxes, and spending, the greatest increases in recent years have been at the state and local levels. And it is there, too, where one finds the most significant programs in education and transportation.

* An *executive agreement* has the same legal status as a treaty, but does not have to be ratified by the Senate.

Innovative Programs and Policies   Many new programs have originated with state and local governments. States have provided parks, hospitals, schools, and other services—often in rather innovative ways. In some cases state action has preceded national action. A few examples will suffice:

- Georgia pioneered in giving eighteen-year-olds the right to vote. (Kentucky and Alaska also lowered voting ages before the national government did so.)
- California imposed stricter air pollution control programs than those mandated by federal law.
- New York, Massachusetts, Oregon, and Wisconsin were some of the states initiating fair employment practices legislation.
- Roughly one fourth of the states abolished the death penalty before the Supreme Court acted to limit its application.
- Several states relaxed their abortion laws before Supreme Court action.
- State experiences with highway safety paved the way for the Federal Highway Safety Act of 1967.
- Some constitutional amendments, such as the Twenty-fourth prohibiting a poll tax as a qualification for voting in federal elections, have merely ratified what most states had already done.
- Several states led the way in personal rehabilitation, to be followed by the Federal Rehabilitation Act of 1965.
- Wyoming, followed by several other western states, provided for women's suffrage long before the federal government did.

Innovative state programs have paved the way not only for the national government but also for other states. California, for example, is noted for its system of higher education. South Carolina is known for its vocational and technical education, and for its educational television. New York and California have provided their legislative branches with high-level scientific and technical personnel.

The success stories of states and cities are often overshadowed by rhetoric describing the seemingly insoluble problems confronting them. Writing about solid accomplishments by local governments, David Broder of the *Washington Post* notes:

> It [success] was achieved by innovative state and local officials who, unlike some of their contemporaries, did not assume that they had exhausted their remedies when they returned empty-handed from a foraging trip to Washington.
> The story can be duplicated elsewhere: In Peoria, where a university medical school project has been the key to a dramatic downtown re-

newal effort. In Hoboken, N. J., where rehabilitation and home improvement loans have been used to save existing neighborhoods. In Berkeley,
Calif., where an intensive program of building code enforcement not
only halted the deterioration of a 47-block area, but reduced its crime
rate from the second-highest in the city to the second-lowest. In Pittsburgh, which has managed to reduce both its city payroll and its crime
rate. And even in Gary, that one-time symbol of approaching ruin,
whose mayor, Richard Hatcher, now is convinced it has turned the corner to better days.[19]

Yet another positive side of federalism is the exciting manner in
which it has provided a way for persons from the militant and radical
movements of the late 1960s and early 1970s to participate construc-
tively in government. Says one writer: "The mellowing militants
... may feel events proved them right, but guerrilla rhetoric about trash-
ing the establishment has given way to the drafting of 'progressive' programs for states, counties and cities."[20] This observer concludes that the
four hundred or so alumni of radicalism now working in state and local
governments may provide a healthy progressive spirit for the continuing
restoration of states and cities.

Former radicals are not the only ones who have changed their
minds about the value of state and local governments. Said a New Jersey
public official who oversees a newly created department aimed at giving
citizens a chance to cut through bureaucratic red tape:

> Philosophically, I came out of the New Deal liberalism and looked to the
> federal government as the place to solve the problems. I don't know
> whether advancing age has made me more conservative, or whether ex-
> perience has made me more skeptical about the ability of the federal gov-
> ernment to solve these problems, but I arrive at the point where I think
> the state could do a hell of a lot better with the problems affecting it
> than the federal government had demonstrated the ability to do over the
> last ten or fifteen years.[21]

Compacts   Interstate compacts, aimed at achieving common solutions
to regional problems, have made real contributions. An example is the
Southern Regional Education Compact, which has allowed several
southern states to pool educational resources on behalf of the whole region. For instance, a South Carolina student may attend the University
of Georgia veterinary school without paying out-of-state tuition since
South Carolina does not have a veterinary school. Other subjects of
compacts in various parts of the nation include water pollution, flood
control, port operations, recreation and parks, and oil conservation.

Federal Aid   Federalism enables one unit of government to utilize the
strength of others. A primary method for doing this is federal aid,

Federal aid enables the states to tap the vast revenue supplies of the national government. Federal money helped finance the new Bay Area Rapid Transit (BART) system in San Francisco, California.

through which state governments benefit from the extraordinary revenue resources of the national government.

As needs have changed, so too have the methods for distributing federal revenue. Until the late 1960s, most grants, called *conditional grants* or *matching grants*, were earmarked for a specific purpose. The state government had to match a certain portion of the national grant. For example, federal funds might be set aside for a specific highway construction project; the state would supply a certain percentage of the money needed. Thus, if the federal government provided 90 percent of the funds, the matching percentage from the state would be 10 percent. (These grants have also been called *categorical grants*, because they are available for only one category or type of project.) Whatever the name, this type of grant entails a contract between two governments.

FIG. 1. Flow of Federal Education Dollars

Before Consolidation
($3.0 Billion in Budget Authority in 1976)

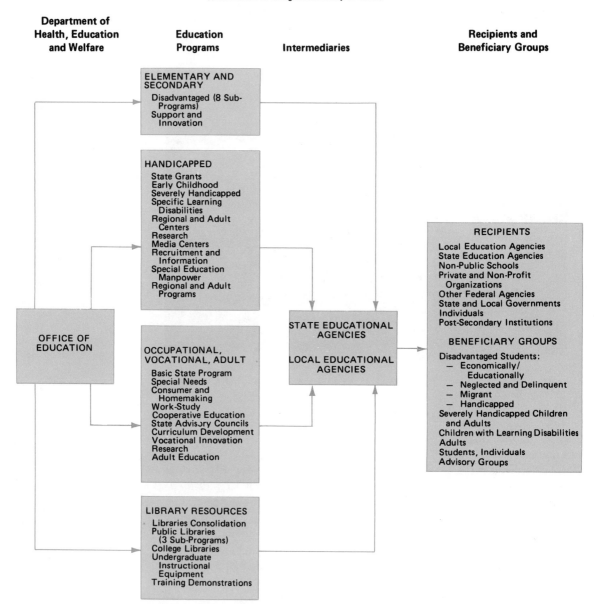

SOURCE: *The Budget of the United States Government: Fiscal Year 1977* (Washington, D.C.: U.S. Government Printing Office, 1976), p. 119.

Beginning in the 1960s, *project grants* came into use. With these, the national government decides where money is most needed; it can bypass state governments, placing its funds directly on the target with local government, or even with private groups or individuals as shown in Figure 1.

In the late 1960s two other forms of federal aid were developed to counteract the lack of flexibility of conditional grants, where money must be spent on specific projects. In one form, *block grants,* the recipient government may use the money for any of a variety of purposes that fall under a general heading. For example, with "701" funds (provided by the Department of Housing and Urban Development) a state can determine its own criteria for distributing the money within certain general guidelines established by HUD. These guidelines might include land use planning, recreation, and government reorganization.

The proposed budget for fiscal year 1977 as submitted to the Congress by President Ford provides many illustrations of the diverse and flexible intergovernmental uses of federal money. For example, the flow of federal education dollars to state and local agencies is shown in Figure 1. Some federal programs provide funds for the development of experimental or pioneering efforts, such as those in curriculum development and in innovative vocational programs, also shown in Figure 1.

The second innovation to increase flexibility was *revenue sharing,* which provides that a portion of national government revenue will be returned to state and local governments. The 1972 Fiscal Assistance Act specified that two thirds of the revenue-sharing funds should go to local government and one third to state governments. These funds are given with practically no strings attached, although there are a few qualifications. The funds cannot be used to support programs that discriminate against any person because of race, national origin, or sex. The funds cannot be used as matching funds for other national government programs. In the case of local governments, the funds must be spent on generally defined goals outlined by the federal government, such as public safety, environmental protection, public transportation, health, recreation, libraries, social services for the poor or aged, and financial administration.

In President Gerald Ford's 1977 Budget Message, he made these comments:

> General revenue sharing has become a significant element in the fiscal relationship between the federal government and state and local governments. Outlays in 1977 will be $6.7 billion, with one third going to state governments and two thirds to local governments. . . . Over the 5-year authorized life of the current program, $30.2 billion of federal funds will have been distributed. These payments are made to states and localities

FIRST ALLOWANCE

with minimal federal restrictions and controls, thus allowing regional and local decision making to address regional and local needs. The principal federal requirements of the program address such concerns as assuring nondiscrimination and public participation in spending decisions.[22]

It is generally conceded that federal programs have stimulated improved performance among state and local governments, have increased citizen participation, and have made the states more innovative and responsive to the public interest.[23] Recognizing the new capabilities of state and local governments, a leading student of federalism, Daniel J. Elazar, says they are just as able to do the job as the federal government.[24] By including state and local governments in problem solving through grant-in-aid programs, the federal government has contributed to a new sense of responsibility among those governments. The 1976 law that extended revenue sharing through 1980 included provisions for enhancing citizen participation and local government responsibility. The law requires:

- state and local government reports to the Treasury Secretary at the close of the local fiscal year on the actual use of the shared revenues, as well as their relationship to the local budget and to the proposed use of the funds;
- information on the proposed use of the grant to be published in local newspapers before budget hearings and after budget adoption and to be available for public inspection;
- public hearings on the proposed use of the revenue sharing funds and also on the local budget;
- information on local compliance with the public participation and nondiscrimination provisions in the Treasury Secretary's annual report to Congress on the program; and
- that senior citizens and their organizations be given an opportunity to comment, to the extent possible, on the use of revenue-sharing funds.

A VALUABLE TRADITION

Opponents of federalism offer improbable alternatives to our system. Who can realistically advocate regional governments or the consolidation of states? Who can realistically advocate a unitary system of government? Such solutions seem visionary, given our historic ties to existing state boundaries and the entire federal system of government.

Many criticisms of federalism are poorly founded. To say that it allows elite interests to capture control of government is a spurious argument. Under any form of democracy that retained an economic structure like that in the United States, the same interests would still exist. Moreover, there is ample evidence to demonstrate that economic elites have not had the control some theorists claim. For a example, although the Dupont interests have opposed reciprocal trade, the Delaware congressional delegation has favored it. Indeed, some politicians have made their political careers by running against established interests in their constituencies.

Division of power is the basis of civilized government. It is what is meant by constitutionalism.— Carl J. Fredrick

Table 2. Citizens' Perceptions of Government's Impact on Their Lives*

GOVERNMENT	IMPROVED	WORSE	NO CHANGE
Federal	23	37	34
State	27	14	52
Local	28	11	54

*In percent.

Source: "Confidence and Concern: Citizens View American Government," a survey of public attitudes by the Subcommittee on Intergovernmental Relations of the Committee on Government Relations, United States Senate (Washington, D.C.: U. S. Government Printing Office, December 1973).

To say that the federal government is more responsive to the public defies survey data on what the public thinks. In a 1973 nationwide survey of public opinion concerning the effect of federal, state, and local governments on people's lives, state and local governments were perceived to have a more beneficial impact than the federal government. As shown in Table 2, 37 percent of the public believes the federal government has made their lives worse, while only 14 percent and 11 percent, respectively, believe the same for state and local governments.[25]

To suggest that federalism aids and abets racism overlooks the fact that racism would exist regardless of whether federalism existed. Unitary governments have problems with racism, too. Certainly the abolition of state governments would not eliminate discrimination in the United States.

Critics have overlooked the fact that federalism has been an ideal system for the United States. It is a middle ground between centralized and decentralized systems. We must remember that when the American Constitution was drafted, public opinion simply would not have permitted the adoption of a unitary form of government, and confederation had already demonstrated its weaknesses. Federalism has been adaptable to changing conditions in the United States, and an essential tool for nation building. Without it, a people opposed to centralization and disenchanted with decentralization might well have ended up by dismembering a nation of states into a balkanized collection of small nations.

Not only is federalism not guilty of many of the sins of which it has been accused, but more importantly, it enhances democracy in a number of ways. Perhaps the most vital is that it inhibits the rise of dictatorships by dividing and diffusing power, thereby making it more difficult for one person or a small group to seize control. James Madison took note of this in No. 10 of *The Federalist:*

> The influence of factious leaders may kindle a flame within their particular States, but will be unable to spread a general conflagration through the other States. A religious sect may degenerate into a political

This nation was founded by men of many nations and backgrounds. It was founded on the principle that all men are created equal, and that the rights of every man are diminished when the rights of one man are threatened. We preach freedom around the world, and we mean it. And we cherish freedom here at home. But are we to say to the world—and much more importantly to each other—that this is the land of the free, except for the Negroes, that we have no second-class citizens, except Negroes, that we have no class or caste system, no ghettos, no master race, except with respect to Negroes.—*John F. Kennedy*

faction in a part of the Confederacy; but the variety of sects dispersed over the entire face of it must secure the national councils against any danger from that source. A rage for paper money, for an abolition of debts, for an equal division of property, or for any other improper or wicked project, will be less apt to pervade the whole body of the Union than a particular member of it; in the same proportion as such a malady is more likely to taint a particular county or district than an entire State.

In the extent and proper structure of the Union, therefore, we behold a republican remedy for the diseases most incident to republican government. And according to the degree of pleasure and pride we feel in being republicans, ought to be our zeal in cherishing the spirit and supporting the character of Federalists.[26]

Federalism not only guards against a minority takeover, it also protects Americans against tyranny by the majority.

A happy result of the federal system is that it prevents a majority from fully exercising its power arbitrarily and thereby preserves for the individual the possibility of a greater degree of self-government. The very existence of a large number of units of government and the exercise of power by them, [former New York] Governor Rockefeller has said, "stands as one of the principal barriers to the creation of a monolithic national bureaucracy that would stifle local initiative and regional creativity."[27]

Federalism also offers distinct advantages for the individual citizen. It enhances what might be called "preparatory democracy," by providing a training ground for public officials. After serving at state and local levels, they may then move up the governmental ladder to national government offices. Many members of Congress previously served in state legislatures or on city councils. A dramatic example of this process in action is Senator Hubert Humphrey, who was mayor of Minneapolis before being elected to national office.

Federalism promotes participatory democracy because, with over 78,000 units of government in the United States, there are so many positions to be filled. Citizens have the opportunity to participate in the democratic process at all levels, whether on a park commission or school board, or in a city council, state legislature, or the United States Congress.

Because of the many units of government, the individual citizen has many points of access through which to approach the government—another distinct advantage of federalism. These multiple access points help to broaden the base of democracy. In an era of bigness, when Americans are increasingly troubled by impersonalization, the multiplicity of governmental jurisdictions offers a way for people to identify with and take pride in their own municipality, county, and state. Federalism allows individual citizens to have a greater sense of control over their own destinies.

Glossary

Block grants: federal grants that the recipient government may use for a variety of purposes falling under a general heading.

Categorical grants: see *conditional grants.*

Concurrent powers: powers that can be exercised by both the states and the national government, such as the power to levy taxes.

Conditional grants (also called **categorical grants** and **matching grants**): national grants, earmarked for a specific purpose, requiring state recipients to match with their own funds a specified portion of the federal money.

Confederation: an alliance among constituent governments operating from delegated and quite limited authority.

Conservatives: those who believe that political, economic, and social changes should occur gradually and within existing institutions of government and society.

Cooperative federalism: a relatively modern view of the federal system in which the federal government and state and local governments function cooperatively as related divisions of a single system.

Dual federalism: a traditional view of the federal system in which the federal government and state and local governments are responsible for performing various functions within specific areas in which each is autonomous.

Executive agreement: an agreement with a foreign country having the legal status of a treaty but not requiring Senate approval.

Express powers: powers specifically enumerated by the Constitution.

Extradition: the return for trial of an alleged criminal to the state having jurisdiction.

Federal: a system of government in which powers are divided among a central government and various local governments.

Implied powers: powers, not specifically enumerated by the Constitution, which may be logically inferred from the express powers.

Inherent powers: powers that a national government has in foreign affairs by virtue of its existence as a government.

Interstate compact: an agreement through which two or more states with a common interest or problem establish a legally binding relationship aimed at a common solution.

Interposition: an act whereby a state could impede a federal law by interposing its own authority.

Liberals: those who believe that political, economic, and social change should occur at a faster rate of speed (than conservatives would allow) and outside existing institutions of society and government, if necessary, to enhance individual development and well-being.

Matching grants: see *conditional grants.*

National preemption: doctrine whereby action by the national government takes precedence over state action in cases involving concurrent powers.

Nullification: a doctrine whereby a state declares null and void a federal law within its boundaries.

Project grants: federal grants that bypass state governments and are distributed directly to state or local agencies or to private groups or individuals that prepare applications for funds.

Reserved powers: powers belonging to the states alone.

Revenue sharing: federal money returned to state and local governments with few specifications for its use.

Secession: withdrawal from the Union.

States' rights: a term expressing opposition to increasing the national government's power at the expense of the states.

Unitary: a system of government in which all power is vested in the central government.

Notes

1. Harold J. Laski, "The Obsolescence of Federalism," *New Republic* 98 (May 3, 1939):367.

2. Edward S. Corwin, "American Federalism—Past, Present, and Future," Princeton University Bicentennial Address, October 7, 1946, as cited in James MacGregor Burns et al., *Government By the People*, 9th ed. (Englewood Cliffs, N.J.: Prentice-Hall, 1975), p. 78.

3. *United States* v. *Darby* (1941).

4. *McCulloch* v. *Maryland* (1819).

5. *United States* v. *Maine* (1975).

6. *National League of Cities* v. *Usery, California* (1976).

7. *Wichard* v. *Filburn* (1942).

8. *Heart of Atlanta Motel* v. *United States* (1964); see also *Perez* v. *United States* (1971).

9. Terry Sanford, *Storm Over the States* (New York: McGraw-Hill, 1967), pp. 91–93.

10. William H. Riker, *Federalism: Origin, Operation, Significance* (Boston: Little, Brown, 1964), pp. 140, 142.

11. Charles D. Tarlton, "Symmetry and Asymmetry as Elements of Federalism: A Theoretical Speculation," *Journal of Politics* 27 (November 1965):871.

12. *Washington Post*, July 1, 1975, p. 3.

13. *National Observer*, October 2, 1976, p. 19.

14. Clinton Rossiter and James Lare, eds., *The Essential Lippmann* (New York: Random House, 1963), p. 221.

15. Henry Cabot Lodge, ed., *The Federalist* (New York: G. P. Putnam's Sons, 1902), p. 94.

16. Ibid., p. 95.

17. *Pennsylvania* v. *Nelson* (1956).

18. *Washington Post*, April 8, 1975, p. 18.

19. *Washington Post*, July 13, 1975, p. C6.

20. *Washington Post*, June 27, 1975, p. 30.

21. *Washington Post*, May 11, 1975, p. C4.

22. U. S. Government, *The Budget of the United States Government: Fiscal Year 1977* (Washington, D.C.: U. S. Government Printing Office, 1976), p. 159.

23. Morton Grodzins, "The Federal System," in Aaron Wildavsky, *American Federalism in Perspective* (Boston: Little, Brown, 1967), p. 275.

24. Daniel J. Elazar, "The New Federalism," *Public Interest*, 34–37 (1974):102.

25. "Confidence and Concern: Citizens View American Government," a survey of public attitudes by the Subcommittee of Intergovernmental Relations of the Committee on Government Relations, United States Senate (Washington, D.C.: U. S. Government Printing Office, December 1973).

26. Lodge, *The Federalist*, pp. 59–60.

27. Richard H. Leach, *American Federalism* (New York: Norton, 1970), p. 240.

Recommended Rebuttal Reading

On Theory

Hamilton, Alexander, John Jay, and James Madison. *The Federalist*, ed. Valerie Earle. New York: Random House, Modern Library, n.d. See especially Numbers 9, 37, 39, and 43–46.

Leach, Richard H. *American Federalism*. New York: Norton, 1970.

On Cooperative Federalism

Clark, Jane Perry. *The Rise of the New Federalism*. New York: Columbia University Press, 1938.

Connery, Robert H., and Richard H. Leach. *The Federal Government and Metropolitan Areas*. Cambridge, Mass.: Harvard University Press, 1960.

Elazar, Daniel J. *American Federalism: A View from the States*. New York: Thomas Y. Crowell, 1972.

Martin, Roscoe. *Cities and the Federal System*. New York: Atherton Press, 1965.

On Federalism Generally (Short Studies)

Elazar, Daniel J., et al. *Cooperation and Conflict*. Itasca, Ill: F. E. Peacock, 1969.

Goldwin, Robert A., ed. *A Nation of States*. Skokie, Ill.: Rand McNally, 1962.

Reagan, Michael. *The New Federalism*. New York: Oxford University Press, 1972.

On the History of Federalism

Cushman, Robert F. *Leading Constitutional Decisions*. Englewood Cliffs, N. J.: Prentice-Hall, 1977.

Graves, W. Brooke. *American Intergovernmental Relations*. New York: Charles Scribner's Sons, 1964.

Mason, Alpheus T. *The States Rights Debate*. Englewood Cliffs, N. J.: Prentice-Hall, 1964.

On Comparative Federalism

Macmahon, Arthur W. *Administering Federalism*. New York: Oxford University Press, 1972.

Riker, William H. *Federalism: Origin, Operation, Significance*. Boston: Little, Brown, 1964.

RESOLVED THAT: Civil Liberties Are Inadequate Safeguards

4

At Issue: Civil Liberties

Should Angela Davis be allowed to teach in a college or university? Should states provide financial aid for private and parochial schools? Should the Ku Klux Klan be allowed to march in opposition to the rights of black Americans? Should radical and revolutionary groups like the Weathermen be permitted to organize and advocate the overthrow of the United States government? Should it be permissible for high school principals to establish dress codes for students, including how long boys may wear their hair? Should everyone have the right to own guns? Is a law or medical school guilty of reverse discrimination when it admits minority group applicants with credentials inferior to those of white applicants? Should college students have access to all of their college records—admission test scores, letters of reference, and so on—or should these be kept confidential? Should a campus police officer be required to advise a student of his or her rights before an arrest if the student has just been seen selling hard drugs? Should a university bookstore be allowed to sell pornographic literature?

All these questions involve civil liberties. And, clearly, civil liberties pertain to the daily life of all citizens. In fact, no other area of government may be quite as important to individuals. Consider for a moment the incident that occurred in March of 1976 at Long Island City High School. The principal, Dr. Howard L. Hurwitz, was suspended by his superiors for refusing their instructions to readmit a seventeen-year-

No fight for civil liberty ever stays won.—*Roger Baldwin*

It is of great importance in a republic not only to guard the society against the oppression of its rulers, but to guard one part of the society against the injustice of the other part.—*No. 51 of The Federalist*

105

REBELS OR RAIDERS

Pensacola, Florida. March 6 [1976]. Years of racial animosity in this Florida panhandle city have erupted into violence in recent weeks on the issue of whether athletic teams at a local high school will be called the Rebels or the Raiders.

The controversy over the name, simmering for several years in and out of court, caused a riot at Escambia County High School Feb. 5.

Subsequently, crosses were burned in the yards of school board members, a shot was fired through the window of a black member and the homes of a human relations board member and a state legislator were burned by arsonists.

This afternoon, 120 Ku Klux Klansmen in full regalia, but with faces uncovered in accordance with law, paraded through the streets of Milton, a small town about 20 miles east of here. They had come into town in an 80-vehicle caravan outside Pensacola and called the march an "organizational effort."

Three Klan leaders from Alabama, Georgia and Florida attended the rally, which drew 450 persons. . . .

The school riot occurred as a result of a school election the day before on whether to change the nickname of the athletic teams from the Raiders back to their old name, The Rebels.

The nickname Rebels, chosen by students when the school was built in 1958, and used thereafter, first became the focus of racial trouble in 1973 when black students, attending the school under a court-ordered desegregation plan since 1969, protested that the name, along with the Confederate battle flag, flown at games and other school functions, was a direct insult to blacks.

Several fights and protests resulted from the controversy, and on July 24, 1973, a United States District Court permanently enjoined the use of the name, the flag and related symbols on the grounds that they were "racially irritating."

However, the school board and a group of white students appealed the court order and on Jan. 25, 1975, the United States Court of Appeals overturned the injunction and returned the matter to the school board to make its own decision on the name.

Source: *New York Times*, March 7, 1976, p. 33. © 1976 by The New York Times Company. Reprinted by permission.

old girl he had suspended as uncontrollable. The suspension of Hurwitz touched off a three-day boycott by parents and students supportive of Hurwitz, which finally ended in a compromise: The principal returned (but would later face departmental trial on charges of insubordination) and the student was readmitted.[1]

A series of recent court decisions have dealt with this problem of the rights of students. The Supreme Court held in 1975 that students could not be suspended without a notification of the charges and evidence against them and an opportunity to present their own evidence. Later it ruled that school administrators who are unfair in disciplining students cannot protect themselves against lawsuits by claiming ignorance of students' constitutional rights.[2]

The principal constitutional sources for civil liberties in the United States are the Bill of Rights and the Fourteenth Amendment. Even a cursory look at these guarantees raises crucial questions. In the First Amendment, what do freedom of speech and freedom of the press mean? Are you free to shout "fire!" in a crowded theater—when there is no fire? Are you free to print a libelous statement about someone? In the Fifth Amendment, what is "due process of law"? Does this phrase mean that murderers can be acquitted because they were not advised of their rights by the arresting police officers? What is "equal protection of the laws," as guaranteed by the Fourteenth Amendment? Does it mean that minority groups should have a preferred status in admission to professional schools because these groups have been discriminated against for so long?

As C. Wright Mills has pointed out, "It is much safer to celebrate civil liberties than to defend them."[3] Perhaps you believe in freedom of speech; do you believe that someone can publicly vilify your character? Perhaps you believe in the right to "keep and bear arms"; do you believe that your neighbors can keep a rifle in their den, within reach of your younger brother?

Our civil liberties are exceedingly difficult to define. They are enumerated in the Constitution in general statements that require specific application. To know their meaning requires at a minimum that we examine relevant decisions of the Supreme Court, which has ultimate jurisdiction over interpreting civil liberties. Civil liberties are also defined by departments and agencies of federal, state, and local governments as they apply these guarantees. Civil liberties may be defined loosely or strictly, broadly or narrowly. That is, freedom of speech may be defined so as to permit all types of speech, or it may be limited to a narrow set of circumstances.

That civil liberties are important is obvious, and so too is it obvious that they are susceptible to a variety of interpretations. More important, however, is the issue of their adequacy. Are civil liberties *adequately supported* and *adequately understood* by the American people? Do civil liberties guarantees *adequately protect* all groups of people in a complex and sophisticated society? The issue of their adequacy necessarily raises some very important questions.

That all men are born to equal rights is true. Every being has a right to his own, as clear, as moral, as sacred as any other being has. This is as indubitable as a moral government in the universe. But to teach that all men are born with equal powers and faculties, to equal influence in society, to equal property and advantages through life, is as gross a fraud, as glaring an imposition on the credulity of the people as ever was practised by monks, by Druids, by Brahmins, by priests of the immortal Lama, or by the self-styled philosophers of the French Revolution.—*John Adams*

"Something in civil rights must cover this."

- Do civil liberties guarantees encroach on the rights of the majority to rule?
- Or are certain kinds of rights so important that they must be protected from being impinged on by the majority?
- Is there any justification for governmental interference in citizens' religious practices? Or for invasion of the privacy of citizens' communications?

The Affirmative Case

Yes, civil liberties are inadequate safeguards.

I want our Bill of Rights implemented in fact. We have been trying to do this for 150 years. We are making progress, but we are not making progress fast enough. This country could very easily be faced with a situation similar to the one with which it was faced in 1922. That date was impressed on my mind because I was running for my first elective office—county judge of Jackson County—and there was an organization in that county that met on hills and burned crosses and worked behind sheets. There is a tendency in this country for that situation to develop again, unless we do something tangible to prevent it.[4]–Harry S. Truman

The guarantees of civil liberties are a hallmark of American democracy, and Americans pay them a great deal of lip service. What we revere most, however, deserves our closest scrutiny, lest we maintain something we really do not want or something that is not what we think it is. Constitutionally guaranteed civil liberties have several inadequacies, to wit:

- Civil liberties lack substantial public support.
- Vagueness in interpreting civil rights guarantees has created confusion in American society.
- Civil liberties have protected citizens in the middle and upper classes more than those in the lower class.
- Civil liberties are irrelevant in today's world.

LACK OF PUBLIC SUPPORT

A fundamental premise of democracy, majority rule, poses serious problems for those who support civil liberties. Many public opinion surveys have shown that civil liberties do not have consistent support from a majority of Americans. According to a 1970 CBS television network survey:

1. 55 percent of all Americans believe that "newspapers, magazines, and television should not have the right to report any story if the government feels it's harmful to our national interest."
2. 75 percent believe that "any person who hides behind the laws when he is questioned about his activities doesn't deserve much consideration."

The struggle for civil rights . . . involves the whole of our struggle for world peace. Nothing is more damaging to the United States in the battle of ideas and ideals . . . than our failures and our shortcomings in this area.—*Richard M. Nixon*

3. 75 percent believe that "if someone is suspected of treason or other serious crimes, he shouldn't be entitled to be let out on bail."
4. 50 percent believe that "a book that contains wrong political views cannot be a good book and does not deserve to be published." [5]

What such surveys reveal is that, while Americans say they support civil liberties, they frequently do not when faced with the realities of specific provisions. In other words, rights like freedom of the press, freedom from self-incrimination, and the right to bail are, in the minds of many, laudable in the abstract but not when granted to individuals with whom they disagree.

The strength of our civil liberties depends on adequate public support for judicial decisions that apply these rights. American history is replete with examples of how civil liberties have been rendered inadequate through court action or inaction or because the public did not support judicial rulings.

During the Civil War, President Lincoln denied the writ of habeas corpus to all people arrested for disloyalty to the Union. He also ordered

The civil liberties of Japanese Americans were violated by the government during World War II when thousands of Nisei living near the Pacific coast were moved inland to relocation camps where they could be kept under surveillance. Here army troops oversee part of the relocation process.

that their trials had to be held before military tribunals, even where civilian courts were functioning. The Supreme Court did not declare Lincoln's actions unconstitutional until after the Civil War.[6]

During World War II, the governor of Hawaii suspended the writ of habeas corpus and even declared martial law, again despite the fact that civilian courts remained open. His steps were ruled unconstitutional near the end of the war.[7] Also during World War II, Americans of Japanese descent were placed in relocation camps in the western United States. In reviewing this action in 1944, the Supreme Court upheld it, saying: "We 'cannot—by availing ourselves of the calm perspective of hindsight—now say that at that time these actions were unjustified."[8]

These three examples illustrate the inadequacy of significant civil liberties, in this instance, rights guaranteed in the Fifth and Sixth Amendments. The Supreme Court either did not declare the violations unconstitutional until a time when public opinion was more likely to support its decisions or, as in the third case, actually upheld the government's violation of civil liberties.

Another example is the issue of school desegregation. In 1954, in *Brown* v. *Board of Education*, the Supreme Court unanimously declared the doctrine of "separate but equal" unconstitutional, a violation of the Fourteenth Amendment's equal protection clause.* School segregation, said the Court, was inherently unequal and integration was to begin with "all deliberate speed." By 1969, however, only 20 percent of black children in the South were attending integrated schools. Except for trying to control violence in places like Little Rock, Arkansas (1957), Oxford, Mississippi (1962), and Tuscaloosa, Alabama (1963), the executive branch of the national government—which has the responsibility for carrying out judicial decisions—waited some ten to fifteen years before seriously beginning to enforce the unanimous 1954 mandate. In the meantime, thousands of black children awaited the opportunity to receive an education equal to that of white children.

Over twenty years after the *Brown* case, school boards were continuing to resist the full scope of the Court's ruling. Throughout much of that time, lower courts floundered, trying to interpret imprecise directions from the Supreme Court as to how "separate but equal" was to be abolished and what "all deliberate speed" meant. Why did the court refrain from saying simply that integration must take place "now"?

Another critical issue in terms of civil liberties involves the rights of black Americans. Writing in 1964, a former assistant attorney general for civil rights, Burke Marshall, declared that the whole system of denying blacks the vote was protected by failure of the government to

---

* An 1896 decision, *Plessy* v. *Ferguson*, had ruled that facilities segregating blacks and whites were not discriminatory so long as accommodations were equal.[9]

Table 1. Selected Civil Rights Decisions Not Fully Enforced Until After the Mid-1960s

DATE	CASE	DECISION
1935	*Norris* v. *Alabama*	Prohibited racial discrimination in jury selection
1938	*Missouri ex rel. Gaines* v. *Canada* (official of the University of Missouri)	Provided that blacks must have equal access to higher education and professional schools in a state
1950	*Sweatt* v. *Painter*	
1950	*McLaurin* v. *Oklahoma*	
1941	*Mitchell* v. *U.S.*	Accommodations must be substantially equal in interstate transportation
1944	*Smith* v. *Allwright*	Blacks have a right to vote in primary elections
1946	*Morgan* v. *Virginia*	Banned segregation in interstate travel
1948	*Shelley* v. *Kraemer*	Decreed that racially restrictive convenants* could not be enforced by state courts
1950	*Brotherhood of Railroad Trainmen* v. *Howard*	Provided that blacks could join labor unions

* A restrictive covenant is a clause entered in a deed to protect the value of property by restricting its use. For example, some covenants prohibit the sale of property to blacks or other minority groups.

enforce federally guaranteed rights because of inadequate public support.[10] Many Supreme Court decisions that theoretically protected other rights of black people were more often ignored than followed, as shown in Table 1.

In spite of decisions like these, it was not until the Civil Rights Act of 1964 and the Voting Rights Act of 1965 that the rights of black Americans were strengthened in a meaningful way. In other words, civil liberties are truly enforced only when the branches of government closer to the people than the judiciary—that is, the legislature and the executive—step in. Civil liberties cannot exist independently of the political process except as an abstraction. Although advances have been made in guaranteeing civil liberties for blacks, inadequate public support still precludes their receiving the full benefit of these guarantees in the Constitution.

Lack of adequate public support has limited the extension or protection of civil rights in many other instances. In the 1962 case of *Baker* v. *Carr*, the Supreme Court began to rule in favor of state legislative districts becoming more equal in population by redrawing district lines. Despite forceful statements that districts should approximate the criterion of "one person, one vote," i.e., be roughly equal in population, nine

ROTHCO

© Punch

"Our token Black - is that really how you think of yourself, Ms Corwin? You're much more than that, I assure you. You're also our token woman."

states still had not complied with the Court's decree seven years later (see page 118). Although the Court in 1966 spelled out very specifically the rights of arrested persons and the obligations of arresting officers,[11] a veritable avalanche of data confirm continued police violations of these rights.[12] Despite the fact that the Court in 1962 declared unconstitutional officially sanctioned prayer in public schools,[13] one survey showed that three years later nearly 13 percent of the nation's schools (and almost 50 percent of those in the South) were violating the ban.[14] In the 1970s, efforts were being made in some states—New Hampshire for one—to require or at least allow Bible reading and prayer. Difficulties in implementing each of these decisions illustrate the fact that civil liberties lack adequate public support and are, therefore, frequently violated.

VAGUENESS AND CONFUSION

Unquestionably the wording and interpretation of civil liberties are vague and imprecise, which results in their being inadequate safeguards. As noted by constitutional law scholar Jay Sigler:

> For many Americans their rights appear to spring from the Constitution
> and especially from the Bill of Rights, but even though most Americans
> are exposed to the Constitution many times during their schooling, few
> are able to say with any accuracy which they may in fact enjoy, and
> what the meaning of these rights may be. On the surface the task of de-
> scribing American rights seems simple enough. But no one can con-
> fidently draw up a list of American rights in outline form to be carried
> around by all citizens (and some aliens) because an accurate under-
> standing of the scope and impact of American rights requires a keen ap-
> preciation of the definitions which courts and public officials have given
> to certain key phrases in the Constitution.[15]

The Bill of Rights and other civil liberties guarantees are like putty
that never hardens but is always subject to manipulation and molding.
The result is a confusing array of decisions in which the Supreme Court
seems to come down on both sides of essentially the same issue. To illustrate this imprecision, let us examine five areas in which the Court
has handed down what appear to be contradictory rulings: freedom of
religion, obscenity, legislative redistricting, rights of the accused, and
evidence admissable at a trial.

Freedom of Religion   Here the opening clauses of the First Amendment are crucial—the so-called "establishment" and "free exercise"
clauses. These state: "Congress shall make no law respecting an establishment of religion, or prohibiting the free exercise thereof." What do
these clauses mean? They mean what the courts say they mean, and various courts have interpreted them in different ways. Realistically can
the public be expected to have an adequate understanding of their civil
liberties when civil liberties are subject to confusing and conflicting
interpretations?

In a number of decisions involving freedom of religion, the Supreme Court has seemingly strengthened the "establishment" clause to
reinforce the "wall of separation." It has ruled that public schools cannot permit religious instructors (even volunteers) to provide religious
instruction in public school buildings during the school day.[16] It has
held that tax funds may not be used to reimburse church-operated ele-

It is obvious that an individual
should not have the final say on
what is "religion" within the
meaning of the First Amendment. Some review and
expression of disinterested judgment are necessary. Otherwise
minor things, such as obeying
traffic signals, or important civic
duties, such as the payment of
taxes, could be blown up into forbidden exactions by calling them
infringements on religious liberty. Likewise practices that are
abhorrent to civilized people,
such as human sacrifices, are beyond the pale. None would go so
far as to include them in religion.
Polygamy, to which many millions of people in the Middle
East and Asia are committed,
may be more debatable. It is,
however, alien to the moral code
of the West. To our community
it does no violence to place polygamy outside the scope of
religious practices so far as First
Amendment rights are con-
cerned.—*William. O. Douglas*

Although it has been said that the First Amendment was designed
to build "a wall of separation between Church and State," the wall has
crumbled in places, leaving its demarcations fuzzy. Consider these facts:
some thirty states have "blue laws" that require the closing of business
establishments on Sundays; the armed forces employ chaplains; legislative bodies typically begin each day's session with prayer; and our currency affirms "In God We Trust."

mentary and secondary schools or otherwise supplement their financial resources in order to pay for the salaries of teachers, even if they teach secular subjects.[17] According to another ruling, a state cannot reimburse parochial and other private schools for the maintenance and repair of school facilities and equipment or for the cost of testing pupils in secular subjects.[18] Parents cannot be reimbursed by the state for tuition costs for private schools;[19] nor can they deduct such payments from their state income taxes.[20] The Court has also held that public schools cannot lend instructional equipment to nonpublic schools.[21]

On the other hand, the Supreme Court has handed down a number of decisions that tend to blur the "establishment" clause. It has ruled that parents may be reimbursed for bus fares to send children to church schools.[22] Another decision held that public schools may release students from part of the compulsory school day to obtain religious instruction outside the school building.[23] State bonds, said the Court, may be used to finance the construction of nonreligious buildings on church-related college campuses.[24] A state may lend textbooks to church-related schools,[25] and it may furnish secular textbooks to pupils in private schools (except institutions that exclude students because of race or religion).[26]

Justice Lewis F. Powell has noted: "We are not unaware that . . . those who have endeavored to formulate systems of state aid to nonpublic education may feel that the decisions of this Court have, indeed, presented them with the 'insoluble paradox.' "[27] (The paradox is between the conclusion that aid is permissible and the criteria that make the granting of the aid almost constitutionally impossible.) But, said Powell, "if novel forms of aid have not readily been sustained by this Court, the 'fault' lies not with the doctrines which are said to have created a paradox, but rather with the Establishment Clause itself."[28]

Actually, a basic reason for the seemingly contradictory decisions of the Supreme Court is the principle of "no excessive entanglement with religion." A threefold test to determine whether a law violates the "establishment" clause, developed by the Court in two of its decisions,* requires that the law (1) have a clear secular legislative purpose; (2)

---

* In another decision, *Wolman* v. *Walter* (1977), the U.S. Supreme Court again applied the threefold test and found four kinds of aid to private and parochial schools permissible and two kinds impermissible. The four kinds of aid that are permissible are: (1) the loan of circular textbooks to nonpublic school students or their parents; (2) the provision of standardized test and scoring services to nonpublic schools; (3) the provision of speech and hearing and sociological diagnostic services to nonpublic schools; and (4) the provision of therapeutic guidance and remedial services for nonpublic schools. The two kinds of aid that are impermissible are: (1) state supplied instructional materials for nonpublic schools and their students; and (2) state supplied field trips—transportation and services.

have the primary effect of neither advancing nor inhibiting religion; and (3) avoid "excessive government entanglement with religion." [29]

The principal hurdle for those seeking state aid to parochial and other private schools is to design aid plans so that their effect is solely to serve secular purposes. One obstacle, however, is that a plan may excessively entangle government with religion by supporting religious instruction indirectly: For instance, public financing of a teacher in a church school may allow the school to use the money thus saved for religious purposes. The seemingly conflicting decisions and doctrines devised by the Court concerning "no establishment of religion" present the public with an unclear picture of their civil liberties guarantees, thereby making it more difficult for the public to understand their rights.

There is even more evidence. What happens if a law requires people to do something that conflicts with the "free exercise" of their religion—when to exempt them from abiding by the law would favor their religion and thus violate the "establishment" doctrine? The Court and the legislatures have recognized the conflict between these two clauses and have struggled to resolve it, often stirring widespread controversy. The question is whether neutral ground exists between the "free exercise" and "establishment" clauses. To date, it has not been found.

Generally, the Court has ruled that religious convictions do not confer any right for a person to violate otherwise valid and nondiscriminatory laws. However, as long as the law is not violated, an individual's freedom of worship should be unrestricted.[30]

Some decisions have restricted the "free exercise" clause. The Court has forbidden the practice of polygamy by Mormons;[31] required the vaccination of school children who are Christian Scientists;[32] and upheld a Massachusetts criminal law forbidding boys under twelve and girls under eighteen from selling merchandise on the streets (the merchandise at issue was Jehovah's Witness literature).[33]

Other Court decisions have upheld the "free exercise" doctrine. The Court has upheld parents' rights to send their children to nonpublic schools;[34] declared that a state may not require Jehovah's Witnesses to participate in a public school flag-salute ceremony;[35] denied states the right to deny unemployment compensation to those who refuse on principle to accept positions requiring them to work on Saturday;[36] and ruled that Amish parents could not be compelled to send their children to any kind of school beyond the eighth grade.[37]

Another confusing area has to do with draft laws. Here the Supreme Court has defined the word "religious" in such a way that any deeply held opposition to war, based upon either humanistic or religious considerations, furnishes constitutional grounds for draft exemption. (It should be pointed out, however, that those who object to one war but not all wars are *not* qualified for draft exemption.) [38]

Obscenity   Although the First Amendment unequivocally grants freedom of speech and freedom of the press, the meaning of these guarantees has presented many problems in relation to the public's understanding of obscenity. A confusing array of Supreme Court decisions adds to the problem. What does the word itself mean? In 1957 the Court for the first time held that "obscenity is not within the area of constitutionally protected speech or press." [39] Its definition of obscenity then was material that is "utterly without redeeming social importance." To determine what is of "redeeming social importance," the Court applied this test: "whether to the average person, applying contemporary community standards, the dominant theme of the material taken as a whole appeals to prurient interests." Justice Potter Stewart said that he would not attempt to define "hard-core" pornography, but added: "I know it when I see it." [40]

In 1966 the Court specified that material could be considered obscene only if (1) its dominant theme as a whole appealed to a "prurient interest in sex"; (2) it was "patently offensive" to contemporary community standards; and (3) it was "utterly without redeeming social value." [41] All three elements have to be present, the Court declared, before material could be banned as obscene. The result was to remove almost all restrictions on the content of books and motion pictures, since even the slightest "social value" might redeem them.

In 1973 the Court set up new standards in the case of *Miller* v. *California*. Now a work might be regarded as obscene if (1) the average person, "applying contemporary community standards," found that, taken as a whole, it appealed to "prurient interest"; (2) it depicted "in a patently offensive way" sexual conduct prohibited by state law; and (3) if, as a whole, it lacked "serious literary, artistic, political, or scientific value." [42]

While the 1966 decision aimed to set a nationwide standard, the effect of the 1973 decision—theoretically, at least—was to allow local communities to set their own standards. In justification, Chief Justice Burger contended that it was unrealistic and constitutionally unsound to impose the standards of Las Vegas or New York City on the people of Maine or Mississippi.[43]

In 1974, however, the Court appeared to qualify its own decision when it declared: "It would be a serious misreading of *Miller* to conclude that juries [in local communities] have unbridled discretion in determining what is patently offensive." [44] The Court stated that appel-

In a democracy, who should decide what is obscene? What standards should be imposed? Where should the line be drawn between free expression and pornography? Are shows featuring naked performers such as the ones advertised in this photo obscene or are they valid forms of entertainment? Would banning them violate the civil liberties of the performers and the patrons? Questions such as these continue to perplex the Supreme Court, Congress, and the general public.

late courts should review decisions of local juries carefully to make certain that constitutional standards are not violated. However, federal courts are not to review state civil proceedings until state court action ends.[45]

Legislative Redistricting In 1946 the Supreme Court declined to rule in a congressional redistricting case brought to establish a more equitable distribution of districts between urban and rural populations. The Court ruled that this was a political question which legislative and executive branches should resolve.[46] By the early 1960s the Court had changed its mind and had begun to concern itself with such questions at both the state and federal levels. In the case of *Baker* v. *Carr*, it held that federal courts had the power to judge the validity of a state's districting for legislative seats. The Court thus began to move toward the idea that each person's vote was to count for as much as anyone else's—"one person, one vote." [47]

The principal criterion applied by the Warren Court* was population equality; this was ultimately defined to mean exact population equality as nearly as possible among all districts. This principle—applied to both state and federal legislative districts in 1969 [48]—stood for only a brief period of time. In 1973, the Burger Court upheld a redistricting plan with a population deviation of 16.4 percent,[49] and recognized criteria other than population.

The Fourteenth Amendment's right to "equal protection of the laws" has led to much confusion because of the Supreme Court's changing interpretation and application of the clause to legislative redistricting.† Opposition in state legislatures to the Court's legislative redistricting decisions became so great that the late U.S. senator Everett M. Dirksen (Rep. Ill.) sponsored an unsuccessful constitutional amendment that would have allowed each state to have districts for one of its two legislative houses to be based upon considerations other than population equality.

Rights of the Accused   What are the rights of an accused person? Between 1966 and 1976, the Supreme Court changed its mind three times.

The Court ruled in 1966, in *Miranda* v. *Arizona*, that evidence given by suspects could not be used in either a federal or state trial unless the suspects had been notified that (1) they were free to remain silent; (2) what they said might be used against them in court; (3) they had a right to have an attorney present during the questioning; (4) if they could not afford to hire a lawyer, an attorney would be provided; and (5) they could terminate the police interrogation at any stage. If the prosecution failed to comply with these requirements, a conviction

---

* In certain periods, the Supreme Court is identified through its chief justice. Thus the Court from 1953 to 1969—when Earl Warren was chief justice—is frequently referred to as the Warren Court. Likewise, the highest tribunal came to be known as the Burger Court after the advent of Chief Justice Warren Burger. For a list of Supreme Court chief justices, see the appendix.

† In congressional redistricting cases, the court has relied on Article I, Section 2, rather than the Fourteenth Amendment. Article I, Section 2, of the Constitution provides that representatives shall be elected "by the people" and shall be apportioned among the states "according to their respective numbers," i.e., population.

would be reversed even if other independent evidence were sufficient to establish guilt.[50]

A 1971 decision somewhat modified the *Miranda* provisions. It held that, although the prosecution could not introduce evidence of guilt obtained contrary to the 1966 ruling, it could introduce statements illegally obtained from suspects to attack their credibility if they took the stand and made statements contrary to what they had told the police.[51]

In a 1974 case the Court further modified the 1966 ruling. The testimony of a witness could be used, it decided, even though police had learned the identity of the witness by questioning defendants without advising them of all their rights pursuant to the 1966 decision. Here the Court decided that a "fair trial" does not mean a perfect trial, thus police officers may make some errors in criminal investigations.[52]

In 1976 the Court further relaxed the *Miranda* standards by condoning some use of statements made to police by suspects in custody, statements made after the suspect had asked for a lawyer but before the lawyer was present. Writing for the majority on the Court, Justice Harry A. Blackmun said: "The shield provided by *Miranda* is not to be perverted to a license to testify inconsistently, or even perjuriously, free from the risk of confrontation with prior inconsistent utterances." [53]

Admissible Evidence   Created by a unanimous Court in 1916, the *exclusionary rule* originally barred from use in federal criminal trials any evidence seized in violation of the Fourth Amendment's ban against unreasonable searches and seizures. In 1961 the exclusionary rule was extended to cover state as well as federal criminal trials.[54] Since then, the rule has been heatedly attacked. Critics say it permits clearly guilty persons to go free if the police have violated their rights while acquiring evidence against them. Also, they contend, it does not distinguish between violations that are deliberate abuses by the authorities and those that entail accidental or minor mistakes by officers in the field or judges on the bench.

In a 1975 case, the Court modified the exclusionary rule, stating: "If the purpose of the exclusionary rule is to deter unlawful police conduct, then evidence obtained from a search should be suppressed only if it can be said that the law enforcement officer had knowledge, or may properly be charged with knowledge, that the search was unconstitutional." [55]

Once again in 1976 the Court further relaxed the exclusionary rule. Lloyd C. Powell, convicted in a 1968 California murder, claimed that evidence used to convict him was unconstitutionally obtained through a defective loitering ordinance. David L. Rice, convicted in a 1971 Ne-

Table 2. 1976 U.S. Supreme Court Decisions Showing Retreat from Enforcement of Bill of Rights

CASE	AMENDMENT	RIGHT/FREEDOM	DECISION
Boyd v. U.S.	Fifth	Self-Incrimination	Seizure and use of personal business records for use in trial is not the same as persons being compelled to testify against themselves
South Dakota v. Opperman	Fourth	Unreasonable Search and Seizure	Evidence (marijuana) obtained through a routine search of the contents of a car impounded for parking violation may be used against the car's owner in a subsequent drug prosecution
U.S. v. Martinez-Fuerte	Fourth	Unreasonable Search and Seizure	Police officers at fixed border patrol traffic checkpoints (not at actual border itself) may question occupants of cars without a judicial warrant and without an articulable reason to believe the cars contain illegal aliens
U.S. v. Santana	Fourth	Arrest Warrant	Police may arrest suspect at home without obtaining an arrest warrant if the arrested person has merely stepped inside the house after being seen by police in doorway
Ludwig v. Massachusetts	Sixth	Jury Trial	A state may decline to allow trial by jury for persons charged with certain offenses even though jury trial would be required in federal courts
U.S. v. MacCollom	Fifth and Fourteenth	Equal Protection/ Trial Transcript	Indigent prison inmates do not have a constitutional right to a transcript of their trial provided at public expense when they challenge their conviction as unconstitutional

braska murder of a police officer, claimed that a defective search warrant provided the prosecution with evidence to obtain his conviction. Both contended that their Fourth Amendment right of *habeas corpus** had been violated by state law enforcement officers. In rejecting the claims of Powell and Rice, Justice Lewis F. Powell said:

> Application of the exclusionary rule . . . deflects the truthfinding process and often frees the guilty. The disparity in particular cases between the error committed by the police officer and the windfall afforded a guilty

* The writ of *habeas corpus* is a court order directing an official who has a person in custody to bring the prisoner to court and to show cause for that person's detention. It is generally considered to be the most important civil liberty, because it prevents an arbitrary arrest and imprisonment. Prisoners serving sentences can seek to have their cases reopened based upon alleged illegal detention, such as the denial of rights before or during their trials, which was the plaintiffs' charge in the 1976 cases before the Court.

defendant by application of the rule is contrary to the idea of proportionality that is essential to the concept of justice.[56]

In several other decisions in 1976, as shown in Table 2, the Supreme Court retreated from clearly and fully enforcing certain provisions of the Bill of Rights, including the right to trial by jury.

Such contradictory decisions naturally result in confusion about what laws mean. Religious groups steer cautiously between the pillars of "establishment" and "free exercise." Among both distributors of pornography and citizens who want to ban it, there is uncertainty about the law on obscenity. Guidance is lacking for state legislators who, within a four-year period, were given two decidedly different standards for legislative redistricting. In law enforcement agencies, confusion reigns as to what portions of the *Miranda* decision might be further altered, what with three changes having been made within ten years. Of course, the exclusionary rule has been weakened twice in a one-year period.

PROTECTION OF WHOSE LIBERTIES?

What criminal cases reveal . . . is that there is one law for the poor, another for the organized criminal with the expensive name lawyers.—*Herbert Mitgang*

. . . to the poor man, "legal" has become a synonym for technicalities and obstruction, not for that which is to be respected. The poor man looks upon the law as an enemy, not as a friend. For him the law is always taking something away.—*Robert F. Kennedy*

Suppose that you are poor and your best friend is wealthy. Each of you commits a serious crime. Who is more likely to obtain bail, to be acquitted, or, if convicted, to receive a reduced or suspended sentence? Your friend! To whose case will the judge be likely to devote more time, effort, and interest? That of your friend! Thorough studies have documented the conclusion that, in practice, the law favors the rich.[57] The Eighth Amendment states: "Excessive bail shall not be required, nor excessive fines imposed, nor cruel and unusual punishments inflicted"; the Fourteenth guarantees that no person shall be denied "equal protection of the laws." What can these rights mean, given the favoritism shown to the privileged?

Of course it should be pointed out that indigent defendants did not even have a constitutionally guaranteed right to counsel under the U. S. Constitution until 1963.[58] (In *Powell* v. *Alabama* in 1932 the Supreme Court held that several adverse circumstances, such as illiteracy, made the right of counsel essential.) Before then a poor defendant was frequently convicted solely because he or she had no counsel at all. Even now, however, there is no assurance that the court-appointed counsel for a defendant will be as good as the attorney for the prosecution.

Judicial discrimination against the poor is most evident in cases involving black people. Some Americans feel that the Supreme Court has been a bastion of strength in the defense of black people's rights. Not so, says civil rights attorney Lewis M. Steel. According to him the Court

has time and again taken the position that racial equality should be sub-
ordinated—or at least balanced against—white America's fear of rapid
change, which would threaten its time-honored prerogatives. Only where
racial barriers were overtly obnoxious—and therefore openly contradictory to the American creed of equality—has the Court deigned to
move. Yet its decisions have allowed a confused, miseducated, and
prejudiced white public to believe that its black fellow citizens have
been given their full rights.[59]

Not only did the Supreme Court call for integration with "all deliberate speed," which led to years of foot-dragging by white authorities. It
also, according to Steel, "waltzed in time to the music of the white majority—one step forward, one step backward and sidestep, sidestep"—on
a variety of other issues. Examples of the Court's "backward" steps are
shown in Table 3.

Table 3. Selected Civil Rights Cases Illustrating Supreme Court's Unwillingness to Apply Rights Fully

DATE	CASE	DECISION
1965	Swain v. Alabama	Allowed Alabama prosecutors to challenge and remove all blacks from a jury
1965	Cox v. Louisiana	Limited peaceful demonstrations by blacks against courthouses
1966	Georgia v. Rachel	Allowed Georgia to inflict a heavy fine on the NAACP for picketing
1967	Green Street Association v. Daley	Refused to review a lower court decision that had the effect of removing blacks from their homes without provision for adequate replacement housing
1968	Cameron v. Johnson	Refused to review a Mississippi decision against civil rights workers who had maintained an orderly and peaceful picket line
1976	Washington v. Davis	Held that challenges to employment tests must be supported by more evidence than the fact that more minority applicants than white applicants failed to pass

INADEQUATE FOR OUR TIMES

Our civil liberties as guaranteed by the Constitution can truly be termed inadequate for the era in which we live. Ironically it may be argued (1) that they do not provide enough protection and (2) that they provide too much protection.

     Concerning their inadequate protection, it is difficult to see how civil liberties drafted some 190 years ago, as was the Bill of Rights, can

Taped

from Herblock's State of the Union (Simon & Schuster, 1972)

be wholly adequate in today's society. Realistically, how could they be expected to protect citizens against a government that now maintains such intelligence agencies as the Federal Bureau of Investigation, Central Intelligence Agency, Secret Service, Defense Intelligence Agency, and National Security Agency? The Watergate scandal revealed the widespread use of equipment designed for surveillance. Among the types of equipment now available are electronic sensors, wall-penetration devices, surveillance radar, voice-print equipment, and night-vision devices. If civil liberties guarantees have been grossly violated in the past—as they have—what hope is there that they will be upheld in the future?

Given the technology, nature, and needs of contemporary American society, some civil liberties guarantees are more straight jacket than shield. Should a society which experienced three major political assassinations in five years, and which also has a soaring crime rate, be bound by a constitutional provision guaranteeing people the right to "keep and bear arms"? Should people be permitted total privacy in their communications when our nation is threatened by subversive groups in its midst? Should criminals be allowed to traffic in drugs without fear of electronic surveillance?

That such questions can be raised is a clear indication that our civil liberties are inadequate safeguards. Harry Truman saw the danger in 1947; it looms larger than ever today.

In the future, I don't think we will see much in terms of legislation with regard to civil rights. I think blacks have begun to recognize that our future is in the political process and that the gains will be made there. . . . It is now an accepted legitimate way to achieve gains for black people, and I think this is what we are going to see more and more.—*Barbara Jordan*

In the councils of Government, we must guard against the acquisition of unwarranted influence, whether sought or unsought, by the military-industrial complex. The potential for the disastrous rise or misplaced power exists and will persist.

We must never let the weight of this combination endanger our liberties or democratic processes.—*Dwight D. Eisenhower*

The Negative Case

No, civil liberties are not inadequate safeguards.

What use then, it may be asked, can a bill of rights serve in popular Governments? I answer the two following which, though less essential than in other Governments, sufficiently recommend the precaution: (1) The political truths declared in that solemn manner acquire by degrees the character of fundamental axioms of free Government, and as they become incorporated with the national sentiment, counteract the impulses of interest and passion. (2) Altho it be generally true as above stated that the danger of oppression lies in the interested majorities of the people rather than in usurped acts of Government, yet there may be occasions on which the evil may spring from the latter source; and on such, a bill of rights will be a good ground for appeal to the sense of the Community.[60]–*James Madison*

Admittedly our civil liberties are not perfect. They have been sometimes violated, sometimes ignored. Their history is certainly unsure and unstable—like the history of the United States itself. Oscillations in the application of civil liberties reflect nothing more than changes in the American experience, for the history of our civil rights is part of our larger history.

In many ways, it is the Bill of Rights that makes American democracy operate. Just one example is the relationship between the political process and the First Amendment's freedom of speech guarantee:

> Discussion, the exchange of views, the ventilation of desires and de-
> mands—these are, of course, crucial to our politics. And so, for much the
> same reason, is the effectiveness of law embodying the wishes of the
> greatest number, or at any rate, their chosen representatives. It would fol-
> low that the First Amendment should protect and indeed encourage
> speech so long as it serves to make the political process work.[61]

Freedom of expression carries with it substantial risks that threaten the very foundations of governmental order. For this reason this right has sometimes been unduly circumscribed; for example, Socialists Eugene V. Debs and Victor L. Berger were imprisoned for their vocal opposition to World War I. It is simplistic, however, to conclude that for this reason civil liberties guarantees are inadequate. No society has ever fully achieved all these rights. The key is whether a society is moving toward their achievement. As noted by Senator Sam Ervin:

> Our founding fathers were wise enough to know that there is no way to
> give freedom of speech and press to the wise and deny it to the fools and
> the knaves. Certainly they did not intend for the government to decide
> who were the fools and the knaves.[62]

Rather than dismiss civil liberties as inadequate safeguards, we should take great pride in them and their meaning in American history, for several reasons.

- Civil liberties serve as the conscience of the nation.
- Through their adaptability, civil liberties perform many vital functions in our society.
- Civil liberties protect all Americans.
- The continuing relevance of the democratic experience in the United States depends in large measure on civil liberties.

THE CONSCIENCE OF THE NATION

The affirmative case suggests there is inadequate public support for civil liberties by citing survey research data and wartime examples of failure to enforce them. What the affirmative case overlooks is the normal daily acceptance of civil liberties by the American people. For example, the First Amendment freedoms of speech, press, assembly, and religion are upheld daily in lecture halls, newspapers, streets, and churches. Similar examples could also be cited for each of our civil liberties. In fact it would be difficult to find another society that observes and supports civil liberties as much as the United States.

Despite the normal daily observance of and support for civil liberties, we must recognize the nature of civil liberties. What are they? Very simply they are abstract declarations of goals to be attained. Dotting American history are many examples of struggles to attain these goals, and undoubtedly much progress has been made, most notably in the civil rights struggles of the 1950s and 1960s. Psychologist Kenneth Clark notes that the civil rights movement would not have existed had there not been the "equal protection of the laws" clause in the Fourteenth Amendment which the Supreme Court relied on to declare school segregation unconstitutional.

> This movement would probably not have existed at all were it not for the 1954 Supreme Court school desegregation decision, which provided a tremendous boost to the morale of Negroes by its clear affirmation that color is irrelevant to the rights of American citizens. Until this time the Southern Negro generally accommodated to the separation of the black from the white society.[63]

In recognizing that civil liberties guarantees are abstract declarations, one places them in their proper perspective: namely that they are in a sense the conscience of the nation. They aim society in the right direction and spur it toward broadening its humanitarian goals.

American democracy has been strengthened through application of our civil liberties. For example, quantum leaps were taken toward achieving equal protection of the laws when indigent defendants were guaranteed the right to legal counsel;[64] when urban and suburban populations were guaranteed their proportion of legislative representation through the doctrine of "one person, one vote";[65] and when black Americans obtained equal access to public accommodations and transportation through the Civil Rights Act of 1964. Similarly, due process gained added meaning when laws regarding police investigations, free speech, and rights to a fair trial were applied to the states as well as to the federal government (see Table 5, p. 142).

Granting such rights in specific situations serves two functions: (1) it redresses wrongs for the person or group adversely affected; and (2) it educates the public at large about the meaning of general phrases and principles.

One might note, too, that judicial decisions based on application of civil liberties have been cited by Congress and the president as reasons

Labor activist Cesar Chavez used constitutionally protected civil liberties such as freedom of speech and freedom of assembly to alert the American public to the terrible working conditions suffered by migrant farm workers. Here Chavez participates in a demonstration on behalf of the National Farm Workers Association (NFWA).

for their own actions. This was the case with the Civil Rights Act of 1964, the Voting Rights Act of 1965, and the Housing Act of 1968—to name but three. In such instances, the legislative and executive branches were in part taking steps to enforce civil liberties as interpreted by the judiciary.

THE ADVANTAGES OF ADAPTABILITY

If the meaning of our civil liberties had been fixed for all time in the constitutional amendments, the protection afforded by these rights would have been greatly circumscribed. Being adaptable—even to the point of vagueness and imprecision—has had many advantages.

Neither civil liberties guarantees nor the judges who interpret and apply them exist in a vacuum. They change as society changes. In interpreting and applying civil liberties guarantees, judges may be expected to reflect the world they live in. The meaning of civil liberties cannot be absolute; as Oliver Wendell Holmes once said, "The right to swing my fist ends where the other man's nose begins." The aim is balance, difficult to obtain and tenuous at best.

Balancing Order and Freedom According to Oliver Wendell Holmes, "The best test of truth is the power of the thought to get itself accepted in the competition of the market." Some decades later law professor Alexander Bickel noted that "a marketplace without rules of civil discourse is no marketplace of ideas, but a bullring." [66]

The shade of difference between Holmes and Bickel illustrates the balance that must be obtained between order and freedom—the government's need to maintain order and the individual's right to freedom. Where only order exists, freedom is stifled; where only freedom exists, anarchy reigns.

Standards and principles embodied in our civil liberties provide a way to establish a proper balance between government and the individual. The government must have the power to investigate and to maintain order in society; the individual must be free from unusual searches and seizures. The government must be able to acquire land by exercising its right of eminent domain; the individual cannot be deprived of property without due process of law.

Changing with the Times Adaptation to changing times is necessary in a dynamic society, in civil liberties as in other respects. A society under stress is clearly going to be more concerned about maintaining order than a peaceful society. Thus individual freedom may well be somewhat restricted in time of war. In such situations it is understandable that government executives may suspend the writ of habeas corpus or the guarantee of a civilian trial.

An example is the case of *Schenck* v. *United States*. During World War I, Congress passed an Espionage Act, which, among other things, prohibited actions leading to insubordination in the armed forces. When Socialist Charles T. Schenck mailed out pamphlets opposing the war, the government accused him of violating the act. This case pitted the rights of free speech and press against the government's need to protect itself in time of war. The Supreme Court ruled unanimously in favor of the government. Wrote Justice Oliver Wendell Holmes: "When a nation is at war many things that might be said in time of peace are such a hindrance to its effort that their utterance will not be endured so long as men fight, and that no court could regard them as protected by any constitutional right." [67]

American democracy should not be judged solely by what happens to civil liberties in times of war. One should also consider the less stressful times of peace—for example, parts of the 1950s and 1960s when the Supreme Court significantly extended the application and meaning of basic human rights in American society.

Civil liberties have been sufficiently flexible to allow the Supreme Court both to lead and to follow public opinion. The Warren Court in the 1950s and 1960s led public opinion on the issue of race relations by declaring segregation in the schools unconstitutional. The Burger Court in the 1970s has followed public opinion on the issues of police investigatory powers and obscenity by modifying Warren Court decisions that had strengthened the rights of the criminal and allowed obscenity greater protection. Supreme Court decisions have also helped to set national standards for civil liberties by applying the Bill of Rights to the states through the due process clause of the Fourteenth Amendment. Application of the Bill of Rights to the states is shown in Table 5 (page 000); note that almost all of these extensions of civil liberties occurred during peacetime.

It is a myth to say that any person has a constitutional right to say what he pleases, where he pleases, when he pleases.—*Justice Hugo Black*

Flexibility: Freedom of Speech   The stability of American society has been preserved by flexible application of the Bill of Rights. This is best seen in reference to freedoms of speech, press, and assembly.

Should all speech receive absolute protection, according to the First Amendment? A quick reading of the amendment suggests an affirmative answer. But what about speech that might incite a riot or defame another person's character? What about the depiction of sex on television? Careful thought about some applications of freedom of speech might suggest a few necessary limitations or guidelines. Protection of all speech, press, and assembly might completely undermine democracy. As indicated by Justice Lewis F. Powell, Jr., "First Amendment rights are not absolute in all circumstances. They may be circumscribed when necessary to further a sufficiently strong public interest." [68] The stability of society is obviously enhanced by flexible interpretation and application of freedom of speech.

Another First Amendment controversy involved *Hair*, the rock musical. Chattanooga, Tennessee, city officials refused to allow the musical to be shown in the municipal auditorium. The Court ruled: "Only if we were to conclude that live drama was unprotected by the First Amendment—or subject to a totally different standard than that applied to other forms of expression—could we possibly find no prior restraint here." A dissenting opinion held that Chattanooga should be able to "reserve its auditorium for productions suitable for exhibition to all the citizens of the city, adults and children alike," thus excluding *Hair*.[69] Clearly a flexible interpretation and application of civil liberties is necessary for society's stability in view of such divergent opinions.

The Court has developed several doctrines in testing whether speech should be constitutionally protected. The doctrines reveal the Court's flexible interpretation and application. These may be summarized as follows: absolutist, clear and present danger, dangerous tendency, preferred position, and balancing of interests. Depending upon the condition of society, e.g., whether at war or peace, one might choose which doctrine to apply.

Absolutist According to this doctrine, the First Amendment means just what it says and cannot be qualified. Justices Hugo Black and William Douglas have taken this position, Black arguing that "there are 'absolutes' in our Bill of Rights" that cannot be weakened by judicial decisions. He argued that obscenity and libel cannot be constitutionally limited because they are types of speech. Few justices have agreed with this view.

Clear and Present Danger Perhaps the best way to define this doctrine is through the words of Oliver Wendell Holmes. In the *Schenck* case, he contended that speech loses its constitutional protections if it presents an immediate threat—"a clear and present danger." [70] The First Amendment would not protect the speech of someone falsely yelling "fire" in a crowded theater, because that person would be creating the immediate threat of a riot. If there were no danger of immediate disturbance harmful to the public, speech would be protected. To use a modern example: Communist Angela Davis might be allowed to speak on a college campus, because her doing so would not constitute a "clear and present danger."

Dangerous Tendency According to this doctrine, speech loses its constitutional protection if it has a tendency to lead to a substantive evil. Application of this doctrine would lead to more infringement on freedom of speech than the "clear and present danger" test, since speech would only have to tend to be dangerous, not present an actual threat. According to this doctrine, Angela Davis might not be allowed to speak if she advocated communism, because this might present a "dangerous tendency."

Preferred Position Justices holding this doctrine contend that the First Amendment freedoms have the highest priority in our constitutional hierarchy. Courts bear a special responsibility to scrutinize with extra care any laws that appear to trespass on these freedoms. The point is that when freedom of speech is diluted or denied, the channels for correcting errors in the political process are clogged or closed. Any limitation on free speech is presumed unconstitutional unless there is some overriding justification. This doctrine, of course, might be used to uphold Angela Davis' right to advocate communism in a campus speech.

Balancing of Interests Does the interest of society in limiting speech outweigh the interest of the person speaking? This doctrine, instead of placing the First Amendment freedom of speech guarantee on a pedestal, weighs it against the interests of society in maintaining order. Turning once again to Angela Davis, the Court would ask whether her

I am persuaded myself that the good sense of the people will always be found to be the best army. They may be led astray for a moment but will soon correct themselves. . . . The basis of our governments being the opinion of the people, the very first object should be to keep that right; and were it left to me to decide whether we should have a government without newspapers or newspapers without a government, I should not hesitate a moment to prefer the latter. But I should mean that every man should receive those papers and be capable of reading them.—*Thomas Jefferson*

If all mankind minus one were of one opinion, and only one person were of the contrary opinion, mankind would be no more justified in silencing that one person, than he, if he had the power, would be justified in silencing mankind. Were an opinion a personal possession of no value except to the owner; if to be obstructed in the enjoyment of it were simply a private injury, it would make some difference whether the injury was inflicted only on a few persons or on many. But the peculiar evil of silencing the expression of an opinion is, that it is robbing the human race; posterity as well as the existing generation; those who dissent from the opinion, still more than those who hold it. If the opinion is right, they are deprived of the opportunity of exchanging error for truth: if wrong, they lose, what is almost as great a benefit, the clearer perception and livelier impression of truth, produced by its collision with error.—*John Stuart Mill*

right to freedom of speech in espousing communism is outweighed by society's need to maintain order. Since speaking on a college campus poses no immediate threat to the order of society, her speech might be protected under this doctrine.

Flexibility: Freedom of the Press   One of the principal reasons for civil liberties, especially the First Amendment, is the belief that truth is more likely to be found when freedom of expression is greatest. John Milton put it this way in an oration addressed to Parliament in 1644:

> Give me the liberty to know, to utter, and to argue freely according to conscience, above all liberties. . . . Though all the winds of doctrine were let loose to play upon the earth, if Truth is in the field we do wrong by licensing and prohibiting to doubt her strength. Let her and Falsehood grapple; who ever knew Truth put to the worse, in a free and open encounter? . . . For Truth is strong next to the Almighty; she needs no policies, nor stratagems, nor licensings to make her victorious.[71]

How absolute is freedom of the press? One area worth investigating is *prior restraint*—that is, forbidding publication, a type of censorship, or not allowing a movie to be shown. A historic Supreme Court decision in 1931 contended that although freedom of the press might be abused by "purveyors of scandal," the press should customarily be immune from "previous restraint."[72] The Court did add, however, that exceptions might be necessary in instances concerning national security. The famous Pentagon Papers case of 1971 presented the Court with an opportunity to decide whether national security did require prior restraint under these circumstances, since many of the documents were classified.*

Although ruling against censorship in this instance, the Court did not settle the basic issue of when, if ever, the government can prevent publication of a newspaper story by claiming the national security is endangered.[73]

Classified documents also figured in the case of CBS correspondent Daniel Schorr, who arranged for publication of classified material in *The Village Voice*. After Congress began an investigation of the matter, he was suspended from his job. When Schorr appeared before the Ethics Committee of the U.S. House of Representatives to testify as to the source that "leaked" the classified materials to him, he refused to disclose the source, citing First Amendment guarantees of freedom of the

* In June 1971 the *New York Times* began publishing excerpts from a 47-volume government analysis of the decision-making process in the Vietnam war. These so-called Pentagon Papers had been secretly taken from Defense Department files. Two days later a court issued a temporary restraining order, which was shortly thereafter overturned by the Supreme Court.

press. By a vote of 6 to 5, the Ethics Committee refused to recommend to the House of Representatives that Schorr be prosecuted for refusing to turn over his copies of the classified material obtained from the Intelligence Committee. The need for flexibility in approaching civil liberties is apparent from the committee's vote. Substantial difference of opinion exists among people in and outside of government concerning the extent to which freedom of the press, for example, should be extended. The Ethics Committee said in its majority report: "It is not axiomatic . . . that the news media is always right and the government is always wrong." [74] The fact that Schorr was suspended by his employer, CBS, indicates that not all of the media support a fully extended application of freedom of the press.

Another test of freedom of the press arises when pretrial and courtroom publicity might endanger a defendant's right to a fair trial. This situation dramatizes a clear conflict between two elements of the Bill of Rights, freedom of the press and the right of an accused person to a fair trial. Instantaneous communication by television, which complicates the problem, led the Supreme Court in 1961 to reverse convictions of two defendants whose televised confessions presumably influenced the jury.[75] In 1966 it reversed the conviction of Samuel H. Sheppard (who had been found guilty of bludgeoning his wife to death) because of excessive news coverage.[76]

Could jurors be unbiased in the trial of Charles Manson or that of Patty Hearst, both of which received extraordinary pretrial publicity? To have been immune from the barrage of news in these cases would have entailed virtual isolation at the time of the Manson murders or the Hearst kidnapping. Clearly, there is no easy solution to this problem. It should be noted, however, that extensive trial coverage does not necessarily result in a conviction. Such radical political figures as Angela Davis and Bobby Seale were acquitted after trials that received widespread publicity. To insure a defendant a fair trial, a judge may delay the trial, transfer it to another location, or sequester the jury.

As recently as 1976, the Supreme Court ruled that a judge could not place a "gag" order on the press in covering pretrial proceedings of a mass murder case. In upholding freedom of the press, Chief Justice Warren Burger wrote:

> Pretrial publicity—even pervasive, adverse publicity—does not inevitably lead to an unfair trial. The capacity of the jury eventually impanelled to decide the case fairly is influenced by the tone and extent of the publicity, which is . . . often in large part, shaped by what attorneys, police, and other officials do to precipitate news coverage.
>
> Prior restraints on speech and publication are the most serious and the least tolerable infringement on First Amendment rights. A prior re-

straint . . . has an immediate and irreversible sanction. If it can be said
that a threat of criminal or civil sanctions after publication "chills"
speech, prior restraint "freezes" it at least for the time.

The damage can be particularly great when the prior restraint falls
upon the communication of news and commentary on current events.
Truthful reports of public judicial proceedings have been afforded special protection against subsequent punishment. For the same reasons the
protection against prior restraint should have particular force as applied
to reporting of criminal proceedings."

The Court confronted two alternatives in the 1976 case of the *Nebraska Press Association* v. *Stuart*. Would it favor freedom of the press
or a fair trial? The Court is placed in the situation of not always being
able to uphold fully one civil liberty because of its conflict with another. Recognizing that a flexible approach is necessary to resolve such
conflict, the Court said that "guarantees of freedom of expression are
not an absolute prohibition [against "gag" orders] under all circumstances, but the barriers to prior restraint remain high, and the pre-
sumption against its use continues intact." [78]

Electronic Media   A special application of freedom of the press involves the electronic media, radio and television. Limited air frequen-
cies restrict the number of radio stations and television channels. As a
result, the government regulates these media more than it does the print
media. The FCC assigns stations and channels, and reviews licenses at
regular intervals (although it seldom revokes them). Of necessity the
First Amendment must be applied differently to the electronic media
than it is to the print media.

The FCC has established general standards for the electronic media
to follow. One of these, the *fairness doctrine*, enjoins fairness in reporting all sides of community issues. The Supreme Court upheld this doctrine in 1969, declaring that "it is the right of viewers and listeners, not
the right of broadcasters, which is paramount." A licensed broadcaster,
said the Court, cannot use the First Amendment to "monopolize a radio
frequency to the exclusion of his fellow citizens." [79]

Recognizing the need to approach this issue flexibly, the Court
ruled in 1971 that broadcasters were protected by the First Amendment
in reporting news events. In this case, a distributor of nudist magazines
had sued a radio station after it had reported his arrest.[80] The Court
ruled in favor of the radio station.

Access to Information   Should government information be freely
available to private citizens? Should the government be allowed to restrict information through a security classification system or executive
privilege? Should reporters be required to testify about information they
possess? These perplexing questions defy easy solutions and require a
flexible approach by the courts.

At present, private citizens are entitled to government information unless it falls within one of several categories exempted from the Freedom of Information Act, such as secret or top secret records relating to national security information, personal and medical files, investigatory records such as certain FBI files, and the "internal" communications of an agency. The Freedom of Information Act (1966) grants citizens the right to go into federal district courts if necessary to force the government to release information.

A somewhat related issue is the exercise of *executive privilege,* when a president withholds information by invoking the doctrine of separation of powers. The Court ruled in 1974 that a president is subject to subpoena for materials relevant to a criminal prosecution. Although the Court thereby limited executive privilege, it did protect the president's interests by requiring that the materials be reviewed in secret by the trial judge, who would release only materials relevant to the case, returning the remainder to the president.[81]

In several cases, the Supreme Court has ruled that the First Amendment does not exempt news reporters from appearing and testifying before grand juries.[82] The Court contended that the grand jury's investigation of possible crimes was more important to the public than the protection of news sources.

Libel Should you be able to say what you want to about another person? If you are speaking about a public official, yes. If you are speaking about a private citizen, no. The Supreme Court has ruled that in a free society "debate on public issues should be uninhibited, robust and wide-open, and . . . may well include vehement . . . attacks on government officials."[83] This ruling and subsequent application of it to include political candidates, some former public officials, and persons involved in events of general or public interest make it almost impossible for a person to be convicted for libeling a public official.[84] Thus, the public can appraise public officials and candidates more fully.

Flexibility: Freedom of Assembly Basically three Supreme Court decisions govern this First Amendment freedom, and they illustrate the Court's flexible approach. One held that a city can require a permit for the "use of public grounds."[85] Another ruled that this right is "equally fundamental" to the rights of free speech and free press.[86] However, said the Court in a third case, in requiring a permit or license for parades, demonstrations, and sound trucks, a city must be exercising control over traffic and regulating the use of public streets and parks, not suppressing free speech.[87]

If you want to assemble or stage a march in your community, you know that this right is protected in the First Amendment; local officials

In the conduct of my newspaper, I carefully excluded all libelling and personal abuse, which is of late years become so disgraceful to our country. Whenever I was solicited to insert any thing of that kind, and the writers pleaded, as they generally did, the liberty of the press . . . in which any one who would pay had a right to a place, my answer was, that I would print the piece separately if desired, and the author might have as many copies as he pleased to distribute himself, but that I would not take upon me to spread his detraction. . . . Now, many of our printers make no scruple of gratifying the malice of individuals by false accusations of the fairest characters among ourselves . . . and are, moreover, so indiscreet as to print scurrilous reflections on the government of neighboring states, and even on the conduct of our best national allies, which may be attended with the most pernicious consequences.—*Benjamin Franklin*

Freedom of assembly as guaranteed by the First Amendment is exercised by these demonstrators at a senior citizens' rally in Boston, Massachusetts. They are protesting the soaring costs of health care. The Supreme Court has developed a flexible position on freedom of assembly; it has set up appropriate guidelines that protect the public interest as well as the rights of groups to assemble.

may require that you have a permit, but they cannot deny the permit in order to suppress free speech. If the Court had taken a rigid rather than a flexible position on freedom of assembly, it might have allowed all assemblies, regardless of whether they affected parks and traffic flow adversely. By upholding the right to assemble freely within appropriate guidelines, the Court promoted both the general public interest and the rights of smaller groups.

PROTECTION OF ALL CITIZENS

Have American civil liberties aided only a few—the rich, educated, or otherwise favored? Hardly. Throughout our history, they have safeguarded all Americans. To demonstrate the breadth of their protection, this discussion will focus on just two aspects of civil liberties guarantees: their function as a bulwark for minorities, and their use in restraining potential government abuses.

Minority Groups Throughout most of American history, if you were white, Anglo-Saxon, Protestant, and male, the executive and legislative branches of the national government and most state and local authorities were relatively responsive to your interests. But the situation was likely to be different if you were a member of a racial, religious, or political minority. In this case, your best guarantee of freedom and equality would have been—and has been—American civil liberties as interpreted by the judiciary.

Black Americans During this century the Supreme Court responded to black group interests long before either the president or Congress began to address the problem of inequality and racial discrimination. By acting against a host of racial abuses, the Court paved the way for the executive and legislature to follow. It might well be argued that without judicial action in interpreting civil liberties, the cause of racial equality would have made much less progress than it has made.

After the 1954 decision in *Brown v. Board of Education*, southerners exerted substantial pressures on the legislative and executive branches to slow down even the "deliberate speed" of integration. Southern influence was strongest in Congress, where black interests were weakest. Black Americans would have had little access to the political process without civil liberties and judicial action. With them, they had the means of exerting pressure within established governmental structures. Had this safety valve not existed, our society might well have witnessed much more racial turmoil in the late 1960s than it did.

The Montgomery bus boycott of 1956, the Selma-to-Montgomery march of 1965, the sit-ins and freedom rides of the 1960s—all had their fundamental and basic support in civil liberties guarantees, especially the First and Fourteenth Amendments, which protect the rights of assembly and petition and provide for equal protection of the laws. Integration of educational facilities at Tuscaloosa, Alabama (1956), Little Rock, Arkansas (1957), and Oxford, Mississippi (1962)—despite the defiance of local governors—stand out in American history as landmarks in the extension of equal protection of the law under the Fourteenth Amendment. Without constitutionally guaranteed civil liberties, especially the equal protection and due process clauses of the Fourteenth Amendment, it would have been difficult if not impossible for blacks to gain access to housing, education, voting, and public accommodations.

Religious Minorities Suppose you were the only Jewish student in a Christian community. In your public schools, teachers taught the Christian faith, recited prayers to the Trinity, and read the New Testament. Would not this be a violation of separation of church and state under the First Amendment and a violation of your own freedom of religion? Although allowing personal and informal group prayer and Bible read-

ing in the public schools, the Supreme Court has ruled as unconstitutional officially composed prayers,[88] recitation of the Lord's Prayer,[89]
and daily Bible reading.[90]

Some religious groups find other aspects of public school education
offensive, and the Court has been responsive to their needs. For example, Jehovah's Witnesses do not believe in saluting the flag. Walter
Barnette had seven children who were expelled from West Virginia public schools because they would not salute the flag. The Court held that a
state may not require anyone, including Jehovah's Witnesses, to participate in a school flag salute ceremony.[91] The Amish generally do not approve of public school education at all, especially past grade school. The
Court bowed to three centuries of Amish religious tradition by holding
that the state of Wisconsin could not require Amish children to attend
school beyond the eighth grade.[92] Without the Bill of Rights, these
groups would have little, if any, opportunity for redress of their grievances. Certainly state and local governments were unresponsive in re-
dressing their grievances; for this reason their cases were brought before
the federal courts, where their rights were finally upheld.

Communists The Constitution is not only color-blind, but also
party-blind. Actually, as you have read, it does not even mention political parties. This fact, however, has not deterred those who would like to
deny certain benefits to Americans who are also members of the Communist party. Three major acts of Congress—the Smith Act of 1940, the
Internal Security (McCarran) Act of 1950, and the Communist Control
Act of 1954—have tried to limit activities of the Communist party and
its members.

The Smith Act prohibited anyone from advocating the violent
overthrow of the government. Through several decisions, the Supreme
Court determined that advocacy cannot be prevented unless lawless action is imminent. The Internal Security Act prescribed several limitations on Communists, such as preventing Communist aliens from entering or remaining in the United States; none of its sanctions, however,
has been upheld by the Court. For example, denying Communists the
right to obtain passports was declared unconstitutional in 1965. The
Communist Control Act of 1954 tried to outlaw the Communist party
specifically. The act has rarely been enforced and has never been tested
before the Supreme Court; in many states, Communist party candidates
regularly run for office. (A summary of these and other actions is found
in Table 4.)

From this discussion of the relationship between civil liberties and
racial, religious, and political minority groups, we can see that civil liberties have aided minority groups as well as persons in other strata of
society.

Table 4. Selected Actions of the Supreme Court, Congress, and the President
on Anti-Communist Legislation

LAW	BRANCH OF GOVERNMENT	DATE	ACTION/DECISION
1940 Smith Act	Supreme Court	1951	Upheld the constitutionality of the Smith Act, which made it unlawful for any person to advocate "overthrowing or destroying any government in the United States by force or violence" (*Dennis* v. *United States*)
		1957	Qualified the *Dennis* decision by holding unconstitutional only the advocacy of "doing" something, not merely "believing" or asking someone to believe in overthrowing the government (*Yates* v. *United States*)
		1961	Upheld provision making it a crime to be a member of the Communist party (*Scales* v. *United States*)
		1961 and 1966	Held that a Communist party member cannot be prosecuted unless the person holds "active membership" and joined the party with "specific intent" of overthrowing the government (*Noto* v. *United States* and *Elfbrandt* v. *Russell*)
		1969	Advocacy of violent overthrow of government is unconstitutional only when lawless action is imminent (*Brandenburg* v. *Ohio*)
1950 Internal Security	Supreme Court	1961	Held that the Communist party could be compelled to register with the attorney general (*Communist Party* v. *Subversive Activities Control Board*)
		1965	Ruled that to require individual Communists to register would violate the Fifth Amendment (*Albertson* v. *Subversive Activities Control Board*)
	Congress/President	1971	Abolished provision allowing president to declare an "internal security emergency" and order the detention of persons suspected of espionage or sabotage
1954 Communist Control Act	Congress	1973	Abolished the Subversive Activities Control Board

Restraints on the Government   The poorest among us, or those representing the least popular causes, can protest the unfairness of a procedure or the denial of a right. Any person or group can challenge the legislative or executive branch when it appears to be exercising arbitrary power. A key provision underlying such challenges is due process of law, which has its constitutional basis in the Fifth and Fourteenth Amendments. Due process of law means protection against arbitrary deprivation of life, liberty, or property. Generally it is thought of in one of two ways: *substantive due process* means that laws must be reasonable and fair; *procedural due process* means that laws must be administered in a fair manner. The former focuses on what the law says; the latter, on how it is implemented. To understand due process, let us see how it restricts the government in searches and seizures, personal privacy, and the rights of the accused or how it contributes to making our civil liberties more adequate.

Searches and Seizures   According to the Fourth Amendment, individuals must "be secure in their persons, houses, papers, and effects, against unreasonable searches and seizures." This generally means that a home cannot be searched without a search warrant signed by a judicial officer and issued on "probable cause" that the evidence to be seized is in the place to be searched. Without a warrant, police can still enter a place to make a valid arrest and conduct a limited search.

The Supreme Court has strengthened this right by stating that police without a warrant cannot ransack a home but must confine their search to the suspect and his or her immediate surroundings.[93] However, other decisions have served to protect the interests of society against criminals. For example, the Court has held that police can search an automobile without a warrant if they have probable cause to believe it contains illegal articles.[94] They can stop and "frisk" a suspect on the street without a warrant if there is reasonable suspicion that the person is armed or dangerous.[95] Police can also stop and frisk a suspect on suspicion of criminal conduct based upon an informant's tip considered to be reliable.[96] However, a police officer who does stop someone on the street must observe the restrictions of the Fourth Amendment relating to searches and seizures. These are, of course, examples of procedural due process.

Privacy   The Court upheld the best-known invasion of privacy, wiretapping, in 1928.[97] In 1967, however, it set limits on its use, declaring that a wiretap or bugging device did not have to involve "physical trespass" to violate the Fourth Amendment and that police could not wiretap without a court warrant.[98]

When the Nixon administration claimed that it had the power to use electronic surveillance without court approval on domestic groups it considered a threat to internal security, the Court unanimously ruled against this as a denial of due process of law. Speaking for the Court, Justice Powell said: "The danger to political dissent is acute where the government attempts to act under so vague a concept as the power to protect 'domestic security.' " [99]

Rights of the Accused The Bill of Rights and judicial decisions based on it guarantee several rights, i.e., procedural due process, to persons accused of a crime. They must be indicted by a grand jury if the crime is serious. They cannot be tried twice for the same offense (*double jeopardy*) nor be forced to testify against themselves (*self-incrimination*). They have a right to "a speedy and public trial" by jury, to be informed of their legal rights, to summon and cross-examine witnesses, and to be represented by counsel. They cannot be held for "excessive bail," nor be inflicted with "cruel and unusual punishments."

These rights, based on the Fifth through the Eighth Amendments, have been expanded, particularly during the 1950s and 1960s. After criticism that these later decisions sometimes hamstrung police, the Burger Court adopted some modifications, while still retaining their basic thrust (see page 119).

THE CONTINUING RELEVANCE OF CIVIL LIBERTIES

Democracy as we know it means majority rule, with guaranteed safeguards for the minority. Historically, rights of the majority have been protected principally in the legislative and executive branches, whereas those of the minority have been protected chiefly by the judiciary through application of civil liberties. It is probable that no other nation in history has protected human freedoms as much as the United States—certainly no nation as developed and complex as ours. The continuing relevance of civil liberties is evident particularly in extending the Bill of Rights, in citizenship, and in the increasingly important role played by the executive branch.

Extension of the Bill of Rights As noted earlier, the Bill of Rights originally applied only to the federal government. The key case in setting this policy was *Barron* v. *Baltimore* (1833), in which the Court concluded that the Constitution was established by the people of the United States for their own government, not for the government of the individual states. Thus the situation remained for several decades.

The Fourteenth Amendment includes a provision specifying that "no State shall . . . deprive any person of life, liberty, or property, without due process of law." In 1925 the Supreme Court interpreted this provision to mean that the "fundamental personal rights" protected by the amendment could not be abridged by the states. [100] With this action, the

Table 5. Applicability of Bill of Rights to States via Due Process Clause of Fourteenth Amendment

RIGHT	WHETHER APPLICABLE	CASE AND DATE
FIRST AMENDMENT		
Freedom of speech*	yes	*Gitlow v. New York* (1925)
		Fiske v. Kansas (1927)
		Stromberg v. California (1931)
Freedom of the press*	yes	*Near v. Minnesota* (1931)
Freedom of assembly	yes	*DeJonge v. Oregon* (1937)
Freedom of religion	yes	*Cantwell v. Connecticut* (1940)
Establishment clause	yes	*Everson v. Board of Education* (1947)
SECOND AMENDMENT	no	
THIRD AMENDMENT	no	
FOURTH AMENDMENT	yes	*Wolf v. Colorado* (1949)
		Mapp v. Ohio (1961)
FIFTH AMENDMENT		
Grand jury clause	no	
Just compensation clause	yes	*Chicago, Burlington & Quincy Ry. v. Chicago* (1897)
Self-incrimination clause	yes	*Malloy v. Hogan* (1964)
Double jeopardy clause	yes	*Benton v. Maryland* (1969)
SIXTH AMENDMENT		
Notice	yes	In re *Oliver* (1948)†
Assistance of counsel clause	yes	*Gideon v. Wainwright* (1963)
Public trial clause	yes	In re *Oliver* (1948)
Confrontation clause	yes	*Pointer v. Texas* (1965)
Compulsory process clause	yes	*Washington v. Texas* (1967)
Speedy trial clause	yes	*Klopfer v. North Carolina* (1967)
Jury trial clause	yes	*Duncan v. Louisiana* (1968)
SEVENTH AMENDMENT	no	
EIGHTH AMENDMENT		
Cruel and unusual punishment clause	yes	*Robinson v. California* (1962)
Excessive fines and bail clause	no	

* There is disagreement on when freedom of speech and freedom of the press were nationalized; it is probably most accurate to say this occurred in a series of cases beginning with *Gitlow* in 1925 and ending with *Near* in 1931.

† Adequate notice of the charges is a traditional requirement of due process in a criminal case; in *Oliver*, the Court indicated that the due process clause requires notice in state criminal proceedings, without formally nationalizing the Sixth Amendment notice requirement.

Source: Reprinted from *The Supreme Court and Civil Liberties Policy* by Richard C. Cortner, by permission of Mayfield Publishing Company. Copyright © 1975 by Richard Cortner.

Court began a process of "selective incorporation"—application of the Bill of Rights to the states—as shown in Table 5. With the enormous growth of state and local governments during recent decades, extending the application of the Bill of Rights to the states becomes even more important.

Citizenship   Another area where rights have been broadened relates to citizenship. One is born a citizen of the United States through one of two principles: *jus soli* (right of soil) or *jus sanguinis* (right of blood). The former confers citizenship by place of birth; the latter, by parental citizenship. Except for the children of foreign diplomats, all persons born in the United States are citizens. Children born abroad of one or more American parents also qualify for American citizenship. An individual who wishes to become an American citizen can do so through the process of naturalization.

A number of Court decisions have strengthened citizenship rights. The Court held that desertion from the armed forces during wartime was not grounds for deprivation of citizenship, as such a penalty would constitute cruel and unusual punishment.[101] Nor would leaving the country in wartime to evade the draft result in automatic loss of citizenship.[102] Naturalized citizens enjoy the same rights as native-born Americans.[103] Furthermore, Congress cannot take away American citizenship unless it is freely renounced.[104]

One of the most significant changes in citizenship law took place when the Immigration Act of 1965 abolished the national origins quota system and substituted a new annual ceiling of 120,000 immigrants from the Western Hemisphere and 170,000 from other nations, with a limit of 20,000 persons from any one nation. The national origins system had favored northern Europeans over immigrants from southern and eastern Europe. Under this system, 70 percent of all immigrants came from three countries—Great Britain, Ireland, and Germany. Since 1965 people from other nations can more easily come to the United States and establish citizenship, yet another example of the increasing relevance of civil liberties.

Executive Action   The executive branch of the government is becoming more important than it used to be in defining and applying civil liberties. One controversial area has been affirmative action guidelines concerning women's rights, as set forth in Department of Health, Education, and Welfare administrative regulations. Some of these regulations concern athletics, requiring—among other things—that a fairer proportion of athletic funds be expended on women's athletic programs. Other regulations involve employment. A member of a minority group can file a complaint with HEW requesting an investigation into the reasons why he or she was not employed for a position. In some instances, federal funds have been withheld from colleges and universities until they complied with federal guidelines. HEW also has school desegregation guidelines, and the Equal Employment Opportunity Commission (EEOC) stipulates employment guidelines.

The Department of Labor also conducts investigations of college and university pay practices to determine whether women and minorities are being treated fairly. Some institutions have been forced to make restitution to employees found to be discriminated against because of sex or ethnic origin. Student rights are also being enforced by the federal bureaucracy, and one of the most interesting regulations is that the posting of grades by any given personal identifiable form, such as social security number or name of student, is in violation of the law unless consent of the student has been obtained.

In the definition and application of civil liberties, executive agencies are an important link in a complicated process:

> To a large extent these rights have been prescribed by the Constitution, interpreted by the Courts, enforced by the various portions of the bureaucracy, but subject more and more to the wishes and policy needs of the president or the governor. Within the framework of this complex policy-making establishment, the various groups which comprise American society must promote their claims of right. Rights policies eventually emerge from the interplay between these various groups, official decision-makers and the occasional individual who can gain recognition of a particular claim.[105]

Civil liberties by themselves are inadequate because they are abstractions. They become adequate only as the governmental policy-making process defines and enforces them, and, as has been shown, the governmental process has been actively defining and expanding civil liberties guarantees.

Glossary

Double jeopardy: being tried twice for the same offense.

Exclusionary rule: bars use in criminal trials of evidence obtained in violation of constitutional prohibition against unreasonable searches and seizures.

Executive privilege: doctrine based on constitutional separation of powers whereby a president withholds information from the other two branches of government.

Fairness doctrine: principle established by the FCC that electronic media should report all sides of community issues fairly.

Habeas corpus: a court order directing an official who has a person in custody to bring the prisoner to court and to show cause for that person's detention.

Jus sanguinis: principle conferring citizenship by parental citizenship.

Jus soli: principle conferring citizenship by place of birth.

Prior restraint: a form of censorship that forbids in advance the publication or the showing of a movie or play.

Procedural due process: the principle that laws must be administered in a fair manner.

Self-incrimination: the Fifth Amendment provision that individuals do not have to testify against themselves in criminal prosecutions.

Substantive due process: the principle that laws must be reasonable and fair.

Notes

1. *New York Times*, March 27, 1976, p. 19.

2. Ibid.

3. C. Wright Mills, *The Power Elite* (New York: Oxford University Press, 1956), p. 334.

4. Mark Goodman, ed., *Give 'em Hell, Harry* (New York: Award Books, 1974), p. 190.

5. For other surveys supporting the results of the CBS survey, see also: James W. Prothro and Charles M. Grigg, "Fundamental Principles of Democracy: Bases of Agreement and Disagreement," *The Journal of Politics* 22 (1960):276–294; and Herbert McClosky, "Consensus and Ideology in American Politics," *American Political Science Review* 64 June 1964):361–382.

6. *Ex Parte Milligan* v. *United States* (1866).

7. *Ex Parte Endo* v. *United States* (1944).

8. *Korematsu* v. *United States* (1944).

9. *Plessy* v. *Ferguson* (1896).

10. As cited in Robert Sherrill, *Why They Call It Politics* (New York: Harcourt Brace Jovanovich, 1974), p. 176.

11. *Miranda* v. *Arizona* (1966).

12. Ramsey Clark, *Crime in America* (New York: Simon & Schuster, 1970), pp. 115–270.

13. *Engel* v. *Vitale* (1962).

14. *New York Times.* March 26, 1969, p. 1.

15. Jay A. Sigler, *American Rights Policies* (Homewood, Ill.: Dorsey Press, 1975), p. 11.

16. *Illinois ex rel. McCollum* v. *Board of Education* (1948).

17. *Lemon* v. *Kurtzman* (1971).

18. *Committee for Public Education* v. *Nyquist* (1973); *Levitt* v. *Committee for Public Education* (1973).

19. *Committee for Public Education* v. *Nyquist* (1973).

20. *Sloan* v. *Lemon* (1973).

21. *Meek* v. *Pittinger* (1975).

22. *Everson* v. *Board of Education* (1947).

23. *Zorach* v. *Clausen* (1952).

24. *Tilton* v. *Richardson* (1971).

25. *Meek* v. *Pittinger* (1975).

26. *Board of Education* v. *Allen* (1968); *Norwood* v. *Harrison* (1973).

27. *Sloan* v. *Lemon* (1973).

28. Ibid.

29. *Waltz* v. *Tax Commission* (1970); *Lemon* v. *Kurtzman* (1971).

30. *Wisconsin* v. *Yoder* (1972).

31. *Davis* v. *Deason* (1890); *Cleveland* v. *United States* (1946).

32. *Jacobson* v. *Massachusetts* (1905).

33. *Prince* v. *United States* (1944),

34. *Pierce* v. *Society of Sisters* (1925).

35. *West Virginia Board of Education* v. *Barnette* (1943).

36. *Sherbert* v. *Verner* (1963).

37. *Wisconsin* v. *Yoder* (1972).

38. *Welsh* v. *United States* (1970); *Gillette* v. *United States* (1971).

39. *Roth* v. *United States* (1957).

40. *Jacobellis* v. *Ohio* (1964).

41. *Memoirs* v. *Massachusetts* (1966).

42. *Miller* v. *California* (1973).

43. Ibid.

44. *Jenkins* v. *Georgia* (1974).

45. *Huffman* v. *Pursue Ltd.* (1976).

46. *Colegrove* v. *Green* (1946).

47. *Baker* v. *Carr* (1962).

48. *Kirkpatrick* v. *Preisler* (1969); *Wells* v. *Rockefeller* (1969).

49. *Mahon* v. *Howell* (1973).

50. *Miranda* v. *Arizona* (1966).

51. *Harris* v. *New York* (1971).

52. *Michigan* v. *Tucker* (1974).

53. *Oregon* v. *Hass* (1976).

54. *Mapp* v. *Ohio* (1961).

55. *United States* v. *Peltier* (1975).

56. *Stone* v. *Powell* (1976); *Wolff* v. *Rice* (1976).

57. See generally Marvin E. Frankel, *Criminal Sentences: Law Without Order* (New York: Hill & Wang, 1973); Ray Bloomberg, "Court Justice Tied to Middle-Class Values," *Quaker Service Bulletin* 54 (Spring 1973):8; Stuart Nagel, "Disparities in Criminal Justice," *UCLA Law Review* 14 (August 1967):1272–1305.

58. *Gideon* v. *Wainwright* (1963).

59. Lewis M. Steel, "Nine Men in Black Who Think White," *New York Times Magazine*, October 13, 1968, p. 56.

60. Quoted by Edmond Cahn in "Can the Supreme Court Defend Civil Liberties," a pamphlet issued by the Sidney Hillman Foundation (undated), pp. 11–12, as cited in Duane Lockard, *The Perverted Priorities of American Politics* (New York: Macmillan, 1971), p. 224.

61. Alexander M. Bickel, "The 'Uninhibited, Robust, and Wide-Open' First Amendment," *Commentary* 54 (November 1972):61.

62. Herb Altman, ed., *Quotations from Chairman Sam* (New York: Harper & Row, 1973), p. 51.

63. Kenneth B. Clark, "The Civil Rights Movement: Momentum and Organization," in Talcott Parsons and Kenneth B. Clark, eds., *The Negro American* (Boston: Beacon Press, 1966); p. 610.

64. *Gideon* v. *Wainwright* (1963).

65. *Baker* v. *Carr* (1963); *Reynolds* v. *Sims* (1964); *Wesberry* v. *Sanders* (1964).

66. Bickel, "The 'Uninhibited, Robust, and Wide-Open' First Amendment," p. 66.

67. *Schenck* v. *United States* (1919).

68. *Congressional Quarterly Weekly Report*, April 17, 1976, p. 911.

69. *Southeastern Productions* v. *Conrad* (1976).

70. *Schenck* v. *United States* (1919).

71. John Milton, *Aeropagitica*, in Merritt Y. Hughes, ed., *John Milton: Complete Poems and Major Prose* (Indianapolis, Ind.: Odyssey Press, 1957), pp. 732, 746.

72. *Near* v. *Minnesota* (1931).

73. *New York Times Co.* v. *United States* (1971).

74. *Congressional Quarterly Weekly Report*, October 16, 1976, pp. 3019–3021.

75. *Irvin* v. *Dowd* (1961); *Rideau* v. *Louisiana* (1963).

76. *Sheppard* v. *Maxwell* (1966).

77. *Nebraska Press Association* v. *Stuart* (1976).

78. Ibid.

79. *Red Lion Broadcasting Co.* v. *Federal Communications Commission* (1969).

80. *Rosenbloom* v. *Metromedia* (1971).

81. *United States* v. *Nixon* (1974).

82. *United States* v. *Caldwell* (1972); *Branzburg* v. *Hayes* (1972); *In the Matter of Paul Pappas* (1972).

83. *New York Times Co.* v. *Sullivan* (1964).

84. *Curtis Publishing Co.* v. *Butts; Associated Press* v. *Walker* (1967); *Rosenbloom* v. *Metromedia* (1971).

85. *Davis* v. *Massachusetts* (1897).

86. *De Jonge* v. *Oregon* (1937).

87. *Hague* v. *C.I.O.* (1939).

88. *Engel* v. *Vitale* (1962).

89. *Abington School District* v. *Schempp* (1963).

90. *Murray* v. *Curlett* (1963).

91. *West Virginia Board of Education* v. *Barnette* (1943).

92. *Wisconsin* v. *Yoder* (1972).

93. *Chimel* v. *California* (1969).

94. *Terry* v. *Ohio* (1968).

95. Ibid.

96. *Adams* v. *California* (1972).

97. *Olmstead* v. *United States* (1928).

98. *Katz* v. *United States* (1967).

99. *United States* v. *United States District Court for the Eastern District of Michigan* (1972).

100. *Gitlow* v. *New York* (1925).

101. *Trop* v. *Dulles* (1958).

102. *Kennedy* v. *Mendoza-Martinez* (1963).

103. *Schneider* v. *Rusk* (1964).

104. *Afroyim* v. *Rusk* (1967).

105. Sigler, *American Rights Policies*, p. 286.

Recommended Rebuttal Reading

On Balancing Freedom and Order

Mill, John Stuart. *On Liberty*. New York: Appleton-Century-Crofts, 1947.
Westin, Alan F. *Privacy and Freedom*. New York: Atheneum, 1967.

On Compliance with Civil Liberties Decisions

Becker, Theodore L., and Malcolm M. Feeley, eds. *The Impact of Supreme Court Decisions*, 2nd ed. New York: Oxford University Press, 1973.

Dolbeare, Kenneth M., and Philip E. Hammond. *The School Prayer Decisions: From Court to Local Practice*. Chicago: University of Chicago Press, 1971.

Johnson, Richard M. *The Dynamics of Compliance*. Evanston, Ill.: Northwestern University Press, 1967.

Wasby, Stephen L. *The Impact of the United States Supreme Court: Some Perspectives*. Homewood, Ill.: Dorsey Press, 1970.

Case Studies of Civil Liberties Decisions

Berman, Daniel M. *It Is So Ordered.* New York: Norton, 1966.

Cortner, Richard C. *The Jones and Laughlin Case.* New York: Alfred A. Knopf, 1970.

Lewis, Anthony. *Gideon's Trumpet.* New York: Vintage Books, 1964.

Vose, Clement E. *Caucasians Only: The Supreme Court, the NAACP, and the Restrictive Covenant Cases.* Berkeley: University of California Press, 1959.

On Judicial Review and Civil Liberties

Bickel, Alexander M. *The Least Dangerous Branch.* Indianapolis, Ind.: Bobbs-Merrill, 1962.

———. *The Supreme Court and the Idea of Progress.* New York: Harper & Row, 1970.

Black, Charles L., Jr. *The People and the Court.* New York: Macmillan, 1960.

Commager, Henry Steele. *Majority Rule and Minority Rights.* New York: Oxford University Press, 1943.

Hand, Learned. *The Bill of Rights.* New York: Atheneum, 1965.

Jackson, Robert H. *The Struggle for Judicial Supremacy.* New York: Vintage Books, 1960.

Mason, Alpheus T., and William M. Beaney. *The Supreme Court in a Free Society.* New York: Norton, 1968.

McCloskey, Robert G. *The American Supreme Court.* Chicago: University of Chicago Press, 1960.

Murphy, Walter F. *Congress and the Court.* Chicago: University of Chicago Press, 1962.

Rodell, Fred. *Nine Men.* New York: Random House, 1955.

Shapiro, Martin. *Freedom of Speech: The Supreme Court and Judicial Review.* Englewood Cliffs, N. J.: Prentice-Hall, 1966.

On Civil Liberties Generally

Cushman, Robert F. *Leading Constitutional Decisions.* Englewood Cliffs, N.J.: Prentice-Hall, 1976.

Etzkowitz, Henry, and Peter Schwab. *Is America Necessary? Conservative, Liberal and Socialist Perspectives of United States Political Institutions.* St. Paul, Minn.: West, 1976.

Peter, Charles, and James Fellows, eds. *Inside the System.* New York: Praeger, 1976.

TWO

WHAT
ARE
AMERICAN
POLITICS
REALLY
LIKE?

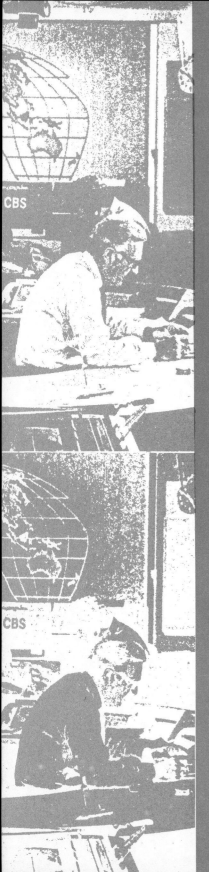

AT ISSUE: PUBLIC OPINION

Structure of Public Opinion

Stages of Public Opinion

Measuring Public Opinion

THE AFFIRMATIVE CASE

THE NEGATIVE CASE

**Mass Media Monopoly
  Concentration
  Commercialism
  Conservatism**

The Benefits of Monopoly

Molding Public Opinion

**How is Public Opinion
  Shaped?
  Family and School
  Other Factors**

**Mass Media and Govern-
  ment Collusion
  Lying
  Manipulation of Media
  Personnel
  Abuse of Government
  Policies**

Resistance to Media Control

Propaganda

Propaganda Limitations

RESOLVED THAT: Mass Media and Government Control Public Opinion

5

At Issue: Public Opinion

What is public opinion? Does it influence government decision making? Should it? How is it developed?

These are important questions for a country that calls itself a democracy. After all, how can a nation claim to be democratic if there is no public opinion, or if its citizens' views are manipulated? In the words of a leading political scientist, V. O. Key, Jr., "It is too early to conclude that governments can ignore public opinion or that democratic government amounts only to a hoax, a ritual whose performance serves only to delude the people and thereby to convert them into willing subjects of the powers that be." [1]

Public opinion has been defined in many different ways. Key writes that it consists of "those opinions held by private persons which governments find it prudent to heed." [2] His definition limits the concept only to those opinions that influence governments. Thus, private opinion becomes public opinion when it relates to government and politics; another term for it might be political opinion. An opinion on the proper roles in marriage would most likely be a private opinion, whereas an opinion on the government's birth control policy would be a public, or political, opinion. By referring to political opinion, we can distinguish between public opinion on detergents and on defense policy.

Because the term *public opinion* is so broad, political scientists have devised the concept of *special publics*. Key describes them as

Public opinion polls are the last refuge for the little guy.—*Richard Scammon*

155

"those segments of the public with views about particular issues, problems, or other questions of public concern."[3] Not everyone has an opinion on every question, but each is concerned with his or her own problem. Labor union members may be interested in collective bargaining, but not in farm subsidies. Feminists may be interested in divorce law, but not in foreign trade.

THE STRUCTURE OF PUBLIC OPINION

After defining public opinion, how do we describe it? Those who specialize in this aspect of politics clarify its structure in terms of six characteristics: salience, stability, fluidity, intensity, latency, and distribution.[4]

Salience—the quality of standing out, of being important—is the characteristic that determines special publics. For each one a certain issue or subject is "at the focus of attention, crowding out other items, a pivot for organizing one's thoughts and acts."[5]

Opinion on some issues is very stable; on others, very fluid. For example, most people do not change their political party preferences quickly or often. But opinions on issues not necessarily related to party preference—such as the performance of a president, war, or inflation—may change rapidly. Richard Nixon, for example, won a resounding victory in the presidential election of 1972; after the Watergate scandal developed, his public support dwindled.

The public reacts to issues with varying degrees of intensity. People directly affected by a problem usually feel more strongly about it than those who are unaffected. Thus, parents of school-age children are more likely to have an intense opinion about busing than a childless seventy-year-old couple living in a retirement community.

Latency is one factor that sets limits or boundaries within which public officials make decisions. During ordinary times, public opinion on a given issue may well be unexpressed; if a crisis occurs, latent attitudes become focused and active. A community may exhibit no visible opposition to school busing. If a court order imposes busing, however, latent public opinion may become aroused. Many politicians owe their careers in whole or in part to their ability to tap latent public opinion. In his presidential campaigns, George Wallace tapped the latent public feeling of alienation from and hostility toward government bureaucracy, focusing on such issues as school busing. More recently, Jimmy Carter and Ronald Reagan tapped the reservoir of a latent anti-Washington feeling among the electorate.

How widely is an opinion held among the various divisions of the public, whether one considers racial, geographic, age, sex, or occupational categories? Answers to questions involving distribution are important to political candidates, who seek to build winning coalitions by taking positions that will appeal to certain definite groups. To be victorious, national parties have usually tried to balance their tickets by accounting for variables like geography, ideology, and religion.

THE STAGES OF PUBLIC OPINION

How much freedom do public officials have in regard to public opinion? When can they ignore it? When must they yield to it? These questions lead us to examine briefly what might be called the three types of public opinion: permissive, directive, and supportive.

The permissive type occurs when there is a high degree of latency. The public is not aroused and therefore allows public officials a wide degree of latitude in making decisions. In most cases involving foreign affairs, the public either does not know about the issue, is not interested enough to put pressure on the government, or simply trusts Washington to do what is right and best. In the early stages of the Vietnam war, foreign policy decision making occurred in a permissive stage of public opinion. Even members of Congress rarely questioned presidential leadership.

In a directive type, public opinion plays a much greater role. As the Vietnam war aroused the public, opposition mounted to the point that demands were made to withdraw American troops. This directive type of public opinion probably led to the troop withdrawal program initiated by President Nixon prior to his campaign for reelection in 1972.

Supportive public opinion, as the term suggests, serves to uphold officials or decisions. Nixon mounted a troop withdrawal program in 1972, pulling American forces out of Vietnam as the election drew near. Supportive public opinion, eager to end the war, approved his decision—and helped him win reelection.

MEASURING PUBLIC OPINION

How do we find out what public opinion is? This issue confronts both scholars and public officials. Actually, experts have developed rather reliable ways for determining public opinion, using a sequence of steps. We see their results in the surveys of public opinion known as *polls*.

First, what group is it whose opinion on an issue is desired? This group, known as the *universe*, defines the boundary lines within which attitudes will be measured. Let us say that the universe consists of all Americans above the age of seventeen living in the United States. Second, it is usually impossible to ask all the people in a given universe

"NOW THINK ABOUT THIS ONE...DO YOU REALLY THINK THE PUBLIC NEEDS SIX-DAYS-A-WEEK, HOME DELIVERED MAIL SERVICE?"

what their opinion is. Therefore, pollsters work with a portion, a *sample*, of the universe. Third, pollsters must take care that their sample is representative of the universe.

How can we be sure that a sample is sufficiently representative to be reliable? The mathematical law of probability provides the answer. According to this principle, a coin tossed in the air a thousand times should come up heads about five hundred times. When a sample is large enough and properly selected, the law of probability operates; the result obtained is customarily accurate within a 4 percent margin of error. National polling organizations, such as Gallup and Harris, may use a sample of 1,200 to 2,000 persons to represent the entire American population of over 210 million. The history of opinion polls in recent

Table 1. Presidential Polls: 1960–1976*

	ACTUAL VOTE	GALLUP	HARRIS
1960			
Nixon	49.3	49	41
Kennedy	49.5	51	49
1964			
Goldwater	38.5	36	36
Johnson	61.1	64	64
1968			
Nixon	43.4	44	40
Humphrey	42.7	31	37
Wallace	13.5	20	16
1972			
Nixon	60.8	59	59
McGovern	38.0	36	35
1976			
Ford	48.0	47	45
Carter	51.0	46	46

*Figures in percent.

Source: Compiled from the Gallup Opinion Poll and the Harris Poll.

presidential campaigns, as summarized in Table 1, suggests their general reliability within a relatively small margin of error.

With this background in the structure, stages, and measurement of public opinion, let us now consider the role played by the mass media and the government. Our debate proposition suggests that the mass media and the government control public opinion. If that is the case, democracy has little meaning in the United States, because the public would be responding to government and the media rather than directing their actions and opinions at definite political goals. Accordingly, it would be more important for us to study the opinions of governmental leaders and the mass media rather than public opinion. Is this really the situation?

The concentration of economic power, opinion power, and political power creates a sort of closed loop. Politicians must raise money from corporations in order to pay the networks the enormous cost of television time. Corporate advertisers call the network tune. And the networks must curry favor with the successful politicians to assure their franchise. The open society seems to be closing—not by conspiracy, but by mutual dependence.—*Kingman Brewster, Jr.*

- Do public officials respond to public opinion?
- Is the information provided by the media and by government adequate to create an educated public opinion?
- Should the media devote large amounts of their resources to investigative reporting?
- What are the linkages between public opinion and public policy?

The Affirmative Case

Yes, the mass media and the government control public opinion.

Media owners stand to lose money when viewpoints or proposals they dislike gain public acceptance. This of course creates conflicts of interest; media owners are not about to give equal treatment to threatening viewpoints. The conflicts of interest for media owners exist in three areas.

The first concerns the communications system itself. Broadcasting stations and newspapers are very profitable businesses. Any laws or regulations aimed at changing present practices regarding postal subsidies, cable television, advertising, license renewal, cross-media ownership, antitrust regulation, the Fairness Doctrine, or the Equal Time Provision can mean not only a loss of money, but the loss of a business. . . .

The second conflict for some mass media owners concerns the possibility of the loss of vast sums of money if the people demand a change in some of our domestic or foreign policies. Westinghouse, AVCO, General Tire and Rubber, RCA (owner of NBC), and CBS provide services or goods for the nation's defense or space programs. A cutback in defense or space spending could mean a loss of profit for these companies. . . .

Policies concerning pollution and labor can also affect a media agency's profit. The New York Times *and the* Los Angeles Times *are two newspapers that own pollution-producing paper mills; many others own mills also.*[6]–Robert Cirino

For a nation to be truly democratic, its people should have an important, indeed preeminent, role in determining what the government does. Obviously, democracy is endangered if people are denied the right to express their opinions, as in totalitarian regimes. But it is also in trouble if opinion is controlled or unduly influenced by mass media and/or government. This is what is happening in the United States.

- Because the mass media have a virtual monopoly, the amount and types of information communicated to the public are limited.
- The mass media mold public opinion in crucial ways.
- The mass media and government are not independent of each other, but rather engage in collusion, with the government using several techniques to control the media.
- What results from this "collaboration" is more like propaganda than sound information.

MASS MEDIA MONOPOLY

Journalist A. J. Liebling once said that "the American newspaper industry has become a series of local elimination tournaments, like Golden Gloves boxing." He also noted that "a large number of competing newspapers, permitting representation of various shades of thought, are a country's best defense against being stampeded into barbarism." [7] The United States no longer has this defense, for virtual monopolies exist in all phases of mass communications.

Concentration   Television, with its enormous potential for educating and informing the public, reaches into some 85 million American homes. But the three major networks—CBS, ABC, and NBC—have a virtual monopoly on the industry. Only the National Educational Television network provides any significant nation-wide competition, and, at the local level, only scattered religious and independent channels with limited viewing audiences offer alternatives to the public.

News is what I say it is. It's something worth knowing by my standards.—*David Brinkley*

Although there is not as much concentration in radio ownership, local stations customarily depend upon national networks for national and international news. Besides the three major networks, the Mutual Broadcasting System and the wire services—AP and UPI—also provide news for local affiliates. It is not uncommon for the same corporation to own both radio and television stations as well as a daily newspaper in the same city. For example, in Chicago, Illinois, *The Chicago Tribune* newspaper owns both WGN radio and WGN TV as well as media outlets in other cities, including *The New York Daily News*, which has a larger circulation than any other paper in the United States. In a November 1976 multimillion-dollar purchase, the Newhouse chain of media outlets made the largest purchase ever of newspapers when it bought the large chain of Booth newspapers.

Daily newspapers, once the major source of news in the United States, are disappearing. In 1909 there were 2,600 dailies; by 1955 the number had fallen to 1,785; in 1975 the total was 1,713. Of the fifty largest cities in the country, twenty-three are served by only one newspaper. It is estimated that some 97 percent of all American cities, regardless of size, have only one newspaper. And approximately 44 percent of all daily newspapers are controlled by chains. [8]

Some people might argue that magazines provide many more channels of information for the public, but do they really? The fact is that relatively few people read magazines. Of some 200 million citizens, less than 5 percent read magazines. Table 2 (p. 162) provides circulation data for national weekly or monthly public affairs publications.

162 WHAT ARE AMERICAN POLITICS REALLY LIKE?

Table 2. Circulation Data of National Weekly or Monthly Publications Dealing with Public Affairs (Circulation Figures for 1975)

GENERALLY CONSIDERED RADICAL OR VERY LIBERAL		GENERALLY CONSIDERED LIBERAL, MIDDLE OF THE ROAD, OR CONSERVATIVE		GENERALLY CONSIDERED VERY CONSERVATIVE OR FAR RIGHT	
Black Panther	40,000	Atlantic	325,000	*American Legion	2,500,000
Guardian	25,000	Atlas	10,000	American Mercury	18,000
Liberation	10,000	Commentary	62,000	American Opinion	44,000
Los Angeles Free Press	100,000	Commonweal	27,000	Barron's	225,000
Militant	30,000	*Ebony	1,300,000	Battleline	80,000
Ms.	400,000	Fortune	600,000	Christian Beacon	118,000
Muhammad Speaks	900,000	Harper's	340,000	Citizen	13,000
New York Review of Books	89,000	Nation	30,000	Human Events	70,000
People's World	8,000	National Observer	545,000	Liberty Letter	125,000
Progressive	40,000	New Republic	95,000	Life Lines	5,000
Progressive Labor	3,000	*Newsweek	2,917,982	National Review	110,000
Ramparts	90,000	*Reader's Digest	17,550,000	New Guard	25,000
Village Voice	150,000	Saturday Review	100,000	Twin Circle	92,000
Washington Monthly	30,000	Senior Scholastic	472,000	*V.F.W. Magazine	1,800,000
Weekly People	9,449	*Time	4,388,471	Wanderer	47,800

*Mass circulation (over 1,000,000)

Source: Classification of publications has been made by the author. Circulation data have been provided by *Ulrich's International Periodicals Directory*, 1975–76, copyright © 1975, R. R. Bowker and *'76 Ayer Directory of Publications* (Philadelphia: Ayer Press, 1976).

Commercialism Television is geared more to selling deodorants than to educating viewers. The profit motive is illustrated in several brief glimpses of decisions on television programming.

1. Described as "witty, thoughtful, and attractive" by *Newsweek* magazine, Dick Cavett was told by ABC management that he had three months to improve the Nielsen rating for his late-night talk show or the show would be dropped. . . .
2. The *Red Skelton* and *Jackie Gleason* shows were dropped by CBS for the 1970–1971 season even though they had very high ratings. But these ratings also showed they were attracting mainly juveniles and people over fifty, groups that are harder to sell to advertisers. . . .
3. In 1970, station WTOP TV in Washington, D.C., complained that advertisers were not supporting its black-oriented programming because the ratings were slight for such programs. . . .
4. Testifying at a January 1973 FCC hearing on children's television, an NBC attorney frankly admitted that over the past few years his

network had tried to be innovative and imaginative and had lost money as a result. . . .

5. Network emphasis on football is understandable; in a two-week period in January 1973, five of the eight programs that topped the Nielson audience ratings were football games or game previews. The Super Bowl, number one in the ratings, brought in $200,000 per minute of advertising money. *All in the Family*, number two in the ratings, brought in $120,000 per minute.[9]

In 1976 when ABC TV sought to improve its third place standing behind CBS TV and NBC TV in their Nielson ratings for the evening news, Barbara Walters was hired from NBC. Significantly, she is not a professionally trained journalist, and some professional journalists criticized ABC for this move. In effect, ABC was seeking to use her entertainment drawing power developed as co-anchorperson of the NBC *Today* show rather than her journalism skills to improve its Nielson ratings. ABC TV news now has more of an entertainment flavor rather than the "hard news" approach taken by the other networks. Why did ABC turn to a well-known television personality rather than a professionally trained journalist to improve its Nielson ratings? An improvement of just a few points on the Nielson rating means millions of dollars in advertising revenue.

Obviously radio stations, except for the few all-news stations in the big cities, do not consider news programming too profitable, since only five minutes out of every sixty are customarily devoted to news and at that a mere news summary, not an in-depth analysis.

Newspapers, except for such papers as the *New York Times* and the *Christian Science Monitor*, tend to feature local and sensational stories that have more reader appeal. Advertisers, of course, want to have the widest possible circulation, so it behooves newspapers to concentrate on those stories that will increase their circulation. In covering the state legislature and other state government news, an overwhelming number of daily newspapers rely solely on AP and UPI news services rather than sending at least one reporter to cover state-house activities. Typically, a newspaper that does send a reporter to cover state government has only one reporter to cover all three branches as well as regulatory agencies. Clearly the commercial motive is the principal determinant in causing newspapers not to send one or more reporters to cover state government. In Illinois, which has one of the larger state governments, the large Chicago papers have historically had only one reporter in Springfield, the state capital, except during a legislative session, when an additional reporter might be dispatched. The *Peoria Journal-Star*, a large downstate newspaper, has had one reporter covering state government, and the Bloomington Daily Pantagraph sends a reporter to cover the legislative session. As a result, most of state government receives little attention from reporters on a continuing basis. In technical areas, the one reporter who may cover state government could hardly be expected to write knowledgeably about all of state government.

Conservatism   While concentration of ownership creates a dearth of alternative points of view, and commercialism makes independent journalism nearly impossible, conservatism in bias further underscores monopoly control of the media. In 1976, 411 of the nation's daily newspapers editorially endorsed Gerald Ford, and only 80 endorsed Jimmy Carter. This conservative bias has important ramifications.

> The January 1973 issue of the *Columbia Journalism Review* published the results of a study on how fairly the press covered the Watergate scandal—one of the major stories of the 1972 presidential campaign. . . . Examining thirty major newspapers, the study found that those endorsing President Nixon minimized or refused to print the Watergate disclosures at a much higher percentage than those that made no endorsement for president. . . .
>   A study, by Congressman Bob Eckhardt in 1971, of nearly one hundred of the largest newspapers showed that the two thirds of the newspapers that regularly endorse Republican candidates also endorsed the conservative position on the ABM system, the Carswell Supreme Court nomination, the Cambodian invasion, the McGovern-Hatfield antiwar amendment, and Spiro Agnew's statements against dissenters.
>   In 1948, papers accounting for 80 percent of daily circulation supported the Republican, Thomas E. Dewey; and only 10 percent supported the Democrat, Harry Truman. In 1952, 80 percent backed Republican Dwight Eisenhower against 10 percent for Adlai Stevenson, the Democrat. Stevenson got 10 percent again in 1956, and Eisenhower received endorsement from 60 percent. In his first try for the presidency in 1960, Richard Nixon received 71 percent compared to John Kennedy's 16 percent; and in 1968 Nixon again received more newspaper support in terms of circulation than his opponent, Hubert Humphrey, by a five-to-one margin. Only in the 1964 election did most of the normally Republican press endorse the Democrat, Lyndon Johnson, over the very conservative Republican, Barry Goldwater, by more than a three-to-one margin.[10]

According to Ben H. Bagdikian, a student of American journalism, the investigative reporting of earlier days has largely faded into oblivion. The pioneers in popular journalism—Hearst, Pulitzer, and E. W. Scripps—protected the ordinary citizen from giant corporations, utilities, unfeeling governments, and even from the status quo. Now news corporations are prominently respectable. Many journalistic outlets served by the descendants of these pioneers would not publish the articles and editorials their founders did, "some because they are not good stories and editorials, but also because they would be too radical and would sound too hostile to corporate leadership." [11]

The public in a supposedly democratic country where there is little competition among the mass media lacks one of the most important safeguards of democracy—the right to be fully informed. Various reforms have been suggested to remedy the monopoly situation. (1) The government might subsidize newspapers to compete with journals in one-newspaper communities. (2) A board or commission with enforcement powers could be established to serve as a watchdog of media fairness. (3) Corporations that own more than one media outlet in a city might be required to relinquish all but one outlet.

MOLDING PUBLIC OPINION

The mass media influence people's attitudes in a variety of ways.[12] They may do so directly, in such forms as newspaper editorials. They may do so more subtly, through placement of a story in a newspaper (on page 1 versus page 15) or emphasis on television (three-minute versus thirty-second coverage). Covert influence may have a greater impact than overt appeals. V. O. Key, Jr., has noted that, between elections, the public is less alert to public issues and therefore more responsive to propaganda. He says that "at these times people are more likely to be blown about by the winds of the media than when political interest is more completely activated." [13]

One particularly powerful technique of the media is one of the simplest—to ignore an issue. To illustrate: Where were the mass communications when the United States became involved in Vietnam? Did they raise questions about our involvement? According to Tom Wicker of the *New York Times*, the mass media did not

> adequately question the assumptions, the intelligence, the whole idea of America in the world—indeed the whole idea of the world—which led this country into the Vietnam war in the 1960s. It is commonplace now, when the horse has already been stolen, to examine those assumptions. But where were we at the time we might have brought an enlightened view to bear on that question? [14]

The first senator to call for a pullout of American troops from Vietnam was Ernest Gruening of Alaska. When he delivered his speech on the Senate floor on March 10, 1964, the press was silent. One Washington reporter, Jules Witcover, reflected on this omission in 1971:

A cursory examination of news sources leads to the conclusion that citizens have a great number of opportunities to become well informed. They can view programs on the various television channels. Most radio stations give the news at least hourly—some continuously—and there are many talk shows. Newspapers and newsweeklies attempt to carry on their traditional function.

Yet a closer examination reveals that the news media are not effective in presenting balanced news in depth, but are to a degree contributing to a malfunctioning of society. They have participated in creating and exacerbating a series of crises by overconcentrating attention on particular topics. Typically, after a period of concentrated attention, the media suddenly drop one topic as they rush to indulge in overkill of the next one.— *Science*

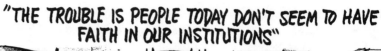

This single incident tells much about the performance of the Washington press corps in covering the Vietnam war. It represents not simply the misreading of the significance of a single event; more critically, it pinpoints the breakdown of a cardinal principle of newsgathering, especially early in the war: *pursuit of all points of view.*[15] [Emphasis supplied.]

Witcover's assessment also took the media to task for their one-sidedness during the early stages of America's involvement in Vietnam:

> While the Washington press corps in those years diligently reported what the government said about Vietnam, and questioned the inconsistencies as they arose, too few sought out opposing viewpoints and expertise until very late, when events and the prominence of the Vietnam dissent no longer could be ignored. Gruening and other early dissenters from official policy in and out of the Senate attest that they found very few attentive ears among Washington reporters in the early 1960s.[16]

Another technique of the media is to tell the public how to react to news.[17] When Harrison Salisbury, an assistant managing editor of the *New York Times*, traveled in North Vietnam in 1967, his reports questioned the veracity of official U.S. government information. Fellow journalists responded like this:

- Crosby Noyes of the *Washington Star* said Salisbury showed an "utter lack of identification . . . with what the government defines as the national interest."
- Chalmers Roberts in the *Washington Post* referred to Salisbury as an "instrument" of Ho Chi Minh.
- William Randolph Hearst, Jr., saw similarities between Salisbury's stories and treasonable broadcasts by Lord Haw Haw and Tokyo Rose during World War II.
- The *Washington Post*, noting similarities with a "Communist propaganda pamphlet," denounced Salisbury's casualty data.

University of Notre Dame psychologist Lloyd R. Sloan concluded that the 1976 post-presidential debate news analyses by television commentators had a substantial impact on public opinion as measured by his study of 254 potential voters who were divided into three groups. Immediately after the second debate between Jimmy Carter and Gerald Ford, Professor Sloan asked one group which candidate had won. In this group, "there occurred an overall shift of 20 per cent in favor of Ford." Two other groups watched the television commentary on the debate on ABC and CBS, respectively. Sloan said that "the network news analyses by themselves produced overall net changes of 27 per cent (CBS) and 22 per cent (ABC) in the direction of Carter." In his summary of television news analyses, Sloan said: "Those who viewed the post-debate news analyses saw both [ABC and CBS] as being biased in favor of Carter. There is bias in the news media, whether intended or not, and that bias has had a powerful effect on viewers and their voting preferences."[18]

MASS MEDIA AND GOVERNMENT COLLUSION

Public opinion on many issues reflects the limited or biased information released by the press. One of the most important factors in limiting and slanting information is the government itself. To continue with the example of press coverage of the Vietnam war, one fact that emerges is that the press industrialists did not commit their resources—namely, enough reporters—to obtain the necessary information. Throughout most of the war, only about a dozen reporters were assigned to the Pentagon despite the fact that its budget was approximately $80 billion and its decisions affected 3 million people in the service and several million civilians. Of all the newspapers west of the Appalachian Mountains, only the *Chicago Tribune* assigned a reporter full time to the Pentagon.

Far more important than the number of reporters was the willingness of the press quietly to accept Pentagon restrictions on its reporters, restrictions that severely hampered their ability to report the news. Reporters could not (1) interview people in private; (2) make interview appointments on their own; and (3) go to their interview appointments without being escorted.

Numerous examples can be adduced to illustrate the collusion between the mass media and the government. Presidents have taken network officials, disguised as technicians, on foreign trips. When President Nixon visited China in 1972, the limited number of seats on the press planes were to be occupied by news reporters, camera operators, and technicians, but top media officials were substituted for many of them. The media have responded to government pressures not to air certain programs or report certain stories. In 1973, for example, CBS canceled the showing of a controversial drama about a Vietnam war veteran.

President Kennedy's handling of the Bay of Pigs episode is a classic example of manipulation. Several press people, including representatives of the *New York Times*, the *New Republic*, and the *Miami Herald*, knew that the CIA was training Cuban exiles for an invasion. At the request of the government, however, they did not report this until too late to stop American involvement. After the debacle, Kennedy told the managing editor of the *New York Times:* "If you had printed more about the operation, you would have saved us from a colossal mistake." [19]

In this case, reporters had kept silent out of consideration for national security, at least as it was presented to them. In other instances, motives may be less patriotic. Corporate interests may play a part. The Chandler family, which owns the *Los Angeles Times*, also has substantial investments in television stations, lumber companies, steel, railroads, airlines, food stores, banking, farming, publishing, and oil. Since federal regulation can be vital in such enterprises, it behooves the *Times* to tread carefully where the government is concerned.

Observers have studied television and television news and their relationship to newspapers. They conclude that television, unlike newspapers, is more trusted by the public, provides more political campaign news, has a captive audience, and reaches people of all ages, educational backgrounds, income levels, and ethnic groups.[20] The president of the United States commands television time at will. Surely this situation creates enormous potential for collusion between television and the government.

The government has numerous ways of controlling the mass media.[21] Among them are blatant lying, the manipulation of media personnel, and abuse of government policies governing information.

Lying   Does the government lie to the press and public? American involvement in the Vietnam war, which ultimately claimed over 45,000 American lives, began without acceptable factual evidence of a provocation against the United States. According to President Johnson, three North Vietnamese PT boats attacked two American destroyers, the *Maddox* and the *Turner Joy*, in the Tonkin Gulf on August 2, 1964. Actually, the first shots were fired by the *Maddox*; there were no American casualties; only one machine gun bullet fired by a PT boat struck the *Maddox*.

On August 4, the *Maddox* and the *Turner Joy* claimed to be under "continuous torpedo attack." This report was based solely on information from one person, a twenty-three-year-old sonarman who had been in the navy two years. It was later discovered that he had mistaken the sound of the *Maddox's* own propellers for torpedoes.

Indeed, the commanding officer wired the Pentagon that "REVIEW OF ACTION MAKES MANY RECORDED CONTACTS AND TORPEDOES FIRED APPEAR DOUBTFUL. FREAK WEATHER EFFECTS AND OVEREAGER SONARMAN MAY HAVE ACCOUNTED FOR MANY REPORTS. NO ACTUAL SIGHTINGS BY MADDOX. SUGGEST COMPLETE EVALUATION BEFORE ANY FURTHER ACTION." Soon afterward, the United States was at war provoked by one bullet hole and evidence full of holes.[22]

President Johnson stated piously that "we don't want our American boys to do the fighting for Asian boys." On another occasion he put it this way: "We are not about to send American boys nine or ten thousand miles away from home to do what Asian boys ought to be doing for themselves."[23] Ultimately 536,000 Americans served in Vietnam.

The Watergate episode provides a rich trove of examples of government lying. For ten months after the initial break-in, President Nixon

We are even being told at exalted levels that the American press has something of a Marxist function—that it is our duty to serve the interests of the state. Let's make it clear, and I believe we never have fully done so, that the press of America is not an adjunct of politics or an appendage of the government, but an estate of its own, with its own responsibilities and its own commitments.—*Tom Wicker*

The credibility gap today is not the result of honest misunderstanding between the President and the press in this complicated world. It is the result of a deliberate policy of artificial manipulation of official news. The purpose of this manipulation is to create a consensus for the President, to stifle debate about his aims and his policies, to thwart deep probing into what has already happened, what is actually happening, what is going to happen. In its press relations, the administration does not hold with the fundamental American principle that true opinion arises from honest inquiry and open debate and that true opinion is necessary to free government. In this administration, the right opinions are those which lead to consensus with the leader, and to create such true opinion it is legitimate to wipe out the distinction between patriotism and patrioteering and to act on the assumption that the end justifies the means.—*Walter Lippmann*

The American public cannot believe everything it sees, reads, and hears about its government through the mass media. For example, former President Richard M. Nixon, who was eventually forced to resign, maintained through the various media that the White House was not involved in the Watergate break-in and cover-up. Nixon made frequent use of his presidential power to command television time in order to state his innocence.

and his aides denied that either he or his White House staff were aware of the planning and execution of the incident or that they had participated in a cover-up of the resulting scandal. When the White House later acknowledged some involvement, it termed previous misstatements on the subject "inoperative."

In the first chapter of his book *The Politics of Lying*, David Wise states:

> The consent of the governed is basic to American democracy. If the governed are misled, if they are not told the truth, or if through official secrecy and deception they lack information on which to base intelligent decisions, the system may go on—but not as a democracy. After nearly two hundred years, this may be the price America pays for the politics of lying.[24]

Manipulation of Media Personnel   Reporters depend on government sources for news stories. Recognizing this fact, many departments and agencies of the government exercise substantial control by rewarding media personnel with information if they write favorable reports and punishing them by withholding information if stories are unfavorable. This situation may substantially impair a reporter's professional standards. The granting and withholding of favors often works like this, according to Robert Walters, a *Washington Star* reporter:

> You get invited to the agency's parties. Not that the bureaucrats are consciously trying to co-opt you. They just want to get to know you better and make you feel more kindly toward them. But then if you get into a shoving match with them over some story, you get the stick instead of the carrot. You not only don't get invited to the background briefings. The same goes for reporters covering for Wyoming or Nebraska or Connecticut papers at the Capitol. It becomes a totally symbiotic relationship.[25]

The nature of this symbiotic relationship—one in which both sides need and help each other—is further illustrated by Jerry Greene, chief of the *New York Daily News* bureau: "Send a young reporter to the White House and let him indulge in a presidential trip or two and he isn't worth a damn for six months. He gets on a first-name basis with these clowns, he gets to indulge in fancy drinks and big hotel rooms that he couldn't otherwise afford, and he's wiped out.[26]

Reporters may be used to satisfy grudges or further quarrels. Some have received praise for their investigative reporting when the real credit belonged to disgruntled bureaucrats who simply "blew the whistle" on their bosses by leaking information to the press. Robert Walters says that newspapers and the public should realize that investigative reporting is largely a fraud. When the Department of Justice wants to go after someone, it has innumerable resources at its command that are totally unavailable to newspapers—subpoena power, almost unlimited personnel, the FBI that can request and get data on the bank account of anyone in the country. In contrast, newspapers generally have one reporter on a story—perhaps as many as five if the story is really big. That is not investigating. Although the *New York Times* credited Neil Sheehan's "investigative reporting" for the Pentagon papers story, an unhappy Daniel Ellsberg actually gave the story to the newspaper. This is how newspapers usually get most of their best stories—somebody wants the story out. Investigative reporters are not really out getting material nobody wants them to have.[27]

Government information released officially may be handled in such a way that the press connives in its own manipulation. A major

Its [the American press] biggest weakness is its reliance on and its acceptance of official sources—indeed, its "objectivity" in presenting the news. That is, that the fundamental reliance of the American news media in my experience has been, with rare and honorable exceptions, on the statement by the official source, be it government or business or academic or whatever. And much of what we mean by objectivity in American journalism concerns whether due credit is given to the official statement, the official explanation, the background explanation from the official source.—*Tom Wicker*

technique in this exercise is the *backgrounder*. Here government officials provide information to reporters on condition that it be relayed without attribution; that is, when the news is released, the identity of the government official must not be revealed. (Hence, stories attributed to "a high government official" or "White House informants.") Bill Moyers, formerly an aide to President Johnson, put the matter pungently:

> The backgrounder permits the press and the government to sleep together, even procreate, without getting married or having to accept responsibility for any offspring. It's the public on whose doorstep orphans of deceptive information and misleading allegations are left, while the press and the government roll their eyes innocently and exclaim: *"non mea culpa!"* ["It's not my fault!"] I know. I used to do a little seducing myself. The objects of this chase—members of the Washington press corps—were all consenting adults.[28]

A classic example of the government's manipulation of the press through a backgrounder occurred in January 1964. At a background news conference, a group of reporters were told that President Johnson would not be able to hold the next budget below $100 billion. The papers dutifully reported that a "high White House source" had disclosed this information. Within a few days, the Johnson budget as submitted to Congress totaled $97.7 billion. The public, cushioned by the media to expect a budget over $100 billion, had little choice but to look upon the President as a fiscal wizard. In the words of one reporter: "Mr. Johnson looked like a fiscal Houdini—and the press, which had been used, looked ridiculous." [29] James Reston of the *New York Times* has written:

> The power of the President to use the free press against itself is . . . very great. If, for example, an influential columnist or commentator criticizes him for landing 23,000 marines in the Dominican Republic to put down a rebellion, it is very easy for him to call in several other carefully selected commentators and give them the detailed argument for landing the marines. He has all the vivid facts of the situation, and if he wants to put them out, he does not have to announce them himself. Other reporters will be perfectly willing to accommodate him, even though they know they are being used to knock the story of a colleague.[30]

Still another factor strengthens the government's hand in dealing with reporters, namely their lack of specialized training. Most journalists are liberal arts majors. A major in journalism, English, or political science, for example, does not qualify a reporter, who is a generalist, to assess complex or technical issues in many specialized fields such as economics, space and nuclear science, or military strategy.

Abuse of Government Policies According to the 1966 Freedom of Information Act, the public is to have relatively easy access to government information, except that protected by security regulations. To protect itself—and also to prevent the public from acquiring data—the government has classified a good deal of material. A 1971 study showed that four departments and agencies alone spend $60 million a year just to stamp documents "secret" and keep them out of general circulation.

Even with information that is available to the press and public, the government can use delays to avoid releasing it. It can deny that information exists, or maintain that it is being compiled, thus preventing it from being published. In the case of the Pentagon Papers—which had already been leaked—the government succeeded in delaying their publication for fifteen days through court action.

Another abuse is the so-called "exception trap" to freedom of information. The government can refuse to release certain information on the grounds that its release would violate an individual or company's right to its "trade secret" on which the government has records. According to Ralph Nader: "The more I look into the trade secret area, the more I realize that it isn't a trade secret between competitors—they know all about it—it's a trade secret against consumers or against the public." [31]

PROPAGANDA

Propaganda may be defined as the deliberate selection and manipulation of information with the purpose of helping one's own cause or damaging one's opponent's cause. If what the public receives from the government through the media is the "story" the government wants the public to know, isn't this propaganda?

The hallmarks of propaganda are repetition, insistent exaggeration, identification with the persons being persuaded, appeal to authority, false association, and appeal to the herd instinct.[32] If you read back over this discussion, you can see that many of the instances cited are indeed propaganda.

One example is the Johnson administration's strategy regarding Vietnam; repetition and insistent exaggeration about the Tonkin Gulf incident led to widespread public support for the initial American involvement. The Departments of State and Defense and the President continued to repeat the same evidence as grounds for American involvement even though there was conflicting evidence; they exaggerated the ability of the United States to intervene and "win the war"; they appealed to the authority of the Tonkin Gulf resolution passed by Congress, the SEATO (Southeast Atlantic Treaty Organization) treaty, and the President's constitutional prerogative as commander in chief without asking for a declaration of war from Congress, which would most likely have provoked a more thorough public debate on the subject; they associated North Vietnamese leader Ho Chi Minh with other communist leaders, failing to point out that he was an American ally during World War II against the Japanese and that he often acted independently from other communist leaders; and they used the overwhelming congressional vote in favor of the Tonkin Gulf resolution as evidence of broad public support for American involvement. In effect, the government appealed to the "anticommunist" impulse of the people without fully exploring the gravity of the issue with them.

The Negative Case

No, the mass media and the government do not control public opinion.

In every country where man is free to think and to speak, differences of opinion will arise from difference of perception and the imperfection of reason; but these differences, when permitted, as in this happy country, to purify themselves by free discussion, are but as passing clouds overspreading our land transiently and leaving our horizon more bright and serene. That love of order and obedience to the laws, which so remarkably characterize the citizens of the United States, are sure pledges of internal tranquility; and the elective franchise, if guarded as the ark of our safety, will peaceably dissipate all combinations to subvert a Constitution dictated by the wisdom and resting on the will of the people. That will is the only legitimate foundation of any government, and to protect its free expression should be our first object.[33]–Thomas Jefferson

The mass media, as influenced by the government, are convenient targets for people in search of scapegoats on which to blame society's problems. A thorough and balanced assessment of the formation of public opinion will show that the reality is not as painted by the affirmative case.

Before turning to a point-by-point analysis, however, we might briefly consider another issue: How large a role *should* the public have in determining government decisions? At least two experts have felt that its role has definite limitations. Walter Lippmann wrote:

What, then, are the true boundaries of the people's power? The answer cannot be simple. But for a rough beginning let us say that the people are able to give and to withhold their consent to being governed—their con-

Two widespread myths about the unknown god public opinion found striking refutation in President Carter's telephone chats with ordinary Americans. . . . First there is the myth, dear to the narcissists of the media, that television and press determine public opinion. Then there is the myth, dear to populist believers in participatory government, that public opinion offers good policy guides. . . . The calls to the President amply demonstrated the relative weakness of the papers and television in determining what's on people's minds. Only 3 of the 42 calls . . . were on the mind of Big Think subjects which dominate the front pages and nightly news shows. The other 34 calls reflected the intense primacy of personal experience. . . . [Furthermore,] as a policy guide the session was useless. None of the ordinary citizens offered ideas for measures to be taken in dealing with health costs or Uganda or higher taxes. In fact the one positive policy suggestion called for moving snow from the East by railway to alleviate the drought in California.—*Joseph Kraft*

sent to what the government asks of them, proposes to them, and has done in the conduct of their affairs. They can elect the government. They can remove it. They can approve or disapprove its performance. But they cannot administer the government. They cannot themselves perform. They cannot normally initiate and propose the necessary legislation. A mass cannot govern. The people, as Jefferson said, are not "qualified to exercise themselves the Executive Department; but they are qualified to name the person who shall exercise it. . . . They are not qualified to legislate; with us therefore they only choose the legislators.[34]

E. E. Schattschneider, commenting on whether the public knows enough to make crucial government decisions, was even more sweeping: "Nobody knows enough to run the government. Presidents, senators, governors, judges, professors, doctors of philosophy, editors and the like are only a little less ignorant than the rest of us." [35]

The affirmative case implicitly assumes that in a democracy the public should have a major impact on governmental decision making on a day-to-day basis. Obviously, this is fallacious, if for no other reason than its impossibility. Such a course would be wholly unrealistic. This

United States government officials can be forced out of office when the tide of public opinion turns against them. Senator Joseph R. McCarthy of Wisconsin, shown here wearing glasses and seated at the head of the table, fell into public disfavor because of the tactics he used to expose alleged communist infiltration of the government and the arts.

is not to underrate the efficacy of public opinion. In recent years it has driven two presidents from office: Lyndon Johnson, over the Vietnam war issue, and Richard Nixon, over the Watergate scandal. Moreover, government officials have the obligation, since they have access to more information than the public, to try to persuade citizens that a particular decision or policy is correct.

Conservatives attack "liberal" reporters for biased news stories; liberals attack "conservative" ownership of the media. Both camps from time to time attack the government's role in forming public opinion. A true picture of the situation can be summarized as follows:

- The argument that media monopolies threaten the public because of concentration, commercialism, and conservatism is largely bogus.
- Public opinion is shaped by many factors other than mass communications.
- Even if the mass media and the government act together, public opinion is not at their mercy.
- Propaganda has significant limitations in forming public opinion.

THE BENEFITS OF MONOPOLY

The argument that monopolistic ownership patterns in the media adversely affect public opinion has another side. Is concentration really bad? If two newspapers are competing for the same market and therefore for the same advertising, won't they tend to report news in any way (including slanting) that will enhance sales and increase advertising? On the other hand, if only one newspaper controls a given market, won't it have more freedom from this type of competition, which may warp the quality of reporting? The public and the advertisers in the latter instance would have no place to go but to the one newspaper outlet; in the former they could use economic leverage to force the newspapers into a particular editorial position or stance on news.

Commercialism, as reflected in sales of advertising space and copies of publications, is an indicator of public preferences. If neither space nor copies are sold in sufficient quantity, there is reason to believe that the public does not particularly favor the medium—or, at least, its message. This situation itself reflects the mass media's inability to control public opinion. No one is forcing the public to buy what the media industries produce.

While the owners of the mass media tend to be conservative, their reporters tend to be liberal. This is the argument of Daniel P. Moynihan, who suggests that this liberalism provides a substantial counter-balance to conservative ownership. Moynihan notes that many journalists are college graduates with hostile attitudes toward middle-class Americans.[36] He reinforces his point by assessing the special role of the *New York Times* and the *Washington Post,* two liberally oriented newspapers. Moynihan argues that readers of these two journals are generally "more liberal than the rest of the nation," which causes the two papers "to set a tone of pervasive dissatisfaction with the performance of the national government, whoever the presidential incumbent may be and whatever the substance of the policies." [37]

The *Times* and *Post* aside, liberals who argue that conservative ownership unfairly skews public opinion may take solace from the outcome of some important political races. In all four of Franklin D. Roosevelt's campaigns, newspaper owners were overwhelmingly opposed to him, but he won every time. In 1960 John F. Kennedy won against this same type of widespread opposition. In 1976, Jimmy Carter won despite editorial support overwhelmingly in favor of Gerald R. Ford.

Given the fact that the public may choose among television, radio, newspaper, and magazine sources for its news, alternatives are available. What need then is there for reform? Besides, if the government were to break up media concentration or subsidize alternative media outlets, wouldn't such actions raise significant questions concerning our First Amendment freedoms of speech and the press? Couldn't similar questions be raised if a national body were set up to police media reporting?

A case could be made that in large cities with many media outlets the fairness doctrine of the Federal Communications Commission should not require that each station report a diversity of views. This is hardly a necessary requirement in major urban centers, where citizens can choose among alternative views offered by several different stations.

The affirmative case suggests implicitly that the news media should devote vast amounts of their resources to investigative reporting. Upon reflection, however, one realizes that there are at least two reasons why this should not be done. First, most media outlets do not have the financial resources to undertake an extensive amount of investigative reporting. Second, why should the media seek to duplicate information already provided by the government through such activities as criminal investigations and congressional hearings? Clearly there is a role for the media to play in investigative reporting, but it should be a supplementary and complementary role rather than a duplicating one. Of course, there are the relatively few instances when its role should be as adversary to governmental interests, such as revealing scandals like Watergate and the congressional sex scandal involving former U.S. Representative Wayne Hays (Dem. Ohio).

The affirmative case also implies that the media should educate the public against its will. To what extent is the media really obligated to impose education on the public? Would it be democratic, for instance, to have the three national television networks abandon most or all of their entertainment programs in favor of news programs? If we assume that the people govern in a democracy, should not the public's tastes and interests dictate more to the media than the reverse?

HOW IS PUBLIC OPINION SHAPED?

There is substantial evidence that the public does not regard its opinions as being controlled by the press. (People who agree with former Vice-President Spiro Agnew that the media are biased may well be in a minority.) In a Gallup survey in 1970, 67 percent of those responding rated television news "good" to "excellent" and 62 percent rated newspapers the same way. A 1971 nationwide Louis Harris survey revealed two points of interest: (1) 59 percent of the respondents said they regarded news coverage from Washington as "good" to "excellent" compared with only 37 percent who said it was "poor" or "so-so"; (2) in assessing the fairness of newspapers and television networks in their news reporting, a substantial majority of respondents in each instance said they were fair—59 percent and 64 percent, respectively.[38]

Of course the public could underestimate the effect of the mass media on its views. But even if we agree that mass communications do have a powerful effect, they are by no means the sole determinants of public opinion. Its shaping is much more sophisticated and complex than the affirmative case indicates.

The affirmative case naively assumes a unified governmental position on issues. Are the president, the bureaucracy, the Congress, and the courts unified on public policy? During the Nixon years, for example, what was the government's position on welfare—that of Congress, the President, or civil servants in the Department of Health, Education and Welfare? How can government control public opinion if it is divided on public policy?

Family and School   Scholars point out that public opinion on political subjects begins very early in life, at a time when a child's awareness and knowledge of mass media are quite limited.[39] The two principal sources of public opinion formation in this early period of life are the family and the school.

It is in the family where a child is inculcated with basic attitudes that will later shape his or her specific political opinions. One study shows a high correlation between political party identification of par-

News personalities such as CBS News's Walter Cronkite (right, wearing glasses) write and report the stories that help shape public opinion. However, other factors, such as family, school, social class, religion, sex, and ethnic background are important determinants of how one views current events.

ents and their twelfth-grade children; this correlation tends to exist throughout a person's life.[40] Other research shows that children tend to identify more closely with the political views of the parent with whom they have a closer personal relationship.[41]

Some scholars believe that the school may be even more important than the family in developing political attitudes.[42] The principal role of elementary and secondary schools, they argue, has been to strengthen and reinforce faith in American government.[43]

As children become older, they are more subject to mass media and government influences in forming their opinions. Even so, however, their attitudes toward these influences have been conditioned by family and educational experiences.

Other Factors   If, as the affirmative case argues, the mass media and government control public opinion, then it should be assumed that most Americans would hold the same opinions regardless of class, race, or ethnicity. This is simply not true. Along with family and school, several other factors help determine public opinion. One is social class. On such issues as social welfare programs, economically deprived persons are more likely to favor them, the affluent to oppose them.[44] Another finding is that community leaders are less tolerant of persons of lower socioeconomic status than they are of nonconformists, such as atheists and communists.[45]

Religious affiliation, sex, and ethnic factors may also affect public opinion. For instance, Jews and Roman Catholics are more likely to vote Democratic, while Protestants are more likely to vote Republican.[46] Geography may affect public opinion on economic issues; the industrialized Northeast, for example, has different ideas about union labor than the rural South. Party philosophy plays a part, too. A Republican will tend to oppose an enlarged role for government, while a Democrat will tend to support it.[47]

RESISTANCE TO MEDIA CONTROL

No two institutions in the country have a more important relationship than the government of the United States and the press. Each is powerful and each has almost inexhaustible resources. . . . The basic reason for the controversy between press and President is the fact that the objectives of the two institutions collide. The press, rooted in American history and tradition of freedom, attempts to find and report every single piece of information. The government naturally wishes to present its programs and positions in the best possible light. It therefore resists—sometimes rightly and sometimes wrongly—the pressures brought on it by the press.—*Pierre Salinger*

How much collusion is there between the media and the government? Certainly a hand-in-glove relationship did not characterize the Watergate affair. Even if one does concede a certain amount of complicity, whether overt or not, the actual effect on public opinion may be exaggerated. Four factors help limit responsiveness to the media.

First, the public is not like an "unfilled pot" ready to be filled by the media and government, but rather it exercises selective perception. In other words, people tend to listen to those speeches and to read those newspapers that agree with their conceptions. The mere fact that people have been exposed to a particular point of view does not mean that they accept it.[48]

Second, what might be called popular skepticism toward the government and the media is fairly widespread, making it difficult for these forces to control public opinion. In fact, the more the public knows about an event, the more skeptical it is of media accuracy.[49] This was true before Watergate, which only added to the distrust already felt for public officials and the government. For example, the percentage of Americans who believe the government is run for the few increased from 18 percent in 1958 to 52 percent in 1970, to 57 percent in 1972, and to 67 percent in 1973.[50]

Third, primary groups—family, neighborhood, peers, and other person-to-person contacts—are effective filters in the public opinion process. These groups generally have more influence on public opinion than televised speeches. And even if the media promote a certain view, it is often conveyed through, and altered by, a primary-group intermediary. Parents, for example, often interpret the meaning of an election for their children.

Fourth, lack of public awareness may inhibit the potential of the media and government to influence public opinion. The public may simply have a "non-opinion." In 1969 there was national debate on abolishing the electoral college, with heavy media support in favor of replacing it with direct popular election. Four out of every five Americans indicated that they preferred direct popular election.[51] However, although the House of Representatives approved a constitutional amendment providing for the change, the Senate did not. And there was no groundswell of public sentiment directed at the Senate. Why not? Despite the fact that an overwhelming number of Americans said they wanted to abolish the electoral college system, public opinion research showed that only about a third actually knew what it was.[52] In this instance, lack of public awareness undoubtedly inhibited opposition to Senate inaction. This was an issue where there was not enough intensity of public opinion to affect the legislative outcome.

Admittedly, lack of public awareness may allow the government more latitude to do as it pleases without reference to public opinion. It must, however, face the danger that latent public opinion will be aroused in opposition to its decisions and policies. The Vietnam war offers a case in point. Certainly the fact that the American people had little knowledge of the realities concerning American involvement did tend to give the government more power. As public awareness and knowledge increased, however, government latitude decreased. In other words, a permissive stage of public opinion became a directive stage.

Opinion is divided on whether public awareness is a danger or an asset to democracy. Walter Lippmann has noted the dangers of the public's being too aware and too active.

> Where mass opinion dominates the government, there is a morbid derangement of the true functions of power. The derangement brings about the enfeeblement, verging on paralysis, of the capacity to govern. This breakdown in the Constitutional order is the cause of the precipitate and catastrophic decline of Western society. It may, if it cannot be arrested and reversed, bring about the fall of the West.[53]

On the other hand, Robert E. Lane argues that the liabilities of nonparticipation may be greater than the liabilities of participation.[54] Lack of public awareness is clearly of debatable significance, but at least it suggests that the public is not waiting with baited breath for the next pronouncement from the mass media, whether or not government inspired.

Have Washington and the media *prevented* issues from being raised about government performance? Hardly. The media may have neglected to raise important questions, but others, such as Ralph Nader and John Gardner, have stepped in to take up the slack. Says Tom Wicker of the *New York Times:*

> Why has it been left mostly to people outside the press to raise the great issue of consumerism in America? Until Ralph Nader came along and began making challenges . . . little was done. I was one of a long line of reporters hired by the *New York Times* Washington bureau to look into and cover the regulatory agencies. I can name at least eight reporters who have been in our bureau who were hired precisely to do that, and the only one who has ever done it is the man who is there now, Christopher Lydon.[55]

"Of course the economy is improving --
it's an election year, ain't it?"

Wicker's very indictment of media weakness is further evidence that mass communications do not exercise undue control over public opinion, especially when it is aroused in opposition to governmental policy.

It is implicitly assumed in the affirmative case that the government (the different branches and agencies) should compete with its own position by putting out information adverse to its interests and that backgrounders are bad in that they involve government-media collusion. What degree of confidence could the public have in its government if the government constantly released information conflicting with existing policy? Its ability to govern would be undermined in such a situation. In addition, the public actually benefits from "backgrounders" since more information is provided than if the government and the press did not cooperate. There are times when government officials want the public to have information which they do not feel free to release. By anonymously releasing such data which would not otherwise be given the public, the government official makes available more information for a fuller debate of the issue at stake.

PROPAGANDA LIMITATIONS

Although skill in propaganda may help one acquire and hold power, it has substantial limitations. These are suggested by experiences in two political campaigns.

Richard Nixon began the 1968 presidential campaign some 16 percentage points ahead of Hubert Humphrey. Despite a campaign that was very well organized, compared to Humphrey's somewhat haphazard effort, Nixon's victory was narrow indeed. In 1970 New York Representative Richard L. Ottinger ran for the United States Senate. In the primary, his heavily financed campaign—publicized with the latest Madison Avenue techniques—led to a substantial victory. Ottinger lost in the general election, however, despite another equally professional advertising effort.

Why? Political advertising experts now tell us that the advertising was too slick. It presented an unrealistic image in both cases. When the public saw Nixon and Ottinger in press conferences, the two men projected very different images than those presented by their advertising. The public was not fooled.

These two campaigns illustrate the limitations of fundamental aspects of propaganda, namely repetition of "slick" advertising on television and exaggeration of a candidate's qualifications. Repetition and exaggeration harmed rather than helped Nixon and Ottinger. Other aspects of propaganda also have their limitations, particularly concerning the war in Vietnam. Although Presidents Johnson and Nixon continually appealed to their presidential authority to gain support for their actions and sought to create the impression of overwhelming public support for their policies, the public still became more and more disenchanted with the war.

Glossary

Backgrounder: news story supplied by the government on condition that the source not be revealed.

Polls: surveys designed to measure public opinion.

Propaganda: the deliberate selection and manipulation of information with the purpose of helping or harming a cause.

Public opinion: expressed views and attitudes of citizens about government, politics, or public issues.

Sample: in polling, a portion of a larger group being examined.

Special publics: special groups of citizens having views on particular issues, especially those affecting them directly.

Universe: in polling, a specific group whose opinions are to be measured and analyzed.

Notes

1. V. O. Key, Jr., *Public Opinion and American Democracy* (New York: Alfred A. Knopf, 1961), p. 7.

2. Ibid.

3. Ibid., p. 10.

4. For studies of the structure of public opinion, see V. O. Key, Jr., *Public Opinion and American Democracy* (New York: Alfred A. Knopf, 1961); Robert E. Lane and David O. Sears, *Public Opinion* (Englewood Cliffs, N. J.: Prentice-Hall, 1964); and Norman R. Luttbeg, "The Structure of Beliefs Among Leaders and the Public," *Public Opinion Quarterly* 32 (Fall 1968): 308–400.

5. Lane and Sears, *Public Opinion*, p. 15.

6. Robert Cirino, *Power to Persuade: Mass Media and the News* (New York: Bantam Books, 1974), pp. 208, 209. Copyright © 1974 by Bantam Books, Inc. Reprinted by permission of Bantam Books, Inc.

7. *Washington Post*, September 17, 1975, p. B8.

8. See Hearings, Senate Judiciary Committee, Subcommittee on Antitrust and Monopoly, U. S. 90th Congress, Vol. 243, Part I, p. 202; and Ben H. Bagdikian, *The Effete Conspiracy* (New York: Harper & Row, 1972), p. 10.

9. Robert Cirino, *Power to Persuade: Mass Media and the News* (New York: Bantam Books, 1974), pp. 113–115. Copyright © 1974 by Bantam Books, Inc. Reprinted by permission of Bantam Books, Inc.

10. Ibid., pp. 187–190.

11. As quoted in Robert Sherrill, *Why They Call It Politics* (New York: Harcourt Brace Jovanovich, 1974), p. 289.

12. See Sherrill, *Why They Call It Politics*, pp. 284–313; and David Wise, *The Politics of Lying* (New York: Vintage Books, 1973), pp. 406–493.

13. Key, *Public Opinion and American Democracy*, p. 403.

14. Tom Wicker, "The Greening of the Press," *Columbia Journalism Review* 10 (May/June 1971):7–12.

15. Jules Witcover, "Where Washington Reporting Failed," reprinted in *Congressional Record*, February 2, 1971, pp. 1383–1385.

16. Ibid.

17. See James Aaronson, *The Press and the Cold War* (Indianapolis, Ind.: Bobbs-Merrill, 1971).

18. *Washington Post*, November 6, 1976, p. A4.

19. Victor Bernstein and Jesse Gordon, "The Press and the Bay of Pigs," *The Columbia University Forum* (Fall 1967):4–15.

20. Gary L. Wamsley and Richard A. Pride, "Television Network News: Rethinking the Iceberg Problem," *Western Political Quarterly* 25 (September 1972):434–450.

21. Excellent discussions of these techniques may be found in Wise, *The Politics of Lying*; and Sherrill, *Why They Call It Politics*.

22. Wise, *The Politics of Lying*, pp. 62–66.

23. Ibid., p. 66.

24. Ibid., p. x.

25. As quoted in Sherrill, *Why They Call It Politics*, p. 309.

26. Ibid., p. 308.

27. Ibid., pp. 299–300.

28. *New York Times*, January 6, 1972, p. 37.

29. Chalmers Roberts, "Fearsome Antagonist," *The Nation*, October 24, 1966, pp. 406–411.

30. James Reston, *The Artillery of the Press* (New York: Harper & Row, 1967), p. 54.

31. *New York Times*, January 24, 1971, Sec. 3, p. 1.

32. "Propaganda Techniques," in Reo M. Christenson and Robert O. McWilliams, eds., *Voice of the People* (New York: McGraw-Hill, 1967), pp. 331–339.

33. Letter to Benjamin Waring, Edward Dumbauld, ed., *The Political Writings of Thomas Jefferson* (Indianapolis, Ind.: Bobbs-Merrill, 1955), pp. 79–80.

34. Walter Lippmann, *Essays in the Public Philosophy* (Boston: Little, Brown, 1955), p. 14.

35. E. E. Schattschneider, *The Semisovereign People* (New York: Holt, Rinehart and Winston, 1960), p. 136.

36. "The Presidency and the Press," *Commentary* 50 (March 1971):43.

37. Ibid., p. 44.

38. *Newsweek*, November 9, 1970, p. 22.

39. Bernard Berelson and Gary A. Steiner, *Human Behavior* (New York: Harcourt Brace Jovanovich, 1967), p. 105.

40. M. Kent Jennings and Richard G. Niemi, "The Transmission of Political Values from Parent to Child," *American Political Science Review* 68 (March 1968):179.

41. M. Kent Jennings and Kenneth P. Langton, "Mothers and Fathers: The Formation of Political Orientations Among Young Americans," *Journal of Politics* 31 (May 1969):357.

42. Robert D. Hess and Judith V. Torney, *The Development of Basic Attitudes and Values Toward Government and Citizenship During the Elementary School Years*, Part I (Washington, D.C.: U. S. Office of Education, 1965), p. 193.

43. Jennings and Niemi, "The Transmission of Political Values," p. 178.

44. Lloyd A. Free and Hadley Cantril, *The Political Beliefs of Americans* (New Brunswick, N.J.: Rutgers University Press, 1967), p. 147.

45. Samuel A. Stouffer, *Communism, Conformity and Civil Liberties* (Gloucester, Mass.: Peter Smith, 1963), pp. 188–219.

46. Free and Cantril, *The Political Beliefs of Americans*, p. 147.

47. Angus Campbell et al., *The American Voter* (New York: John Wiley & Sons, 1960), pp. 168–187.

48. Kurt Lang and Gladys Engel Lang, *Politics and Television* (New York: Quadrangle Books, 1968), p. 303.

49. *Newsweek*, November 9, 1970, pp. 22–25.

50. Survey Research Center studies, Institute for Social Research, University of Michigan, and National Opinion Research Center study, University of Chicago.

51. *Gallup Opinion Index*, October 1969, p. 22.

52. Hazel Gaudet Erskine, "The Polls: Textbook Knowledge," *Public Opinion Quarterly* 27 (Spring 1963):139.

53. Clinton Rossiter and James Lare, eds., *The Essential Lippmann* (New York: Random House, 1963), p. 241.

54. Robert E. Lane, *Political Life* (New York: The Free Press, 1959), p. 344.

55. Wicker, "The Greening of the Press," pp. 7–12.

Recommended Rebuttal Reading

On Public Opinion Generally

Berelson, Bernard, and Morris Janowitz, eds. *Reader in Public Opinion and Communication*. New York: The Free Press, 1966.

Bogart, Leo. *Silent Politics: Polls and Awareness of Public Opinion*. New York: John Wiley & Sons, 1972.

Campbell, Angus, et al. *Elections and the Political Order*. New York: John Wiley & Sons, 1966.

Erikson, Robert S., and Norman R. Luttbeg. *American Public Opinion*. New York: John Wiley & Sons, 1973.

Hennessy, Bernard. *Essentials of Public Opinion*. North Scituate, Mass.: Duxbury, 1975.

Ippolito, Dennis. *Public Opinion and Responsible Democracy*. Englewood Cliffs, N. J.: Prentice-Hall, 1975.

Jennings, M. Kent, and Richard G. Niemi. *The Political Character of Adolescence*. Princeton, N. J.: Princeton University Press, 1975.

Katz, E., and P. E. Lazarsfeld. *Personal Influence: The Part Played by People in the Flow of Mass Communications*. New York: The Free Press, 1955.

Key, V. O., Jr. *Public Opinion and American Democracy*. New York: Alfred A. Knopf, 1963.

Lippmann, Walter. *Public Opinion*. New York: Macmillan, 1922.

Mendelsohn, Harold, and Irving Crespi. *Polls, Television, and the New Politics.* Scranton: Chandler, 1970.

Monroe, Alan. *Public Opinion in America.* New York: Harper & Row, 1975.

Pomper, Gerald, et al. *The Election of 1976.* New York: David McKay, 1977.

"Public Opinion and Voting Behavior," in *The Handbook of Political Science,* Vol. 4, eds., Fred I. Greenstein and Nelson W. Polsby. Reading, Mass.: Addison-Wesley, 1975.

On the Mass Media

Balk, Alfred, and James Boylan, eds. *Our Troubled Press.* Boston: Little, Brown, 1971.

Liebling, A. J. *The Press.* New York: Ballantine, 1961.

MacDougall, A. Kent. *The Press: A Critical Look from the Inside.* Princeton, N. J.: Dow Jones, 1972.

MacNeil, Robert. *The People Machine: The Influence of Television on American Politics.* New York: Harper & Row, 1968.

Talese, Gay. *The Kingdom and the Power.* New York: Bantam, 1970.

On the Relationships of Mass Media and Government

Dunn, Delmar. *Public Officials and the Press.* Reading, Mass.: Addison-Wesley, 1969.

McGaffin, William, and Ervin Knoll. *Anything but the Truth.* New York: G. P. Putnam's Sons, 1968.

McGinniss, Joe. *The Selling of the Presidency.* New York: Trident Press, 1968.

Nimmo, D. D. *Newsgathering in Washington.* Englewood Cliffs, N. J.: Prentice-Hall, 1964.

Rivers, William. *The Opinion Makers.* Boston: Beacon Press, 1967.

Safire, William. *The New Language of Politics.* New York: Collier, 1972.

AT ISSUE: INTEREST GROUPS

Types of Interest Groups

Operation of Interest Groups

THE AFFIRMATIVE CASE

**Predominance of Business
    and Industry
    Money
    Knowledge
    Built-in Constituencies**

**Weakness of Countervailing
    Forces**

Serving the Public Interest?

THE NEGATIVE CASE

A Variety of Interest Groups

**Checks on Influence
    Emerging Interest Groups
    Preserving First Amend-
        ment Freedoms
    Role Theory**

**Democracy and the Public
    Interest
    A Supplement to Checks
        and Balances
    Additional Representa-
        tion
    Aiding an Open Society
    Helping the Public
        Understand
    Stabilization of Society**

RESOLVED THAT:
Interest Groups Undermine Democracy

6

At Issue: Interest Groups

Alexis de Tocqueville once noted that America is a nation of joiners par excellence. On almost any conceivable subject, one or more groups represent varying shades of opinion. Some of the best-known organizations are the National Association of Manufacturers and the Chamber of Commerce, both representing business and industry; the AFL-CIO, representing labor; the American Farm Bureau Federation and the Farmers Union; and, representing consumer or citizen interests, Common Cause and various groups associated with Ralph Nader, such as Congress Watch.

Each of these organizations is an *interest group,* defined as an organized group representing a special segment of society that seeks to influence governmental policies directly affecting its members. Interest groups—also called *lobbies* or *pressure groups*—are important because they are considered to be legitimate representatives of public opinion. That is, they are special publics that take definite positions on specific issues. Labor groups represent the interests of working people, the highway lobby is concerned chiefly with transportation, and so on. *Lobbyists* are persons who represent such an interest group.

TYPES OF INTEREST GROUPS

There are various ways of distinguishing among interest groups. One is to characterize them by the principal reason for their existence—their

A striking feature of American politics is the extent to which political parties are supplemented by private associations formed to influence public policy. These organizations, commonly called pressure groups, promote their interests by attempting to influence government rather than by nominating candidates and seeking responsibility for the management of government. The political interests of agriculture, for example, may be advanced through lobbying and propaganda activities of pressure groups, such as the American Farm Bureau Federation. Such groups, while they may call themselves nonpolitical, are engaged in politics; in the main theirs is a politics of policy. They are concerned with what government does either to help or to harm their membership. They do not attempt to assume, at least openly, the party's basic function of nominating candidates and seeking responsibility for the conduct of government, although the division of labor in the political system between parties and pressure groups is not always clear-cut. Pressure groups may campaign for party candidates and may even become, in fact if not in form, allied with one or the other of the parties. Yet by and large, pressure groups, as they seek to influence the exercise of public power, play a distinctive role: they supplement the party system and the formal instruments of government by serving as spokesmen for the special interests within society.— *V. O. Key, Jr.*

common interest. Four main categories are professional, economic, political, and consumer interest groups.

Professional interest groups include the American Medical Association, formed by doctors, and the American Bar Association, organized by lawyers. In some instances, professionals have spawned more than one interest group: teachers are represented by both the National Education Association and the American Federation of Teachers, and professors, by the American Association of University Professors.

Interest groups organized along economic lines are many and varied. Among the leading business organizations are the Chamber of Commerce of the United States, the National Small Business Association, and the National Association of Manufacturers. Some business groups have much more specialized interests, such as the American Bankers' Association. Representing farmers are the American Farm Bureau Federation, the National Farmers' Union, and the National Farmers' Organization. Specialized farm groups include the National Livestock Feeders Association, the National Wool Growers Association, and the American Meat Institute. Labor's major interest group is the AFL-CIO, which represents a 1955 merger between the American Federation of Labor and the Congress of Industrial Organizations. The former grouped craft unions, such as those of bricklayers or carpenters. The industrial unions of the latter organized all the workers in a given industry, such as steel. These many separate groups still exist within the AFL-CIO. Two other powerful labor organizations are the International Brotherhood of Teamsters and the United Auto Workers.

Political interest groups are typified by Americans for Democratic Action, a liberal organization, and Americans for Constitutional Action, a conservative association. Both the ADA and the ACA rate members of Congress according to how they vote on critical issues. These ratings may play a key role in election campaigns. In a conservative district, for example, a member of Congress can use a high ACA rating to advantage. U.S. Senator Strom Thurmond (Rep. S. C.), for example, publicizes his very high rating by the ACA, while U. S. Senator Jacob Javits (Rep. N. Y.) does the same with his ADA rating.

Consumer interest groups represent a wide range of issues and frequently do not have immediate economic interests at stake. Common Cause and the Ralph Nader groups are prime examples. Although not concerned with as broad a range of issues, both the National Association for the Advancement of Colored People and the American Civil Liberties Union meet the second criterion.

A second way to distinguish interest groups is by their position on the ideological spectrum, from far left to far right. Most groups would be located somewhere near the middle, in the moderate category. Most business groups can be classified as conservative, most labor groups as liberal. The sprinkling of radical organizations range from the Weathermen on the left to the Minutemen and the John Birch Society on the right. Typically, the moderate, conservative, and liberal groups in the United States believe in working within the established political system, while radicals are more apt to advocate violence as a tactic.

A third way to view interest groups is to distinguish between private and governmental interest groups. All those mentioned so far are private. It is important to note, however, that the various departments and agencies of government may also constitute interest groups. For example, the Office of Education in the Department of Health, Education and Welfare seeks to influence Congress on educational issues, while the Department of Defense constitutes a kind of lobby concerned with military affairs. State and local governments may also have lobbying interests, such as through the National League of Cities, the U.S. Conference of Mayors, the National Governors' Conference, and the National Association of Counties. These groups have been very instrumental in gaining congressional support for federal revenue sharing to assist state and local governments.

OPERATION OF INTEREST GROUPS

Interest groups use a variety of methods to achieve their goals, including (1) testimony before congressional committees, (2) personal meetings with members of Congress, (3) mass media advertising to build grassroots pressure and support, (4) demonstrations, (5) petitions, and (6) lawsuits. These and other methods will be discussed in the debate.

What is the public interest? Realistically, the public interest is determined by the result of interest group competition. The law that emerged from compromises made among the groups concerned with the issue of revenue sharing became the public interest. This practical or realistic definition of the public interest, of course, does not address the question of what should be the public interest. As we will see, some scholars contend that the public interest should be distinguished from the result of interest group competition.

The impact of interest groups on American democracy is heatedly debated. Some observers believe that they undermine our democracy; others contend that they are its very essence and lifeblood. Gabriel Almond and Sidney Verba state that interest groups permit the individual "to relate himself effectively and meaningfully to the political system." [1] On the other hand, Theodore Lowi argues that interest groups do not lead to "... strong, positive government ... but impotent government." [2] According to Lowi, to the extent that the public interest

The pluralist component has badly served interest-group liberalism by propagating and perpetuating the faith that a system built primarily upon groups and bargaining is perfectly self-corrective. This is based upon assumptions which are clearly not often, if ever, fulfilled—assumptions that groups always have other groups to confront them, that "overlapping memberships" will both insure competition and keep competition from becoming too intense, that "membership in potential groups" or "consensus" about the "rules of the game" are naturally and inevitably, scientifically verifiable phenomena that channel competition toward a public interest. It is also based on an impossible assumption that when competition does take place it yields ideal results.—*Theodore Lowi*

is determined by the resolution of conflict among private interest groups, government is amoral. And it depends on this resolution for its ideals and values in forming public policy. Thus, as pointed out by C. Wright Mills:

Mass democracy means the struggle of powerful and large-scale interest groups and associations, which stand between the big decisions that are made by state, corporation, army, and the will of the individual citizen as a member of the public. Since these middle-level associations are the citizen's major link with decision making, his relation to them is of decisive importance. For it is only through them that he exercises such power as he may have.[3]

Which position is right? That is the focus of our debate.

- Have citizens groups really proved effective as lobbyists?
- Should citizens groups attack or support specific candidates or simply stick to issues alone?
- Are activities of interest groups and the ways in which they work harmful to the well-being of the general public?
- Are there large numbers of citizens who are not represented by interest groups?

The Affirmative Case

Yes, interest groups undermine democracy.

When decision-making power is parceled out, it goes to special public-private interest groups—quasi-autonomous, entrenched minorities that use public authority for unaccountable private purposes of low visibility. The fragmentation of power is the pocketing of power, a way of insulating portions of the political process from the tides of popular sentiments.[4]—Michael Parenti

In other words, says Parenti, "the diffusion of power does not necessarily mean the democratization of power." Indeed, the proliferation of interest groups has been harmful to American democracy. One observer notes: "Year after year, there are new scandals about the operations of unethical lobbyists. Cases of payoffs, threats, and blackmail have been made regularly since the early years of the nation." [5] One of the principal reasons for this is the undue influence of business and industrial interest groups.

- Business and industry dominate interest group representation; through their money, access to knowledge, and weight in local communities, they wield a disproportionate influence.

Contrary to tradition, against the public morals, and hostile to good government, the lobby has reached such a position of power that it threatens government itself. Its size, its power, its capacity for evil, its greed, trickery, deception, and fraud condemn it to the death it deserves.—*Hugo Black*

● Countervailing forces have been ineffectual.
● The public interest is not served through the present method of resolving conflict and competition among interest groups.

PREDOMINANCE OF BUSINESS AND INDUSTRY

We have a problem. American government, both state and federal, is in disrepair. Few but the rich are assured access to elected officials. Campaign costs make politics a rich man's game. Lobbyists operate unobserved and unregulated. Legislators pass laws from which their friends derive personal financial gain. And all this goes on beneath a shroud of secrecy. The government is just not responsive or accessible to the people.—*John Gardner*

Economic power in the United States is increasingly concentrated. Although there are over 200,000 industrial corporations in the nation, 100 of them control half of all the country's assets—$290 billion out of $554 billion. (This proportion increased from 39.8 percent in 1950 to 52.8 percent in 1970.) Moreover, 10 percent of all industrial assets are controlled by the five largest industrial corporations—Exxon (Standard Oil of New Jersey), General Motors, Texaco, Ford Motors, and Gulf Oil.

Nor is concentration limited to industry. Just 33 corporations out of 67,000 control half the nation's assets in transportation, communications, and utilities. In banking, 50 banks out of 13,500 control 48 percent of all assets. In insurance, two companies, Prudential and Metropolitan, control one fourth of all assets.[6]

It is thus not surprising that industrial and business lobbies predominate both in number and expenditures. Table 1 shows that in 1973, 159 interest groups represented business alone, while professional, labor, farm, and military interest groups totaled only 73. As might be expected, business organizations spent more money on lobbying than did any other groups.[7] It should be noted that there are many expenses which, if reported, would only strengthen the conclusions already drawn. Only expenditures used to influence public policy directly must be reported as lobbying expenses. This would exclude an oil company's television commercial that focuses on the search for new energy sources.

Not only do business and industry have powerful lobbies. They are aided by representatives of their interests, elected and appointed, within the government itself. Many leading state and national officials have come from corporate management, prominent law firms, and large banking and other financial institutions. According to one view: "Elected and appointed . . . policy makers are overwhelmingly from the more favored classes; in the federal government 60 percent of them come from business and professional families."[8]

Between 1945 and 1947, during the Truman administration, 125 top appointments included 49 bankers and industrialists, 31 military officers, and 17 lawyers. "The effective locus of government" noted one commentator, "seemed to shift from Washington to some place equidistant between Wall Street and West Point."[9] In Eisenhower's first administration, 50 top appointments came primarily from industry, finance, and corporate law firms.

Table I. 1973 Lobbying Report

CATEGORY	NO. OF GROUPS	AMOUNT REPORTED
Business and Industry	159	$3,287,561.89
Professional	22	732,633.35
Labor	27	1,886,793.86
Agriculture	18	672,838.74
Military and Veteran	6	249,899.74
Miscellaneous	129	2,634,095.69
Total	361	$9,463,823.27

Source: *Congressional Quarter Weekly Report,* July 27, 1974, pp. 1947–1955. Reprinted by permission.

Sometimes it is thought that business dominance is peculiar to Republican presidential administrations, but the Carter appointments have business connections dispelling this theory. Among the six lawyers in the Carter cabinet, just a few of their clients are Gulf and Western, Revlon, Warner Communications, Occidental Petroleum, Northwestern Industries, American Electric Power Company, and Colonial Penn Insurance. A law firm in which Attorney General Griffin Bell served before his appointment represented General Motors.

The Coca-Cola connection is very pervasive in the Carter cabinet. Attorney General Bell's law firm in Atlanta represents Coca-Cola. The Washington law firm of Secretary of Health, Education and Welfare Joseph Califano represents Coca-Cola there. When he served as president of the California Institute of Technology, Secretary of Defense Harold Brown had the chairman of the board of Coca-Cola on his board of trustees.

In the corporate world of the media, Secretary of State Cyrus Vance served as a director of the *New York Times;* HEW Secretary Califano represented the *Washington Post;* and Defense Secretary Brown served on the board of the *Los Angeles Times.*

Beyond this, however, is the interesting tie of several Carter appointees to David Rockefeller, chairman of the board of the Chase Manhattan Bank. The Trilateral Commission, established by David Rockefeller with the aid of Carter's national security adviser, Zbigniew Brzezinski (then of Columbia University), worked to chart a new American course in foreign affairs. Carter appointees who served on the Trilateral Commission were State and Defense Secretaries Vance and Brown and UN Ambassador Andrew Young.

Rockefeller connections do not stop there. Vance and Treasury Secretary Michael Blumenthal served on the executive committee of the

Table 2. Business and Governmental Experience of Defense, State, and Treasury Secretaries: 1953–1977

SECRETARY	NAME	POSITION PRIOR TO NOMINATION	GOVERNMENT EXPERIENCE	BUSINESS EXPERIENCE
DEFENSE	Harold Brown 1977–	Pres., California Institute of Technology	Sec. of Air Force	Dir. Schroders Ltd, IBM, Times-Mirror Corp.
	Donald Rumsfeld 1975–1977	Member, U.S. Congress		
	James R. Schlesinger 1973–1975	Director, Central Int. Agency	Chairman, Atomic Energy Comm., Ass't Dir., Office of Management and Budget	
	Melvin Laird 1969–1973	Member, U.S. Congress		
	Clark Clifford 1967–1969	Clifford and Miller (law firm)	Special Counsel to Pres. (1946–50)	Dir., National Bank of Washington, Sheridan Hotel Corp.
	Robert S. McNamara 1961–1967	Pres., Ford Motor Co.		Dir., Scott Paper Co.
	Thomas S. Gates 1959–1960	Sec. of Navy	Pres., Morgan Guaranty Trust Co.	Dir., General Electric, Bethlehem Steel, Scott Paper Co., Campbell Soup Co., Ins. Co. of N.A., Cities Service, Smith, Kline & French
	Neil H. McElroy 1957-1959	Pres., Procter & Gamble		Dir., General Electric, Chrysler Corp., Equitable Life
	Charles E. Wilson 1953–1957	Pres., General Motors		Dir., General Motors
STATE	Cyrus Vance 1977–	Simpson Thatcher & Bartlett (law firm)	Sec. of Army, Deputy Sec. of Defense, Sec. of Defense	Dir., IBM, Pan-Am. World Airways, New York Times Co. Bd. of Directors
	Henry Kissinger 1973–1977	Spec. Ass't. to President		
	William P. Rogers 1969–1973	Royall, Koegal, Rogers and Wells (senior partner)	U.S. Attorney General	
	Dean Rusk 1961–1968	Pres., Rockefeller Foundation	Dep. Under Sec. of State	
	John Foster Dulles 1953–1960	U.S. Ambassador	Variety of foreign relations positions with U.S. government	Dir., Bank of New York

SECRETARY	NAME	POSITION PRIOR TO NOMINATION	GOVERNMENT EXPERIENCE	BUSINESS EXPERIENCE
TREASURY	Michael Blumenthal 1977–	Pres., Bendix Corp.	Deputy Asst. Sec. of State for Economic Affairs, Dept. of State, appointed Pres.'s dep. special rep. for trade negotiations with rank of ambassador	Dir., Crown Cork Int. Corp., Dir., Overseas Affiliated Cos., Bendix Corp., Vice-Chairman, Bendix Corp.
	William E. Simon 1974–1977	Dir., Federal Energy Office	Deputy Sec. of Treasury	Senior Partner, Salomon Brothers (investment firm)
	George P. Schultz 1972–1974	Sec. of Labor		Dir., Borg-Warner Corp., General Am. Transportation Co., Stein, Roe & Farnham
	John B. Connally 1971–1972	Attorney, Murcheson Brothers Investment Co.	Sec. of Navy, Gov., Texas	Dir., N.Y. Central Railroad
	David Kennedy 1969–1971	Pres., Continental Illinois Bank and Trust Co.		Dir., International Harvester, Commonwealth Edison, Pullman Co., Abbott Laboratories, Swift and Co., U.S. Gypsum, Communications Satellite Corp.
	Douglas Dillon 1961–1963	Under Sec. of State	Under Sec. of State for Econ. Affairs	Dir., Dillon, Reed and Co., N.Y. Stock Exchange, U.S. Foreign Securities Corp., U.S. International Securities Corp.
	Robert B. Anderson 1957–1961	Deputy Sec. of Defense	Sec. of Navy	Dir., Goodyear Tire & Rubber, Pan-Am. World Airways
	George M. Humphrey 1953–1957	Chm. of Board, M. A. Hanna Co.		Dir., M. A. Hanna Co., National Steel Corp., Consolidated Coal Co., Dominion Sugar Co.

Source: Compiled from data in *Who's Who in America*, (Chicago: Marquis Who's Who, Inc., 1953–1977).

Rockefeller Foundation as well as on the board of directors of the Chase Manhattan Bank and IBM where Rockefeller money is also important.[10]

A close look at the experience of the secretaries of defense, state, and the treasury since 1953 reveals the close ties between corporate wealth and governmental decision makers (see Table 2). Even when a man's previous experience has been largely academic, corporate financial power may have figured largely. James Schlesinger, for example, was an economics professor with close ties to the corporate world, while Henry Kissinger served as project director for the Rockefeller Brothers Fund and as personal adviser to Nelson Rockefeller on foreign affairs.

There are three main reasons why interest groups representing business and industry are able to exert such strong influence. (1) They are affluent. (2) They have access to information. (3) They have built-in constituencies because of their importance to communities' well-being.

Money With huge funds at their disposal, business and industrial interest groups can finance the best lobbyists. employ the best minds, and conduct the best campaigns to influence public opinion.

For example, in 1976 business and industry won eight of ten statewide votes on energy and environmental issues in ten states. In six states—Arizona, Colorado, Montana, Ohio, Oregon, and Washington—voters overwhelmingly rejected efforts to regulate the growth of nuclear power plants. Significantly, the Sierra Club estimates that industry spent $6 million to defeat these nuclear regulatory proposals. In four states, there were elections on whether to phase out disposable bottles and cans for beverages and to require refunds for returnable containers. Although the proposal won in Maine and Michigan, it lost in Massachusetts and Colorado, and industry funds were substantial in each instance.[11]

Another example involves a labor-management dispute. In 1975 Congress passed the so-called common-sites picketing bill, allowing all construction unions to picket a building site in protest against a single contractor working at the site. President Ford had promised to sign the bill, but the National Right to Work Committee, a lobbying organization generally opposed to labor unions, organized a blitz campaign. In sixteen days it spent $800,000 to send direct mail appeals to 4 million Americans, requesting that they write the President about their opposition. The result was a barrage of over 700,000 cards and letters—and a presidential veto early in 1976. This lobbying effort appeared to be a major factor in changing the President's mind. The White House indicated that no issue since the Vietnam war had sparked such a volume of mail.[12]

Table 3. 1972 Illegal Corporate Campaign Contributions

CORPORATION	NIXON	McGOVERN
American Airlines	$ 55,000	
Ashland Petroleum Gabon, Inc.	100,000	
Braniff Airways	40,000	
Diamond International Corporation	5,000	$1,000
Goodyear Tire and Rubber Company	40,000	
Gulf Oil Corporation	100,000	
Lehigh Valley Cooperative Farmers	50,000	
Minnesota Mining & Manufacturing Company	30,000	
Northrop Corporation	150,000	
Philips Petroleum Company	100,000	

Source: *Congressional Quarterly Weekly Report,* July 20, 1974, pp. 1857–1858. Reprinted by permission.

While money may be legitimately used to finance lobbying activities, corruption may result from the illegal use of money. During the 1972 presidential campaign, corporations made substantial contributions (see Table 3)—a practice forbidden by federal law. Several business leaders were later fined or imprisoned, including executives from American Airlines, Ashland Petroleum, and Gulf Oil. Some campaign finance operations may be less obvious. The Associated Milk Producers, Inc.—a dairy lobby—has contributed hundreds of thousands of dollars to a host of politicians in attempts to raise milk price supports. During the 1972 presidential campaign, a commitment of $2 million from AMPI was followed the next day by a presidential decision to allow increases.

The subtle forms of lobbying that corrupt even honest people are perhaps more dangerous. When businesses and industries lend politicians planes for their travel needs or personnel for their campaign staffs, they may not be directly buying votes or support, but they have certainly furthered their cause. At the very least, politicians so aided will be receptive to representatives of the company that has helped them.

Knowledge Gathering information requires time and money. Here again business and industry have an advantage. A 1976 study of interest group activity concerning the 1973 debate on the Federal Housing Subsidy Programs suggests there are several factors contributing to interest group success: number of members, size of staff, total expenditures, communications with key decision makers, and the ability to participate in congressional hearings.[13] Data on several of these factors are given in Table 4. Although each factor may contribute to interest group success, it is not of equal importance to all groups. An interest group

Table 4. Groups Interested in Federal Housing Subsidy Programs

GROUP	NUMBER OF MEMBERS	TYPE OF MEMBERS	STAFF SIZE
American Bankers Association (ABA)	13,500	Commercial banks	300
American Institute of Planners (AIP)	6,000	Individual urban planners	20
Mortgage Bankers Association of America (MBA)	2,200	Firms in mortgage banking	50
National Association of Home Builders (NAHB)	54,000	Builders and associates, individuals and firms	180
National Association of Housing and Redevelopment Officials (NAHRO)	10,000	8,200 individuals and 2,000 organizations	38
National Association of Mutual Savings Banks (NAMSB)	500	Mutual savings banks	54
National Association of Real Estate Boards (NAREB)	94,000	Individual realtors (in over 1,500 boards)	190
National Housing Conference (NHC)	4,000	Individuals and organizations	3
National League of Cities (NLC)	15,000	Municipalities and state municipal leagues	124
United States Conference of Mayors (USCM)	500	Mayors of cities of more than 30,000 and state capitals*	
U.S. Savings and Loan League (USS & LL)	4,814	Savings and loan companies	195

* Joint staff with National League of Cities.

Source: Randall B. Ripley, "How to Map Interest Group Environments," *DEA News*, Spring 1976, pp. 2–5. Reprinted by permission of The American Political Science Association.

with a small membership may more than compensate for its size by its larger staff or, of course, the opposite may be true. An examination of the interest groups listed in Table 4 reveals that financial and local government interests predominate. The interests of beneficiaries of the Federal Housing Subsidy Programs appear to be underrepresented except as they may be represented by the local government groups or the National Housing Conference. As we can see from this example, allowing the public interest to be determined by the result of interest group competition may ignore important segments of the population that are not organized and able to compete with the dominant interest groups.

Another dramatic example of this problem is the continuing debate over energy policy. For many years the oil lobby has controlled information on oil reserves and oil production, making it the dominant influence in determining the public interest on this crucial issue. Only since the energy crisis of the 1970s has the government begun to develop information that may be used to challenge the oil lobby's information monopoly. Understandably an organization with superior information resources may be expected to provide better testimony in congressional committee hearings.

Not only can interest groups often influence public policy through expert testimony, government officials may also call on business and industry leaders for their advice. The latter can employ the best minds to work on their behalf, and may actually lend such talent to work for the government itself. Not infrequently, close relationships develop between business interests and governmental decision makers.

Another aspect of "knowledge collusion" is the appointment of industry and business personnel to federal regulatory agencies, such as the Federal Trade Commission and the Federal Communications Commission, charged with regulating these same industries and businesses (see Table 5). An Associated Press study in 1975 revealed the following: (1) More than 100 of the government officials who decide what drugs can be sold and what chemicals can be added to food once worked for drug or chemical companies. (2) More than 300 top-level regulatory officials are now making the rules for sale of stocks and bonds to the public by their former employers—including brokerage firms and stock exchanges. (3) At least 41 high-level officials have left federal regulatory agencies in the last five years to take posts (often more lucrative) with companies in the same regulated industries.[14] (For further development of this point, see Chapter 10.)

To illustrate the problem specifically, Common Cause has cited data showing that 429 (or 65 percent) of the top-level officials of the Nuclear Regulatory Commission come from private enterprises holding licenses, permits, or contracts from the NRC and that 28 (or 6.5 percent) of the other top-level employees come from other private-energy enterprises. Following up on this data, Ralph Nader charged on October 25, 1976, that the NRC promotes nuclear power even though its role is solely to regulate it. He noted that the NRC had advocated subsidies of

Table 5. Business/Industry Professionals Now Employed
in Policy Positions in Selected Regulatory Agencies
Governing Professionals' Prior Employer

REGULATORY AGENCY	NUMBER EMPLOYED
Food and Drug Administration	115
Securities and Exchange Commission	36
Environmental Protection Agency	51
Federal Power Commission	30
Federal Communications Commission	20
Interstate Highway Commission	15
National Highway Traffic Safety Administration	14

Source: The Associated Press, September 7, 1975. Reprinted by permission.

Consumer advocates such as Ralph Nader, shown here addressing a "People Power" conference in Minneapolis, Minnesota, in 1974, help alert the American public to ways in which interest groups representing business and industry can shape public policy to suit their own special needs.

utilities that expand their nuclear power potential and also legislation to limit the liability of utilities in the event of a nuclear accident.[15]

Built-in Constituencies   Another factor in favor of business and industry is the basic constituency of many a large firm. It is not uncommon for a company to advise town officials that if they act against its interests, it will leave the community. In such a case the company is aided by its own employees, whose livelihood is at stake. As the constituency of the company, they are forced to lobby on behalf of the firm, even when they disagree with company policy. The company is also aided indirectly by other local businesses or individuals that stand to lose money in case of a move.

Many small towns are dominated by one industry. And even in larger communities the importance of a major firm, with a constituency of thousands, is immeasurable. Boeing in Seattle and Du Pont in Delaware, to name but two, command resources that make them formidable members of any interest group.

In their use of all three weapons—money, information, and built-in constituencies—interest groups have become increasingly subtle over the years.

> The "old" NAM [National Association of Manufacturers] bribed congressmen and employed legislative spies; the "new" prefers to work in public, openly offering advice and assistance to politicians. The "old" NAM sent paid intermediaries to "influence" the drafting of the Republican Convention Platform; the "new" prepares a "Platform of American Industry" and offers to testify at both party conventions. ... Today the NAM refers to its "bank account" theory of public relations, which "necessitates making regular and frequent deposits in the Bank of Public Good-Will so that valid checks can be drawn on this account when desirable." [16]

WEAKNESS OF COUNTERVAILING FORCES

Among interest groups, none has sufficient authority to balance the overwhelming power of business and industrial interests. The two groups most often regarded as *countervailing forces* are labor and agriculture. Labor leaders, however, are certainly not consulted by government officials as business leaders are. In any case, organized labor has had problems with an unfavorable public image and the erosion of its power as white-collar workers have grown in numbers. The number of small farmers has declined steadily in this century. While there were 6.5 million farms in 1925, it is estimated that there will be only about 2 million in 1980. At the same time farming is becoming big business, and so-called agribusiness has more in common with industry giants than with the individual farmer.

One problem is that although Americans are thought of as joiners, this phenomenon is more common at higher socioeconomic levels than at lower ones. One study of group membership showed that 80 percent of persons with some college education belonged to at least one group, while only 46 percent of those with a primary education or less were members of any association.[17] Political scientist V. O. Key, Jr., has written:

[The general will] instead of being the united opinion of the whole community is usually nothing more than the voice of the strongest interest or combination of interests, and not infrequently a small but energetic and active portion of the people.—*John C. Calhoun*

> Studies of the members of organized groups and of their potential members in different times, places, and circumstances uniformly show that persons who belong to organizations are, on the average, distinguishable from the nonjoiners. The better-off and better-educated in almost any category of potential members are more likely to be members than are those not so well off or those with less education. The prosperous, the alert, the informed, and the educated join together in organizations to promote their concerns.[18]

"TSK TSK—ACCIDENTS **WILL** HAPPEN"

Although the federal government has tried to regulate lobbying, its controls are ineffectual. In 1946 Congress passed the Federal Regulation of Lobbying Act, which required lobbyists to register and to report their lobbying expenses. As interpreted a few years later by the Supreme Court, the law was severely limited in scope. For instance, organizations need register only if lobbying is their "principal purpose." This exempts many groups that do lobby, even if it is not their main goal. Lobbyists are required to report only those expenses incurred in direct contact with members of Congress. Thus they need not report money spent contacting members of the executive department. This provision also effectively exempts overhead expenses and the major portion of lobbyists' salaries.

Political parties are no more effective than the government at counteracting the power of business and industry interests groups. In the American system, political parties do not exert sufficient control over legislators and other elected officials to force them to follow established party positions and thus lessen their susceptibility to interest group pressure. The high cost of campaigns, coupled with ineffective campaign finance laws, makes parties peculiarly vulnerable to influence by the wealthy (see Chapter 8).

What might be called a *cozy triangle* often develops among key members of Congress, bureaucrats, and interest groups. To cite only one example: Representative Mendel Rivers, at one time chairman of the House Armed Services Committee, strongly supported large defense budgets—which also happened to be a primary concern of the Department of Defense and of military weapons contractors. In effect, Rivers was a major spokesman in Congress for both the Pentagon and defense suppliers.

The weakness of forces that might counteract business and industry interest groups has led to a counterreaction among many people. In the 1960s and 1970s large numbers of Americans felt they could not influence the government's position because they lacked resources. To them, violence became a justifiable technique of persuasion. The radical actions of those thus alienated from the American system of government illustrate the frustration people feel in the face of massive pressure from affluent interest groups.

> Yet full realization of the American ideal of government by elected representatives depends to no small extent on their ability to properly evaluate . . . pressures. Otherwise, the voice of the people may all too easily be drowned out by the voice of special-interest groups seeking favored treatment while masquerading as proponents of the public weal.—*Earl Warren*

SERVING THE PUBLIC INTEREST?

Was it in the public interest for oil companies to have a depletion allowance higher than that set for any other type of production? * After all, it is the public that is thus subsidizing oil producers. Is it in the public interest for tariffs on some products to be set at artificially high levels, thus protecting industries that cannot produce as efficiently as their for-

---

* Adopted in the 1920s, the oil depletion allowance permitted oil producers a tax write-off of 27.5 percent of their gross income to compensate for the reduction in oil reserves. In 1969, the allowance was cut to 22 percent and then removed entirely in 1975 except for independent producers who retained the 22 percent allowance.

Strip mining is an economical and effective method that benefits business and industry. But is the environmental destruction it causes really in the public interest? Here a hillside in Cumberland, Ohio, is ravaged by strip mining.

eign counterparts? After all, it is the public that pays the higher prices that result from lack of competition. Is it in the public interest for car safety and pollution control standards to be waived or reduced for certain periods of time in order to help the automobile industry? After all, it is the public that suffers from resulting highway accidents and polluted air.

These are the kinds of things that happen when the public interest is determined through interest group conflict, defined by whoever wins the battle of lobbyists. Nearly 50,000 Americans lost their lives in Vietnam because the dominant interests of the military-industrial complex supported the war there.

A most revealing comment was made in 1966 by Senator Russell Long of Louisiana on the question of scientific patents growing out of the space program (a program funded by tax dollars). It had been suggested that these patents be placed under private control.

> I submit that there is no more outrageous thing that can be done to the public interest. Many of these [corporate] people have much influence. I, like others, have importuned some of them for campaign contributions for my party and myself. Nevertheless, *we owe it to the people, now and then, to save one or two votes for them.* This is one such instance. If any Senator should suspect that he might lose his campaign contributors by voting with me today, I might assure him that I have been able to obtain contributions from some of those people, even though they knew I voted for the public interest as I see it on such issues as this. We Democrats can trade on the dubious assumption that we are protector of the public interest only so long if we permit things like these patent giveaways [emphasis supplied].[19]

The Negative Case

No, interest groups do not undermine democracy.

[Interest groups] represent a healthy democratic development. They rose in answer to certain needs. . . . They are part of our representative system. . . . These groups must be welcomed for what they are, and certain precautionary regulations worked out. The groups must be understood and their proper place in government allotted, if not by actual legislation, then by general public realization of their significance.[20]–Pendleton Herring

If there were no interest groups, they would most likely be invented because they are essential to the effective working of democracy. The public depends on them for representation of group interests, and elected officials depend on them for information on which to make decisions.

The weight of the evidence . . . suggests that there is relatively little influence or power in lobbying per se.—*Lester Milbraith*

- Interest groups represent many segments of society; business and industry do not dominate.
- The influence of interest groups is sufficiently restricted by limitations built into the system.
- Democracy depends upon interest groups for a definition of the public interest.

A VARIETY OF INTEREST GROUPS

While there are more interest groups representing business and industry than any single segment of our society, it should be noted that total expenditures by other groups far exceed those by business and industrial lobbies—$6,176,261.38 to $3,287,561.89 during the year 1973.[21] This substantial amount may well prompt us to examine the success of other interest groups in the determination of public policy.

It is natural to expect that business and industrial interest groups would figure largely in a capitalist economy, but this does not necessarily mean that such groups dominate public policy. The major social and economic innovations of the twentieth century did not originate with the Chamber of Commerce or the NAM. The New Deal, for instance, forged a coalition of labor unions, big cities, and the South largely through a "brain trust" of liberal intellectuals, including men like Rexford Guy Tugwell and Tommy Corcoran. Similar influences lay behind the Fair Deal, New Frontier, and Great Society programs.

Another indication that business and industry do not dominate the scene is the "war chests" put together by several types of interest groups for political campaigns. In 1974, 526 special interest groups raised $16.7 million in campaign funds; significantly, organized labor raised the largest share, $6.1 million. Fully a year before the 1976 campaign, labor had already outstripped other categories of interest groups in raising funds.

Labor	$4,807,996
Agriculture	2,705,489
Health	2,185,936
Business	1,844,809
Finance	649,530
Other	324,971[22]

The effect of organized labor on the electoral process can be illustrated by election results from 1972 (not a vintage year for labor-supported candidates). The Committee on Political Education (COPE), the political action arm of the AFL-CIO, raised $2.8 million for congres-

Table 6. 1976 Interest Group Endorsements of
House and Senate Candidates

INTEREST GROUP	CANDIDATES ENDORSED		CANDIDATES WINNING	
	HOUSE	SENATE	HOUSE	SENATE
AFL-CIO (Committee on Political Education)	368	28	258	19
Business-Industry (Political Action Committee)	105	18	45	10
National Education Association	323	26	272	19
National Rifle Association	279*		204*	
Consumer Federation of America	89	5	34	5

* Separate breakdown for House and Senate not given.

Source: *Washington Post*, November 14, 1976, p. A3. © Washington Post. Reprinted by permission.

sional candidates; the result was victory for 391, or 57.1 percent of all labor-backed candidates. In 1976, of course, labor support was crucial to Jimmy Carter's victory in key states like Ohio and New York. Also in 1976, as shown in Table 6, labor, gun, education, and liberal interest groups fared better in congressional elections. For example, of the 28 Senate candidates and 362 House candidates endorsed by the AFL-CIO Committee on Political Education, 19 and 258 won, respectively, while the Business-Industry Political Action Committee had only 10 of 18 Senate candidates who won and 45 of 105 House candidates.

Labor may also work in direct opposition to business and industry. For instance, multinational corporations like International Telephone and Telegraph and Shell Oil are checked by multinational labor unions like the International Longshoremen's Union.

It is not only organized labor that wields power. For example, teachers and religious groups demonstrated their influence when they backed a 1965 education bill. The National Education Association favored the bill because it made large amounts of federal money available to elementary and secondary schools. The United States Catholic Conference lobbied for the bill because it aided parochial schools. Pressure

EVOLUTION OF TWO GROUPS

Public Citizen and Common Cause are the creations of two figures who are influential in their own right—Ralph Nader and John W. Gardner.

Nader, 42, first attracted public attention in November 1965 with the publication of his bestselling book, "Unsafe at any Speed," charging that the General Motors' Chevrolet Corvair was dangerous to drive.

The Connecticut lawyer testified at Senate hearings in 1966 on auto safety legislation, and on March 22 of that year, GM President James M. Roche admitted to a Senate Government Operations subcommittee that the company had hired private detectives to spy on Nader and apologized for it. Subcommittee Chairman Abraham Ribicoff (D Conn.) depicted the Nader-GM episode as "a David-Goliath confrontation, and David won." (*Background, 1965 Almanac p. 266*)

Building on his personal triumph, Nader formed the Center for the Study of Responsive Law in 1969, staffing it with young lawyers. With the aid of student summer volunteers (dubbed "Nader's Raiders" by the press) they produced books criticizing, among other things, the Food and Drug Administration, the Federal Trade Commission, the Interstate Commerce Commission and antitrust policy.

Nader focused his attention on Congress in 1971 and 1972 with his mammoth "Congress Project," which was to profile every member of Congress running for reelection in 1972. He has since described the project as "my C-5A," a less-than-successful endeavor. But Joan Claybrook, who was one of the project's coordinators, defends it as "about 75 percent better than anything which had been done before."

One result of the project was Nader's decision to establish a permanent lobbying operation on Capitol Hill and to institutionalize his activities. Public Citizen was the name given the umbrella organization which raises and distributes money for Nader's activities. Its operating groups actually started in 1973.

Common Cause was established in 1970, an outgrowth of the Urban Coalition Action Council headed by Gardner (now 63), a former president of the Carnegie Foundation. He was Secretary of Health, Education and Welfare from 1965 to 1968, resigning to head the Urban Coalition. Because of federal tax laws, the coalition established the action council as a separate lobbying arm.

Common Cause sources give two reasons for the decision to form an entirely new organization to replace the action council. First, Gardner and other council leaders wanted to work on a wider range of issues such as opposing the Vietnam War and advocating political reforms. Secondly, the group sought a wider base of support in terms of both citizen involvement and money.

From an initial membership of fewer than 100,000, Common Cause grew to more than 325,000 members, reaching its peak in 1974 at the height of the Watergate crisis. Its membership since has declined to 265,000. The group [made] a major organizational effort in 1976 to halt the decline and stabilize its membership at a minimum of 250,000.

Source: "Evolution of Two Groups," *Congressional Quarterly Weekly Report*, May 15, 1976, p. 1200. Reprinted by permission.

by these groups, among others, aided in the passage of the Elementary and Secondary Education Act.

Another lobby, Common Cause—with an annual budget exceeding $4 million—has proved to be a strong force. In 1974 it led an effort to oust from their committee chairmanships two powerful legislators— Edward Hebert of Louisiana, chairman of the House Armed Services Committee, and William Poage of Texas, chairman of the House Agriculture Committee. Common Cause objected not only to the close ties of these legislators with military suppliers and agribusiness, respectively, but also to the fact that they were not open in their conduct of committee business. Common Cause lobbied in Washington and conducted a direct mail campaign to influence the votes of members of Congress. Its efforts succeeded, and both Hebert and Poage lost their positions as chairmen.

CHECKS ON INFLUENCE

Certain limitations on interest groups are built into our system. The most important of these are (1) public opinion and (2) the government itself. The president and the bureaucracy, with their large staffs and budgets, have especially strong lobbying resources; in fact, they may be more powerful than all lobbyists combined.

What he [John Gardner] and Common Cause have done these last seven years has been rather extraordinary. They have played a leading role in the weakening of the congressional seniority system, the passage of public financing for presidential campaigns and other major campaign-reform legislation, and in the enactment of ethics, conflict-of-interest and "open government" statutes at both state and federal levels.

Another way of measuring their impact is to note that among their chief antagonists were former President Richard Nixon and former Rep. Wayne Hays. . . .

And I have to like the orneriness Common Cause showed in making life miserable for the defenders of the old devices for dodging responsibility. It's badgered them with law suits, publicity, and threats of political reprisal. Gardner said . . . "I'd been through some rough issues—race and poverty—but I never knew what real slugging was until I got into the ways people in power preserved their power." For seven years, he has given as good as he has got.— *David S. Broder*

The importance of both forces can be seen in actions involving the American Medical Association in the 1960s. For years the AMA had resisted what it considered to be forms of socialized medicine that might threaten the independence of medical doctors. In 1965, however, after Lyndon Johnson's landslide victory and the election of an overwhelmingly Democratic Congress, public opinion and interested public officials paved the way for Medicare and Medicaid. AMA pressure was not strong enough to kill these key proposals in Johnson's Great Society program. In 1969, the AMA successfully resisted the nomination of John Knowles to be assistant secretary for health in the Department of Health, Education and Welfare becauee it opposed some of his policies. But it could not prevent the nomination of Roger O. Egeberg, whose views were similar to those of Knowles, and who was backed by groups representing nurses and hospitals.

Emerging Interest Groups   David Rosenbaum notes that the system of checks on interest groups has improved through the emergence of new interest groups.

> . . . invariably, as their agents [oil companies, shippers, and medical associations] leave a congressman's office, they pass a young lobbyist going in who represents the Energy Action Committee or the Sierra Club or the Tax Reform Research Group or the Health Research Group. Laws regulating campaign finance, automobile safety, air pollution, and government secrecy are, among others, their legislative monuments.[23]

Preserving First Amendment Freedoms   Another point to be considered is the danger of excessive regulation of lobbying. What if interest groups were to be abolished or substantially restricted? The result would be catastrophic for the First Amendment freedoms of speech, press, and assembly, which are fundamental to any democracy. Realistically, if we do not accept interest groups, we must necessarily allow a single "truth" to prevail over all others. And that is dangerous. As James Madison wrote:

> No man is allowed to be a judge in his own cause, because his interest would certainly bias his judgment, and, not improbably, corrupt his integrity. With equal, nay with greater reason, a body of men are unfit to be both judges and parties at the same time; yet what are many of the most important acts of legislation, but so many judicial determinations, not indeed concerning the rights of single persons, but concerning the rights of large bodies of citizens? And what are the different classes of legislators but advocates and parties to the causes which they determine? . . .
> It is vain to say the enlightened statesmen will be able to adjust these clashing interests, and render them all subservient to the public

good. Enlightened statesmen will not always be at the helm. Nor, in many cases, can such an adjustment be made at all without taking into view indirect and remote considerations, which will rarely prevail over the immediate interest which one party may find in disregarding the rights of another or the good of the whole.[24]

Role Theory The affirmative case simplistically suggests that just because a government employee previously worked for a business or industry which that person is now charged with helping to regulate, the business or industry benefits. This analysis overlooks some very important considerations. For example, just as President Lyndon Johnson did not represent the view of the Old South on civil rights (though he was from that region), so a government employee does not necessarily represent the interests of a previous business or industrial employer. In fact, the business or industry may be adversely affected by the employee's desire to avoid even the appearance of benefitting the previous employer. We must also recognize that generally the individuals cited in the affirmative case are professional people who are employed because of their knowledge and skills. Peer-group pressure to maintain high professional standards would help to counteract an employee's desire to benefit a previous employer.

DEMOCRACY AND THE PUBLIC INTEREST

Sometimes public policy or the public interest is considered to be the balance achieved in the competition among interest groups. This definition provides a clue to five significant contributions interest groups make to American democracy: (1) they supplement the constitutional system of checks and balances; (2) they provide a form of representation; (3) they help maintain an open society by offering alternatives to government policies; (4) they aid the public in understanding the complexities of government; and (5) they stabilize American society.

A Supplement to Checks and Balances Although James Madison did not consider factions the ideal, he did provide a rationale for allowing group interaction and conflict to operate freely:

> By a faction, I understand a number of citizens, whether amounting to a majority or minority of the whole, who are united and actuated by some common impulse of passion, or of interest, adverse to the rights of other citizens, or to the permanent and aggregate interests of the community. . . .
>
> The latent causes of faction are . . . sown in the nature of man; and we see them everywhere brought into different degrees of activity, according to the different circumstances of civil society. A zeal for differ-

ent opinions concerning religion, concerning government, and many other points, as well of speculation as of practice; and attachment to different leaders ambitiously contending for pre-eminence and power . . . have, in turn, divided mankind into parties, inflamed them with mutual animosity, and rendered them much more disposed to vex and oppress each other than to co-operate for their common good. . . .

The influence to which we are brought is, that the cause of faction cannot be removed, and that relief is only to be sought in the means of controlling its effects.[25]

Group competition and conflict is a natural way to control the "effects" of faction. As groups challenge each other, they serve as an informal supplement to the constitutional system of checks and balances.

Competition between conflicting interest groups serves to supplement the constitutional system of checks and balances as groups vie for the support of the public and the government. Here conflicting views are evident as marchers demonstrate for and against legalized abortion.

Competing interests vie with each other for the support of public opinion and the various branches of government. The Sierra Club and other environmental groups are often opposed by real estate development interests. So-called Right to Life groups advocate a constitutional amendment to prohibit abortion; they are opposed by the National Organization of Women and other interest groups. State aid to parochial schools, supported by many Roman Catholic and Lutheran groups, has frequently been challenged by some Jewish and other Protestant groups.

Indeed, where one interest may have the upper hand with the legislature, another interest may have the upper hand with the executive. No one group can dominate the development of public policy on a permanent basis. During the Ford administration, interest groups that wanted to reduce the federal budget, such as the National Association of Manufacturers, frequently lost on crucial votes in Congress. However, they often prevailed in helping to obtain presidential vetoes of some public jobs and education bills that had been supported in the Congress by other groups such as the AFL-CIO and the National Education Association. Interest groups that have lost in the congressional and executive branches may also contest the issue in the courts. A vivid example occurred during the early New Deal period when President Franklin D. Roosevelt obtained passage of major legislation only to have the Supreme Court declare much of the legislation unconstitutional.

Elections do not usually decide issues in America; the interaction of interest groups does that, and the election is only one part—perhaps a relatively minor part—of the political process.—Charles Adrian and Charles Press

Additional Representation   In a democratic society based on republican principles, representation is crucial in enabling the citizen's point of view to be heard in the councils of government. Obviously, political parties and the electoral system provide representation, but it is usefully supplemented by interest groups. Unlike political parties, interest groups generally represent persons with similar concerns about a narrow range of interests.

In many respects, interest group representation is superior to party and electoral representation, because the bond holding interest group members together is stronger. For example, blacks stood to gain more by working through the National Association for the Advancement of Colored People and seeking to win their rights in the courts than they did by working through political parties. After all, party affiliation had no meaning until they could vote.

Most powerful special interest groups of all kinds have limited legislative goals. Generally, self-protection is the first goal. Special advantage is the next objective. They see their positions as just, and they are willing to pay to get done what they see as important.—Larry L. Berg et al.

Aiding an Open Society   As Madison said, groups will exist in any form of government that allows people some measure of freedom to express their views. There is a danger to a free and open society if all information begins to come from one or a few sources, or if there are no alternatives to government policies and decisions. All kinds of groups need the liberty to express their opinions and to try to influence government about their needs and interests. Only this way can we prevent the stagnation of ideas that would result from the dominance of one or a few groups.

A relevant example concerns the funding of public schools. Traditionally they have been supported almost entirely by local property taxes, with the result that the wealthier the community, the better the schools. This method of financing was challenged in the courts by groups in California and Texas, contending that it was a denial of equal protection of the laws under the Fourteenth Amendment. The California supreme court and a three-judge federal court in Texas ruled in favor of the challengers, but the Supreme Court reversed the decision in the Texas case.[26] Several state courts, however, have since declared the property-tax financing unconstitutional, as a violation of purely state-constitutional provisions.

Without interest group agitation, there would have been no alternative to the Vietnam war policies of Johnson and Nixon. In this instance, several interest groups organized for the specific purpose of opposing the war. Among them were the Vietnam Veterans Against the War. They marched and picketed in the streets, petitioned the government, gave testimony in congressional hearings, and challenged the Presidents' actions in the courts.

With interest groups providing a challenge, the government must constantly evaluate and defend its policies. The public benefits from this constant interchange. Consider the NAACP's challenge to race discrimination, the Ralph Nader challenge to auto manufacturers, and the Sierra Club's challenge to lumbering interests. Without the work of these groups, it is safe to say that white supremacy, automobiles "unsafe at any speed," and unchecked cutting of trees would be far bigger problems than they are today.

Helping the Public Understand   The public, looking at a mass of 535 persons serving in the Congress, finds it hard to distinguish the "bad guys" from the "good guys." One way in which interest groups help people cope with this problem is through their ratings of members of Congress. As shown in the box, a variety of organizations—liberal and conservative, business and labor—rate members of Congress. Their ratings have had a substantial impact on public thinking. A special instance of rating is the listing of the "Dirty Dozen"—twelve members of Congress rated as especially poor on environmental issues by an interest group known as Environmental Action, Inc. After compiling its list, Environmental Action sends organizers into the congressional districts involved to campaign actively against each of the "Dirty Dozen" at elec-

I define the normal American political process as one in which there is high probability that an active and legitimate group in the population can make itself heard effectively at some crucial state in the process of decision. . . . When I say a group is heard "effectively" I mean more than the simple fact that it makes a noise; I mean that one or more officials are not only ready to listen to the noise, but expect to suffer in some significant way if they do not placate the group, its leaders, or its most vociferous members.—*Robert A. Dahl*

RATING ORGANIZATIONS

The number of organizations that rate members of Congress on their votes has increased steadily in recent years. More than 50 groups are now in the ratings business, compared with only a handful a few years ago.

Some of the newer raters are established organizations that have decided to adapt the ratings techniques successfully used for years by labor and political groups such as the Americans for Democratic Action, Americans for Constitutional Action and the AFL-CIO's COPE (Committee on Political Education).

Another reason for the increase is the proliferation of public interest groups, many of which issue congressional ratings. One of the most recent entrants to this field is Ralph Nader's Public Citizen organization.

Listed below are some of the major organizations that regularly compile congressional ratings:

Business. Chamber of Commerce of the United States, National Association of Businessmen, National Federation of Independent Businessmen.

Conservatives. American Conservative Union, Americans for Constitutional Action, Liberty Lobby.

Consumer Affairs. Consumer Federation of America, Public Citizen.

Defense/Foreign Policy. American Security Council, Coalition for a New Foreign and Military Policy, Friends Committee on National Legislation, SANE [a citizen's organization for a sane world].

Education. American Federation of Teachers, Committee for Full Funding of Education Programs, National Education Association, National Student Lobby.

Environment. Environmental Action, League of Conservation Voters.

Labor. AFL-CIO Committee on Political Education; Amalgamated Clothing Workers of America; American Federation of Government Employees; American Federation of State, County and Municipal Employees; Building and Construction Trades Department, AFL-CIO; Communications Workers of America; International Association of Machinists; International Brotherhood of Teamsters; United Auto Workers, United Mine Workers.

Liberals. Americans for Democratic Action, *The New Republic*, Ripon Society.

Rural/Farm. American Farm Bureau Federation, National Farmers Organization, National Farmers Union.

Other. American Parents Committee, Common Cause, Council on National Priorities and Resources, League of Women Voters, National Council of Senior Citizens, National Taxpayers Union, Taxation With Representation, Women's Lobby.

Source: "Rating Organizations," *Congressional Quarterly Weekly Report*, May 22, 1976, p. 1286. Reprinted by permission.

tion time. When House Minority Leader John Rhodes of Arizona made the list in 1974, he did win reelection, but by an unusually small number of votes.

Stabilization of Society   Because of the plethora of interest groups, change in American society occurs gradually. Interest groups face competition from other groups. They must also convince the government about the validity of their positions. All of this takes time, so the evils of too rapid change are avoided.

Preceding most major public policy innovations is an "incubation period" of several years during which the new idea is discussed. With issues like federal aid to education and federal medical programs, this period may last several decades. In the latter instance, the first proposals even remotely resembling Medicare and Medicaid were made by President Theodore Roosevelt around the turn of the century. Approximately a decade passed between the time revenue sharing was first introduced in the Congress and when it became law in President Nixon's first administration. The "incubation period" allows groups to present their views before Congress. During this time the public benefits by receiving news media accounts and analyses of the on-going national debate on major new proposals.

Glossary

Countervailing forces: checks on interest groups, such as opposing influence of other interest groups and governmental action.

Cozy triangle: self-interest relationship among interest group, bureaucratic agency, and congressional committee that helps to secure favorable action on what the interest group wants.

Interest group: an organized group, representing a special segment of society, that seeks to influence governmental policies directly affecting its members. (Also called *lobbies* or *pressure groups*.)

Lobbyist: a person who represents an interest group.

Notes

1. Gabriel Almond and Sidney Verba, *The Civic Culture: Political Attitudes and Democracy in Five Nations* (Boston: Little, Brown, 1965), p. 245.

2. Theodore Lowi, *The End of Liberalism* (New York: Norton, 1969), p. x.

3. C. Wright Mills, *The Power Elite* (New York: Oxford University Press, 1956), p. 307.

4. Michael Parenti, *Democracy for the Few* (New York: St. Martin's Press, 1974), p. 277.

5. *New York Times*, September 12, 1976, p. E3.

6. Thomas R. Dye, *Who's Running America: Institutional Leadership in the United States* (Englewood Cliffs, N. J.: Prentice-Hall, 1976), p. 20.

7. *Congressional Quarterly Weekly Report*, July 27, 1974, pp. 1947–1955.

8. Charles Lindbloom, *The Policy-Making Process* (Englewood Cliffs, N. J.: Prentice-Hall, 1968), p. 68.

9. Howard K. Smith, *The State of Europe* (New York: Alfred A. Knopf, 1949), p. 83.

10. *Washington Post*, December 26, 1976, p. C2.

11. *Congressional Quarterly Weekly Report*, November 13, 1976, p. 3164.

12. *Washington Post*, May 17, 1976, p. 1.

13. Randall B. Ripley, "How to Map Interest Group Environments," *DEA News* (Spring 1976):2–5.

14. Associated Press, September 7, 1975.

15. *Washington Post*, November 14, 1976, p. A3.

16. Douglass Cater, *Power in Washington* (New York: Random House, 1964), p. 208.

17. Almond and Verba, *The Civic Culture*, p. 249.

18. V. O. Key, Jr., *Public Opinion and American Democracy* (New York: Alfred A. Knopf, 1965), p. 504.

19. As quoted in Parenti, *Democracy for the Few*, p. 185.

20. Pendleton Herring. *Group Representation Before Congress* (Baltimore, Md.: The Johns Hopkins Press, 1929), p. 268.

21. *Congressional Quarterly Weekly Report*, July 27, 1974, pp. 1947–1955.

22. *Washington Post*, September 21, 1975, p. 2.

23. *New York Times*, September 12, 1976, p. E3.

24. Henry Cabot Lodge, ed., *The Federalist* (New York: G. P. Putnam's, 1902), pp. 52–55.

25. Ibid., pp. 54, 55.

26. *San Antonio School District* v. *Rodriguez* (1973).

Recommended Rebuttal Reading

Interest Group Theory

Dye, Thomas R. *Who's Running America: Institutional Leadership in the United States.* Englewood Cliffs, N. J.: Prentice-Hall, 1976.

Lowi, Theodore. *The End of Liberalism.* New York: Norton, 1969.

Truman, David. *The Governmental Process: Political Interests and Public Opinion.* New York: Alfred A. Knopf, 1951.

Zeigler, Harman, and G. Wayne Peak. *Interest Groups in American Society.* Englewood Cliffs, N. J.: Prentice-Hall, 1972.

Group Representation

Bauer, Raymond A., et al. *American Business and Public Policy.* Chicago: Aldine, 1972.

Greenstone, J. David. *Labor in American Politics.* New York: Random House, 1970.

Lobbying Methods

Congressional Quarterly Service. *The Washington Lobby,* 2nd ed. Washington, D. C.: Congressional Quarterly, 1974.

Dexter, Lewis A. *How Organizations Are Represented in Washington.* Indianapolis, Ind.: Bobbs-Merrill, 1969.

Viewpoints on Interest Groups

Berg, Larry L., Harlan Hahn, and John R. Schmidhauser. *Corruption in the American Political System.* Morristown, N. J.: General Learning Press, 1976.

Etzkowitz, Henry, and Peter Schwab. *Is America Necessary? Conservative, Liberal and Socialist Perspectives of United States Political Institutions.* St. Paul, Minn.: West, 1976.

Peter, Charles, and James Fellows, eds. *Inside the System.* New York: Praeger, 1976.

General Reference

Salisbury, Robert H., ed. *Interest Group Politics in America.* New York: Harper & Row, 1970.

Smith, Judith G., ed. *Political Brokers: People, Organizations, Money and Power.* New York: Liveright, 1972.

Wilson, James Q. *Political Organizations.* New York: Basic Books, 1973.

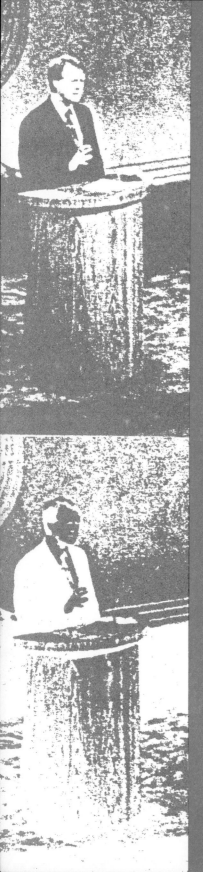

AT ISSUE: POLITICAL PARTIES

Historical Summary
 The First Parties
 Democrats and Whigs
 Democrats Versus
  Republicans

Transferring Party Power

THE AFFIRMATIVE CASE

Distinctions Without
  Difference

A Barrier to Change
 Lack of Responsiveness
 "Safe" Candidates
  Preferred
 Discouragement of Minor
  Parties

A Harmful Holdover

THE NEGATIVE CASE

Substantial Party
  Differences
 Composition
 Ideology
 Organization

Change—Within Limits
 Modernization and
  Reform
 Minor Party Contribu-
  tions

Values of the Two-Party
  System
 Simplification of Voter
  Choice
 Promotion of Stability
 A Bridge for Commu-
  nication
 Diversity in Local Systems

7 RESOLVED THAT: The Two-Party System Is Irrelevant

At Issue: Political Parties

The Constitution makes no provision for political parties, but they have become a vital force in our government. Indeed, some would argue that parties have been the glue holding together the American system.

What is a *political party*? If we confine our definition to the two major parties, we may say that a party is an organization with diverse membership that seeks to control government by winning elections and placing party members in office. The many *minor* or *third parties* in the United States do not generally fit this definition, because they have little, if any, chance of winning an election, except occasionally in state or local elections. Their chief purpose is rather to raise the flag of an issue or ideology that is not being dealt with by either of the major parties.

A party consists of the voters who identify with that party; party activists, who solicit votes and do other work to maintain the organization; party leaders outside of government such as party chairpersons; and party leaders inside government, such as elected officials. Minor parties may have the first three of these components but generally not the fourth, since almost all government positions are held by Democrats or Republicans. There are two principal ways of determining party identification. One is to consider those who identify affiliation through public opinion polls. Another is to consider those who officially register to vote in the primary election of a party. The *majority party* has the

The saddest life is that of a political aspirant under democracy. His failure is ignominious and his success is disgraceful.—*H. L. Mencken*

225

largest number of people identifying with it; the *minority party* has the second largest number.

The main difference between a party and an interest group has to do with their role in elections. A party exists to elect its candidates to office. An interest group exists to influence the policies and decisions made by the candidates who are elected. A party runs candidates, which an interest group may or may not endorse. A party addresses a broad range of interests, while an interest group is usually concerned with only a narrow range of issues. Once again, minor parties must generally be distinguished from major parties on this point; often they are concerned only with one or a few issues. An example is the 1948 States' Rights Party, whose principal concern was opposition to racial integration.

The two major parties—and to some extent minor parties as well— perform several functions. They provide a peaceful and orderly way to transfer power. They offer voters a choice between rival candidates on issues, character, personality, and so on. They recruit persons to campaign for public office or to serve as appointees in nonelective positions. They reconcile conflicts in society by bringing diverse groups of people together in the common interest of winning office and making public policy. Finally, they link together the several branches and levels of government by establishing some common bonds between, say, Democratic mayors and representatives, or between Republican governors and a Republican president.

HISTORICAL SUMMARY

We shall very soon have parties formed, a court and country party, and these parties will have names given them. One party in the house of representatives will support the president and his measures and ministers; the other will oppose them. A similar party will be in the senate; these parties will study with all their arts, perhaps with intrigue, perhaps with corruption, at every election to increase their own friends and diminish their opposers. Suppose such parties formed in the senate, and then consider what factious divisions we shall have there upon every nomination.—*John Adams*

Many leaders of the early Republic disliked the idea of political parties. George Washington warned against "the baneful effects of the spirit of party" in his farewell address, while John Adams said, "There is nothing I dread so much as the division of the Republic into two great parties, each under its leader."[1] Perhaps prophetically, however, James Madison had already foreseen the emergence of parties when he wrote in *The Federalist* that the job of resolving conflicting interests would necessarily involve "the spirit of party and faction in the necessary and ordinary operation of the government."

The First Parties   The first American parties emerged out of the continuing debate over a strong versus a weak central government. Those who favored a strong central government formed the Federalist party, under the leadership of Alexander Hamilton. In the other camp were the Democratic-Republicans, under Thomas Jefferson's leadership. The former party appealed primarily to banking, commercial, and financial interests. The latter drew support from small farmers, debtors, southern planters, and frontier settlers.

Federalist ideas were in the ascendancy during the administration of Washington and that of John Adams. The party went into decline, however, when Jefferson's election in 1800 began a twenty-eight year period of Democratic-Republican dominance. After 1816, the Federalists no longer even offered a candidate for the presidency.

Democrats and Whigs Democratic-Republican strength began to wane when irreconcilable factions developed within the party. On the one hand, there were the Jacksonians, who stood for popular rule and the hopes of common people. They were opposed by Henry Clay, William Henry Harrison, and Daniel Webster, who formed the new Whig party from a coalition of bankers, merchants, and southern planters. Thus the two dominant parties between 1824 and the coming of the Civil War were the Democratic-Republicans (generally called Democrats after 1828) and the Whigs.

Both parties successfully competed for the presidency during this period. Out of their competition grew the modern party system with its concerted emphasis on winning the presidency, the intermittent rise of third parties, patronage, national nominating conventions, and party bosses.[2]

Democrats Versus Republicans With the coming of the Civil War, both the Democrats and the Whigs experienced the same divisions that were tearing asunder American society in general. After passage of the Kansas-Nebraska Act in 1854 (which permitted slavery in the territories), a group of Whigs, antislavery Democrats, and others formed a new party to fight the further expansion of slavery. This organization, the Republican party, quickly became the chief rival of the Democrats, as the Whig party disintegrated. Following a North-South split among Democrats over slavery, the Republicans elected their first president, Abraham Lincoln, in 1860.

Although the Republicans represented mainly the North and the West, they remained the majority party in the United States until the Great Depression of the 1930s. Then Franklin D. Roosevelt, elected in 1932, formed the New Deal Democratic coalition, a majority composed of southern interests, big city voters, and labor. Since the 1930s, Republicans have had a majority in Congress in only two periods, 1947–1948 and 1953–1954, and have occupied the White House for only sixteen years. Beginning in the 1960s, Democrats witnessed critical battles between inheritors of the New Deal tradition, such as Hubert Humphrey, and others less concerned with New Deal policies, such as George McGo-

There is an opinion that parties in free countries are useful checks upon the administration of the government, and serve to keep alive the spirit of liberty. This within certain limits is probably true; and in governments of a monarchial cast patriotism may look with indulgence, if not with favor, upon the spirit of party. But in those of the popular character, in governments purely elective, it is a spirit not to be encouraged. From their natural tendency it is certain there will always be enough of that spirit for every salutary purpose; and there being constant danger of excess, the effort ought to be by force of public opinion to mitigate and assuage it. A fire not to be quenched, it demands a uniform vigilance to prevent its bursting into a flame, lest, instead of warming, it should consume.—*George Washington*

vern and George Wallace. In the Republican party, ideological conflict split conservatives, such as Ronald Reagan, from the more moderate elements typified by Gerald Ford. In both parties, public identification and loyalty declined, with more and more people becoming independents.

TRANSFERRING PARTY POWER

What may seem like a confusing seesaw between Republicans and Democrats makes more sense when we characterize the election-transferring power as belonging to one of four categories: realigning, deviating, reinstating, or maintaining.

In a realigning election, a party comes to the fore to assume a lasting majority position. This happened in 1860, when the coming Civil War paved the way for the new Republican party. It happened again in 1932, when the Great Depression helped sweep the Republicans out and made the Democratic party dominant. The minority party remained competitive during both periods, however. Thus there occurred deviating elections, in which the minority party won the presidency. Such were the victories of Democrat Woodrow Wilson in 1912 and 1916 and Republican Dwight Eisenhower in 1952 and 1956.

It is common, after such minority party victories, for the majority party to return to its dominant position in a reinstating election. The Republicans won in 1920 with Warren Harding, the Democrats with John F. Kennedy in 1960. Finally, maintaining elections simply continue the status quo between the parties. Examples are the 1924 Republican victory of Calvin Coolidge and the 1964 Democratic victory of Lyndon Johnson.[3]

The American two-party system is constantly under attack. Some contend it is on the decline because of the rising number of independents. Others believe the two major parties should represent clearly ideological positions. Still others would like to see a multiparty system in its place. With the defeat of Gerald Ford in 1976, some argue that the Republican party should become a genuinely conservative party and change its name. Is the two-party system as we know it irrelevant?

- Should political parties be committed to specific ideologies rather than be loose coalitions crossing ideological lines?
- Do you feel that American political parties nominate the best-qualified candidates to run for national, state, and local offices?
- Would a one-party or multiparty system be preferable to our two-party system?

Candidates representing both major parties campaigned vigorously before the 1976 presidential election. Here the Republican incumbent, President Gerald R. Ford (right), faces the challenger, Democrat Jimmy Carter, in the first of several televised debates. Party power was transferred from the Republicans, who had occupied the White House since 1968, to the Democrats when Carter won the election. Future candidate debates would look very different if the two-party system were abandoned.

The Affirmative Case

Yes, the two-party system is irrelevant.

It is by no means clear that political parties are competent, efficient or appropriate institutions for the formation of policy which is to be binding upon legislators and executive leaders. They lack sufficient expertise to devise solutions to our complicated problems.[4]*–Evron Kirkpatrick*

Americans are increasingly dissatisfied with political parties. An escalating percentage identify themselves as independents rather than as Republicans or Democrats. Indeed, independents now outnumber Republicans, who constitute a bare 20 percent of the population. This dissatisfaction has a harmful effect, contributing to the disintegration of

The first lesson that any European has to learn about American politics is that they are not "issue oriented"—and that is certainly only too clear this year [1968]. When former Governor George Wallace of Alabama announces that "there's not a dime's worth of difference between those two big parties of ours," he may not be speaking the literal truth, but it is hard to fault his use of politician's license.... There is scarcely an area of public policy in which Nixon and Humphrey do not make the same soothing noises. What division there is between them is not ideological or philosophical. It is purely personal—a Tweedledum-Tweedledee argument between the two of them as to which is better qualified to occupy the White House.—
Anthony Howard

society. As public confidence in parties and candidates weakens, so does faith in the government itself. This lack of confidence makes it more difficult for government to govern. Political parties have become irrelevant for our time.

- There is essentially no difference between the parties.
- Political parties are a barrier to significant change.
- The two-party system harms democracy.

DISTINCTIONS WITHOUT DIFFERENCE

What really is the difference between the parties besides their names? On basic and fundamental issues, there is little, if any. Both parties uphold the sanctity of private property, advocate a free enterprise economy, support individual freedom, view government's role as limited, and adhere to majority rule and due process of law. Do not both parties support the major domestic policies developed since 1930—Social Security, a graduated income tax, and welfare and unemployment compensation? Have not both parties supported the same foreign and military policies in this period?

The basic purpose of American political parties is to win office, not to raise issues. Little wonder, therefore, that the parties advocate positions only on issues that fit an already established view of what is

acceptable. Parties would lose rather than gain votes by advocating positions outside the areas of consensus.

In a very real way, the parties are like twins with essentially the same definition of the public interest. Both advocate programs to maintain a private corporate economy. Both utilize deficit spending and tax advantages to bolster the economy. Both attack public problems like poverty by giving tax dollars to private companies to perform job training. Both defend multinational corporations. The Democrats and Republicans disagree mainly over which party is better qualified to achieve the goals both accept. The chief competition is therefore not between policies, but between different types of packaging.

Party agreement on fundamental issues restricts the alternatives presented to the electorate. Rather than having a wide range of choices, Americans are presented with a very limited selection.

Differences between the parties appear to be decreasing. Evidence is provided by congressional roll-call votes during the period 1921–1967. As shown in Table 1, the percentage of party votes (where 90 percent of one party voted against 90 percent of the other party) declined during this period from 28.6 percent to 3.3 percent.

Several conclusions may be drawn about the similarity between the parties. One is that party identification has been decreasing, as more people identify themselves as independents. In addition, the party identification that does exist is at a rather crude level of understanding. It is frequently based upon influences like family and socioeconomic class rather than a rational assessment of issue differences. Nor can party identification be relied on to predict the behavior of either the electorate or those elected. In 1972, one third of all registered Democrats voted for Richard Nixon; an extremely large number voted for Dwight Eisenhower in 1952 and 1956. Also, as indicated, the party attachment of legislators appears to be declining. Finally, whatever differences do appear between the parties tend to be relatively minor and to reflect disagreement over means, not ends.

A BARRIER TO CHANGE

Not only do the major parties present no meaningful alternatives to voters. They also prevent change in a number of ways. (1) They are unresponsive to the electorate. (2) They favor middle-of-the-road candidates with few new ideas. (3) They discourage minor parties and thus the articulation of differing views.

Lack of Responsiveness   By far the most frequent criticism of the two major parties is their lack of responsiveness to the electorate. A

Table 1. Proportion of Party Votes Cast in Selected Sessions of the U. S. House of Representatives, 1921–1967

YEAR	PERCENTAGE OF PARTY VOTES 90% v. 90%
1921	28.6
1930–31	31.0
1933	22.5
1937	11.8
1944	10.7
1948	16.4
1950	6.4
1953	7.0
1959	8.0
1963	7.6
1964	6.2
1965	2.8
1966	1.6
1967	3.3

Source: Julius Turner, *Party and Constituency: Pressure on Congress,* rev. ed. by Edward V. Schneier, Jr. (Baltimore: Johns Hopkins University Press, 1970), pp. 16–17. Reprinted by permission.

committee of the American Political Science Association has reported that parties lack the discipline and organization to insure that their programs are passed by Congress and signed by the president.[5]

The Republican and Democratic parties are not truly national parties. Rather, they are loose coalitions or confederations of fifty state parties. Power in the parties tends to flow up to rather than down from the national leadership. State and local party organizations function relatively free from national party direction. Mayor Richard Daley of Chicago ruled the Cook County Democratic party; he did not take orders from the head of either the state or the national party.

At the national level, the president cannot dictate to members of his party in Congress, nor can the national party chairman. During the 1950s, Democratic National Chairman Paul Butler tried to establish a policy council in the Democratic party that would include the Senate Democratic leader (then Lyndon Johnson) and the Speaker of the House (at the time Democrat Sam Rayburn). Both men declined to participate. Voters have no rational way of determining the responsiveness of national party leadership to policy positions. Indeed, neither party *has* a policy position except for a rather vaguely worded platform and other statements emanating from the national convention and national

No American political institution is more visible than the convention or more often visibly shoddy, and none is less visibly constituted and managed—*Alexander M. Bickel*

committee meetings. And neither the president nor the congressional
leaders are bound by such statements.

Political scientist James MacGregor Burns has argued that our national parties are not two, but four—the congressional Republican and
Democratic parties and the presidential Republican and Democratic
parties. He holds that the two "congressional parties" are generally
much more conservative than the two "presidential parties." He contends, for example, that both Democratic and Republican presidents
have been far ahead of their congressional party leadership in advocating civil rights legislation.

In this situation compromise becomes the dominant theme. In order to implement a policy requiring action from both Congress and the
president, it is sometimes necessary to reconcile and thus dilute the effect of what was originally intended. Compromise tends to force differences to the center and to eliminate major change or reform.

"Safe" Candidates Preferred   To achieve a party nomination and
then win an election requires that a candidate offend as few people as
possible, especially party leaders. To the extent that candidates deviate
from this policy, they encounter resistance and opposition, and lose financial support. Charles Goodell of New York, running for the Senate
in 1970, alienated Republican regulars with his opposition to the Vietnam war. This cost him dearly in party organization and financial back-
ing, and he lost the election in a three-way race. In 1972 George
McGovern offended many party leaders including Richard Daley of
Chicago with his support for party reform. This unpopular stand—
among others—was a factor in his defeat for the presidency.

Historically, the candidate with unusual views has more difficulty
in winning—whether he is William Jennings Bryan and his "free silver"
platform, Barry Goldwater and his plan to abolish Social Security, or
George McGovern and his tax proposals.

Even if elected, persons with original ideas may face ostracism, assignment to obscure tasks or committees, or redistricting out of their
jobs. These possibilities often force public officials to trim their sails by
softening their positions and becoming more conformist.

Discouragement of Minor Parties   One observer has commented
that each party "views with suspicion the third-party movements in
America. Each in effect is committed to the preservation of the other." [6]
The status quo is maintained chiefly by the election laws, and occasionally even by physical harassment, such as FBI surveillance of the Socialist party headquarters in New York City during the 1960s and early
1970s.

Neither party has anything definite to say on the issues; neither
party has any principles and distinctive tenets. . . . Tenets and
policies, points of political doctrine, and points of political
practice have all but vanished.—
Lord Bryce

In the American federal system, most election laws are made by the fifty states. Although the standards for party organization differ, one uniform thread runs through the fifty sets of election laws—the obstacles confronting minor parties in organizing and challenging the major parties. Some states require exorbitant filing fees for minor party candidates. In Louisiana, the filing fee is $5,000. Others demand an extraordinarily large number of signatures on third-party petitions before allowing candidates to run for office. In Pennsylvania in 1972, third-party candidates for statewide office had to obtain the signatures of 36,000 registered voters within a three-week period. And in some states, such as Illinois, the signatures must come from a large number of counties and not just one or a few.

Perhaps the major protection for the two-party system in the United States is the *single-member district.* Whoever wins a plurality of votes in a given district (whether it is a small congressional district or a whole state) wins all of the representation. The winner-take-all system forces people to coalesce into two dominant groups in order to be competitive. The result is the need for substantial compromises. Without compromises how else could the Democratic party bring blacks and southern whites, Edward Kennedy and George Wallace, under the same party banner?

Any group that endeavors to compete as a third or minor party in the single-member district, winner-take-all system faces the futility of rarely or never winning. It should be added that the voter who casts a ballot for a minor-party candidate is in effect throwing away his or her vote unless the minor party has enough strength to affect major-party positions on issues, as did George Wallace's American Independent party in 1968.

Although multimember districts exist in some states for legislative and local government races, they have not led to the development of competitive third parties. In a *multimember district,* more than one person is elected.

Actual physical harassment has been the fate of some minor parties advocating radical ideas, among them the Populist party of the late 1800s and the Black Panthers of the mid-1960s. This is especially apt to occur when a party achieves some success, as did the Socialists in the early 1900s. After the Socialists won control of some thirty-two municipal governments, their headquarters in several cities were ransacked, their funds confiscated, their leaders jailed, and their newspapers denied mailing privileges. Some immigrant members were deported. Winning candidates were even denied seats in state legislatures and Congress.

More recently, according to the *New York Times*, the FBI allegedly burglarized the New York City offices of the Socialist Workers Party ninety-two times between 1960 and 1966.

> The burglaries by specially trained teams of Federal agents in the early morning hours, occurred, on the average, once every three weeks in a 6½ year period, the reports show. They produced about 10,000 photographs of documents and correspondence concerning virtually every aspect of the party's business, including the defense strategies of members involved in Federal legal proceedings.[7]

A HARMFUL HOLDOVER

Not only does the two-party system fail to perform useful functions. This outdated relic from earlier days actually impairs the democratic process. The lack of alternatives presented to American voters means that elections are determined primarily by factors other than party differences on issues. This result ill serves the voter. Disadvantaged groups are underrepresented, elections are determined by useless publicity contests, and national party conventions merely rubber stamp status-quo platforms and nominate middle-of-the-road candidates.

There is a striking ... lack of ideological or programmatic commitment in both the front and the rear ranks of the two major parties. ... The parties ... are interested in the votes of men, not in their principles.—*Clinton Rossiter*

The national convention, in fact, illustrates much that is wrong with the two-party system. William Seward once likened a political party to "a joint stock association, in which those who contribute most direct the action and management of the concern." This monopoly is especially obvious at a convention. Since the two major parties tend to represent the rich more than the poor and the white more than the black, national conventions are composed largely of a select audience of middle- and upper-class delegates. In leading the effort to reform the Democratic party by increasing representation from disadvantaged groups, Senator Harold Hughes of Iowa said: "It is no secret that we are in trouble, especially with significant groups that have traditionally been identified with the Democratic Party. . . . For much too long now, national conventions have largely been the private domain of the rich, the white, and the party regular."[8]

With parties controlled by an elitist leadership that takes centrist positions, voter apathy is widespread (see Chapter 8). Lacking a keen awareness of politics and public issues and not being encouraged to assume leadership, the electorate retreats to the sidelines. Since it is impossible to maintain party responsibility, interest groups assume more and more power. In effect, interest groups dominate the making of public policy because parties are too weak, inept, and divided to stand up against them.

. . . the American party system as it now exists performs a role of great usefulness in our national politics and government; that, judged by the criterion of our conception of democracy, that role is of great value and deserving of high praise; and that the price America would probably have to pay for more centralized and disciplined national parties is, from the standpoint of democracy and in the light of the present nature of the American community, too high.—*Austin Ranney and Willmore Kendall*

The rise of political parties is indubitably one of the principal distinguishing marks of modern government. The parties, in fact, have played a major role as makers of government, more especially they have been the makers of democratic government. It should be stated flatly at the outset that this volume is devoted to the thesis that the political parties created democracy and that modern democracy is unthinkable save in terms of the parties. As a matter of fact, the condition of the parties is the best possible evidence of the nature of any regime. The most important distinction in modern political philosophy, the distinction between democracy and dictatorship, can be made best in terms of party politics. The parties are not therefore mere appendages of modern government; they are in the center of it and play a determinative and creative role in it. The two-party system is the Rock of Gibraltar of American politics.—*E. E. Schattschneider*

The Negative Case

No, the two-party system is not irrelevant.

The American party system . . . gets very high marks indeed. By sustaining and refreshing the consensus on which our society and governmental system are based, it makes possible our characteristic brand of pluralistic bargaining—compromising discussion of public issues, which is probably about as close to the model of creative democratic discussion in the nation-state as a community like the United States can hope to get.[9]–Austin Ranney and Willmore Kendall

American political parties have been much maligned, especially by those who want well-disciplined party organizations or more ideologically oriented factions. Their complaints, however, overlook important contributions of the two-party system. It is not irrelevant for the following reasons:

- There are substantial differences between the major parties.
- The two major parties have allowed for change—insofar as the American people want it.
- The two-party system serves a real need in the American political system.

SUBSTANTIAL PARTY DIFFERENCES

Critics enjoy arguing that Democrats and Republicans are like fraternal twins, but the evidence substantiates meaningful differences between the two parties. According to one journalist: "When times get tough, it turns out that there really is more than a minute difference between Republicans and Democrats. There is a whole lot of difference—and there is going to be more."[10] These differences exist in the composition of each party, in ideology, and in organization.

Composition   In 1917 the economic historian Charles Beard said that the "center of gravity of wealth is on the Republican side while the center of gravity of poverty is on the Democratic side."[11] Membership of the two parties differs not only in wealth, but also in education, occupation, religion, and race (see Table 2). Moreover, as shown in Table 3, a study of delegates to the national conventions of the two parties in 1976 shows differences in income, ideology, race, sex, political experience, and religion. Clearly both parties attract support from all groups, but the base of power in the two parties differs.

DEMO OR GOP?
HERE'S A CHECKLIST

Dew James of the *Florence Morning News* has passed along a handy set of rules for making positive identification of Republicans and Democrats.

James, who apparently doesn't subscribe to the theory that "There's not a dime's worth of difference" in the two parties, lists the following criteria for determining political loyalties:

1. DEMOCRATS buy most of the books that have been banned somewhere. Republicans form censorship committees and read them as a group.

2. Republicans consume three-fourths of all the rutabaga produced in this country. The remainder is thrown out.

3. Republicans usually wear hats and almost always clean their paint brushes.

4. DEMOCRATS give their worn-out clothes to those less fortunate. Republicans wear theirs.

5. Republicans employ exterminators. Democrats step on the bugs.

6. Democrats name their children after currently popular sports figures, politicians and entertainers. Republican children are named after their parents or grandparents, according to where the most money is.

7. Democrats keep trying to cut down on smoking but are not successful. Neither are Republicans.

8. REPUBLICANS tend to keep their shades drawn, although there is seldom any reason why they should. Democrats ought to, but don't.

9. Republicans study the financial pages of the newspaper. Democrats put them in the bottom of the bird cage.

10. Most of the stuff you see alongside the road has been thrown out of the car window by Democrats.

11. Republicans raise dahlias, Dalmations and eyebrows. Democrats raise Airedales, kids and taxes.

12. DEMOCRATS eat the fish they catch. Republicans hang them on the wall.

13. Republican boys date Democratic girls. They plan to marry Republican girls, but feel they're entitled to a little fun first.

14. Democrats make up plans and then do something else. Republicans follow the plans their grandfathers made.

15. Republicans sleep in twin beds—some even in separate rooms. That is why there are more Democrats.

Source: Florence Morning News, February 16, 1975, p. 5A. Originally published in the Sterling Bulletin.

Table 2. Group Presidential Voting, 1952–1976

GROUP	1952		1956		1960		1964		1968			1972		1976	
	D%	R%	D%	R%	D%	R%	D%	R%	D%	R%	A*%	D%	R%	D%	R%
Grade school	52	48	50	50	55	45	66	34	52	33	15	49	51	58	41
High school	45	55	42	58	52	48	62	38	42	43	15	34	66	54	46
College	34	66	31	69	39	61	52	48	37	54	9	37	63	42	55
Manual	55	45	50	50	60	40	71	29	50	35	15	43	57	58	41
White Collar	40	60	37	63	48	52	57	43	41	47	12	36	64	50	48
Professional and Business	36	64	32	68	42	58	54	46	34	56	10	31	69	42	56
Catholic	56	44	51	49	78	22	76	24	59	33	8	48	52	57	42
Protestant	37	63	37	63	38	62	55	45	35	49	16	30	70	46	53
Non-White	79	21	61	39	68	32	94	6	85	12	3	87	13	85	15
White	43	57	41	59	49	51	59	41	38	47	15	32	68	46	52

* American Independent Party led by George Wallace.

Source: *Gallup Opinion Index*, November 1976. Reprinted by permission.

A study of candidate support during the 1976 presidential primaries, shown in Table 4, also indicates geographic and ideological differences between the parties. Geographically, Democrats have more strength in the South; Republicans, in the Midwest. There are ideological differences as well.

Ideology There are very clear policy and ideological differences between the two parties. They are evident among party members and their legislative representatives, among the judiciary, among party leaders, and in party platforms. David Broder, a journalist for the *Washington Post*, has detailed the policy differences between the two parties. (See Table 5.) In analyzing these differences, Broder concludes:

> There is not just a dime's worth of difference between the parties. There are dollars and livelihoods at stake, to say nothing of the balance between private enterprise and government in our economy and the reliance on public officials or private citizens to decide the basic issues that affect all our lives.
> If voters won't turn out and make such a choice, then we might as well admit that politics is what pollster Pat Caddell called it—one of the less popular spectator sports.[12]

Lest anyone think that the differences summarized in Table 5 are the product of very recent history, consider the following data from presidential elections: In 1948, most of those persons opposed to the Taft-Hartley Act voted Democratic. In 1952, most of the Americans who thought the government had gone too far in dealing with problems of unemployment and housing voted Republican. In 1960, most persons who favored greater government involvement to stimulate the economy voted Democratic. In 1964, those who thought the government should do more to advance the cause of civil rights voted overwhelmingly Democratic. In 1968 and 1972, those who believed that more concern should be shown for victims of crime than for the rights of the accused voted heavily Republican.[13]

Table 3. Comparisons Between Republican and Democratic Delegates*

	REPUBLICANS	DEMOCRATS
ANNUAL FAMILY INCOME		
Less than $10,000	2%	6%
$10,000-$17,999	13%	19%
$18,000-$29,999	29%	34%
$30,000-$49,999	29%	22%
$50,000 and more	26%	19%
IDEOLOGY (SELF-DESIGNATED)		
Very liberal	1%	14%
Somewhat liberal	6%	42%
Moderate	31%	31%
Somewhat conservative	46%	12%
Very conservative	16%	1%
Age 30 and under	7%	19%
Women	32%	33%
Blacks	3%	9%
Have held party office	85%	68%
Have held public office	61%	58%
RELIGION		
Protestant	76%	48%
Catholic	17%	39%
Jewish	2%	8%
Other or none	5%	5%
Average age	49 yrs.	43 yrs.

* Figures based on *Washington Post* surveys of 449 Republican delegates and 407 Democratic delegates.

Source: *Washington Post*, August 15, 1976, p. A6. © The Washington Post. Reprinted by permission.

Table 4. Composition of 1976 Presidential Primary Candidate Support* (In Percent)

	ALL DEMO-CRATS	UDALL	HUMPHREY	CARTER	JACKSON	WALLACE	ALL REPUB-LICANS	FORD	REAGAN
IDEOLOGY									
Liberal	29%	38%	33%	37%	27%	12%	13%	17%	7%
Moderate	41	50	42	36	47	42	32	34	28
Conservative	29	12	25	28	26	46	55	50	65
OCCUPATION									
Professional and Managerial	22	35	20	35	22	11	33	32	35
Other White Collar	9	3	9	3	5	9	10	9	14
Blue Collar	45	34	43	34	49	46	31	31	33
AGE									
18-29	25	29	22	27	16	29	27	27	29
30-44	23	21	21	28	13	27	25	24	26
45-64	34	26	37	33	37	37	29	26	34
65 and Over	19	24	20	13	34	7	20	22	11
RELIGION									
Protestant	55	52	50	57	56	56	74	73	75
Catholic	33	40	39	32	34	35	17	17	16
Jewish	3	8	3	3	6	0	1	1	1
REGION									
North East	27	22	41	25	31	35	28	30	23
Midwest	20	33	21	19	16	17	30	30	28
South	36	5	31	42	31	36	23	23	24
West	17	40	17	14	22	13	20	17	25
RACE									
White	81	95	81	79	86	90	94	93	98
Black	16	2	16	19	13	5	4	5	0

* Based on a *New York Times*/CBS News Survey of 1,524 adults.

Source: *New York Times*, March 29, 1976. © 1976 The New York Times Company. Reprinted by permission.

In a 1976 study the *Washington Post* and the Harvard Center for International Affairs found substantial differences between Democratic and Republican party workers (state, city, and county officials) in their ranking in importance ten national goals, as shown in Table 6. This national survey of 155 Republican and 128 Democratic workers shows that they do not agree on the priority of any one of the ten goals. For example, Republican party workers consider reducing the role of government as the second highest goal, but Democratic party workers view the same goal as last in order of importance.

The same *Washington Post*-Harvard survey also shows that party workers, as well as the rank-and-file, differ ideologically in that Democrats are more liberal and Republicans are more conservative. Rank-and-

Table 5. Party Differences

ISSUE	MOST REPUBLICANS	MOST DEMOCRATS
Social programs	See a serious threat in the rapid expansion of government benefits to individuals and urge that "caps" be placed on such programs as Social Security and food stamps.	Think beneficiaries of programs are being squeezed by the recession and need more, not less, federal help. They are willing to risk inflation to deliver it.
Federal spending	See a danger of recurring inflation and emphasize discipline and restraint in federal spending.	See a danger of deep recession and high unemployment and call for greater economic stimulus through higher federal spending.
Business profits	Are concerned about the profits squeeze on business limiting the availability of funds for the capital investment needed to overcome the shortage of energy and basic commodities.	Are angry about exorbitant corporate profits, particularly in the energy area, and want to sock it to the companies while cutting taxes for consumers.
Oil	Want to use the market mechanism to allocate scarce oil supplies, even if it means higher prices, and will let the profits provide incentives for higher domestic production of oil and other forms of energy.	Favor some form of government controls—quotas, allotments or rationing—to distribute scarce oil, and would have the government go into the energy business to produce larger supplies of nonfossil fuels from public investment.

Source: David Broder, "Widening Party Differences," *Washington Post*, February 9, 1975, p. B6. © Washington Post. Reprinted by permission.

Table 6. How Party Officials View the Importance of 10 National Goals

QUESTION: Party officials were asked to rank, in order of importance, solutions to 10 major problems.

REPUBLICANS	DEMOCRATS
1. Curbing inflation	1. Reducing unemployment
2. Reducing role of government	2. Curbing inflation
3. Maintaining a strong military defense	3. Protecting freedom of speech
4. Developing energy sources	4. Developing energy sources
5. Reducing crime	5. Achieving equality for blacks
6. Reducing unemployment	6. Reducing crime
7. Protecting freedom of speech	7. Giving people more say in govt. decisions
8. Giving people more say in govt. decisions	8. Achieving equality for women
9. Achieving equality for blacks	9. Maintaining a strong military defense
10. Achieving equality for women	10. Reducing the role of government

* Based on a survey by the *Washington Post* and the Harvard University Center for International Affairs.

Source: *Washington Post*, September 27, 1976, p. A2. © Washington Post. Reprinted by permission.

file Democrats and Republicans are shown to be more moderate than party workers (see Figure 1).

Historically, Democrats and Republicans have differed most in the legislative arena on the issues of the tariff, agriculture, labor, and social legislation. They have differed least on public works, states' rights, civil service, and women's rights. Republicans have tended to favor higher tariffs, less government support for agriculture, less assistance to labor, and fewer new social programs than the Democrats. In foreign policy, the two parties had very different views between 1933 and 1948 and very similar views from 1948 to the 1960s. During the last few years, a divergence seems to be emerging. Most Republicans want to continue the strong anticommunist foreign and defense policy of the post-World War II years, while Democrats increasingly desire a foreign policy less concerned with the containment of communism.[14] *source : (pub. 1968*

Although party cohesion on congressional roll-call votes declined between 1921 and 1967 (Table 1), there has been a recent rise in party cohesion. David Broder makes the following observations about the 93rd Congress (1973–1974):

The majority of Democrats opposed the stand taken by the majority of Republicans more often on roll-call votes than they had in the two previous Congresses. The changes are relatively small—from 33 percent in 1969–70 to 36 percent in 1971 and 39 percent in 1973–74—but the direction of the trend toward increased partisanship is plain. . . .

The degree of cohesion within each party . . . has increased, gaining roughly 5 or 6 points on both sides of the aisle in the past three Congresses. In the most recent Congress, roughly two thirds of the Democrats and Republicans voted with their party stand on the issues where the two parties diverged. . . .

As the cohesion has grown, there has been a marked decrease in the most famous of the intra-party quarrels, that between the northern and southern Democrats. They split on only 29 percent of the roll calls in the last Congress, compared to 38 and 35 percent in the two previous Congresses.[15]

Among judges, clear and decided differences may be seen between Republicans and Democrats. Studies show that "Democratic judges are more likely than Republican judges to vote for the defense in criminal cases, for the claimant in unemployment cases . . . for the government in tax cases, for the tenant in landlord-tenant cases, for the consumer in sale-of-goods cases . . . and for the employee in employee injury cases." [16]

A landmark study of party leadership, done in 1956, documented sharp differences between the leaders of the two parties. Herbert

FIG. 1. How Party Officials Compare to Public in Political Ideology

QUESTION: State and local Democratic and Republican party officials and the general public were asked to position themselves on a liberal-conservative scale.

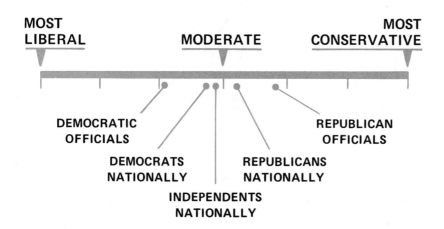

SOURCE: *Washington Post*, September 27, 1976, p. A2. © Washington Post. Reprinted by permission.

McClosky studied delegates to the two national conventions. He concluded that the leadership or active members of the two parties "are obviously separated by large and important differences. The differences, moreover, conform to the popular image in which the Democratic party is seen as the more 'progressive' or 'radical,' the Republican as the more 'moderate' or 'conservative' of the two." [17]

Are there differences in the subjects addressed by the *platforms* (the policy positions on which a party or candidate runs for office) of the parties? Are platforms specific? Are they implemented? The answer in each case is yes.

A study by Gerald Pomper of platforms between 1944 and 1964 shows that Republicans make more pledges about defense and government; Democrats emphasize labor and welfare. As to the language of platforms, pledges tend to be very specific: 60 percent have to do with continuing or repealing an existing and very specific program or policy. As to implementation, Pomper ascertained that, of the 2,245 pledges made in party platforms between 1944 and 1964, 72 percent had been implemented by 1966. He concluded that "Democrats and Republicans are not 'Tweedledee' and 'Tweedledum.' " [18]

Organization   The national conventions and committees of the two parties reveal striking differences. The Democratic national convention is more complex and the national committee larger than Republican counterparts. Power in the Democratic party is also much more centralized. The national committee now has the right to impose certain rules on both state and local party organizations. In 1972, Democratic rules requiring proportional representation for various minority groups helped George McGovern capture control of the convention and win the presidential nomination. Table 7 shows party committee and convention organization.

CHANGE—WITHIN LIMITS

Throughout most of American history, there have been two major parties, with a sprinkling of minor parties. The major parties, organized on a decentralized, or federated, basis (perhaps one might more properly term it a confederated basis), have been rather loosely knit organizations at the national level, coming together primarily every four years to nominate a candidate for president. Power in the two parties has resided in state and local organizations and in some of the party representatives at the national level. In short, power is diffused—in keeping with the federal system itself.

Also in keeping with the American governmental system is the nonideological orientation of the two parties. The mass of the American public is in the center of the ideological spectrum, neither to the left nor to the right. It is significant that whenever a major party has nominated a presidential candidate with a pronounced ideological bias, the party has been defeated. After all, the majority of American voters are, as one book put it, "unyoung, unpoor, and unblack." Naturally, candi-

In classical democratic theory, political parties are supposed to bridge the gap between people and government. They are to be the principal policymakers, presenting contrasting choices to the electorate so that, by voting, people can participate in the choice of government programs. . . . Although political parties in an ideal situation are suited to presenting meaningful and realistic policy choices for the electorate, they also serve the personal goals of their active members, which may have nothing at all to do with implementing one public policy instead of another.—*Peter Woll*

Table 7. Party Committee and Convention Organization

COMMITTEES		CONVENTIONS
National	**NATIONAL LEVEL**	**National Convention**
Republicans: Committeeman and woman plus state chairman from each state, D.C., Guam, Puerto Rico and Virgin Islands. Total, 162 members. Nomination by various methods. Election at National Convention.		Delegates elected by State or Congressional District Conventions, by primary elections or by State Committee.
Democrats: 360 members with 351 votes. 104 state chairpersons and ranking officer of opposite sex; 200 additional members apportioned to state on National Convention formula; 12 members from territories; 3 members Democratic Governors Conference; 4 Congressional representatives; 6 Democratic National Committee officers; 3 members Democratic Mayors Conference; 3 members Young Democrats; 25 At-Large members selected by Democratic National Committee.		
State Committee **(Chairman)**	**STATE LEVEL**	**State Convention**
Varying sizes, made up of members from counties. Congressional or other Districts. Elected at primaries, conventions or by Committees, or serve ex-officio.		Delegates from Congressional Districts, Counties or other districts, or made up of all Party nominees for State office. Elected at lower conventions, primaries or caucuses—plus holdover state and national officers.

Source: From *The Republicans and the Democrats—Similarities and Differences* prepared by Arthur L. Peterson and William C. Louthan for The Robert A. Taft Institute of Government, 1976, p. 8.

dates who take moderate positions on issues—close to the "political center"—are more likely to be elected than those advocating more extreme positions.[19] The two-party system is like the American people in being nondoctrinaire and pragmatic.

According to two students of government, the American party system

as it now exists performs a role of great usefulness in our national politics and government; . . . judged by the criterion of our conception of de-

Table 7. Party Committee and Convention Organization (continued)

COMMITTEES		CONVENTIONS
District Committee: Congressional, Senatorial, Judicial Circuit (Chairman) Number varies with State and size of Congressional District. Elected by County Committees or in primaries or appointed jointly by nominee and state executive committee or set up by nominee.	**CONGRESSIONAL DISTRICT LEVEL**	**Congressional District Convention** Delegates elected from County or other conventions or caucuses.
County Committees (Chairman) Number varies with State and size of County. Generally composed of all Precinct Committeemen and women elected at primary or caucus.	**COUNTY LEVEL**	**County Convention or Caucus** Delegates selected from precinct, ward or other district caucuses or County caucus open to all Party members of delegates elected in primary.
City, Ward, District (Chairman) Number varies with city, ward and district. **Composed of all Precinct committeemen and women or of separate members—sometimes selected by State Committee or by party candidates for State legislative offices—or elected in primary.**	**CITY, WARD OR DISTRICT LEVEL**	**City, Ward or District Caucus City, ward or district caucus open to all Party members.**
Precinct Committee Precinct Committeeman and/or Precinct Committeewoman. Elected at primary elections, precinct caucuses or appointed by County Committee.	**PRECINCT LEVEL**	**Precinct Caucus** Precinct caucus open to all Party members.

mocracy, that role is of great value and deserving of high praise; . . . the price America would probably have to pay for more centralized and disciplined national parties is, from the standpoint of democracy and in the light of the present nature of the American community, too high.[20]

Modernization and Reform   In spite of their loose organization and ideological moderation—in keeping with the American tradition—the major parties are by no means averse to change. The parties themselves are constantly undergoing modernization and reform. In the past, they

Neither party convention in 1976 could be called merely an exercise in rubber stamping—both Democrat Jimmy Carter and Republican Gerald R. Ford had to compete strenuously for their party's nomination. As can be seen from these photos, convention delegates waved signs and campaigned energetically for the candidate of their choice.

absorbed immigrants from Europe and helped them adapt to the United States. More recently, they have purged themselves of bosses, such as Carmine De Sapio of New York's Tammany Hall, and have assimilated blacks into leadership roles. They are now modernizing their procedures and organization, especially in the Democratic party. The Republican party, although now addressing reform issues, has not progressed as far. Unlike the Democratic party, which has mandated changes at the national level, the Republican party has suggested procedures for state and local party organizations to follow.

Recently adopted procedural reforms in the Democratic party include forbidding proxy voting in state party organizations; prohibiting the use of the unit rule (whereby a majority determines how the entire party delegation will vote); and making certain that party meetings are planned with adequate notice and conducted with proper procedures. Participation is being broadened through efforts to insure that minorities, youth, and women take part in party meetings and national conventions. In the Democratic party, national party conferences are now being utilized to develop continuity in the national organization during the years between presidential elections.

Minor Party Contributions Although the two-party system is eminently suitable for the American people and their government, this does not mean that it has prevented meaningful contributions by minor parties. Their principal benefit has been to bring the voters' attention to issues avoided by the major parties. Their names alone are a clue to this function: the Free Soil party advocated the abolition of slavery; the Greenback party urged the government to print more paper money.

Minor parties have also provided an important political fulcrum for leaders who were frozen out of the two-party system: Eugene Debs, Robert La Follette, Norman Thomas, Henry Wallace, and George Wallace. Each of these men articulated positions that challenged those taken by the major parties. Their success in calling attention to issues has been nothing short of phenomenal. Norman Thomas, the Socialist party standard bearer for many years, remarked in his later years that he was proud of his political achievements. Most of the proposals he had advocated through his party had ultimately been adopted into law through the efforts of the two major parties.

Third parties also provide a way for interest groups to organize on a key issue. Both the 1948 States Rights party and the 1968 American Independent party attracted support from those who opposed the federal government's role in enforcing civil rights legislation.

VALUES OF THE TWO-PARTY SYSTEM

Far from indicating what is wrong with the two-party system, national conventions perform a very useful function. They are not mere rubber stamps for selecting presidents, but make meaningful and responsible decisions. The Brookings Institution analyzed sixty-five national conventions held between 1832 and 1960 and identified five types of nominations:

1. *Confirmation*—An existing president or party titular leader is confirmed as the party's choice.
2. *Inheritance*—A political understudy or previous leader inherits the party mantle.
3. *Inner group selection*—Dominant party leaders get together and agree on the nominee.
4. *Compromise in stalemate*—A deadlocked convention turns to a dark horse or unexpected candidate.
5. *Factional victory*—One of several competing factions within the party succeeds in nominating its candidate.[21]

As shown in Table 8, only twenty-two conventions were of the "confirmation" type. Almost as many—nineteen—were in the category of "factional victory." This is evidence that genuine competition has characterized national nominating conventions a good part of the time. Since 1960, there have been four factional victories (Republicans in 1964 and 1968, Democrats in 1972 and 1976), three confirmations (Republicans in 1972 and 1976, Democrats in 1964), and one inheritance (Democrats in 1968).

The two-party system has numerous other values. It simplifies choice, promotes stability, bridges divisions, and allows for diversity in local party systems.

Simplification of Voter Choice   In a multiparty system, voters would confront a bewildering array of choices that would tend to confuse rather than simplify the democratic process. With only two major

Table 8. Patterns in Major-Party Presidential Nominations, 1832–1976

| TYPE OF NOMINATION | NUMBER OF PRESIDENTIAL NOMINATIONS | | | | | | |
| | DEMOCRATIC | | REPUBLICAN* | | MAJOR-PARTY TOTAL | | |
	1832–1892	1896–1960	1832–1892	1896–1960	1832–1892	1896–1960	1964–1976
Confirmation	4	8	3	7	7	15	3
Inheritance	1	1	2	3	3	4	1
Inner group selection	5	1	2	2	7	3	0
Compromise in stalemate	3	1	2	1	5	2	0
Factional victory	3	6	6	4	9	10	4
Total	16	17	15	17	31	34	8

* Includes National Republican and Whig parties.

Sources: Paul T. David, Ralph M. Goldman, and Richard C. Bain, *The Politics of National Party Conventions* © 1960 by The Brookings Institution, Washington, D.C., p. 123; and analyses of 1964–1976 national conventions.

parties, voter choices are limited to two principal candidates and options on issues. This is especially important in a nation with diverse racial, geographic, and social interests. To compete effectively and successfully within the system of single-member districts, American parties must unite a variety of groups behind one candidate and position. Thus the parties ease group differences. Each one, in trying to achieve a broad base of support, becomes generally representative of all groups in American society.

Promotion of Stability   Compromising differences at the party level reduces the amount of time the government might otherwise have to spend on conflict resolution (already an enormous task). Suppose the United States had a multiparty system with strong ideological orientation. The government would undoubtedly have to devote more time to resolving disputes among parties than it presently does. Also, in such a system, there is a greater potential for too-rapid, even chaotic, change when one party replaces another in office. The pragmatic and nonideological American two-party system insures that changes occur gradually and incrementally.

A Bridge for Communication   As it is organized, the two-party system serves as a bridge between and among the branches of the national government and between the national government and state and local governments. It helps to foster *bipartisanship*—cooperation between Democrats and Republicans. During the 1940s and 1950s, Democratic President Truman turned to certain Republican congressional leaders, notably Senator Arthur Vandenburg, to obtain passage of crucial foreign policy legislation. Similarly, Republican President Eisenhower called upon Democrats Sam Rayburn and Lyndon Johnson for support in Congress. What would result from the constitutional separation of powers structure if there were no two-party system to provide this kind of interaction?

Diversity in Local Systems   The loosely structured American two-party system allows for different types of organization in different regions. In the large northern states like Illinois, Ohio, New York, and Michigan, a very competitive two-party system exists. In other states, although the two parties compete, one party is dominant. In Maryland, for example, the Democratic party controls politics, but the Republican party wins enough offices to be competitive on a statewide basis. In much of the South until recent years, the Republican party hardly existed, and the Democratic party elected all officials. In some localities there is a powerful central party organization, such as that of the

The party is intended to be an organization for "getting or keeping the patronage of government." Instead of seeking "principles," or "distinctive tenets," which can only divide a federal union, the party is intended to seek bargains between the regions, the classes, the other interest groups. It is intended to being men and women of all beliefs, occupations, sections, racial backgrounds, into a combination for the pursuit of power. The combination is too various to possess firm convictions. The members may have nothing in common except a desire for office. . . . They tend to ignore any issue that rouses deep passion. And by doing so they strengthen the Union.—*Herbert Agar*

Chicago Democratic machine that was put together by Mayor Richard Daley; in others there is a loosely knit structure, such as the California Democratic party.

Glossary

Bipartisanship: cooperation between Democrats and Republicans.

Majority party: presently the Democratic party in the American two-party system; that party which has the largest number of people identifying with it.

Minority party: presently the Republican party in the American two-party system; that party which has the second largest number of people identifying with it.

Multimember district: a district in which more than one candidate is elected.

Platform: the policy positions on which a party or candidate runs for office.

Political party: organization with diverse membership that seeks to control government by winning elections and placing members in office.

Single-member district: a district in which only one candidate is elected.

Third party: a party that runs candidates for office but seldom, if ever, wins elections. (Also called *minor party.*)

Notes

1. As quoted in Wilfred E. Binkley, *American Political Parties* (New York: Alfred A. Knopf, 1965), p. 19.

2. Clinton Rossiter, *Parties and Politics in America* (Ithaca, N. Y.: Cornell University Press, 1960), pp. 73–74.

3. See generally Angus Campbell et al., *Elections and the Political Order* (New York: John Wiley, 1966).

4. As quoted in David S. Broder, *The Party's Over* (New York: Harper & Row, 1972), p. 183.

5. American Political Science Association, *Toward a More Responsible Two-Party System* (New York: Holt, Rinehart and Winston, 1950).

6. Douglass Cater, *Power in Washington* (New York: Random House, 1964), p. 180.

7. *New York Times,* March 29, 1976, p. 1.

8. *Congressional Quarterly Weekly Report,* March 7, 1969, p. 330.

9. Austin Ranney and Willmore Kendall, *Democracy and the American Party System* (New York: Harcourt Brace Jovanovich, 1956), p. 1.

10. David S. Broder, "Widening Party Differences," *Washington Post,* February 9, 1975, p. B6.

11. *National Municipal Review* 6 (1917):204.

12. Broder, "Widening Party Differences," p. B6.

13. Arthur L. Peterson and William C. Louthan, *The Republicans and the Democrats—Similarities and Differences* (New York: The Robert A. Taft Institute of Government, 1976), p. 10.

14. William J. Keefe and Morris S. Ogul, *The American Legislative Process* (Englewood Cliffs, N. J.: Prentice-Hall, 1968), pp. 300–304.

15. Broder, "Widening Party Differences," p. B6.

16. Herbert Jacob, *Justice in America* (Boston: Little, Brown, 1972), pp. 117–118; see also Stuart Nagel, "Political Party Affiliation and Judges' Decisions," *American Political Science Review* 55 (1961):843–850.

17. Herbert McClosky et al., "Issue Conflict and Consensus Among Party Leaders and Followers," *American Political Science Review* 54 (June 1960):409.

18. Gerald M. Pomper, *Elections in America* (New York: Dodd, Mead, 1968), p. 200.

19. This is the thesis of Richard M. Scammon and Ben J. Wattenberg in *The Real Majority* (New York: Coward, McCann & Geoghegan, 1970).

20. Ranney and Kendall, *Democracy and the American Party System,* p. 1.

21. Paul T. David, Ralph M. Goldman, and Richard C. Bain, *The Politics of National Party Conventions,* Kathleen Sproul, ed. (New York: Vintage Books, 1964), Chapter 7.

Recommended Rebuttal Reading

Party Systems

Chambers, William N., and Walter Dean Burnham, eds. *The American Party Systems.* New York: Oxford University Press, 1975.

Herring, Pendleton. *The Politics of Democracy: American Parties in Action.* New York: Norton, 1968.

Sundquist, James L. *Dynamics of the Party System: Alignment and Realignment of Political Parties in the United States.* Washington, D. C.: The Brookings Institution, 1973.

Presidential Party Politics

Barber, James David, ed. *Choosing the President.* Englewood Cliffs, N. J.: Prentice-Hall, 1974.

Sayre, Wallace S., and Judith H. Parris. *Voting for President: The Electoral College and the American Party System.* Washington, D. C.: The Brookings Institution, 1970.

Viewpoints on Parties

Berg, Larry L., Harlan Hahn, and John R. Schmidhauser. *Corruption in the American Political System.* Morristown, N. J.: General Learning Press, 1976.

Etzkowitz, Henry, and Peter Schwab. *Is America Necessary? Conservative, Liberal and Socialist Perspectives of United States Political Institutions* St. Paul, Minn.: West, 1976.

Nie, Norman H., et al. *The Changing American Voter.* Cambridge, Mass.: Harvard University Press, 1976.

Peter, Charles, and James Fellows, eds. *Inside the System.* New York: Praeger, 1976.

Party Reform

Parris, Judith H. *The Convention Problem: Issues in Reform of Presidential Nominating Conventions.* Washington, D. C.: The Brookings Institution, 1972.

Ranney, Austin. *Curing the Mischiefs of Faction: Party Reform in America.* Berkeley: University of California Press, 1975.

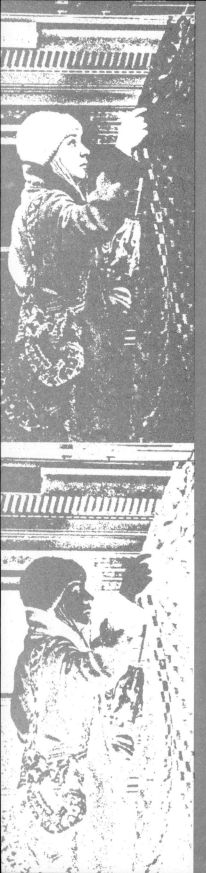

AT ISSUE: VOTING

A Brief History

8

RESOLVED THAT: Voting Is a Futile Exercise

At Issue: Voting

Millions of Americans vote each year in local, state, and national elections. They cast their ballots for council members, state legislators, mayors, governors, and members of Congress, and for propositions, amendments, and referendums. If voting is a criterion for a democracy, then surely the United States passes the test. Probably no other nation has as many different types of elections and elective offices as the United States.

But what is the significance of all of this voting? Does it really make any difference? Before assessing the many conflicting opinions on this issue, let us take a look at the historical background.

A BRIEF HISTORY

Voting has not been taken lightly in American history. The suffrage has been considered sufficiently important for major political debates to have been dominated by it. Its extension has focused on four major issues: abolition of property qualifications, women's suffrage, suffrage for black Americans, and voting rights for those under twenty-one.

Property qualifications were originally required for the obvious purpose of protecting property rights: Someone who owned property was thought to have a more legitimate stake in governmental affairs than someone who did not. The poor, it was argued, might sell their votes to

People say we spend too much money on politics. But the total spent on all political campaigns for all public offices over a four-year span is about one tenth of one per cent of all the budgets of all local, state and federal governments. If you were forming a business corporation and selecting your top personnel and directors, you might be willing to spend something more than one tenth of one per cent of your annual budget to make sure you had the right people running your corporation. We don't spend too much on politics. Perhaps we spend too little, and we do not spend it as wisely and effectively as we might. To take all private money out of politics would professionalize it. But volunteerism has been tremendously important in American life. It is one of the most robust facets of the American political system.—*Stewart Mott*

the rich. These attitudes were modified by the increasingly egalitarian mood exemplified by Jacksonian democracy—and by the desire of politicians to win additional votes. By the mid-1800s, property restrictions on voting had been abolished.

Women were denied the right to vote for many and various reasons; one premise held that a man voted the interests of his whole family. Agitation for women's suffrage eventually involved parades, petitions, the organization of a Washington lobby, White House picketing, arrests, and hunger strikes in jail. Women won the right to vote in some state elections in the 1890s, and finally gained national suffrage with passage of the Nineteenth Amendment in 1920.

In recent history, the most significant broadening of the vote broke down barriers to Negro suffrage. Although black Americans theoretically gained the right to vote with the Fifteenth Amendment, adopted in 1870, numerous restrictions, such as the *grandfather clause*, effectively kept most of them from the polls.* Only some hundred years later—after extensive litigation, sit-ins, marches, passage of the Civil Rights Act of 1964 and the Voting Rights Act of 1965, and the abolition of the poll tax by the Twenty-Fourth Amendment—were they able to vote in large numbers.

The fourth extension of the suffrage centered on the movement to lower the voting age from twenty-one to eighteen. Proponents argued that young people had enough education to vote intelligently and that it was undemocratic to require youths to enter military service, perhaps to die, without allowing them the right to vote. (This movement took place when there was a draft to meet Vietnam war needs.)

Many political battles have been waged over the right to vote. The question still remains, however, whether these battles and this right have really changed anything.

- Are voters significantly influenced by factors other than issues?
- Does the outcome of an election really have an impact on public policy?
- Do political campaigns affect voting?

*The "grandfather clause" prevented a person from voting unless one's grandfather had voted before the Civil War; naturally, this provision excluded black Americans. Various literacy tests were also used by voter registration officials, ostensibly to gauge citizens' knowledge of government. In effect, these were administered in ways that required only perfunctory answers from whites, while demanding extensive knowledge (such as memorizing whole sections of the state constitution) on the part of blacks.

The Affirmative Case

Yes, voting is a futile exercise.

So what carried us into a big undeclared war? Did anyone vote for Lyndon Johnson to start it? Obviously not. And who would have voted for Richard Nixon to keep it going except someone with foreknowledge that his fervent promise to stop it was hollow? [1]–Frank Trippett

Is the voter supreme in a democracy? The affirmative case directly challenges this assumption, for several reasons.

- The electorate is unqualified to make rational choices between candidates and parties.
- The people who vote tend to be of higher socioeconomic status and therefore unrepresentative of the population.
- Political campaigns are wasteful and often counterproductive towards the goal of informing the voter.
- Elections have little effect on public policy.
- The electoral college system for choosing our nation's highest official is undemocratic.

In analysis after analysis of opinions on specific issues, sizable proportions of persons have been shown to lack an opinion. For most Americans issues of politics are not of central concern.—*V. O. Key, Jr.*

THE UNQUALIFIED ELECTORATE

For a variety of reasons, the American electorate is unable to make rational choices. Voters do not know enough to vote intelligently. They make irrational decisions, and they are easily manipulated.

Over the long run party identification has more influence on a person's vote decision than any other single factor.—*Robert E. Lane*

Ignorance What is more important in determining how a person votes: party loyalty, identification with a candidate, or position on an issue? The Survey Research Center at the University of Michigan concluded that one of the greatest limits on political participation in presidential elections in the 1950s was "sheer ignorance" of major social and economic problems.[2] Indeed, according to one observer, "large portions of the electorate do not have meaningful beliefs, even on those issues that have formed the basis for intense political controversy among elites for substantial periods of time."[3]

Nor is lack of knowledge where issues are concerned the only impediment. It is a natural assumption that for elections to be meaningful, the electorate must have some basic knowledge not only about the issues, but also about the structure of government within which issues are decided and policies established. But the American people are amazingly ignorant about the structure of their government. As shown

Table 1. Proportion of Adult Americans Informed About Various Aspects of the American Political System

	PERCENTAGE OF CORRECT RESPONSES
How many senators are there in Washington from your state?	55
When someone is elected to the United States House of Representatives, how many years does that person serve in one term of office?	47
Do you happen to know whether all United States Senators come up for reelection this fall?	46
Can you tell me how many justices there are normally on the United States Supreme Court, including the Chief Justice?	40
Do you happen to know whether federal or state governments make the laws about who can vote in a presidential election?	33
What do you know about the Bill of Rights? Do you know anything it says?	23

Source: Fred I. Greenstein, *The American Party System and the American People,* © 1970, pp. 26–27. Reprinted by permission of Prentice-Hall, Inc., Englewood Cliffs, New Jersey. National surveys were conducted by the University of Michigan Survey Research Center. The 1948 and 1956 data are reported in Austin Ranney, *The Governing of Men* (New York: Holt, 1958), pp. 291–293. The 1964 data were furnished by the SRC.

in Table 1, less than a majority of those questioned knew the answers to several basic and fundamental questions; a bare 55 percent knew that each state has two senators.

Ignorance increases as the level of education decreases, as Table 2 indicates. Only 21 percent of those with less than eight years of schooling had some familiarity with a variety of national and international issues, while those who had attended college made a better showing.

Table 2. Education and Familiarity with Policy Issues

FAMILIARITY WITH ISSUES	LESS THAN 8 YEARS OF SCHOOL	HIGH SCHOOL	COLLEGE
High	21%	31%	50%
Medium	37	47	44
Low	42	22	6
Total	100	100	100

Source: A. Campbell, P. Converse, W. Miller, and D. Stokes, *The American Voter* (New York: John Wiley, 1960), p. 175. Reprinted by permission.

ROTHCO

© PUNCH

"People get the government they deserve. I must be a terrible. terrible person."

Irrational Decisions   American voting patterns are contradictory, to say the least. As a candidate for president in 1964, Lyndon B. Johnson received support from 63 percent of those favoring withdrawal from Vietnam, from 52 percent of those favoring a stronger stand in Vietnam, and from 82 percent of those who wanted the United States to keep soldiers in Vietnam but try to end the fighting.

Studies have been conducted to determine the degree of change in public opinion over a period of time. These show that, except for party identification, public opinion is very unstable. Statistically it has been shown that only about thirteen out of twenty persons may be expected consistently to take the same position on the same issue. Of these thirteen, ten may be expected to take the same position merely because of

What really goes on in a national nominating convention is the attempt by the party leaders to forecast the intangible and uncertain will of the people, as it will be registered in the state pluralities, and to shape the party policies in conformity with it.—*Carl Becker*

chance rather than an understanding of and commitment to a principle.[4]

Moreover, public opinion contradicts itself on the fundamental principles of democracy, as shown in Chapter 1. While Americans uphold democratic principles such as freedom of speech and the press in the abstract, they tend to be less supportive of these rights when confronted with specific instances where they are to be applied.

Nor do voters necessarily make rational decisions based on analysis of information. For one thing, people are highly selective in accepting political messages; they reject "too strenuous an overload of incoming information." [5] Other factors also enter in. How was Dwight Eisenhower able to defeat Adlai Stevenson in 1952 and 1956, considering that Democrats outnumbered Republicans in those years by about 45 to 33 percent? One reason is that Eisenhower's personal appeal—his smile, his image as an outstanding military hero of World War II—helped offset normal party loyalties.

Some might argue that voters did make rational decisions based on the issues when presented with clear choices in 1964 and 1972. In the first instance, Barry Goldwater's brand of Republican conservatism ("A Choice, not an Echo," was his campaign theme) was clearly at odds with Lyndon Johnson's Democratic liberalism. In the latter instance, Democrat George McGovern's position and policies had little in common with those of Republican Richard Nixon. But did the elections actually indicate thoughtful decision making? Two analysts who assessed the 1972 vote saw it not as a choice on issues but rather as a rejection of change

> that takes place in a non-traditional manner. . . . The basic threat perceived by the electorate in the McGovern candidacy was not so much to existing social arrangements as to the social order itself. And especially to due process. That is the "extremism" which voters finally rejected, not any liberal social or economic policy per se.[6]

Why then do we persist in the view that democracy depends on the idea that the people can make rational choices about public issues? The idea, says one scholar,

> is as inverted as it is reassuring. This model, avidly taught and ritualistically repeated, cannot explain what happens; but it may persist in our folklore because it so effectively sanctifies prevailing policies and permits us to avoid worrying about them. . . . The public is not in touch with the situation, and it "knows" the situation only through the symbols that engage it.[7]

Are We Like Sheep? If voters reject an overload of information and are influenced by factors other than issues, several questions are in or-

Is this voter participating in the working of democracy by casting her ballot, or is she merely engaging in a futile exercise? Although the United States probably has more types of elections and more elective offices than any other country, serious doubts exist about the relevance and effectiveness of the electoral process.

der: Is the great mass of American voters like sheep, manipulated by Madison Avenue? Does a candidate's image and personality so captivate our minds that we vote against our own interests? Do elites control the decision-making process because of electoral apathy? At least one student of the subject thinks so.

> Mass publics respond to currently conspicuous political symbols; not to "facts," and not to moral codes embedded in the character or soul, but to the gestures and speeches that make up the drama of the state. . . . It is therefore political actions that chiefly shape men's political wants and "knowledge," not the other way around. . . .
> The mass public does not study and analyze detailed data about secondary boycotts, provisions for stock ownership and control in a proposed space communications corporation, or missile installation in Cuba. . . . It ignores these things until political actions and speeches make them symbolically threatening or reassuring and it then responds to the *cues furnished* by the actions and speeches, not to direct knowledge of the facts.[8]

Substantial portions of the campaign dollar go into television because it reaches so many people. And it is precisely this medium where issues can very easily be blurred, as pointed out by Marshall McLuhan:

> The TV image is of low intensity or definition, and therefore, unlike film, it does not afford detailed information about objects. . . .
> The TV producer will point out that speech on television must not have the careful precision necessary in the theater. . . .
> Instead of a political viewpoint or platform, the inclusive political posture or stance. Instead of the product, the process. In periods of new and rapid growth there is a blurring of outlines. In the TV image we have the supremacy of the blurred outline, itself the maximal incentive to growth and new "closure" or completion.[9]

It is significant that after his loss to John F. Kennedy in 1960, Richard Nixon felt that he had devoted too much time to issues and too little time to his physical appearance. With the increasing influence of advertising and public agency executives, the electorate is asked to choose not between candidates, but rather between prepackaged images.

The low level of appeals to voters is indicated by campaign slogans. No better and no worse than most were the relatively meaningless phrases shouted by Nixon supporters in 1972: "Nixon's the One" and "Four More Years."

THE UNREPRESENTATIVE ELECTORATE

Who votes? The answer is quite clear, at least historically: persons of higher, rather than lower, socioeconomic status (see Table 3). As cyni-

Table 3. Nonvoters Classified by Group Characteristics

GROUP CHARACTERISTIC	PERCENTAGE OF ELIGIBLE VOTERS NOT VOTING*
EDUCATION	
Grade school	33
High school	19
College	10
OCCUPATION	
Professional and managerial	12
Other white collar	16
Skilled and semiskilled	22
Unskilled	32
Farm	23
COMMUNITY	
Metropolitan area	18
Towns and cities	22
Rural areas	23
RACE	
White	19
Black	46
LABOR	
Union	23
Nonunion	20
RELIGION	
Protestant	24
Catholic	15

*The exact percentages may change from one election to another, but the general pattern remains very stable.

Source: Fred I. Greenstein, *The American Party System and the American People*, © 1970, pp. 26–27. Reprinted by permission of Prentice-Hall, Inc., Englewood Cliffs, New Jersey. National surveys conducted by the University of Michigan Survey Research Center. The 1948 and 1956 data are reported in Austin Ranney, *The Governing of Men* (New York: Holt, 1958), pp. 291–293. The 1964 data were furnished by the SRC.

cism and distrust become more widespread, however, we may assume that nonvoting will become more common in all groups. It is a premise of democratic theory that voting reflects the individual's feeling of having a stake in the political system. Nonvoting, therefore, may to some extent be interpreted as representing alienation from the system.

Not only does voting decrease as we move from national to state and then to local elections, but also those of lower socioeconomic status are increasingly less likely to vote. One scholar who studied a municipality of 13,000 residents concluded that 810 voters, primarily from the middle class, elected the city council:

FIG. 1. Thermometer of Degrees of Political Activity Among Americans

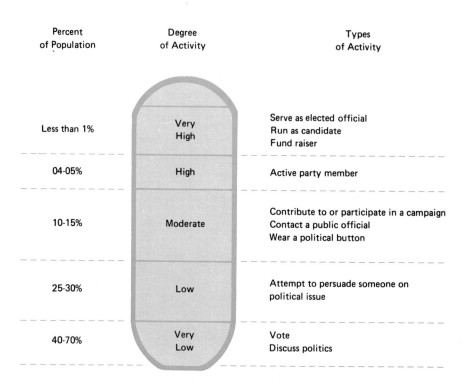

Percent of Population	Degree of Activity	Types of Activity
Less than 1%	Very High	Serve as elected official Run as candidate Fund raiser
04-05%	High	Active party member
10-15%	Moderate	Contribute to or participate in a campaign Contact a public official Wear a political button
25-30%	Low	Attempt to persuade someone on political issue
40-70%	Very Low	Vote Discuss politics

SOURCE: L. W. Milbrath, *Political Participation*, © 1965 by Rand McNally College Publishing Company, Chicago, p. 18, figure 3.

Such figures sharply question the validity of thinking that "mass electorates" hold elected officials accountable. For these councilmen, even if serving in relatively sizable cities, there are no "mass electorates"; rather there are the councilman's business associates, his friends at church, his acquaintances in the Rotary Club, and so forth which provide him the electoral support he needs to gain office.[10]

What about participation in other forms of political activity? Figure 1 shows that, while up to 70 percent may vote in an election, other forms of political activity drop off dramatically. Again persons of lower socioeconomic status are less likely than middle- and upper-class persons to have a high degree of political activity.

Difficulties of Voting The mechanics of voting are bothersome if not intimidating to many would-be voters. Registering to vote often requires that a citizen go to the courthouse or some other public building unfamiliar to most people, especially those of lower socioeconomic status. Moreover, the period for registration often begins, and ends, well before an election, when political interest is at a low level.

The voting process itself may present problems. Someone unfamiliar with voting machines will probably require instruction, and this may cause embarrassment. Another stumbling block is the *long ballot*, used in localities with numerous elected officials. Appropriately named,

ROTHCO

Pearson-Knickerbocker News, Albany, New York.

"No vacant houses, no out-of-towners on our nominating petitions — we only want bona fide residents."

the long ballot may list everyone from dogcatcher to president. The most bizarre example of the long ballot confronted Illinois voters in 1964, when by court order, all candidates for the state house of representatives had to be elected on a statewide basis. The ballot was a yard long to accommodate the names of over a hundred candidates for each major party.

Voters may also be confused by the various ways candidates are nominated, whether by caucus, convention, or primary. A *caucus* is a small group of party leaders or other members who may well meet in closed session. A *convention* is a larger meeting of party members held at the county, state, or national level. In a *primary*, a party's nominee is decided by election. There are two types of primaries. In a *closed primary*, only a party's members may vote for their candidate. In an *open primary*, a Democrat may vote for a Republican, and vice versa. Although more people participate in the primary than in the caucus or convention methods of nomination, the percentage of primary voters is generally well under 50 percent. Many people do not like to vote in the primary because most states require that voters declare their party affiliation at this time.

Primaries may discourage voters simply by their number. In 1976 there were thirty-one presidential primaries, with as many as six on some days. While candidates flew from state to state, voters were constantly bombarded with results and predictions, often inconclusive and confusing.

In some states, delegates to the national conventions were selected by caucus and convention; in others, by the primary; and in still others, by a combination of caucus, convention, and primary. Voters in some states cast ballots in a *presidential preference primary*, which merely records a preference—not binding on anyone—among prospective presidential candidates. Meanwhile convention delegates were chosen by caucus and local convention.

Other factors that may affect the level of voting include weather and the degree of partisanship in an election. If the weather is bad, voter turnout generally declines, but more so among voters of lower socioeconomic status. (Republicans usually benefit from poor weather because lower-status Americans are more likely to vote Democratic.) And if the election is in a one-party area, voter turnout will decline because of a low level of competition; this too enhances the voting strength of upper-income voters.

A Downward Trend   It is little wonder why even in presidential elections the number of eligible voters who vote has fallen dramatically. A glance at Figure 2 will reveal that, after consistently high turnouts in the

FIG. 2. Voter Turnout in Presidential Elections, 1824-1976
(Percent of Eligible Voters)

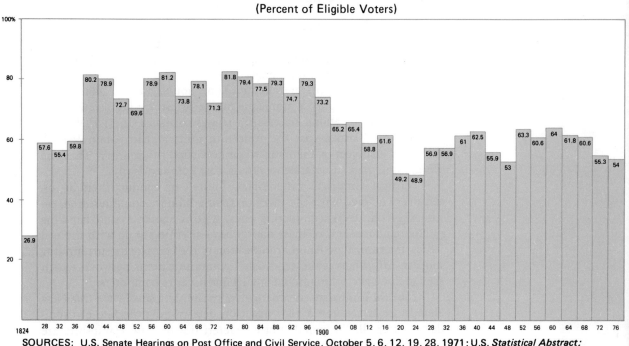

SOURCES: U.S. Senate Hearings on Post Office and Civil Service, October 5, 6, 12, 19, 28. 1971; U.S. *Statistical Abstract;* and Gerald M. Pomper, *The Election of 1976* (New York: David McKay, 1977), p. 72.

late 1800s, the trend has been generally downward ever since. Indeed the United States has the lowest voting turnout among the leading democratic countries of the world (see Table 4).

Table 4. Voter Participation in Leading Democratic Countries

NATION	ELECTION	TURNOUT
Australia[1]	1972	97%
Italy[2]	1972	93
West Germany	1972	91
France	1973[3]	82
Canada	1972	74
Great Britain	1970	71
United States	1972	55

[1] Compulsory registration and voting.
[2] Compulsory voting.
[3] Runoff assembly elections.

Source: Adapted from the *Congressional Record*, April 10, 1973, p. 7030.

POLITICAL CAMPAIGNS

Most elections take place after political campaigns, which theoretically illuminate and clarify issues. Does this actually happen? How important is money? What role do public opinion and the press play? Have campaign reforms made any difference?

Political campaigns are chaotic. Long hours, fatigue, momentous decisions made at only a moment's notice—these are but a few of the hazards, none of which necessarily relates to issues. In 1967, George Romney complained that the American military had "brainwashed" him on the subject of Vietnam, when he visited the country. That one word, implying a susceptible weakness, cost Romney dearly.

Political campaigns are complex. Those who conduct them are often overwhelmed with the tasks of raising money, doing research, organizing volunteers, conducting polls, writing speeches, and handling public relations. Few of these chores have anything to do with the real issues of a campaign. Another indication of the complexity surrounding modern campaigns is the candidate's communications network, which may include everything from copying machines to computers.

Political campaigns are chancy. Why should a small state like New Hampshire have such a big impact on determining the fate of candidates? After all, the population characteristics of New Hampshire are decidedly different from those of pivotal states like California, New York, and Michigan. Yet the fate of a presidential candidate may hinge on this electorate, unrepresentative of either party, let alone the entire nation.

If the old practice of taking kickbacks on public contracts was corrupt, what name will we invent for the new one of receiving the "donated" services of a public relations agency during a campaign and later giving that agency a city contract?—*Stephen Weissman*

Candidates for Sale   Candidates for office have a wide variety of needs that require ample funds. At the national level, requirements usually include a professional campaign firm, a computer expert, a polling organization, an advertising agency, a film-making specialist, and a direct-mail organization. Fees for these professionals may consume 20 percent of the total cost of a campaign.

At the very least, distortion may result from their advertising campaigns. Joe McGinniss wrote about Richard Nixon's 1968 campaign in a book with the revealing title, *The Selling of the President.*

> It was as if they were building not a President but an Astrodome, where the wind would never blow, the temperature never rise or fall, and the ball never bounce erratically on the artificial grass. . . .
> And it worked. As he moved serenely through his primary campaign, there was new cadence to Richard Nixon's speech and motion;

"YOUR HONOR, MY CLIENT BELIEVES THAT CAMPAIGN SPENDING
LIMITATIONS ARE A CURB ON FREE SPEECH BECAUSE EVERYBODY
KNOWS MONEY TALKS."

new confidence in his heart. And a new image of him on the television
screen.[11]

Prior to 1976, a major problem with presidential elections proved to
be ties between candidates and their financial supporters, especially interest groups (see Chapter 7). Table 5 shows labor union contributions
to presidential candidates McGovern and Nixon in 1972 while Table 6
lists major contributions over $100,000.

Table 5. 1972 Labor Union Contributions to Presidential Candidates

UNION	MCGOVERN	NIXON
United Auto Workers	$307,000	
Communications Workers of America (AFL-CIO)	223,000	
International Ladies Garments Workers Union (AFL-CIO)	64,000	
International Assoc. of Machinists and Aerospace Workers (AFL-CIO)	274,000	
Brotherhood of Railway, Airline, and Steamship Clerks (AFL-CIO)	5,000	$ 10,000
Retail Clerks International Union (AFL-CIO)	71,000	
Laborers International Union (AFL-CIO)		25,000
Seafarers International Union		100,000
International Brotherhood of Teamsters		6,000

Source: *Congressional Quarterly Weekly Report*, March 17, 1973, pp. 570–588. Reprinted by permission.

Table 6. Major Contributions (over $100,000) for Presidential Candidates in 1972

CONTRIBUTOR	STATE	OCCUPATION	NIXON	MCGOVERN
W. T. Duncan	Tex.		$ 300,000	
R. J. Carver	Ia.		279,000	
S. Schulman	Calif.		253,000	
R. A. Kroc	Ill.		237,000	
F. L. Cappaert	Miss.		234,000	
J. Dreyfus	N. Y.		150,000	
E. P. Helfaer	Wis.		160,000	
M. Riklis	N. Y.		141,000	
J. DuPont	Pa.		141,000	
J. C. Newington	Conn.		144,000	
G. Farkas	N. Y.		138,000	
N. A. McConnell	N. Y.		113,000	
E. J. Daly	Calif.		105,000	
G. Stephenson	N. Y.		104,000	
E. Dixon	Pa.		102,000	
E. J. Frey	Mich.		102,000	
E. Barwick	Ga.		100,000	
H. Hughes	Tex.		100,000	
Employees at Gulf Corp.			100,000	
J. P. Humes		Ambassador to Ireland	100,000	
P. Kiewit		Pres., Nebraska Constr. Co.	100,000	
R. Kleberg		Pres., King Ranch	100,000	
J. Massey		Chairman, Hosp. Ownership Co.	250,000	
J. Meyerhoff		Chairman, Baltimore Real Estate Co.	104,000	
J. Moran		Chairman, Texas Co. Med. Lab. Equip.	101,000	

CONTRIBUTOR	STATE	OCCUPATION	NIXON	MCGOVERN
J. A. Mulcahy		Pres., Steel Furnace Subsidiary Co.	573,000	
J. M. Olin		Chairman, Olin Corp.	100,000	
F. Ourisman		Wash., D.C., Real Estate Developer	150,000	
T. Pappas		Head, Food & Liquor Import Co.	100,000	
Employees of Philips Pet. Co.			100,000	
J. W. Rollins		Pres., Delaware Conglomerate	254,000	
J. H. Safer		Maryland Real Estate Developer	250,000	
R. Scaife		Heir, Mellon Fortune	1,000,000	
C. A. Smith		Chairman, California Co.	200,000	
K. H. Smith		Ret. Chairman, Food & Chem. Co.	244,000	
J. Stein		Chairman, MCA	117,000	
S. Steinberg		Chairman, N. Y. Computer Ser. Co.	250,000	
W. C. Stone		Chairman, Combined Ins. Co. of Amer.	2,000,000	
TAPE-Assoc. Milk Prod. Inc.			187,000	
D. J. Terra		Chairman, Printing Co.	250,000	
R. L. Vesco		Chairman, Ht'l Controls Corp.	200,000	
E. Walker, Sr.		Heir, Investment Co.	100,000	
D. Wallace		Founder of *Reader's Digest*	100,000	
J. L. Warner		Motion Picture Executive	100,000	
A. K. Watson		Former Ambassador to France	300,000	
C. V. Whitney		Chairman, Whitney Ind.	300,000	
S. Mott	N. Y.			$724,000
M. Palersky	Calif.			308,000
A. Zaffereni	Calif.			210,000
N. Noyes	Ind.			203,000
D. Noyes	Ind.			196,000
R. Saloman	N. Y.			137,000
L. Davis	N. Y.			124,000
B. Allen	Ill.			102,000
R. Allen		Pres., Gulf Resources & Chem. Corp.	100,000	
W. Annenberg		Ambassador to England	250,000	
T. Ashley		Pres., Warner Brothers	137,000	
O. Atkins		Chairman, Ashland Oil	100,000	
L. Berry		Chairman, Ohio Tel. Direc. Ad. Co.	102,000	
E. Bobst		Chairman, Warner-Lambert Pharm. Co.	100,000	
E. W. Brown, Jr.		Chairman, Lumber, Shipbldg. Co.	150,000	
S. Davis		Ambassador to Switzerland	100,000	
L. Firestone		Director, Firestone Tire and Rubber Co.	100,000	
M. M. Fisher		Chairman, Detroit Real Estate Co.	125,000	
K. Gould, Jr.		Ambassador to Netherlands	100,000	
R. R. Guest		Virginia Horse Breeder	200,000	

Source: *Congressional Quarterly Weekly Report*, October 6, 1973, pp. 2656–2660. Reprinted by permission.

Such largesse does not go unrewarded. A business firm may receive government aid of one sort or another. During the administration of Illinois Governor Richard Ogilvie (1969–1973), a major advertising contract went to a firm headed by one of his top political advisers. Individuals have been compensated by judgeships and other high appointments. This has led to many scandals about the "sale" of diplomatic posts, most recently in the Nixon administration, which made several appointments in exchange for campaign contributions (see Table 6). It has been well known for years that the best ambassadorial appointments, such as those to Britain and France, are usually awarded to persons who contribute large sums to the victorious presidential candidate.

If one candidate has a good deal more money than his or her opponent, the campaign may be decided simply on the basis of contributions. A prime example is the 1968 presidential campaign. Hubert Humphrey's effort lacked "early money"; Nixon had it in sufficient quantity to design and execute a thorough public relations campaign. Only during the last two weeks of the campaign did Humphrey have enough funds to surpass Nixon's spending for network television advertising. By then it was too late.

Beginning in 1976, new campaign finance laws changed the financial groundrules for presidential campaigns (see the appendix). However, new problems, perhaps equally as serious, arose.

First, relatively little money was available to involve the general public in the campaign. Most of the public funds had to be spent on the candidates' travel and the mass media, leaving little money for door-to-door canvassing, leaflets, or campaign headquarters in counties, cities, and towns.[12]

Second, labor unions and other organizations were not restricted by the law in their campaign expenditures, just in their contributions to candidates. As a result, labor unions could engage in door-to-door canvassing to pass out campaign leaflets, to register new voters, and to take voters to the polls. In effect, organizations like labor unions and black groups supplanted the traditional role of the Democratic party, because the former had the funds to spend that were not available to the party.

Third, Gerald Ford's incumbency provided him with a substantial advantage in that the White House could be used as a forum to generate major publicity through press conferences and policy announcements without expending limited campaign funds. Since the challenger, Jimmy Carter, was limited to his public funds, he could not raise private funds to try to overcome Ford's advantage.

Fourth, Carter's campaign was severely hampered financially as the election drew nearer because it had expended most of its funds and had little left for the mass media, buttons, bumper stickers, and rallies. Ford, on the other hand, had husbanded his funds by relying on White House exposure so that he had more to spend near the close of the campaign.

Fifth, the low level of voting in the 1976 election (see Figure 2) was at least in part caused by the limited campaign funds available to stimulate interest in the campaign.

Sixth, party organization is weakened by the campaign finance law in that public funds are given to the candidate, not to the party. Jimmy Carter, after winning the Democratic presidential nomination by defeating entrenched and well-known Democratic party leaders and then collecting $25 million from the U.S. Department of the Treasury to finance his campaign, really owed the party organization little.

Polls and the Press   Now a sophisticated art, if not indeed a science, public opinion polling may determine the positions candidates take on issues. If candidates find themselves running behind in the polls, they may switch positions on a crucial issue in order to enhance prospects for winning. Candidates pay thousands of dollars for sophisticated polls, so it is logical that they will be prone to heed them, rather than taking a conscientious position on an issue, especially if winning is their goal.

A candidate can be made or unmade by a news story. In early 1972 during the New Hampshire presidential primary, the press reported that U. S. Senator Edmund Muskie (Dem. Maine) cried about a newspaper's attack on his wife. Much of the electorate perceived this as a sign of weakness, and as a result, his ratings dropped in public opinion polls.

Television is vital, too, but the print media can set a mood for a campaign among those who influence what occurs on television. Candidates typically emerge after having received favorable reviews in the press. It should also be noted that there are some 62,000,000 daily newspaper readers in the United States. This big readership is especially important, since people who read newspapers are more likely to vote than those who do not. According to Frank Shakespeare, a top campaign advisor to Richard Nixon, the antagonism of the print media toward Nixon influenced him to use television as a medium to reach the public and thereby to undercut the force of the print media.[13]

The Mirage of Reform   On many occasions Congress has tried to reform campaign spending. So far it has had only limited success. One method of reform is to limit the amount of campaign money given, received, or spent. The 1925 Corrupt Practices Act stated that a candidate for the House of Representatives could not spend more than $2,500, while a candidate for the Senate had a $10,000 ceiling. Even though the bill allowed for larger amounts in larger states or districts, it was quickly and easily circumvented. Subsequently, this act was amended to set spending limits by any political committee to $3 million per year and contributions by individuals to each candidate or nationally affiliated party committee to $5,000 annually. Neither limitation proved effective.

Another method of reform relies on disclosure. In 1971 Congress passed the Federal Election Campaign Act. Its provisions included the following: (1) Any political committee that anticipated spending more than $1,000 on behalf of a candidate for federal office had to register with the government. (2) Such committees had to file information on every contributor of more than $100, and on each expenditure over $100. (3) Contributions could not be made in the name of another person. (4) Ceilings on political contributions would be abolished except for what candidates, or their immediate families, contributed to their own campaigns. (5) Candidates for national office would be limited in the amounts they could spend on campaign advertising to ten cents per registered voter.

In another 1971 law, Congress turned to a third alternative of campaign reform, subsidizing. The bill allowed political donors to claim a nominal income tax credit of $12.50 on a single return ($25 on a joint return) or an income tax deduction of $50 on a single return ($100 on a joint return). This law also allowed taxpayers to specify that $1 of their tax obligation could go to a fund to subsidize presidential election campaigns.

In 1974, another campaign reform law returned to limitations on campaign expenditures and contributions, continued to tighten existing disclosure laws, and established public financing for presidential campaigns. The Supreme Court, however, overturned the campaign expenditure limitations, except for publicly financed presidential campaigns, on the grounds that they violate First Amendment freedoms of speech and the press.[14] In brief, the 1974 law (1) sets limits on how much individuals and political committees may contribute to candidates; (2) provides for the public financing of presidential primary and general election campaigns; and (3) requires the disclosure of campaign contributions of more than $100 and campaign expenditures of more than $10. A guide to this highly complex law, found in the Appendix, reveals the enormous obstacles in regulating campaign finance.

Despite all these efforts, campaign finance reform may well be a mirage. Does the national government have any business establishing yet another bureaucracy to regulate campaign finance? Should tax dollars be used for political campaigns when there are more important uses for this money? Is the government restricting freedom of speech and the press by limiting the amount of money a person can contribute to a political candidate? Will contributions to candidates, rather than parties,

further weaken political parties, making campaigns even more fragmented and personalized?

ARE ELECTIONS RELEVANT?

There is a very real question about whether elections change anything
at all.

> Just as nobody "voted in" the New Deal, the New Deal government
> didn't "govern out" the Great Depression it strove so hard to overcome.
> That particular social ailment was cured only by the enormous produc-
> tion effort demanded by World War II—which also was scarcely a con-
> sequence of popular mandate.
>   Examples of the irrelevance of elections to crucial tides and events
> are easy to turn up. What may be the biggest social event of the last 20
> years—the outlawing of racial segregation in schools—resulted from no-
> body's vote or election. And elections hardly started the related black
> liberation or civil rights movement.
>   No election stopped it either. It was stopped by the Vietnam war,
> which students generally credit with also wrecking the economy.[15]

The decreasing rate of voter participation, described earlier, reflects
Americans' dissatisfaction with the efficacy of elections. Nonvoting has
risen dramatically in recent years, reaching as high as 55 to 60 percent
in congressional elections and 40 to 45 percent in presidential elections.
One cannot deny a pervasive feeling of frustration or, at best, apathy:
"Elections come and go, and the life of poverty goes on pretty much as
before, neither dramatically better nor dramatically worse. The postur-
ing of candidates and the promises of parties are simply irrelevant to the
daily grind of marginal existence."[16]
   Current feelings of futility and distrust began to intensify about
1965 and appear to be on the rise. As shown in Table 7, distrust and
cynicism have increased greatly in recent years among adults, that is,
parents.

An estimated 10 million Americans have dropped out of the
political system since 1968.
. . . The decline in voter participation is regarded as a clear
danger to the future of democracy and one of the most
significant developments in
American politics. . . . Their reasons for not voting spanned a
wide range of causes. Sixty-eight
percent said "candidates say one
thing and do another," 55 percent said it doesn't make any
difference who's elected, and 52
percent said Watergate proved to
them that elected officials are
only out for themselves. In contrast, only 18 percent said they
couldn't get to the polls and 12
percent said it was too difficult to
register.—Jim Squires

THE ELECTORAL COLLEGE ANACHRONISM

Delegates to the Constitutional Convention in 1787 designed the electoral college to prevent the people from voting directly for president.
The electors were originally designated by the state legislatures but are
now chosen by popular election and reflect the number of members
each state has in Congress. In a presidential election, one's vote is cast
for a slate of electors and not directly for the presidential candidate. (In
states where the slate of electors does not appear on the ballot, votes go

Table 7. Political Trust and Cynicism Among American Parents 1965—1973

PERCENT WHO BELIEVE	1965	1973
1. They can trust government in Washington only some of the time.	20	40
2. Government wastes a lot of money.	46	66
3. Government is run by a few big interests.	23	53
4. Quite a few people running the government don't know what they are doing.	25	38

Source: Adapted from M. Kent Jennings and Richard G. Niemi. "Continuity and Change in Political Orientation: A Longitudinal Study of Two Generations." Paper presented to the 1973 meeting of the American Political Science Association, New Orleans, p. 25. © 1973 by The American Political Science Association. Reprinted by permission.

A shift of a few thousand votes in Ohio and Hawaii last November would have left Jimmy Carter with a majority of the popular vote—and elected Gerald Ford President. That quirk of the electoral-college system was perhaps the most personal factor in Carter's support . . . of a landmark package of election reforms. He endorsed the idea of a constitutional amendment abolishing the electoral college. . . . Carter proposed the change to prevent a President from taking office even though his opponent wins more popular votes.—*David M. Alpern, Henry W. Hubbard, and Hal Bruno*

to a presidential candidate whose slate of electors has previously been chosen by the candidate's party.) The electoral college has serious defects as a method of electing our nation's highest official.

First, if a presidential candidate wins a state by even one popular vote, he receives all the state's electoral votes. This winner-take-all system distorts the will of the voters, in that votes for the losing candidate mean nothing. It may even result in the election of a president who has lost the total popular vote. This has indeed happened three times: in 1824, with John Quincy Adams; in 1876, with Rutherford B. Hayes; and in 1888, with Benjamin Harrison.

Second, the electoral college system does not fairly represent all states. In the North, substantial minority groups may exert undue influence. This occurs because large northern states are often fairly evenly divided between parties, at least in close presidential elections. In this case minority groups have the pivotal strength to determine to whom all of the state's electoral votes will be given. Significantly, the NAACP opposed the direct popular election amendment, because it would have reduced the political power of black voters in key northern states. The electoral college system also overrepresents the nation's smallest states; each has three electoral votes regardless of its population (two for its senators and one for its representative). Although direct popular election of the president has the support of a substantial majority of the population, the Senate failed to approve such an amendment to the Constitution in 1970 despite the fact that the House of Representatives had already approved this amendment, which had the support of such groups as the American Bar Association and the AFL-CIO. In 1977 President Carter proposed abolition of the electoral college.

A third defect of the electoral college is that electors in some states do not have to vote for the candidate to whom they are pledged. In our nation's history, a total of ten electors have defected from their pledge. A Virginia elector in 1972 who was pledged to Nixon voted for the Libertarian party candidate. Then in 1976, a Washington state elector pledged to Ford voted for Reagan.

Fourth, the system can result in deadlock, with an election being decided by the House of Representatives (as happened in 1824). In 1968 many people feared that George Wallace would receive enough electoral votes to deprive either Nixon or Humphrey of their necessary majority of electoral votes. A deadlock would then lead to bargaining for votes and determination of the winner in either the electoral college or Congress. If the president were chosen in the House of Representatives, each state would have one vote, thereby placing the least populated states on an equal plane with the most populous.

The Negative Case

No, voting is not a futile exercise.

What difference does one vote make? It can make a lot. In most elections, those who fail to vote could have changed the result had they gone to the polls. For every vote in Richard Nixon's plurality over Hubert Humphrey in 1968, 150 people did not vote. The 1960 presidential election was decided by less than one vote per precinct.[17]–John Gardner

Far from being futile, voting is useful and meaningful for several persuasive reasons:

- The electorate votes in a responsible and rational manner.
- Voting has value whether or not there is a high rate of participation.
- Voting effectively influences the behavior of public officials and candidates for office.
- The electoral college performs a useful function.

THE RESPONSIBLE ELECTORATE

Voting is not an irrational and irresponsible act. In the 1976 presidential election, 94 percent of the black voters cast their ballots for Jimmy

Table 8. Social Groups and the Presidential Vote, 1972 and 1976
(in percent)

	1972		1976	
	NIXON	MCGOVERN	FORD	CARTER
PARTY				
Republicans	94	6	89	11
Independents	66	34	52	48
Democrats	42	58	20	80
IDEOLOGY				
Liberal	31	69	26	74
Moderate	69	31	47	53
Conservative	87	13	70	30
OCCUPATION				
Professional/managerial	68	32	57	43
White collar	63	37	49	51
Blue collar	61	39	41	59
UNION HOUSEHOLDS				
Members	57	43	38	62
Nonmembers	67	33	52	48
COMMUNITY				
Cities over 500,000	42	58	40	60
Suburbs—small cities	63	37	47	53
Rural—5,000 and less	71	29	53	47
RELIGION				
Protestant	69	31	54	46
Catholic	60	40	45	55
Jewish	37	63	32	68
RACE				
White	70	30	52	48
Black	13	87	17	83
Other	32	68	18	82

Carter.[18] They perceived that the Democratic party and its candidate would better represent black interests. Logically this would be the proper perception inasmuch as major civil rights legislation, e.g., the 1964 Civil Rights Act and the 1965 Voting Rights Act, bear the principal imprint of the Democratic party. Moreover, the Republican administrations beginning in 1969 had frequently sought to abolish or to limit programs, such as the Office of Economic Opportunity (OEO) programs, in which blacks were especially interested. This illustration of black voting behavior in the 1976 presidential election indicates that segments of the electorate know how a specific government policy affects

Table 8. Social Groups and the Presidential Vote, 1972 and 1976
(continued)

	1972		1976	
	NIXON	**MCGOVERN**	**FORD**	**CARTER**
SEX				
Male	68	32	48	52
Female	62	38	48	52
AGE				
18–21	46	54	51	49
22–29	55	45	44	56
30–44	66	34	48	52
45–59	68	32	52	48
60 and over	71	29	52	48
INCOME*				
(Under $5,000)				
Under $8,000	57	43	38	62
($5,000–$10,000)				
$8,000–$12,000	62	38	43	57
($10,001–$15,000)				
$12,001–$20,000	67	33	50	50
(Over $15,000)				
Over $20,000	69	31	62	38
REGION				
East	59	41	48	52
Midwest	61	39	51	49
South	72	28	46	54
Far West	61	39	53	47

*Figures in parentheses are income categories for 1972.

Sources: For 1972, the election survey of the Center for Political Studies, University of Michigan; for 1976, *New York Times*, November 4, 1976, p. 25, © 1976 by The New York Times Company. Reprinted by permission. In both years regional data are based on the actual vote. Copyright © 1977 by David McKay Company, Inc. From the book *The Election of 1976: Reports and Interpretations*, by Gerald Pomper with colleagues. Reprinted by permission of David McKay Company, Inc.

them; are aware of how the parties stand on government policies that affect them; know whether the major group or groups to which they belong will benefit more from one party or another; and are aware of whether the condition of the nation merits the retention of the incumbent party, administration, or candidate.

V. O. Key, Jr., describes three types of voters, all of whom he believes conduct themselves rationally. The "standpatters," who stick with one party election after election, tend to do so because they understand its policies and perceive them as favorable to their own interests. The "switchers" are generally people of more than average education,

It is often noted that the vote of those below thirty tends to be more conservative than that of their elders. But commentators tend to overlook the fact that it is precisely those young people on the left who tend to be so disaffected as not to vote. Those below thirty with whom "the movement" is most in touch are those who ignore electoral politics.—*Michael Novak*

information, and interests; they base their voting decisions on a rational set of premises and thus vary their choices. The "new voters"—that is, those who enter or reenter after not voting for some years—do so because of rational considerations related to their personal interests. Of course, rational conduct is not limited to the act of voting; people who do not vote rationally may know how to get the political process to work for them in other ways—for instance, through appeals to their legislators.[19]

People tend to vote in ways that reflect their group memberships, party affiliation, socioeconomic class, religion, or race. These are obviously rational considerations. The increasing number of independents (Table 8) may also be seen as a sign of rational decision making. Quite properly, a large segment of voters are not influenced by predetermined party ties or established positions on issues. It is this group that often determines the outcome of an election and to which parties and candidates must pitch their campaign in order to win.

Also recent research in *The Changing American Voter*[20] suggests that the increasing number of independents results from increased awareness of issues and ideologies among the electorate. Traditionally, American voters by and large have been more pragmatic, frequently being called "centrists" or "moderates." Between 1956 and 1973, middle-of-the-road voters have declined from 41 to 23 percent of the electorate, while those on the left of the political spectrum have increased from 12 to 21 percent, and those on the right from 13 to 23 percent (see Figure 3). This increasing issue and ideological awareness may lead to major changes in the two parties. Certainly the Republican party in 1964 and the Democratic party in 1972 made significant shifts to the right and left, respectively (see Figure 4). No longer can the two major parties blindly count on party affiliation by itself to produce electoral victories. They may have to adjust their approaches to the voters by becoming more sensitive to issues and ideological concerns. According to Figure 5 more voters identify themselves as independents than either as Democrats or Republicans.

Contrary to data cited in the affirmative case, more recent research by Professors Norman H. Nie, Sidney Verba, and John R. Petrocik show that the American electorate is taking more consistent positions on issues and making more use of issues to evaluate candidates (see Figure 6). The American electorate now appears to be much better informed than the affirmative case indicates.

Manipulation of voters should not be assumed to occur simply because campaign ads appear on television and in other media. As pointed out in Chapter 5, the public is not necessarily fooled by slick appeals.

FIG. 3. Distribution of Population on Political Beliefs, 1956 and 1973

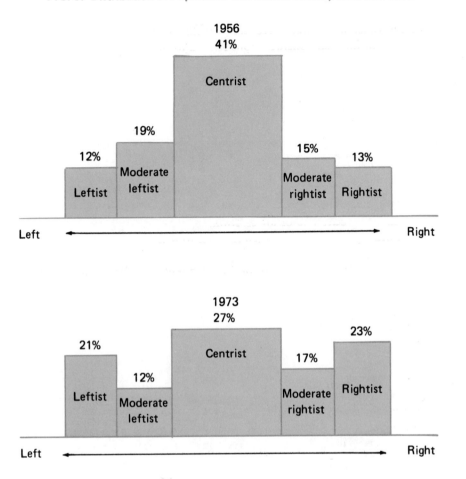

SOURCE: Reprinted by permission of the publishers from *The Changing American Voter* by Norman H. Nie, Sidney Verba, and John R. Petrocik, Harvard University Press, © 1976 by the Twentieth Century Fund, p. 143.

Political consultants have come to recognize that the electorate can see through campaign advertising that does not reveal the genuine character of the candidate. In fact, the latest research as conducted by two Syracuse University political scientists, Thomas Patterson and Robert McClure, concludes that "what the voters are reacting to is substance. The most effective campaign ad is based on substance, not flimsy image appeal." [21]

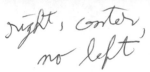
right, center, no left!

FIG. 4. Distribution of Democrats and Republicans on the Issue Position Scale, 1956 and 1972

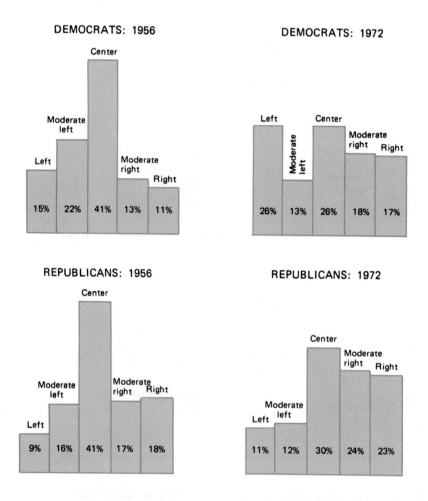

SOURCE: Reprinted by permission of the publishers from *The Changing American Voter* by Norman H. Nie, Sidney Verba, and John R. Petrocik, Harvard University Press, © 1976 by the Twentieth Century Fund, p. 199.

Voting is the key mechanism of consensus in democratic society.—*Seymour Martin Lipset*

VOTING: QUALITY, NOT QUANTITY

Statistics indeed indicate that many Americans who could vote do not do so. A number of points may be raised to throw further light on this issue.

First, it should be stressed that the majority of voters in the United States do vote in presidential elections. Second, although voting levels in the United States are presently lower than those in several other demo-

FIG. 5. Partisan Affiliation, 1952-1974

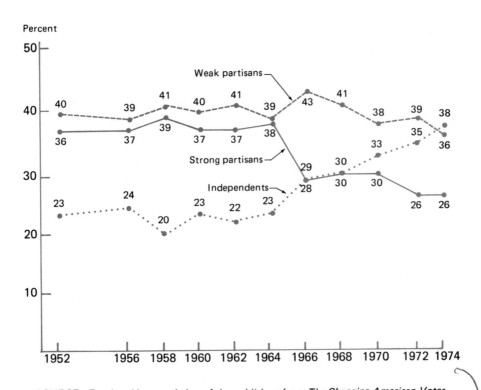

SOURCE: Reprinted by permission of the publishers from *The Changing American Voter* by Norman H. Nie, Sidney Verba, and John R. Petrocik, Harvard University Press, © 1976 by the the Twentieth Century Fund, p. 49.

cratic countries, they have not been so consistently. In the presidential election of 1876, 81.8 percent of those eligible voted, but voting rates dropped from then on until the 1920s. They rose in the late 1920s, declined in the 1940s, climbed in 1952 and 1956, and have decreased since 1960 (see Figure 2). History thus shows a cyclical pattern, which suggests that voting levels will most likely rise again, just as they have in the past.

Nor should we regard nonvoting necessarily as an indication of alienation from the political system. People may abstain from voting simply because they are satisfied with the status quo. Indeed, high levels of voting may be a bad sign rather than a good one. Exceedingly high voter participation existed in Weimar Germany, where Hitler attained office through the electoral process.

FIG. 6. Proportion Consistent in Attitudes and Proportion Referring to
Issues to Evaluate Candidates, 1956-1972

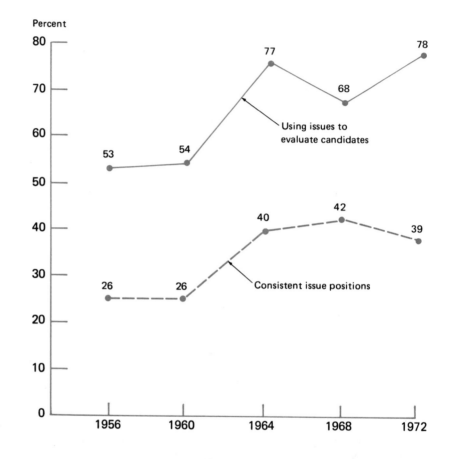

Another interesting point is suggested by a theory advanced by
Walter Lippmann. Many years ago he noted the importance of deference as a prerequisite for effective democratic leadership. He pointed
out that if everyone exhibited the same high level of political interest
and participation, it would be extremely difficult for leaders to govern.
Everyone would be seeking leadership; no one would be a follower.[22]

Using this criterion, low voting levels may be seen as a positive
sign, indicating that deference is accorded democratic leaders in the

United States. Americans as political beings may be divided into three categories: apathetics, participants, and leaders. Most are either apathetics or participants (voting being the principal function of the latter).

At any rate the actual level of participation is not necessarily the most important feature of voting; the stabilizing and symbolic values afforded by the institution itself may be much more important. For example, as long as Eugene McCarthy and Robert Kennedy remained in the 1968 presidential race, violence was not a principal method of the antiwar movement. After both men were eliminated from the contest, violence became more widespread, escalating most vividly at the Democratic national convention in Chicago. It may be argued, therefore, that voting, especially insofar as the electorate is presented with alternatives, creates a stabilized atmosphere.

Nonvoting itself is conducive to stabilization, in that persons with nondemocratic values are more likely to be among the nonvoters. With a low level of political sophistication, they are more likely to be intolerant of those with whom they disagree, and tend to respond positively to authoritarian leadership.[23] A dramatic rise in voter participation, if it led more such people to the polls, might well be a cause for alarm, not rejoicing.

Finally, voting has enormous symbolic value. Murray Edelman contends that voting provides "symbolic reassurance," thereby enabling elections to "quiet resentments and doubts about particular political acts, reaffirm belief in the fundamental rationality and democratic character of the system, and thus fix conforming habits of future behavior."[24]

VALUES OF POLITICAL CAMPAIGNS

If the 1976 presidential election had been held in late August, Jimmy Carter would have beaten Gerald Ford by a landslide. The same was true of the 1968 presidential race between Richard Nixon and Hubert Humphrey. During these two campaigns, the front-runner lost substantial ground and very nearly lost the election. In both elections, the months of September and October prior to the November election allowed the electorate an opportunity to assess the two candidates and their running mates of the major parties as they were tested in the political heat of a campaign. In 1968 the slick, Madison-Avenue-like campaign of Richard Nixon contributed to the resurgence of Hubert Humphrey, who very nearly overcame a 16 percentage point deficit in public opinion polls. Then in 1976, Jimmy Carter's effort to be "all things to all people" nearly cost him a lead that had once been pegged at 33 percent. As it was, he narrowly squeaked to victory by approximately

The Swiss have a lower voter turnout than we [in the U.S.] have, and almost everybody in the Western world regards Switzerland as a stable, well-governed democracy. The idea that high voter turnout necessarily means good government and low turnout means bad government is nonsense. It's something that we've been fed in high-school civics class. We've salivated over this thing like a Pavlovian dog, and it just isn't true. The Soviet Union, Hitler's Germany, Italy under Mussolini—all had very high participation, but not many people would hold them up as examples to be emulated. What it boils down to is that freedom means the freedom not to vote, as well as the right to vote.— *Richard M. Scammon*

For the voters are very important people . . . and despite what one may read about back-room political machinations, it is the voters who choose presidents and lesser political leaders. It is the voters who in large measure shape the men they elect and, in shaping the men, shape ultimately the policies of the nation. Political leaders are leaders only insofar as they can lead voters. The leaders are in office only insofar as they can win elections.—*Richard M. Scammon and Ben J. Wattenberg*

3 percentage points. In fact, the shift of just 8,000 to 10,000 votes in a few states, such as Ohio, would have given Gerald Ford the victory. A campaign lasting one week longer in either 1968 or 1976 might well have produced a different result, given the momentum of the Humphrey and Ford campaigns, respectively.

One value of the political campaign is that it tests candidates' organizational skills, including their ability to attract competent people to work for them. In 1960, Richard Nixon's campaign suffered because he failed to delegate sufficient responsibilities to subordinates. As a result, Nixon spent too much time worrying about campaign strategy and not enough time being the candidate. By 1968, he had rectified this problem by delegating substantial authority to his campaign manager and a top group of advisors. These organizational tests are important to help determine if a candidate is able to cope with administering the largest government in the world.

Another value of the campaign is to test physical endurance. Candidates who are not equipped to withstand the rigors of intensive campaigning could hardly be expected to endure well the extraordinary demands of the presidential office. Vice-President Walter Mondale withdrew from the 1976 Democratic presidential primaries because he was not prepared for this extraordinary physical undertaking. It is common for newspapers to print pictures of presidents showing the impact of the office on their countenances. Even a youthful and vibrant John F. Kennedy revealed the wear and tear of this office.

How capable is a president in making sound judgments and decisions, especially under pressure? A campaign provides a good test for this capacity as illustrated in the 1976 Carter campaign. Both supporters and opponents of Jimmy Carter agreed that he made several poor decisions during his campaign, particularly his decision to grant an interview with *Playboy* magazine. Obviously, this interview cost him support from a large portion of the electorate opposed to pornography, a portion very crucial to Carter's primary election successes when he had campaigned as a "born again" Christian. This interview created a credibility gap among these people, particularly in the South, that helped the Ford campaign to contest a region that had earlier been conceded to Carter. Other elements of the population, such as college and university professors, also generally took a dim view of the *Playboy* interview, but

Political campaigns give voters the valuable opportunity to assess how candidates hold up under intense pressure and close public scrutiny. Here presidential hopefuls Eugene McCarthy, Edmund Muskie, and George Wallace confront microphones, cameras, and outstretched hands along the campaign trail.

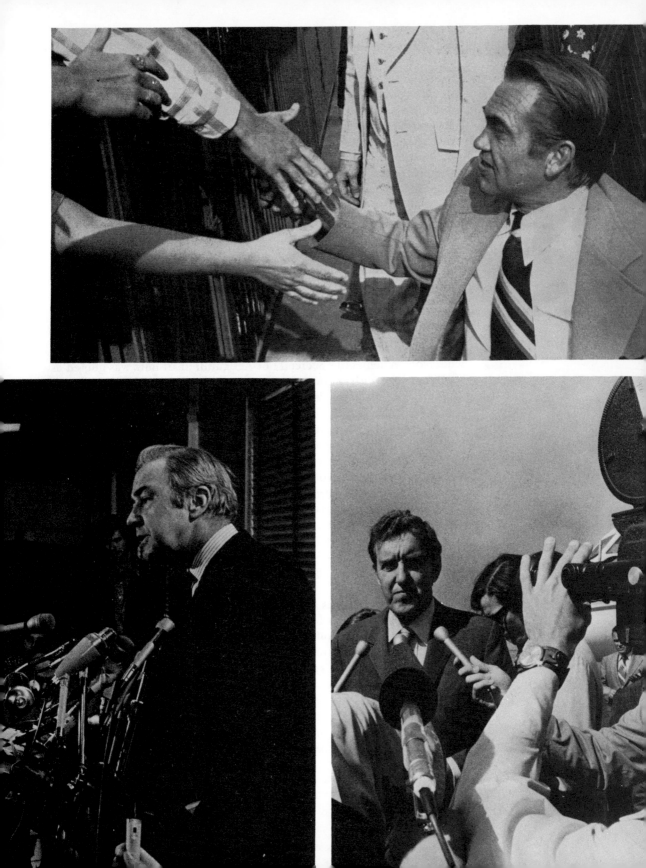

not necessarily for the same reasons. They felt that it revealed poor judgment about the type of image a presidential candidate should create, particularly a candidate who had projected himself in a manner that could easily lead voters to perceive him to be opposed to the very publication in which the interview was printed. In other words, the Carter decision was not "smart politics" and thus cost him support among many voters in this group.

Still another value of the campaign is to test timing—when to do something. The 1976 Ford campaign was timed to expend more resources later in the campaign, a strategy that appeared to be working, but which ultimately did not overcome the extraordinary Carter lead. The Ford campaign managers felt that large numbers of voters were undecided and that a major advertising campaign during the final days of the campaign would attract their support and overcome Carter's lead.

In administering the government, a president needs to have what is called a good sense of timing, when to do something in order to have the desired result. A good decision improperly timed can become a bad decision. When Ford's Secretary of Agriculture Earl Butz was quoted as telling a joke with serious racial overtones, Ford delayed firing him, allowing Butz to resign. If Ford had acted immediately to fire Butz, he might have had a much better opportunity to garner black votes which, as it turned out, led Carter to victory in at least ten states, according to the Joint Center for Political Studies.[25] In seven of these states, the Carter margin of victory was between 7,586 votes in Ohio and 207,334 in Texas. The black vote for Carter was substantially more than the margin of victory in each instance—285,000 black votes in Ohio and 295,000 black votes in Texas. The other states where this was true were Pennsylvania, Missouri, Louisiana, Maryland, and Mississippi. Black support was also crucial to Carter's victory in North Carolina, South Carolina, and Florida. A strong case, therefore, can be made that Ford's poor timing in handling the Butz case helped pave the way for his defeat.

Political campaigns test candidates' knowledge. During the second debate with Carter, Ford suggested that there was no Soviet domination of Eastern European countries. Whether a misstatement or not, Ford's pronouncement cost him support among many voters, particularly immigrants from Poland, Yugoslavia, Hungary, and Czechoslovakia. It was generally conceded that Ford would have won the second debate if it had not been for this statement. As it was, the loss of the debate checked the growing momentum of the Ford campaign.

How effective is a president in communicating with diverse groups of people? Political campaigns easily reveal candidates' skills in this area.

During the 1976 campaign, Mr. Carter demonstrated greater skill at communicating effectively with diverse groups than did Mr. Ford. Once again, the black vote is instructive. Had Ford been able to communicate more effectively to black people, he would have easily won the presidency.

Political campaigns cannot be lightly dismissed as either of no consequence or counterproductive. They are very constructive in that the public benefits by having prospective presidents tested under very rigorous circumstances.

THE EFFECTIVENESS OF VOTING

As pointed out in the introduction, the franchise has continuously been extended throughout American history. It should be remembered that constitutional amendments were required in several instances. This fact alone should demonstrate the importance with which Americans regard the vote, since adopting an amendment requires a great deal of time and effort.

Not only was suffrage deemed sufficiently important to wage these political battles, but the results also indicate the importance of voting. Since the 1960s, for instance, women and blacks have won elective office in increasingly larger numbers. Representatives Shirley Chisholm, Elizabeth Holtzman, Bella Abzug, and Barbara Jordan became national figures. (Chisholm, in 1972, was the first black woman to campaign for the presidency.) Blacks now occupy the mayor's office in many large cities, including Atlanta, Cleveland, Newark, and Gary. Andrew Young, a black, was named by President Carter as ambassador to the United Nations, and a black woman, Patricia Roberts Harris, was appointed Secretary of Housing and Urban Development.

The history of voting in the United States shows that the electoral process has influenced public policy since the beginning of our history. Indeed, it was the electoral victory of the Democratic-Republicans over the Federalists in 1800 that showed what happens when a party disregards the masses. Other crucial elections include the Republican defeat of the Democrats in 1860; the Democratic win over the Republicans in 1932; and the Republican landslide of 1972. All of these contests substantially affected political power and public policy in this country. To put it another way: If we look back and speculate, we could never assume that Hoover would have pursued the same policies in 1933 that Roosevelt did, or that McGovern would have followed the same course as Nixon did in 1973. Voting has indeed brought major shifts in political power and public policy.

John Stuart Mill cogently points out why voting is efficacious:

> Rulers in ruling classes are under a necessity of considering the interests
> of those who have the suffrage; but of those who are excluded, it is in
> their option whether they will do so or not. However honestly disposed,
> they are in general too fully occupied with things they must attend to, to
> have much room in their thoughts for anything which they can with im-
> punity disregard.[26]

Now that the United States has universal suffrage, to all intents and
purposes, politicians cannot afford to disregard the interests of any
group of citizens. If people consider themselves disregarded, they can do
what many others have done—namely, organize with those of similar interests to achieve their common objectives.

American voters may be said to exercise their influence in two
chief ways, prospectively and retrospectively.

Prospective Influence   Who could argue that Richard Nixon did not
have the 1972 election in mind when he began withdrawing American
troops from Vietnam in 1969? Who could argue that Gerald Ford did not
have the 1976 Republican primaries in mind when, early in the year, he
accepted Nelson Rockefeller's assurance that he would not be a candidate for the vice-presidency? Clearly, the prospect of an election shapes
the actions of government officials.

Parties and candidates carefully consider many aspects of their appeal to the public. They try to provide geographic, religious, or ideological balance on presidential tickets. They take policy positions on some
issues, but not on others, to gain votes. Richard Nixon, for example, advocated federal aid to parochial schools when he spoke before the
Knights of Columbus in New York City.

Conversely, failure to be cognizant of prospective electoral judgment may lead to resounding defeat. Barry Goldwater advocated abolition of the Social Security system in the retirement city of St. Peters-
burg, Florida, and urged abolition of the Tennessee Valley Authority in
Tennessee. George McGovern proposed changes in federal tax policy
that would have been to the disadvantage of the middle class—the dominant voting group.

The vast bulk of the American electorate is in the center ideologically; policies that conflict with this orientation may be expected to
run into trouble. Nor is it just the majority of which politicians must be
aware. They must remember that a minority can organize with other
minorities to *become* a majority. A minority may be disregarded for a
while, but it has the potential of building a coalition to fight for its
interests.

The two major parties have been adept at assimilating minority group and minor party interests. Much of the Populist party platform of the 1890s was absorbed by the Republicans and Democrats in the early 1900s. It can also be argued that the views of George Wallace on school busing affected the positions of leaders in both parties in the late 1960s and early 1970s.

Retrospective Judgment   When voters elected Eisenhower in 1952, they were indicating, among other things, their disenchantment after twenty years of Democratic presidents. Likewise, the 1974 congressional elections indicated that the electorate was less than happy with Republicans because of the Watergate scandal. Many scholars claim that such retrospective judgment may be the most important purpose of voting:

> The voters employ their powerful sanction *retrospectively*. They judge the politician after he has acted, finding personal satisfactions or discontents as the results of these actions. . . . The issue of Vietnam is illustrative. . . . For their part, critics of the war did not emphasize their own alternative policies, but instead concentrated on retrospective and adverse judgments. . . . Declining public support of the war brought all major candidates to promise its end. The Republican party, and particularly Richard Nixon, joined in this pledge, but provided no specific programs, instead seeking the support of all voters inclined to criticize past actions.[27]

The power of retrospective judgment forces politicians to listen to the demands of the enfranchised, who hold a weapon of substantial force. Gerald Pomper says: "The ability to punish politicians is probably the most important weapon available to citizens. It is direct, authoritative, and free from official control."[28]

THE ELECTORAL COLLEGE ADVANTAGES

Although criticized by many, the electoral college system has several advantages. First, since the winner of a state receives all its electoral votes, candidates do not waste much time campaigning in states where they are fairly likely to win or lose. Rather, they concentrate on states where the partisan balance between the two major parties appears to be about even. Typically these are populous states—Illinois, New York, California, Pennsylvania, and the like—with a cross section of voters: rich and poor, black and white, industrial and agricultural, urban, suburban, and rural. Candidates thus project their platforms to voters representing divergent interests rather than appealing to a narrow ideological or geographic spectrum.

Defenders of the electoral college are defending not an eighteenth-century artifact, but a system that has evolved, shaping and shaped by all the instruments of politics, especially the two-party system. It is an integral part of a constitutional system with premises too subtle and purposes too varied to be summed up in slogans like "one man, one vote." [Birch] Bayh insists that the electoral college "is, by simple definition, undemocratic." But this constitutional democracy was not devised by, and should not be revised by, persons addicted to simple definitions of democracy.—*George F. Will*

Second, the electoral college system has worked for nearly two hundred years. Why change an existing system for something that might be less stable?

Third, direct popular election, the principal alternative to the electoral college, has many disadvantages. It would increase the likelihood of minority parties, thereby fragmenting American politics and endangering the two-party system. The proposal under consideration in 1969–1970 required that a candidate receive at least 40 percent of the vote in order to win. This provision would encourage more candidates to run. With the knowledge that denying a major candidate 40 percent of the vote could force a run-off election, fringe candidates might well enter simply to enhance their bargaining power. The electoral college helps the two-party system resolve social conflict and manage the transfer of power by forcing serious presidential candidates to develop a national base of support.

The electoral college system tends to create stability and therefore give the voter more confidence in the government and its ability to govern. It avoids the kind of trouble that would probably have resulted in 1960 when Kennedy narrowly edged Nixon by less than one vote per precinct. With direct popular election, a vote recount would have been likely, and a cloud would have hung over the American government at least until the recount was completed, if not for long afterward.

As pointed out in one study of the electoral college:

> Although imperfect, as Hamilton predicted, the electoral college system has at least been excellent. It has worked well. It has evolved along with the nation and has in every era produced presidents accepted as legitimate and capable of governing effectively. It has been a salutary force in American politics, in ways of which Hamilton never dreamed. It has encouraged political leaders to wage their struggles within two great parties. It has provided a point of access for metropolitan interests that are often ignored elsewhere. It has promoted national stability in the battle for the presidency. We see no reason to abandon, and many reasons to support, an institution whose assets have been very tangible and whose liabilities have been largely conjectural.[29]

Glossary

Caucus: a closed meeting of party leaders to choose party candidates.

Convention: a meeting of party delegates at the national, state, or local levels to decide on party policy and to nominate candidates for office.

Grandfather clause: voting requirement that granted the franchise to persons whose ancestors had voted prior to 1867.

Long ballot: a voting sheet that includes a large number of offices to be filled, candidates to be selected, and issues to be decided.

Presidential preference primary: an election held in a state to determine voter preferences among prospective presidential candidates; it is binding in some states in that a state's delegates to the national conventions must support the victorious candidate in the state's primary.

Primary: an election held to nominate a party's candidates to run in the general election. There are two types of primaries: closed (for party members only) and open (for registered voters regardless of party affiliation).

Notes

1. Frank Trippett, "The Shape of Things as They Really Are," *Intellectual Digest* 3(December 1972):25.

2. Angus Campbell, et al., *The American Voter* (New York: John Wiley, 1960), p. 175.

3. Philip Converse, "The Nature of Belief Systems in Mass Publics," in David E. Apter, ed., *Ideology and Discontent* (New York: The Free Press, 1964), p. 210.

4. Ibid., p. 240.

5. Murray Edelman, *The Symbolic Uses of Politics* (Urbana: University of Illinois Press, 1964), pp. 171–172.

6. Seymour Martin Lipset and Earl Raab, "The Election and the National Mood," *Commentary* 55(January 1973):44.

7. Edelman, *The Symbolic Uses of Politics*, p. 172.

8. Ibid., p. 172.

9. Marshall McLuhan, *Understanding Media: The Extensions of Man* (New York: McGraw-Hill, 1964), pp. 276, 280.

10. Kenneth Prewitt, "Political Ambitions, Volunteerism, and Electoral Accountability," *American Political Science Review* 64(March 1970):9.

11. Joe McGinniss, *The Selling of the President* (New York: Trident Press, 1969), pp. 39, 40.

12. *Congressional Quarterly Weekly Report*, July 31, 1976, p. 2306.

13. Ibid., p. 58.

14. *Buckley* v. *Valeo* (1976).

15. Trippett, "The Shape of Things," p. 25.

16. Penn Kimball, *The Disconnected* (New York: Columbia University Press, 1972), p. 17.

17. John Gardner, Common Cause *Report from Washington*, 1, No. 1(November 1970).

18. *Washington Post*, November 11, 1976, p. A22.

19. V. O. Key, Jr., *The Responsible Electorate* (Cambridge, Mass.: Harvard University Press, 1966), pp. 9–28.

20. Norman H. Nie, et al., *The Changing American Voter* (Cambridge, Mass.: Harvard University Press, 1976), chapters 4–6, 8–10, and 12–14.

21. *Washington Post*, July 30, 1976, p. A9.

22. Walter Lippmann, *The Phantom Public* (New York: Harcourt Brace Jovanovich, 1927), pp. 54–62.

23. Seymour M. Lipset, "Working-Class Authoritarianism," in Seymour M. Lipset, *Political Man* (New York: Doubleday, 1960), pp. 97–130.

24. Edelman, *The Symbolic Uses of Politics*, p. 17.

25. *Washington Post*, November 11, 1976, p. A22.

26. John Stuart Mill, *Considerations of Representative Government* (Chicago: Henry Regnery, Gateway Edition, 1962), p. 144.

27. Gerald Pomper, *Elections in America: Control and Influence in Democratic Politics* (New York: Dodd, Mead, 1968), pp. 255–256.

28. Ibid., pp. 254–255.

29. Wallace S. Sayre and Judith L. Parris, *Voting for President* (Washington, D. C.: The Brookings Institution, 1970), pp. 150–151.

Recommended Rebuttal Reading

On Voting

Campbell, Angus, et al. *The American Voter.* New York: John Wiley, 1960.

Converse, Philip E. "Change in the American Electorate," in *The Human Meaning of Social Change*, eds. Angus Campbell and Philip E. Converse. New York: Russell Sage Foundation, 1972.

Converse, Philip E., et al. "Continuity and Change in American Politics: Parties and Issues in the 1968 Election." *American Political Science Review* 69 (December 1969).

———. "Electoral Myth and Reality: The 1964 Election." *American Political Science Review* 75(June 1975).

McClosky, Herbert. "Issue Conflict and Consensus Among Party Leaders and Followers." *American Political Science Review* 60 (June 1960).

Miller, Arthur H., et al. "A Majority Party in Disarray: Political Polarization in the 1972 Election." *American Political Science Review* 76 (March 1976).

Nie, Norman H., Sidney Verba, and John R. Petrocik. *The Changing American Voter.* Cambridge, Mass.: Harvard University Press, 1976.

Popkin, Samuel L., et al. "Comment: What Have You Done for Me Lately? Toward an Investment Theory of Voting." *American Political Science Review* 76 (March 1976).

On Campaign Finance and Political Participation

Adamany, David. *Campaign Financing in America.* North Scituate, Mass.: Duxbury, 1972.

Alexander, Herbert E. *Financing the 1972 Election.* Lexington, Me.: Lexington Books, 1976.

——. *Money in Politics.* Washington, D. C.: Public Affairs Press, 1972.

——. *Financing Politics.* Washington, D.C.: Congressional Quarterly Press, 1976.

Tolchin, Martin, and Susan Tolchin. *To the Victor.* New York: Random House, 1971.

Verba, Sidney, and Norman H. Nie. *Participation in America: Political Democracy and Social Equality.* New York: Harper & Row, 1972.

General Reference

Berg, Larry L., Harlan Hahn, and John R. Schmidhauser. *Corruption in the American Political System.* Morristown, N. J.: General Learning Press, 1976.

Dunn, Delmar. *Financing Presidential Campaigns.* Washington, D. C.: The Brookings Institution, 1972.

Etzkowitz, Henry, and Peter Schwab. *Is America Necessary? Conservative, Liberal and Socialist Perspectives of United States Political Institutions.* St. Paul, Minn.: West, 1976.

Peter, Charles, and James Fellows, eds., *Inside the System.* New York: Praeger, 1976.

PART

THREE

ARE
POLICY
MAKERS
REALLY
EFFECTIVE?

RESOLVED THAT:
The Presidency Is Too Powerful

At Issue: Presidential Power

Has the American presidency become too powerful? Are there enough controls on presidential power? How much executive power can a democracy afford? Questions like these suggest that the presidency is too powerful. Others suggest the opposite. Does the presidential office have adequate powers to cope with the burdens placed on it? Are other branches of the government sufficiently responsive to presidential guidance in solving national problems?

Beneath these questions is the fundamental but unresolved issue: How much power should a president have? Many scholars and others have argued that presidential power should be broadly construed. This view has been held by most presidents. Theodore Roosevelt said:

I decline to adopt the view that what was imperatively necessary for the nation could not be done by the president unless he could find some specific authorization to do it. My belief was that it was not only his right but his duty to do anything that the needs of the nation demanded, unless such action was forbidden by the Constitution or by the laws. Under this interpretation of executive power I did and caused to be done many things not previously done by the president and the heads of departments. I did not usurp the power, but I did greatly broaden the use of executive power.[1]

Others have held a narrow view of the presidency, contending that the chief executive can exercise only those powers explicitly spelled out

We know what an election is in the United States for President of the Republic.... Every four years there springs from the vote created by the whole people a president over that great nation. I think the whole world offers no finer spectacle than this; it offers no higher dignity; and there is no greater object of ambition on the political stage on which men are permitted to move. You may point, if you will, to hereditary rulers, to crowns coming down through successive generations of the same family, to thrones based on prescription and conquest, to sceptres wielded over veteran legions and subject realms,—but to my mind there is nothing more worthy of reverence and obedience, and nothing more sacred, than the authority of the freely chosen magistrate of a great and free people; and if there be on earth and amongst men any divine right to govern, surely it rests with a ruler so chosen and so appointed.—*Clinton Rossiter*

301

in the Constitution or derived from laws passed pursuant to it. One of the classic statements of this position was made by William Howard Taft:

> The true view of the executive function is, as I conceive it, that the president can exercise no power which cannot be fairly and reasonably traced to some specific grant of power or justly implied and included within such express grant as proper and necessary to its exercise. Such specific grants must be either in the federal constitution or in the pursuance thereof. There is no undefined residuum of power which can be exercised which seems to him to be in the public interest.[2]

Most presidents can be placed in one of these two categories. In the twentieth century those holding the broad view have been Wilson, both Roosevelts, Truman, Kennedy, Johnson, and Nixon. Those adhering to the narrower view have been Taft, Harding, Coolidge, Hoover, and Eisenhower.

What of the Constitution itself? As in many other instances, its provisions on presidential power represent a compromise among those at the Convention. At one extreme was Alexander Hamilton, who wanted a lifetime chief executive. At the other extreme were delegates who advocated a plural executive or wanted Congress to select the executive, as in the parliamentary system. There was no proposal even remotely suggesting a kingship. On the other hand, there was too much fear of a popularly chosen legislature not to have executive power substantial enough to check it.

Early advocates of a single, powerful executive were James Wilson and Gouverneur Morris; their camp was strengthened with the addition of the influential voice of James Madison. What emerged was a presidency consisting of one person, who would be independently elected to head the executive branch of government for a four-year term. Constitutionally, the scope of presidential power was restricted by the system of checks and balances built into the three branches of government. The precise definition of this power was left to history.

THE FUNCTIONS OF THE PRESIDENT

Article II of the Constitution deals with the five major functions of the president—head of state, chief executive, diplomatic leader, commander in chief, and legislative leader. In each of these constitutional functions, the president's power has increased enormously since the days of Washington. A sixth function, that of party chieftain, was not even envisioned by the framers of the Constitution.

In one day, a president may hold a state dinner as head of state; sign a bill into law as chief executive; order the movement of American troops as commander in chief; sign a treaty as a diplomatic leader; submit a bill to Congress as legislative leader; and deliver a campaign speech as party chieftain. This mere listing of presidential roles gives some idea of the awesome burden of the office. Harry Truman said: "The Presidency is a killing job—a six man job. ... It requires young men—young in physical and mental ability, if not necessarily young in age." [3] What does each of these major roles entail?

Head of State   In many democracies, such as Great Britain, there is a ceremonial national leader, the monarch, and a governmental leader, the prime minister. In the United States, both the ceremonial and governmental functions are combined in the president as head of state, who combines the mystique of monarchy with the power of political leadership.

As head of state, the president lays wreaths on the tomb of the unknown soldier, entertains visiting dignitaries, issues proclamations on holidays, presents awards, lights the White House Christmas tree, and throws out the first ball of the baseball season. These functions may appear trivial, but they have ceremonial value. Failure to perform them would offend many people; performing them well enhances a president's stature.

The symbolic, almost mystical, power of the presidency is revealed when a president dies in office. Even the death of a mediocre figure like Warren Harding brought an outpouring of grief, with the public turning out in droves merely to see the train carrying his body back to Ohio. The deaths of presidential giants like Abraham Lincoln and Franklin Roosevelt had an even greater impact. And anyone old enough to remember the assassination of John F. Kennedy in 1963 will not soon forget the sights and sounds of that November weekend. It is not surprising that a mere medical checkup for a president can affect the stock market.

Chief Executive   According to Article II of the Constitution, "The executive Power shall be vested in a President. ... [who] shall take Care that the Laws be faithfully executed." To assume the office of chief executive, one must be at least thirty-five years of age, fourteen years a resident of the United States, and a "natural-born" citizen. Administratively, of course, the president is responsible for seeing that the laws are "faithfully executed," which means that as chief executive the president not only signs bills into law, but he also implements them. For example, a law providing for additional federal judges would oblige the president to nominate persons to the judgeships.

The president has an annual taxable salary of $200,000, with an additional $50,000 for expenses (taxable) and $40,000 for travel expenses (tax free), together with a lifetime pension of $60,000 a year.

The president should obey and enforce the laws, leaving to the people the duty of correcting any errors committed by their representatives in Congress.—*Thomas Paine*

Richard M. Nixon epitomized the roles of head of state and chief executive. Detractors often referred to his tenure as the "imperial presidency" and criticized his concern with protocol and ceremony.

The chief executive wields power over a huge bureaucracy, including eleven cabinet departments, the Executive Office of the President, and more than fifty independent agencies,. boards, and commissions. He nominates or appoints people to fill upper echelon positions: the secretaries and other top personnel in the cabinet departments, members of the Executive Office of the President, and upper level executives in regulatory agencies. The principal statutory limitation on this broad power of appointment involves regulatory agencies; appointees must be representative of both major parties. (And, of course, once hired, they do not report to the president.) Senate confirmation of high-level presidential nominations or appointments is generally required except for most positions in the Executive Office of the President.

The president also has broad powers to remove officials. He can remove without cause anyone he has appointed, except for persons named to regulatory agencies.

Diplomatic Leader Article II also provides that the president "shall have Power, by and with the Advice and Consent of the Senate, to make Treaties, provided two thirds of the Senators present concur; and he shall nominate, and by and with the Advice and Consent of the Senate, shall appoint Ambassadors, other Public Ministers and Consuls." Inherent in this language is the president's role as diplomatic leader.

Although Congress plays an important part in foreign policy, the president has the upper hand because of his access to more information through the Department of State, the Pentagon, and the Central Intelligence Agency; and his ability to negotiate executive agreements. And, according to one observer, "Presidents prevail not only because they may have superior resources but because their potential opponents are weak, divided, or believe that they should not control foreign policy." [4]

As diplomatic leader, the president also has sole power to recognize foreign governments, a power that gives him substantial leverage in executing American foreign policy. One far-reaching instance of diplomatic recognition occurred in 1933 when Franklin Roosevelt recognized the Soviet Union, sixteen years after the Russian Revolution. Another occurred in 1972 when Nixon's historic trip to Peking precipitated a new era of diplomatic contacts between the United States and China.

Our president must always henceforth be one of the great powers of the world, whether he act greatly and wisely or not.
. . . We have not begun to see the presidential office in this light, but it is the light which will more and more beat upon it.
. . . We can never hide our president again as a mere domestic officer.—*Woodrow Wilson*

The presidential role of diplomatic leader was especially important at the end of World War II as heads of states gathered to negotiate peace treaties. Here U.S. President Harry S Truman (center) meets with Britain's Prime Minister Clement R. Atlee (left) and the USSR's Generalissimo Joseph Stalin at the Berlin Conference in August 1945.

The president's function as commander in chief of the armed forces is, of course, a vital one during wartime. Here President Franklin D. Roosevelt (in white shirt) *plans strategy with leaders of the army and navy during World War II.*

Commander in Chief An important principle of American government, civilian supremacy over the military, finds its constitutional basis in Article II, Section 2, which says that "the President shall be Commander in Chief of the Army and Navy of the United States." The president's power as commander in chief of the armed forces was perhaps most dramatically illustrated by Truman's firing of General MacArthur during the Korean War.

Other examples indicate further the broad ramifications of this prerogative:

● Truman's order to drop the atomic bomb on Hiroshima and Nagasaki in 1945;
● Truman's decision to commit troops in the Korean War;
● Kennedy's authorization of the Bay of Pigs invasion of Cuba;
● Johnson's personal approval of bombing targets during the Vietnam war;

● Nixon's decisions to bomb Cambodia in secret in 1969, to send American troops into Cambodia in 1970, to bomb North Vietnam and to mine its seaports in 1972, and to bomb Cambodia once again in 1973.

Perhaps the most ominous reminder of the president's role as commander in chief is the locked briefcase sometimes called the "black box" or "football." This briefcase, always kept near the president, contains the coded orders he would need in order to authorize nuclear retaliation.

Legislative Leader   Article II, Section 3, reads in part that the president "shall from time to time give to the Congress Information of the State of the Union, and recommend to their Consideration such Measures as he shall judge necessary and expedient." The president's function as legislative leader has evolved into one of his principal sources of power, though this did not happen until this century.

The initial step to dramatize the president's legislative role occurred when Woodrow Wilson became the first president in modern times to deliver his State of the Union messages to Congress personally. He and his predecessor, Theodore Roosevelt, also developed legislative

During the past century the president's role of legislative leader has evolved into a major source of power. Here President Dwight D. Eisenhower addresses a joint session of Congress in February 1953. Richard M. Nixon, then vice-president, is seated behind Eisenhower.

programs for congressional action. The second step was the requirement, adopted after World War II, that the president submit an annual budget message as well as an annual economic message. The practice of submitting a detailed legislative program to Congress also began after World War II.

Now, by commanding prime television time to deliver these addresses on all networks, presidents communicate their legislative ideas not only to Congress, but also to the American public. Voters can be mobilized on behalf of the president's program as its specific components are submitted to Congress in special follow-up legislative messages.

The president's legislative power, however, does not end here. He also has a highly trained group of skilled legislative technicians who monitor the flow of legislation through the Congress on a day-by-day basis. The congressional liaison office, another post-World War II phenomenon, helps make the president not only the chief legislator, but also the chief lobbyist in Washington.

The Constitution also gives the president the power to *veto* (refuse to sign) bills passed by Congress; Congress can override an ordinary veto by a two-thirds vote in each house. Another presidential weapon is the *pocket veto*, by which a bill is automatically vetoed if the president chooses to take no action on it within a ten-day period while Congress is adjourned. Since with a pocket veto the president does not return the bill to Congress, the latter has no opportunity to override it. As shown in Table 1, only about 3 percent of all presidential vetoes have been overridden by Congress. As a result, a veto threat alone is generally sufficient to force Congress to modify legislation to accommodate the president's wishes.

Other constitutional powers allow the president to adjourn Congress if the House and Senate disagree about when to do so (a power no president has ever exercised), and to call Congress into special session. Although seldom used, the power to call a special session can be a great advantage to a president. When Truman called Congress into special session in 1948 to act on his legislative proposals, the Republican majority failed to give him what he wanted. In his presidential campaign that year, Truman attacked the "do nothing" Congress, a political stratagem that many credit as the main reason for his unexpected election victory.

Theoretically, Congress cannot delegate legislative authority to the president. Practically, however, the chief executive can establish guidelines through administrative law that will implement and enforce acts of Congress (see page 353); critics contend that this gives him substantial legislative authority. In addition, Congress has granted the presi-

Table 1. Presidential Vetoes, 1789–1975*

	REGULAR	POCKET	TOTAL	OVERRIDDEN	SUSTAINED
Washington	2	—	2	—	
Madison	5	2	7	—	
Monroe	1	—	1	—	
Jackson	5	7	12	—	
Tyler	6	3	9	1	
Polk	2	1	3	—	
Pierce	9	—	9	5	
Buchanan	4	3	7	—	
Lincoln	2	4	6	—	
A. Johnson	21	8	29	15	
Grant	45	49	94	4	
Hayes	12	1	13	1	
Arthur	4	8	12	1	
Cleveland	304	109	413	2	
Harrison	19	25	44	1	
Cleveland	43	127	170	5	
McKinley	6	36	42	—	
T. Roosevelt	42	40	82	1	
Taft	30	9	39	1	
Wilson	33	11	44	6	38
Harding	5	1	6	—	6
Coolidge	20	30	50	4	46
Hoover	21	16	37	3	34
F. Roosevelt	372	261	633	9	626
Truman	180	70	250	12	238
Eisenhower	73	108	181	2	179
Kennedy	11	9	21	—	21
L. Johnson	16	14	30	—	30
Nixon	24	16	40	4	15
Ford	53	11	42	13	10
Total	1370	979	2328	90	1243
Average	45.67	36.26	77.60	4.74	113.00

*Lists only Presidents vetoing bills.

Source: U. S. Bureau of the Census, *Statistical Abstract of the United States: 1971* (Washington, D. C., 1971), p. 356. Congressional Quarterly, *Annual* (1972–1976).

dent the power to restructure the executive departments and agencies; if one house of the Congress does not disapprove such a reorganization plan within sixty days, it becomes effective.

Electioneering for the presidency has spread its contagion to the President himself, to his now only competitor, to his immediate predecessor. . . . The principal leaders of the political parties are travelling about the country . . . and holding forth, like Methodist preachers, hour after hour to assembled multitudes under the canopy of heaven.—*John Quincy Adams*

Party Chieftain　Of the six major functions of the president, that of party chieftain is the only one not mentioned in the Constitution, yet in some respects it is the most important. No president has ever been elected without first obtaining support of his party. After being nominated, it is customary for a presidential candidate to name his own national party chairman; if the candidate is elected, he thus continues to control most, if not all, of his party's affairs.

Beyond being nominated and elected through the party process, a president also relies on his party to obtain support in Congress and among state governors. A president who commands overwhelming support among his party in Congress, as did Lyndon Johnson, can impose major changes in national policy. On the other hand, a president who lacks such support, like Kennedy, may have difficulty pushing through major or innovative legislation. The same is true of presidents whose party is in the minority in Congress, such as was true with Nixon.

A president becomes the nation's foremost political figure whether he likes it or not. It is a role he cannot shirk. Teddy Roosevelt pro-

Although the presidential function of party leader is not mentioned in the Constitution, it is vital to an effective presidency. John F. Kennedy often had difficulty getting Congress to pass important legislation because he lacked strong support among fellow Democrats in Congress.

claimed, "No President has ever enjoyed himself as much as I have enjoyed myself." [5] Not so Dwight Eisenhower, who announced flatly, "I do not like politics." [6] As the principal spokesman for his party, the president plays an important role in mobilizing the opinion of party members. Of course he has no assurance of total support from them, but they will usually form a solid foundation on which he can build a wider consensus.

Perhaps more than any other president—certainly more than any other modern president—Franklin Roosevelt utilized each of the presidential functions to maximum advantage. For this reason political scientist Richard Neustadt regards him as a prime example of how a president should use his power.

> Roosevelt's methods were the product of his insights, his incentives, and his confidence. No president in this century has had a sharper sense of personal power, a sense of what it is and where it comes from; none has had more hunger for it, few have had more use for it, and only one or two could match his faith in his own competence to use it. Perception and desire and self-confidence, combined, produced their own reward. No modern president has been more nearly master in the White House. [7]

ORGANIZATIONAL STRUCTURE

Presidential power is exercised through a complex structure of subordinate offices: the independent agencies (discussed in Chapter 10), the twelve executive departments, and the Executive Office of the President (see Figure 1). The total executive structure employs nearly 5 million persons, including military personnel.

Before examining the organizational structure of the presidency, we should make note of an office that does not even appear on the organizational chart, that of vice-president. A vice-president, whose only constitutional duty is to preside over the Senate, is generally chosen for political reasons. Kennedy, for example, chose Johnson, a Protestant and southerner, to balance his own Roman Catholic, northern background. As a result, vice-presidents do not necessarily bring with them administrative skill or experience. Moreover, vice-presidents typically have their own political ambitions, which may not be consistent with the president's.

It is natural, then, that few chief executives have given their vice-presidents much more than ceremonial functions. Richard Nixon, as Eisenhower's vice-president, did assume more substantial duties, being sent on a variety of foreign affairs missions. Eisenhower admitted late in his administration, however, that Nixon knew little about the day-to-day operations of the presidency. Even so, the Nixon vice-presidency may well be regarded as a watershed. Each vice-president since then—

FIG. 1. Executive Branch of the United States Government*

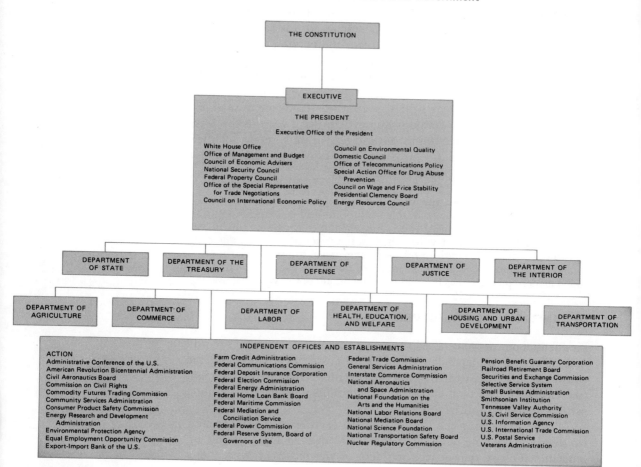

*Partial listing only. (The Department of Energy was added in 1977.)

SOURCE: *U. S. Government Manual*, 1975-76, p. 21.

Lyndon Johnson, Hubert Humphrey, Spiro Agnew, Gerald Ford, Nelson Rockefeller, and Walter Mondale—has been assigned at least a few important functions. It is perhaps significant that since 1952, when Nixon was elected vice-president, only Agnew and Rockefeller never received their party's nomination for president. Three of the six—Nixon, Johnson, and Ford—served as president. Walter Mondale appears to be the beneficiary of three decades of increasing responsibility for vice-presidents. Under President Carter, Mondale seems to have been given the most significant role to date in policy development and implementation.

The Cabinet The *cabinet* includes the vice-president and the head of each executive department. Beginning with the Departments of State and Treasury in 1789, the cabinet has generally grown in response to societal pressures and problems. It mirrors to some degree the growth of the United States itself. Westward expansion led to creation of the Department of the Interior in 1849; housing problems in the twentieth century resulted in a new Department of Housing and Urban Development, formed in 1965 (see Table 2). In 1977 Congress created a new Department of Energy to coordinate the principal energy functions of the executive branch. This new department combines functions and powers formerly held by the Federal Energy Administration (FEA), the Federal Power Commission (FPC), and the Energy Research and Development Administration (ERDA). It also inherits certain functions from the Departments of Housing and Urban Development, Commerce, Defense, and Interior as well as from the Interstate Commerce Commission (ICC).

The cabinet, as a body of advisers, exists for the president to utilize as he sees fit. He is not required by law to hold cabinet meetings. (For information on how the executive departments function, see Chapter 10.)

Table 2. Creation of Executive Departments

1789	State
1789	Treasury
1849	Interior
1870	Justice[1]
1889	Agriculture[2]
1913	Commerce[3]
1913	Labor[3]
1947	Defense[4]
1953	Health, Education, and Welfare
1965	Housing and Urban Development
1966	Transportation
1977	Energy

The office of Postmaster General, created in 1789, received cabinet rank in 1829 and was made a cabinet department in 1872. In 1970 Congress abolished the Post Office as a cabinet department and replaced it with the United States Postal Service, an independent federal agency.

[1] The office of Attorney General, created in 1789, became the Department of Justice in 1870.
[2] Originally created in 1862; made an executive department in 1889.
[3] The Department of Commerce and Labor, created in 1903, was divided into two separate departments in 1913.
[4] The Department of War (the Army), created in 1789, and the Department of Navy, created in 1798, were consolidated along with the Air Force under the Department of Defense in 1949.

Reproduced by permission of Harcourt Brace Jovanovich, Inc. from *Democracy Under Pressure*, 2nd ed., by Cummings and Wise, copyright © 1971, 1974, by Harcourt Brace Jovanovich, Inc.

The Executive Office of the President   As government became bigger during the New Deal, questions arose about the president's ability to manage and administer an ever-growing bureaucracy. A study commissioned in the late 1930s determined that "the president needs help." [8] The answer was the creation of the Executive Office of the President, the staff arm of the presidency.

Like the cabinet, the Executive Office has grown in response to national problems. In the mid-1970s it had sixteen members (see Figure 2). The six principal components are the White House Office, the National Security Council, the Central Intelligence Agency, the Domestic Council, the Office of Management and Budget, and the Council of Economic Advisers.

The White House Office   Personal presidential assistants have had an enormous impact on American history through the years—Wilson's Colonel House, Franklin Roosevelt's Harry Hopkins, Eisenhower's Sherman Adams, Kennedy's Theodore Sorenson, Johnson's Bill Moyers, and Nixon's Robert Haldeman and John Ehrlichman. The authority of such men flows from that of the president; they hold their positions at his pleasure, and their purpose is to help the president coordinate and administer the executive branch.

The power of the White House staff has been dramatized in recent years by Henry Kissinger, who served as foreign policy adviser to Nixon and later as secretary of state to both Nixon and Ford. As foreign policy adviser he was generally regarded as having more power than Secretary of State William Rogers.

The National Security Council   This council, created pursuant to the National Security Act of 1947, includes the president, vice-president, the secretaries of state and defense, and the director of the Office of Emergency Preparedness. When Kissinger served as staff director of NSC, it was this position that represented the fulcrum of power.

The National Security Council coordinates day-to-day security policy and administers crises as well. Its meetings were the focus of national attention during the Cuban missile crisis of 1962. President Kennedy established the so-called Executive Committee of the National Security Council; ExComm—some sixteen top officials and advisers in the foreign, military, and intelligence fields—met every day to help resolve the emergency.

The Central Intelligence Agency   A product of the post-World War II era, the CIA is one of several executive agencies gathering intelligence. The CIA's intelligence function is theoretically confined to overseas operations, but during the Watergate episode, congressional hearings revealed that it had exceeded its mandate and had become involved in domestic intelligence work.

FIG. 2. Executive Office of the President

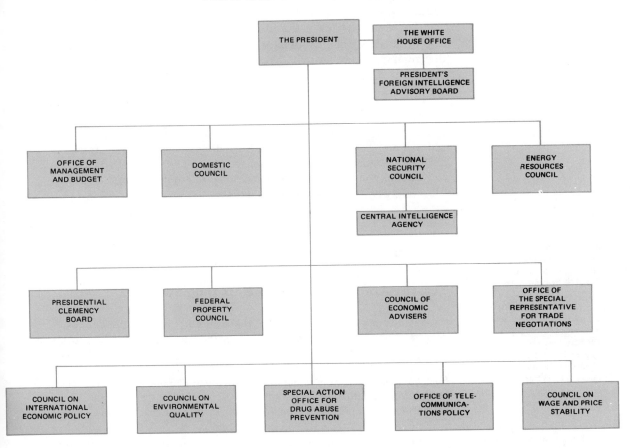

SOURCE: *U. S. Government Manual*, 1975-76, p. 80.

The Domestic Council Planned as the domestic counterpart of the National Security Council, the Domestic Council has never attained comparable power. Merely an advisory body, it has at best only coordinating authority. Most of its members, such as the secretaries of agriculture and transportation, belong to the cabinet as well, and it is in that capacity that they carry out Domestic Council recommendations.

The Office of Management and Budget Formerly the Bureau of the Budget in the Treasury Department, the OMB has two principal tasks—preparing the federal budget (its original function) and assisting the president with his management chores (a function added by Nixon).

The Council of Economic Advisers This council was created to help combat post-World War II economic problems. It advises the president on such matters as wage and price controls, taxes, spending, and unemployment.

These summaries of the functions of the president and the structure of his department provide a broad outline of the office. The question remains, however, whether the roles and structure have provided presidents with too much power.

- Is it wise, much less realistic, to reduce presidential power?
- If presidential power should be limited, how could this purpose be accomplished?
- Have the events surrounding the Watergate scandal downgraded the presidency too much?

The Affirmative Case

Yes, the American presidency is too powerful.

Those who tried to warn us back at the beginnings of the New Deal of the dangers of one-man rule that lay ahead on the path we were taking toward strong, centralized government may not have been so wrong. . . . The presidency—by nature remote from the people, monolithic in structure and with a huge bureaucracy at its command—is the one branch most in danger of degenerating into dictatorship. Especially in these days of vast governmental controls over and interference in the lives of our citizens.[9]–Senator Alan Cranston

It is now almost taken for granted that too much power rests in the presidential office. Senator Cranston's fears are shared by many, for a variety of reasons:

- The presidency has expanded out of all reasonable proportions.
- Excessive presidential power may be dangerous.
- Attempts to limit the presidency have had little success.
- It is all but impossible to remove a president from office.
- Only reforms of the presidency can remedy the situation.

EXPANSION OF POWER

Domestic and foreign crises, the weakening of Congress, a changing society, and the chief executives themselves have all served to enlarge presidential power. No longer can one man oversee the entire govern-

We hear praise of a power-wielding, arm-twisting president who "gets his program through Congress" by knowing the use of power.

Throughout the course of history, there have been many other such wielders of power. There have even been dictators who regularly held plebiscites, in which their dictatorships were approved by an Ivory-soap-like percentage of the electorate. But their countries were not free, nor can any country remain free under such despotic power.

Some of the current worship of powerful executives may come from those who admire strength and accomplishment of any sort. Others hail the display of presidential strength . . . simply because they approve of the *result* reached by the use of power. This is nothing less than the totalitarian philosophy that the end justifies the means. . . . If ever there was a philosophy of government totally at war with that of the Founding Fathers, it is this one.

To be a constitutionalist, it is at least as important that the use of power be legitimate as that it be beneficial.—*Barry Goldwater*

NEWS ITEM: *TRUMAN REQUESTS MORE POWERS*

Chicago Tribune-Chicago Historical Society

ment. With some 2.5 million civilian employees, almost as many armed forces personnel, and a budget of some $400 billion, the executive establishment is gigantic indeed. How did it get so big?

Domestic Crises   The Civil War offers a prime example of how presidential power grew to resolve a domestic crisis:

> Unquestionably, the high-water mark of the exercise of the executive power in the United States is found in the administration of Abraham Lincoln. No President before or since has pushed about the degrees of executive power so far into the legislative sphere. . . . Under the war power he proclaimed the slaves of those in rebellion emancipated. He devised and put into execution his peculiar plan of reconstruction. With dis-

regard of law he increased the army and navy beyond the limits set by statute. The privilege of the writ of habeas corpus was suspended wholesale and martial law declared. Public money in the sum of millions was deliberately spent without congressional appropriation. Nor was any of this done innocently. Lincoln understood his Constitution. He knew, in many cases, just how he was transgressing, and his infractions were consequently deliberate. It is all the more astonishing that his audacity was the work of a minority president performed in the presence of a bitter congressional opposition even in his own party.[10]

Another watershed in domestic policy making was the crisis of the Great Depression and the measures taken to overcome its effects. Many would agree with the scholar who noted that the New Deal created "social acceptance of the idea that government should be active and reformist, rather than simply protective of the established order of things." [11] Thus today the executive establishment, under presidential leadership, has been granted broad powers to solve problems in race relations, health care, education, and a host of other fields.

Foreign Crises   In the aftermath of World War II, the United States played a more active role in world affairs than ever before. For the first time in its history, the country maintained a large peacetime army. It formed a variety of alliances, among them the North Atlantic Treaty Organization (NATO) and the Southeast Asia Treaty Organization (SEATO). Foreign projects grew out of the Truman Doctrine and the Marshall Plan. All these programs originated with the president, who was also responsible for their overall direction. Their essential purpose was to assist American allies in containing communism. As a result, the American president, head of state of one of the two most powerful countries, became leader of the "free world" nations and thus an international figure with far-reaching influence.

Crises like the Berlin blockade of 1948–1949, the Korean War, the Lebanon landing of 1958, the Bay of Pigs invasion, and the Cuban missile crisis further aggrandized presidential power. Presidents have ranged widely in foreign affairs, broadly interpreting treaty commitments and the president's power as commander in chief, and confident that they are better informed than anyone else. (Not for nothing are Lyndon Johnson's memoirs called *The Vantage Point.*)

With the escalation of presidential power in international affairs, foreign policy making has tended to overshadow domestic policy making. "Foreign policy concerns tend to drive out domestic policy," notes one observer. "Once, when trying to talk to President Kennedy about natural resources, Secretary of the Interior Stewart Udall remarked, 'He's imprisoned by Berlin.' " [12] One reason for the dominance of international affairs in the presidential calendar is the interrelationship of events in different parts of the world. A mistake in Vietnam could have disastrous effects on American policy toward China, for example. Another reason is the speed with which such events can move. A president must devote extraordinary time and energy just to keep abreast of them.

Congressional Capitulation Congress, intended by the framers of the Constitution to be the most powerful of the three branches of government, has increasingly during the twentieth century yielded power to the president. Even if the pendulum now swings back, it is highly unlikely that the balance will ever revert to what it was before. The president, to put it bluntly, can use his power to keep his power.

The president commands levers of power in both foreign and domestic matters that allow the Congress no alternative except to follow his leadership. For one thing, he controls management and budgeting. For another, he has thousands of specialized administrators on whom he can call for help, as contrasted with Congress' rather anemic resources in such areas. It should be pointed out that almost all major legislation approved by Congress has received its major boost from the president and that few pieces of legislation become law without presidential approval.

Congresssional capitulation occurred because Congress, seeking solutions to problems, took the easy way out by simply extending to the president broad grants of authority. One of the standard jokes about Franklin Roosevelt's first hundred days in office was that a representative stood on the floor of the House waving a blank piece of paper, which he claimed was a bill that the president wanted in his New Deal program; the House passed it. During the heyday of Lyndon Johnson's Great Society, both the Speaker of the House, John McCormack, and the chairman of the Education and Labor Committee, Adam Clayton Powell, took the floor to say that Johnson did not want any changes in the Elementary and Secondary Education Act. Except for one minor change, the bill passed the House of Representatives as the president wanted it.

Social and Technological Changes In coping with the social tensions of modern America, the logical place to look for help became the presidency and the courts. It is easier to identify with a single individual than with the judiciary or a Congress of 535 members. For instance, black Americans have looked primarily to the presidency and the courts for relief of their grievances. It was easier and quicker to move the president and the courts as levers of governmental power than a rural- and southern-dominated Congress. In addition, presidents—especially liberal Democrats—turned to such minority groups in building coalitions to win presidential elections.

Even American technology has helped increase presidential power. The executive has made maximum use of highly centralized information and communications mechanisms, such as computers, while Congress and the courts have been slow to take advantage of such devices. Especially in a crisis, it is obvious that obtaining and controlling information becomes a formidable tool of power.

The mass media have been powerful forces in making the president larger than life. Television, newspapers, and magazines try to cover his every move, revealing even his personal habits and idiosyncrasies. This magnification of the president's image affects the national mood and shapes the times, to the extent of causing fluctuations in the stock market. And, with access to prime television time on request, a president has the means to influence vast numbers of people in a way that no other public official can.

All presidents start out pretending to run a crusade, but after a couple of years they find they are running something much less heroic, much more intractable: namely, the presidency.—*Alistair Cooke*

Presidential Initiative   No assessment of the expansion of presidential power would be complete without mentioning the role of presidents themselves. Most of those in the modern era have had a rather aggressive attitude toward their role. Woodrow Wilson said that the president's office is "anything he has the sagacity and force to make it. . . . The President is at liberty, both in law and conscience, to be as big a man as he can." [13] Kennedy stated boldly that the president "must be prepared to exercise the fullest powers of his office—all that are specified and some that are not." [14]

Presidents have forged power for themselves by force of personal philosophy and will, engaging in new activities and venturing into uncharted terrain. Like a snowball going downhill, their power has been increased by sheer momentum.

DANGERS, REAL AND POTENTIAL

The previous discussion has suggested some of the disadvantages of a presidency bloated with power: a chief executive distracted from domestic problems by foreign concerns; an imbalance in the governmental system, with a weakened Congress trying vainly to recover lost authority; and an unhealthy reliance on a larger-than-life executive to solve all the nation's ills. There are other dangers as well, including unrealistic hero worship, undue influence by special interests, and hasty—possibly unconstitutional—interference in the affairs of foreign nations.

Man or Superman?

Alexander Hamilton himself, who wanted a strong executive, said that the president could not become a monarch "decorated with attributes superior in dignity and splendor to those of the king of Great Britain ... with the diadem sparkling in his brow and the imperial purple flowing in his train ... seated on a throne surrounded with minions and mistresses, giving audience to the envoys of foreign potentates, in all the supercilious pomp of majesty." [15] In many respects, Hamilton was wrong.

Several hyperbolic statements about the presidency indicate the veneration in which the office has been held. According to one, the president is the "great engine of democracy." Another states that the president is the "American people's one authentic trumpet." A third extols presidential government as "a superb planning institution," while a fourth reverently declares that the White House "is the pulpit of the nation and the president is its chaplain." [16]

Americans have placed the president on a pedestal of power far above what the Founders ever intended or imagined. They have invested the president with almost supernatural qualities. In the words of Woodrow Wilson:

> The nation as a whole has chosen him, and is conscious that it has no other political spokesman. His is the only national voice in affairs. Let him once win the admiration and confidence of the country, and no other single force can withstand him, no combination of forces will easily overpower him. His position takes the imagination of the country. He is the representative of no constituency, but of the whole people. When he speaks in his true character, he speaks for no special interest. If he rightly interprets the national thought and boldly insists upon it, he is irresistible; and the country never feels the zest for action so much as when its President is of such insight and calibre.[17]

This reverential attitude can have negative consequences. With so much power committed to one person, the risk of failure is too great. If he fails, we all fail. If Watergate had been looked on as a failure of one man and less as a failure of the presidential office, the whole affair could probably have been resolved in a shorter period of time. However, because of the public's presidential attachment and worship, there was extreme reluctance to act against Richard Nixon, since the man and the office are so closely linked in the public's mind.

Second, there is the "big daddy" or "father knows best" syndrome, with the president looking on the people like children. Indeed Nixon said that "the average American is just like the child in the family."[18] And a third is the "king and his court" syndrome, with the president growing increasingly out of touch with American life.

> The President, needing "access to reality" in order to govern effectively, too often has access, instead, only to a self-serving court of flunkeys, knights, earls, and dukes in business suits, whose best chances of advancing their separate fortunes usually lie in diverting reality before it can reach the President. The result is a dangerous presidential isolation, which may be compounded in its peril because court life works to persuade the President that he is more closely in touch with reality than anyone else in the realm.[19]

The Role of Special Interests   Those who become presidents have made compromises to gain the votes necessary for nomination and election. They are captives of their compromises; their power is exercised on behalf of those who helped them become president. As a result, a president's power tends to be used only in one way—to protect the interests that gained him his election. Primary among these are the rich corporations that control such a large share of American wealth. Some may think of the president as being more responsive to the needs of the poor and downtrodden, but this is not true. Even Kennedy, considered a champion of the have-nots in American society, capitulated to the special interests. According to one writer, "In every significant area—wage policy, tax policy, international trade and finance, federal spending—the

President showed a keen understanding and ready response to the essential corporate program." [20]

To make a successful bid for the presidency, candidates have to obtain enormous sums of money or other aid from the corporate elites, who can thus buy the soul of their candidate. As has been pointed out, campaign contributions by special interests (discussed in Chapter 7) and individuals (discussed in Chapter 8) create obligations which are honored in one way or another after a candidate's victory.

Foreign Intervention   Since World War II, American presidents have increasingly involved the United States in overseas entanglements. They have done so through the two chief means: executive agreements and unilateral military action.

It would appear from a reading of the Constitution that its framers intended that the United States establish relationships with other nations only by treaty, which requires Senate ratification. If so, their intention has been subverted; executive agreements between a president and another nation are now much more common than treaties (see Table 3). Some of the foremost examples of executive agreements are the Atlantic Charter of 1941, the Yalta Agreement of 1944, and the Potsdam Agreement in 1945—all of which established major portions of American foreign policy during World War II.

Table 3. Treaties and Executive Agreements: 1940–1945 and 1963–1968

YEAR	TREATIES	EXECUTIVE AGREEMENTS
1940	12	20
1941	15	39
1942	6	52
1943	4	71
1944	1	74
1945	6	54
1963	9	248
1964	13	231
1965	5	197
1966	10	242
1967	10	218
1968	57	266

Source: Hans J. Morgenthau, "Congress and Foreign Policy," *The New Republic*, June 14, 1969, p. 18. Reprinted by permission of *The New Republic*, ©1969, The New Republic, Inc.

The president, as commander in chief, has all the American military establishment at his disposal. And he uses it. As early as the Korean War, President Truman gave congressional leaders only perfunctory notice of his intentions just moments before he publicly announced his decision to commit troops. At least five times in the past fifteen years, presidents have militarily intervened in foreign countries without previously consulting with Congress: the Bay of Pigs, the invasion of the Dominican Republic, and the attacks on North Vietnam, Cambodia, and Laos. It is questionable if any of these incidents was really an emergency.

When public outcry against the Vietnam war became intense, congressional leaders tried to recoup their lost leadership and power in international crises. The Constitution gives Congress the power to declare war; from this it would seem to follow that presidential deployment of troops without a declaration of war is unconstitutional. Such may not be the case.

> [This presidential power] is not patently unconstitutional. There is nothing in the Constitution that says that the President may not *wage war abroad at his discretion.* The Constitution merely states that only Congress can "declare" war. But it does not say that a war has to be "declared" before it can be waged.
>
>   Vietnam is the culmination of this long-accumulating executive power in the military domain. Where it differs from preceding presidential commitments of armed forces abroad without war declaration is in scale—in numbers of troops committed, worldwide consequences, and soaring casualties. There is obviously a considerable difference between the three small frigates and one sloop of war that Jefferson dispatched against the Barbary pirates in 1801, and the current deployment [of half a million men] in Vietnam. However, the principle of presidential discretion in the use of force abroad remains the same [emphasis supplied].[21]

Whether or not such presidential discretion is constitutional, the fact remains that it gives the chief executive enormous resources.

Much has already been said to suggest that the American people have contributed greatly to the rise of presidential power. In his conduct of foreign affairs, the president may be hasty or aggressive, not out of mere whim, but out of a sense of responsibility to the electorate. Historian Henry Steele Commager notes:

> Abuse of power by presidents is a reflection, and perhaps a consequence, of abuse of power by the American people and nation. . . .
>
>   As we have greater power than any other nation, so we should display greater moderation in using it and greater humility in justifying it. . . . In the long run, the abuse of the executive power cannot be separated from the abuse of national power.[22]

ARE LIMITS POSSIBLE?

Until recent years, the American intellectual community has generally praised strong presidents. It has admired men like Lincoln, the Roosevelts, and Truman, and scorned such weak presidents as Coolidge, Hoover, and Eisenhower, During the 1950s conservatives sought to curtail the president's power in foreign affairs through the Bricker Amendment (named after Senator John Bricker of Ohio); it would have curbed the president's treaty-making power and also given Congress control over executive agreements. Advocates of a strong presidency prevailed, and the Bricker Amendment failed to get the necessary two-thirds approval in the Senate, though by only one vote.

In 1960 political scientist Richard Neustadt published a book, *Presidential Power*, in which he admonished presidents to conduct themselves in ways that would maximize their power.[23] Americans were taught that the president, the only official elected by all the people, would use his authority to "do good."

Then, in quick succession, two presidents challenged almost everything the liberal intellectual community had been saying about a strong presidency. First came Lyndon Johnson and the Vietnam war. Next it was Richard Nixon and Watergate. As a result, serious questions were asked about the advisability of a strong presidency. In the words of George McGovern: "Many of us in the Congress understood how Dr. Frankenstein must have felt when *his* creation ran amok."[24] Steps were taken to limit the presidency in the areas of foreign affairs and executive privilege—with dubious results.

Foreign Affairs   The principal challenge to presidential power in the field of foreign affairs was the War Powers Act of 1973. It was designed to prevent a president from committing troops for extended periods of time without the approval of Congress, and thus reassert congressional authority to declare war. The act has four main provisions:

1. If Congress has not declared war, military force may be committed to "situations where imminent involvement in hostilities is clearly indicated by circumstances" only to repel an armed attack on the United States or to forestall the "direct and imminent threat of such an attack"; to repel an armed attack on American armed forces outside the United States or forestall the threat of one; to protect American citizens in another country if their lives are threatened; or to carry out specific statutory authorization by Congress.
2. The president is to report promptly to Congress the commitment of forces for such purposes.

3. Forces may be committed for a period of up to sixty days unless Congress authorizes their continued use, or for an additional thirty days if the president certifies that the time is needed for their safe withdrawal.
4. Congress is authorized to terminate a presidential commitment by a concurrent resolution (which does not require presidential approval).

There is a very real doubt that this act decreased the power of the president in foreign affairs, despite what its proponents say. There are also questions about its constitutionality.

The president can commit troops for up to sixty days without congressional approval. If he takes this step, how can Congress force him to remove the troops, especially if he claims his action was made to protect the national interest and was based on his constitutional authority as commander in chief? Theoretically, Congress can cut off funds, but practically this is not a realistic alternative.

The War Powers Act may be unconstitutional. It has the effect of preempting the president's constitutional authority as commander in chief. (Constitutional law is superior to congressional statutes.) It also denies the president's constitutional right to act on legislation approved by Congress in that he cannot veto a war-powers resolution.

In the final analysis, it would appear that the War Powers Act, if it accomplished anything at all, merely strengthened the president's power to commit troops. This power could have been questioned more effectively if Congress had pitted its right to declare war against the president's right as commander in chief. Congress has now in effect given the president carte blanche to do what he wants for sixty days—during which time he may rally public support for his actions.

Executive Privilege First invoked against Congress by Washington in 1796, *executive privilege* is an assertion of the right of the president to withhold information, documents, or testimony from either Congress or the courts in the interest of national security or proper functioning of the executive branch. The president's right of executive privilege has also been extended to presidential advisers and cabinet members to insure that they can be completely candid in their conversations with the president.

The Constitution has no specific provisions dealing with executive privilege; it is a right predicated on the independence of the branches. Though invoked by presidents many times, the doctrine did not come under severe attack until the Watergate scandal when Nixon declined to give presidential tapes to either the courts or Congress. In the case of *United States* v. *Nixon* (1974), the Supreme Court unanimously ruled that executive privilege is constitutional, although it does not extend to criminal cases in which the public interest in a fair trial outweighs the necessity for presidential confidentiality. Thus executive privilege has been held constitutional, and even in the very limited area where it does not apply, we do not know what a strong president, unencumbered by a scandal like Watergate, might do if challenged. It would be difficult to imagine the Court employing sanctions against a president as strong and popular as Franklin Roosevelt if he utilized executive privilege as he chose.   *

The Budget   Although the Constitution gives Congress the "power of the purse," the president has had the upper hand in making budgets since the 1920s. Budgetary recommendations originate with executive departments and agencies, are channeled through the Office of Management and Budget, and are submitted to Congress in the president's budget message. Because of this one package backed by enormous research, the chief executive in effect takes the offensive, with Congress placed in the position of reacting to proposals.

The president also has another budgetary weapon at his disposal. This is *impoundment*—the refusal to spend certain funds appropriated by Congress in a given fiscal year. Before the twentieth century, only Jefferson and Grant made use of impoundment, but it has become more common since Franklin Roosevelt's time. Nixon practiced impoundment more freely than any of his predecessors, withholding millions of dollars from social-welfare programs of which he disapproved.

THE IRREMOVABLE OBJECT

Can a president be removed from office? It is almost impossible. The simplest way is through defeat in an election, but presidents have a way of being reelected. In this century, only three incumbents who ran for reelection have been defeated—Taft, Hoover, and Ford.

The Constitution provides that a president (and certain other federal officials) may be removed by *impeachment*. In this case the House of Representatives adopts an impeachment resolution (brings charges) by a majority vote; conviction requires a two-thirds vote in the Senate. The grounds are "Treason, Bribery, or other high Crimes and Misdemeanors." Only one president—Andrew Johnson, in 1868—has ever been impeached by the House and tried by the Senate. The Senate fell one vote short of conviction and he remained in office.

Congress has been reluctant to use impeachment, the only means it has for removing the highest official in the nation. There is a fear that the process might become a political weapon used by the opposition party to remove a president on slight provocation. Time is another factor. A Congress must be willing to commit a substantial amount of time and energy to the issue of impeachment, and to sacrifice other important business—as was shown in the case of Nixon. Nixon resigned before he was impeached, a move that undoubtedly avoided several months of agonizing debate in the Senate.

Not only is impeachment a laborious process, but, as spelled out in the Constitution, it is far from precise in its meaning and implications. Can a president be indicted by a court before he is impeached? Does the phrase "high crimes and misdemeanors" mean that a president can be impeached and convicted only for actual crimes, or may he be removed for serious abuses of the office that fall short of indictable crimes? Opinion is divided on both questions. The most commonly held view is that judges and other officials, including the vice-president, may be indicted and convicted in judicial proceedings before Congress impeaches. This view holds, however, that a president must first be impeached and removed before prosecution, lest the nation find itself with its president behind bars while still in office. As to the second question, several authorities feel that impeachable offenses should be limited to actual crimes, arguing that if a president can be impeached and convicted for something other than an actual crime, there is greater likelihood of his being removed for purely political reasons.

The result is that the president is almost completely safe from the prospect of removal by Congress, at least for his political actions. His power is enhanced because the means for removal, uncertain as it is, remains essentially unused.

What if a president becomes mentally ill while in office? The Twenty-fifth Amendment, ratified in 1967, provides that the vice-president will become acting president (a) if the president informs Congress in writing that he is unable to perform his duties; or (b) if the vice-president and a majority of the cabinet or some other congressionally created body make this decision. If the president should reclaim his office against the wishes of a majority of the cabinet, Congress has to vote (by a two-thirds majority of both houses) within three weeks to support the vice-president as chief executive. In essence, the balance of power rests with the president.

If the office of vice-president becomes vacant, the president nominates someone to fill the position—as Nixon nominated Ford, and as Ford nominated Nelson Rockefeller. When Rockefeller was designated, the nation had as its top two officials a president and a vice-president who had not been elected by the people. The extraordinary power in the hands of the president is obvious. Richard Nixon could name the man who would ultimately succeed (and later pardon) him. Gerald Ford in turn named the man to succeed him. The resemblance to a royal dynasty is disquieting.

REFORMING THE PRESIDENCY

Only by reforming the presidency can the executive office be restored to its proper role. Several alternatives are possible.

One possibility is a constitutional amendment allowing the president to serve only one six-year term. This would free the president to be president instead of spending so much time, energy, and money (at least in his first term) running for reelection. Power could be concentrated on constructive ends rather than on the pettiness of party politics.

Another possibility is a constitutional amendment allowing Congress a *vote of no confidence.* As in a parliamentary system, a new election would be called in which the incumbent president would have the right to run for reelection. Thus, the putrid air of an event like Watergate could be cleared without the extensive and counterproductive consequences of impeachment proceedings. People, in the election following a majority vote of no confidence, could remove a president (or restate their faith in him) without the storm clouds of impeachment hanging in the air.

A third alternative is a multiple executive, which could also be established by a constitutional amendment. It is obvious that too much power is now concentrated in one person, who cannot fulfill all of his duties properly and who often sacrifices domestic interests in concentrating on foreign policy. There could, for example, be one president for foreign affairs and another for domestic affairs. The concept of a multiple executive is not new. Many state governments have several statewide elected officials performing different functions. The multi-headed executive would reduce the concentration of power in the hands of one president.

A fourth alternative would be a new amendment to provide for an election when the vice-presidency falls vacant. This would prevent the awesome power of the presidency from being concentrated in the hands of one person who had never been popularly elected. Richard Nixon designated Gerald Ford to replace Spiro Agnew as vice-president, and Ford, upon becoming president, named Nelson Rockefeller to replace him in that office.

The Negative Case

No, the American presidency is not too powerful.

The nation badly needs to change the lens. Everyone, especially the press, would see things quite differently if they could draw back from the presidency

No man who ever held the office of president would congratulate a friend on obtaining it. . . . He will make one man ungrateful, and a hundred men his enemies, for every office he can bestow.— *John Adams*

*and consider it at a distance. It would then look, not like the ultimate throne
of power, but as one important piece in a very complicated machine. Often it
is not even the most important gear. Presidents, we would discover, do things
or don't do them for complicated reasons, including their personal impulses—
but also including many factors which are beyond their control.*

*Much of what Presidents do—maybe even most of what they do—is in re-
sponse to a stream of history that is utterly beyond their manipulation. They
do not shape it so much as they react to it. Events and cycles of events create
certain imperatives over time, which confront government and, in the long
run, presidents must react to them, wisely or ineptly but inevitably.*[25]—
William Greider

The affirmative case leaves us with the impression that presidents are
practically omnipotent. Nothing could be further from the truth. The
American presidency is not too powerful for several reasons:

- There are too many built-in restrictions and restraints on the
  president.
- Presidential power can have positive value.
- Congress has taken steps to limit presidential authority.
- As recent history has shown, presidents can be removed from
  office.
- Reforming the presidency is neither practical nor necessary.

RESTRICTIONS AND RESTRAINTS

Nixon's presidency was not an aberration but a culmination. It carried to reckless extremes a compulsion towards presidential power rising out of deep-running changes in the foundations of society. In a time of the accelera-tion of history and the decay of traditional institutions and val-ues, a strong presidency was both a greater necessity than ever be-fore and a greater risk—necessary to hold a spinning and distracted society together, necessary to make the separation of powers work, risky because of the awful temptation held out to override the separation of powers and burst the bands of the Con-stitution.—*Arthur M. Schlesinger, Jr.*

The president of the United States is indeed a powerful executive, but it
is far from correct to portray him as an autocrat. The American system
of government, with its checks and balances, makes it impossible for
him to do just as he pleases. Other restraints, subtler but no less effective, include a president's personality and goals, and such factors as economic and social change.

Governmental Curbs   Governmental power in the United States is
shared, not concentrated in the hands of one man or one office. The
Constitution provides several very important checks on presidential
power, including those exercised by Congress and the courts. State and
local governments and the two-party system provide additional curbs.

Congressional Checks   Congress has several means at its disposal for
checking presidential actions. Probably the most important is the
"power of the purse," the budgetary power. The president can spend
money only if it has been appropriated, and Congress alone can do this.
Nor can taxes be raised or lowered without congressional action. Therefore a president who needs funds to finance his programs must go to
Congress hat in hand.

Because congressional power is diffused among many committees and leaders, the president has to deal, not with the legislative branch as a unit, but with many smaller fiefdoms. Clashes with recalcitrant representatives and senators are not infrequent. Richard Nixon, for instance, sought major new legislative programs from Congress with very little success. He recognized that the Republican party was in a distinct minority in Congress and that he simply lacked the votes to accomplish a major domestic agenda. His attention turned more to foreign affairs where he could innovate with less restraint in achieving such objectives as renewed relations with the government of mainland China.

Another congressional weapon is the veto override. A president's veto is not the last word on whether a bill will become a law. Congress can and does override presidential vetoes (see Table 1) and has done so with important legislation. In 1975 alone, Congress overrode President Ford's vetoes of bills involving education, health services, and school lunches.

A third check Congress can use is its constitutional privilege to vote on presidential nominations. The Senate has frequently either rejected nominations made by a president or forced him to withdraw them. When Richard Nixon began to appoint his top governmental officials in 1969, he encountered stiff opposition from the Senate Republican leader, Everett M. Dirksen of Illinois. Dirksen had in effect been the second most powerful Washington politician during the administrations of Kennedy and Johnson, who had relied heavily on him for crucial support. When Nixon came to Washington, Dirksen had to reestablish his authority with the new administration. His strategy was to use his Senate leadership position to force the President to deal with him. His opposition to Nixon appointees forced the President to back down on some of his appointments, such as John Knowles, who was nominated to be assistant secretary for health in the Department of Health, Education, and Welfare.

Nixon was twice rebuffed in the case of candidates he had named to the Supreme Court: The Senate turned down Clement Haynsworth in 1969 and G. Harrold Carswell in 1970.

When Gerald Ford wanted to appoint an old friend, Richard Poff, to the federal bench in Virginia, Republican Senator William Scott of Virginia, a political foe of Poff, held up the nomination through *senatorial courtesy*. According to this custom, the Senate will not confirm a presidential appointment of an official in or from a state if one or both senators (if they are of the president's party) oppose it. In the end, Ford had to back down.

The Senate can also use its power to win concessions from nominees before confirming them. In 1976, before confirming George Bush as director of the Central Intelligence Agency, it exacted a promise from him that he would not be a vice-presidential candidate in the 1976 election.

Yet a fourth congressional check on the president is the constitutional amendment. If the presidency is too powerful an institution, what is there to prevent Congress from limiting it by amendment? This right to propose amendments to the Constitution—restricting presidential power if need be—provides an ample safeguard against an authoritarian president.

A fifth important congressional power, the right to investigate presidential performance, has been used many times. Beginning in 1974, for example, Senator Edward Kennedy held hearings on the performance of the Food and Drug Administration in testing new drugs. In 1976 Senator Frank Church conducted hearings on the Central Intelligence Agency. These were but two of many investigations of agencies under the president's jurisdiction. Such investigations remind the president of his limitations and that he himself can be held accountable for abusing his power.

In sum, it is useful to remember what historian Arthur Schlesinger, Jr., wrote about the president, comparing him with European parliamentary leaders:

> Where a parliamentary prime minister can be reasonably sure that anything he suggests will become law in short order, the president of the United States cannot even be sure that his proposals will get to the floor of Congress for debate and vote. And no executive in any other democratic state has so little control over national economic policy as the American president.[26]

The Courts Throughout history, presidents have had to face the possibility that their actions would be tested in the courts. Roosevelt saw several of his early New Deal programs declared unconstitutional by the Supreme Court. The Court also ruled against Truman's seizure of the nation's steel mills in 1952. In the 1970s, several lower federal courts held that Nixon could not impound congressionally appropriated funds. In the 1975 case of *Train* v. *City of New York*, the Supreme Court held unanimously that President Nixon exceeded his authority when he refused in 1972 to allocate to the states $9 billion in water pollution funds. The Court, however, did not address the issue of whether all impoundments are necessarily unconstitutional.[27] Although this power has been used sparingly by the judiciary, it has been an effective check on abuses by the executive.

The special role of the judiciary was dramatically illustrated in the 1930s. After his 1936 election triumph, Roosevelt proposed that the number of Supreme Court justices be increased from nine to fifteen; in this way he hoped to have a majority of justices who would be loyal to his New Deal programs. Public and congressional opposition to this "court-packing" scheme led to a crushing defeat for Roosevelt's effort.

State and Local Interests Although the national government and its executive branch are very powerful, they must reckon with state and local governments throughout the country. Some of these are centers of power that cannot be ignored. What president would have dared disregard the wishes of Mayor Daley of Chicago, especially if that president were a Democrat? The diffusion of governmental power among state and local governments makes it mandatory for a chief executive to take into account the wishes and needs of state and local political officials. This is especially true when nominations and elections are at stake.

The Two-Party System The diffused nature of the two-party system, with more power at the bottom than at the top, makes it difficult for a president to control his party. With no way to discipline it or force its members to support his policies, a president must use compromise, thus sacrificing some power in order to achieve his ends. For example, when Kennedy made judicial appointments, he appointed some segregationists, even though he publicly opposed segregation. The party system required that he reward the southern Democrats who had supported him.

Personality and Goals Every president has a unique personality that affects how he does his job. A passive president like Eisenhower will not try to accomplish as much as an active president like Franklin Roosevelt. Eisenhower, with a distaste for political battles, refrained from acquiring power. Roosevelt, with a great zest for politics, took the opposite tack. Thus the character of a president will help determine the extent of his leadership, since the strength of the office must be nurtured and developed by each incumbent. No one inherits all the authority of his predecessor—witness Truman, who, without the commanding voice and presence of Roosevelt, had to build a power base through his own force of will.

A president who wants to establish a progressive record in domestic affairs has much greater difficulty than a president who wants to keep things as they are. The very nature of federalism and the separation of powers works against rapid change and favors the utilization of authority to preserve the status quo or actually to retrench. To put it another way, power checks power. For example, Kennedy, even with a Democratic majority in Congress, had great difficulty getting progressive legislation adopted. Nixon had much more success in limiting the passage of liberal legislation. He could use impoundment, the veto (or the threat of the veto), and slowing down the processing of federal grants to ac-

I told my aides [when polls showed Carter 30 points ahead in the campaign], "Remember Harry Truman. He did it in 1948, and we can do it in 1976." And sure enough, just like in 1948, we got a Democrat elected President.—*Gerald R. Ford*

The informal style of Jimmy Carter's presidency was evident as early as inauguration day. He and First Lady Rosalynn Carter passed up the customary limousine and strolled hand in hand from the inaugural ceremony at the foot of Capitol Hill to the White House.

complish his objective; programs in the Office of Economic Opportunity were among those that felt the sting of these weapons.

The Need to Persuade   A quick glance at Figure 1 (p. 312) shows that the president is at the top of the executive branch and suggests therefore that he is in command of those below him. This is hardly the case. The essence of presidential power, according to Richard Neustadt, is not command, but persuasion.[28] Harry Truman put it well: "The principal

power the president has is to bring people in and try to persuade them
to do what they ought to do without persuasion. That's what I spent
most of my time doing. That's what the powers of the presidency
amount to." [29]

Why? The answer lies in the nature of relationships between presidents and their subordinates, and between presidents and other political leaders. No other person or group has the same perspective as the
president. Even cabinet members have their own political ambitions, as
well as the particular viewpoint of their own departments. They have
different interests and loyalties. A president's appointees are also responsible to Congress, to the groups and individuals that helped them
get their appointments, and to the people working in their departments
or agencies as well as to themselves. The president is only one of five
masters. As a result, cabinet secretaries are sometimes referred to as a
president's natural enemies. The president's job is not so much one of
commanding subordinates as of persuading them that what he wants
done is what they should do despite their own interests or loyalties.
When former Secretary of the Interior Walter Hickel consistently held
differing views from the President that the President and his aides could
not change by persuasion, Hickel had to be replaced.

In cultivating the art of persuasion, a president is aided by his public reputation throughout the nation and by his professional reputation
in Washington. Eisenhower had tremendous prestige among the people
but lacked a Washington reputation as a professional who could manipulate effectively. By contrast, Johnson was esteemed in the capital as a
practiced politician but lost favor in the country at large with his Vietnam policy. When he referred to "the awesome power and the immense
fragility of executive authority," he spoke as one who had witnessed the
collapse, like a row of dominoes, of all that had gone into constructing
his power base. Among the dominoes were relations with the public,
with Congress, with the bureaucracy, and with the press. Presidential
power is built on the shaky foundations of relationships that necessitate
persuasion, not command.

Other Limitations   How can a president master economic and societal
forces in the United States? He may influence them, but he cannot truly
command them. If Johnson could have controlled the demonstrations
that ignited urban ghettos and campuses in the 1960s, we can safely assume that he would have done so.

Nor are presidents free agents in effecting basic social change. They
must share power with elected officials, bureaucrats, interest groups,
elites, and politicians. Public opinion prescribes boundaries for the exercise of presidential power. So does the Twenty-second Amendment,

which precludes a president from succeeding himself more than once. After one term he is in effect a four-year *lame duck* who cannot go to the polls again to rally widespread public support for his cause.

Still another restraint on the president is posited by the ebb-and-flow, or tide, theory of presidential power. This theory holds that the flow of history itself places limits on the chief executive; activity or passivity seems to run in cycles (see Table 4). According to this argument, Eisenhower's times in part shaped him as a passive president. The American people, having lived through the Great Depression, World War II, and the Korean War, were tired of the activity of the New Deal and the Fair Deal. They wanted tranquillity. If Eisenhower had tried to be an active and powerful president like his predecessors, he would have been cutting against the grain of public feelings.

Another limitation on presidential power—at least on the power to act wisely—is simply inadequate information. One reason for the Bay of Pigs fiasco was Kennedy's lack of sufficient, correct data to make the proper decision about American involvement in Cuba. The CIA had provided an exaggerated assessment of the potential of the Cuban insurgents, at the same time underestimating the strength of Castro's forces to withstand an attack on the island. Similar incidents, of course, occurred during the Vietnam war. Knowledge is power. Clearly a president does not have all the information or the best information available, so the proper and wise exercise of his power is limited accordingly.

Finally, presidential power is restricted by American allies. Although the United States saw itself as the premier world power in the World War II era, in later decades it had to modify its actions because of balky allies who did not share this view. In resolving American economic problems, for example, presidents have been forced to accept measures they did not necessarily want in order to keep the support of American allies. A balance of payments deficit during Nixon's first administration could not be solved unilaterally by the President, but only

Table 4. Ebb-and-Flow Theory: Active and Passive Presidents, 1905–1977

	1905–1909	1909–1913	1913–1921	1921–1933	1933–1953	1953–1961	1961–1974	1974–1977
Active	Roosevelt		Wilson		Roosevelt Truman		Kennedy Johnson Nixon	Carter?
Passive		Taft		Harding Coolidge Hoover		Eisenhower		Ford?

Source: Charles W. Dunn, ed., *The Future of the American Presidency* (Morristown, N. J.: General Learning Press, 1975), p. 339. Updated to 1977.

with cooperation from allies like Germany and Japan, which had balance of payments surpluses.

PRESIDENTIAL POWER: THE PLUS SIDE

In a time of complex change and rapid communications, the United States needs an executive who has the authority to act decisively. A few questions will illustrate the necessity for a strong president. Could another nation negotiate in confidence with an American president who lacked the power to follow through on the results of the negotiations? Can we rely on 535 members of Congress to make fast decisions in the midst of a critical energy crisis? Should Congress be entrusted with data gathered by our intelligence agencies?

Each of these questions can be answered only with a ringing no. A president without the power to implement international agreements would soon lose the respect of other nations and their leaders. During the energy crisis of the early 1970s, Congress spent months debating and haggling with the President without solving the problem. Much intelligence data gathered by the CIA and other agencies must remain confidential; the likelihood of information leaks increases as Congress is apprised of this data—which of course undermines the future effectiveness of intelligence officers.

Foreign Versus Domestic Power It is important to understand that presidents do not have the same amount of strength in domestic as in foreign affairs. Nor should they.

> It takes great crises, such as Roosevelt's hundred days in the midst of the depression or the extraordinary majorities that Barry Goldwater's candidacy willed to Lyndon Johnson, for presidents to succeed in controlling domestic policy. From the end of the 1930s to the present (what may roughly be called the modern era), presidents have often been frustrated in their domestic programs. From 1938, when conservatives regrouped their forces, to the time of his death, Franklin Roosevelt did not get a single piece of significant domestic legislation passed. Truman lost out on most of his intense domestic preferences, except perhaps for housing. Since Eisenhower did not ask for much domestic legislation, he did not meet consistent defeat, yet he failed in his general policy of curtailing governmental commitments. Kennedy, of course, faced great difficulties with domestic legislation.
>
> In the realm of foreign policy there has not been a single major issue on which presidents, when they were serious and determined, have failed. The list of their victories is impressive: entry into the United Nations, the Marshall Plan, NATO, the Truman Doctrine, the decisions to stay out of Indochina in 1954 and to intervene in the 1960s, aid to Poland and Yugoslavia, the test-ban treaty, and many more. Serious setbacks to

In persuading the country to adopt the Twenty-second Amendment, which forbids a third term, the opponents of the strong presidency have struck a mighty blow for their cause. Their cause, I am bound to say, is ill-considered and ill-starred . . . because any major reduction now in the powers of the President would leave us naked to our enemies, to the invisible forces of boom and bust at home and to the visible forces of unrest and aggression abroad. In a country over which industrialism has swept in great waves, in a world where active diplomacy is the minimum price of survival, it is not alone power but a vacuum of power that men must fear.— *Clinton Rossiter*

the president in controlling foreign policy are extraordinary and unusual.[30]

Although Congress began acting in the mid-1970s to check presidential power, even critics admit the need to maintain a strong presidential position in foreign affairs (including a major role for the Central Intelligence Agency). It is precisely in the area where the president is more powerful that he *should* be more powerful. Presidents must act quickly in protecting the national interest.

You cannot return all the power to the people.—*Richard M. Nixon*

What Americans Want Studies of the presidency consistently show that active and more powerful presidents like Lincoln and Truman rank higher with the public than do passive, less powerful ones like Taft and Eisenhower, at least in historical perspective. This does not mean that active and powerful presidents are always popular while in office. (Certainly Lincoln and Truman were often very unpopular.) Typical of presidential rankings is a study made by Arthur Schlesinger, Sr., who polled fifty-five political scientists and historians to determine their opinions.[31] Although the American public does not have as well-defined views of presidential greatness, it is generally assumed that their views are fundamentally the same.

The United States Historical Society recently asked historians at 100 colleges and universities to list the 10 greatest of our 38 Presidents. Lincoln was a unanimous choice, followed closely by Washington and Franklin D. Roosevelt. Theodore Roosevelt, Jefferson, Wilson, and Jackson crowded closely behind, while Truman, whose star is now in the ascendant, stood higher than any of FDR's successors. These 8 were the only Presidents who commanded over half the votes. . . . There is one essential common denominator that transcends all others: All the great Presidents were men of principle, prepared to sacrifice popularity to what they thought was right. . . . In short, what makes for Presidential greatness in the eyes of both contemporaries and posterity—and in truth, too—is integrity of character.—*Henry Steele Commager*

GREAT

1. Abraham Lincoln
2. George Washington
3. Franklin Roosevelt

4. Woodrow Wilson
5. Thomas Jefferson
6. Andrew Jackson

NEAR GREAT

7. Theodore Roosevelt
8. Grover Cleveland

9. John Adams
10. James K. Polk

AVERAGE

11. John Quincy Adams
12. James Monroe
13. Rutherford B. Hayes
14. James Madison
15. Martin Van Buren
16. William Howard Taft

17. Chester A. Arthur
18. William McKinley
19. Andrew Johnson
20. Herbert Hoover
21. Benjamin Harrison

BELOW THE AVERAGE

22. John Tyler
23. Calvin Coolidge
24. Millard Fillmore

25. Zachary Taylor
26. James Buchanan
27. Franklin Pierce

FAILURES

28. Ulysses S. Grant

29. Warren G. Harding

A 1975 study surveyed the opinions of political scientists, economists, and historians on the presidents from Franklin Roosevelt through Richard Nixon. The results shown in Table 5 reveal that activist presidents are generally more highly regarded.[32] Both Republicans and Democrats ranked Roosevelt and Truman at the top.

Significantly, the presidents regarded as great have been those who reached outside the established political and interest group structure to obtain support from the rank and file of the electorate. Andrew Jackson allied himself with immigrants and pioneer farmers, and Abraham Lincoln established rapport with black Americans that was to aid the Republican party in the North till the 1930s. Franklin Roosevelt, though a man of wealth, was certainly no captive of big business interests. On the contrary, public support for his New Deal programs was concentrated largely in the lower and middle classes; it was the upper class that opposed them.

Because of the strong measures they take, powerful presidents receive a good deal of criticism. All activist presidents have been vilified during their terms in office. Many have engaged in undemocratic actions: Lincoln's suspension of habeas corpus, Kennedy's wiretapping of Martin Luther King. Unpopular measures, such as the impounding of funds and the use of executive privilege, have a long history among presidents. Thus it may take time to give a president his just due. Truman left office with minimal support among voters, yet today he ranks high in public esteem. For this reason, some critics are now arguing that Johnson and Nixon too may rank higher in the long run than they do now—Johnson because of his domestic accomplishments and Nixon because of his achievements in foreign affairs.

It is very important to understand that arguments about presidential power are inextricably linked to a much larger debate about the future of the nation. Clinton Rossiter put it this way:

Table 5. Partisan Influence in Presidential Ratings

DEMOCRATS	REPUBLICANS
1. Roosevelt	1. Roosevelt
2. Truman	2. Truman
3. Kennedy	3. Nixon
4. Johnson	4. Eisenhower
5. Eisenhower	5. Kennedy
6. Nixon	6. Johnson

Source: Malcolm B. Parsons, "The Presidential Rating Game," in Charles W. Dunn, ed., *The Future of the American Presidency* (Morristown, N. J.: General Learning Press, 1975), p. 82.

> The struggle over the powers of the presidency, fierce though it may seem, is only a secondary campaign in a political war . . . over the future of America. Few men get heated up over the presidency alone. Their arguments over its powers are really arguments over the American way of life and the direction in which it is moving.[33]

The presidency, linked to the future of the United States more closely than any other governmental institution, must necessarily be involved in debates about the direction of the country. Will presidential powers be used for war or peace? Will a president's economic program benefit one class more than another? Such questions underline the importance of not allowing our distaste for a given president's policies to color our view of presidential power itself; the same authority used by a different president may bring about great accomplishments in what we regard as the public interest.

"SENATOR! IS THAT A WHITE FLAG I SEE FLYING OVER THE WHITE HOUSE?"

IMPOSING LIMITS

The Vietnam war and the Watergate scandal provoked Congress to an intense reexamination of its relationship to the president, with a view to restoring congressional power to be more in balance with that of the presidency. As a result, Congress took action in the areas of emergency authority, the budget, confirmations, military intervention, and intelligence.

With the Depression and the New Deal, presidents began to acquire grants of authority to act in emergencies without the specific consent of Congress. Congressional acts giving the president this power were never repealed. When a special committee of the Senate catalogued national emergency acts in 1974, it found there were 470 such statutes still on the books. Since then, Congress has acted to repeal them so that presidential power will be exercised in a manner consistent with specific congressional authority rather than broad mandates.

In the area of budget making, Congress took action in 1974 by creating a streamlined budgetary process, complete with a Congressional Budget Office and budget committees in each house. Congressional leaders hoped that these moves would provide efficient expertise in dealing with presidential budget and tax proposals.

As you have read, congressional confirmation is an important check on the president. Congress made the director and deputy director of the Office of Management and Budget subject to Senate confirmation, which now allows the Senate to interrogate this most important budget officer before the nominee takes office.

The War Powers Act, as discussed earlier in this chapter, was passed by Congress in 1973. Although its effectiveness has been questioned by some, others believe that it will give Congress leverage to control presidential military commitments. Among those who feel this way is Senator Javits of New York.

> It would not "deprive the President of authority essential to the security of our country." It would permit him to follow his own judgment in responding to emergencies, but would subject unauthorized action to a time limit of sixty days. The important thing is that at some stage . . . [a presidential decision] ceases to be repelling or retaliating against an attack and becomes a basic commitment to war. . . . That requires the concurrence of Congress.[34]

After extensive investigations of intelligence agencies in 1976, especially the CIA, the Senate created a committee to oversee intelligence operations. Its intent was to monitor these functions in order to prevent abuses of intelligence, such as occurred in the Watergate affair when the CIA assisted the White House in some domestic political intelligence work. Among the charges contained in the investigation conducted by the House Intelligence Committee were that up to $10 billion annually of the intelligence budget had not been reported to Congress in recent years; thousands and perhaps millions of dollars had been added to the cost of bugging equipment purchased by the FBI; and the CIA was secretly advised by U.S. Senator Henry M. Jackson (Dem. Wash.) on how to thwart an investigation of its relationships with the International Telephone and Telegraph Corporation in Chile.[35]

These actions of Congress suggest that whatever abuses of presidential power might have existed can be rectified through congressional action. It might be argued that what we have witnessed is not so much the abuse of presidential power as the atrophy of congressional power. Presidential power grew with the explicit or implicit blessing of Congress.

A REMOVABLE OBJECT

No one can know how it feels to resign the presidency of the United States. Is that punishment enough? Oh, probably not.—*Richard M. Nixon*

If the presidencies of Lyndon Johnson and Richard Nixon demonstrate nothing else, they show that presidents can be removed from office. Lyndon Johnson announced his retirement in 1968 after recognizing he had lost substantial public support even in his own party. Richard Nixon resigned from office in 1974 when it became apparent that votes were available to convict him in the Senate if the House of Representatives impeached him.

Impeachment may be an arduous and time-consuming task, but should the nation's highest elected official be removed without a thorough investigation? Removal of the only official other than the vice-president who is elected by all the people should not be anything other than an awesome undertaking. In the post-Civil War era, President Andrew Johnson was impeached in the House of Representatives, but the Senate failed by one vote to convict him. The lengthy deliberations helped to exonerate and to protect Johnson from extremists who wanted him removed from office because of his refusal to deal as harshly as they would have liked with the South.

Impeachment, if taken lightly and acted upon quickly, might lead to the removal of presidents for solely political reasons rather than for violations of the law. In the case of Richard Nixon, a clear and overwhelming majority in favor of impeachment in the House of Representatives was obtained only after Judiciary Committee hearings demonstrated his constitutional and legal violations. Because the impeachment process requires substantial time, the president is more likely to get a fair and impartial investigation in which partisan prejudice is minimized.

THE CASE AGAINST REFORM

Carrying out structural reforms to limit the power of the presidency would be extremely difficult. Reforms tend to come only when there is a crisis focusing continuing attention on the need to make major changes. As far as the presidency is concerned, this time passed when the momentum generated by Watergate died down. Realistically, discussion of reform is wishful thinking. But even if it were not, of what constructive value are the reform proposals in the affirmative argument?

The adoption of one six-year term could certainly remove a president from partisan politics, i. e., the necessity to prepare for reelection, but what about its negative impact? A president who must keep reelection in mind is more likely to respond to public and congressional pressures as well as to the interests of his own party. In preparing for the 1972 election, Richard Nixon made Vietnam troop withdrawal decisions that helped to eliminate that issue during the campaign. Looking at the one six-year term in another way, if members of Congress recognize that an incumbent cannot be reelected, they will have greater freedom not to support the president's legislative program, thereby making it more difficult for the president to govern. The Twentieth Amendment was ratified to keep the president from being a lame duck for four months, and many people now have doubts about the wisdom of the lame-duck feature of the Twenty-second Amendment. Would we want a lame duck as president for six years?

The idea of a vote of no confidence, while appealing, would mix parliamentary and presidential systems, thereby creating a hybrid whose prospects for success would be unknown. Certainly, a no-confidence vote could be used frequently for purely partisan purposes in such a way as to hamper the proper functioning of our government.

A multiple executive would only add more confusion to our highly complex and diffuse governmental structure. Where would the power of one president end and the power of another president begin?

In sum, it would be far better to keep the existing structure of the presidency than to impose reforms that might cause more harm than good. What *is* needed, however, is a more realistic attitude toward the presidency. We need to remove the president from the pedestal of greatness, which has led Americans to expect too much from an executive whose power is limited. And we need to understand the difference between what makes an appealing candidate and what makes a good president. If Americans come to recognize that the president is not a magician who can wave a magic wand, we will be in a position to evaluate performance better and more fairly.

Glossary

Cabinet: a body of advisers composed of the principal departments of the executive branch whose heads (secretaries) are nominated by the president, subject to senatorial confirmation.

Executive privilege: power claimed by presidents to withhold information from the Congress or the courts based upon the separation of powers doctrine.

Impeachment: the calling to account by the House of Representatives of a public official upon a charge of wrongdoing while in office; a two-thirds vote of the Senate is necessary to convict.

Impoundment: power of the president to refuse to spend appropriated funds.

Lame duck: a president who cannot succeed himself in office.

Pocket veto: an automatic veto if Congress adjourns within ten days after passing a bill and the president has not signed it.

Senatorial courtesy: a custom whereby senators of the president's party exercise a veto power over presidential appointments in their states.

Veto: the president's refusal to sign a bill that subsequently can become law only by a·two-thirds vote of the Congress.

Vote of no confidence: device used in parliamentary systems when parliament votes "no confidence" in the executive branch, i.e., the prime minister and his party; election follows. This differs from impeachment in that the chief executive can run for office again.

Notes

1. Arthur B. Tourtellot, *Presidents on the Presidency* (Garden City, N. Y.: Doubleday, 1964), pp. 55, 56.

2. William Howard Taft, *Our Chief Magistrate and His Powers* (New York: Columbia University Press, 1938), p. 138.

3. Mark Goodman, ed., *Give 'em Hell, Harry!* (New York: Award Books, 1974), p. 108.

4. Aaron Wildavsky, "The Two Presidencies." *Transaction*, December 1966, p. 9.

5. Thomas A. Bailey, *Presidential Greatness* (New York: Appleton-Century-Crofts, 1966), p. 157.

6. Richard E. Neustadt, *Presidential Power* (New York: John Wiley, 1960), p. 166.

7. Ibid., p. 161.

8. Ibid., p. 152.

9. *Congressional Record*, June 29, 1973, pp. 22261–22263.

10. Wilfred E. Binkley, *President and Congress* (New York: Alfred A. Knopf, 1947), p. 127.

11. Edward S. Corwin, *The President, Office and Powers 1787–1957* (New York: New York University Press, 1957), p. 311.

12. Wildavsky, "The Two Presidencies," pp. 13–14.

13. Emmet John Hughes, *The Living Presidency* (New York: Coward, McCann and Geoghegan, 1973), p. 52.

14. Ibid, p. 57.

15. Henry Cabot Lodge, ed., *The Federalist* (New York: G. P. Putnam's, 1902), p. 419.

16. For a full assessment of these and similar quotations about the American presidency, see Thomas E. Cronin, "The Textbook Presidency and Political Science," *Congressional Record*, October 5, 1970, pp. S17102–S17115.

17. James MacGregor Burns, *Presidential Government* (Boston: Houghton Mifflin, 1965), p. 96.

18. *Washington Post*, Marquis Childs' Syndicated Column, November 17, 1972.

19. Russell Baker and Charles Peters, "The Prince and His Courtiers: At the White House, the Kremlin, and the Reichchancellery," *The Washington Monthly*, March 1971, p. 34.

20. Bernard Nossiter, *The Mythmakers* (Boston: Beacon Press, 1964), p. 40.

21. Saul K. Padover, "The Power of the President," *Commonwealth*, August 9, 1968, p. 524.

22. Henry Steele Commager, "Can We Limit Presidential Power?" *New Republic*, April 6, 1968, p. 18.

23. Neustadt, *Presidential Power*, p. vii.

24. George McGovern in *Progressive*, May 1973, pp. 11–14.

25. *Washington Post*, November 7, 1976, p. C1.

26. Arthur M. Schlesinger, Jr., "The Limits and Excesses of Presidential Power," *Saturday Review*, May 3, 1969, pp. 18–19.

27. *Train v. City of New York* (1975).

28. Neustadt, *Presidential Power*.

29. Goodman, *Give 'em Hell, Harry*, p. 111.

30. Wildavsky, "The Two Presidencies," pp. 7–8.

31. Arthur M. Schlesinger, Sr., *Paths to the Present* (New York: Macmillan, 1949), pp. 94–99.

32. Malcolm B. Parsons, "The Presidential Rating Game," in Charles W. Dunn, ed., *The Future of the American Presidency* (Morristown, N. J.: General Learning Press, 1975), p. 82.

33. Clinton Rossiter, *The American Presidency* (New York: Harcourt Brace Jovanovich, 1960), p. 257.

34. "The Power of the Pentagon," *Congressional Quarterly* (Washington, D. C.: Congressional Quarterly, Inc., 1972), p. 42.

35. *Congressional Quarterly Weekly Report.* January 31, 1976, p. 203.

Recommended Rebuttal Reading

Personality and Power

Barber, James David. *The Presidential Character.* Englewood Cliffs, N. J.: Prentice-Hall, 1972.

Evans, Rowland, Jr., and Robert D. Novak. *Lyndon B. Johnson: The Exercise of Power.* New York: New American Library, 1968.

——. *Nixon in the White House: The Frustration of Power.* New York: Vintage, 1972.

Hargrove, Erwin C. *The Power of the Modern Presidency.* New York: Alfred A. Knopf, 1974.

Mullen, William F. *Presidential Power and Politics.* New York: St. Martin's Press, 1976.

Neustadt, Richard E. *Presidential Power: The Politics of Leadership.* New York: John Wiley, 1976.

Organization and Administration

Hess, Stephen, *Organizing the Presidency.* Washington, D. C.: The Brookings Institution, 1976.

Kessel, John H. *The Domestic Presidency.* North Scituate, Mass.: Duxbury, 1975.

Nathan, Richard. *The Plot That Failed: Nixon and the Administrative Presidency.* New York: John Wiley, 1975.

Woodward, Bob, and Carl Bernstein. *All the President's Men.* New York: Simon & Schuster, 1974.

Journalists' Accounts

Hughes, Emmet John. *The Living Presidency.* New York: Coward, McCann and Geoghegan, 1973.

Reedy, George E. *The Twilight of the Presidency.* New York: New American Library, 1970.

General References

Cronin, Thomas F. *The State of the Presidency.* Boston: Little, Brown, 1975.

Dunn, Charles W., ed. *The Future of the American Presidency.* Morristown, N. J.: General Learning Press, 1975.

James, Dorothy. *The Contemporary Presidency.* Indianapolis, Ind.: Bobbs-Merrill, 1974.

Lammers, William W. *Presidential Politics: Patterns and Prospects.* New York: Harper & Row, 1976.

McConnell, Grant. *The Modern Presidency.* New York: St. Martin's Press, 1976.

Selected Readings

Etzkowitz, Henry, and Peter Schwab, eds. *Is America Necessary? Conservative, Liberal and Socialist Perspectives of United States Political Institutions.* St. Paul, Minn.: West, 1976.

Peters, Charles, and James Fellows, eds. *Inside the System.* New York: Praeger, 1976.

AT ISSUE: BUREAUCRACY

Organization

Functions

RESOLVED THAT:
Bureaucracy Subverts Democracy

At Issue: Bureaucracy

Bureaucracy, especially the federal bureaucracy, has come under almost constant attack in recent years. In the 1976 presidential primaries, both Jimmy Carter and Ronald Reagan—outsiders in terms of the federal establishment—gained substantial voter support by lashing out at the Washington bureaucracy. Nor were they alone. Liberal Democratic governors like Jerry Brown of California and Michael Dukakis of Massachusetts joined ranks with conservatives like Senator Barry Goldwater in doing the same thing.

Just what is bureaucracy and who are the bureaucrats? Scholars generally agree that a *bureaucracy* is any administrative system, but particularly a governmental agency, that implements policy pursuant to law, that follows standardized procedures, and that allocates specialized duties to its employees. Bureaucracies generally try to have their employees perform routine tasks that are carefully prescribed by a personnel office as defined by management in program agencies, such as bureaus and branches.

In the case of the federal bureaucracy (and that is the one on which this chapter will concentrate), this personnel office is the United States Civil Service Commission. Created by the Pendleton Act of 1883, this commission adopted a *merit system*, so that employees would be hired on the basis of ability rather than political allegiance. Employees hired in this way make up the *civil service*. Thus bureaucrats are *civil servants*.

349

Within a civil service system, positions are classified according to the type of work performed. In the federal civil service, positions have a GS (General Schedule) rating, such as GS-5 or GS-14. Persons with the same rating and in the same position class (for example, secretary) do essentially the same work.

Several benefits are claimed for the civil service system: (1) simplified recruitment and selection of personnel, with similar tests being administered for similar positions; (2) payment of equal salaries for equal work; (3) well-understood lines of authority and responsibility among employees; (4) clear avenues of promotion and transfer; and (5) treatment of all cases alike when their situations are similar.

The main purpose for creating civil service was to overcome the ills of the *patronage system,* which allowed elected political officials to hire and fire employees at will. The president can still appoint persons to approximately five thousand non-civil service positions (about one half of which are in policy-making positions). Except for these, however, personnel in the federal bureaucracy generally remains the same from one president to another.

ORGANIZATION

The ideal type of bureaucracy is a conceptual construction of certain empirical elements into a logically precise and consistent form, a form which in its ideal purity, is never to be found in concrete reality.—*Max Weber*

Beneath the president, at the apex of the bureaucracy, is the Executive Office of the President. Included in the Executive Office—as you read in Chapter 9—are some fifteen organizations, including the White House Office, the Office of Management and Budget, the National Security Council, and the Council of Economic Advisers.

A second major element of the bureaucracy is made up of the twelve executive departments, each headed by a cabinet secretary (see Table 1). Typically, each secretary has an undersecretary and several assistant secretaries, all of whom serve at the president's pleasure.[1] Beneath them are the directors of bureaus and other offices within the department. (Figure 1 shows the structure of a typical executive department.) Cabinet secretaries are nominated by the president and are subject to senatorial confirmation.

A third element in the bureaucracy is formed by the administrative or service agencies, such as the Veterans' Administration, the National Aeronautics and Space Administration, and the General Services Administration. The directors of these agencies are nominated by the president, subject to senatorial confirmation.

Finally, there are the regulatory commissions and the government corporations, which do not report directly to the president. The commissioners or board members, although nominated by the president and confirmed by the Senate, are not responsible to the chief executive for

Table 1. Executive Departments in the National Government

DEPARTMENT	NUMBER OF EMPLOYEES
State	32,120
Treasury	119,962
Interior	73,351
Justice	49,936
Agriculture	104,549
Commerce	36,177
Labor	13,710
Defense	1,038,071
Health, Education, and Welfare	143,528
Housing and Urban Development	16,785
Transportation	72,426
Energy*	

*Created in 1977.

Source: U. S. Bureau of the Census, *Statistical Abstract of the United States 1975*, p. 243.

FIG. 1. Department of Health, Education, and Welfare

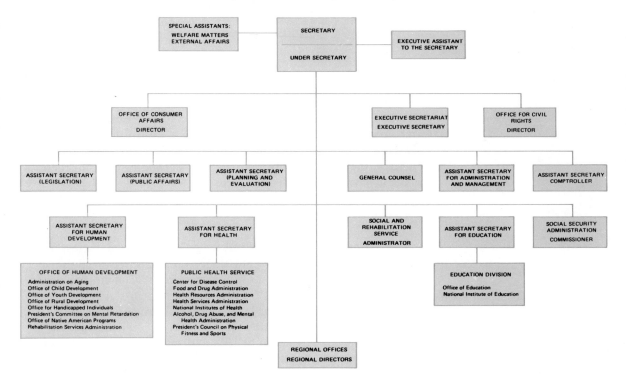

SOURCE: *U.S. Government Manual*, 1975, p 230.

Modern technology has become an integral part of government bureaucracy, giving agencies access to vast data supplies at a moment's notice. These computers at the National Computer Center in West Virginia verify and store tax-return information of all U.S. taxpayers.

their decisions, and he cannot remove them from office, except for cause as specified by Congress.[2]

Increasingly in recent years, many government activities, such as research, have been contracted out to private institutions like the RAND Corporation. Although not formally and officially a part of the bureaucracy, they are certainly adjuncts of it, depending on it for their survival and providing it with assistance.

FUNCTIONS

Federal government departments and agencies perform a variety of functions that might be categorized under the headings of administration, legislation, adjudication, and enforcement. Constitutionally, each of these functions derives from Article II, which states that the president "shall take care that the laws be faithfully executed."

In its administrative function, the bureaucracy carries out laws. Thus, when the Civil Rights Act of 1964 and the Voting Rights Act of 1965 became law, the Department of Justice had the primary responsibility for implementing them. Almost any law requires a measure of administrative implementation from some part of the bureaucracy.

In the field of legislation, the bureaucracy performs two tasks. One is to recommend legislative proposals to the president, which are customarily filtered through the Office of Management and Budget. The second legislative function is to implement statutory law through administrative law. Bills passed by Congress are called *statutory law;* they are usually general in nature. Spelling out more specific rules, guidelines, and regulations is the job of *administrative law.*

How is administrative law created? A common method is for an agency, upon request, to provide more detail about the provisions of a given law. The Federal Election Commission was established in 1973 in order to develop rules and regulations for a new federal election law. When NBC News consultant Walter Pincus did some checking a few years later, he found that the commission was being asked a number of questions.

> Senator Gary Hart of Colorado wants to purchase a mobile van to make "constituent services more accessible to Colorado residents." Will the funds used for that purchase (asks Hart's lawyer) be considered political contributions? Senator Strom Thurmond of South Carolina has a campaign committee, which during non-election years makes what the Senator terms "non-campaign expenditures," paying for lunches in Washington for South Carolina constituents and also for paperweights and letter openers with Thurmond's name on them, which are passed out to visitors as gifts. Are these to be considered "ordinary and necessary expenses incurred in connection with [Thurmond's] duties as a federal officeholder?" the Senator asked.
>
> Along with administration of the campaign fund laws, the commission was also given responsibility for handling the new congressional limitations on honorariums. With that has come an opportunity for the commissioners to get into another personal aspect of public life. Representative Barbara Jordan of Texas has been asked by CBS to do monthly commentaries for that network's morning news program, for which she will be paid $150 each. Jordan felt it necessary to get the commission's approval on the deal since a congressman is limited to $1000 in honorarium from a single source. Representative Jordan's position is that the fee is for services rendered and, therefore, should not be included when computing honorariums for the year.
>
> Ways and Means Committee chairman Al Ullman has written in to ask if organizations seeking his appearance at conventions could make contributions to charities in lieu of honorariums to him, and not have that money counted against his honorarium limit. Ullman also inquired about an even more intriguing proposal. Would money that organizations contribute to a "scholarship fund" be counted against the honorarium limit when such donations are made "only if they wished and not as a condition for [Ullman's] appearance?" [3]

The decisions made by the Federal Election Commission on these (and other) matters form just one part of a huge body of administrative law. They are, of course, a principal reason for the bureaucracy's power.

Adjudication means simply that a department or agency resolves conflict between parties. For example, the National Labor Relations Board issues decisions on disputes between labor and management. In a dispute between a consumer group and a manufacturer, the Federal Trade Commission may rule whether a television advertisement advertises a product honestly.

Enforcement is an extremely important task, especially for the Justice Department. In enforcing federal criminal law, the Department of Justice maintains a large staff to investigate and prosecute violators. Other departments also have enforcement powers. For example, the Bureau of Customs—part of the Treasury Department—enforces laws against importing drugs and other illegal goods.

With its complex organization and numerous functions, the bureaucracy obviously has substantial power. Is it used to subvert democracy, or to further its ends?

The Federal bureaucracy has evolved into a fourth non-Constitutional branch of the government with a thick tangle of regulations that carry the force of law without the benefit of legislative considerations.—*Eliott H. Levitas*

- Could democracy survive without bureaucracy?
- Does the bureaucracy engage in policy making that normally ought to be in the hands of the political branches of government?
- Can citizens realistically expect a president to institute new programs when career bureaucrats who administer such programs resist change?
- Does the bureaucracy perform more effectively for some groups of citizens than for others? If so, which groups are favored and why?

The Affirmative Case

Yes, bureaucracy subverts democracy.

The federal government now employs over 100,000 people whose sole responsibility is the writing, reviewing, and enforcing of some type of regulation. One hundred thousand people whose principal job is telling you how to do your job. It's a bureaucrat's dream of heaven, but it's a nightmare for those who have to bear the burden. Just to list all of the rules and regulations established last year required 45,000 pages of very small print in the Federal Register. *I mourn for the trees that were felled in America's forests to make this exercise in governmental nagging possible.*[4]—Gerald Ford

The bureaucracy was established to implement and administer public law as passed by Congress. Yet it has become vast, impersonal, and dangerous. To be more specific:

- In its seemingly uncontrollable growth, the bureaucracy is like an octopus grasping for total power over society.
- Bureaucrats, unrepresentative of the population they supposedly serve, are allied with special interests.
- The bureaucracy suffers from inertia and incompetence.

UNCONTROLLABLE GROWTH

The growth of the federal bureaucracy has been nothing short of phenomenal. Between 1790 and 1976, it increased in size from 780 people to nearly 3 million. Of all these employees of the national government, approximately 8,000 work for the judicial branch and 30,000 for the legislative branch. The rest work for the executive branch; of these, over a million and a quarter are civilian employees in the Department of Defense and the Veterans' Administration.

As shown in Table 2, the number of civilians employed by the federal government has increased over sevenfold since the early twentieth century. This staggering growth requires an increasingly larger share of the tax dollar to support salaries, equipment, buildings, retirement funds, and other items. To give a few examples: Between 1958 and 1971, the number of engineers and other comparable employees in the top five ranks of the federal bureaucracy increased by 300 percent. The minimum salary for a GS-14 was $11,355 in 1958; it had increased to $20,815 by 1971 and to $23,088 by 1973. The number of employees receiving this salary had increased to over 73,000 by 1973.

I believe it is time for us to declare our independence from governmental bureaucracies grown too large, too powerful, too costly, too remote, and yet too deeply involved in our day-to-day lives. Even though there are many things government must do for people, there are many more things that people would rather do for themselves.— *Gerald R. Ford*

Table 2. Increase in Civilian Federal Employees

1910	388,708
1920	655,265
1930	601,319
1940	1,042,420
1950	1,960,708
1960	2,398,704
1970	2,921,909

Source: For 1910–1950, *Historical Statistics*, p. 710; for 1960–1970, *Statistical Abstract of the United States 1975*, p. 243.

A classic example of bureaucratic growth has occurred in the military. In 1945 there were 139 three-, four-, and five-star generals and admirals to command armed forces exceeding 8 million. By the early 1970s—with only 2.5 million in uniform—there were 190 three-, four-, and five-star generals and admirals. During the same period the number of colonels, majors, and commanders increased from 52,000 to 58,000.

In terms of growth, it is instructive to see what happened in a single year. The government's civilian payroll in May 1975 was $3.3 billion, more than $100 million higher than in May 1974.

Although it is important to note the bureaucracy's growth in budget and employees, its most dangerous growth has been in the issuance of administrative laws. As President Ford notes at the beginning of the Affirmative Case, over 100,000 people are now employed by the federal government just to write, review, and enforce some type of regulation. He also notes that in 1974, 45,000 pages of very small print were required to publish these rules and regulations in the *Federal Register.*

Presidents, who are supposed to govern the bureaucracy, come and go; the bureaucracy remains. Arthur M. Schlesinger, Jr., writes of the Kennedy administration:

> The permanent government soon developed its own stubborn vested interests in policy and procedure, its own cozy alliances with committees of Congress, its own ties to the press, its own national constituencies. It began to exude the feeling that presidents could come and presidents go, but it went on forever.
>
> The permanent government was, as such, politically neutral; its essential commitment was to doing things as they had been done before. This frustrated the enthusiasts who came to Washington with Eisenhower in 1953 zealous to dismantle the New Deal, and it frustrated the enthusiasts who came to Washington with Kennedy in 1961 zealous to get the country moving again.[5]

Why Employment Expansion?   It is important to understand why bureaucracy grows in a seemingly unstoppable fashion. Theories of employment growth have been advanced by C. Northcote Parkinson and Norman John Powell.

Parkinson is most noted for his development of *Parkinson's Law,* which holds that work expands to fill the amount of time available. Parkinson argues that since rigid boundary lines do not exist, bureaucracy will continue to expand. Bureaucracies tend to be self-perpetuating and self-protecting; they expand in order to perpetuate and protect. There is always something more to be done and therefore more employees needed to do it. Parkinson points out that bureaucrats would rather multiply subordinates than rivals. As new subordinates are

Government by bureaucratic decree threatens freedom itself. The pursuit of no goal justifies the destruction, or even the erosion, of freedom.—*Sam J. Ervin, Jr.*

added, they make work for others. Employees will make work merely to justify their existence; as they make work, more employees are needed to handle the work they have created.[6]

A modification of Parkinson's law, devised by Norman John Powell, holds that (1) bureaucratic employment and expenditures rise in relationship to increases in community needs; and (2) bureaucratic growth necessitates more personnel to help manage the employees.[7] For example, the Executive Office of the President was created in the late 1930s to help the president manage the bureaucracy. Since then, it too has expanded in response to community needs. One of many additions is the Energy Research and Development Administration, created by President Ford to help solve the nation's energy crisis. (In 1977, ERDA was made a part of the Department of Energy.) The Executive Office of the President has become so large that it creates management problems which, ironically, it was supposed to solve.

In effect, the bureaucracy expands in a never-ending spiral. Each executive needs subordinates. Each subordinate needs work in order to justify his or her existence. With more work, more employees are hired. And so on.

Why Budgetary Expansion?   Budgetary growth, obviously affected by employment growth, involves two important principles. The first is that bureaucrats fight against rival agencies for funds. The second is that each unit wants an annual increase, an increment over its previous year's budget. To compete effectively, departments and agencies may propose new programs that require new personnel and a larger budget. Even if no new programs are proposed, however, bureaucratic units still want more money every year.

In seeking budgetary increments, the strategy is (1) to assume that the increment will be added to last year's budget and (2) to ask for more than what is needed in order to be sure of obtaining the amount actually desired. Bureaucracies tend to spend most of their budget preparation time not in justifying their existing budget but rather in justifying their need for more money. If a budget proposal must pass through three channels—for example, an executive department, the White House, and Congress—the budget request is inflated to allow for the possibility of three cuts. Bureaucracies expend an inordinate amount of time justifying their expansion rather than their accomplishments. They subtly shift the focus of debate from the past, which is known, to the future, which is unknown. This ploy makes it difficult for opponents to deny their requests, since they have to argue against prospective plans as well as past performance.

IN THE SERVICE OF SPECIAL INTERESTS

Studies of the top 1,000 bureaucrats (not a part of the Civil Service) appointed by Presidents Truman, Eisenhower, Kennedy, Johnson, and Nixon reveal that they were primarily white Protestants born and reared in the East.[8] Most were between the ages of 40 and 60 and had graduated from the more prestigious colleges and universities. A majority had at one time been employed by a major business; 44 percent held law degrees. This is hardly a picture of the average American.

Even at the lower levels of the bureaucracy, where one would expect personnel to be more nearly representative, statistics are revealing. As of 1974, approximately 21 percent of all civil service positions were held by members of minority groups (see Table 3), but most of these were custodial and menial jobs.

If the bureaucrats charged with implementing and enforcing our laws are not representative of the public as a whole, it is natural to assume that there is a potential for tension between the public and its bureaucratic servants. The most common place for this tension to occur is in the field of social welfare legislation. Here the interests of poor and otherwise deprived Americans, the beneficiaries of such laws, differ from the interests of middle- and upper-class Americans who implement and enforce the laws (and pay a large proportion of the taxes to support their programs). One study concludes that "bureaucratic systems are the key medium through which the middle class maintains its advantaged position vis-à-vis the lower class."[9]

Within the executive bureaucracy one finds a great deal of closed politics, that is, competition for power and influence among small groups of policy-makers, advisers, and bureaucrats without direct reference to any larger political arena.—Erwin C. Hargrove

The "Cozy Triangle" Bureaucracy can perform quite efficiently, contrary to common belief, but its efficiency and effectiveness are related to the groups it serves. The bureaucracy is not politically neutral. It responds more quickly and favorably to business interests than to those of

Table 3. Federal Civilian Employment

	TOTAL	PERCENT OF TOTAL
Male	1,896,000	70
Female	828,000	30
Minority Groups*	510,061	21
Total**	2,724,000	

*Includes both males and females of Negro, American Indian, and Oriental extraction and persons with Spanish surnames; these persons are also included in the male and female categories.

**Total is computed by adding males and females.

Source: *Statistical Abstract of the United States 1975*, pp. 242, 245.

the poor. For example, the Department of Housing and Urban Development is better attuned to the needs of realtors and contractors than to the situation of the ghetto residents for whom many housing laws were designed.

By establishing close relationships with special interests, the bureaucracy has allowed portions of public authority to be given over to private groups seeking only to benefit themselves. As you read in Chapter 6, there is a "cozy triangle" among the bureaucracy, key members of Congress, and special interest groups. This interaction enables the bureaucracy to defy the public interest, as interpreted by the nation's highest elected official, the president.

One would like to think that the Department of Agriculture (and all other executive departments) serves what we vaguely call the "public interest." In reality, it has conferred portions of national sovereignty on private groups, who in turn dictate public policy. Every American has a legitimate stake in farm production and prices. But the Department of Agriculture has allowed farming to become neither a public nor a private enterprise.

> It is a system of self-government in which each leading farm interest controls a segment of agriculture through a delegation of national sovereignty. Agriculture has emerged as a largely self-governing federal estate within the federal structure of the United States . . . through a line [of power] unbroken by personality or party in the White House.[10]

It is not surprising that Agriculture Department decisions have not always been in the public interest. Take the content of meat products like hot dogs or hash. As pointed out by one critic, "standards are ordinarily based on prevailing industry practices," not on what is best for consumers. Thus the department decides according to commercial, private considerations rather than according to the needs of the public.[11]

A *New York Times Magazine* article about former Secretary of Agriculture Earl Butz notes that when nominated, he served on the boards of three large agribusiness corporations. One was Ralston Purina to which his predecessor was going as vice-chairman. When Butz named an eight-member departmental advisory committee, the consumer representative on the committee happened to be a vice-president for consumer affairs of Jewell Food Stores, a major supermarket chain.[12]

Clientelism   The special relationship between industries and the federal commissions that regulate them—*clientelism*—is prevalent and potentially harmful. Because of it, cases can drag on for years without resolution. A glaring example involved the patent medicine Geritol. A case accusing the maker of misleading advertising was pending against it for nearly a decade. Through a combination of Federal Trade Commission timidity and the legal and financial resources available to the manufacturer, the company was able to stall a final decision until it had subtly changed its advertising program (from a claim that Geritol provides strength to one implying that it would keep users young). However, clientelism can best be illustrated through a series of pointed questions: Why have large numbers of high-ranking employees in the Food and Drug Administration come from regulated industries; why do so many of them return to regulated industries?[13] Why have more than half of the top 573 officials in the Energy Research and Development Administration and the Nuclear Regulatory Commission previously worked for private companies holding contracts, licenses, or permits from these two agencies?[14]

These questions clearly lead to the conclusion that public government has become private government, that the public interest has been sold out to private interests.

Tools of Control   Of the bureaucracy's many devices for achieving control, two especially useful in maintaining the "cozy triangle" are administrative law and the provision of information.

Administrative law results from the political process, and its effectiveness depends on the political strength of the groups involved in implementing it. Statutory law affecting housing, for example, may theoretically benefit the poor, but the superior organization of realtors and contractors works in their favor. The huge and complex sources for administrative law are statutory law and the *Federal Register*, which contains the rules and regulations for implementing statutory law. Little wonder that groups with superior education and greater political sophistication can understand and manipulate them better. Perhaps at least part of the reason for the failure of poverty programs has to do with bureaucrats who fail to comply with the intent of statutory law.

Information, or its absence, is an important weapon. A foremost student of bureaucracy, Max Weber, holds that the first line of defense for any bureaucracy is the ability to withhold information. It has already been noted (Chapter 6) that an awkward situation resulted when the government was dependent on the oil industry for data on oil reserves. But the bureaucracy itself may control information and release it only on a selective basis. For instance, the Federal Aviation Administration for years would release its reports on airline accidents and mechanical defects only to the airline industry.[15]

In the United States today, information may take the form of propaganda, also a significant bureaucratic weapon. According to estimates, the Department of Defense spends some $30 million a year to influence

By Mike Peters for The Dayton Daily News

"Oh good, we're early.... The next postal hike's at 5:25...."

public opinion. Included is the Defense Information School at Fort Benjamin Harrison, Indiana. It has trained over 30,000 persons since World War II as information "specialists" to help communicate the Defense Department story to the public.[16] Large public information budgets are common throughout the bureaucracy.

INERTIA AND INCOMPETENCE

Even if the bureaucracy were not so involved with special interests, it could not accomplish a great deal. Inherent defects render it weak, if not actually harmful. Among the most important of these are inertia and downright incompetence.

Fighting a Marshmallow   The natural bureaucratic tendency is to resist change, especially when it is perceived as a threat to position and

Government leaders sit on top of a conglomerate of bureaucratic organizations each of which has folkways of its own, an organizational culture that reflects concern with certain kinds of policy problems to the exclusion of others, the possession of habitual strategies for dealing with problems, and stock solutions. The chief problem for the top policymaker is that the organization develops a life of its own that is difficult for him to alter should he seek to do so.—*Graham T. Allison*

power. Matthew P. Dumont, Assistant Commissioner for Drug Rehabilitation in the Massachusetts Department of Mental Health, minced no words:

> Can you imagine trying to fight a revolution against a huge, righteous marshmallow? Even if you had enough troops not to be suffocated by it, the best you can hope for is to eat it. And, as you all know, you become what you eat. And that is the point. For a revolution to be meaningful it must take into account the nature of organizational life. . . . If a revolution harbors the illusion that a reign of terror will purify a bureaucracy of scoundrels and exploiters, it will fail. It matters little whether bureaucrats are Royalist or Republican, Czarist or Bolshevik, Conservative or Liberal, or what have you. It is the built-in forces of life in a bureaucracy that result in the bureaucracy being so indifferent to suffering and aspiration.[17]

Even if one's hopes for change are less than revolutionary, the bureaucracy is likely to be unresponsive. This is seen most clearly in its relationship to the presidency. Of the nearly 3 million federal employees, the president appoints only about 5,000, of whom some 3,000 are stenographers, chauffeurs, and other minor employees. Quite simply, the chief executive lacks the necessary leverage through policymaking personnel appointments to insure that the bureaucracy responds to the national interest. It may take two or three years for a pres-

"Congratulations! I've been dying to meet you—!"

idential directive to be translated into agency guidelines and reach the action level.

There are several reasons for this delay, not the least of which is that a new presidential policy is a threat to the way the bureaucracy has been doing things. One of the reasons why Lyndon Johnson wanted his poverty programs administered primarily by a new agency (the OEO) in the Executive Office of the President was that he feared what existing bureaucratic organizations in the executive departments might do to them. The Department of Health, Education, and Welfare, for example, had its own programs and policies, and the new poverty programs would have threatened the status quo.

The bureaucracy has a built-in asset in resisting or subverting presidential (and congressional) initiatives: its continuing identity. The bureaucracy was there before the president and will be there after he has gone; it can outwait him. Moreover, the president, encumbered with many interests and problems, cannot focus his entire attention on persuading foot-dragging bureaucrats to be more cooperative. If his interest wanes, there is no one to prod the bureaucracy. The department secretaries and other political appointees usually do not have a lifetime career commitment. If they attempted to make major changes or to control the bureaucracy more effectively, the result might well be a battle that bureaucrats would be more likely to win by virtue of their longevity in office. When one considers that a president has no more than eight years to accomplish his objectives and that a bureaucracy has until eternity to resist them, it is remarkable that presidential authority has any meaning at all.

The ties that bureaucrats have developed over the years with interest groups and Congress also serve as a weapon in resisting presidential initiatives. To illustrate: during the Nigeria-Biafra civil war in the late 1960s, the State Department bureaucracy, with a long history of ties to the federal government of Nigeria, displayed little interest in relieving starvation in Biafra. The White House office of Henry Kissinger had extraordinary difficulty in implementing a humanitarian program to assist Biafra. Ultimately, the president had to establish the position of special ambassador for the Nigeria-Biafra conflict to overcome bureaucratic recalcitrance.*

Bureaucratic Bungling Inertia is bad enough. Even worse is the massive problem of bureaucratic ineptitude and bungling. One example: in

*Information provided by the State Department itself revealed its historic ties to the Nigerian government. As a member of a study mission to Nigeria and Biafra in 1969, the writer learned through discussions with the American ambassador that the ambassador knew little about the problems of malnutrition and starvation—and seemed to care less.

THE LEFT HAND AND THE RIGHT HAND

1969, the Department of Health, Education, and Welfare spent $8 million to discourage smoking; meanwhile the Department of Agriculture was spending $30 million to subsidize tobacco growing.[18] Here are three other examples:

1. Why did the Department of Defense produce twelve different movies on how to brush your teeth?

2. Why did the Department of Health, Education, and Welfare spend $19,300 for a study about why children fall off tricycles?
3. Why did the Department of the Interior spend $6 million for a study of citizen recreation habits—and then throw the study away? [19]

These examples suggest that everybody is somewhat responsible for everything, and nobody is completely responsible for anything. The result is mindless bureaucracy without cohesive and well-planned action. Citizens and institutions alike become frustrated and alienated.

At best, the continuing growth of bureaucracy results in astronomical costs. One senator who has taken an interest in the staggering amount of paperwork required by government bureaucracy is Thomas J. McIntyre of New Hampshire. A Wisconsin farmer recently sent him a fat package of blank government forms. Every year, the farmer wrote the Senator, he must fill out:

> W-2s and W-3s, to report on employees' wages; 940s and 941s, to report on Social Security and unemployment taxes; 1099s, dividend reporting forms; 1096s, to report on the number of 1099s filed; WT-7s and W-2s, for the state tax bureau; corporate income tax forms, capital stock transfer forms, and quarterly stock withholding tax forms for household employees.

> "That's a stack half an inch thick right there," said an aide in the Senator's office. "And that's only the income tax forms." For the farmer . . . there are also Equal Employment Opportunity Commission reports, census reports, pension plan reports and Department of Agriculture reports.

> . . . Ten billion sheets [of paper] flow into federal offices from across the nation every year, according to testimony by McIntyre at a 1972 hearing in Chicago (testimony that found its way, predictably, into a printed report). Four and a half million cubic feet. Enough paper to fill a major league baseball stadium from the playing field to the top of the bleachers 50 times. [20]

According to an Office of Management and Budget study, it takes Americans 143 million hours annually to fill out almost 13 million forms despite President Ford's campaign to slash bureaucratic paperwork. [21]

At worst, continuing bureaucratic growth creates the potential for a welfare state, with the government controlling most phases of American life. With more bureaucrats managing more programs, more power will be concentrated in the hands of the federal government. This could well result in the demise of individual initiative and private enterprise. The bureaucracy, says Senator Barry Goldwater,

Government inefficiency is becoming today's Number 1 villain. Until we bring what programs we now have under control, we simply may not have the resources we need, either in the budget or the public's trust, to pursue new legislative solutions to pressing national problems.—*Edmund S. Muskie*

is so massive that it literally feeds on itself. It is so large that no one in or out of government can accurately define its power or scope. It is so intricate that it lends itself to a large range of abuses, some criminal and deliberate, others unwitting and inept. The government is so large that institutions doing business with it or attempting to do business with it are forced to hire trained experts just to show them around through the labyrinthine maze made up of hundreds of departments, bureaus, commissions, offices and agencies. . . . It would be downright laughable if it were not so serious to consider how many of our people actually believe that a national administration firmly controls the federal government. It is true that broad overall policy is determined at the White House level or at the cabinet level in the government bureaucracy. But its implementation is too often left to the tender mercies of a long-entrenched bureaucracy.[22]

Why the low level of competence in the bureaucracy? Laurence J. Peter and Raymond Hull would respond that it is simply the application of what they call the *Peter Principle*—the theory that "in a hierarchy, every employee tends to rise to his level of incompetence." Peter and Hull hold that there are two main reasons for promoting and one for retaining employees in a bureaucracy. Promotion occurs either to get rid of people by "kicking them upstairs" or to advance them because of merit; in the latter case, a person ultimately reaches a position that he or she cannot handle. Incompetents are retained primarily because civil service regulations protect employees to such an extent that getting rid of anyone is not worth the effort. Clearly, if these conditions apply, every position will sooner or later be occupied by an incompetent.[23]

Bureaucratic growth accelerates the increase in the number of employees to whom the Peter Principle applies.

Limitless are the public servants who are indolent and insolent; military commanders whose behavioral timidity belies the dreadnaught rhetoric, and the governors whose innate servility prevents their actually governing. In our sophistication, we virtually shrug aside the immoral cleric, corrupt judge, incoherent attorney, author who cannot write and English teacher who cannot spell.[24]

Incompetence also results from the personality type most favored by the bureaucracy. Since bureaucratic organizations have long life spans, it is not surprising that the institution is more important than the individual. In this context, the successful bureaucrat is the one who fits into the agency's expected mold of behavior, neither too far to the left not too far to the right, with no desire for personal publicity—in short, a person in tune with the aim of perpetuating the agency. One critic has outlined five rules of behavior that successful bureaucrats follow:

Rule number one is to *maintain your tenure.* . . . The second rule of behavior in the government, and clearly related to the sustenance of your own tenure, is to *keep the boss from getting embarrassed.* That is the single most important standard of competence for a federal official. . . . The third unwritten rule of federal behavior is to *make sure that all appropriated funds are spent by the end of the fiscal year.* . . . The fourth unwritten rule of behavior in government is to *keep the program alive.* It is not appropriate to question the original purposes of the program. Nor is it appropriate to ask if the program has any consonance with its original purposes. . . . The fifth and final unwritten rule of federal behavior is to *maintain a stable and well-circumscribed constituency.* With so great a concern for survival in the government, it is necessary to have friends outside of it.[25]

To the bureaucrat, the important thing is not individualism and the right to personal creativity (which are threatening), but protection of one's job and prospects for advancement. The result of this process throughout the bureaucracy is massive depersonalization. Talent that might otherwise be used imaginatively to solve national problems is suppressed into a mold of mediocrity.

The motto of the bureaucracy is simply: "To get along, go along." Bureaucrats who do exert themselves may well end up in trouble. When Pentagon official A. Ernest Fitzgerald "blew the whistle" in 1968 on cost overruns for Defense Department weapons systems that were making fortunes for defense contractors, he lost his job until 1973 when congressional pressure forced his return. (See pp. 13–14). One observer has noted that there really are no incentives for a bureaucrat to achieve excellence.

The best we get from government in the welfare state is competent mediocrity. More often we do not get even that: we get incompetence such as we would not tolerate in an insurance company. . . . And the more we expand the welfare state, the less capable even of routine mediocrity does it seem to become.[26]

Bureaucracy is the major administrative vehicle of industrial society in the United States as well as in the rest of the world. Thus the solution of almost every specific practical problem in the United States involves the extension of bureaucracy and a broader and deeper penetration of its effects in all areas of personal, social, and cultural experience. Bureaucracy deprives individuals of freedom and autonomy, not necessarily by coercion but rather by creating a favorable system of rewards for compliance with dehumanized, technical, and efficient patterns of performance. The development of the bureaucratic machine, nationally and internationally, results in a kind of bureaucratic ideology which would deprive all individuals of any independence from it. Bureaucrats develop a sense of their power and have a tendency to affirm their bureaucratic function by exercising this power against the individual and his unique, personal creativity. When the bureaucrat expresses himself through the exercise of the bureaucratic function, he opposes the personal inclinations of others to express themselves.— *Joseph Bensman and Arthur J. Vidich*

The Negative Case

No, bureaucracy does not subvert democracy.

The legislative programs of administrative agencies . . . tend to incorporate the objectives of private groups and to temper and to modify them in the public interest. Indeed, in many situations of policy parturition it seems that the bureaucracy is the only participant animated by a devotion to the common welfare.[27]*–V. O. Key, Jr.*

The bureaucracy and the people that serve within it may not seem as dynamic and forceful as the charismatic leaders that populate the political scene elsewhere, but the personalities and styles of bureaucratic leaders have had a profound effect on the political system and public policy over the years.—*Peter Woll*

Criticizing the bureaucracy seems to be an American pastime. There is even a nationally syndicated radio program that satirizes its shortcomings. But every point in the argument against it can be countered by one equally as effective.

- The bureaucracy is large, but not disproportionately so.
- Substantial limitations check the bureaucracy's exercise of power.
- Though operating under difficult conditions, the bureaucracy has made a number of noteworthy achievements.

MYTHS ABOUT SIZE

The common impression is that the federal bureaucracy is like an octopus extending its tentacles everywhere. Actually, however, the principal bureaucratic growth today is in state and local governments as shown in Figure 2. Since 1947, the ratio of federal government employ-

FIG. 2. Government Civilian Employment

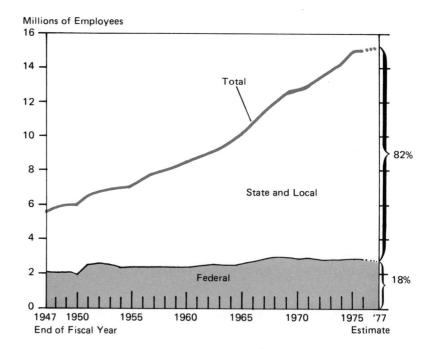

SOURCE: *Special Analyses, Budget of the United States, Fiscal Year 1977* (Washington, D.C.: U.S. Government Printing Office, 1976), p. 156.

ees to the total population has actually decreased from 14.4 to 13.3 per thousand.[28]

Most government growth that has occurred has been in response to demand, as our society has become more complex and plagued with more problems. Government programs do not originate without public support. We, the American people, ask our government for services. That is the main reason why bureaucracy grows, not because bureaucrats demand programs. Think about any government program, even one you may dislike, and you will find substantial public support for it. That is why we have a Federal Communications Commission, a Food and Drug Administration, a Federal Elections Commission, and a Social Security Administration—among many others.

Myths about the Washington bureaucracy are legion. George Wallace of Alabama could count on applause when he promised that, if elected, he would go to the capital and throw the "pointy-head" bureaucrats' briefcases into the Potomac River. Wallace's comments were directed implicity at people who worked for social welfare programs (which he regards as left wing).

Actually the Washington metropolitan area contains only a small proportion of the federal government's civilian employees—about 12 percent. To get rid of bureaucrats' briefcases, Wallace would have to travel throughout the United States; in California alone he would find over 250,000 federal bureaucrats. Wallace would also discover that a mere 10 percent of all bureaucrats work for welfare agencies like the Social Security Administration. Of this number, over half work for the Veterans' Administration—hardly a bureaucracy the Alabamian would want to eliminate. (The frequently condemned federal regulatory agencies employ an even smaller proportion of the federal work force than do the social welfare agencies.)

BUREAUCRATIC LIMITATIONS

The affirmative case espouses the theory that a "cozy triangle" exists among the bureaucracy, interest groups, and Congress. Indeed, it is argued that interest groups shuffle top personnel into and out of the bureaucracy to serve their interests. Certainly this occurs, but why not? Should the bureaucracy be denied the right to employ the best-trained personnel available? Should bureaucrats be denied the freedom to earn a livelihood in the private sector that they previously helped to regulate? To answer "yes" to these questions is to acknowledge that one does not want the bureaucracy to benefit from the enormous expertise of such groups; bureaucrats to have the right to obtain the best possible positions for themselves; or the private sector, desiring to employ former bureaucrats, to have the right to hire the best-informed applicants.

The American bureaucracy is a frequent target for criticism. Yet could the United States maintain its position as a major world power without a large bureaucratic system? The impressive diplomatic entrance to the State Department, one of the bastions of the bureaucracy, is shown here.

The "cozy triangle" argument also suffers for other reasons. First, not all interest groups have the same concerns in the same department. For example, the Farmers' Union and the American Farm Bureau Federation have distinctly different interests in the Department of Agriculture. The former is more concerned with the small farmer and the latter with the larger enterprises. Second, not all members of a congressional committee share the same interests in the department or agency overseen by the committee. To illustrate, liberal Democrats and conservative Republicans on the House and Senate Armed Services Committees differ in their views concerning the budget for the Department of Defense. Liberal Democrats are more likely to support cuts and conservative Republicans, increases.

Bureaucrats are not unrepresentative, nor are they unrestrained advocates of special interests. As pointed out earlier by V. O. Key, Jr., bureaucrats are sometimes the only participants in the policy-making process who are devoted to the public interest. Contrary to what many Americans believe, bureaucrats are not of any one political or ideological persuasion. Indeed, one study shows that they are more representative of the general public in education, religion, and other characteristics than are legislators or politically appointed executives.[29]

It would be seriously misleading to regard the bureaucracy as performing in a vacuum without curbs. Professional ethics, the advice and criticism of experts, and the views of political figures, interest groups, and private citizens restrain bureaucracy. In addition, Congress, the president, and the courts all operate to limit the bureaucracy. Whether or not these institutions exercise their rights of control is not the fault of the bureaucracy.

Concerning professional ethics, there are thousands of lawyers and doctors throughout the bureaucracy, but especially in the Departments of Justice and Health, Education, and Welfare, respectively. These civil servants must adhere not only to civil service standards of performance but also to the ethical standards specified by their respective professions.

Consider for a moment lawyers in the Department of Justice who are conducting criminal investigations. Should they fail to conduct a thorough and fair investigation, they would likely be criticized by experts in that department as well as by lawyers outside. Or if doctors with the Food and Drug Administration neglect to seek and consider advice from professionals outside the FDA concerning whether a given drug should be marketed, they would also be subject to criticism.

Congressional Controls   The chief job of the bureaucracy is to interpret, implement, and enforce acts of Congress. Whenever it fails to do so properly, Congress has numerous remedies. It may amend the law to make its intent clearer. It may call on the courts to require the bureaucracy to implement a law properly, or to enjoin it from interpreting a law contrary to congressional intent. For example, individual members of Congress have sued to enjoin an agency to interpret a law a certain way as Senator Edward Kennedy did with respect to presidential impoundment of congressionally appropriated funds (see discussion of impoundment on p. 327). Congress may conduct a public investigation of the bureaucracy; this is especially useful in bringing public opinion to bear on the matter of appropriations or to focus public attention on a specific issue. For example, on December 28, 1976, Senator Richard Schweiker (Rep. Pa.) asked that the Senate investigate germ warfare tests conducted by the Army in American cities during the 1950s and 1960s. Schweiker contended that these tests were a violation of the ideals of human liberty and that they led to significant increases in the incidence of illness and death from pneumonia in the test areas, which included eight cities.[30] Bureaucrats who participated in the decision making that approved these tests would obviously be the focus of Schweiker's attack.

Federal employees, well aware of their dependence on Congress for funds, are not likely to abuse their power if Congress asserts itself. Finally, Congress may ask the General Accounting Office to conduct a special investigation to determine whether an agency is functioning properly. The GAO's principal technique is the post-audit of expenditures, but it may also investigate the effectiveness of several alternative systems designed to achieve essentially the same goals.

Through the Administrative Procedures Act of 1946, Congress has specified several procedures that the bureaucracy must follow: Government agencies must make public their administrative organizations. They must provide interested persons with advance information on proposed rules, allow them to present information and arguments on pending cases, and allow their counsel to cross-examine witnesses.

Presidential Controls Through the Office of Management and Budget, the president can review the budget and administrative operation of each agency and make appropriate recommendations to Congress. OMB, together with the president's annual budgetary recommendations to Congress, can serve as a strong restraint on the bureaucracy.

The president also has the power to propose changes in the organizational structure, subject only to a veto by either house of Congress. If neither house votes against the proposal within sixty days, the president's proposed changes take effect.

The president's influence on public opinion and his ability to create new agencies give him further opportunities to control the bureaucracy. To avoid having his programs lost in the bowels of the bureaucracy, Franklin Roosevelt created many new agencies outside the structure of existing departments and agencies. In fact, most of the New Deal's so-called "alphabet" agencies were so established.

Court Checks Citizens who believe they have been wronged by bureaucratic action have judicial recourse. A private citizen may seek an injunction against a bureaucratic agency to stop a particular action or seek enforcement of a law not being enforced. The United States Court of Claims and the United States Tax Court are examples of special courts designed to adjudicate citizen complaints against bureaucratic decisions. A citizen with an income tax complaint, for instance, can take the case to the Tax Court.

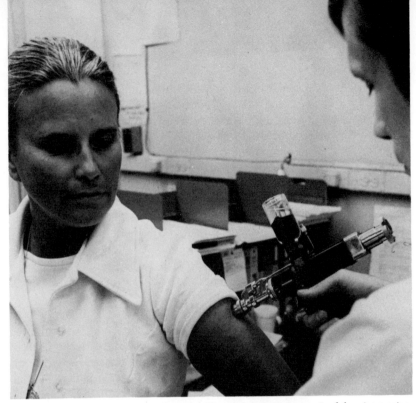

Bureaucracy at work—in 1976 and 1977 millions of Americans received free immunizations against swine flu through a well-run, well-publicized government-sponsored program.

The bureaucracy is hardly an island unto itself, but rather it is a part of a whole political process with numerous and diverse relationships and restraints among competing private groups and other government agencies and departments.

ACHIEVEMENTS IN SPITE OF DIFFICULTIES

Bureaucrats, much maligned today by both public and private citizens, are human beings like the rest of us. Understanding why they resist change and knowing something about the special pressures under which they operate will place their very real accomplishments in truer perspective.

Understanding Resistance to Change   There are reasons why bureaucrats behave as they do, especially as regards change and reform. It is a natural human tendency, especially for people working in a complex organization, to concentrate their energies on activities that may garner praise and promotion. Bureaucrats understand that to change a program, even to improve it, is to change the status quo. This presents threats not only to them but to other persons as well. In other words, pure selfishness is not the only factor. Risks may threaten one's superiors, subordinates, and peers.

Like most people, bureaucrats do not want others to control them. Reform proposals (and, of course, other types of proposals as well) may be opposed because of the possibility of an agency's becoming controlled by another organization. One reform proposal would, for example, move the Federal Trade Commission, now an independent regulatory agency, to the Department of Justice. The reason for this proposal is that the Federal Trade Commission has allegedly become the captive of regulated interests and thus insensitive to the public interest. If placed under the Attorney General in the Department of Justice, it would be in a clear line of accountability to the president, who could more effectively respond to the public pressures concerning actions of this agency. Since the FTC is an independent regulatory commission, the president can appoint members of the commission with the consent of the Senate for seven-year terms, but he cannot remove them except for cause (i.e., a specific violation of statutory law as provided by Congress). Within the Department of Justice, the president has removal powers over the directors of principal bureaus, such as the Federal Bureau of Investigation, regardless of whether there is cause for removal. This power would in all likelihood apply to the Federal Trade Commission if it were dissolved and transferred to the Department of Justice.

Special Pressures   The federal bureaucracy, unlike private business, functions under public scrutiny. Its actions are subject to analysis and criticism by journalists, scholars, and politicians. This scrutiny is not only public, it is political, and thus subjects the bureaucracy to the vicissitudes of political fortune. The same decision may be praised at one time and later condemned. This uncertain bureaucratic environment is illustrated by the Federal Bureau of Investigation. For most of the FBI's history, it was seen as the epitome of efficiency, and much esteemed by the public. Who dared criticize it? But as the public attitudes toward the role of intelligence became more critical, the FBI's position diminished accordingly. Evidence suggests that the FBI was the same agency making the same kind of decisions, with but one difference—the political environment had altered.

Besides functioning in a very open and intensely political environment, bureaucrats must make decisions on the most controversial of issues and problems. After all, one reason the bureaucracy exists is to help solve problems that have not been solved by private business or any other institution. The bureaucracy, a sort of agency of last resort, confronts issues and problems that are not easily soluble. As a result of public pressure and the conflicting demands of interest groups, Congress places problems in the hands of the bureaucracy. But doing so does not mean that the pressures will disappear. For example, merely because Congress abolished the United States Post Office Department and created the United States Postal Corporation did not reduce the problems of the postal service; authority for solving them was simply transferred from an executive department to a public corporation.

Naturally, bureaucrats' decisions, made to help solve previously insoluble problems, face adverse criticism from those whom their actions do not favor. Attacks on bureaucracy are one way the public has of "letting off steam."

> Frustrated clients can relieve their pent-up aggression in discussions of bureaucratic stupidity and red tape. Whereas the organization's ruthlessness, not its inefficiency, is the source of their antagonism, by expressing it in the form of an apparently disinterested criticism of performance, clients derive a feeling of superiority over the "blundering bureaucrats" that serves as psychological compensation for being under their power.[31]

Politicians can run for reelection to seek vindication for their decisions. What can a bureaucrat do? He or she has no place to appeal for protection from the public's natural inclination to criticize.

Bureaucracy's Accomplishments People often complain that only bad news makes news. To a considerable extent this is true of bureaucracy. We hear about its failures and shortcomings, but pay less attention to the many government programs that are run efficiently and in the public interest.

A few examples will suffice: (1) Our exceedingly complex tax laws are administered by the Internal Revenue Service with great dispatch. (2) The Social Security Administration enrolled 19 million people in Medicare and set up the organizational procedures to pay their medical bills in all fifty states in less than a year's time. (3) An innovative and successful space program was directed by the National Aeronautics and Space Administration; as one man put it, "The feat of landing men on the moon was not only a scientific achievement but a bureaucratic one as well."[32] (4) The interstate highway system, run by the Federal Highway Administration, has made travel for all Americans much easier and economical. (5) Year after year, the Bureau of the Census (part of the Social and Economic Statistics Administration) provides detailed and reliable data on almost every facet of American society. (6) Also the National Bureau of Standards and the National Institutes of Health are highly regarded for their contributions to the quality of American life.

The natural base for the bureaucracy's role as policy counselor is found in its exceptional resources. It is a gatherer of facts that constantly accumulate as a byproduct of administrative activities. It is a surveyor of public needs as well as of governmental performance in meeting such needs. It is a recorder of interest pressures and public sentiments affecting the political course. It is an inaugurator of organizational devices and technical procedures suitable for attaining the government's ends. It is a fountain of ideas about what ought to be done to redress conditions that cry for remedy. Finally, it is a knowledgeable and skillful draftsman in converting broad understandings about desirable goals into the detailed language of regulatory measures.—*Fritz Marstein Marx*

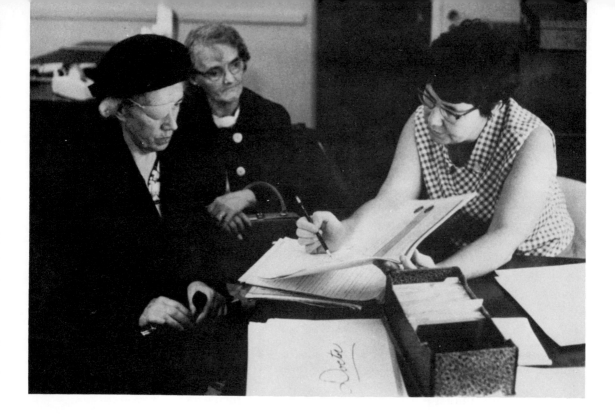

Despite complaints of inefficiency and bureaucratic red tape, government agencies provide much-needed assistance to millions of Americans each week. Here a senior citizen is helped to file a claim by a worker in a Social Security Administration office, and out-of-work Americans line up to receive checks and job referrals at an unemployment office.

Admittedly some bureaucratic programs fail or are abused, but the proportion is not large. Putting the issue another way, we might ask ourselves just what governmental programs we would like to abolish. The answer is probably very few.

It is interesting that, when all is said and done, Americans think rather highly of the work of bureaucrats. Four psychologists who carried out a study reported:

> Bureaucrats have had a bad press. The vision is of a petty tyrant who wraps the cloak of office around inadequate shoulders, dominates those below him, and crouches sheepishly before those above him. That image has been with us a long time. . . .
>
> It turns out, however, that for all the snickering at the stereotype, Americans like the bureaucrats they deal with pretty well.[33]

In looking at a range of government services, these psychologists found that the percentage of people who are satisfied with bureaucracy far exceeds those who are dissatisfied.

There is a prevailing myth that somehow private business is much more efficient than government. If this is so, why do major corporations have huge cost overruns in executing military contracts? Clearly, business produces its share of Edsels and blockbuster movie flops.

Certainly the federal bureaucracy does not present a threat to private capitalism. The principal areas of public ownership and administration in the United States are the postal service, the Tennessee Valley Authority, very limited public housing, and Social Security. There is also government aid to education, and public television programming (which does not compete substantially with the commercial networks). In other nations, it is common for government to own and operate not only the postal service, public housing, and all radio and television communications but also the railroads, airlines, all utilities, and full health and medical insurance programs. In the United States, government ownership is thus quite limited. Socialism is not just around the corner.

Reforms Under Consideration   Any organization as large as the federal bureaucracy could be improved. To its credit, the bureaucracy itself has experimented with a variety of new organizational techniques. One is program budgeting, commonly called PPBS (Planning, Programming, Budgeting System). Under this plan, agencies must put a price tag on what they are trying to accomplish before they request new programs and appropriations. Continued experimentation with interdepartmental committees—such as the Domestic Council in the Executive Office of the President—and coordinating bodies may also improve bureaucratic efficiency. Perhaps nothing would bring a more welcome breath of fresh air than for bureaucrats to be candid about their failures and short-comings instead of trying to cover them up. George Romney, former Secretary of the Department of Housing and Urban Development, set a high standard when he said of his own department that it was rife with "incompetence, conflict of interest, favoritism, graft, bribes, and fraud." [34]

A number of proposals for reform, some specific and some general, are at present under consideration both inside and outside the bureaucracy.

Sunset Laws   One dramatic bureaucratic reform proposal, first conceived in Colorado by that state's chapter of Common Cause, would provide for the automatic abolition of every governmental agency within a prescribed time period unless there were substantial justification for continuing it. The purpose of the so-called *"sunset laws,"* supported by both conservatives (such as Senator Barry Goldwater) and liberals (such as Senator Edmund Muskie), is to fight bureaucratic obesity through (1) automatic termination, (2) shifting the proof of an agency's value to the agency, and (3) encouraging the legislature to perform its oversight function better by requiring legislative hearings on the continuation of agencies (with the public having a voice in determining whether an agency should live or die).

Zero Budgeting   Traditionally, every governmental agency has assumed that the funds received the previous year will be provided for the next year. The agency's task has been not to justify the past year's budget but to justify an increase. *Zero budgeting* forces an agency to justify the previous year's budget before seeking an increase. That is, its budget for the coming year is assumed to be zero until the agency's rationale for its expenditures convinces the Congress.

Shifting Senior Bureaucrats   Another reform idea is to rotate senior bureaucrats periodically from one agency to another. Such shifts would help prevent abuses of power, freshen the perspectives of civil servants, and lessen the ties that bureaucrats develop with members of Congress and interest groups.

Party Leadership   V. O. Key, Jr., once said that "the problem of bureaucracy is in part not a problem of bureaucracy at all. It is rather a question of attracting into party service an adequate supply of men competent to manage and control the bureaucracy from their posts as the transient but responsible heads of departments and agencies. . . . It is through such persons who owe their posts to the victorious party that popular control over government is maintained." [35] Key places the burden of controlling the bureaucracy on the parties that elect the presidents who are supposed to administer the government. If parties placed more emphasis on recruiting and placing in top administrative positions outstanding administrative talent rather than outstanding political tal-

[On controlling the growth of government bureaucracy] The steps that need to be taken would fall into three general categories: first of all, the reorganization of the structure of government to make it simple, efficient, economical, purposeful and manageable for a change. The second principle is proper budgeting. We had throughout my own term as Governor a concept instituted called zero-based budgeting. Every program that spends the taxpayers' money has to rejustify itself annually. You have an automatic reassessment of priorities; you have an automatic detection with the possibility of eliminating duplication and overlapping of functions. And you have an automatic screening out of obsolete and obsolescent programs. And the third general principle is long-range planning or, to be expressed more simply, the careful delineation of purposes and goals so that the government knows what it hopes to accomplish at the end of a year, two years, five years or twenty-five years in every realm of human life which is determined by or affected by government.—*Jimmy Carter*

ent, the party process could do much to improve relationships between bureaucracy and democracy.

Ombudsman   To help average citizens by making the bureaucracy more responsive to their needs, many experts have suggested establishing the office of *ombudsman* (from the Swedish word for "commissioner"). This office, by investigating citizen complaints against government, would give people an alternative to accepting (as most often happens) the decision of a faceless bureaucrat. It should be noted, however, that members of Congress already perform the role of ombudsman in a major way (see Chapter 11).

Public Confrontation   Another means of making the bureaucracy responsive is to allow citizens to confront bureaucrats personally and to levy penalties on public servants for being derelict in their duties.

Under former Secretary F. David Matthews of the Department of Health, Education, and Welfare, a special effort was made in 1976 to obtain public comment on projected regulations, i.e., administrative law, before it was actually written and to train bureaucrats to write administrative law so the public could more easily read and interpret it. Previously, administrative law was written, and then the public was given an opportunity to respond. By taking suggestions before the regulations are actually proposed and written, the public interest should be better protected.[36]

Decentralization   Efforts have been made to decentralize bureaucratic decision making so that the public can participate in or at least be much closer to choices that affect their lives. Some of Johnson's Great Society programs, with their Community Action Councils, embodied this goal. Richard Goodwin, a former aide to Presidents Kennedy and Johnson, noted that "the general guide should be to transfer power to the smallest unit [of government] consistent with the scale of the problem."[37]

Improving Presidential Control   If the regulatory agencies, which exist in a kind of "no man's land" as quasi-judicial and quasi-executive bodies, were brought under the president's direct control, the public would at least have an opportunity to express disapproval of their actions at the polls by holding the president accountable. As it is, the commissioners on these bodies cannot be removed by the president. They are thus in a highly independent position and aloof from control by the political process.

It is also difficult for the president to control existing agencies because of the "cozy triangle." Several of the proposals already discussed would help overcome this difficulty. James MacGregor Burns has noted that "the line of command between the White House and action agencies must be drawn taut" in order to eliminate the problem of special interests, which weakens presidential control.[38]

> The bureaucratic organization must try to act instrumentally and rationally because it is designed as a tool for achieving a goal of an external owner. It searches for alternatives and consequences, for better ways of doing things, and makes choices between the alternatives (decides) by reference to its goal.— *Victor A. Thompson*

Glossary

Administrative law: rules and guidelines made and carried out by the various federal agencies and commissions.

Bureaucracy: any administrative system, but particularly a governmental agency, that daily implements policy pursuant to law, that follows standardized procedures, and that allocates specialized duties to employees.

Civil servants: employees in the civil service.

Civil service: refers to governmental employees hired and promoted on the basis of merit; first adopted in the United States with the Pendleton Act of 1883.

Clientelism: the special relationship between industries and the federal agencies or commissions that regulate them.

Merit system: the hiring of governmental employees on the basis of ability rather than political allegiance.

Ombudsman: official charged with investigating citizen complaints about the bureaucracy.

Parkinson's law: a theory that work expands to fit the amount of time available.

Patronage system: the practice of allowing elected political officials to hire and fire employees at will.

Peter Principle: persons tend to rise to the level of their own incompetence so that in time, every position tends to be occupied by an employee who is incompetent to carry out its duties.

Statutory law: law enacted by Congress or other legislative bodies.

Sunset law: reform proposal providing for automatic abortion of a governmental agency after a specified time period unless the legislature reestablishes it.

Zero budgeting: type of budgeting requiring governmental agencies to justify all of their budget, not just their proposed increase.

Notes

1. *Myers* v. *United States* (1926).

2. *Humphrey's Executor* v. *United States* (1935); *Wiener* v. *United States* (1958).

3. *Washington Post*, September 15, 1975, p. 22.

4. Speech on September 5, 1975, in Sacramento, California, as reported in the *National Journal*, September 13, 1975, p. 1308.

5. Arthur M. Schlesinger, Jr., *A Thousand Days* (Boston: Houghton Mifflin, 1965), pp. 680–681.

6. C. Northcote Parkinson, *Parkinson's Law* (New York: Ballantine Books, 1957), p. 17.

7. Norman John Powell, *Responsible Public Bureaucracy in the United States* (Boston: Allyn & Bacon, 1967), pp. 175–176.

8. For more information on the Truman, Eisenhower, Kennedy, and Johnson administrations, see David T. Stanley, Dean E. Mann, and Jameson W. Doig, *Men Who Govern: A Biographical Profile of Federal Political Executives* (Washington, D. C.: The Brookings Institution, 1967). For details on the Nixon administration, see Dom Donafede, "Nixon's First-Year Appointments Reveal Pattern of His Administration," *National Journal*, January 24, 1970, pp. 182–192.

9. Gideon Sjoberg, Richard A. Brymer, and Bufore Farris, "Bureaucracy and the Lower Class," in Francis Rourke, ed., *Bureaucratic Power and National Politics* (Boston: Little, Brown, 1972), pp. 395–396.

10. Theodore Lowi, *The End of Liberalism* (New York: Norton, 1969), pp. 103–104.

11. Michael Jacobson, *Eater's Digest* (Garden City, N. Y.: Doubleday, 1972), p. 200.

12. James Risser and George Anthan, "Why They Love Earl Butz," *New York Times Magazine*, June 13, 1976, pp. 49, 52.

13. Morton Mintz and Jerry S. Cohen, *America Inc.: Who Owns and Operates the United States* (New York: Dell, 1972), pp. 305–306.

14. David Burnham, "Conflict of Interest, Clear Yet Fuzzy," *New York Times*, June 20, 1976, p. E5.

15. James Ridgeway, "How Government and Industry Keep Secrets from People," *New Republic*, August 21 and 28, 1971, pp. 17–19.

16. David Wise, *The Politics of Lying* (New York: Random House, 1973), p. 266.

17. Matthew P. Dumont, "Down the Bureaucracy!" *Transaction*, October 1970, p. 14.

18. As cited in Leonard Freedman, *Power and Politics in America* (North Scituate, Mass.: Duxbury Press, 1974), p. 242.

19. As cited in Robert Sherrill, *Why They Call It Politics* (New York: Harcourt Brace Jovanovich, 1974), p. 197.

20. *Washington Post*, August 12, 1975, p. A15.

21. *The Greenville* [S. C.] *News*, December 15, 1976, p. 5A.

22. Barry Goldwater, speech on Senate floor, *Congressional Record*, July 14, 1970, pp. 24103–24107.

23. See generally Laurence J. Peter and Raymond Hull, *The Peter Principle* (New York: Bantam Books, 1969).

24. Ibid., pp. 2–3.

25. Dumont, "Down the Bureaucracy!" pp. 10–12.

26. Peter Drucker, *The Age of Discontinuity* (New York: Harper & Row, 1969), pp. 212–220.

27. V. O. Key, Jr., *Politics, Parties and Pressure Groups*, 5th ed. (New York: Crowell, 1964), p. 710.

28. Robert Samuelson, "Good-for-Nothing Government," *New Republic*, May 15, 1976, p. 10.

29. Norton Long, "Bureaucracy and Constitutionalism," *American Political Science Review* 52 (1952):808–818.

30. *Washington Post*, December 18, 1976, p. A3.

31. Peter Blau, *Bureaucracy in Modern Society* (New York: Random House, 1956), p. 103.

32. Duane Lockard, *The Perverted Priorities of American Politics* (New York: Macmillan, 1971), p. 282.

33. Robert L. Kahn et al., "Americans Love Their Bureaucrats," *Psychology Today*, June 1975, p. 66.

34. *New York Times*, April 2, 1972, pp. D1, D12.

35. Key, *Politics, Parties and Pressure Groups*, pp. 711–712.

36. *The Chronicle of Higher Education*, December 20, 1976, p. 5.

37. Richard Goodwin, "Reflections: Sources of Public Unhappiness," *New Yorker*, January 4, 1969, p. 50.

38. James MacGregor Burns, *Uncommon Sense* (New York: Harper & Row, 1972), p. 127.

Recommended Rebuttal Reading

The National Bureaucracy

Altshuler, Alan A., ed. *Politics of the Federal Bureaucracy*. New York: Dodd, Mead, 1968.

Gawthrop, Louis C. *Bureaucratic Behavior in the Executive Branch.* New York: The Free Press, 1969.

Rourke, Francis E., ed. *Bureaucratic Power in National Politics.* Boston: Little, Brown, 1972.

Bureaucracy and Public Policy

Berkman, Richard L., and W. Kip Viscusi. *Damming the West: The Report on the Bureau of Reclamation.* New York: Grossman, 1973.

Rourke, Francis E. *Bureaurcacy, Politics, and Public Policy.* Boston: Little, Brown, 1969.

Organization Theory

Blau, Peter M. *On the Nature of Organizations.* New York: John Wiley, 1974.

Parkinson, Cyril N. *Parkinson's Law.* Boston: Houghton Mifflin, 1957.

Budget and Personnel

Mosher, Frederick C. *Democracy and the Public Service.* New York: Oxford University Press, 1968.

Wildavsky, Aaron, *The Politics of the Budgetary Process.* Boston: Little, Brown, 1974.

Bureaucratic Issues

Etzkowitz, Henry, and Peter Schwab, eds. *Is America Necessary? Conservative, Liberal, and Socialist Perspectives of United States Political Institutions.* St. Paul, Minn.: West, 1976.

Jacoby, Henry. *The Bureaucratization of the World.* Berkeley: University of California Press, 1973.

Peters, Charles, and James Fellows, eds. *Inside the System.* New York: Praeger, 1976.

Rourke, Francis E. *Secrecy and Publicity.* Baltimore, Md.: Johns Hopkins University Press, 1966.

General Reference

Seidman, Harold. *Politics, Position, and Power.* New York: Oxford University Press, 1970.

Thompson, Victor. *Bureacracy and the Modern World.* Morristown, N. J.: General Learning Press, 1976.

Tullock, Gordon. *The Politics of Bureaucracy.* Washington, D. C.: Public Affairs Press, 1965.

RESOLVED THAT: Congress Is Archaic

At Issue: Congress

Mark Twain once referred to members of Congress as "probably the only indigenous American criminal class." Twain was indulging in a favorite American pastime, mocking the national legislature. Stephen Vincent Benét did it more elegantly in *John Brown's Body*, when he described the legislators who went to watch the Civil War battle of Bull Run:

> The congressmen came out to see Bull Run,
> The congressmen who like free shows and spectacles.
> They brought their wives and carriages along,
> They brought their speeches and their picnic-lunch,
> Their black constituent-hats and their devotion:
> Some even brought a little whiskey, too.
> (A little whiskey is a comforting thing
> For congressmen in the sun, in the heat of the sun.)
> The bearded congressmen with orators' mouths,
> The fine, clean-shaved, Websterian congressmen,
> Come out to see the gladiators' show
> Like Iliad gods, wrapped in the sacred cloud
> Of Florida-water, wisdom and bay-rum,
> Of free cigars, democracy and votes,
> That lends such portliness to congressmen.

To any student of government, it is eminently clear that the role of the Congress in determining national policy, defense or otherwise, has deteriorated over the years. More and more the role of Congress has come to be that of a sometimes querulous but essentially kindly uncle who complains while furiously puffing on his pipe but who finally, as everyone expects, gives in and hands over the allowance, grants the permission, or raises his hand in blessing, and then returns to the rocking chair for another year of somnolence broken only by an occasional anxious glance down the avenue and a muttered doubt as to whether he had done the right thing.—*House Report 1406*

385

You are the people and the voice of the people
And, when the fight is done, your carriages
Will bear you safely, through the streaming rout
Of broken troops, throwing their guns away.
You come to see the gladiators' show,
But from a high place, as befits the wise.[1]

No other institution of American government, unless it be that of dogcatcher, has been ridiculed as much as the Congress of the United States. One must naturally wonder why. After all, as a representative body, it is in many ways the keystone of our democratic system. Its roots go back very far indeed.

THE ROOTS OF CONGRESS

James Mill, father of John Stuart Mill, once wrote that "representation is the grand discovery of modern times." If it is, then the American Congress is one of the foremost examples of this "discovery." For, serving as a substitute for the meeting of individual citizens that characterizes a direct democracy, a gathering of representative lawmakers is the prime institution of indirect democracy, and the Congress of the United States has fulfilled this function for over two hundred years.

Assemblies of lawmakers go back at least as far as ancient Greece. The immediate antecedents of the American legislature, however, were the British parliament and the colonial assemblies. When newly independent Americans adopted the Articles of Confederation, they established a strong national legislative body in reaction to the enormous power of the British executive (the monarchy). Government without an effective executive did not function well, however, so the Constitution created a balance of power among legislative, executive, and judicial branches. Even so, the framers still looked upon the legislature as the most powerful branch and the one closest to the people. Before amendments changed the system, the House of Representatives was the only component of the federal government directly affected by the will of the people through direct popular election.

Born out of a conflict between proponents of a strong executive and others favoring a strong legislature, Congress is still one focus of disagreement on this issue. And its members—fixed since 1929 at 435 representatives, plus, of course, the two senators from each state—have been praised, ridiculed, and even feared. An overview of the functions played by Congress may contribute to an understanding of such attitudes.

THE FUNCTIONS OF CONGRESS

What are the functions of Congress? What is it about them that has led to the continuing conflict between the legislative and executive branches?

Constitutional Functions Constitutionally prescribed functions include some for both House and Senate combined and others for just one of the two houses. Both the House and the Senate together must act to propose constitutional amendments, declare war, pass legislation, and determine presidential disability. In handling impeachment proceedings, the House of Representatives impeaches the official and the Senate acts as a trial court. In the case of elections, if the electoral college fails to provide a majority for president and vice-president, the House elects the former and the Senate, the latter. Each house has the constitutional authority to regulate the conduct of its members and to determine whether a prospective member has been properly elected or should be seated.

Certain functions are specified for one house only. The Senate has sole authority to ratify treaties proposed by the president and to con-

... the prime function of the Congress is to be much more than an arena of competing interests, more than a cacophony of many spokesmen. Its imperative function should be to achieve coherent, effective national policy. That is why the Congress is best described as [a] process, essentially a process intended to achieve understanding and at least majority agreement out of disagreement. And that is largely a conceptual process, requiring long periods of time and varied means to obtain basic information and advice, in the search for understanding ... long sessions of taking testimony, of probing questions, of intensive study, analysis and synthesis, of discussion and argument, argument, argument; of skillfully writing decisions into legislative form; and also of bargaining, amending, accommodating, compromising ... moving the bills through cumbersome, tortuous parliamentary procedures and levels to that point of final agreement by both houses, and then the President's signature which makes these decisions an Act, the law.—*Charles A. Mosher*

The Senate was [for Lyndon Johnson] faith, calling, club, habit, relaxation, devotion, hobby, and love.—*Theodore H. White*

firm presidential nominations. Since the Senate has confirmation power, it developed the custom of senatorial courtesy. The House has the power to originate all money bills; this authority is based on the theory that the branch of government closest to the people should exercise the closest control over tax dollars.

The predominant and controlling force, the centre and source of all motive and of all regulative power is Congress. . . . The legislature is the aggressive spirit.—*Woodrow Wilson*

Legitimizing Function Individuals and groups have conflicting ideas on public policy. For instance, Roman Catholics and Lutherans generally support aid to private and parochial schools, while most Baptists and most Jews oppose it. Should there be a national health insurance program? Should railroads be nationalized? Should there be a national land-use policy? One of the principal functions of Congress is to help resolve such questions through compromise, thus legitimizing public policy—that is, devising a solution that competing groups will accept.

Another phase of the legitimizing function occurs during military emergencies in which the president commits military forces, as happened since World War II in Korea, Lebanon, the two Cuban crises, and Vietnam. Typically, Congress through its leaders announces its support for the president's action. Only on rare occasions have rank-and-file members differed with such endorsements of presidential actions.

Investigatory Function One of the most visible congressional functions is that of investigating the executive branch. Congress conducts such inquiries to determine whether the executive is functioning properly and spending money wisely. The most dramatic contemporary example of this role was the Senate Watergate hearings of 1973, chaired by Senator Sam Ervin of North Carolina. Other much-publicized investigations of the 1970s probed the Central Intelligence Agency, including the alleged cover-up of facts about the assassination of President Kennedy, and the Federal Food and Drug Administration, particularly its alleged unethical or illegal relationship to the food and drug industry. Then in 1976, the House of Representatives began a thorough investigation of political assassinations, particularly those of John F. Kennedy and Martin Luther King, Jr., to determine if all the facts about those assassinations had been revealed. It was alleged, for example, that Cuban Premier Fidel Castro had played a role in the 1963 Kennedy assassination.

Ombudsman Function Voters write to their legislators when they have problems with other government agencies; these may range from Social Security checks to draft exemptions to immigration visas. Of course, members of Congress also represent cities, counties, states, groups, and institutions in such matters as obtaining federal grants or contracts. In this ombudsman role, a legislator acts as an agent representing constituent interests against the bureaucracy. Staff caseworkers help carry out this role.

THE ORGANIZATION OF CONGRESS

The several functions of Congress are carried out in a complex organizational setting. For our purposes the two most important aspects of this structure are party leadership and the committee framework.

Party Leadership Formal party organization in Congress is shown in Table 1. In the House of Representatives, this organization is headed by the Speaker, who is the presiding officer and most powerful member. The Speaker is theoretically chosen by all members of the House but is in reality elected by the majority party. His powers derive not only from his position as parliamentary leader, who can recognize persons on the

So long as the Speaker remains a weak king surrounded by strong dukes, the House cannot organize itself to lead. A strong Speaker is crucial to the House. He is the indispensable man for its legislative and political health, education, and welfare.—*Richard Bolling*

Table 1. Party Organization in Congress
(When the Democratic Party Is in the Majority)

	HOUSE	SENATE
DEMOCRATS	Speaker	Majority Leader
	Chairman of Caucus*	Majority Whip
	Majority Leader	Chairman of Caucus*
	Majority Whip	Policy Committee
	(Deputy and Assistant	Steering Committee
	Whips)	Senatorial Campaign
	Steering and Policy	Committee
	Committee	
	Democratic National	
	Congressional Committee	
	Patronage Committee	
REPUBLICANS	Minority Leader	Minority Leader
	Chairman of Conference*	Minority Whip
	Minority Whip	Chairman of Conference*
	(Regional Whips)	Policy Committee
	Committee on Committees	Committee on Committees
	Policy Committee	Senatorial Campaign
	National Republican	Committee
	Congressional Campaign	Personnel Committee
	Committee	

*Caucus and conference include all members of party.

floor and thus influence the flow of legislation, but also his control over appointments to the Rules Committee, which governs the flow of legislation coming to the House. The Speaker also serves as a member of the Steering and Policy Committee, which allocates committee assignments.

Each party in the House also has a majority (or minority) floor leader and whip. They are responsible for party leadership in debate and for attempting to line up members' votes on issues on which there is a party position.

Other important elements in the formal party organization of the House are the Democratic caucus and the Republican conference. All party members belong to one of these organizations. Each group has a chairman.

The Senate is presided over by the vice-president. In the vice-president's absence the presiding officer is the president pro tempore of the Senate. Though the senior member of the majority party, the president pro tempore does not have the power of the House Speaker. The majority leader in the Senate is the principal party spokesman in that body and as a result has considerably more power than the majority leader in the House. Because the Senate has only 100 members, compared to 435 in the House, the floor leadership in the House has more power. In the Senate power is much more diffused among individual members.

In addition to formal party organization, there are also informal groups that have a great deal of influence on member behavior. Republicans have the Wednesday Club, the Chowder and Marching Society, the SOS, and an organization of conservative members. The Wednesday Club consists of moderate to liberal Republicans in the House (a similar organization exists for Senate Republicans); they develop and sponsor legislation as a group. Two of the best-known Democratic organizations are the Democratic Study Group, which has been in the forefront of efforts to modernize the House of Representatives, and the Black Caucus, which consists of all black members of the House.

Congress is a collection of committees that come together in a chamber periodically to approve one another's actions.—*Clem Miller*

Committees The most crucial unit in legislative organization is the committee. It is in committees that the fate of the thousands of bills and resolutions introduced each year is determined. *Standing committees* are permanent, continuing their work from one session to the next. There are twenty-two standing committees in the House and fifteen in the Senate, as shown in Table 2. Although committees dealing with appropriations and finance (the Ways and Means Committee handles finance in the House) are among the most powerful in both the House and Senate, the prestige of other committees varies between the two houses. The House of Representatives, with its large and complex

Table 2. Standing Committees of Congress (Ranked in Groups, by Order of Importance) with Membership and Subcommittees

	HOUSE			SENATE		
	COMMITTEE	MEMBERS	SUB-COMMITTEES	COMMITTEE	MEMBERS	SUB-COMMITTEES
1	Appropriations	55	13	Appropriations	25	13
	Rules	16	0	Finance	18	10
	Ways and Means	37	6	Foreign Relations	16	9
2	Agriculture	46	10	Agriculture, Nutrition and Forestry	18	7
	Armed Services	40	7	Armed Services	18	8
	Budget*	25	0	Budget*	16	0
	Government Operations	43	7	Commerce, Science and Transportation	18	6
	International Relations	37	10			
	Interstate and Foreign Commerce	43	6			
	Judiciary	34	7	Judiciary	17	10
3	Banking, Finance and Urban Affairs	46	10	Banking, Housing and Urban Affairs	15	8
	Education and Labor	37	8	Energy and Natural Resources	18	6
	Interior and Insular Affairs	43	7	Human Resources	15	8
	Public Works and Transportation	43	6	Environment and Public Works	15	6
	Science and Technology	40	7			
4	Merchant Marine and Fisheries	40	5	Governmental Affairs	17	7
	Post Office and Civil Service	25	7			
	Standards of Official Conduct	12	0			
	Veterans' Affairs	28	5	Veterans' Affairs	9	3
	Small Business	37	6			
5	District of Columbia	19	3	Rules and Administration	9	0
	House Administration	25	8			

*New committees with important formal powers but not as yet clearly established policy influence.

Source: Membership and subcommittees based on data from *Congressional Quarterly Weekly Report,* April 30, 1977. Rankings based on data from several sources, including Donald H. Matthews, *U. S. Senators and Their World* (New York: Vintage, 1960); and H. Douglas Price, as cited in Stephen K. Bailey, *The New Congress* (New York: St. Martin's Press, 1966).

organization, has a powerful Rules Committee. In the Senate, because of constitutional obligations to confirm ambassadors and ratify treaties, the Foreign Relations Committee occupies a preeminent position. Committees can change in status over time. For instance, when the House Committee on Science and Technology was first created, it was relatively unimportant and thus consisted of relatively new and uninfluential members. Later, however, as its subject matter became more important to American society, it gained in prestige and desirability.

In addition to standing committees, there are also several *joint committees*, with members from both the House and Senate. In the mid-1970s these consisted of the following: Atomic Energy, Defense Production, Economic, Internal Revenue, Taxation, and Reduction of Nonessential Federal Expenditures. Each house also creates special *select committees* from time to time to explore subjects of extraordinary interest. The Senate Watergate Committee, to name just one, was a select committee.

THE LEGISLATIVE PROCESS

Congress is, first and foremost, a legislative body. Through a complex set of procedures, it enacts proposals, which may be in the form of either resolutions or bills.

Resolutions are of three types. A *simple resolution* requires the action of only one house, does not have the force of law, and merely expresses the opinion of that house. Also without the force of law is a *concurrent resolution*, which requires action by both houses and expresses the opinion of both houses. A *joint resolution*, passed by both houses, has the force of law, but does not require the president's signature.

There are two kinds of bills. A *private bill* involves the private interests of an individual or corporation. A *public bill*, as the name suggests, deals with matters of concern to the whole population.

There are eight basic stages in the legislative process, as shown in Figure 1. First, a bill is developed and prepared for introduction. This stage may take from several hours to several years. The idea for the bill may come from constituents, a lobby, the president or an executive agency, one or more representatives or senators, or congressional staff members. Both the House and Senate offer services to members, doing research to provide background data for bills and putting bills into proper form. Figure 2 shows what a bill looks like.

Second, the bill is introduced and referred to a committee, in the House by the Speaker, in the Senate by the presiding officer. Committee jurisdictions are fairly well defined, so that there is seldom a controversy about where a bill is assigned. On very rare occasions, the refer-

FIG. 1. Stages in the Legislative Process*

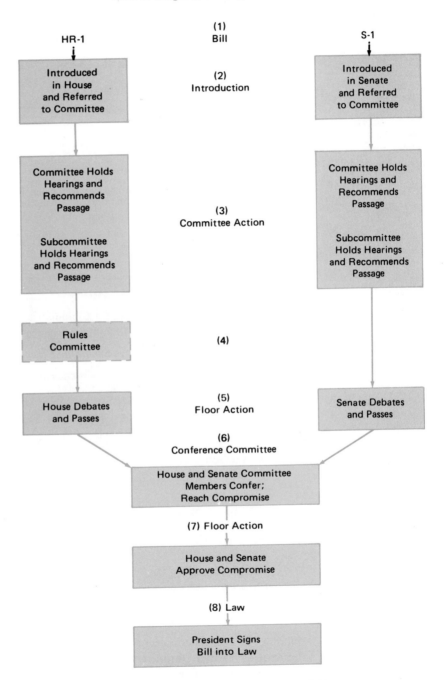

*For a nonappropriations bill introduced in similar form in both Houses.

FIG. 2. A Sample Bill

Union Calendar No. 644

91st CONGRESS
2d Session

H. R. 18434

[Report No. 91–1347]

IN THE HOUSE OF REPRESENTATIVES

July 13, 1970

Mr. MacDonald of Massachusetts (for himself, Mr. Van Deerlin, Mr. Rooney of Pennsylvania, Mr. Ottinger, Mr. Tiernan, Mr. Broyhill of North Carolina, Mr. Harvey, Mr. Brotzman, and Mr. Brown of Ohio) introduced the following bill; which was referred to the Committee on Interstate and Foreign Commerce.

July 29, 1970

Committed to the Committee of the Whole House on the State of the Union and ordered to be printed

---

A BILL

To revise the provisions of the Communications Act of 1934 which relate to political broadcasting.

1   *Be it enacted by the Senate and House of Representa-*

2   *tives of the United States of America in Congress assembled,*

3   That (a) the first sentence of section 315(a) of the Com-

4   munications Act of 1934 (47 U.S.C. 315(a)) is amended

5   by inserting before the colon the following: ", except that

6   the foregoing requirement shall not apply to the use of

7   a broadcasting station by a legally qualified candidate for

8   the office of President or Vice President of the United

9   States in a general election".

I

NOTE: A bill receives a number based upon when it introduced. The first bill introduced in each Congress always receives the number *1.*

ral of a bill may be contested, and on equally rare occasions, a bill may be referred to two committees. If contested, the House or the Senate would vote on the matter.

Table 3. Calendars in the House of Representatives

CALENDAR	BILLS
Private	For private bills affecting specific persons.
Union	Bills that pertain to the appropriation of money or the raising of revenue.
House	Bills that do not appropriate money or raise revenue.
Consent	Noncontroversial bills.
Discharge	Rarely used; bills that have been removed from a committee by a discharge petition, which must have the signatures of 218 members.

Third, the appropriate committees and/or subcommittees hold hearings and make recommendations. If they recommend passage, a bill is "marked-up"—that is, put in final form for presentation to the full House or Senate. A bill that has been radically altered by the committee may be redrafted by the committee; it is then known as a *clean bill.*

The fourth stage applies only in the House. There a bill (unless it deals with appropriations) customarily goes to the Rules Committee to be scheduled and assigned a rule to be followed in debate (see page 402).

In the fifth stage, a bill is placed on the appropriate calendar and then scheduled for debate. Although there is only one legislative calendar in the Senate, there are five in the House (see Table 3). The chairman (or person the chairman assigns) and the ranking minority members on the committee (or persons the minority member assigns) are in charge of the majority and minority positions on debate.

Assuming that the two houses have passed a bill in different form, there is now a sixth stage. A conference committee—usually consisting of ranking members from the committees that handled the bill earlier—is appointed to compromise differences.

In the seventh stage, the conference committee reports the bill back to both houses for final action.

In the eighth and final stage, the bill goes to the president. As you read in Chapter 9, he has various options for dealing with it.

The Congress is a highly complex and cumbersome institution in which compromise between two houses and among 535 members is the norm. The complex structure and slow movement of Congress raise crucial questions about its role in a world of crises and instant communication.

- Can Congress act quickly enough?
- How can Congress try to restore public confidence in the wake of widely publicized corruption and other wrongdoing among its members?
- Is Congress a representative body?

The proper office of a representative assembly is to watch and control the government, to throw the light of publicity on its acts, to compel a full exposition and justification of all of them which anyone considers questionable, to censor them if found condemnable, and if the men who compose the government abuse this trust, or fulfill it in a manner which conflicts with the deliberative sense of the nation, to expel them from office. . . . This is surely ample power and security enough for the liberty of the nation.—*John Stuart Mill*

Congress has become an inert body which is creaky in its functions, arrogant in its disregard for ethics and morals, a pitiful, helpless giant that cannot even act when it wants to act.—*John J. Rhodes*

The Affirmative Case

Yes, Congress is archaic.

It has become increasingly clear that responsibility for coming up with new ideas in public policy as well as administering established government programs lies within the jurisdiction of non-elected officials who operate not in the open forum of public or congressional debate but in the cloistered recesses of executive offices and committee rooms. The role of government has expanded steadily in American society since the New Deal of Franklin D. Roosevelt in the 1930s, and the chief beneficiaries of this expansion have been the executive agencies and officials who carry on the day-to-day tasks of government.[2]*—Francis E. Rourke*

Congress, once the principal reservoir of governmental power, has fallen from its exalted position. It is no longer the innovator, but rather the reactor, in the American national government. The intention of the Founders has been reversed, and there is now little reason to restore Congress to its position of preeminence.

- Congress is not a representative body.
- Clumsy, time-consuming rules and procedures inhibit legislative action.
- Members of Congress spend too much of their time playing politics.

- Congress has betrayed the public through corruption and other forms of wrongdoing.

CONGRESS AS UNREPRESENTATIVE

It is natural to assume that in a representative democracy, those who do the representing—the legislature—would be a cross section of the whole population. Race, sex, age, religion, and other groupings should be reflected in the legislative body in at least a roughly proportionate way. If this is not the case, some question can be raised as to how much of a representative democracy exists.

In the United States Congress, there are three gross distortions in representation. Some groups are seriously underrepresented. Others are overrepresented. And influential constituents receive better representation than do others.

Underrepresentation Blacks, women, and youth get short shrift in Congress. Although at least 10 percent of the American population is black, only 1 percent of the Senate (one member) and 4 percent of the House (seventeen) are black. Slightly more than half the population is female; yet only seventeen women serve in the House (some 4 percent of the membership); there are none in the Senate. Although the average age of all Americans is under thirty, the average age of representatives is 46.8; that of senators is 54.6, a disparity explainable in part, but not in full, by two facts—persons under eighteen cannot vote, and one must be twenty-five and thirty respectively to serve in the House and the Senate.

If blacks and women were represented in proportion to the population, there would be approximately forty-five blacks in the House and ten in the Senate; women would constitute half of both houses. If Congress were more representative in terms of age, the median age of House members would be closer to the median age for all Americans.

Overrepresentation An examination of congressional backgrounds reveals overrepresentation in several categories. Members of Congress come largely from middle-class and upper-class families, with fathers who were primarily professionals or business executives. More than half of those in Congress are lawyers, with banking and business being heavily represented as well. In 1977 lawyers made up 51 percent of the House and 68 percent of the Senate. Over four fifths of the senators and representatives are college graduates, compared to one fifth of the voting-age population.

In religion, too, Congress is not representative. According to the 1970 census, of those Americans having a religious affiliation, some 55

The principal difficulty lies, and the greatest care should be employed, in constituting this representative assembly. It should be in miniature an exact portrait of the people at large. It should think, feel, reason, and act like them. That it may be the interest of this assembly to do strict justice at all times, it should be an equal representation, or, in other words, equal interests among the people should have equal interests in it. Great care should be taken to effect this and to prevent this and to prevent unfair, partial, and corrupt elections.—*John Adams*

percent were Protestant, 37 percent were Roman Catholic, and 4 percent Jewish. Yet Congress has 33 (6 percent) Jewish members, 132 (24 percent) Roman Catholics, and over 350 (approximately 65 percent) Protestants. In other words, its image is that of a predominantly white, Anglo-Saxon, Protestant body.

As late as the early 1970s, only six of the standing committee chairmen in the House of Representatives came from urban centers with more than 100,000 people. Indeed, for most of the last hundred years, committee leadership has been dominated not only by rural but also by southern members of Congress. For example, for most of the last twenty-five years, the three most powerful committees in the House of Representatives have been chaired by rural, southern members:

- Appropriations: George Mahon of Texas, 1964–
- Rules: Howard Smith of Virginia, 1955–1965
  William Colmer of Mississippi, 1966–1973
- Ways and Means: Wilbur Mills of Arkansas, 1958–1974

The requirements for membership in what has been called the "Congressional Club" are high social status, experience in interpersonal relations and public contacts, and a great deal of free time to pursue a political career. Lawyers are more likely than any other occupational group to meet these criteria. In the Senate, an inner circle, the "Senate Club," has exercised substantial power. Senators who never "arrived" in this august group—which has had a decidedly southern bias—have lacked the influence the others had. In general, to be a congressional leader, it helps to be from an area that rather consistently reelects its members to Congress (generally these are rural and/or southern areas).

This brings us to the issue of seniority. According to the *seniority system*, committee chairmanships go to those of the majority party with the longest service on the committee. The Democratic Study Group in the House noted in a 1970 study that the seniority system had "in the past fifteen years resulted in giving committee and subcommittee chairmanships to fifty-nine members who in 1956 signed the 'Southern Manifesto' pledging that they would employ 'every available legal and parliamentary weapon' at their disposal to reverse the Supreme Court's school desegregation decision and defeat all civil rights legislation coming before Congress."[3] In 1975 the South, considered here as the nine deep South states,* not only had the six most senior representatives, but also five senators and twenty-one representatives with over twenty years

---

* Alabama, Arkansas, Florida, Georgia, Louisiana, Mississippi, North Carolina, South Carolina, and Virginia.

of seniority; the rest of the nation had only five senators and twenty-eight representatives with the same level of seniority.

Historically, until the 1970s, there has been a decline in the percentage of first-term members of the House, thereby increasing the seniority of those from areas that consistently return the same people. These areas have tended to be southern, rural, and conservative. Data show that between 1789 and 1887 over 40 percent of all representatives were serving their first term. Between 1949 and 1965, however, the proportion of first-termers had decreased to under 20 percent.[4] In fact, 96 percent of all House incumbents who sought reelection in 1972 were reelected. A slightly higher percentage of first-termers was elected in 1974, but this increase reflected more a reaction to Watergate than a trend toward higher turnover. (Where there were forty incumbents defeated in 1974, only thirteen lost in 1976.)

Service on the more prestigious and powerful committees is almost universally the prerogative of more senior members. It is the senior members who dominate the committee selection process and look for trustworthy members, i.e., those loyal to the party, to place on committees. Obviously, a member generally needs an apprenticeship in Congress to be judged for trustworthiness by senior members. For House Republicans a Committee on Committees, dominated by the senior members from states with large numbers of Republican representatives, controls the committee assignment process. If a state has twelve Republican representatives, the senior Republican from that state has twelve votes in the Committee on Committees. House Democrats have a Steering and Policy Committee chaired and generally controlled by the Speaker of the House. In the Senate, committee assignments are made by veteran-dominated steering committees for both parties.

Policy Misrepresentation What if Congress were dominated by women instead of men? Would this make any difference in national policies? A leading voice in the women's movement, former Representative Bella Abzug (Dem. N. Y.), says it would.

> Would we rank 14th in infant mortality among the developed nations of the world? Would we allow a situation in which thousands of kids grow up without decent care because their mothers have to work for a living and have no place to leave their children, or else that condemns women to stay at home when they want to work, because there are no facilities for their children? . . . Would women allow the fraudulent packaging and cheating of consumers that they find every time they shop? Would they consent to the perverted sense of priorities that has dominated our government for the past few decades, appropriating billions of dollars for war and plunging our cities into crises of neglect? Would they vote for

ABM's instead of schools, MIRV's instead of decent housing or health centers? And does anyone think they would have allowed the war in Vietnam to go on for so many years, slaughtering and maiming our young men and the people of Indochina? [5]

Although no definitive studies are available to prove her contention, this analysis certainly provides a good speculative hypothesis for further study. In addition, one might want to examine if better balanced representation, which would include more youth and blacks, might make a difference in congressional policy making.

Tunnel Vision   Who is important to members of Congress? Special interests! It is easy to understand why, because these are the people and groups who know more about politics and how to influence politicians. Two scholars have written that "the communication most congressmen have with their districts inevitably puts them in touch with organized groups and individuals who are relatively well informed about politics. ...As a result, [a congressman's] sample of contacts with a constituency ... is heavily biased." [6]

A national survey has shown that only 59 percent of those surveyed could identify one senator from their state; only 46 percent could identify their own representative in the House. Indeed, 20 percent believed that Congress also included the United States Supreme Court! [7]

It is usually a small percentage of people who know about Congress and how to influence it. Little wonder that members of Congress pay more attention to them than to the masses. Tunnel vision makes political sense.

IMPEDIMENTS TO LEGISLATIVE ACTION

Even if Congress were a more representative body, real accomplishments would be more difficult given the nature of the legislative process. Figure 1 is in many ways a simplification. Every one of its eight stages also represents an opportunity for delay.

Through the Maze   Congressional representatives who want to accomplish something are frustrated at almost every turn by a maze of rules and procedures. Success may seem to lie just ahead but, like a mirage, vanishes in the face of obstacles. For example, with an ordinary bill (one that does not involve appropriations), there are at least eleven potential roadblocks:

1. The chairman of the House committee may try to prevent the committee from considering the bill.

2. The House committee may decide not to move the bill along to the chamber.
3. The Rules Committee chairman may neglect to act on the bill.
4. The House Rules Committee may decline to act.
5. The House of Representatives may vote against the bill.
6. The chairman of the appropriate Senate committee may refuse to have the bill considered.
7. The Senate committee may fail to act favorably on the bill.
8. The Senate may vote against the bill.
9. A Senate filibuster may prevent action on the bill.
10. The conference committee between the two houses may not be able to resolve the differences between the two versions of the bill.
11. Either the House or the Senate (or both) may decline to approve the conference committee's action on the bill.

At each stage, a new majority must be developed in the bill's favor or it will die. Every program that involves appropriations must pass through the eight stages shown in Figure 1 twice—first to have funds authorized, e.g., Judiciary Committee action authorizing appropriations for the Department of Justice, and second to have funds appropriated, e.g., Appropriations Committee action on the authorization legislation. To fund a program, therefore, the number of obstacles is approximately doubled.

Two particularly undemocratic features of this maze should be pointed out. First, although a committee chairman acting alone can no longer unilaterally kill legislation by *pigeonholing* it—that is, by refraining from scheduling committee work on it, the chairman still retains disproportionate power to affect the outcome of committee work. Second, in the Senate a minority of members may carry on a *filibuster*—talking a bill to death. Some senators have talked over twenty hours nonstop in efforts to kill a bill. A filibuster may be ended only by a form of termination called *cloture:* Sixteen senators introduce this by petition, and it must be approved by sixty members. Without cloture, the Senate simply cannot act on a bill that is the subject of a filibuster, even though it may have already passed every other stage in the legislative process.

Committee Roadblocks   In the House of Representatives alone, eighteen committees have jurisdiction over one or more programs of aid to education; no more than half the education bills are referred to the Education and Labor Committee itself. This is merely one example of the problem of conflicting and competing committee jurisdiction. The elaborate subcommittee system further confuses and complicates the problem. Each standing committee generally has several subcommittees. (See Table 2.) These may also serve as roadblocks since a bill referred to a committee is customarily then referred to a subcommittee. Sometimes jurisdictional conflicts develop between subcommittees of different standing committees as, for example, between the Health subcommittees of the House Ways and Means Committee and the House Interstate and Foreign Commerce Committee.

One committee that deserves special attention here is the conference committee for a bill. Here a few senators and representatives—generally the ranking members of the two committees concerned with the bill—can sit down and undo in a few minutes what the two houses have taken months to accomplish. When the conference committee reports its action back to the two houses, its report must be accepted or rejected without amendment. There is generally little debate on the report. A majority of the two houses may be forced to accept what a few senior members want, simply because the senior members are more likely to serve on the conference committee.

Another extremely important committee is the Rules Committee of the House. It monitors the flow of legislation to the House floor, and

ROTHCO   The Hartford Times   Ed Vallman '74

'But, but . . .'

Many Americans feel that members of Congress spend too much time "playing politics" and campaigning for reelection and not enough time legislating. Here former California Senator John Tunney (right) is shown waging an unsuccessful campaign for reelection against Republican challenger S. I. Hayakawa in 1976.

it can refuse to schedule a bill for consideration. If it does schedule a bill, it determines the rule of procedure to be followed. A *closed rule* prevents any amendment from being offered on the House floor; an *open rule* allows amendments; a *modified closed rule* allows amendments on some but not other portions of a bill. Each rule also specifies how much time may be devoted to debate.

PLAYING POLITICS

According to one representative: "Although legislative matters theoretically consume most of a congressman's time, this is rarely true in

The most pressing day-to-day demands for the time of senators and congressmen are not directly linked to legislative tasks. They come from constituents.—*Hubert H. Humphrey*

practice. The energies of a great many of us are spent primarily in feath-
ering the elective nests. Many members of Congress use their official facilities and staff help for various forms of constant campaigning." [8] The
situation is especially bad in the House where members must run for
election every two years.

The situation smacks of a "misdirection play" in football, when
the ball is apparently going one way but is really being carried in another direction. Members of Congress appear to be legislating when they
are really playing politics, and this can be a demanding chore.

> Infant-care booklets, provided free, may be mailed to all new mothers
> along with rhapsodical notes on the subject of motherhood. Home-
> district newspapers may be so carefully clipped that no new Tenderfoot
> Boy Scout, bathing beauty, or bake-off contest winner goes unremarked
> by the Congressman. . . . Sometimes there is no rest even for the dead:
> their survivors may be sent weepy letters of condolence.[9]

Such attentions win votes. So do *pork-barrel projects*—local dams,
rivers, and harbors projects financed by the federal government. The annual public works bill allotting these projects benefits members who
have seniority and have not bucked the system. They have lived long
enough and have been orthodox enough to be rewarded with "goodies."
Needless to say, a bill involving pay raises for Congress attracts almost
everyone to the floor; a representative urging better care for the aged
may speak to a nearly empty chamber.

While the president is elected from a national constituency, senators and representatives are elected by states and districts. Logically,
therefore, one would expect members of Congress to be more concerned
with the interests of their own constituencies than with larger, national
concerns—and one would be correct. Since congressional campaign
money and other help come almost entirely from localities, members
are practically forced to concentrate on local issues. As one senator put
it, "Local matters come first and global problems a poor second." [10]

Examples of congressional myopia are legion. Harley Staggers, chairman of the House Interstate and Foreign Commerce Committee, insisted on a major Amtrak train to serve his own (rural) district when it
would have better aided more densely populated areas. The chairman
and ranking members of the Armed Services Committee in the House
work hard to obtain prime military contracts and bases for their localities. And the Department of Defense has difficulty closing down bases
in the districts of ranking members even though they may no longer
serve the national interest. In 1977 President Carter's proposal to eliminate a large number of federal water projects met almost universal opposition from the affected senators and representatives.

In essence, Congress is a sort of mutual benefit society in which back scratching dominates the scene. The syndrome is "I'll vote for your bill if you'll vote for mine." This description shows how congressional voting often takes place.

> After whispered consultation ... the debate ends and the voting bell sounds, reverberating through the vast Senate complex of Capitol Hill buildings. Scores of senators begin to converge upon the chamber.
> Possessed of the prima donna's disdain for peers, compelled by their profession to fight one another on issues, they have often measured each

other as enemies. But they are conscious, too, that they are brothers, that ambition makes them endure the same indignities, wage the same lonely struggle for career survival. And so they compensate for the mutual hostility inherent in their situation with the kind of exaggerated cordiality that is evident as they enter the doorways together.

But, as the senators approach their desks, the cordial glow is fleetingly interrupted by a look of perplexity—what the hell is the vote about this time? ... To men so skilled, the minute remaining before the roll call should be adequate to identify the issue and divine the safe vote.

Covertly, they case the situation through the particular stratagem each has worked out over the years. Some have aides who now come forward to whisper a 30-second summary of the 3-hour debate. Some just follow their party leader, who has minions stationed about the floor to pass the word "aye" or "nay" to the faithful. Some, who are not faithful, follow the lead of their particular Senate guru. ... Some, particularly those who are committee chairmen or near-chairmen, automatically support the position of the chairman who has jurisdiction over the measure—for they expect the same hierarchical support when they are piloting their own bills through the Senate.

And, too, there is a last-second vote hustling on the floor. "Give me a vote, Bill, if you can," the sponsor of the pending amendment will say to an undecided senator he has given a vote to in the past; and, if this is not one of those red-flagged issues of particular interest back home, the vote may well be given for "friendship's sake," with the donor carefully filing the incident away in his memory for future repayment.

Thus, by a variety of means most of them substitute for personal study and decision, the senators work their will, and the votes are counted.[11]

In this mutual admiration society, members treat other members with the most genteel courtesy even though they may despise them.*

CONGRESSIONAL WRONGDOING

Edward Everett Hale, chaplain to the Senate in the early 1900s, was once asked if he prayed for the senators. "No," he replied, "I look at the senators and pray for the country." Congressional wrongdoing has ranged from the slightly shady to the downright illegal.

Some common and well-documented types of congressional wrongdoing include *junketing*, or traveling for pleasure at government

* While serving as a young staff aide to a member of Congress, the author observed a bitter debate between two senior members, Representative Mendel Rivers and George Mahon. The next morning he anticipated reading about how these two southern gentlemen had almost come to blows on the House floor. Much to his surprise, the printed proceedings of their debate in the *Congressional Record* gave one the impression that they were the best of friends and that nothing out of the ordinary had taken place. The *Congressional Record*—in which members may edit their speeches or insert whatever they please—mirrors the unreality of congressional proceedings.

expense; *nepotism*, or placing relatives on the payroll; and having committee staff aides work on an election campaign. Some members of Congress have also used their *franking privilege*—sending mail free—to mail campaign literature.

The New York City Bar Association, in a study of Congress, outlined the ties between the practice of law and corruption. Lawyers represent clients, and the single largest occupational category among members of Congress is lawyers. The Bar report said: "It is hard to escape the conclusions ... that law practice has demonstrated a special potential for actual and alleged congressional improprieties, and that law practices have played a disproportionate role in the history of congressional scandals." [12] Former Senator Thomas J. Dodd (Dem. Conn.) allegedly helped a client acquire a Small Business Administration loan, and allegedly accepted legal and loan-finder's fees from insurance companies while conducting an investigation of the insurance industry as chairman of the Antitrust and Monopoly Subcommittee. *Life* magazine reported in 1968 that Representative Cornelius Gallagher (Dem. N. J.) accepted $50,000 from Anthony "Tino" De Angelis, later imprisoned for a multimillion dollar swindle. [13] In the 1970s several members of Congress have been convicted for crimes committed while in office including Frank Brasco (Dem.) and Bertram Podell (Dem.) of New York, John Dowdy (Dem. Tex.), J. Irving Whalley (Rep. Pa.), and Andrew Hinshaw (Rep. Calif.).

Members of Congress are also easy prey for lobbyists, as has been pointed out in Chapter 6. Wrote one observer:

> The main part of a lobbyist's job in practice is ... to get priorities and preferences for clients who have no legal rights to them. To achieve this, he needs the cooperation of one or more members of Congress—the more influential they are, the fewer he needs—who will write the letter or make the telephone call to the government department or agency handling the matter. He gets this cooperation by paying for it—preferably in cash. [14]

It is interesting to note the possible conflicts of interest between a representative's financial interests and the committee on which he or she serves. Membership on the Ways and Means Committee, which has jurisdiction over tax policy, is a plum for House members, yet George Bush of Texas received an appointment during his first term in Congress. Bush had formerly been an oil company executive. One might reasonably wonder whether there was any relationship between the oil lobby of the Southwest and this choice assignment.

Some members of Congress have used their offices for private gain and pleasure. A powerful member of the House, Wayne Hayes of Ohio,

The distinctive Capitol Building in Washington, D.C., the meeting place of the House and Senate, is known throughout the world as a symbol of American democracy.

had two payrolls, one as a representative and one as chairman of the House Administration Committee. One of his top political advisers received salaries from both payrolls, though he never worked for the committee. And one Elizabeth Ray, allegedly Hayes' mistress, was paid $14,000 a year, though she rarely showed up at the office—and could not even type.

But corruption does not stop there. Staff members have also been convicted. Martin Sweig, former top aide to House Speaker John McCormack, was convicted of perjury. Bobby Baker, a key aide to Lyndon Johnson when he was Senate majority leader, was convicted on counts of tax evasion, theft, and conspiracy to defraud the federal government. Both men used their staff positions for financial gain, either for their friends or for themselves. Sweig, for example, is said to have imitated McCormack's voice when telephoning officials in executive departments to obtain favors for friends.

Still another type of corruption is the misuse of power for public purposes as distinguished from private financial or other gain. Perhaps the worst example of this type of wrongdoing in recent times was the character assassination of the McCarthy era, during the 1950s. In their search for communists in government, Senator Joseph McCarthy and the House Committee on Un-American Activities harrassed innocent witnesses and ruined the careers of several American citizens who refused to testify against associates. Later the Supreme Court rebuked Congress: "Protected freedoms should not be placed in danger in the absence of a clear determination by the House or the Senate that a particular inquiry is justified by a specific legislative need. . . . There is no congressional power to expose for the sake of exposure." [15]

The Negative Case

No, Congress is not archaic.

The popular critical image of Congress as a static or decaying institution with archaic forms is, in our estimate, highly inaccurate. While scholars have structured and restructured power in Congress, much of their analysis has ignored the steady incremental thrust of change within Congress itself.[16]*–John S. Saloma, III*

Congress, a highly complex institution, can easily be used as a scapegoat. All the pressures of society impinge upon it. If Congress adopts legislation, it loses favor with groups that opposed the law, and vice versa. If Congress takes no action, it is charged with delay and insensitivity. Congress is damned if it does, damned if it doesn't.

As one might expect, the branch of government that is supposed to be closest to and most representative of all the people will also reflect both the liabilities and assets of society. Congress is molded by the forces of the society it represents. To point the finger of accusation at Congress is like blaming a mirror. Congress, reflecting the character of the American people, is "Main Street, U.S.A." writ large.

Congress does not need so much to be defended as to be explained. As people come to understand its complexities, they will see its very real assets.

- Congress, though perhaps not strictly representative, is responsive to the public interest.
- Congressional delays aid the government and society by helping to prevent too rapid change.
- Congress does its job by dealing with a large volume of legislation.
- Congress continually adapts and changes.

It often seems to me that we have better political leadership in this country than we have any right to expect. The legislators, the congressmen . . . and senators whose campaigns and whose work I have reported are not more venal, crass, selfish, short-sighted or crooked than their predecessors of earlier generations. On the contrary, they are, as a whole, as well educated, well motivated, and as earnest in their pursuit of the elusive public good as anyone could reasonably expect them to be.— *David Broder*

REPRESENTATION AND RESPONSIVENESS

It has been charged that Congress is not a representative body because some groups, such as blacks and women, are underrepresented. If one is looking for neat and tidy statistics that show a perfect relationship between groups in the population and their numbers in Congress, there might be a problem. But is such perfect congruence really necessary? Can only blacks represent blacks? Must only women represent women? Clearly, important laws favoring both groups have been enacted by members of Congress who were neither black nor female. Arguments involving representation can be carried to ludicrous extremes. After all, who represents the handicapped? the housewife? the handicapped

CHARACTERISTICS OF MEMBERS OF 95TH CONGRESS

The average member of the 95th Congress is younger and a bit more likely to be a lawyer and a Roman Catholic than the average member of the 94th Congress.

The elections of 1976 that brought 18 new members to the Senate and 67 new members to the House made no radical changes in the demographics of Congress, but they did reinforce trends that had been under way for several years.

The shift toward youth continued. The average age of House members dropped to 46.8 from 49.8, making the 95th House the youngest since World War II. The Senate also received a heavy transfusion of younger blood, and the average age of the senators dropped to 54.6 from 55.5.

Had incumbent Sen. John V. Tunney (D Calif.), 42, not lost his seat to 70-year-old S.I. Hayakawa, the change in the average Senate age would have been even more dramatic.

The average age of Congress as a whole dropped to 48.1 from 50.9.

Thomas J. Downey (D N.Y.), 27, handed over the title of youngest member of the House to Nick Joe Rahall (D W.Va.), who was born on May 20, 1949, four months after Downey.

W. R. Poage (D Texas), 77, became the oldest House member and the only one to have been born before 1900.

John L. McClellan (D Ark.) was the only senator to have passed his 80th birthday before the new Congress opened. He will be 81 Feb. 25. Milton R. Young (R N.D.) at 79 was the oldest Republican senator. Joe Biden (D Del.), 34, remained the youngest senator.

The elections also brought changes in the occupational and religious makeup of Congress. There were, for example, 20 fewer businessmen or bankers in the 95th Congress and 16 fewer farmers. (Continued, p. 411.)

housewife? the handicapped Italian-American housewife? the handicapped Italian-American housewife on Social Security?

Are members of Congress too old? It is true that the average age of our legislators is above the national average. This is true partly because the Constitution specifies minimum ages (twenty-five for the House and thirty for the Senate). In addition, it takes time to develop enough experience and reputation to be successful as a candidate and as an effective member of Congress. Learning how the federal government functions requires time. It is not wise for a district or state to change lawmakers too frequently.

What about the charge that some groups, such as lawyers, southerners, and rural areas, are overrepresented? (Table 4 shows the occu-

Law remained by far the most common profession. The number of members with law degrees increased by three to 291. The number of educators increased by 12.

Certainly the most overrepresented group in Congress was astronauts. Harrison H. Schmitt (R N.M.), was the Senate's second veteran of space flight. The first was John Glenn (D Ohio).

The number of House members listing their profession as congressional aide also took a quantum leap as three former Capitol Hill aides were elected in 1976 to join the two already in Congress.

Congress' only self-professed riverboat captain, Rep. Don Young (R Alaska), was back in the 95th as were three former professional athletes—Morris K. Udall (D Ariz.), basketball; Gus Yatron (D Pa.) boxing, and Jack F. Kemp (R N.Y.), football.

The number of Catholics in Congress increased by eight, to 132, and Catholics remained the single largest religious group in Congress. Methodists remained in second place with 86 after a pickup of five and Episcopalians remained in third place with 64, a drop of two.

The number of Jewish members increased to 23 from 23. There were also 57 Baptists and 54 Presbyterians in the 95th.

The number of women in Congress declined by one, to 17, all in the House, as three women House members left Congress and only two new ones were elected: Mary R. Oakar (D Ohio) and Barbara A. Mikulski (D Md.).

The number of black members remained the same at 17. However, this statistic, like most others, could change after special elections are held to fill posts of three members of Congress selected to serve in top posts in the Carter administration.

Source: *Congressional Quarterly Weekly Report*, January 1, 1977, p. 19. © 1976(7) by Congressional Quarterly Inc. Reprinted with permission.

Table 4. Occupations of Members of the 95th Congress

OCCUPATION	HOUSE D	HOUSE R	HOUSE TOTAL	SENATE D	SENATE R	SENATE TOTAL	CONGRESS TOTAL
Agriculture	6	10	16	3	6	9	25
Business or Banking	69	49	118	14	10	24	142
Education	57	15	72	8	4	12	84
Engineering	0	2	2	0	0	0	2
Journalism	10	4	14	3	1	4	18
Labor Leader	6	0	6	0	0	0	6
Law	155	68	223	46	22	68	291
Law Enforcement	7	0	7	0	0	0	7
Medicine	1	1	2	1	0	1	3
Public Service/Politics	34	26	60	12	14	26	86
Clergyman	4	2	6	0	1	1	7
Scientist	2	0	2	0	1	1	3

Source: *Congressional Quarterly Weekly Report,* January 1, 1977, p. 20. © 1976(7) by Congressional Quarterly Inc. Reprinted with permission.

pational makeup of the 95th Congress.) Surely it makes sense for a body that drafts legislation to contain many lawyers. As far as southern and rural strength in Congress, that situation is caused by "safe districts," which are now declining in number. For example, southerners no longer chair the Ways and Means or Rules Committees of the House.

The Public Interest   What matters most is that Congress is responsive to the public. While the president and vice-president are elected by a national constituency, members of Congress represent smaller constituencies closer to group and individual interests. The American public is not a large, shapeless mass. Its differing values and concerns all merit representation in a democracy.

One of the strong tendencies of a bureaucracy is to establish uniform rules for everyone overlooking individual, regional, and group differences. In a society with over 200 million citizens, the standards relevant for some may not be the best for all. Unity and uniformity have their virtues, but so does diversity, especially in the United States.

Congress is uniquely equipped to represent diversity. Because of their local concerns, members of Congress are well suited to balance the interests of heterogeneity against the forces of homogeneity.

And the legislature is a much more accessible institution than either the judiciary or the executive. Its members must campaign for office every two (or six) years in a district or state where they are held accountable for their actions—or inaction. Federal judges do not have to face the public in this way and, in the executive branch, only the president and vice-president are similarly accountable. The courts are solemn and the executive bureaucracy is impersonal, but Congress is open. A citizen may incur tremendous costs in bringing a lawsuit, and enormous frustration in getting a response from the bureaucracy, while a simple letter or phone call to his or her representative or senator frequently produces the help needed.

The Congressional Balancing Act What should affect a legislator's vote: the views of constituents? advice from colleagues? party loyalty? the president and the executive? conscience? These are just five of the more important influences on congressional voting, and they illustrate the balance a member of Congress must maintain. To vote every time according to party loyalty, for instance, would indicate a crippling inflexibility. Likewise, if one's constituents were the most important influence on each vote, then a legislator might too often be voting against the national interest.

The manner in which these forces are weighed is determined largely by a legislator's perception of his or her role. Three types of roles have been ascribed to members of Congress: delegate, trustee, and politico.[17] The *delegate* tries to determine what constituents want and vote accordingly. The *trustee* attempts to work out a position through factual analysis and conscience, even though this may conflict with constituent interests. The *politico* votes as a trustee on some issues and as a delegate on others.

Definitions of the first two roles are well grounded in the classic statement of Edmund Burke to the English Parliament:

> Certainly, gentlemen, it ought to be the happiness and glory of a representative to live in the strictest union, the closest correspondence, and the more unreserved communication with his constituents. . . . It is his duty to sacrifice his repose, his pleasure, his satisfactions to theirs; and, above all, ever and in all cases to prefer their interest to his own. But his unbiased opinion, his mature judgment, his enlightened conscience, he ought not to sacrifice to you, to any man, or to any set of men living. These he does not derive from your pleasure; no, nor from the law and the constitution. They are a trust from Providence, for the abuse of which he is deeply answerable. . . . Parliament is not [where] local prejudices ought to guide, but the general good, resulting from the general reason of the whole.[18]

The three congressional roles are most easily seen in operation when lawmakers vote on a bill. In the South where support for both high tariffs on textiles and a large defense budget are strong, a southern representative would be a delegate by consistently representing constituents' views on these and other issues. However, if this same southern representative sometimes represented constituent wishes and sometimes did not, this would be an example of the politico. A trustee would consistently take an independent position regardless of constituent desires. A trustee's support for constituent wishes would come only from reasoned judgment, not because of constituents' views. Most members of Congress are either delegates or politicos inasmuch as the trustee role is fraught with more dangers for reelection.[19, 20]

THE VALUE OF DELAY

In a democracy issues are supposed to be thoroughly debated so that voters can make intelligent decisions based on the best data available. Research to get the facts, debate to determine the alternatives, and compromise to achieve agreement on issues require a good deal of time. A people obsessed with productivity often fail to recognize that the legislative process is designed not just to produce results but to insure that the results are the best possible. Assembly-line speed is not necessarily a virtue when applied to the resolution of serious social and economic problems.

Two features of Congress show how beneficial the legislature's emphasis on deliberation, rather than speed, can be: the Rules Committee in the House and the filibuster in the Senate.

What would the House of Representatives be like without a traffic cop to monitor the flow of legislation originating with 435 members? The Rules Committee provides an invaluable service. If every bill had an equal right to the House floor, and if all bills were subject to amendments from members of the House, chaos would always be just around the corner. The Senate, with only a hundred members, does not have the same need for a traffic cop.

What would the Senate be like without the right to filibuster? It might be a more efficient body, but efficiency has never been a hallmark of democracy. The filibuster represents one way of protecting minority rights. It has been used by both conservatives and liberals to protect their interests. The former have used it to oppose civil rights legislation, while the latter have used it to oppose antibusing laws. Strom Thurmond of South Carolina talked for twenty-four hours and eighteen minutes against the Civil Rights Act of 1957. Wayne Morse of Oregon talked for twenty-two hours and twenty-six minutes against the Tidelands oil bill in 1953. It should be noted that the filibuster does not necessarily stop the majority from acting. Even though there were southern filibusters against civil rights legislation, the majority was still able to pass the laws in question.

I think Congress has changed. I'm not sure it has changed for the better. At one time, Congress simply disposed of things that the President proposed. . . . I think that has changed, beginning with the wave of consumer and environmental legislation in the mid-1960s, almost all of which was conceived of in the legislative branch and not in the executive branch. Congress began for the first time to sense its own power to initiate and carry through legislation without executive leadership. . . . Congress now, I believe, passes legislation far too quickly. It develops new programs, conceives of new subsidies, supports new forms of regulation really without any careful deliberation, scarcely even offering an opportunity for the effective parties to be heard on the matter. Congress has lost the central leadership that it long had—a strong Speaker, a strong Senate Majority Leader—and has weakened the power of the committee chairmen. The result has been an increased tendency, in my view, for it to ride off in 12 different directions at once.—James Q. Wilson

The internal structure of Congress is a rational way to maintain our legislative system. Without it, stability would be threatened. Perhaps even more important, society's acceptance of legislative decisions would be seriously questioned. By deliberating at length on legislation, Congress performs the useful function of gradually educating society, of preparing people for change. One has only to imagine what could have happened throughout the country if there had not been extensive debates on civil rights laws. Debate and deliberation help cushion the impact of change, an aid in stabilizing our society with its diversity of volatile interests.

Checking Executive Power   Overlooked by many in their haste to criticize Congress is its important role in checking executive power. This role was considered extremely important by the Founders, who wanted to guard against a monopoly of governmental authority in the hands of any one branch. Congress has the power to bring even a strong executive to heel, as its severest critics would admit in the light of the Vietnam war and the Watergate scandal. Without congressional criticism of his Vietnam policy, would Nixon have carried out troop withdrawal? Without the threat of congressional impeachment and conviction, would he have resigned from office?

In the words of one political scientist:

> The Congress no longer expects to originate measures but to pass, veto, or modify laws proposed by the chief executive. It is the president, not the Congress, who determines the content and substance of the legislation with which Congress deals. The president is now the motor of the system; the Congress applies the brakes. The president gives what forward movement there is in the system; his is the force of thrust and innovation. The Congress is the force of inertia—a force, it should be said, that means not only restraint, but stability in politics.[21]

The Congress looks more powerful sitting here [in the presidency] than it did when I was there in Congress. But that is because when you are in Congress, you are one of a hundred in the Senate or 435 in the House, so that power is divided. But from here I look at Congress, and I look at the collective power of the Congress, particularly the bloc action, and it is a substantial power.—*John F. Kennedy*

Table 5. Growth of Congressional Staffs

YEAR	HOUSE	INCREASE	SENATE	INCREASE
1955	3,623		1,962	
1960	4,148	+ 525	2,643	+ 681
1965	5,672	+ 1,524	3,219	+ 576
1970	7,134	+ 1,462	4,140	+ 921
1975 (April)	9,951	+ 2,817	5,543	+ 1,403

Note: The House Administration Committee on March 6, 1975, increased the maximum number of staff for each member from 16 to 18, adding a possible 870 staffers to the total House employment.

Source: *Congressional Quarterly Weekly Report*, July 12, 1975, p. 1477. Reprinted by permission.

In Defense of Committees The committee system divides the workload and provides for specialists to develop expertise in subject matter areas. Committee members and their staffs are often the most knowledgeable people in the United States about the subjects under their jurisdiction, and Congress has been increasing its staff to provide more assistance. (See Table 5.) The custom of seniority, which allows members to stay on one or a few committees for most of their congressional careers, enables them to develop expertise and leadership, two very desirable qualities in the legislative branch, especially when checking the enormous resources available to the executive.

Of course both the House and the Senate have modified their seniority system in the 1970s. Except for three instances in 1975, seniority has been strictly observed in the selection of committee chairmen. Indeed, what better way could there be to select committee chairmen and ranking minority members? Would it be preferable to have hotly contested elections? These would subject committees to selecting leaders best able to make the right deals. The seniority system enables committees to avoid the conflicts that could occur every two years if chairmen were elected in hard-fought contests. In short, seniority provides continuity.

The committee assignment process is also quite rational. Why should freshmen members be placed in substantial numbers on the most powerful committees? Surely it is better for senior members to have an opportunity to assess the abilities of new members before giving them committee assignments they might not be able to handle. A study of committee assignments in the House of Representatives concluded:

> A responsible legislator is . . . one who does not believe that the Congress is the proper place to initiate drastic and rapid changes in the direction of public policy. On the contrary, he is more inclined to be a gradualist, and to see public policy as a sort of synthesis of opposing viewpoints. . . . Even in an instance in which party leaders feel compelled to appoint a member of a dissident wing of the party in order to gain greater cooperation, they will tend to select the member who most closely conforms to the norms of responsibility.[22]

This analysis reveals that the responsible legislator is like the average American; neither believes in rapid and drastic change. It is logical and rational, therefore, that the committee assignment process would favor such individuals and that senior members and party leaders would have substantial influence in making committee assignments.

Testifying before congressional committees is one of the principal ways for citizens to influence the legislative process. Anti-Vietnam war hearings, conducted by the Senate Foreign Relations Committee, allowed citizens in opposition to the war to obtain national press atten-

Table 6. Major Differences Between House and Senate

	HOUSE	SENATE
Size	435	100
Formality	More	Less
Hierarchical Organization	More	Less
Action	Faster	Slower
Power Distribution	Very Uneven	More Even
Apprenticeship	Longer	Shorter
Relationships	More Impersonal	More Personal
Constituency Importance	Less	More
Prestige	Lesser	Greater
Ideology	More Conservative	More Liberal

Source: Adapted from Lewis A. Froman, Jr., *The Congressional Process: Strategies, Rules, and Procedures*, p. 7. Copyright © 1967 by Little, Brown and Company. Reprinted by permission.

tion for their views. Some might also argue that Ralph Nader made his national reputation in large measure by testimony on automobile safety before congressional committees. Since these hearings often receive exposure on network television news programs, they are excellent vehicles for molding public opinion, which in turn influences the legislative process.

PRODUCING RESULTS

To say that members of Congress are too busy playing politics to fulfill their real duties is unfair. For one thing, there are numerous differences between the House and Senate that affect how its members approach their jobs. For another, the major business of Congress—handling legislation—does get accomplished, and both houses contribute in achieving this goal.

Different Approaches   Blanket characterizations of members of Congress are misleading. The two houses are different in many ways, ways that balance and complement each other (see Table 6). For instance, there is an ideological balance between liberals and conservatives. The Senate tends to be more liberal for several reasons. First, senators have a larger constituency (except in those states with only one representative) and thus naturally deal with a wider range of interests. Senators from metropolitan areas especially confront diverse racial, social, and other

Table 7. Average Turnover in the House of Representatives

DATE	AVERAGE TURNOVER (NUMBER)	PERCENT OF HOUSE MEMBERSHIP
1940–1948	96	22
1950–1958	68	16
1960–1968	66	15
1970–1974	73	17

Source: From *The United States Congress in Comparative Perspective* by John E. Schwarz and L. Earl Shaw. Copyright © 1976 by The Dryden Press, a Division of Holt, Rinehart and Winston. Reprinted by permission of Holt, Rinehart and Winston.

pressures, a situation that tends to encourage a more liberal position. Second, senators are more likely than representatives to have significant competition for reelection. This is indicated by the number of *safe seats*—that is, those for which there is little or no competition. In the House, at least until the 1970s, the number of safe districts has been increasing (see Table 7). Meanwhile the number of safe Senate seats has been decreasing. It is more difficult to measure turnover of Senate seats because of staggered terms; since 1968, however, approximately a third of all senators elected have been new members.

Another way in which the two houses balance each other has to do with the role of *mavericks*—legislators with unorthodox views or positions—who have challenged congressional leadership on important issues. The House, a large body with a need to restrain freedom of its members, has produced few effective mavericks. The Senate, on the other hand, has boasted many such people; they have made important

Table 8. Congressional Bills, Acts, and Resolutions: 1957 to 1976

ITEM	85th CONG.	86th CONG.	87th CONG.	88th CONG.	89th CONG.	90th CONG.	91st CONG.	92d CONG.	93d CONG.	94th CONG.
Period of session	1957–58	1959–60	1961–62	1963–64	1965–66	1967–68	1969–70	1971–72	1973–74	1975–76
Measures										
introduced	19,112	18,261	18,376	17,480	24,003	26,460	26,303	22,969	23,396	21,096
Bills	18,205	17,230	17,230	16,079	22,483	24,786	24,631	21,363	21,950	19,762
Joint resolutions	907	1,031	1,146	1,401	1,520	1,674	1,672	1,606	1,446	1,334
Measures enacted	1,854	1,292	1,569	1,026	1,283	1,002	941	768	772	729
Public	1,009	800	885	666	810	640	695	607	649	588
Private	845	492	684	360	473	362	246	161	123	141

Source: *Statistical Abstract of the United States 1975*, p. 444; and *The Congressional Record*, October 26, 1976, p. D1397.

contributions, especially in championing minority views. (Former Senator Charles E. Goodell of New York even had the courage to attack his Republican floor leader, Everett M. Dirksen, for holding up key presidential appointments.) This situation indicates that, although the so-called "Senate Club" has been accused of running the upper house, mavericks have actually been free to challenge the establishment with unusual and unique ideas. The size of the Senate is not the only factor here. Senators have large staffs, much social prestige in Washington, and a high degree of visibility. These assets enable them to address issues and develop a following outside the Senate hierarchy.

Legislative Accomplishments   Critics, quick to point out all the legislation on which Congress does not act, are slow to praise the legislature for the number of laws it does pass (see table 8). In 1975, 17,015 public bills and resolutions were introduced. Congress passed 158 bills that were signed into law by the President. Of another 15 bills vetoed by the President, 3 became law after Congress overrode his veto. Included among the important pieces of legislation that year were bills on fair trade, voting rights, criminal procedure, tax cuts, debt limit, the securities industry, aid to the jobless, energy policy, pesticide regulation, education for the handicapped, emergency housing, lending practices, and railroad revitalization.

It should never be forgotten that Congress can represent the public interest just as much by killing a bill as by passing one. Many bills have no future, and should have none. Some are introduced by legislators simply to appease a person or group. Others represent pet interests of legislators and may be introduced each year just to show members' continued concern in the subjects. A member may introduce a bill for its publicity value alone. And some members have been known to introduce legislation solely to upstage another member who is planning to introduce a bill on the matter.

The president is often given the credit for his legislative accomplishments without a full understanding of where the ideas originated. In many if not most instances, a president's program, especially for major, innovative legislation, has had an incubation period in Congress. For example, Great Society legislation proposed and enacted during the Johnson administration had been culled in part from bills developed and introduced earlier by members of Congress. And the concept of revenue sharing was introduced in the House of Representatives by Melvin Laird and Charles E. Goodell long before it was enacted during the Nixon administration.

Table 9. Comparison of Public and Congressional Opinion
on Key Policy Issues, 1970

	PUBLIC	U. S. HOUSE MEMBERS	U. S. SENATORS
1. Vietnam: Percent say "speed up withdrawal"	27	30	45
2. Defense: Percent say "place less emphasis" on military weapons programs	30	37	45
3. Guaranteed Income: Percent approve of "at least $1600 for a family of four or more"	48	65	76
4. Civil Rights: Percent say "government should go farther to improve blacks' conditions"	53	58	76
5. Supreme Court: Percent deny it gives "too much consideration to rights of people suspected of crimes"	29	36	56

Source: Robert S. Erickson and Norman Luttbeg, *American Public Opinion* (John Wiley, 1973), p. 257. Reprinted by permission.

Congress has been unfairly charged with not acting on legislation demanded by the public, but research, as shown in Table 9, reveals quite a different story. Congress is often ahead of the public on key policy issues. Liberal critics of Congress should take stock of Table 9. Perhaps they should direct their criticism toward the public for lagging behind congressional opinion.

THE CHANGING CONGRESS

As Congress adjourned in 1973, one of its premier critics, Common Cause, declared: "Congress in 1973 has done more to make itself an effective and responsible institution than has any preceding Congress since the days of Speaker Cannon*. . . . The overall changes are so far-reaching that the Congress—particularly the House—is at last in a posi-

* "Uncle Joe" Cannon, a longtime representative from Illinois, was noted for his extreme conservatism and for his arbitrary rule as Speaker of the House. He served in this post from 1901 until 1911 when fellow representatives overthrew his rule.

tion to recapture its role as a co-equal branch of government." [23] It now appears that the events of 1973 constitute a part in a continuing effort to change and revitalize the Congress. Both the House and the Senate adopted codes of ethics in 1977 to guide the behavior of members. These regulations ban private, unofficial office accounts (commonly called "slush funds"), limit outside income from speaking engagements, articles, and other sources, restrict gifts to members from lobbyists, prohibit foreign travel by lame duck members, and widen financial disclosure. Major changes and improvements during the past several years have involved seniority, committees, the filibuster, and budget reform.

Seniority   There are several important indicators of change in this area. Moderate and liberal members are gaining positions on many strategic committees as "safe districts" are decreasing. The seniority system has been modified to allow challenges to the automatic ascension of the senior member of a committee to chairmanship. In 1971, House Republicans determined that their ranking committee members would be elected in the Republican Conference by secret ballot. In 1973, House Democrats passed a rule requiring that Democratic committee chairmen be elected by secret ballot in the Democratic Caucus. Three Democratic committee chairmen were removed in 1975 by this modification of the seniority system. Senate Republicans in 1973 began the practice of having the Republican membership of a committee choose its ranking member. Then, in 1975, Senate Democrats required that committee chairmen be chosen by secret ballot in the Democratic Caucus whenever one fifth of the Senate Democrats requested it.

Committee Reform   Committee proceedings are now open to the public unless there is a (public) vote to close them. Since important legislative work takes place in "mark-up" sessions, where language is put in final form, opening these sessions may have made the Congress more responsive to the public interest. The decline in closed meetings in both houses is shown in Table 10. Between 1953 and 1975, the overall proportion of closed meetings has been reduced from 35 percent to 7 percent.

Committees in the House of Representatives are the main legislative forces, and it is there that many reforms have been implemented. Seven new rules or procedures implemented in the 1970s have improved committee processes in the House.

1. No House member may chair more than one legislative subcommittee. This change breaks the lock that senior conservative Democrats had on key subcommittees.

I will be leaving Congress in the belief that it is now a more enlightened and responsive body than when I first arrived in 1966. Then it was an institution caught within the grip of a rigid seniority system and dominated by a cabal of powerful aging committee chairmen. . . . A new member was expected to adjust to his small spot in the Congressional solar system and let time slowly, through the deaths and defeats of his seniors, push him toward the hub of power. New voices striving to be heard were hidden and suppressed. Much has changed. . . . The undue centralization of power has been broken. Younger members are now free to participate far more freely in the forming of policy in committees dealing with policy. . . . While the seniority system still reigns on Capitol Hill, it has been modified. Three chairmen were passed over last year, and this in itself has tended to make chairmen more responsive to the membership. . . . On the other hand, I am disturbed at the growing tendency of polarization of rhetoric on the complex domestic and international issues before us.—*Thomas M. Rees*

Table 10. Open and Closed Standing Committee Meetings, 1974–1975

	PERCENT CLOSED	
	1974	**1975**
SENATE COMMITTEES		
Aeronautical and Space Sciences	17	4
Agriculture and Forestry	35	8
Appropriations	28	25
Armed Services	64	54
Banking, Housing, and Urban Affairs	10	1
Budget	—	3
Commerce	24	5
District of Columbia	0	0
Finance	37	4
Foreign Relations	42	38
Government Operations	4	1
Interior and Insular Affairs	5	0
Judiciary	9	8
Labor and Public Welfare	22	13
Post Office and Civil Service	50	18
Public Works	35	0
Rules and Administration	52	9
Veterans' Affairs	24	0
HOUSE COMMITTEES		
Agriculture	0	1
Appropriations	10	6
Armed Services	34	19
Banking, Currency and Housing	0	0
Budget	—	2
District of Columbia	0	0
Education and Labor	0	0
Government Operations	1	1
House Administration	32	9
Interior and Insular Affairs	0	0
International Relations	6	6
Interstate and Foreign Commerce	4	1
Judiciary	20	1
Merchant Marine and Fisheries	0	0
Post Office and Civil Service	0	1
Public Works and Transportation	6	0
Rules	0	0
Science and Technology	1	0
Standards of Official Conduct	20	0
Veterans' Affairs	0	0
Ways and Means	5	2

Source: *Congressional Quarterly Weekly Report,* January 24, 1976, p. 154. Reprinted by permission.

2. According to a "bill of rights" for committees, chairmen must share authority with other party members, since all of them select subcommittee chairmen and establish subcommittee jurisdictions, among other things. Committee chairmen can no longer "pocket veto" legislation by ignoring it. They must refer all bills to subcommittees within two weeks.

3. There must be at least four subcommittees for all committees with over twenty members, a requirement that prevents chairmen from concentrating power in their own hands.

4. Written rules are required for all committees. This requirement provides another way to check the arbitrary exercise of power by committee chairmen.

5. Each subcommittee must have at least one staff member each for the chairman and ranking minority member.

6. Senior Democrats may belong to only two of a committee's subcommittees. This reform reduces the conservative and Southern dominance of key Appropriations Committee subcommittees.

7. The chairmen of all Appropriations subcommittees must be approved by the House Democratic Caucus.[24]

In addition, House Democrats as of 1973 allow each Democrat to have one major committee assignment before allowing any member to have two major committee assignments. This rule increases the opportunity of junior members to serve on important committees. In 1975, House Democrats also mandated that each committee member could choose a subcommittee assignment before any member could have two subcommittee memberships.

In February of 1977, the Senate restructured its committee system by (1) reducing the number of committees, (2) limiting the number of committees on which a senator could serve, (3) providing the minority party with one third of each committee staff, and (4) establishing a computerized scheduling of committees to reduce the number of overlapping meetings. The new committee system immediately decreased the number of committees to twenty-five from thirty-one, including joint, special, select, and standing committees, with plans to eliminate three more committees by January 1978. Before the restructuring, some members had as many as thirty committee and subcommittee assignments, but now the maximum is eleven.

The Filibuster   Senate Rule 22, originally adopted in 1917, required two thirds of the senators present and voting to terminate a filibuster. In 1949, the requirement was increased to two thirds of all senators. Ten years later, under Lyndon Johnson's leadership, the number in the original Senate Rule 22 was restored, with the proviso that a vote on ending a filibuster would be taken two days after a cloture petition was submitted by sixteen senators. If successful, debate would be limited to one hour for each senator on the bill itself and all amendments and motions affecting it. The most recent revision of Senate Rule 22 requires that three fifths (60 percent) of all senators vote to terminate debate two days after the filing of a cloture petition. The number of successful cloture votes has increased markedly in recent years. Between 1917 and 1970, cloture votes succeeded only eight times; between 1971 and 1975, they were successful on fourteen occasions.[25]

Budget Reform   One of the most severe charges levied at Congress has been that it is unable to challenge the president on budgetary matters. The Congressional Budget Reform Act of 1974 created a standing Budget Committee for each house, plus a Congressional Budget Office. Through the efforts of these new organizations, Congress can more effectively determine the government's revenue and appropriations needs each year. The legislature can put together its own data without relying on the executive branch and thus establish priorities for revenue and spending within its budget timetable. Before the 1974 act, Congress acted on each appropriations bill separately without establishing the relationship between all appropriations bills and anticipated federal revenues. By establishing a spending ceiling, Congress can now relate appropriations bills to the entire revenue and expenditure picture.

Glossary

Clean bill: a bill written by a congressional committee; when reported out of committee it receives a new number.

Closed rule: A rule preventing amendments in the House; also known as a "gag" rule.

Cloture: the closing of debate on a bill.

Concurrent resolution: resolution without the force of law that requires action by both the House and the Senate.

Delegate: a member of Congress whose major goal in voting is to reflect constituents' desires.

Filibuster: unlimited debate on a bill intended to delay or prevent its passage.

Franking privilege: legislators' privilege to send official mail free.

Joint committee: committee having members from both the House and the Senate.

Joint resolution: resolution passed by both houses of Congress that has the force of law.

Junketing: traveling for pleasure at government expense.

Maverick: legislator with unorthodox views or positions.

Modified closed rule: a rule allowing amendments from the House floor on some but not on other portions of a bill.

Nepotism: the placing of relatives on the payroll.

Open rule: a House rule permitting amendments to a bill from the floor.

Pigeonholing: a method of killing legislation whereby a committee chairman acting on his own refrains from scheduling committee work on a bill.

Politico: member of Congress who votes as a delegate on some issues and as a trustee on others.

Pork-barrel projects: local projects, not of overriding importance, to be financed by federal money.

Private bill: bill involving the private interests of an individual or corporation.

Public bill: bill dealing with matters of concern to the whole population.

Safe seat: seat in Congress for which there is little or no competition.

Select committee: special committee created to explore subjects of extraordinary interest.

Seniority system: the method of selecting chairmen for congressional committees by which the chairmanships go to those of the majority party with the longest service on the committee.

Simple resolution: resolution that requires the action of only one house of Congress and does not have the force of law.

Standing committee: committee that is permanent, continuing its work from one session to the next.

Trustee: a member of Congress who tries to vote according to his or her own judgment, experience, and information, rather than mirroring constituent desires.

Notes

1. Stephen Vincent Benét, *John Brown's Body* (New York: Holt, Rinehart and Winston, 1928), pp. 79–81.

2. Francis E. Rourke, "Bureaucracy: Some Case Studies," *National Journal Reprints*, p. 1.

3. Democratic Study Group, *The Seniority System in the U. S. House of Representatives*, February 25, 1970.

4. Nelson W. Polsby, "The Institutionalization of the U. S. House of Representatives," *American Political Science Review* 68(March 1968):147.

5. As cited in Theodore L. Becker, *American Government* (Boston: Allyn & Bacon, 1976), pp. 218, 219.

6. Warren Miller and Donald Stokes, "Constituency Influence in Congress," *American Political Science Review* 57(March 1963):55.

7. U. S. Congress, Committee on Government Operations, Subcommittee on Intergovernmental Relations, *Confidence and Concern: Citizens View American Government* (Washington, D. C.: U. S. Government Printing Office, 1973), pp. 72–77.

8. Paul N. McCloskey, Jr., *Truth and Untruth: Political Deceit in America* (New York: Simon & Schuster, 1972), p. 107.

9. Ibid.

10. In Samuel P. Huntington, "Congressional Responses to the Twentieth Century," in David B. Truman, ed., *The Congress and America's Future* (Englewood Cliffs, N. J.: Prentice-Hall, 1965), p. 15.

11. James Boyd, "A Senator's Day," in Charles Peters and Timothy J. Adams, eds., *Inside the System* (New York: Praeger, 1970), pp. 101–103.

12. Report of the Association of the Bar of the City of New York Special Committee on Congressional Ethics, *Congress and the Public Trust* (New York: Atheneum, 1971), p. 85.

13. Ibid., pp. 84, 85.

14. Robert Winter-Berger, *The Washington Pay-Off* (New York: Dell, 1972), p. 14.

15. *Watkins* v. *United States* (1957).

16. John S. Saloma, III, *Congress and the New Politics* (Boston: Little, Brown, 1969), p. 276.

17. See Heinz Eulau et al., "The Role of the Representative: Some Empirical Observations on the Theory of Edmund Burke," *American Political Science Review* 59(September 1959):742–756.

18. Edmund Burke, "Speech to the Electors of Bristol (1774)," *Works* (New York: Somerset, 1899), II, 11.

19. Eulau et al., "The Role of the Representative," p. 753.

20. Roger H. Davidson, *The Role of the Congressman* (Indianapolis, Ind.: Bobbs-Merrill, 1969), p. 128.

21. Robert Dahl, *Pluralist Democracy in the United States* (Skokie, Ill.: Rand McNally, 1967), p. 136.

22. Nicholas Masters, "Committee Assignments in the House of Representatives," *American Political Science Review* 56(June 1961):352.

23. Common Cause, *Editorial Memorandum on Common Cause and Congressional Reform*, 1973, p. 2.

24. *Congressional Quarterly Weekly Report*, November 8, 1975, p. 2407.

25. *Congressional Quarterly Weekly Report*, March 1, 1975, pp. 450–451.

Recommended Rebuttal Reading

On Criticisms of Congress

Berg, Larry L., et al. *Corruption in the American Political System.* Morristown, N. J.: General Learning Press, 1976.

Bolling, Richard W. *House Out of Order.* New York: E. P. Dutton, 1965.

Burns, James MacGregor. *Congress on Trial.* New York: Gordian Press, 1966.

Clark, Joseph S. *Congress: The Sapless Branch.* New York: Harper & Row, 1964.

Etzkowitz, Henry, and Peter Schwab, eds. *Is America Necessary? Conservative, Liberal and Socialist Perspectives of United States Political Institutions.* St. Paul, Minn.: West, 1976.

Peters, Charles, and James Fellows, eds. *Inside the System.* New York: Praeger, 1976.

On Reforming Congress

Bailey, Stephen K. *Congress in the Seventies.* New York: St. Martin's Press, 1970.

Davidson, Roger H., et al. *Congress in Crisis: Politics and Congressional Reform.* Belmont, Calif.: Wadsworth, 1966.

Dodd, Lawrence, and Bruce I. Oppenheimer, eds. *Congress Reconsidered.* New York: Praeger, 1977.

Liston, Robert A. *We the People? Congressional Power.* New York: McGraw-Hill, 1974.

Ornstein, Norman, ed. *Congress in Change.* New York: Praeger, 1975.

On Congressional Power

Ripley, Randall B. *Power in the Senate.* New York: St. Martin's Press, 1969.

Truman, David B., ed. *Congress and America's Future.* Englewood Cliffs, N. J.: Prentice-Hall, 1973.

On Congressional Leadership

Bolling, Richard W. *Power in the House.* New York: E. P. Dutton, 1968.

Peabody, Robert L. *Leadership in Congress.* Boston: Little, Brown, 1976.

Ripley, Randall B. *Majority Party Leadership in Congress.* Boston: Little, Brown, 1969.

On Congress Generally

Bibby, John F., and Roger H. Davidson. *On Capitol Hill.* New York: Holt, Rinehart and Winston, 1972.

Ferejohn, Jonn A. *Pork Barrel Politics: Rivers and Harbors Legislation.* Stanford, Calif.: Stanford University Press, 1974.

Huitt, Ralph K., and Robert L. Peabody. *Congress: Two Decades of Analysis.* New York: Harper & Row, 1969.

Jewell, Malcolm E., and Samuel C. Patterson. *The Legislative Process in the United States.* New York: Random House, 1977.

Keefe, William J., and Morris S. Ogul. *The American Legislative Process.* Englewood Cliffs, N. J.: Prentice-Hall, 1977.

Kingdom, John W. *Congressmen's Voting Decisions.* New York: Harper & Row, 1973.

Mayhew, David R. *Congress: The Electoral Connection.* New Haven, Conn.: Yale University Press, 1974.

Vinyard, Dale. *Congress.* New York: Charles Scribner's Sons, 1968.

Vogler, David J. *The Politics of Congress.* Boston: Allyn & Bacon, 1977.

On Congressional Committees

Fenno, Richard F. *Congressmen in Committees.* Boston: Little, Brown, 1973.

Ornstein, Norman J., ed. *Changing Congress.* Philadelphia: American Academy of Political and Social Science, 1974.

AT ISSUE: THE JUDICIARY

Organization

Procedure

RESOLVED THAT:
The Judicial
System
12 Is Undemocratic

At Issue: The Judiciary

The judiciary has always been controversial. Its precise nature was never clearly defined by the Founders, and its role has been heatedly debated throughout American history. Alexis de Tocqueville wrote that "scarcely any political question arises in the United States that is not resolved, sooner or later, into a judicial question." [1]

Indeed, the judiciary has had to render a decision on almost every major controversy in American history: the scope of the national government's power in economic, political, and social matters; the rights of black Americans and other minorities; the war powers of the president; and the definition of justice itself.

Cases presented to the courts must involve real and not theoretical questions. Courts will not issue advisory decisions on speculative issues; a genuine controversy must be involved.[2] In other words, the American system of justice is based on the *adversary process*, with two sides opposing each other. Another limitation is that the courts will not decide cases in which an individual fails to show direct personal injury or damages (actual or prospective).[3]

The courts, of course, aim to clarify and interpret the law. Here some definitions of types of law may be in order. *Constitutional law* is based on a constitution and court decisions that interpret and apply it. As you read in Chapter 10, *statutory law* results from action by a legislature and the signature of an executive, while *administrative law* is

Thugs and federal judges have just about taken charge of this country.—*George C. Wallace*

We have an imperial judiciary—intruding into people's lives in a manner unparalleled in our history.—*Nathan Glazer*

The judiciary has become the primary lawmaker of our society.—*Philip Kurland*

431

promulgated by executive agencies to implement statutory law. *Common law* is made by judges. It customarily develops according to the principle of *stare decisis* (Latin for "to stand by things already decided"). This means that a judge renders a decision using decisions in earlier, similar cases as precedents. *Civil law* pertains to relationships between individuals or organizations. *Criminal law* concerns crimes against the government or society as a whole. *Admiralty and maritime law* is the law of the sea.

ORGANIZATION

At the apex of the American judicial system is the United States Supreme Court, which has both original and appellate jurisdiction. (See Figure 1 and Table 1.) Its *original jurisdiction* covers cases that come directly to it. These cases—involving foreign diplomats or one of the states, for example—are listed in Article III of the Constitution. Many more cases, however, come through *appellate jurisdiction*—the right to review decisions of lower courts. All these cases originating in lower courts are concerned with constitutional issues. A case may come to the Supreme Court through appeal or through a *writ of certiorari*. In the latter instance, a litigant who has lost a case requests that the Court issue the writ (*certiorari* is Latin for "made more certain"). If the Court issues the writ, it indicates its willingness to be "made more certain"—to hear the case. If the request is denied (as it is in over 85 percent of the cases), the Court is in effect upholding the decision of the lower court.

Beneath the Supreme Court are the eleven United States courts of appeals. Each state and territory falls within the jurisdiction of one of these courts. They have only appellate jurisdiction, reviewing appeals from lower federal courts and decisions of federal regulatory agencies.

The third principal layer of courts in the pyramid of the federal judiciary is formed by the United States district courts. There are ninety-seven districts; each state has at least one, as do four territories and the District of Columbia. Unlike the courts of appeal, the district courts are trial courts, handling cases involving violations of federal law and disputes between citizens of different states. District courts do have some, albeit limited, appellate jurisdiction.

Four additional courts handle certain specialized cases. The Court of Claims rules on claims (1) against government appropriation of property; (2) for income tax refunds; and (3) of government workers for back pay. The United States Court of Customs hears cases pertaining to civil actions concerning tariff laws. The Court of Customs and Patent Appeals has jurisdiction over trademark, patent, and tariff appeals cases. The Court of Military Appeals is the final appellate court in court-

FIG. 1. Structure of the United States Judicial System

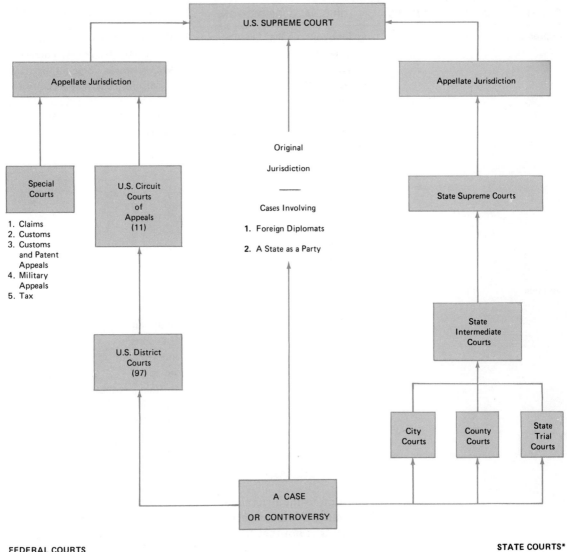

FEDERAL COURTS   STATE COURTS*

*Although state court systems differ, they generally follow the basic pattern outlined above.

martial convictions. The Tax Court, although technically a part of the executive branch, has the judicial function of reviewing decisions of the Internal Revenue Service and is, therefore, a fifth specialized court.

Table 1. Jurisdiction of the Major Federal Courts of the United States □

COURT	NO. OF COURTS	NO. OF JUDGES	ORIGINAL JURISDICTION	APPELLATE JURISDICTION
Supreme	1	9	*1. Actions between the United States and a state 2. Actions between two or more states *3. Cases involving foreign ambassadors, other foreign public ministers, and foreign consuls or their "domestics or domestic servants, not inconsistent with the law of nations" *4. Actions commenced by a state against citizens of another state or aliens, or against a foreign country (See Amendment 11 to the Constitution)	1. All lower federal constitutional courts; most, but not all, federal legislative courts (created by Congress); and the territorial courts 2. The highest state courts when a "substantial federal question" is involved
Appeals	11	97		1. District courts 2. Territorial courts, the U. S. Tax Court, and some District of Columbia courts 3. Independent regulatory commissions 4. Certain federal administrative agencies and departments (for review, but also for enforcement of their actions and orders)

In addition to the federal courts, there are separate systems of state and local courts. It should be noted that the main difference between the two systems is not that federal courts are superior to state and local courts, but rather that the two systems have different jurisdictions. In general, federal courts have jurisdiction over cases involving: (1) the Constitution and federal laws and treaties; (2) admiralty and maritime law; (3) land disputes under titles granted by two or more states; (4) the United States as a party; (5) a state as a party; (6) citizens of different states as litigants; and (7) diplomats. State and local courts have jurisdiction over all other types of legal controversies.

Table 1. Jurisdiction of the Major Federal Courts of the United States (continued)

COURT	NO. OF COURTS	NO. OF JUDGES	ORIGINAL JURISDICTION	APPELLATE JURISDICTION
District**	97	400 (approx.)	1. All crimes against the United States 2. All civil actions arising under the Constitution, laws, or treaties of the United States wherein the matter in controversy exceeds $10,000 (unless the Supreme Court has jurisdiction, as outlined above) *3. Cases involving citizens of different states or citizens and aliens, provided the value of the controversy is in excess of $10,000 4. Admiralty, maritime and prize cases *5. Review and enforcement of orders and actions of certain federal administrative agencies and departments 6. All such other cases as Congress may validly prescribe by law	

ᵃ For purposes of this table, the "special" courts (U. S. Court of Claims, U. S. Court of Customs, U. S. Court of Customs and Patent Appeals, U. S. Court of Military Appeals, and the U. S. Tax Court) are omitted.

* Jurisdiction not exclusive—*i.e.*, while cases, according to Article III of the Constitution, are to originate here, legal arrangements may be made to have them handled by a different level court. For example, Congress has the power to give the federal District Courts concurrent original jurisdiction over cases affecting foreign ambassadors and some cases in which a state is a party to the suit. See *United States* v. *Ravara,* 2 Dallas 297 (1793); *Bors* v. *Preston,* 111 U. S. 252 (1884); and *Ames* v. *Kansas,* 111 U. S. 449 (1884). And in 1964, the Supreme Court declined to review a Ninth Circuit Court decision that federal District Courts have jurisdiction over suits by the United States against a state. (*California* v. *United States,* 379 U. S. 817.)

** An argument can be made that U. S. District Courts also have a measure of appellate jurisdiction, involving certain actions tried before U. S. Commissioners (one of whom is authorized for each federal district).

Source: Adapted from Henry J. Abraham, *The Judiciary* (Boston: Allyn & Bacon, 1977), pp. 16–17. Reprinted by permission of the copyright owner (Allyn & Bacon).

Two other differences between federal and most state judicial systems are (1) the method of judicial selection and (2) judicial tenure. Federal judges are nominated by the president and confirmed by the Senate. They have lifetime tenure during good behavior. These two features of the federal judiciary are meant to free judges from political battles.

In the states, judges are chosen by one of six methods: Judges appoint judges in two states; the legislature appoints judges in four states; the voters elect judges in partisan elections in fifteen states; the voters elect judges in nonpartisan elections in eighteen states; the governor appoints judges in four states; and some form of merit selection is used in twenty-eight states.[4] Most state judges have limited tenure and face reelection or reappointment at regular intervals. The selection and tenure features of state judicial systems are intended to make judges more responsive to public opinion.[5]

PROCEDURE

Although procedure differs between federal and state judicial systems, a typical sequence of steps may be outlined as follows:

CIVIL CASES	CRIMINAL CASES
1. Plaintiff brings suit against defendant	1. Apprehension by government agents
2. Summons to court	2. Preliminary examination
3. Pleadings in court	3. Grand jury indictment
4. Trial	4. Arraignment and pleading in court
5. Verdict	5. Trial
6. Judgment and sentencing	6. Verdict
7. Appeal	7. Judgment and sentencing
8. Enforcement	8. Appeal
	9. Execution of sentence

A civil case involves private parties, with one, the plaintiff, seeking damages from the other, the defendant. If a patient sues a doctor for malpractice, the patient is the plaintiff and the doctor is the defendant. In criminal cases the two parties are the government, or prosecutor, and someone accused of a crime, or defendant. If a patient murders a doctor, the government as prosecutor brings suit against the patient, the defendant.

Since the Supreme Court is a unique body, playing an extremely important role in the judicial system, it may be well to summarize its own special procedures. The highest court is usually in session between October and June to hear cases and render decisions. Every Friday—and frequently on Wednesdays as well—the justices meet in secret to discuss and vote on pending cases, and to determine which cases from lower courts they will hear.

Before the Supreme Court hears a case, lawyers for each side submit written briefs stating their clients' case in full. When the case comes before the Court, each side generally has a half hour to state its

Rich man, poor man

case. It is quite common for this time period to be punctuated by questions from the justices. Although each case presented to the Court has two adversaries, others who are not parties to the case may seek to influence the Court by filing an *amicus curiae* (literally, "friend of the court") *brief*. For example, in a case involving freedom of speech, a special interest organization such as the American Civil Liberties Union may file an *amicus curiae* brief containing arguments it hopes will be persuasive.

After a decision is reached, the senior justice on the prevailing side will assign the writing of the *majority opinion*, and the senior justice on the minority side will assign the writing of the *minority*, or *dissenting*, *opinion*. The Chief Justice is always senior on his side of the issue. Justices may write *concurring opinions*, in which they agree with the majority, but perhaps for different reasons than stated in the majority opinion; and *dissenting opinions*, in which they disagree with the majority position. Sometimes the Court issues *per curiam decisions*. These are decisions without written opinions. Since in essence they state the Court's refusal to review a lower court decision, they serve to reaffirm the lower court's opinion. After opinions are agreed upon in written form, the Court then makes public its decision.

Cases may be appealed directly from the highest state court to the U.S. Supreme Court either if a federal law (or treaty) has been declared unconstitutional or if a state law has been upheld against the challenge that it conflicts with the U.S. Constitution or federal law (or treaty). Also a writ of certiorari may bring a case from the highest state court to the U. S. Supreme Court if there is a "substantial federal question."

In some instances, plaintiffs may decide between bringing suit in either federal or state courts. For example, in 1977 in South Carolina, suits were brought in both federal and state courts to determine if the state constitution's five year residency requirement for governor precluded a candidate from running for governor who had not had an established residence in South Carolina for the preceding five years. The state court suit successfully sought to establish that the candidate did not meet the state constitutional standards, while the federal court suit unsuccessfully sought to establish that the state constitutional provisions violated the U.S. Constitution's "equal protection of the laws" clause of the Fourteenth Amendment.

The American judicial system, from the Supreme Court down to the simplest local court, is regularly criticized for a variety of reasons. Some charge that it is too powerful. Others say it is too slow. Still others contend that it protects the interests of the rich over those of the poor. Many complain that it (especially the Supreme Court) has usurped legislative and executive functions by formulating political, social, and economic policy. Some think that judges are unrepresentative of the general public and therefore unlikely to render decisions fairly and equitably. These and other criticisms raise a crucial question: Is our judicial system really democratic?

The dignity and stability of government in all its branches, the morals of the people, and every blessing of society depend so much upon an upright and skillful administration of justice that the judicial power ought to be distinct from both the legislative and executive, and independent upon both, that so it may be a check upon both, as both should be checks upon that. The judges, therefore, should be always men of learning and experience in the laws, of exemplary morals, great patience, calmness, coolness, and attention. Their minds should not be distracted with jarring interests; they should not be dependent upon any man, or body of men.—*John Adams*

- Is justice really "blind" in the United States?
- Should the Supreme Court "legislate" social policy?
- Could the Missouri Plan be used to improve the selection of federal judges?
- How can the judicial system deal effectively with governmental lawlessness?

The Affirmative Case

Yes, the judicial system is undemocratic.

To the person who waits all day to pay a traffic fine, the young man who spends a few months in jail for possessing marijuana, the woman who finds no remedy in court for an exorbitant rent hike, the black who still cries for implementation of "civil rights" legislation, and the student who resists serving in an illegal war, the judicial process appears to worsen pressing problems rather than solve them.[6]–Robert Lefcourt

What kind of judicial system do we have? It is highly flawed, and its many defects may be summarized under two headings:

- The judiciary is too powerful.
- Justice is inequitable because of the judges themselves and the ways in which justice is dispensed.

THE ALL-POWERFUL COURTS

To put it bluntly, our court system has become too powerful. The chief tool enabling it to gain this power has been the principle of judicial review. The chief result is the unhealthy practice of policy making by the courts.

The only check upon our own exercise of power is our own sense of self-restraint.—Harlan F. Stone

Judicial Review   The foundation of our judiciary's potent authority, especially that of the Supreme Court, is *judicial review*—the power to determine whether a law or action of government is constitutional. How can we reconcile this judicial supremacy with democratic ideals? It is difficult indeed. "Scratch a fervent believer in judicial supremacy," says one observer, "and like as not you will find someone with a bitterness about democracy. The two are as close as skin and skeleton." [7]

Studying judicial review as practiced by the Supreme Court provides us with our best understanding of how this principle makes the judiciary so powerful. Why should a body of nine persons who are not elected by the people have the authority to strike down what the people want? Are not Congress and the president, both elected by the people, capable of judging whether a proposed action is constitutional? Is there any reason to believe that the legislature and the chief executive are less devoted to the Constitution than is the Supreme Court?

The power of judicial review has led to *judicial activism*, with the Supreme Court playing a vigorous role in trying to bring about social change. The Warren Court exemplified this role. It had "a philosophy which held that, when other branches of government are not capable of responding to the rightful demands and grievances of the people, it is the proper role of the Court to exercise leadership and initiate social change." [8] In his 1968 presidential campaign, Richard Nixon stated: "I believe we need a Court which looks upon its function as being that of interpretation rather than of breaking through into new areas that are really the prerogative of the Congress of the United States." [9] Many Americans agree with this view.

As the Supreme Court pursues the course of judicial activism, it loses whatever impartiality it may have had. We know that justice is not blind. Studies have shown that judges bring with them to the bench their personal and political biases, which condition how they will decide cases.[10] For example, Republican judges are more likely than Democrats to vote for the prosecution in criminal cases. In tax cases, Republican judges are more likely to support the government, while Democratic judges are more likely to support private citizens.

When the Court takes an activist stance, it destroys the concept of "settled law," which is based on precedent. The law shifts as the Court shifts in making its decisions. What one court rules is the law, the next may reverse or modify. In key areas of civil rights, civil liberties, and criminal procedures, the Burger Court has frequently reversed or modified Warren Court decisions. (See Chapter 4 for details of these cases.)

One end result is that the language of constitutional law loses its timeless quality. As Senator Sam Ervin said: "Everyone will concede that the Constitution is written in words. If these words have no fixed meaning, they make the Constitution conform to Mark Twain's description of the dictionary. He said the dictionary has a wonderful vocabulary, but no plot." [11]

Five-to-four Decisions   When the Supreme Court hands down a decision, it may have been reached by a mere majority of five to four. In other words, matters of grave national and international import may be decided by the vote of one man.

> Writing in 1941, Attorney General Jackson told how Europeans were astonished that national monetary policy could be determined "in the guise of private lawsuits involving a few dollars"—$15.60 to be exact. He was referring to the gold-clause cases of 1934 in which the court ruled, five to four, that Congress did have constitutional power to declare gold-payments contracts void. A five-man majority had final say on United States monetary policy. Partisan advocacy for private litigants, before judges with built-in predilections, can achieve the "public interest" or "general welfare" only by happenstance. [12]

The problem of five-to-four decisions becomes glaringly obvious when one examines examples like *Escobedo* v. *Illinois* (1964) and *Miranda* v. *Arizona* (1966). In the *Escobedo* case, the Supreme Court allowed a confessed killer to be released, provoking Justice Byron White to comment that the decision allowed "a killer, a rapist, or other criminal [to return] to the streets and to the environment which produced him, to repeat his crime whenever it pleases him." [13] In the *Miranda* case, a confessed rapist and kidnapper was allowed to be released. (See Chapter 4 for more details on these cases.) Technically, of course, the Supreme Court never releases anyone; rather, it reverses a lower court decision and remands (returns) the case to that court for a decision consistent with the Supreme Court decision.

What is the function of the Court—to protect society from confessed criminals or to protect criminals? Would it not be better to require an extraordinary majority of at least six to three in Supreme Court

Do we really believe that judges have any special aptitude which makes them suitable custodians for the solution of our social problems?—*Simon H. Rifkind*

decisions in order to have greater assurance that the proper decision is being made?

Judicial Notice   Although commonly thought to be bound by the constraints of the adversary system, justices do not limit their concern in making decisions to the facts presented to the Court. Rather, they have been known to take *judicial notice* of other facts while ruling on a case and to conduct research for information not provided in the case itself either in oral arguments or in legal briefs. The Model Code of Evidence of the American Law Institute says that judicial notice and independent research are permissible within narrow limits, but there is no clear specification of these limits. Should sociological theory be used by justices in making judicial decisions and writing opinions? More generally, to what extent should any nonlegal information, especially in the social sciences, be used in rendering court verdicts? For example, opponents of the Supreme Court's 1954 school desegregation case, *Brown* v. *Board of Education*, have charged that the Court used sociological theory to interpret and apply the Constitution. Of course, the plaintiffs did submit much of the so-called sociological data as evidence. However, if the Court had limited its decision strictly to judicial research, it would not have eliminated opposition to its decision, but at least it would have given the opposition one less argument. It is easy to see that judicial notice and independent research, if used by some justices and not others, may lead to a hit-or-miss approach to interpretation of the Constitution and may undermine the adversary system, which at least theoretically binds the Court to the facts presented to it.

Making Public Policy   Until the 1950s, the Supreme Court generally applied a decision only to the case before it. The Warren Court, however, began to apply many of its decisions to a wide range of public issues. Thus, a legislative redistricting decision from one state set public policy for other states. Some argue that the Supreme Court should not set public policy but merely interpret and apply the law in the case before it. Others believe that it is quite appropriate for the Court to set public policy, but that the adversary process causes this to be done in an arbitrary fashion; that is, the Court can establish public policy only on the issues that come before it.

The problem of policy making is certainly not limited to the Supreme Court. An examination of the highly unpopular school busing decisions rendered by lower federal courts shows vividly how the judicial process can disregard public opinion. Against a background of strong community opposition, hundreds of thousands of children have been forced to ride buses to schools outside their neighborhoods. Were the courts considering the health and safety of the children? (Many had to board buses before daybreak and return home in the dark.) Did the

The mounting influence of law and lawyers on modern American life constitutes one of the great unnoticed revolutions in U.S. history: the ever-increasing willingness, even eagerness, on the part of elected officials and private citizens to let the courts settle matters that were once settled by legislatures, executives, parents, teachers—or chance. ... So long as modern life grows ever more complex, demands on the law will increase. That much is inevitable. And if Americans want to prevent their system of government from being changed in a fundamental manner, they will have to find ways in which to prevent every buck from being passed to a judge and every problem from being turned over to a lawyer. The U.S. has created the most sophisticated—and the fairest—legal process in the world. But the burdens are becoming intolerable.—*Jerrold K. Footlick*

Drawing by Lorenz; © 1976 The New Yorker Magazine, Inc.

"Warrington Trently, this court has found you guilty of price-fixing, bribing a government official, and conspiring to act in restraint of trade. I sentence you to six months in jail, suspended. You will now step forward for the ceremonial tapping of the wrist."

judges consider the energy crisis? Did they have incontrovertible evidence that either black or white students would benefit from this massive shuffling of human flesh? Evidence shows that the courts generally did not have answers to these questions in rendering their decisions. Such questions suggest that the judiciary is not the place for making public policy.

Considering all the problems attendant on judicial policy making, it is little wonder that one of the most distinguished jurists ever to serve on the Supreme Court, Felix Frankfurter, remarked that "courts are not representative bodies. They are not designed to be a good reflex of a democratic society. Their judgment is best informed, and therefore most dependable, within narrow limits." [14]

JUSTICE FOR SOME

Who dispenses justice? How is it dispensed? The first question focuses on the background of the judges who render decisions. The second has to do with the way in which these decisions are made. The answers in

For myself, it would be most irksome to be ruled by a bevy of Platonic Guardians, even if I knew how to choose them. . . . If they were in charge, I should miss the stimulus of living in a society where I have, at least theoretically, some part in the direction of public affairs.—*Learned Hand*

We can't have a safe America unless everyone agrees to obey the law . . . including those big shots in high public office who also commit crimes. There is nothing more sacred to this country than equality under the law.—*Walter F. Mondale*

The aphorism that "the law is what the judges say it is" needs to be amended to "the law is what the judges say it is after all others have had their say." What is legal at any given moment is what government officials enforce as legal with the sanctions officially available to them.— *Robert Dahl*

both cases will indicate that our system hardly leads to the "justice for all" proclaimed by the Pledge of Allegiance.

Elites in Charge   Most American judges are upper-middle-class white males. Although their background does not necessarily determine how they will decide a case, it does predispose them in certain directions. One may naturally expect that judges will be better able to empathize with litigants who have had experiences like their own. If nothing else, judges can better understand the life-styles, speech, and values of those in their own socioeconomic class.[15]

What this means is that the scope of socioeconomic backgrounds and political attitudes among judges is narrower than that for society generally—and more so in the higher courts than in the lower courts. Summarizing research on this subject, James Eisenstein writes:

> The recruitment process does appear to screen out effectively those whose opinions and life-styles are unusual. Few militant homosexuals, black separatists, or revolutionary anarchists are sitting on the bench. Furthermore, the more important t'.e post, the less likely that anyone holding unusual social and politica' views will occupy it. Individuals recruited for higher posts generally are selected from among those who have previously held less important ones. When an incumbent of a lesser post displays unusual behavior or deviant attitudes, he is usually eliminated from consideration for a higher office. Thus, the breadth of political and social attitudes represented on the bench is narrower than that found in society generally.[16]

Why are persons with uncommon ideas or life-styles unlikely to serve as judges? Why is it that the higher a judgeship, the less likely it is to be occupied by someone with unusual views?

First, most judges are lawyers. This generally means that they have received both college and law school educations. Since most minority groups have not had equal access to higher education, this fact alone has substantially limited the number of persons with diverse viewpoints. Historically, law schools have been populated largely by white males from the middle and upper-middle classes.

Second, the methods of selecting judges effectively screen out persons with unusual views. In the federal courts, most presidential nominees are first approved by a committee of the American Bar Association. It rates prospective candidates prior to Senate confirmation. Thus a president must keep in mind the views of the ABA as well as those of the Senate. In the latter body, senatorial courtesy allows a senator of the president's party to block a nomination from the senator's home state. As a result, a well-qualified judicial candidate may be blocked solely because of one senator's opposition.

In state and local courts, where election is common, it is usually helpful if a judicial candidate has participated in party politics. This is true even where an appointive system is used. A judicial nominating commission may propose a list of prospective judges from which the governor is to name one. But the governor's appointments to the nominating commission itself may be influenced by party officials, who in turn help determine what names appear on the list of prospective judges given to the governor.

In their general background, justices of the Supreme Court are fairly typical of those who administer our laws. With few exceptions, members of the Court have been white, Anglo-Saxon, and Protestant (see Table 2). The first and only black ever to sit on the Court is Thurgood Marshall, appointed by President Johnson. It has been customary to have one Jew on the Court since Louis Brandeis came to the bench in 1916, but currently there is no Jewish representative. The sole Catholic is William Brennan, appointed by President Eisenhower. There has never been a woman justice of the Supreme Court.

As might be expected, Supreme Court justices have generally had some political experience before serving on the court (see Table 3) and are customarily of the appointing president's political party (see Table 4). They are an educated elite with the expected political contacts and commitment to the establishment, which, of course, is why they were considered for nomination in the first place. As one federal judge noted: "If [a judge] was ever a firebrand, he is not discernibly an ember

Table 2. The "Average" Supreme Court Justice: A Profile of 101 Justices

1. Race	Only one black ever appointed
2. Ethnicity	Anglo-Saxon except for six, the last being Felix Frankfurter (appointed by Franklin Roosevelt)
3. Sex	All male
4. Religion	All Protestant except for six Roman Catholics and five Jews
5. Age	Between fifty and fifty-five at time of appointment
6. Education	B.A. and LL.B. from such prestige schools as Harvard and Yale
7. Status	Upper-middle to high social status
8. Career	Generally some public service
9. Hometown	Generally an urban area

Source: Adapted from John R. Schmidhauser, "The Justices of the Supreme Court: A Collected Portrait," *Midwest Journal of Political Science* 3(1959):1–57. Reprinted with permission.

Table 3. Occupations* of Supreme Court
Designees at Time of Appointment†

Federal Officeholder in Executive Branch	22
Judge of Inferior Federal Court	22
Judge of State Court	21
Private Practice of Law	18
U.S. Senator	8
U.S. Representative	4
State Governor	3
Professor of Law	3
Associate Justice of U.S. Supreme Court**	2
Justice of the Permanent Court of International Justice	1

*Many of the appointees had held a variety of federal or state offices, or even both, prior to their selection.

†In general the appointments from state office are clustered at the beginning of the Court's existence; those from federal office are more recent.

**Justices White and Stone, who were *promoted* to the Chief Justiceship in 1910 and 1930, respectively.

Source: Adapted from *Justices and Presidents: A Political History of Appointments to the Supreme Court* by Henry J. Abraham, p. 53. Copyright © 1974 by Oxford University Press, Inc. Reprinted by permission. Updated through 1976.

Table 4. Percentages of Federal Judicial Appointments of Same
Political Party as the President, 1888–1973

PRESIDENT	REPUBLICAN	DEMOCRAT
Cleveland		97.3
B. Harrison	87.9	
McKinley	95.7	
T. Roosevelt	95.8	
Taft	82.2	
Wilson		98.6
Harding	97.7	
Coolidge	94.1	
Hoover	85.7	
F. D. Roosevelt		96.4
Truman		90.1
Eisenhower	94.1	
Kennedy		90.9
L. B. Johnson		93.2
Nixon	93.7	
Ford	82.0	

Source: Adapted from *Justices and Presidents: A Political History of Appointments to the Supreme Court* by Henry J. Abraham, p. 60. Copyright © 1974 by Oxford University Press, Inc. Reprinted by permission. Updated to 1977.

now. If he ever wanted to lick the Establishment, he has long since joined it."[17] Although the WASP background of judges is not quite so pronounced in the lower federal courts, the same general conclusions still apply.[18]

Weaknesses in the System   Even if elitism were eliminated from the judiciary, the American judicial system would still not be fair. Among the most serious weaknessess undermining its effectiveness are incompetence, inequitable policing, bail inequalities, plea bargaining, case overloads, and cost.

Incompetence   Ironically, the public sees and hears most about the Supreme Court, where well-qualified persons serve and where justice appears to be dispensed fairly and rationally. For example, written briefs are filed and oral arguments are made in a routine and competent manner.

> When the legal process becomes visible to the general public, its beliefs in the myths are reinforced. After all, it is the Supreme Court decision, replete with written opinion, cogently argued briefs, and the sanctity of the Court's legitimacy that accounts for much public awareness of the legal process. The notorious crime, which typically is resolved by a full-fledged jury trial rather than negotiated pleas, reinforces the tendency. Notions that all's well in the legal process are perpetuated by the unrepresentativeness of the glimpses the general public sees of its operation.[19]

But it is the lower courts—especially those at the municipal and county levels and below—where most Americans are directly affected by the judicial process. Here less well-qualified persons serve as judges and justice is less equitable. Particularly affected are the poor, whose cases rarely go beyond these local courts. As James Eisenstein points out: "It is the poor man, the immigrant, the minority group member who most often encounters the police, landlord-tenant court, civil commitment proceedings, and misdemeanor court."[20]

By contrast, middle- and upper-class people rarely confront the judicial process at these lower levels except perhaps to pay a traffic fine (often without even appearing in court). They are more likely to have experience with a higher state court or federal District Court. This situation leads to important consequences. First, leaders in state and local bar associations and other powerful lawyers seldom represent clients at the lowest levels of the judicial process; therefore they are not knowledgeable about its inequities. Second, the people least able to challenge and change the judicial process generally confront it at its worst point, precisely where the greatest improvement is needed.

Is there really "equal justice under the law" in the United States, or is police behavior affected by such factors as age, appearance, ethnic background, and socioeconomic status? Critics might argue that the man pictured here would be less likely to be handcuffed and handled roughly, let alone arrested, if he were a prosperous-looking middle-aged man in a well-tailored business suit.

Inequitable Policing Consider just a few inequities having to do with police behavior. Why do country clubs often get away with selling drinks after hours, while lower-class taverns can expect to be raided? Why are affluent-looking drunks generally given a ride home in a taxi, while a "down-and-outer" is usually driven to the police station in a paddy wagon? Why is a well-dressed person less likely to be stopped and frisked than someone who is shabbily dressed?

Such examples of police behavior do little, if anything, to build public confidence in the judicial system, especially among the less fortunate in our society. Rather, these examples breed a callous view that the judicial system exists to help the more fortunate and that there is no such thing as "equal justice under the law."

Bail Inequalities *Bail* is money "posted" as a guarantee that a person will appear in court at the proper time. It is permitted after arrest and before trial, as well as after conviction and prior to sentencing or appeal. The fact that poorer people are less able to put up funds for bail has a marked effect on the judicial process. Statistics show that a person on bail is less likely to be convicted than someone who is not on bail. One reason is that a person on bail has more freedom to help lawyers prepare for a defense in court. As noted in a national study of the bail system: "Those who go free on bail are released not because they are innocent but because they can buy their liberty. The balance are detained not because they are guilty, but because they are poor." [21] If there is a conviction, a person on bail usually receives a lighter sentence than someone who is not on bail.

Plea Bargaining   Amendment Six of the Bill of Rights reads in part that "in all criminal prosecutions, the accused shall enjoy the right to a

Poor Americans frequently are unable to put up funds for bail and thus must spend long periods in prison even before they have been convicted of a crime. Ironically, statistics show that those who cannot raise bail are more likely to be convicted and receive heavier sentences than those who can raise bail money. What does this say about the impartiality of our judicial system?

speedy and public trial, by an impartial jury." According to the Seventh Amendment, "In suits at common law, where the value in controversy shall exceed twenty dollars, the right of trial by jury shall be preserved." What actually happens?

> If every case went to a jury . . . the system would soon be overwhelmed. Jails, already overcrowded in many places, would have to house even more defendants unable to make bail who were awaiting trial. Prosecutors, public defenders, and judges would be inundated. "Our office keeps eight courtrooms extremely busy trying 5 percent of the cases," observed one Manhattan prosecutor. "If even 10 percent of the cases ended in a trial, the system would break down." [22]
>
> Meanwhile, the lag between arrest and trial would rapidly increase. The number of convictions, even if the prosecutor won every trial, would fall dramatically. Private attorneys would encounter financial disaster as they were forced to accept meager fees inadequate to compensate them for the time spent preparing and actually trying cases. [23]

The public image of plea bargaining is terrible. The public sees justice disbursed in terms of deals—that if you get a good lawyer you can get off, not necessarily by winning a trial, but by out-snookering the DA. Sentencing should be determined after a plea is entered and not to get a plea to end a criminal proceeding. It should be a separate function. . . . It doesn't do much good for the criminal-justice system to indict someone for assault with a deadly weapon, then find out that you didn't have any evidence on which to prove the charge; so you end up reducing it to an assault-and-battery misdemeanor with an agreed-upon deal for a suspended sentence. That, I don't think, did anything but send all of us through the motions and convince everybody that the whole thing was basically a sham. Now we don't handle that kind of case any more. If we can't prove them, we don't file them. The police are making better cases for our office because they know that for the most part they're going to have to justify their cases in court. Now we can make more cases stick when we file them.— *Avrum M. Gross*

The result is *plea bargaining*—that is, the plaintiff (or prosecutor) and the defendant, their respective attorneys, and the judge agree that the defendant will plead guilty to a lesser charge in exchange for a reduced sentence. Several unfortunate consequences may result. For one thing, the bargaining skill of defendant and attorney—rather than an examination of the evidence—determine a defendant's guilt and sentence. [24] (Lesser sentences are generally given to experienced defendants and attorneys who know the plea bargaining process. [25]) This means that decisions properly the province of judges and juries are made by lawyers and their clients, and lawyers are often more concerned about case loads, fees, conviction rates, and time spent on a case than with achieving equitable justice. [26]

In a criminal case, the prosecutor may offer the defense a very attractive bargain to avoid presenting poor or illegal evidence in court (such as evidence obtained through an illegal search or unnecessary force), or to keep secret the identity of an informer. [27] Ironically, the pressure on a defendant to plead guilty is greater if the evidence is weak. [28] A prosecutor with a weak case would rather plea bargain than risk losing a case by going to trial.

In sum, imagine that you are wrongly accused of committing a robbery. Defendant X is accused of a similar crime. You plead innocent, are convicted, and receive a ten-year sentence. Defendant X pleads guilty and is sentenced to eighteen months in prison. How would you feel about the fairness of the judicial process?

Case Overloads   A serious weakness in the American judicial system, case overloads, is illustrated by the federal judiciary. Chief Justice Earl Warren himself concluded as early as 1958 that "the delay and choking congestion in the federal courts . . . have created a crucial problem for constitutional government in the United States." [29] Although some improvement has been made during the 1970s with the so-called "speedy trial rule," especially in criminal cases, there remains a backlog of cases. At one point during the early 1970s, about one fourth of some 80,000 cases pending in the federal system were two or more years old. Frequently, case overloads are even greater in state and local courts.

Some 4,000 cases are presented to the Supreme Court each year, but it reviews fewer than 200. Before the Court will review a case, at least four justices must request that it be considered. One scholar has noted:

> Of course, it is true that the justices have much brought to them for decision. More than 4,000 cases are filed each term, which means that an average of about 80 decisions a week must be made. But those raw figures fail to uncover the reality that most cases are dealt with summarily, by discretionary denial of review. Even the court's "original" jurisdiction is discretionary.
>
> Most efforts to get Supreme Court review thus receive mere cursory attention. Even with the help of law clerks, it is impossible for a justice to read carefully and to assimilate everything filed. As a consequence, his views on whether review should be granted are made in a few minutes at most. A former justice has said that he often did it in 15 seconds.[30]

One of the principal causes of this overload is our fragmented judiciary. The system of justice in the United States includes federal, state, and local courts, prosecutors at each of these levels (the United States attorney general, state attorneys general, and states' attorneys), the FBI, state and local police, parole officers and parole boards, and numerous federal, state, and local prisons. It would be unfair to blame the fragmented judiciary for the entire overload. Certainly the increasingly litigious nature of American society, as well as the increased number of laws being passed by the U.S. Congress and state legislatures, has also contributed to this serious problem. However, a more unified system might better organize and make more efficient the distribution of justice in the United States.

Cost A person of low to moderate income can hardly afford to pay the costs of extensive litigation against adversaries like large companies or the government. To illustrate with a person of some financial means, former U.S. Senator Edward Gurney (Rep. Fla.) had the same charges brought against him twice by the U.S. Department of Justice, even though he had been acquitted by a federal jury during the first trial. Despite two acquittals on the same charges, Gurney had to pay several hundred thousand dollars in legal expenses. The legal expenses of the government, of course, were borne by the taxpayers. Although seriously harmed financially, at least Gurney had been a U.S. senator, which

The cost of rendering legal services today has become so high that in modest matters lawyers cannot afford to undertake the work and prospective clients cannot afford to retain lawyers.— *Justin A. Stanley*

should help him to raise funds to pay his legal debts. Persons without Gurney's affluence and prestigious background would most likely be inhibited from seeking vindication of their reputations in legal proceedings. This analysis strongly suggests that justice is more equal for those who are able to bear the costs. Although the government would have provided an attorney for Gurney had he been an indigent defendant, in all likelihood the quality of his defense would not have been as good.

The Negative Case

No, the judicial system is not undemocratic.

[The] judiciary is truly the only defensive armor of the Federal government, or rather of the Constitution and the laws of the United States. Strip it of that armor and the door is wide open for nullification, anarchy, and convulsion.[31]–James Madison

A thorough examination of the American judicial process leads conclusively to the view that it has been vital in preserving democracy. Moreover, our judicial process is indeed responsive to public opinion. To summarize:

- The powers of the courts are necessary but not unlimited.
- The judicial process has strengthened democracy by protecting both minority and majority rights.

POWER: NECESSARY BUT LIMITED

In our judicial system, the courts do indeed have power. But this power, with deep historic roots, is needed to protect and promote democratic government. Whether or not it actually results in the formation of public policy is a debatable point. In any case, limitations on the courts prevent them from exercising their authority in an irresponsible manner.

The Need for Judicial Review   The courts' power of judicial review has a long history. At the Constitutional Convention of 1787, between twenty-five and thirty-two of the forty delegates generally favored judicial review. Such leading delegates as James Madison, Alexander Hamilton, and Gouverneur Morris publicly stated their support for the concept. Judicial review is implied in Article III, Section 2, and in Article VI of the Constitution. Because of these historic roots, it can be argued that the power is a proper one in terms of the intent of the Founders.[32]

Is judicial review undemocratic as exercised by the Supreme Court, whereby a small group of justices, appointed for life, can overturn actions of an elected Congress and president? No, because the courts do not capriciously reverse actions of other units of government. Even in *Marbury* v. *Madison*, the key precedent for judicial review, the Supreme Court recognized its limitations.

Just before leaving office in 1801, President John Adams and his Federalist party majority in Congress created fifty-nine federal judgeships, to which Adams promptly nominated members of the Federalist party. As Adams' Secretary of State, John Marshall was responsible for delivering the commissions for the judgeships, but seventeen went undelivered in the pressure of inaugural preparations for the new president, Republican Thomas Jefferson. Recognizing that the Federalists had attempted to pack the judiciary with members of their party, Jefferson and his Secretary of State, James Madison, ignored the undelivered commissions. In the meantime, John Marhsall had assumed his new position as Chief Justice of the United States.

One of the judges who did not get his commission was William Marbury. He asked the Supreme Court to issue a writ of mandamus (Latin for "we command") ordering Secretary of State Madison to give him his judicial commission. Marbury based his request on Section 13 of the Judiciary Act of 1789, which empowered the Supreme Court to issue such writs. When asked by Marshall to show cause why he would not deliver the commission, Madison did not respond.

Marshall faced a dilemma. If he issued the writ of mandamus, Madison would ignore it, and the Supreme Court would be powerless to do anything. If he did not issue the writ, the Jeffersonian Republicans would triumph by default. Marshall chose a third alternative. He declared Section 13 of the 1789 Judiciary Act unconstitutional, saying that Congress had no right to expand the original jurisdiction of the Supreme Court by a statute; additional powers could be conferred only by a constitutional amendment.

Thus Marshall had his cake and ate it too. He declared that Marbury was entitled to the commission but that the Supreme Court could not act because it lacked jurisdiction. His decision was a reprimand to Jefferson and Madison for not performing their duties, but he avoided a confrontation with them that he could not win. In the process he established the precedent for judicial review. Marshall stated:

> It is emphatically the province and duty of the judicial department to say what the law is. Those who apply the rule to particular cases must of necessity expound and interpret that rule. ... A law repugnant to the

Constitution is void; . . . courts, as well as other departments, are bound by that instrument.[33]

Paradoxically, the power of judicial review was established in the face of judicial weakness, which is the important lesson to learn here. The very power cited by critics of the judiciary as demonstrating its all-powerful nature is fraught with limitations.

To those who worry about the power of the judiciary, one might also respond with a question: Who is going to determine whether the legislative and executive branches have exceeded their powers under the Constitution? In *The Federalist*, Hamilton argues that it is the courts "whose duty it must be to declare all acts contrary to the manifest tenor of the Constitution void." [34] The people must have protection against unconstitutional acts committed by the legislative and executive branches; the judiciary is the proper agency to provide this protection. Who should interpret the laws? Once again, Hamilton argues that "interpretation of the laws is the proper and peculiar province of the courts." [35]

We are sometimes uncomfortable with having courts do these things [filing suits to save wildlife, suing companies that may be selling faulty products, etc.], but people are going to court because of a perception that other institutions for making decisions are hopeless and unresponsive. People have more confidence that the issues will be resolved properly in court.—*Charles Halpern*

Policy Making   Many critics argue that in exercising judicial review, the courts are to judge, not legislate. What this argument does not explain is where judging ends and legislating begins.

It is difficult to draw clear distinctions. Was the Supreme Court judging or legislating when it declared mandated nondenominational prayers in public schools unconstitutional? [36] What was the Court doing when it held that legislative districts that are unequal in population violate the equal protection clause of the Fourteenth Amendment? [37] Did the Court judge or legislate when it ruled that "separate but equal" educational facilities are a denial of equal protection of the laws? [38]

As to praying in public schools, most Jews would contend that doing so violates the separation of church and state and infringes upon their freedom of religion, as guaranteed in the First Amendment. But many Christians would argue that public policy should be determined by a plurality or majority of citizens; thus if enough people want school prayers, they should be permitted.

Increasingly, Congress legislates in broad, general terms. Sometimes because the legislation is not as thoroughly considered as it might be, or because it goes through natural processes of compromise, with resulting ambiguity, the courts are compelled to do the best they can using the accepted rules and canons of statutory construction to try to discern the intent of the Congress. This frequently puts courts in the appearance of engaging in [social, political, and economic reform]. Possibly there are some judges who like that function; but I think most would prefer to have Congress make the basic social, economic, and political decisions. My view is that, under our constitutional system, the elected representatives should make these basic decisions, not tenured judges who cannot be rejected by the people, as senators and Congress members can be.—*Warren E. Burger*

What about the decision affecting legislative redistricting and desegregation? Certainly the Court was setting public policy here, but would it not also have been setting public policy if it had upheld existing practices—or not rendered decisions at all? The answer to whether courts judge or legislate turns on whose ox is being gored.

Checks on the Judiciary   The three main sources of limitations on the judicial system are the president, Congress, and the courts themselves.

ROTHCO

"I CAN'T QUITE FIGURE OUT HER SIGNAL."

Presidential Checks Presidents may refuse to enforce Court decisions (a fact recognized by Marshall in *Marbury* v. *Madison*). Later in *Worcester* v. *Georgia*, the Marshall Court ruled that the laws of Georgia were of no effect inside the boundaries of the Cherokee nation. President Andrew Jackson, who did not like the decision, reportedly said: "John Marshall has made his decision; now let him enforce it." Presidents may also try to rally public opinion against the judiciary. Franklin

Roosevelt sought to obtain public support for his plan to increase the number of justices on the Supreme Court, because of decisions striking down many of his New Deal programs. Although unsuccessful in obtaining approval for the plan, Roosevelt was soon receiving decisions more favorable to his New Deal program.

Another check on the judiciary's exercise of power is provided by the system of presidential nomination. Since federal judges are subject only to confirmation by the Senate, the executive can have enormous influence. During Nixon's presidency, for instance, he made four appointments to the Supreme Court, men who were able to alter the direction of decision making from what it had been during Warren's time. It should be pointed out that Supreme Court justices can become independent of the president who appointed them. Earl Warren, for instance, did not turn out to be an Eisenhower conservative. As a general rule, however, judges follow the thinking of the president who appointed them.

Congressional Checks   Congress has several important checks on judicial power. First, it can limit the Supreme Court's jurisdiction. Article III, Section 2, of the Constitution states that the Supreme Court has appellate jurisdiction "both as to Law and Fact, with such Exceptions, and under such Regulations as the Congress shall make."

Second, the Congress can impeach and try judges, and in the past it has impeached and convicted four judges. The most recent, but unsuccessful, effort was made in 1970 by some House members led by then Representative Gerald Ford to impeach Justice William O. Douglas. There are no well-defined criteria for impeachment, but generally conduct unbecoming to the judiciary is either explicit or implicit in impeachment charges. In the instance of Justice Douglas, his rather eccentric behavior and very liberal political ideology led to impeachment charges against him.

Third, constitutional amendments proposed by Congress can reverse Supreme Court decisions. In 1793, the Court held, in the case of *Chisholm* v. *Georgia,* that a citizen of one state could sue another state; the Eleventh Amendment reversed this decision. The Thirteenth and Fourteenth Amendments in effect reversed the Dred Scott decision of 1857, which had declared that black Americans were ineligible for citizenship. The Sixteenth Amendment reversed *Pollack* v. *Farmer's Loan and Trust Company* (1895), which had declared an income tax unconstitutional. Amendments Nineteen, Twenty-four, and Twenty-six also had the effect of reversing Supreme Court decisions.

Fourth, Congress may modify or abort the impact of a court decision as it did in 1962 after the DuPont Company had twice lost Supreme Court decisions involving a complex and expensive stock acquisition and holding case.[39] In this instance, the Congress passed a bill assisting the DuPont Company in the achievement of its stock acquisition and holding plan.

Fifth, Congress may exercise limitations on the judiciary through its power to determine the number of judges serving on the courts.

Sixth, the Senate has the power to confirm the president's judicial nominations, and it used this power to reject two of President Nixon's nominations to the Supreme Court.

What we may conclude here is that court decisions cannot differ too drastically from opinions of the legislative majority over a long period of time. If this happens, it is likely that court decisions will be modified or reversed in one way or another.

Self-Imposed Checks It is important to remember that courts are presented with controversies that they must decide according to constitutional principles. A jurist, according to Justice Benjamin Cardozo,

> is not to innovate at pleasure. He is not a knight-errant, roaming at will in pursuit of his own ideal of beauty or of goodness. He is to draw his inspiration from consecrated principles. He is not to yield to spasmodic sentiment, to vague and unregulated benevolence. He is to exercise a discretion informed by tradition, methodized by analogy, disciplined by system, and subordinated to "the primordial necessity of order in the social life." [40]

In the case of the Supreme Court, it cannot rule on a case unless (1) there is a genuine legal controversy between two adversaries, (2) one adversary has suffered or will suffer substantial injury, (3) it involves a clear and substantial constitutional question, and (4) the Court can provide a remedy.[41] In addition, a person cannot first benefit from a statute and then ask the court to declare the law unconstitutional. These criteria help the courts determine whether a *justiciable issue* exists—that is, an issue that can be decided by law. These issues are generally applicable to other federal and state courts.

Another strong inhibition on court action is the doctrine of *stare decisis*. It is useful to note that the entire phrase is *stare decisis et quieta non movere*, meaning "stand by things already decided and do not disturb the calm." Commonly courts adhere to precedent except when an error could probably not be corrected by legislative means. Otherwise, as noted by Justice Louis Brandeis, "the Court bows to the lessons of experience and the force of better reasoning, recognizing that the process of trial and error, so fruitful in the physical sciences, is appropriate also in the judicial function." [42]

In addition to these limitations, there are those having to do with presumed constitutionality and judicial restraint. *Presumed con-*

Drawing by Joe Mirachi; © 1974 The New Yorker Magazine, Inc.

"Do you ever have one of those days when everything seems un-Constitutional?"

stitutionality means that a law is presumed to be constitutional as long as there is a constitutional interpretation by which it can be declared valid. Chief Justice Charles Evans Hughes wrote that "as between two possible interpretations of a statute, by one of which it would be unconstitutional and the other valid, our plain duty is to adopt that which will save the act." [43] *Judicial restraint* is an avoidance of the urge to set public policy. As Justice Felix Frankfurter stated:

> It is not the business of the Court to pronounce policy. It must observe a fastidious regard for limitations on its own power, and this precludes the Court's giving effect to its own notions of what is wise or politic. That self-restraint is of the essence in the observation of the judicial oath, for the Constitution has not authorized the justices to sit in judgment on the wisdom of what Congress and the executive branch do. . . . [44]

When a judge makes law, his action is no more final than that of any other lawmaker. Our political system is marked by the constant communication, dissolution, and recombination of various political forces in the process of continuously adjusting the law to changing social needs and political demands.—*Martin M. Shapiro*

What about cases in which the Supreme Court does make policy? For one thing, the Court may subsequently alter its decision. For example, the Burger Court has modified crucial Warren Court decisions in the area of criminal law (see Chapter 4). Second, an earlier decision may be reversed. This occurred in 1941,[45] when the Court reversed a 1918 decision striking down congressional wage-and-hour legislation.[46]

STRENGTHENING DEMOCRACY

Our judicial system exists in a dynamic society. It is not independent of society's problems, but rather inherits many of those problems for resolution. In a perfect society, with no conflicts among people, the judicial process would be unnecessary. We should ask not whether our courts are perfect, but whether they are improving. The answer is that they are.

Administrative Improvements　At the level of lower courts, improvements have taken a variety of forms. One is the unified court system, which allows judges to be assigned where the case load is greatest so that the constitutional guarantee of a speedy trial can be maintained. Numerous states have adopted this system of allowing a senior or higher court judge to assign judges to areas where the case load is greater. In Illinois, for example, rural downstate judges may be assigned to densely populated and heavy case-load areas like Chicago. Other elements of a unified court system are generally the consolidation and simplification of court structure, centralized making of rules for court operations, centralized budgeting, and statewide financing of all courts.[47]

Another reform, merit selection of judges, provides for mixed systems of appointment and election, such as the California and Missouri Plans. Under the California Plan, the governor nominates one prospective judge to a three-member Commission of Qualifications. If approved by the Commission, the judge serves for one year, after which he or she runs unopposed for a twelve-year term. If a majority of the electorate fails to approve, the governor makes another appointment. Under the Missouri Plan, a nonpartisan nominating board selects three candidates for each vacant judgeship. The governor appoints one of the three for a one-year probationary term, after which he or she runs in the same type of election as is held in California. The merit selection of judges does not remove party politics from the scene, but it does allow other interests to have a more effective voice in determining who will serve. For example, under merit selection, a person who is not a native to an area (and who has perhaps graduated from a more prestigious law school) has a greater opportunity to serve as a judge than under purely elective systems.

Still another reform is Judicial Discipline and Removal Commissions. This reform provides for judges to be disciplined or removed by a commission rather than to have the matter resolved by impeachment proceedings in the legislature. Citizens are able to file charges against a judge before the Discipline and Removal Commission.

Even [Warren E.] Burger's opponents are quick to applaud the reforms he has promoted—an Institute for Court Management to train administrators; a National Center for State Courts to develop more effective procedures, and a thorough reorganization of the Supreme Court bureaucracy to improve its efficiency. . . . Says one former high government legal official, "I respect his abilities as a focuser of judicial reform." . . . The Burger Court has even ventured into territory that its predecessors did not reach. It has repeatedly ruled against sex discrimination and has extended the rights of prisoners, aliens, and the mentally ill.—*Jerrold K. Footlick and Lucy Howard*

Police training is another area where improvements are taking place. Criminal justice programs have been instituted in many universities. It is not uncommon to find state and local police personnel with college degrees, especially in such states as California and New York. Impetus for police training efforts has been provided by the Law Enforcement Assistance Act, enacted during the Johnson Administration. LEAA funds have helped finance the development of college and graduate school programs in criminal justice administration, as well as in-service training for police.

Local judges are benefiting from in-service training to assist them with specialized problems associated with family, probate, traffic, and other local courts. Computerization of records has also helped improve justice at the local level.

Federal courts have also received their share of attention. They too have benefited from computerized records. In addition, various proposals to streamline the federal judicial process are under consideration. Congress has been working for several years to modernize the federal criminal code. One of the most controversial proposals involves establishing a new court composed of some appellate court judges between the courts of appeal and the Supreme Court. It would rule on whether a case should come before the highest court. The purpose of such a court would be to reduce the amount of time justices spend determining whether to hear cases, so that they could concentrate more on the actual cases themselves.

Judicial Representation   It is also significant to note that more women and minority group members are being chosen for judgeships. For example, until 1977 no woman or black had ever served on the California State Supreme Court. In two appointments made on the same day, Governor Jerry Brown appointed both a woman, Rose Elizabeth Bird, and a black man, Wiley W. Manuel, to the Supreme Court, and the former as Chief Justice.[48] Because of the very substantial increase in women and minority group enrollment in law schools, the pool of legal talent available from these two groups will increase substantially in the near future, eliminating one of the most significant reasons for the underrepresentation of these groups in the judiciary.

Crucial Decisions   For the less privileged in society, the judicial process represents an important way to seek redress of grievances (see Chapter 4). Two decisions of federal district courts illustrate the importance of the judicial process in assisting the less privileged. In New York a preliminary injunction was granted in 1971 to prevent the state from cutting off Medicaid benefits for 165,000 persons and reducing benefits

The impression made upon the public by the Court's decisions has often had as great an effect upon history as have the decisions themselves.—*Charles Warren*

for another 660,000 through more stringent eligibility standards. In Virginia the state's prison system was told in 1971 to halt "bread and water punishment, unnecessary use of various forms of physical force, forced nudity as punishment, overly small solitary confinement cells, and interference with the legal activities of inmates on their own behalf." [49]

According to one study, four common misconceptions of judicial review—as reflected in many American government textbooks—suggest that this power of the judiciary has not been used as much as it could have been to strengthen democracy. It has been incorrectly assumed that

> (1) judicial review has rarely been used in national cases since 1937; (2) federal laws voided in the recent past are insignificant; (3) the Supreme Court's record of defending civil liberties is [poor]; and (4) the Nixon appointees have fulfilled his 1968 campaign promise "to turn the court around." [50]

There is, however, substantial data to indicate that judicial review has strengthened democracy. First, the Supreme Court has declared fifty-nine federal laws unconstitutional since 1943—as many as in any other comparable period of Supreme Court history. Second, during the same period the Court declared provisions in forty-nine national laws unconstitutional as abridgements of such constitutional rights as equal protection under the law. Third, between 1969 and 1976, the Burger Court ruled provisions in twenty-seven national laws unconstitutional, and it has held more congressional acts unconstitutional on First Amendment and equal protection grounds than all preceding courts combined.[51]

Glossary

Admiralty and maritime law: the law of the sea and shipping.

Adversary process: a system of justice based on two sides opposing each other.

Amicus curiae brief: additional brief presented by special interest organization or individuals not parties to the case but seeking to influence the court in reaching a decision.

Appellate jurisdiction: authority to review case decided by a lower court.

Bail: money "posted" as a guarantee that a person will appear in court at the proper time.

Civil law: law pertaining to relationships between individuals or organizations.

Common law: law made by judges, using similar cases as precedents.

Concurring opinion: an opinion of one or more judges that supports the conclusions of a majority of the court but offers different reasons for reaching that conclusion.

Constitutional law: law based on a constitution and on court decisions interpreting and applying it.

Criminal law: law dealing with crimes against the state or society.

Dissenting opinion: an opinion of one or more judges that disagrees with the decision reached by the majority of the court.

Judicial activism: the philosophy that the Supreme Court should play a vigorous role in bringing about social justice.

Judicial notice: the act of a judge in recognizing the existence of certain facts without making one side in a lawsuit place them in evidence.

Judicial restraint: the philosophy that the Supreme Court should refuse to rule on cases involving political questions.

Judicial review: the power to review laws or executive actions and declare them unconstitutional.

Justiciable issue: an issue that may be decided by legal methods (an issue not involving domestic politics or foreign policy).

Majority opinion: an opinion of a majority of the judges supporting the decision of the court.

Minority opinion: see *dissenting opinion.*

Original jurisdiction: authority to try cases for the first time.

Per curiam decision: a Supreme Court decision without a written opinion that upholds the decision of a lower court.

Plea bargaining: the plaintiff (or prosecutor), the defendant, their attorneys, and the judge agree that the defendant will plead guilty to a less serious charge in exchange for a reduced sentence.

Presumed constitutionality: a law is presumed to be constitutional as long as there is a constitutional interpretation by which it can be declared valid.

Stare decisis: a principle literally saying "to stand by things already decided." A previous decision by a court applies as a precedent in similar cases.

Writ of certiorari: a court order to a lower court to send the record of a case for review.

Notes

1. Alexis de Tocqueville, *Democracy in America*, ed. Phillips Bradley (New York: Alfred A. Knopf, 1944), I, 280.

2. *Muskrat v. United States* (1911).

3. *Massachusetts v. Mellon* (1923).

4. Larry Berkson, "Judicial Selection, Discipline, and Removal in the American States," an address to the National Conference of State Legislatures, Lincoln, Neb., May 6, 1977.

5. James Eisenstein, *Politics and the Legal Process* (New York: Harper & Row, 1973), pp. 26, 27.

6. Robert Lefcourt, "Law Against the People," in Henry Etzkowitz and Peter Schwab, eds., *Is America Necessary? Conservative, Liberal and Socialist Perspectives of United States Political Institutions* (St. Paul, Minn.: West, 1976), p. 337.

7. Max Lerner, *Ideas Are Weapons* (New York: Viking Press, 1939), p. 474.

8. Louis M. Kohlmeier, Jr., *God Save This Honorable Court!* (New York: Charles Scribner's Sons, 1972), p. 44.

9. *Congressional Quarterly Weekly Report*, May 23, 1969, p. 798.

10. Sheldon Goldman and Thomas P. Jahnige, *The Federal Courts as a Political System* (New York: Harper & Row, 1971), p. 194; and Stuart S. Nagel, "Off the Bench Judicial Attitudes," in Glendon Schubert, ed., *Judicial Decision-Making* (New York: The Free Press, 1963), p. 43.

11. Sam J. Ervin, Jr., and Ramsey Clark, *Role of the Supreme Court: Policymaker or Adjudicator* (Washington, D. C.: American Enterprise Institute for Public Policy Research, 1970), p. 52.

12. Arthur Miller, "Supreme Court: Time for Reforms," *Washington Post*, January 11, 1976, p. F1.

13. *Escobedo v. Illinois* (1964).

14. *Dennis v. United States* (1951).

15. Eisenstein, *Politics and the Legal Process*, p. 65.

16. Ibid., pp. 65, 66.

17. Marvin E. Frankel, "An Opinion by One of Those Softheaded Judges," *New York Times Magazine*, May 13, 1973, p. 41.

18. Sheldon Goldman, "Characteristics of Eisenhower and Kennedy Appointees to the Lower Federal Courts," *Western Political Quarterly* 18(December 1965):726–755.

19. Eisenstein, *Politics and the Legal Process*, p. 321.

20. Ibid., p. 314.

21. Daniel Freed and Patricia Wald, *Bail in the United States: 1964 Report to the National Conference on Bail and Criminal Justice* (Washington, D. C.: U. S. Government Printing Office, 1964), p. vii.

22. Quoted by Albert Alschuler, "The Prosecutor's Role in Plea Bargaining," *University of Chicago Law Review* 36(1968):55.

23. Eisenstein, *Politics and the Legal Process*, p. 111.

24. Donald J. Newman, "Pleading Guilty for Considerations: A Study of Bargain Justice," *Journal of Criminal Law, Criminology, and Police Science* 46(1956):790.

25. Ibid.

26. Robert Polstein, "How to 'Settle' a Criminal Case," *Practical Lawyer* 8(1962):35.

27. Arthur Rosett, "The Negotiated Guilty Plea," *The Annals of the American Academy of Political Science* 374(1967):74.

28. Alschuler, "The Prosecutor's Role in Plea Bargaining," p. 62.

29. Earl Warren, "Delay and Congestion in the Federal Courts," *Journal of the American Judicature Society* 42(1958):6.

30. Miller, "Supreme Court: Time for Reforms," p. F1.

31. As quoted by Charles Warren in *The Supreme Court in the United States History* (Boston: Little, Brown, 1937), I, 740.

32. For a discussion of the historic justification of judicial review, see Charles A. Beard, *The Supreme Court and the Constitution* (Englewood Cliffs, N. J.: Prentice-Hall, 1962).

33. *Marbury* v. *Madison* (1803).

34. Alexander Hamilton, John Jay, and James Madison, *The Federalist* (New York: The Modern Library, 1937), p. 505.

35. Ibid., p. 506.

36. *Engel* v. *Vitale* (1962).

37. *Baker* v. *Carr* (1962); *Reynolds* v. *Sims* (1964); *Kirkpatrick* v. *Preisler* (1969).

38. *Brown* v. *Board of Education* (1954).

39. *United States* v. *E. I. du Pont de Nemours and Co.* (1957) and (1961).

40. Benjamin Cardozo, *The Nature of the Judicial Process* (New Haven, Conn.: Yale University Press, 1921), p. 168.

41. *Ashwander* v. *TVA* (1936).

42. *Burnett* v. *Coronado Oil and Gas Co.* (1932).

43. *NLRB* v. *Jones and Laughlin Steel Corporation* (1937).

44. *Trop* v. *Dulles* (1958).

45. *United States* v. *Darby* (1941).

46. *Hammer* v. *Dagenhart* (1918).

47. Larry C. Berkson, "The Emerging Ideal of Court Unification," *Judicature* 60 (March 1977):377–382.

48. *New York Times*, February 13, 1977, p. 1.

49. Eisenstein, *Politics and the Legal Process*, p. 275.

50. P. Allan Dionisopoulos, "Judicial Review in the Textbooks," *DEA News* 11(Fall 1976):1.

51. Ibid.

Recommended Rebuttal Reading *

On the Judicial System Generally

Abraham, Henry J. *The Judiciary*. Boston: Allyn & Bacon, 1977.

Berkson, Larry, Steven Hays, and Susan Carbon. *Managing the State Courts*. St. Paul, Minn.: West, 1977.

Eisenstein, James. *Politics and the Legal Process*. New York: Harper & Row, 1973.

Glick, Henry, and Kenneth Vines. *State Court Systems*. Englewood Cliffs, N. J.: 1973.

Goldman, Sheldon, and Thomas P. Jahnige. *The Federal Courts as a Political System*. New York: Harper & Row, 1971.

Murphy, Walter, and Joseph Tanenhaus. *The Study of Public Law*. New York: Random House, 1972.

History

McCloskey, Robert G. *The Modern Supreme Court*. Cambridge, Mass.: Harvard University Press, 1972.

Mason, Alpheus Thomas, and William M. Beaney. *The Supreme Court in a Free Society*. New York: Norton, 1968.

* See also bibliography in Chapter 4.

Nominations

Chase, Harold W. *Federal Judges: The Appointing Process.* Minneapolis: University of Minnesota Press, 1972.

Judicial Review

Bickel, Alexander M. *The Least Dangerous Branch.* Indianapolis, Ind.: Bobbs-Merrill, 1962.

Black, Charles L., Jr. *The People and the Court.* New York: Macmillan, 1960.

Jackson, Robert H. *The Struggle for Judicial Supremacy.* New York: Vintage Books, 1960.

Policy Making

Bickel, Alexander M. *The Supreme Court and the Idea of Progress.* New York: Harper & Row, 1970.

Murphy, Walter F. *Congress and the Court.* Chicago: University of Chicago Press, 1962.

Shapiro, Martin. *The Supreme Court and Judicial Review.* Englewood Cliffs, N. J.: Prentice-Hall, 1966.

Decision Making

Murphy, Walter F. *Element of Judicial Strategy.* Chicago: University of Chicago Press, 1964.

Schubert, Glendon. *The Judicial Mind.* Evanston, Ill.: Northwestern University Press, 1965.

Spaeth, Harold J. *An Introduction to Supreme Court Decision Making.* San Francisco: Chandler, 1972.

Impact of Court Decisions

Becker, Theodore L., and Malcolm M. Feeley, eds. *The Impact of Supreme Court Decisions.* New York: Oxford University Press, 1973.

Wasby, Stephen L. *The Impact of the United States Supreme Court: Some Perspectives.* Homewood, Ill.: Dorsey Press, 1970.

Others

Etzkowitz, Henry, and Peter Schwab, eds. *Is America Necessary? Conservative, Liberal, and Socialist Perspectives of United States Political Institutions.* St. Paul, Minn.: West, 1976.

Peters, Charles, and James Fellows, eds. *Inside the System.* New York: Praeger, 1976.

EPILOGUE
Policy Choices and American Democracy

There is a question in the air, more sensed than seen, like the invisible approach of a distant storm, a question that I would hesitate to ask aloud did I not believe it existed unvoiced in the minds of many: "Is there hope for man?"

In another era such a question might have raised thoughts of man's ultimate salvation or damnation. But today the brooding doubts that it arouses have to do with life on earth, now, and in the relatively few generations that constitute the limit of our capacity to imagine the future. For the question asks whether we can imagine that future other than as a continuation of the darkness, cruelty, and disorder of the past; worse, whether we do not foresee in the human prospect a deterioration of things, even an impending catastrophe of fearful dimensions.[1]*–Robert L. Heilbroner*

The concern about natural resources and population is wildly exaggerated. There's no shortage of energy resources. That's a myth. We have 400 years of coal and as much unexploited oil as we've extracted in our history. These gloom-and-doom guys are always talking about exponential growth, with the curves ascending at the recent rate into the future indefinitely. But many experts believe population and economic growth have reached their highest rate in history, that both will decline soon.[2]*–Ernest E. Schneider*

American government does not exist in a vacuum. It is closely connected with the future of Western civilization and indeed that of the whole world. Policy choices made by the United States—the oldest and largest democratic nation—ultimately affect all humanity.

Throughout much of American history, the policies pursued by

467

Is our luck or our talent running out on us? More realistically, can we still count on the natural resources, the immunity from outside dangers, a resourceful people, and a leadership enlightened enough to cope with the problems that glare upon us from every quarter of the horizon? Certainly no other nation was born under such auspicious circumstances: a boundless continent with seemingly limitless resources, immunity from the wars and deprivation of other peoples, a rich inheritance, the wisest leadership ever vouchsafed to a single nation, and an enlightened people "advancing rapidly," as Jefferson said, "to destinies beyond the reach of mortal eye." . . . For the first time in our history as a nation we are no longer masters of our own destiny. Every major problem that confronts us now is global and to be solved only through cooperation with other nations. . . . We who heretofore have not been able to face even the possibility of defeat are now required to take the possibility of annihilation into our calculations. . . . Though we cannot save ourselves merely by our own efforts, the world cannot save itself without both our efforts and our leadership. Because we invented modern federalism, because we were chiefly responsible for the League of Nations and the United Nations, we have had longer experience with international cooperation than any other major power. Because we are not blinded by ancient animosities or ideological commitments, we can see what should be done more clearly than can most nations. . . . What is called for is a revival of the wisdom and resourcefulness that presided over the birth of our Republic and gave us those institutions which still serve us so well and have been so widely copied throughout the rest of the civilized (c'td)

the government had little, if any, direct bearing on the rest of the world. But in this century, particularly during the last fifty years, American policy choices have been pivotal in determining, on a worldwide scale, war and peace, food and famine, resource scarcity and abundance.

It is important here to define the word *policy* in order fully to understand the importance of these choices. A policy is a long-range position, taken by a government, which guides day-to-day decision making on a given issue. For example, between 1949 and 1971, United States policy toward China called for nonrecognition of the government on the mainland, along with recognition of and support for the government of Taiwan. Decisions made within the guidelines of this policy allowed for widespread trade and travel with the government of Taiwan, but essentially none with the mainland. President Nixon's 1971 trip to Peking signaled a policy change. This brought about diplomatic recognition of mainland China and increased travel by Americans to the region.

In this epilogue, we shall examine some basic questions pertaining to public policy. The comments by Schneider and Heilbroner typify two opposing attitudes toward the future: Is traditional American optimism, long a fundamental motivating force in shaping policy, giving way to pessimism? What has happened to democracy in the rest of the world? What are some basic policy problems confronting the American government? Within what economic framework should our government try to solve these policy problems? What has American policy making been like in the past, and how may it change in the future?

DESPAIR OR HOPE?

Public policy is deeply affected by Americans' views of the world and their role in it. Fueled by the fires of optimism, the progress of American political history has been marked by brave slogans like "manifest destiny," "the white man's burden," and "a war to make the world safe for democracy"—rallying cries that ignited in the American spirit a desire either to conquer the North American continent or to spread American democracy throughout the world. There seemed to be no obstacle, given the drive and determination of Americans, too big for American ingenuity. Even as late as the 1960s, political campaign slogans promising a "New Frontier" and a "Great Society" reinforced this historic belief in the American dream of spreading the good life as widely as possible.

Today, however, the force of despair competes with what had seemed to be an endless rhetoric and, indeed, reality of hope. Public opinion polls in the 1970s consistently showed that confidence in American institutions of government had decreased. For example, 46 percent of all Americans doubt that a great depression could be prevented by the federal government, while a mere 11 percent believe that the president can maintain a healthy economy.[3]

One factor contributing to an ostensibly growing feeling of gloom is the changing role of developing, or "third world," nations in Africa, Latin America, and Asia. Many such countries—long-time suppliers of raw materials for American industry—now wish to use these scarce resources for their own economic development. Their new-found economic muscle may shift the balance of power away from the West (the United States and Western Europe).

The Middle East poses both an economic and a military threat. American dependence on Arab oil and the American commitment to Israel make it difficult to define our national interest: What would we do in the event of a major war in the Middle East that might cut off our essential oil supplies?

Prophecies foretell population explosions and fuel shortages, pollution from oil slicks and other hazards, and incalculable and permanent damage to our environment. In the face of such threats, there is a very real question about the willingness of the American people to make the sacrifices that might be necessary to solve social, economic, and political problems. Are Americans willing to adopt a somewhat more austere lifestyle, as they did during the Great Depression of the 1930s and during World War II?

Numerous scholars and studies take a pessimistic view of the future.[4] Economist Robert Heilbroner contends that because people are not willing to make the necessary sacrifices, the outlook is for "convulsive change—change forced upon us by external events rather than by conscious choice, by catastrophe rather than by calculation."[5] Heilbroner believes that certain events—race riots, street crime, airplane hijackings, bombings, and assassinations—have created uneasiness and foreboding among Americans, and that we now question how civilized we really are. One symptom of malaise is the discontinuity between generations, exemplified by the drug culture of a younger generation that has not accepted the values of its parents. Another cause for alarm is a basic change in attitude: a loss of assurance and feeling of control over events, coupled with a growing belief that the quality of life is declining rather than improving. Americans generally used to believe that social change and improvements could be rationally engineered; now we have come to realize that massive expenditures to create a "Great Society" or to spread "the American way of life" abroad through foreign aid have serious limitations. As Heilbroner notes, all our efforts have not eliminated poverty or strident racial conflict.

Yet another symptom is a dissatisfaction with civilization itself.

world. . . . That same inventiveness must be invoked to organize the immense but desperately fragmented resources of over 150 independent and competing nations . . . to solve those common problems which simply do not recognize national or even continental boundaries. Now it is up to us, together with other nations . . . to summon up our wisdom and skills to solve the problems that threaten us all.—*Henry Steele Commager*

People have come to wonder whether their ancestors, with far fewer material goods, were happier than they are. Heilbroner calls it the "civilizational malaise," and says that it reflects

> the inability of a civilization directed to material improvements—higher incomes, better diets, miracles of medicine, triumphs of applied physics and chemistry—to satisfy the human spirit. To say as much is not to denigrate its achievements, which have been colossal, but to bring to the forefront of our consciousness a fact that I think must be reckoned with in searching the mood of our times. It is that the values of an industrial civilization, which has for two centuries given us not only material advance but also a sense of elan and purpose, now seem to be losing their self-evident justification.[6]

Optimism is by no means dead, however. Those with a brighter view of the future believe that the prophets of doom have overstated their case and that their prophecies are too much influenced by immediate events and short-term considerations. The optimists feel that the problems we face can be solved through the application of adequate technology and social engineering.

They contend that the resources necessary to continue a respectable rate of economic growth do exist and that the technology necessary to acquire them is within our grasp. While many recent government programs have been aimed at achieving legal equality—for instance, those growing out of the Civil Rights Act of 1964 and the Voting Rights Act of 1965—our next efforts will be devoted to achieving social and economic equality through a more even distribution of material goods. According to these observers, the government will have to be more active in insuring that private groups, corporations, and unions are motivated to serve the public interest rather than striving simply for personal gain or other narrow interests.

Ben J. Wattenberg, a leading student of American society and public opinion, argues that many of the pessimistic forecasts are not backed by solid research.

> We've become a nation of crisis-mongers. We see gloom and doom where there's progress. Overblown rhetoric, dispensed by ambitious politicians and spokesmen for various New Politics causes, gets echoed in the media. It destroys our feeling of self-worth as a nation, distorts our policy judgments, and turns people to six-packs rather than political involvement.[7]

Wattenberg, using a wide array of statistical data, argues that (1) income, education, and housing quality in the cities have increased since 1960, and (2) workers now have more money, more leisure, and more security than ever before.[8] It is his firm conviction that if the American government makes a basic policy change leading to reduced productivity and consumption, the developing nations of the world will suffer; they are now being helped by American economic growth, since it leads to the expenditure of dollars for their raw materials. They can, therefore, consume more goods and services because of our indirect contribution to their economies. Wattenberg also believes that energy scarcity is a myth. The solution, he aruges, is not to reduce consumption and productivity, but rather to allow our technology to develop new energy resources to support a continually expanding economy. After all, coal and uranium were once useless rocks; they became useful because of technological developments.[9]

Still other optimists insist that government programs to alleviate poverty have been successful. The director of the Congressional Budget Office, Alice M. Rivlin, believes that "the nation has come a lot closer to eliminating poverty than most people realize." Economist Sar A. Levitan says that "if poverty is defined as a lack of basic needs, it's almost been eliminated."[10] Because of programs like Medicaid, Medicare, food stamps, housing subsidies, school lunches, and other noncash benefits (to be distinguished from cash benefits like Social Security) totaling almost $40 billion per year, the Congressional Budget Office has concluded that the number of poor people in the United States is only 9 million. (Some studies that do not account for noncash benefits show a much higher proportion of poor people—up to 26 million.)

IS DEMOCRACY RELEVANT?

Regardless of their views of the future, most experts agree on at least one thing: Democracy is on the wane around the world. In terms of public policy, democracy may be defined as the determination of this policy by a government whose political leaders have been chosen by elections in which there is competition between candidates and parties. This definition assumes that the necessary civil liberties, such as freedom of speech and press, exist to protect dialogue and debate about alternatives. Given this definition, democracy is definitely on the decline.

Many nations that preserve the form of public elections are one-party states that do not offer voters any choice between candidates or policies. Many of these are communist countries.

Military dictatorships without even the trappings of democracy have replaced democratic governments in many nations, particularly in Africa and Latin America. The view generally held is that a democratic government would be too unstable in these countries. They lack a large middle class of well-educated people, which has been necessary for the proper functioning of modern democracies.

There is no parliament in the world that has the access to policy making that the Congress of the U.S. has—not in Britain, not in France, not in any of the democracies. The key decisions have to be subjected to congressional approval. The democratic process involves an approval [by Congress] of the general direction in which a country is going, as well as of specific individual steps. But to attempt to subject every single decision to individual approval will lead to the fragmentation of all effort and will finally lead to chaos and no national policy.—*Henry A. Kissinger*

Even in historically democratic nations like the United States, France, and Britain—where competitive elections are still held—the substantive principles of democracy have been partially undermined. For example, in the 1972 presidential campaign, the Nixon forces sought to undermine the Democratic opposition by using bugging devices to acquire private and personal information. The Republicans also published bogus literature in the Democratic presidential primaries designed to breed friction among Democratic candidates, denying voters a fair opportunity to evaluate candidates on the basis of their literature and campaign statements.

If a few incidents like this were all that could be cited, we might conclude that the United States had learned a lesson from these tawdry experiences, which were not likely to be repeated. But the problem of democratic decline is deeper than this. Increasingly in this age of rapid technological advancements, democratic governments find themselves responding to important substantive decisions that are made by special interests of one kind or another. For example, when the United States Steel Company decides to raise its prices, there is little that the government can do—or at least seems willing to do—to reverse a decision that will feed the inflationary spiral. The same situation exists with respect to labor-union demands for higher pay and more fringe benefits. More and more frequently, the policies that vitally affect people are made outside the representative institutions of democracy.

The question naturally arises whether democratic government is relevant in a highly industrialized society. Can democratically elected representatives rationally and thoroughly debate complex technological issues? Can voters rationally and thoroughly communicate with their elected representatives on these issues? Can such questions be properly discussed in political campaigns characterized by brief television commercials and short newspaper advertisements? These questions make dubious the historic premise that the people can govern.

PUBLIC POLICY ISSUES

It would be easy to list a large number of policy issues confronting the institutions of American government. Our purpose here, however, is not to develop an exhaustive list, but rather to indicate the range of policy issues and show how increasingly difficult it will be for the public to influence the decisions made to resolve them. If we are entering an era in which the individual has less control over his or her own destiny, alienation between the government and the people will most likely increase. Democracy will work only if people believe that their government is responsive to their interests. A situation in which they lose the

I believe that an economic growth policy which abandons environmental objectives would be a foolish course. The nation must have clean growth. If the price of that clean growth is to restrain the size of particular activities pending the development of new pollution-control technologies or new production procedures, then new technologies and processes can and will be developed in order to take advantage of the economies of scale. Conversely, if environmental objectives are abandoned simply to accommodate the economies of scale, new pollution-control technologies will not be developed, and the result will be environmental chaos. The facts on the record clearly suggest that subtle and often irrevocable changes are being made in man's basic life-support system as the result of uncontrolled dispersion of pollutants into the environment. Almost without exception, research into the effects of dispersal of these pollutants has given us more, rather than less, reason to be concerned. To ignore these problems because they are not fully understood is to court catastrophe.— *Edmund S. Muskie*

ability to influence governmental policy decisions clearly strikes at the heart of democracy—namely, government by the consent of the governed.

Growth and Its Limits Americans have long been attracted by size, speed, and efficiency. These tastes were particularly obvious in the 1950s and 1960s. The public thirsted after bigger, faster, and fancier cars. The automobile industry was only too happy to oblige, with gas-guzzling monsters that sent profits upward. New houses were bigger and more elaborate; business structures were erected higher and higher; real estate developments devoured larger and larger chunks of farm land, escalating real estate taxes and helping drive farmers off their land. Food and drink processors turned out quantities of chemically treated products in disposable packages.

These developments seemed to ignore the resulting problems: reduced energy supplies, diminishing resources, and increased pollution. Can our present rate of economic growth continue? What is an acceptable rate of economic growth? Should economic growth be tolerated if it threatens the environment?

Energy Should public policy call for (a) rationing scarce energy sources like gasoline, (b) letting the market control supply and demand, or (c) setting price ceilings?

There are problems with any one of these policy alternatives. Gasoline rationing may not always be equitable; how will it provide for those people, such as sales representatives, who need more gasoline than others? Rationing may also lead to black markets, where products are sold illegally outside the existing distribution outlets, usually at higher prices. If the market controls supply and demand, prices tend to rise. Inflation adversely affects those least able to pay, creating an additional burden on the poor. But if price ceilings are set, there is the problem of enforcing compliance, which usually requires a large bureaucratic structure. In this case, too, black markets often develop.

Another factor that must be taken into consideration is that business and industry need substantial energy in order to operate. If energy consumption is reduced, unemployment tends to increase.

Environment In recent years Americans have become increasingly concerned about pollution in many forms. Automobiles, airplanes, buses, and cigarettes cause air pollution. Water pollution results from industrial waste and sewage. Noise pollution is serious in areas of large industries and heavy auto traffic.

Cleaning up the environment is a laudable objective, especially if it

The reason we have cities is because we need them, and we are going to need them all the more as the energy situation grows worse. Even the oil in the Middle East may run out by the end of this century at the present rate of consumption. That is not so far off. Here we go on building highways and big cars—usually one passenger to a car, driving 15 miles one way in the morning and 15 miles the other at night. In an energy shortage it is more efficient for people to live and work in cities. So cities are more needed than ever on that basis. Wait until the real energy crunch comes! The American people haven't realized yet what people in other countries pay for gas and fuel. Wait until it hits! I have just come from a visit to Israel, where gas is $1.50 to $2 a gallon. We thought things were bad a couple of years ago when people had to stand in line for gas [in the U.S.]. I am talking about a crisis when you don't even get in line because there isn't any gas. We don't understand yet what being without energy is like; but, when we do, then cities are going to be very, very attractive because it isn't going to be much fun riding a bicycle 15 miles in the morning and 15 miles out at night, as people can now do in their big cars.—*Kenneth A. Gibson*

I think we have two groups of [environmental] extremists. There are, of course, those people on the one side who would pave the country over in the name of progress. There is an extremist group on the other extreme that wouldn't let you build a house unless it looked like a bird's nest. Now, I think there has to be common sense in-between that recognizes the people are ecology, too.—*Ronald Reagan*

reduces the hazards of such diseases as cancer. But some economists would ask whether it is better to live with some pollution rather than create a possible recession or depression by slowing down industrial productivity in the interest of a clean environment. The trade-offs have to be calculated with care. For example, oil is needed to support industrial growth, but oil slicks contaminate ocean waters and threaten marine life and the fishing industry. Can offshore drilling be allowed for its potential benefit to, say, the transportation industry, even though it threatens potential harm to another industry, like fishing? These are not easy policy choices. In areas short of fuel, many people would accept such a risk. This cycle of relationships possesses another vicious relationship, particularly as it relates to consumer costs, that is, prices and taxes.

Consumer Costs   Automobile manufacturers, forced to comply with Environmental Protection Agency regulations requiring the installation of pollution-control devices, increase car prices. This increase in turn reduces the purchasing power and savings potential of consumers. Pressures are then created to increase salaries in order to compensate for such reductions. Labor unions may seek higher wages and more fringe benefits to help their members, in which case labor-management disputes and negotiations will result. The government, requiring ever more money (for the support of such bodies as the Environmental Protection Agency), contributes to this problem by taking ever higher taxes out of paychecks. Each of these examples illustrates the added burdens on consumers.

Social Welfare   Economic growth creates economic dislocations. When new businesses become more efficient than older ones, some people lose their jobs. Should the government provide alternative work? Should it retrain people for other jobs?

When the American space program began to slow down in the late 1960s, thousands of highly trained and well-educated aerospace workers lost their positions. When college and university enrollment declined during the same period, some Ph.D.'s had to turn to such jobs as driving cabs just to earn a living. Does the government have an obligation to provide unemployed or underemployed people with jobs commensurate with their education and training? To do so creates another tax burden. But not to do so fosters discontent and deprives society of the valuable contributions such people may make.

Social Equality   To what extent and under what circumstances should the government act to guarantee social equality among all people? Official government policy since passage of the 1964 Civil Rights

Act has been to eliminate vestiges of discrimination in a variety of areas, among them education, housing, and employment. But should the government initiate affirmative action on behalf of females and minority groups if such action discriminates against white males? For example, if the government requires a law school to admit a certain proportion of females, this might lead to discrimination against some white males who are better qualified. If the school has room for a hundred new students and is required to admit twenty-five females, it may have to accept some women who are less qualified than men it is forced to reject. The justification for this action is that females and minority groups have been discriminated against for many years; reverse discrimination is necessary to compensate for the past. Once again, the complexities of policy making are indicated. The policy goal of eliminating discrimination can itself lead to discrimination.

Foreign Policy   As developing nations raise prices of their raw materials necessary to feed our industrial machine, the cost per unit produced increases, reducing the buying power of American consumers. When the United States sells wheat to the Soviet Union, American farmers may benefit from higher prices, but American consumers may have to pay more for bread. When the United States intervenes overseas, as in Vietnam, American industry may benefit through contracts for military weapons, but thousands may die and American society may be thrown into turmoil. When the United States keeps thousands of soldiers in Western Europe, it aggravates our balance-of-payments problem—that is, the situation in which American dollars are spent more overseas than in the United States and thereby become cheaper in relationship to other currencies. As a result, costs for Americans to travel overseas and to purchase foreign-made goods have increased substantially. These foreign-policy issues show that policy making, whether domestic or international, is complex.

ECONOMIC POLICY-MAKING MODELS

Politics and economics, as shown in the preceding discussion, are inseparably connected. It is important, therefore, to assess that relationship both in the United States and in other countries. There is a different relationship between politics and economics in each of the following models: communist, socialist, capitalist, mixed, and fascist. A look at each of these models will help us in charting the course of the United States, with its mixed model combining capitalist and socialist features.

The illusion that a nation can escape, if it wants to, from power politics into a realm where action is guided by moral principles rather than by considerations of power is deeply rooted in the American mind.— *Hans J. Morgenthau*

[We pledge] a new American foreign policy . . . based on constant decency in its values and on optimism in its historical vision. [The first plank is] America's commitment to human rights as a fundamental tenet of our foreign policy.— *Jimmy Carter*

To the extent that the heavy dose of moralism now being prescribed from Washington makes Americans "feel very good" about the country's foreign policy (to use Vice-President Mondale's phrase), we are likely to be lulled into forgetting that while moral principles can provide a base for our foreign policy, they are not, in themselves, a policy. They become a policy only when they are applied to the practical problems on international affairs . . . in a manner that not only reflects the values of our country but protects its interests as well. There is no inherent conflict between values and interests; but policy can be fatally flawed when either is ignored. . . . History shows that the more our leaders talk of moral principle, the more important it is that we ask how the transaction will affect America's national interest.—*David S. Broder*

Communist   According to this model, the government owns all farms and industries and rigidly controls all economic decision making. The ultimate objective of this model is to have the government develop the national economy by imposing plans, such as the five-year plans of the Soviet Union. This model is sometimes referred to as an economic democracy because it seeks to apportion wealth relatively evenly throughout the society. But political freedom is submerged in the interest of economic achievement.

Socialist   In this model, the government owns major businesses and industry, but there is usually private ownership as well. The goal is to create maximum economic security for the individual. Most socialist nations allow freedom of expression and other basic human rights. Sweden, for example, allows relatively uninhibited human expression, but follows a generally socialist pattern of government ownership and social-welfare programs.

Capitalist   In this model, all the means of production are in private hands. The government does not interfere with economic decision making. The economic system regulates itself through the free market, which operates according to the laws of supply and demand. This model operates within a political democracy, as did the United States during the early part of its history.

Mixed   The American model today is a mixed economic system containing both socialist and capitalist elements. The American system has certain socialist features, such as government-aided old-age pensions, but it retains such capitalist features as privately owned insurance companies. This model, like the socialist model, is a political rather than an economic democracy, but it does not seek to create a "cradle to the grave" sense of security for the individual.

The role of government, a heatedly debated subject, is an issue of continuing tension between liberals and conservatives in a mixed economy. Liberals believe that government policy should emphasize security over risk for the individual. They favor wide-ranging government programs designed to protect the citizen, such as Social Security, unemployment compensation, Medicare, and Medicaid. Conservatives, on the other hand, believe that a public policy of providing maximum security for the individual creates too great a tax burden. They argue that the government should emphasize risk over security—not to the exclusion of security, but with the aim of limiting programs so that taxes are lower.

Liberals feel that the government should make choices for the indi-

Even in the highly literate nation of our own, we have seen repeated attacks on the incentive system for farmers. We have had such campaigns as the beef boycott, eat-one-less-hamburger-per-week, or meatless Tuesdays. It has only been two years since political pressures forced us into a system of federally imposed price ceilings on meats and other food products. . . . Now we must ask, have we learned our lesson from taking those negative acts? Have we learned that if the United States is indeed to use its great food-productive capacity, then the individual farmer must be free to produce and market his crops as he sees fit? We must *not* dampen the incentives that have made our farmers the producers that they are. We must *not* signal to them in the language of price—the language they understand best—that we want *less,* not more. We must *not* periodically signal to our farmers that they have only limited access to markets beyond their shores. We must *not* periodically throw government controls at them that dampen their plans for investment, their dreams of expansion, their hopes for success.—*Earl L. Butz*

vidual in some cases, while conservatives want to maximize the individual's freedom to make choices. For example, while liberals would require everyone to take part in the Social Security program, conservatives would allow individuals to decide whether they want to participate.

Fascist Under this model, the government is supreme, as in the communist model, but private ownership is allowed. A fascist government does not tolerate political dissent, and hence in that way is like communist states. However, it could not be classified as an economic democracy in that it has no policy to spread wealth evenly. Historically, the fascist model characterized Nazi Germany, Mussolini's Italy, and Spain under Francisco Franco. In more recent years, military dictatorships in several Latin American countries are based on fascist economies.

THE NATURE OF POLICY MAKING IN THE UNITED STATES

Several chapters in this book have provided information on how policy is made in the United States. It is important in assessing policy making, however, to note several central features about its nature and to appreciate their interrelationships.

Incrementalism Policy in the United States tends to be made slowly and to evolve over a long period of time. Many discussions in this book have demonstrated this incrementalism; perhaps the most dramatic examples are in the field of civil rights (see Chapters 4 and 12). Although the Supreme Court declared in 1954 that public schools had to be integrated with "all deliberate speed," well over a decade passed before a concerted effort was made to implement the Court's decision. In the meantime, the president and Congress began to act in other areas of civil rights with the adoption of the Civil Rights Act of 1964 and the Voting Rights Act of 1965. Some civil rights issues, such as reverse discrimination, still await resolution by the policy process.

Multiplicity of Policy Makers One of the factors contributing to incrementalism is the large number of policy makers. Not only were all three branches of the federal government active in determining civil rights policy, but there were many policy makers in each branch. In Congress there were the Judiciary Committees of both houses. In the executive branch, though policy first evolved mainly in the Department of Justice, it was ultimately shared by every other department and agency, as civil rights policy had to be enforced in many areas of society. In the judiciary, the lower courts played a major role in interpreting and applying Supreme Court decisions. State and local governments were also active in reacting to and implementing policy made by the national government.

Complexity   As noted earlier in this epilogue, policies cannot be made in isolation from one another. There are linkages to be considered, such as those between energy and environment. Because of the interrelationships—and the resulting necessity of numerous policy makers—policy making is quite complex. For example, a national policy concerning land use would involve the cabinet departments of Agriculture, Commerce, and Housing and Urban Development, plus the appropriate congressional committees and subcommittees. The courts might become involved, too, as citizens test whether the federal government has the authority to limit use of their own land. Each policy maker would most likely have a different interest in and position on the issue of land use.

Outside Influences   The general public, interest groups, and political parties have often been influential in determining public policy. In the fight over ratification of the Equal Rights Amendment, interest groups were well organized on both sides of the issue. Proponents included the League of Women Voters and the National Organization for Women; opponents formed the STOP-ERA organization. Some legislators also tested general public reaction by taking their own opinion polls.

Impermanence   However official and permanent policies may seem, most bear a stamp of tentativeness. Individuals and groups may work not only to create a new policy but also to change or abolish it. Hardly any American policy seemed more fixed than that of nonrecognition of mainland China after 1949. The same could be said of decisions not to sell wheat to Russia during the 1950s and 1960s.

Dynamism   Because policy making is tentative, it is dynamic and not static. Public policy is the result of a struggle at any given time. In assessing it, observers need to determine which forces want to preserve the status quo, which are advocating change, and what levers of power are available to both sides. For example, until civil-rights groups developed power in Congress and with the president, their efforts to change policy had little impact.

Symbol and Substance   President Carter began his administration with several symbolic acts: walking during the inaugural parade, receiving telephone calls from average citizens, addressing the nation in informal clothing, and reducing the number of limousines for use by administration personnel and the number of television sets in the White House. Though Carter was acting symbolically, his actions had substantive consequences. He was seeking to build public support for his role in the policy-making process in the same way that Franklin Roosevelt did with his famous fireside chats. The symbolic and substantive aspects of policy making cannot be separated. To the extent that a president develops public support through symbolic gestures, he generally strengthens his role in policy making.

The relationship may be shown through another example. During the Eisenhower administration, Public Law 480 was adopted to provide food to needy foreign countries. In 1961 the Kennedy administration renamed the program Food for Peace. The policy was essentially the same, but the Kennedy administration reaped more benefits from it than did its predecessor. The best public policy, if not dressed in the proper attire, will usually accomplish less than policy that is both substantively sound and symbolically stylish.

PUBLIC POLICY AND THE AMERICAN FUTURE

Is our method of shaping public policy relevant to the complex era in which we live? What alternative ways of making public policy should be considered? What fundamental changes should be made in public policy itself? Should our economic model contain more or less socialism, more or less capitalism? Should public policy have more emphasis on risk or on security for the individual? Should the policy-making process be made less incremental and more comprehensive? These are basic and fundamental questions that provoke genuine debates. The political process will ultimately provide answers to these questions. If the past is any indication, those answers will come incrementally and tentatively.

[Inaugural Address] We have learned that "more" is not necessarily "better," that even our great nation has its recognized limits, and that we can neither answer all questions nor solve all problems. We cannot afford to do everything, nor can we afford to lack boldness as we meet the future. So together, in a spirit of individual sacrifice for the common good, we must simply do our best.

Our nation can be strong abroad only if it is strong at home, and we know that the best way to enhance freedom in other lands is to demonstrate here that our democratic system is worthy of emulation.—*Jimmy Carter*

Notes

1. Robert L. Heilbroner, *An Inquiry into the Human Prospect* (New York: Norton, 1974), p. 13.

2. *The National Observer*, February 22, 1975, p. 27.

3. Ibid., p. 1.

4. For a summary of these scholars and studies, see *The National Observer*, February 22, 1975, p. 1.

5. Heilbroner, *An Inquiry into the Human Prospect*, p. 132.

6. Ibid., p. 21.

7. *The National Observer*, February 26, 1977, p. 3.

8. Ben J. Wattenberg, *The Real America* (New York: G. P. Putnam's Sons, 1974), Chapters 3–9.

9. *The National Observer*, February 26, 1977, p. 3.

10. *The National Observer*, February 19, 1977, p. 1.

Bibliography

Policy Process

Lindbloom, Charles E. *The Policy-Making Process.* Englewood Cliffs, N.J.: Prentice-Hall, 1968.

Lowi, Theodore J. *The End of Liberalism.* New York: Norton, 1969.

Wildavsky, Aaron. *The Politics of the Budgetary Process.* Boston: Little, Brown, 1964.

Symbolic Policy Making

Edelman, Murray. *The Symbolic Uses of Politics.* Urbana: University of Illinois Press, 1964.

——. *Politics as Symbolic Action.* Chicago: Markham, 1971.

Policy Implementation

Becker, Theodore L., and Malcolm M. Feeley. *The Impact of Supreme Court Decisions.* New York: Oxford University Press, 1973.

Wildavsky, Aaron. *Implementation.* Berkeley: University of California Press, 1973.

Domestic Policy

Bernstein, Marver. *Regulating Business by Independent Commissions.* Princeton, N.J.: Princeton University Press, 1965.

Peckman, Joseph A., and Benjamin A. Okner. *Who Bears the Tax Burden?* Washington, D.C.: The Brookings Institution, 1974.

Sundquist, James L. *Politics and Policy: The Eisenhower, Kennedy, and Johnson Years.* Washington, D.C.: The Brookings Institution, 1968.

Foreign Policy

Halberstam, David. *The Best and the Brightest.* New York: Random House, 1972.

Hilsman, Roger. *The Politics of Policy Making in Defense and Foreign Policy.* New York: Harper & Row, 1971.

Kahan, Jerome H. *Security in the Nuclear Age: Developing U.S. Strategic Arms Policy.* Washington, D.C.: The Brookings Institution, 1975.

Policy Choices: Domestic and Foreign

Critical Choices for Americans. *Africa: From Mystery to Maze.* Lexington, Mass.: Lexington Books, 1977.

——. *China & Japan: A New Balance of Power.* Lexington, Mass.: Lexington Books, 1977.

——. *Latin America: Struggle for Progress.* Lexington, Mass.: Lexington Books, 1977.

——. *The Middle East: Oil, Conflict & Hope.* Lexington, Mass.: Lexington Books, 1977.

——. *Power and Security.* Lexington, Mass.: Lexington Books, 1977.

——. *Qualities of Life.* Lexington, Mass.: Lexington Books, 1977.

——. *Southern Asia: The Politics of Poverty & Peace.* Lexington, Mass.: Lexington Books, 1977.

——. *The Soviet Empire: Expansion & Detente.* Lexington, Mass.: Lexington Books, 1977.

——. *Trade, Inflation and Ethics.* Lexington, Mass.: Lexington Books, 1977.

——. *Values of Growth.* Lexington, Mass.: Lexington Books, 1977.

——. *Vital Resources.* Lexington, Mass.: Lexington Books, 1977.

——. *Western Europe: The Trials of Partnership.* Lexington, Mass.: Lexington Books, 1977.

Etzkowitz, Henry, and Peter Schwab, eds. *Is America Necessary? Conservative, Liberal and Socialist Perspectives of United States Political Institutions.* St. Paul, Minn.: West, 1976.

Owen, Henry, and Charles L. Schultze, eds. *Setting National Priorities: The Coming Decade.* Washington, D.C.: The Brookings Institution, 1976.

"Where Does the Balance Belong?" *Ripon Quarterly* 1 (Summer 1975).

Attitudes Toward Policy

Critical Choices for Americans. *The Americans: 1976.* Lexington, Mass.: Lexington Books, 1976.

——. *How Others See Us.* Lexington, Mass.: Lexington Books, 1977.

Heilbroner, Robert L. *An Inquiry into the Human Prospect.* New York: Norton, 1974.

Wattenberg, Ben J. *The Real America.* New York: G. P. Putnam's Sons, 1974.

APPENDICES
The Constitution of the United States

We the People of the United States, in Order to form a more perfect Union, establish Justice, insure domestic Tranquility, provide for the common defence, promote the general Welfare, and secure the Blessings of Liberty to ourselves and our Posterity, do ordain and establish this Constitution for the United States of America.

ARTICLE I

Section 1 All legislative Powers herein granted shall be vested in a Congress of the United States, which shall consist of a Senate and House of Representatives.

Section 2 The House of Representatives shall be composed of Members chosen every second Year by the People of the several States, and the Electors in each State shall have the Qualifications requisite for Electors of the most numerous Branch of the State Legislature.

No Person shall be a Representative who shall not have attained to the Age of twenty five Years, and been seven Years a Citizen of the United States, and who shall not, when elected, be an Inhabitant of that State in which he shall be chosen.

Representatives and direct Taxes shall be apportioned among the several States which may be included within this Union, according to their respective Numbers, which shall be determined by adding to the whole Number of free Persons, including those bound to Service for a Term of Years, and excluding Indians not taxed, three fifths of all other Persons. The actual Enumeration

483

shall be made within three Years after the first Meeting of the Congress of the United States, and within every subsequent Term of ten Years, in such Manner as they shall by Law direct. The Number of Representatives shall not exceed one for every thirty Thousand, but each State shall have at Least one Representative; and until such enumeration shall be made, the State of New Hampshire shall be entitled to chuse three, Massachusetts eight, Rhode-Island and Providence Plantations one, Connecticut five, New-York six, New Jersey four, Pennsylvania eight, Delaware one, Maryland six, Virginia ten, North Carolina five, South Carolina five, and Georgia three.

When vacancies happen in the Representation from any State, the Executive Authority thereof shall issue Writs of Election to fill such Vacancies.

The House of Representatives shall chuse their speaker and other Officers; and shall have the sole Power of Impeachment.

Section 3   The Senate of the United States shall be composed of two Senators from each State, chosen by the Legislature thereof, for six Years; and each Senator shall have one Vote.

Immediately after they shall be assembled in Consequence of the first Election, they shall be divided as equally as may be into three Classes. The Seats of the Senators of the first Class shall be vacated at the Expiration of the second Year, of the second Class at the Expiration of the fourth Year, and of the third Class at the Expiration of the sixth Year, so that one third may be chosen every second Year; and if Vacancies happen by Resignation, or otherwise, during the Recess of the Legislature of any State, the Executive thereof may make temporary Appointments until the next Meeting of the Legislature, which shall then fill such Vacancies.

No Person shall be a Senator who shall not have attained to the Age of thirty Years, and been nine Years a Citizen of the United States, and who shall not, when elected, be an Inhabitant of that State for which he shall be chosen.

The Vice-President of the United States shall be President of the Senate, but shall have no Vote, unless they be equally divided.

The Senate shall chuse their other Officers, and also a President pro tempore, in the Absence of the Vice President, or when he shall exercise the Office of the President of the United States.

The Senate shall have the sole Power to try all Impeachments. When sitting for that Purpose, they shall be on Oath or Affirmation. When the President of the United States is tried, the Chief Justice shall preside: And no Person shall be convicted without the Concurrence of two thirds of the Members present.

Judgment in Cases of Impeachment shall not extend further than to removal from Office, and disqualification to hold and enjoy any Office of honor, Trust or Profit under the United States: but the Party convicted shall nevertheless be liable and subject to Indictment, Trial, Judgment and Punishment, according to law.

Section 4   The Times, Places and Manner of holding Elections for Senators and Representatives, shall be prescribed in each State by the Legislature thereof; but the Congress may at any time by Law make or alter such Regulations, except as to the Places of chusing Senators.

The Congress shall assemble at least once in every Year, and such Meeting shall be on the first Monday in December, unless they shall by Law appoint a different Day.

Section 5 Each House shall be the Judge of the Elections, Returns and Qualifications of its own Members, and a Majority of each shall constitute a Quorum to do Business; but a smaller Number may adjourn from day to day, and may be authorized to compel the Attendance of absent Members, in such Manner, and under such Penalites as each House may provide.

Each House may determine the Rules of its Proceedings, punish its Members for disorderly Behaviour, and, with the Concurrence of two thirds, expel a Member.

Each House shall keep a Journal of its Proceedings, and from time to time publish the same, excepting such Parts as may in their Judgment require Secrecy; and the Yeas and Nays of the Members of either House on any question shall, at the Desire of one fifth of those Present, be entered on the Journal.

Neither House, during the Session of Congress, shall, without the Consent of the other, adjourn for more than three days, nor to any other Place than that in which the two Houses shall be sitting.

Section 6 The Senators and Representatives shall receive a Compensation for their Services, to be ascertained by Law, and paid out of the Treasury of the United States. They shall in all Cases, except Treason, Felony and Breach of the Peace, be privileged from Arrest during their Attendance at the Session of their respective Houses, and in going to and returning from the same; and for any Speech or Debate in either House, they shall not be questioned in any other Place.

No Senator or Representative shall, during the Time for which he was elected, be appointed to any civil Office under the Authority of the United States, which shall have been created, or the Emoluments whereof shall have been encreased during such time; and no Person holding any Office under the United States, shall be a Member of either House during his Continuance in Office.

Section 7 All Bills for raising Revenue shall originate in the House of Representatives; but the Senate may propose or concur with Amendments as on other Bills.

Every Bill which shall have passed the House of Representatives and the Senate, shall, before it become a Law, be presented to the President of the United States; if he approve he shall sign it, but if not he shall return it, with his Objections to that House in which it shall have originated, who shall enter the Objections at large on their Journal, and proceed to reconsider it. If after such Reconsideration two thirds of that House shall agree to pass the Bill, it shall be sent, together with the Objections, to the other House, by which it shall likewise be reconsidered, and if approved by two thirds of that House, it shall become a Law. But in all such Cases the Votes of both Houses shall be determined by Yeas and Nays, and the Names of the Persons voting for and against the Bill shall be entered on the Journal of each House respectively. If any Bill shall not be returned by the President within ten Days (Sundays excepted) after it shall have been presented to him, the Same shall be a Law, in like Manner as if he had signed it, unless the Congress by their Adjournment prevent its Return, in which Case it shall not be a Law.

Every Order, Resolution, or Vote to which the Concurrence of the Senate and House of Representatives may be necessary (except on a question of Adjournment) shall be presented to the President of the United States; and before the Same shall take Effect, shall be approved by him, or being disapproved by him, shall be repassed by two thirds of the Senate and House of Representatives, according to the Rules and Limitations prescribed in the Case of a Bill.

Section 8   The Congress shall have Power To lay and collect Taxes, Duties, Imposts and Excises, to pay the Debts and provide for the common Defence and general Welfare of the United States; but all Duties, Imposts and Excises shall be uniform throughout the United States;

To borrow Money on the credit of the United States;

To regulate Commerce with foreign Nations, and among the several States, and with the Indian Tribes;

To establish an uniform Rule of Naturalization, and uniform Laws on the subject of Bankruptcies throughout the United States;

To coin Money, regulate the Value thereof, and of foreign Coin, and fix the Standard of Weights and Measures;

To provide for the Punishment of counterfeiting the Securities and current Coin of the United States;

To establish Post Offices and post Roads;

To promote the Progress of Science and useful Arts, by securing for limited Times to Authors and Inventors the exclusive Right to their respective Writings and Discoveries;

To constitute Tribunals inferior to the supreme Court;

To define and punish Piracies and Felonies committed on the high Seas, and Offences against the Law of Nations;

To declare War, grant Letters of Marque and Reprisal, and make Rules concerning Captures on Land and Water;

To raise and support Armies, but no Appropriation of Money to that Use shall be for a longer Term than two Years;

To provide and maintain a Navy;

To make Rules for the Government and Regulation of the land and naval Forces;

To provide for calling forth the Militia to execute the Laws of the Union, suppress Insurrections and repel Invasions;

To provide for organizing, arming, and disciplining, the Militia, and for governing such Part of them as may be employed in the Service of the United States, reserving to the States respectively, the Appointment of the Officers, and the Authority of training the Militia according to the discipline prescribed by Congress;

To exercise exclusive Legislation in all Cases whatsoever, over such District (not exceeding ten Miles square) as may, by Cession of particular States, and the Acceptance of Congress, become the Seat of the Government of the United States, and to exercise like Authority over all Places purchased by the Consent of the Legislature of the State in which the Same shall be for the Erection of Forts, Magazines, Arsenals, dock-Yards, and other needful Buildings;- And

To make all Laws which shall be necessary and proper for carrying into Execution the foregoing Powers, and all other Powers vested by this Constitution in the Government of the United States, or in any Department or Officer thereof.

Section 9   The Migration or Importation of such Persons as any of the States now existing shall think proper to admit, shall not be prohibited by the Congress prior to the Year one thousand eight hundred and eight, but a Tax or duty may be imposed on such Importation, not exceeding ten dollars for each Person.

The Privilege of the Writ of Habeas Corpus shall not be suspended, unless when in Cases of Rebellion or Invasion the public Safety may require it.

No Bill of Attainder or ex post facto Law shall be passed.

No Capitation, or other direct, Tax shall be laid, unless in Proportion to the Census or Enumeration herein before directed to be taken.

No Tax or Duty shall be laid on Articles exported from any State.

No Preference shall be given by any Regulation of Commerce or Revenue to the Ports of one State over those of another: nor shall Vessels bound to, or from, one State be obliged to enter, clear, or pay Duties in another.

No Money shall be drawn from the Treasury, but in Consequence of Appropriations made by Law; and a regular Statement and Account of the Receipts and Expenditures of all public Money shall be published from time to time.

No Title of Nobility shall be granted by the United States: And no Person holding any Office of Profit or Trust under them, shall, without the Consent of the Congress, accept of any present, Emolument, Office, or Title, of any kind whatever, from any King, Prince, or foreign States.

Section 10   No State shall enter into any Treaty, Alliance, or Confederation; grant Letters of Marque and Reprisal; coin Money; emit Bills of Credit; make any Thing but gold and silver Coin a Tender in Payment of Debts; pass any Bill of Attainder, ex post facto Law, or Law impairing the Obligation of Contracts, or grant any Title of Nobility.

No State shall, without the Consent of the Congress, lay any Imposts or Duties on Imports or Exports, except what may be absolutely necessary for executing its inspection Laws: and the net Produce of all Duties and Imposts, laid by any State on Imports or Exports, shall be for the Use of the Treasury of the

United States; and all such Laws shall be subject to the Revision and Control of the Congress.

No State shall, without the Consent of Congress, lay any Duty of Tonnage, keep Troops, or Ships of War in time of Peace, enter into any Agreement or Compact with another State, or with a foreign Power, or engage in War, unless actually invaded, or in such imminent Danger as will not admit of delay.

ARTICLE II

Section 1 The executive Power shall be vested in a President of the United States of America. He shall hold his Office during the Term of four Years, and, together with the Vice-President, chosen for the same term, be elected, as follows

Each State shall appoint, in such Manner as the Legislature thereof may direct, a Number of Electors, equal to the whole Number of Senators and Representatives to which the State may be entitled in the Congress: but no Senator or Representative, or Person holding an Office of Trust or Profit under the United States, shall be appointed an Elector.

The Electors shall meet in their respective States, and vote by Ballot for two Persons, of whom one at least shall not be an Inhabitant of the same State with themselves. And they shall make a List of all the Persons voted for, and of the Number of Votes for each; which List they shall sign and certify, and transmit sealed to the Seat of the Government of the United States, directed to the President of the Senate. The President of the Senate shall, in the Presence of the Senate and House of Representatives, open all the Certificates, and the Votes shall then be counted. The Person having the greatest Number of Votes shall be the President, if such Number be a Majority of the whole Number of Electors appointed; and if there be more than one who have such Majority, and have an equal Number of Votes, then the House of Representatives shall immediately chuse by Ballot one of them for President: and if no Person have a Majority, then from the five highest on the List the said House shall in like Manner chuse the President. But in chusing the President, the Votes shall be taken by States, the Representation from each State having one Vote; A quorum for this Purpose shall consist of a Member or Members from two thirds of the States, and a Majority of all the States shall be necessary to a Choice. In every Case, after the Choice of the President, the Person having the greatest Number of Votes of the Electors shall be the Vice-President. But if there should remain two or more who have equal Votes, the Senate shall chuse from them by Ballot the Vice-President.

The Congress may determine the Time of chusing the Electors and the Day on which they shall give their Votes; which Day shall be the same throughout the United States.

No Person except a natural born Citizen, or a Citizen of the United States, at the time of the Adoption of this Constitution, shall be eligible to the Office of President; neither shall any Person be eligible to that Office who shall not have attained to the Age of thirty five Years, and been fourteen Years a Resident within the United States.

In Case of the Removal of the President from Office, or of his Death, Resignation, or Inability to discharge the Powers and Duties of the said Office, the Same shall devolve on the Vice-President, and the Congress may by Law Provide for the Case of Removal, Death, Resignation or Inability, both of the President and Vice-President, declaring what Officer shall then act as President, and such Officer shall act accordingly, until the Disability be removed, or a President shall be elected.

The President shall, at stated Times, receive for his Services a Compensation, which shall neither be encreased nor diminished during the Period for which he shall have been elected, and he shall not receive within that Period any other Emolument from the United States, or any of them.

Before he enter on the Execution of his Office, he shall take the following Oath or Affirmation: "I do solemnly swear (or affirm) that I will faithfully execute the Office of President of the United States, and will to the best of my Ability, preserve, protect and defend the Constitution of the United States."

Section 2   The President shall be Commander in Chief of the Army and Navy of the United States, and of the Militia of the several States, when called into the actual Service of the United States; he may require the Opinion, in writing, of the principal Officer in each of the executive Departments, upon any Subject relating to the Duties of their respective Offices, and he shall have power to grant Reprieves and Pardons for Offences against the United States, except in Cases of Impeachment.

He shall have Power, by and with the Advice and Consent of the Senate, to make Treaties, provided two thirds of the Senators present concur; and he shall nominate, and by and with the Advice and Consent of the Senate, shall appoint Ambassadors, other public Ministers and Consuls, Judges of the supreme Court, and all other Officers of the United States, whose Appointments are not herein otherwise provided for, and which shall be established by Law; but the Congress may by Law vest the Appointment of such inferior Officers, as they think proper, in the President alone, in the Courts of Law, or in the Heads of Departments.

The President shall have Power to fill up all Vacancies that may happen during the Recess of the Senate, by granting Commissions which shall expire at the End of their next Session.

Section 3   He shall from time to time give to the Congress Information of the State of the Union, and recommend to their Consideration such Measures as he shall judge necessary and expedient; he may, on extraordinary Occasions, convene both Houses, or either of them, and in Case of Disagreement between them, with Respect to the Time of Adjournment, he may adjourn them to such Time as he shall think proper; he shall receive Ambassadors and other public Ministers; he shall take Care that the Laws be faithfully executed, and shall Commission all the Officers of the United States.

Section 4   The President, Vice-President and all civil Officers of the United States, shall be removed from Office on Impeachment for, and Conviction of, Treason, Bribery, or other High Crimes and Misdemeanors.

ARTICLE III

Section 1   The judicial Power of the United States, shall be vested in one supreme Court, and in such inferior Courts as the Congress may from time to time ordain and establish. The Judges, both of the supreme and inferior Courts, shall hold their Offices during good Behaviour, and shall, at stated Times, receive for their Services, a Compensation, which shall not be diminished during their Continuance in Office.

Section 2   The judicial Power shall extend to all Cases, in Law and Equity, arising under this Constitution, the Laws of the United States, and Treaties made, or which shall be made, under their Authority;-to all Cases affecting Ambassadors, other public Ministers and Consuls;-to all Cases of admiralty and maritime Jurisdiction;-to Controversies to which the United States shall be a Party;-to Controversies between two or more States; between a State and Citizens of another State;-between Citizens of different States;-between Citizens of the same State claiming Lands under Grants of different States, and between a State, or the Citizens thereof, and foreign States, Citizens or Subjects.

In all Cases affecting Ambassadors, other public Ministers and Consuls, and those in which a State shall be Party, the supreme Court shall have original Jurisdiction. In all the other Cases before mentioned, the supreme Court shall have appellate Jurisdiction, both as to Law and Fact, with such Exceptions, and under such Regulations as the Congress shall make.

The Trial of all Crimes, except in Cases of Impeachment, shall be by Jury; and such Trial shall be held in the State where the said Crimes shall have been committed; but when not committed within any State, the Trial shall be at such Place or Places as the Congress may by Law have directed.

Section 3   Treason against the United States, shall consist only in levying War against them, or in adhering to their Enemies, giving them Aid and Comfort. No Person shall be convicted of Treason unless on the Testimony of two Witnesses to the same overt Act, or on Confession in open Court.

The Congress shall have Power to declare the Punishment of Treason, but no Attainder of Treason shall work Corruption of Blood, or Forfeiture except during the Life of the Person attainted.

ARTICLE IV

Section 1   Full Faith and Credit shall be given in each State to the public Acts, Records, and judicial Proceedings of every other State. And the Congress may by general Laws prescribe the Manner in which such Acts, Records and Proceedings shall be proved, and the Effect thereof.

Section 2   The Citizens of each State shall be entitled to all Privileges and Immunities of Citizens in the several States.

A Person charged in any State with Treason, Felony, or other Crime, who shall flee from Justice, and be found in another State, shall on Demand of the executive Authority of the State from which he fled, be delivered up, to be removed to the State having Jurisdiction of the Crime.

No Person held to Service or Labour in one State, under the Laws thereof, escaping into another, shall, in Consequence of any Law or Regulation therein, be discharged from such Service or Labour, but shall be delivered up on Claim of the Party to whom such Service or Labour may be due.

Section 3   New States may be admitted by the Congress into this Union; but no new State shall be formed or erected within the Jurisdiction of any other State; nor any State be formed by the Junction of two or more States, or Parts of States, without the Consent of the Legislatures of the States concerned as well as of the Congress.

The Congress shall have Power to dispose of and make all needful Rules and Regulations respecting the Territory or other Property belonging to the United States; and nothing in this Constitution shall be so construed as to Prejudice any Claims of the United States, or of any particular State.

Section 4   The United States shall guarantee to every State in this Union a Republican Form of Government, and shall protect each of them against Invasion; and on Application of the Legislature, or of the Executive (when the Legislature cannot be convened) against domestic Violence.

ARTICLE V

The Congress, whenever two thirds of both Houses shall deem it necessary, shall propose Amendments to this Constitution, or, on the Application of the Legislatures of two thirds of the several States, shall call a Convention for proposing Amendments, which, in either Case, shall be valid to all Intents and Purposes, as Part of this Constitution, when ratified by the Legislatures of three fourths of the several States, or by Conventions in three fourths thereof, as the one or the other Mode of Ratification may be proposed by the Congress; Provided that no Amendment which may be made prior to the Year One thousand eight hundred and eight shall in any Manner affect the first and fourth Clauses in the Ninth Section of the first Article; and that no State, without its Consent, shall be deprived of its equal Suffrage in the Senate.

ARTICLE VI

All Debts contracted and Engagements entered into, before the Adoption of this Constitution, shall be as valid against the United States under this Constitution, as under the Confederation.

This Constitution, and the Laws of the United States which shall be made in Pursuance thereof; and all Treaties made, or which shall be made, under the Authority of the United States, shall be the supreme Law of the Land; and the Judges in every State shall be bound thereby, any Thing in the Constitution or Laws of any State to the Contrary notwithstanding.

The Senators and Representatives before mentioned, and the Members of the several State Legislatures, and all executive and judicial Officers, both of the United States and of the several States, shall be bound by Oath or Affirmation, to support this Constitution; but no religious Test shall ever be required as a Qualification to any Office or public Trust under the United States.

ARTICLE VII

The Ratification of the Conventions of nine States, shall be sufficient for the Establishment of this Constitution between the States so ratifying the Same.

Done in Convention by the Unanimous Consent of the States present the Seventeenth Day of September in the Year of our Lord one thousand seven hundred and Eighty seven and of the Independence of the United States of America the Twelfth. In witness whereof We have hereunto subscribed our Names.

[The first ten Amendments were ratified December 15, 1791, and form what is known as the Bill of Rights.]

AMENDMENT 1

Congress shall make no law respecting an establishment of religion, or prohibiting the free exercise thereof; or abridging the freedom of speech, or of the press; or the right of the people peaceably to assemble, and to petition the Government for a redress of grievances.

AMENDMENT 2

A well regulated Militia, being necessary to the security of a free State, the right of the people to keep and bear Arms, shall not be infringed.

AMENDMENT 3

No Soldier shall, in time of peace be quartered in any house, without the consent of the Owner, nor in time of war, but in a manner to be prescribed by law.

AMENDMENT 4

The right of the people to be secure in their persons, houses, papers, and effects, against unreasonable searches and seizures, shall not be violated, and no Warrants shall issue, but upon probable cause, supported by Oath or affirmation, and particularly describing the place to be searched and the persons or things to be seized.

AMENDMENT 5

No person shall be held to answer for a capital, or otherwise infamous crime, unless on a presentment or indictment of a Grand Jury, except in cases arising in the land or naval forces, or in the Militia, when in actual service in time of War or public danger; nor shall any person be subject for the same offence to be twice put in jeopardy of life or limb; nor shall be compelled in any criminal case to be a witness against himself, nor be deprived of life, liberty, or property, without due process of law; nor shall private property be taken for public use, without just compensation.

AMENDMENT 6

In all criminal prosecutions, the accused shall enjoy the right to a speedy and public trial, by an impartial jury of the State and district wherein the crime shall have been committed, which district shall have been previously ascertained by law, and to be informed of the nature and cause of the accusation; to be confronted with the witnesses against him; to have compulsory process for obtaining witnesses in his favor, and to have the Assistance of Counsel for his defence.

AMENDMENT 7

In Suits at common law, where the value in controversy shall exceed twenty dollars, the right of trial by jury shall be preserved, and no fact tried by a jury, shall be otherwise reexamined in any Court of the United States, than according to the rules of the common law.

AMENDMENT 8

Excessive bail shall not be required, nor excessive fines imposed, nor cruel and unusual punishments inflicted.

AMENDMENT 9

The enumeration in the Constitution, of certain rights, shall not be construed to deny or disparage others retained by the people.

AMENDMENT 10

The powers not delegated to the United States by the Constitution, nor prohibited by it to the States, are reserved to the States respectively, or to the people.

AMENDMENT 11

[Ratified February 7, 1795]

The Judicial power of the United States shall not be construed to extend to any suit in law or equity, commenced or prosecuted against one of the United States by Citizens of another State, or by Citizens or Subjects of any Foreign State.

AMENDMENT 12

[Ratified July 27, 1804]

The Electors shall meet in their respective states and vote by ballot for President and Vice-President, one of whom, at least, shall not be an inhabitant of the same state with themselves; they shall name in their ballots the person voted for as President, and in distinct ballots the person voted for as Vice-President, and they shall make distinct lists of all persons voted for as President, and of all persons voted for as Vice-President, and of the number of votes for each, which lists they shall sign and certify, and transmit sealed to the seat of the government of the United States, directed to the President of the Senate;-The President of the Senate shall, in the presence of the Senate and House of Representatives, open all the certificates and the votes shall then be counted;-The person having the greatest number of votes for President, shall be the President, if such number be a majority of the whole number of Electors appointed; and if no person have such majority, then from the persons having the highest numbers not exceeding three on the list of those voted for as President, the House of Representatives shall choose immediately, by ballot, the President. But in choosing the President, the votes shall be taken by states, the representation from each state having one vote; a quorum for this purpose shall consist of a member or members from two-thirds of the states, and a majority of all the states shall be necessary to a choice. And if the House of Representatives shall not choose a President whenever the right of choice shall devolve upon them, before the fourth day of March next following, then the Vice-President shall act as President, as in the case of the death or other constitutional disability of the President.-The person having the greatest number of votes as Vice-President, shall be the Vice-President, if such number be a majority of the whole number of Electors appointed, and if no person have a majority, then from the two highest numbers on the list, the Senate shall choose the Vice-President; a quorum for the purpose shall consist of two-thirds of the whole number of Senators, and a majority of the whole number shall be necessary to a choice. But no person constitutionally ineligible to the office of President shall be eligible to that of Vice-President of the United States.

AMENDMENT 13

[Ratified December 6, 1865]

Section 1 Neither slavery nor involuntary servitude, except as a punishment for crime whereof the party shall have been duly convicted, shall exist within the United States, or any place subject to their jurisdiction.

Section 2 Congress shall have power to enforce this article by appropriate legislation.

AMENDMENT 14

[Ratified July 9, 1868]

Section 1 All persons born or naturalized in the United States, and subject to the jurisdiction thereof, are citizens of the United States and of the State wherein they reside. No State shall make or enforce any law which shall abridge the privileges or immunities of citizens of the United States; nor shall any State deprive any person of life, liberty, or property, without due process of law; nor deny to any person within its jurisdiction the equal protection of the laws.

Section 2 Representatives shall be apportioned among the several States according to their respective numbers, counting the whole number of persons in each State, excluding Indians not taxed. But when the right to vote at any election for the choice of electors for President and Vice-President of the United States, Representatives in Congress, the Executive and Judicial Officers of a State, or the members of the Legislature thereof, is denied to any of the male inhabitants of such State, being twenty-one years of age, and citizens of the United States, or in any way abridged, except for participation in rebellion, or other crime, the basis of representation therein shall be reduced in the proportion which the number of such male citizens shall bear to the whole number of male citizens twenty-one years of age in such State.

Section 3 No person shall be a Senator or Representative in Congress, or elector of President and Vice-President, or hold any office, civil or military, under the United States, or under any State, who, having previously taken an oath, as a member of Congress, or as an officer of the United States, or as a member of any State legislature, or as an executive or judicial officer of any State, to support the Constitution of the United States, shall have engaged in insurrection or rebellion against the same, or given aid or comfort to the enemies thereof. But Congress may by a vote of two-thirds of each House, remove such disability.

Section 4   The validity of the public debt of the United States, authorized by law, including debts incurred for payment of pensions and bounties for services in suppressing insurrection or rebellion, shall not be questioned. But neither the United States nor any State shall assume or pay any debt or obligation incurred in aid of insurrection or rebellion against the United States, or any claim for the loss or emancipation of any slave; but all such debts, obligations and claims shall be held illegal and void.

Section 5   The Congress shall have power to enforce, by appropriate legislation, the provisions of this article.

AMENDMENT 15

[Ratified February 3, 1870]

Section 1   The right of citizens of the United States to vote shall not be denied or abridged by the United States or by any State on account of race, color, or previous condition of servitude.

Section 2   The Congress shall have power to enforce this article by appropriate legislation.

AMENDMENT 16

[Ratified February 3, 1913]

The Congress shall have power to lay and collect taxes on incomes, from whatever source derived, without apportionment among the several States, and without regard to any census or enumeration.

AMENDMENT 17

[Ratified April 8, 1913]

The Senate of the United States shall be composed of two Senators from each State, elected by the people thereof for six years; and each Senator shall have one vote. The electors in each State shall have the qualifications requisite for electors of the most numerous branch of the State legislatures.

When vacancies happen in the representation of any State in the Senate, the executive authority of such State shall issue writs of election to fill such vacancies: *Provided,* That the legislature of any State may empower the executive thereof to make temporary appointments until the people fill the vacancies by election as the legislature may direct.

This amendment shall not be so construed as to affect the election or term of any Senator chosen before it becomes valid as part of the Constitution.

AMENDMENT 18

[Ratified January 16, 1919]

Section 1   After one year from the ratification of this article the manufacture, sale, or transportation of intoxicating liquors within, the importation thereof into, or the exportation thereof from the United States and all territory subject to the jurisdiction thereof for beverage purposes is hereby prohibited.

Section 2   The Congress and the several States shall have concurrent power to enforce this article by appropriate legislation.

Section 3   This article shall be inoperative unless it shall have been ratified as an amendment to the Constitution by the legislatures of the several States, as provided in the Constitution, within seven years from the date of the submission hereof to the States by the Congress.

AMENDMENT 19

[Ratified August 18, 1920]

The right of citizens of the United States to vote shall not be denied or abridged by the United States or by any State on account of sex. Congress shall have power to enforce this article by appropriate legislation.

AMENDMENT 20

[Ratified January 23, 1933]

Section 1   The terms of the President and Vice-President shall end at noon on the 20th day of January, and the terms of Senators and Representatives at noon on the 3d day of January, of the years in which such terms would have ended if this article had not been ratified; and the terms of their successors shall then begin.

Section 2   The Congress shall assemble at least once in every year, and such meeting shall begin at noon on the 3d day of January, unless they shall by law appoint a different day.

Section 3   If, at the time fixed for the beginning of the term of the President, the President elect shall have died, the Vice-President elect shall become President. If a President shall not have been chosen before the time fixed for the beginning of his term, or if the President elect shall have failed to qualify, then the Vice-President elect shall act as President until a President shall have qualified; and the Congress may by law provide for the case wherein neither a President elect nor a Vice-President elect shall have qualified, declaring who shall then act as President, or the manner in which one who is to act shall be selected, and such person shall act accordingly until a President or Vice-President shall have qualified.

Section 4   The Congress may by law provide for the case of the death of any of the persons from whom the House of Representatives may choose a President whenever the right of choice shall have devolved upon them, and for the case of the death of any of the persons from whom the Senate may choose a Vice-President whenever the right of choice shall have devolved upon them.

Section 5   Sections 1 and 2 shall take effect on the 15th day of October following the ratification of this article.

Section 6   This article shall be inoperative unless it shall have been ratified as an amendment to the Constitution by the legislatures of three-fourths of the several States within seven years from the date of its submission.

AMENDMENT 21

[Ratified December 5, 1933]

Section 1   The eighteenth article of amendment to the Constitution of the United States is hereby repealed.

Section 2   The transportation or importation into any State, Territory, or possession of the United States for delivery or use therein of intoxicating liquors, in violation of the laws thereof, is hereby prohibited.

Section 3   This article shall be inoperative unless it shall have been ratified as an amendment to the Constitution by conventions in the several States, as provided in the Constitution, within seven years from the date of the submission hereof to the States by the Congress.

AMENDMENT 22

[Ratified February 27, 1951]

Section 1   No person shall be elected to the office of the President more than twice, and no person who has held the office of President, or acted as President, for more than two years of a term to which some other person was elected President shall be elected to the office of the President more than once.

But this Article shall not apply to any person holding the office of President when this Article was proposed by the Congress, and shall not prevent any person who may be holding the office of President, or acting as President, during the term within which this Article becomes operative from holding the office of President or acting as President during the remainder of such term.

Section 2   This article shall be inoperative unless it shall have been ratified as an amendment to the Constitution by the legislatures of three-fourths of the several States within seven years from the date of its submission to the States by the Congress.

AMENDMENT 23

[Ratified March 29, 1961]

Section 1   The District constituting the seat of Government of the United States shall appoint in such manner as the Congress may direct:
    A number of electors of President and Vice-President equal to the whole number of Senators and Representatives in Congress to which the District would be entitled if it were a State, but in no event more than the least populous State; they shall be in addition to those appointed by the States, but they shall be considered, for the purposes of the election of President and Vice-President, to be electors appointed by a State; and they shall meet in the District and perform such duties as provided by the twelfth article of amendment.

Section 2   The Congress shall have power to enforce this article by appropriate legislation.

AMENDMENT 24

[Ratified January 23, 1964]

Section 1   The right of citizens of the United States to vote in any primary or other election for President or Vice-President, for electors for President or Vice-President, or for Senator or Representative in Congress, shall not be denied or abridged by the United States or any State by reason of failure to pay any poll tax or other tax.

Section 2   The Congress shall have power to enforce this article by appropriate legislation.

AMENDMENT 25

[Ratified February 10, 1967]

Section 1   In case of the removal of the President from office or of his death or resignation, the Vice-President shall become President.

Section 2   Whenever there is a vacancy in the office of the Vice-President, the President shall nominate a Vice-President who shall take office upon confirmation by a majority vote of both Houses of Congress.

Section 3   Whenever the President transmits to the President pro tempore of the Senate and the Speaker of the House of Representatives his written declaration that he is unable to discharge the powers and duties of his office, and until he transmits to them a written declaration to the contrary, such powers and duties shall be discharged by the Vice-President as Acting President.

Section 4   Whenever the Vice-President and a majority of either the principal officers of the executive departments or of such other body as Congress may by law provide, transmit to the President pro tempore of the Senate and the Speaker of the House of Representatives their written declaration that the President is unable to discharge the powers and duties of his office, the Vice-President shall immediately assume the powers and duties of the office as Acting President.

Thereafter, when the President transmits to the President pro tempore of the Senate and the Speaker of the House of Representatives his written declaration that no inability exists, he shall resume the powers and duties of his office unless the Vice-President and a majority of either the principal officers of the executive department or of such other body as Congress may by law provide, transmit within four days to the President pro tempore of the Senate and the Speaker of the House of Representatives their written declaration that the President is unable to discharge the powers and duties of his office. Thereupon Congress shall decide the issue, assembling within forty-eight hours for that purpose if not in session. If the Congress, within twenty-one days after receipt of the latter written declaration, or, if Congress is not in session, within twenty-one days after Congress is required to assemble, determines by two-thirds vote of both Houses that the President is unable to discharge the powers and duties of his office, the Vice-President shall continue to discharge the same as Acting President; otherwise, the President shall resume the powers and duties of his office.

AMENDMENT 26

[Ratified June 30, 1971]

Section 1   The right of citizens of the United States, who are eighteen years of age or older, to vote shall not be denied or abridged by the United States or by any State on account of age.

Section 2   The Congress shall have the power to enforce this article by appropriate legislation.

PROPOSED AMENDMENT 27

[Proposed March 22, 1972]

Section 1   Equality of rights under the law shall not be denied or abridged by the United States or by any State on account of sex.

Section 2   The Congress shall have power to enforce, by appropriate legislation, the provisions of this article.

Section 3   This amendment shall take effect two years after date of ratification.

Presidents of the United States

		TERM
1.	George Washington (1732–99)	1789–1797
2.	John Adams (1735–1826)	1797–1801
3.	Thomas Jefferson (1743–1826)	1801–1809
4.	James Madison (1751–1836)	1809–1817
5.	James Monroe (1758–1831)	1817–1825
6.	John Quincy Adams (1767–1848)	1825–1829
7.	Andrew Jackson (1767–1845)	1829–1837
8.	Martin Van Buren (1782–1862)	1837–1841
9.	William Henry Harrison (1773–1841)	1841
10.	John Tyler (1790–1862)	1841–1845
11.	James K. Polk (1795–1849)	1845–1849
12.	Zachary Taylor (1784–1850)	1849–1850
13.	Millard Fillmore (1800–74)	1850–1853
14.	Franklin Pierce (1804–69)	1853–1857
15.	James Buchanan (1791–1868)	1857–1861
16.	Abraham Lincoln (1809–65)	1861–1865
17.	Andrew Johnson (1808–75)	1865–1869
18.	Ulysses S. Grant (1822–85)	1869–1877
19.	Rutherford B. Hayes (1822–93)	1877–1881
20.	James A. Garfield (1831–81)	1881
21.	Chester A. Arthur (1830–86)	1881–1885
22.	Grover Cleveland (1837–1908)	1885–1889
23.	Benjamin Harrison (1833–1901)	1889–1893
24.	Grover Cleveland (1837–1908)	1893–1897
25.	William McKinley (1843–1901)	1897–1901
26.	Theodore Roosevelt (1858–1919)	1901–1909
27.	William Howard Taft (1857–1930)	1909–1913
28.	Woodrow Wilson (1856–1924)	1913–1921
29.	Warren G. Harding (1865–1923)	1921–1923
30.	Calvin Coolidge (1872–1933)	1923–1929
31.	Herbert Hoover (1874–1964)	1929–1933
32.	Franklin Delano Roosevelt (1882–1945)	1933–1945
33.	Harry S. Truman (1884–1972)	1945–1953
34.	Dwight D. Eisenhower (1890–1969)	1953–1961
35.	John F. Kennedy (1917–63)	1961–1963
36.	Lyndon B. Johnson (1908–73)	1963–1969
37.	Richard M. Nixon (b. 1913)	1969–1974
38.	Gerald R. Ford (b. 1913)	1974–1977
39.	James E. Carter (b. 1924)	1977–

Chief Justices of the Supreme Court

John Jay (1789–1795)
John Rutledge (1795)
Oliver Ellsworth (1796–1800)
John Marshall (1801–1835)
Roger B. Taney (1836–1864)
Salmon P. Chase (1864–1873)
Morrison R. Waite (1874–1888)
Melville W. Fuller (1888–1910)
Edward D. White (1894–1921) *
Charles Evans Hughes (1910–1916; 1930–1941) *
William Howard Taft (1921–1930)
Harlan F. Stone (1925–1946) *
Frederick M. Vinson (1946–1953)
Earl Warren (1953–1969)
Warren E. Burger (1969–   )

* Includes previous service as Associate Justice.

Guide
to the Campaign
Finance Law

Following is a summary of how the campaign finance law's provisions, as affected by the Supreme Court decision in *Buckley* v. *Valeo* (1976), applied to the 1976 presidential and congressional elections.

Candidates

Who is a candidate?
An individual officially becomes a candidate in a federal election if he accepts contributions or spends money to seek election or if he authorizes an individual or a committee to raise or spend money on his candidacy.

Contribution Limits

What are the contribution limits for individuals?
An individual may give a candidate $1,000 for each primary, runoff and general election campaign. In addition, an individual may give an unlimited amount of money to a political action committee or a party committee so long as the total amount of his political contributions to federal campaigns does not exceed $25,000 a year.

What are the contribution limits for political committees?

Political committees may give $5,000 to a candidate for each primary, runoff and general election campaign if they:

- Have been registered with the Federal Election Commission for at least six months.
- Have more than 50 contributors.
- Support five or more candidates.

Committees that file with the commission within six months of an election or do not meet the other requirements may contribute only $1,000 to a candidate for each election—the limit that applies to contributions by individuals.

Political committees include national and state party organizations and political action committees (PACs) set up by unions, corporations, groups of individuals and trade associations.

Political action committees established by companies may solicit company employees and stockholders, while union PACs may seek contributions from their members. Contributions raised by a political action committee may be distributed to candidates by the officers of the committee.

In addition, companies may establish payroll deduction plans (also known as trustee plans) that allow an employee to channel donations directly to candidates he selects. Contributions made through those plans are considered individual contributions, since an individual is making the donation.

There is no limit on the overall amount of contributions a political committee may give.

How much of their own funds may candidates contribute to their campaigns?

The Supreme Court struck down the limits for candidates, including their immediate families. But the court attached several strings to the money. A candidate may spend family money if he controlled or had access to it at the time he became a candidate. Immediate family members who control their money independently or who denied the candidate access to it before the election are held to the $1,000 contribution limit.

May individuals spend money for independent activities on behalf of a candidate?

Individuals may spend as much of their own money as they wish to support a candidate, so long as they do not clear or coordinate the expenditures with him or his campaign organization. Thus, an individual may give $1,000 to a candidate, for example, and then spend $100,000 for his own newspaper or television advertising or billboards on behalf of that candidate. Conversely, an individual may spend an unlimited amount of his own money attacking a candidate, so long as the expenditures are not cleared or coordinated with any candidates.

May political committees spend money for independent activities on behalf of a candidate?

As a result of the Supreme Court's January 30 decision, union and corporate political action committees and citizens' committees may spend as much as they wish on behalf of a candidate, so long as the expenditures are not cleared or coordinated with the candidate or his committee.

What contribution limits apply to campaigns of candidates for delegate to the Democratic and Republican national conventions?

The law does not set specific limits. The commission, however, established its own ceilings for delegate candidates, which were revised by the court decision:

- Delegates authorized by a presidential candidate: Individuals may give $1,000 and political committees may give $5,000. Individual contributions to a delegate count as contributions to the candidate authorizing them and are subject to the candidate's contribution limit. Thus, if an individual gives $1,000 to a candidate, he may not give any money to a delegate authorized by that candidate.
- Delegates committed to a candidate without his authorization: Individuals and political committees may give as much money as they want to "pledged but unauthorized" delegates, since these delegates are not treated by the law as candidates.
- Uncommitted delegates: An individual may contribute up to $25,000 (the aggregate annual contribution limit) to an uncommitted delegate candidate.

What types of contributions are prohibited?

The law bars cash contributions of more than $100 (contributions of more than $100 have to be made by check, money order or other written instrument); contributions from foreign nationals who do not have a permanent residence in the United States; and contributions of corporate or union funds (contributions from corporate or union political action committees are permitted).

A contribution made by one person in the name of another person is banned. However, a contribution earmarked through a go-between such as a political committee is treated as a contribution from the original donor. The go-between must report who originally made the contribution and who received it.

How are loans treated?

Loans, whether from banks or individuals, are treated as individual contributions and thus are limited to $1,000. Once the repayment of a loan has started, the individual who guaranteed it may make another contribution as large as the part of the loan that has been repaid.

Spending Limits

Does the campaign finance law include limits on how much candidates may spend?

The Supreme Court struck down the law's spending limits for House and Senate campaigns and for presidential campaigns in which candidates use only private contributions. However, presidential candidates who accept public subsidies for either the pre-nomination campaign or the general election campaign have to abide by the spending limits.

Are the spending limits for campaigns adjusted annually to take into account changes in the cost of living?

The expenditure limits are increased each year in relation to the percentage rise in the consumer price index computed by the Labor Department's Bureau of Labor Statistics. According to the Bureau of Labor Statistics, the consumer price index has risen 9.1 per cent since 1974. Thus, the presidential spending limits have been increased by 9.1 per cent by the Federal Election Commission.

How much money may presidential candidates who accept public funds spend to seek the nomination?

A presidential candidate can spend an overall amount of $10,910,000 in seeking the nomination. If he runs in primary states and caucus states, his expenditures in any state are limited to no more than twice the amount a Senate primary candidate was allowed to spend in that state before the Supreme Court decision removed the ceiling from Senate contests.

Each candidate may spend an additional 20 per cent of the overall pre-nomination spending limit to raise campaign funds. Thus, the real pre-nomination spending limit is $13,092,000.

May a presidential candidate who accepts the spending limits for primary campaigns spend as much of his own money on his campaign as he could if he were privately financed?

Under the Supreme Court ruling, presidential candidates who accept matching public subsidies for their pre-nomination campaigns agree to abide by the pre-nomination spending limits in the law. However, that does not bar a candidate from supplementing his private contributions and matching funds with his own money as long as he does not exceed the overall spending limit. For example, a candidate could raise $4-million in private contributions, receive another $4-million in matching money and then spend $2.9-million of his own money to bring his expenditures up to the $10.9-million pre-nomination spending limit.

How much may presidential candidates who receive public money spend in the general election campaign?

A candidate in the presidential general election campaign may spend $21,820,000. The Democratic and Republican presidential candidates will receive full public financing if each decides to accept it. Candidates who do not receive public funds are not held to any limit.

What spending limits apply to presidential nominating conventions?

The Democrats and Republicans may spend no more than $2,182,000 each on their conventions if they accept public financing. That limit also applies to conventions of minor parties.

However, the commission weakened that spending limit in an advisory opinion that allows parties to accept gratuities and reduced fees for their conventions. Under the advisory opinion, local or state government agencies are permitted to provide facilities or services to the parties so long as the facilities are not leased from corporations, national banks or labor organizations for less than fair market value and the municipal corporations are not conduits for corporate contributions that are banned by law.

The commission held that rate reductions and rent-free facilities ordinarily offered by private corporations to nonpolitical conventions of comparable size should not be considered political contributions.

Local retail businesses that will profit directly from a convention, such as hotels, restaurants and car rental agencies, may donate money to nonprofit civic groups such as the Chamber of Commerce if those groups also seek equally large nonpolitical conventions. These contributions or transactions are defined by the commission as gratuities that do not affect the $2,182,000 spending limit for party conventions.

Are political parties allowed to spend money on behalf of candidates?

The law originally included limits on independent expenditures that political parties could make for House, Senate and presidential candidates in general election campaigns. The Supreme Court did not strike these down, since the challengers of the campaign finance law did not contest them as violations of the First Amendment. According to the law, a party may not give the money to a candidate but must spend it on campaign items such as media time or polling. Parties may coordinate these expenditures with candidates.

National and state parties each may spend money on House and Senate races. For example, the Republican National Committee may spend $10,910 and the New York State Republican Party may spend another $10,910 for a House candidate. Only national parties such as the Democratic and Republican National Committees may make independent political expenditures in the presidential general election campaign. The party spending limits are as follows:

- House, $10,910 per candidate.
- Senate, $21,820 per candidate or two cents per eligible voter, whichever is greater.
- Presidency, two cents per eligible voter.

However, the court ruled the independent expenditure limits for individuals to be unconstitutional. That has the effect of freeing parties from the spending limits on candidates so long as the expenditures are not cleared or coordinated with the candidates.

Exemptions

Are any contributions exempted from the law's contribution limits?
The law allows contributions above the limits in two areas:

- Fund-raising costs of up to 20 per cent of the presidential primary spending limit are exempted. The exemption effectively increases candidate spending limits by up to 20 per cent.
- Individuals do not have to report expenditures of up to $500 for the use of real or personal property, printing of invitations or food and beverages for a campaign. Thus, a coffee party in an individual contributor's home that costs less than $500 is exempted both from the candidate's spending limit and the individual's contribution limit. In addition, individuals and candidates do not have to report unreimbursed expenditures of up to $500 per candidate on volunteer travel by an individual. Finally, a vendor—an individual or a business—who sells food and beverages at cost to a campaign does not have to report the sale as a contribution if the difference between his

normal charge and the charge to the candidate is $500 or less. The cumulative total of this type of contribution is $500 per candidate.

Public Financing

Do candidates receive public funds for their campaigns?
The law provides for optional full public funding for major-party candidates in presidential general election campaigns and for the major parties' national nominating conventions. The Democrats and Republicans began receiving money in January to pay for their national conventions. The parties' presidential candidates will receive federal money to pay for their fall campaign after they are nominated.

Minor parties are eligible to receive public funds for their national conventions and for their presidential general election campaigns. No third party will receive federal money for the 1976 presidential election, however, since the amount the party can receive is based on its performance in the last presidential election. The amount is determined by a formula that takes into account the number of votes the party received. A minor party has to receive more than 5 per cent of the presidential vote in order to receive public financing.

Candidates seeking a party's presidential nomination receive public matching funds for their pre-nomination campaign if they opt to take them instead of using only private funds.

The public money for presidential pre-nomination and general election campaigns comes from the presidential election campaign fund. The fund receives the dollars earmarked by taxpayers on their federal income-tax returns.

What campaigns are not publicly financed?
Congressional campaigns are not publicly financed and have to rely solely on private contributions.

What formula is used to determine how much matching money a presidential candidate may receive for his pre-nomination campaign?
Before a candidate is eligible to receive matching funds, he has to meet a fund-raising requirement of $100,000. That total has to be raised in amounts of at least $5,000 in each of 20 states or more and through contributions of $250 or less.

Once the Federal Election Commission certifies a candidate, he may receive matching public funds of up to $5,455,000 for the primary campaign. Only the first $250 of individual contributions is matched.

What formula is used to determine how much public money minor parties will receive for presidential campaigns?
A minor party has to receive more than 5 per cent of the vote in a presidential election to be eligible for public funds. The law defines a party as a minor party if it receives at least 5 per cent but less than 25 per cent of the vote in a presidential election.

The formula to determine minor-party funding is as follows: The number of votes received by the minor party in the preceding presidential general election is divided into the average popular presidential vote of the major parties. The 1976 general election spending limit of $21,820,000 is then multiplied by the resulting percentage. For example, if a minor party received 10 million votes in 1976 and the average number of votes received by the two major parties were 40 million, then the minor party would receive 25 per cent—or $5,455,000—of the $21,820,000 presidential election spending limit.

The same formula would be used to determine how much a minor party would receive for its national convention. The party would receive a proportional share of the $2,182,000 that major parties receive for their conventions.

Minor parties will not be reimbursed for any of the costs of their 1976 national conventions. However, if a minor party ran a presidential candidate in 1976 who received more than 5 per cent of the vote, it would receive public money for its 1980 convention.

The situation is more complicated for minor-party presidential candidates. A minor-party candidate who ran in 1976 and received more than 5 per cent of the vote could receive public funds after the election only if he had debts remaining from his campaign. Otherwise, his party would receive public money only at the beginning of the 1980 presidential campaign. The amount it received would be based on its performance in the 1976 presidential election.

Disclosure

How should candidates handle campaign contributions and expenditures?
The law requires each candidate to establish a central campaign committee to report all contributions he receives and all expenditures made on his behalf. The committee must have a chairman and a treasurer before it can accept contributions or spend funds on behalf of a candidate.

What must be disclosed by a candidate and a political committee?
The following must be disclosed:

- The total amount of all contributions received in both primary and general elections.
- All contributions of more than $100, including the donor's name, address, occupation and principal place of employment.
- The total amount of all expenditures for both primary and general elections.
- All expenditures of more than $10, including the date, the amount spent, the name and address of the recipient and the purpose of the expenditure.
- All campaign debts.

What do contributions include?
According to the commission, contributions that must be reported include deposits of money; in-kind contributions such as phone banks, postage stamps and use of cars; loans; earmarked funds; and proceeds from mass collections or sales of items.

What do expenditures include?
Expenditures that must be reported include payments of money, transfer

of funds to another political committee or candidate and repayment of loans.

Are some expenditures not counted toward a candidate's spending limit?

There are some categories of expenditures, such as repayment of loans or purchase of Treasury bonds, that must be reported as expenditures but are not counted against a candidate's spending limit.

What do debts include?

According to the commission, debts include guarantees and endorsements of loans, contracts to make expenditures and outstanding bills.

Do officeholders have to file reports on their office accounts?

Senators and representatives and state officeholders who are candidates for federal office have to file quarterly reports if they maintain special office accounts to pay for their official duties. All contributions to and expenditures from the accounts have to be disclosed.

Do any contributors have to file reports on their own?

Individuals whose combined contributions to uncommitted or pledged but unauthorized delegate candidates exceed $100 must report to the commission.

When does a candidate or political committee not have to file a quarterly campaign finance report?

A candidate or committee does not have to file a report if not more than $1,000 was raised or spent in that quarter.

Where do candidates and political committees contributing to them file their campaign finance reports?

Authorized committees of a candidate file reports with the candidate's principal campaign committee. The principal campaign committee then files a single report for that campaign. House candidates file with the clerk of the House of Representatives, Washington, D.C. 20515. Senate candidates file with the secretary of the Senate, Washington, D.C. 20510. Presidential and delegate candidates file with the Federal Election Commission, 1325 K St., N.W., Washington, D.C. 20463.

The House clerk and Senate secretary immediately forward copies of all their reports to the commission. Copies of the reports of all the candidates are kept at the commission's street-floor public records office at 1325 K St. The director of the office is Kent C. Cooper. His telephone number is (202) 382-7012.

Copies of individual candidate and political committee reports may be ordered from the public records office.

Candidates also must file a copy of their campaign finance report with the appropriate state official in the state in which they are running.

When must reports be filed?

Following is the schedule for the filing of campaign finance reports:

- Pre-election reports: Candidates must file reports by the 10th day before an election, covering transactions through the 15th day before the election.
- Post-election reports: Candidates must file reports within 30 days after an election, disclosing all transactions up to 20 days after the election.
- Quarterly reports: Campaign finance reports must be filed four times annually—by April 10, July 10, Oct. 10 and Jan. 31. The reports must disclose

transactions of the preceding quarters ending March 31, June 30, Sept. 30 and Dec. 31. However, if an election falls within 10 days of the filing deadline, the quarterly report is not required, because the candidate already is filing pre-election and post-election reports covering that period.

- Annual report: Candidates or political committees that have not filed the full complement of quarterly reports must file an annual report covering their activities for the year. The report is due Jan. 31.
- Monthly reports: Presidential candidates and their campaign committees must file reports by the 10th of each month (except January, November and December) in the election year disclosing transactions of the preceding months. These reports take the place of the pre-election and post-election primary reports and quarterly reports in the election year.

Political committees that support several candidates also may file monthly reports with the approval of the commission. Otherwise, they have to file pre-election and post-election reports disclosing all their contributions and other transactions.

"Guide to the Law," *Congressional Quarterly Weekly Report*, February 7, 1976, pp. 270–274, © 1976(7) by Congressional Quarterly Inc. Reprinted with permission.

CREDITS

PHOTOGRAPHS

Part opening photographs: *pp. xviii–xix*—Norman Hurst from Stock, Boston. *pp. 152–153*—Eric Kroll from Taurus Photos. *pp. 298–299*—J. P. Laffont from Sygma.

CHAPTER 1: *p. xx*—Benyas/Kaufman from Black Star. *p. 9*—Hugh Haynies © 1975 The Courier-Journal distributed by The Los Angeles Times Syndicate. *p. 13*—Benyas/Kaufman from Black Star. *p. 15 left*—Owen Franken from Stock, Boston; *right*—Elizabeth Hamlin from Stock, Boston. *p. 26 left*—Anne Dockery from Black Star; *right*—Martin Adler Levick from Black Star.

CHAPTER 2: *p. 36*—Jean-Claude LeJeune from Stock, Boston. *p. 47*—Culver Pictures. *p. 60*—Jean-Claude LeJeune from Stock, Boston.

CHAPTER 3: *p. 66*—Frank Wing from Stock, Boston. *p. 76*—Burt Glinn from Magnum. *p. 93*—Frank Wing from Stock, Boston.

CHAPTER 4: *p. 104*—Patricia Hollander Gross from Stock, Boston. *p. 110*—War Relocation Authority, The National Archives. *p. 118*—Patricia Hollander Gross from Stock, Boston. *p. 128*—Paul Fusco from Magnum. *p. 136*—Norman Hurst from Stock, Boston.

CHAPTER 5: *p. 154*—Photo Trends. *p. 158*—Gamble, The Register Tribune Syndicate. *p. 170*—Elizabeth Hamlin from Stock, Boston. *p. 175*—Harris & Ewing from Photo Trends. *p. 179*—Photo Trends.

CHAPTER 6: *p. 190*—UPI. *p. 204*—UPI. *p. 208*—Elizabeth Hamlin from Stock, Boston. *p. 216 left*—Daniel S. Brody from Stock, Boston; *right*—Gerhard E. Gscheidle from Peter Arnold.

CHAPTER 7: *p. 224*—Owen from Black Star. *p. 229*—Owen from Black Star. *p. 248 left* and *right*—Peter Southwick from Stock, Boston.

CHAPTER 8: *p. 256*—Daniel S. Brody from Stock, Boston. *p. 263*—Daniel S. Brody from Stock, Boston. *p. 289 top*—UPI; *bottom left*—Owen Franken from Stock, Boston; *bottom right*—Donald Patterson from Stock, Boston.

CHAPTER 9: *p. 300*—J. P. Laffont/Owen Franken/Sygma. *p. 304*—Photo Trends. *p. 305*—Culver Pictures. *p. 306*—Culver Pictures. *p. 307*—Harris & Ewing from Photo Trends. *p. 310*—Bob Martin from Photo Trends. *p. 321*—Jules Feiffer, The Hall Syndicate. *p. 334*—J. P. Laffont/Owen Franken/Sygma.

CHAPTER 10: *p. 348*—Public Affairs Office-Internal Revenue Service. *p. 352*—Public Affairs Office-Internal Revenue Service. *p. 370*—U.S. Department of State. *p. 373*—Leo Choplin from Black Star. *p. 376 top*—Patricia Hollander Gross from Stock, Boston; *bottom*—Arthur Grave from Stock, Boston.

CHAPTER 11: *p. 384*—Dennis Brack from Black Star. *p. 403*—UPI. *p. 408*—Dennis Brack from Black Star.

CHAPTER 12: *p. 430*—Elizabeth Hamlin from Stock, Boston. *p. 448*—Elizabeth Hamlin from Stock, Boston. *p. 449*—Jeff Albertson from Stock, Boston.

MARGIN QUOTES

CHAPTER 1: *p. 1 top*—*Washington Post*, June 11, 1975, p. A1; *middle*—*New York Times*, March 2, 1975, Sec. 3, p. 5; *bottom*—*Wall Street Journal*, October 16, 1975, p. 20. *p. 2*—*New York Times*, October 29, 1975, p. 41. *p. 4*—George A. Peek, Jr., ed., *The Political Writings of John Adams* (Indianapolis, Ind.: Bobbs-Merrill, 1954), p. xxi. *p. 8 top*—Louis M. Kohlmeier, "The Politics of Deregulation," *National Journal*, April 10, 1975, p. 10; *bottom*—David Wise, *The American Police State: The Government Against the People* (New York: Random House, 1976), p. 30. *p. 9*—Ibid., pp. 403–404. *p. 11*—Alan Wolfe, *The Seamy Side of Democracy* (New York: David McKay, 1973), p. 4. *p. 12*—Archibald Cox, "A Future for American Democracy? If We Have the Will," *Current*, September 1975, pp. 3–4. *p. 14 top—Newsweek*, February 14, 1977, p. 77; *bottom—*Dale Vree, "Intellectuals, Scholars and the Common People," *Freedom at Issue* 31(May–June 1975): 6. *p. 15*—James S. Coleman, "Population Stability and Equal Rights," *Transaction: Social Science and Modern Society* 14(May/June 1977): 35–36. *p. 18*—[Newark] *Star-Ledger*, March 20, 1977, Sec. 3, p. 1. *p. 21*—Alexis de Tocqueville, *Democracy in America* (New York: Vintage Books, 1945), I, 60. *p. 25*—[Newark] *Star-Ledger*, March 20, 1977, Sec. 3, p. 1. *p. 27 top—Washington Post*, November 5, 1975, p. A26; *bottom—*Thomas Griffith, "Reshaping the American Dream," *Fortune*, April 1975, p. 88.

CHAPTER 2: *p. 37*—Richard N. Current et al., eds., *Words That Made American History: Colonial Times to the 1880's*, 3rd ed. (Boston: Little, Brown, 1972), p. 134. *p. 40*—J. C. Fitzpatrick, ed., *Writings from the Original Manuscripts Sources 1745-1799* (Westport, Conn.: Greenwood, 1938), xxviii, 502–503. *p. 42*—William Appleman Williams, *America Confronts a Revolutionary World: 1776-1976* (New York: William Morrow, 1976), p. 25. *p. 44*—Charles Beard, *An Economic Interpretation of the Constitution of the United States* (New York: Macmillan, 1935), p. 324. *p. 45*—Max Farrand, ed., *The Records of the Federal Convention of 1787* (New Haven, Conn.: Yale University Press, 1911), I, 299–300. *p. 48*—Williams, *America Confronts a Revolutionary World*, p. 15. *p. 52*—Max Lerner, *Ideas for the Ice Age* (New York: Viking, 1941), pp. 241–242. *p. 55*—George A. Peek, Jr., ed., *The Political Writings of John Adams* (Indianapolis, Ind.: Bobbs-Merrill, 1954), pp. 106–107. *p. 57—Dallas Times Herald*, April 14, 1974, p. B3. *p. 63*—Glyndon G. van Deusen, ed., *Readings in American History* (New York: Macmillan, 1968), I, 105.

CHAPTER 3: *p. 67*—Richard H. Leach, *American Federalism* (New York: Norton, 1970), pp. 7–8. *p. 69*—South Carolina Department of Wildlife and Marine Resources Memorandum, June 20, 1977, Re Shrimping off the Southern Coast of South Carolina. *p. 70*—William H. Riker, *Federalism: Origin, Operation, Significance* (Boston: Little, Brown, 1964), p. 140. *p. 73 top*—[Newark] *Star-Ledger*, May 12, 1977, p. 1; *bottom*—Ibid., p. 4. *p. 83*—George C. S. Benson, *Essays in Federalism* (Claremont, Calif.: Institute for Studies in Federalism 1961), p. 3. *p. 86*—Daniel J. Elazar, *American Federalism: A View from the States* (New York: Thomas Y. Crowell, 1972), p. 213. *p. 87*—"The Continentalist," in John F. Roche, *Illustrious Americans: Alexander Hamilton* (Morristown, N.J.: Silver Burdett, 1967), pp. 151–152. *p. 97*—Carl J. Fredrick, *Constitutional Government and Democracy* (Waltham, Mass.: Blaisdell, 1950), p. 5. *p. 98*—Gerald Stourzh, ed., *Readings in American Democracy*, 2nd ed. (New York: Oxford University Press, 1966).

CHAPTER 4: *p. 105 top*—Charles L. Markmann, *The Noblest Cry: A History of the American Civil Liberties Union* (New York: St. Martin's Press, 1965), p. 3; *bottom*—Edward M. Earle, ed., *The Federalist* (New York: Modern Library, 1937), p. 339. *p. 107*—George A. Peek, Jr., ed., *The Political Writings of John Adams* (Indianapolis, Ind.: Bobbs-Merrill, 1954), p. 201. *p. 110—New York Times*, February 9, 1960, p. 18. *p. 114*—William O. Douglas, *The Right of the People* (New York: Pyramid Books, 1962), p. 92. *p. 122 top*—Herbert Mitgang, "The Storefront Lawyer Helps the Poor," *New York Times Magazine*, November 10, 1968, p. 34; *bottom*—Victor Lasky, *The Myth and the Man* (New York: Trident, 1968), p. 165. *p. 125 top—The Christian Science Monitor*, March 18, 1974, p. 6; *bottom*—Douglas, *The Right of the People*, p. 8. *p. 130*—Justice Hugo Black, Dissenting Opinion, *Tinker* v. *Des Moines Independent School District* (1969). *p. 132 top*—Edward Dumbauld, ed., *The Political Writings of Thomas Jefferson* (Indianapolis, Ind.: Bobbs-Merrill, 1955), p. 94; *bottom*—Douglas, *The Right of the People*, pp. 13–14. *p. 135—The Autobiography of Benjamin Franklin* (New York: Washington Square Press, 1955), p. 119.

CHAPTER 5: *p. 155—Los Angeles Times*, June 18, 1970, p. 27. *p. 159—Washington Post*, June 15, 1969, p. 3. *p. 161*—Edith Efron, *The News Twisters* (Los Angeles: Nash, 1971), p. 6. *p. 165*—"Media Coverage of Substantive Issues," *Science*, May 1974, p. 941. *p. 169 top—Washington Post*, April 29, 1971, p. F1; *bottom—Washington Post*, March 23, 1967, p. 1. *p. 172*—Tom Wicker, "The Greening of the Press," *Columbia Journalism Review*, May/June 1971, p. 7. *p. 174*—[Newark] *Star-Ledger*, March 10, 1977, p. 20. *p. 180*—Pierre Salinger, *With Kennedy* (Garden City, N.Y.: Doubleday, 1966), p. 109.

CHAPTER 6: *p. 192*—V. O. Key, Jr., *Politics, Parties, and Pressure Groups*, 5th ed. (New York: Crowell, 1964), pp. 18–19. *p. 193*—Theodore Lowi, *The End of Liberalism* (New York: Norton, 1969), p. 294. *p. 195*—Thomas B. Mechling, "Washington Lobbies Threaten Democracy," *Virginia Quarterly Review* 22(Summer 1946): 341. *p. 196*—John Gardner, "Introduction," *Money and Secrecy: A Citizen's Guide to Reform of State and Federal Practices* by Lawrence Gilson (New York: Praeger, 1972), p. ix. *p. 205*—John C. Calhoun, "A Disquisition on Government," in Benjamin F. Wright, ed., *Source Book of American Political Theory* (New York: Macmillan, 1929), p. 537. *p. 207—United States* v. *Harriss* (1954). *p. 209*—Lester Milbraith, *Washington Lobbyist* (New York: Rand McNally, 1963), p. 364. *p. 213*—[Newark] *Star-Ledger*, April 24, 1977, Sec. 3, p. 3. *p. 217 top*—Charles Adrian and Charles Press, *Governing Urban America*, 4th ed. (New York: McGraw-Hill, 1972), p. 148; *bottom*—Larry L. Berg, Harlan Hahn, and John R. Schmidhauser, *Corruption in the American Political System* (Morristown, N.J.: General

Learning Press, 1976), p. 156. *p. 218*—Robert A. Dahl, *A Preface to Democratic Theory* (Chicago: University of Chicago Press, 1956), p. 145.

CHAPTER 7: *p. 225*—H. L. Mencken, *Baltimore Evening Sun*, December 9, 1929. *p. 226*—George A. Peek, Jr., ed., *The Political Writings of John Adams* (Indianapolis, Ind.: Bobbs-Merrill, 1954), p. 172. *p. 227*—George Washington, Farewell Address, 1796. *p. 230*—Anthony Howard, "The Greatest Sham on Earth?" *The* [London] *Observer*, October 6, 1968. *p. 232*—Alexander M. Bickel, *The New Age of Political Reform: The Electoral College, The Convention, and the Party System* (New York: Harper & Row, 1960), p. 23. *p. 233*—James Bryce, *The American Commonwealth*, 3rd ed. (New York: Macmillan, 1904), II, 20. *p. 235*—Clinton Rossiter, *Parties and Politics in America* (Ithaca, N.Y.: Cornell University Press, 1960), p. 7. *p. 236 top*—Austin Ranney and Willmoore Kendall, *Democracy and the American Party System* (New York: Harcourt Brace Jovanovich, 1956), p. 533; *bottom*—E. E. Schattschneider, *Party Government* (New York: Holt, Rinehart and Winston, 1942), pp. 1, 69. *p. 245*—Peter Woll, *Behind the Scenes in American Government: Personalities and Politics* (Boston: Little, Brown, 1977), p. 1. *p. 251*—Herbert Agar, *The Price of Union*, 2nd ed. (Boston: Houghton Mifflin, 1966), pp. 689–690.

CHAPTER 8: *p. 257*—*The Center Magazine*, November/December 1975, p. 26. *p. 259 top*—V. O. Key, Jr., *Public Opinion and American Democracy* (New York: Alfred A. Knopf, 1965), pp. 47, 185; *bottom*—Robert E. Lane, *Political Life* (Beverly Hills, Calif.: Glencoe, 1959), p. 300. *p. 261*—Carl Becker, "The Will of People," *Yale Review*, March 1945, p. 389. *p. 270*—Stephen Weissman, *White Ethnic Politicians and Local Big Business: The New Urban Coalition*, Paper presented at the American Political Science Association meeting September 1973, p. 3. *p. 277*—*Chicago Tribune*, September 5, 1976, p. 6. *p. 278*—*Newsweek*, April 4, 1976, pp. 22, 24. *p. 282*—Michael Novak, "Let a Million Voters Bloom," *Commonweal*, April 2, 1971, p. 80. *p. 284*—Seymour Martin Lipset, *Political Man: The Social Bases of Politics* (New York: Anchor, 1963), p. 12. *p. 286*—*U.S. News & World Report*, October 25, 1976, p. 30. *p. 287*—Richard M. Scammon and Ben J. Wattenberg, *The Real Majority: An Extraordinary Examination of the American Electorate* (New York: Coward, McCann & Geoghegan, 1970), p. 15. *p. 294*—*Newsweek*, April 4, 1977, p. 96.

CHAPTER 9: *p. 301*—Clinton Rossiter, *The American Presidency* (New York: Harcourt Brace Jovanovich, 1956), p. 3. *p. 303*—Harry Hayden Clark, ed., *Thomas Paine: Representative Selections*, rev. ed. (New York: Hill & Wang, 1961), p. 392. *p. 305*—Woodrow Wilson, *Constitutional Government in the United States* (New York: Columbia University Press, 1908), pp. 77–78. *p. 310*—Nathan Sargent, *Public Men and Events* (New York: Da Capo, 1875), I, 258. *p. 316*—*Saturday Review*, October 17, 1964, p. 22. *p. 318*—[Newark] *Star-Ledger*, May 29, 1977, p. 16. *p. 320*—Douglass Cater, *Power in Washington* (London: Collins, 1965), p. 72. *p. 329*—D. C. Coyle, *Ordeal of the Presidency* (Washington, D.C.: Public Affairs Press, 1960), pp. 19–20. *p. 330*—Arthur M. Schlesinger, Jr., *The Imperial Presidency* (Boston: Houghton Mifflin, 1973), p. 417. *p. 333*—[Newark] *Star-Ledger*, May 10, 1977, p. 10. *p. 337*—Rossiter, *The American Presidency*, p. 159. *p. 338 top*—*New York Times*, January 6, 1971, p. 21; *bottom*—Henry Steele Commager, "Our Greatest Presidents," *Parade*, May 8, 1977, pp. 16, 19. *p. 342*—[Newark] *Star-Ledger*, May 29, 1977, p. 16.

CHAPTER 10: *p. 350*—Max Weber, *On Methodology of the Social Sciences* (Glencoe, Ill.: The Free Press, 1949), p. 90. *p. 354*—*Washington Post*, December 27, 1975, p. A2. *p. 355*—*Los Angeles Times*, July 4, 1975, p. 16. *p. 356*—Sam J. Ervin, Jr., "Too Much Government by Decree," *Reader's Digest*, May 1975, p. 108. *p. 358*—Edwin C. Hargrove, *The Power of the Modern Presidency* (Philadelphia: Temple University Press, 1974), p. 123. *p. 362*—Graham T. Allison, *The Essence of Decision: Explaining the Cuban Missile Crisis* (Boston: Little, Brown, 1971), p. 48. *p. 365*—*U.S. News & World Report*, May 17, 1976, p. 39. *p. 367*—Joseph Bensman and Arthur J. Vidich, *The New American Society: The Revolution of the Middle Class* (New York: Quadrangle Books, 1971), p. 276. *p. 368*—Peter Woll, *Behind the Scenes in American Government: Personalities and Politics* (Boston: Little, Brown, 1977), p. 263. *p. 375*—Joseph LaPalombara, ed., *Bureaucracy and Political Development* (Princeton, N.J.: Princeton University Press, 1963), II, 77. *p. 378*—*New York Times*, April 2, 1975, p. 9. *p. 379*—Victor A. Thompson, *Bureaucracy and the Modern World* (Morristown, N.J.: General Learning Press, 1976), p. 86.

CHAPTER 11: *p. 385*—House Report 1406, Eighty-seventh Congress, Second Session (1962), p. 7. *p. 387 top*—*Vital Speeches*, October 1, 1976, p. 741; *bottom*—Theodore H. White, *The Making of the President* (New York: Atheneum, 1961), p. 132. *p. 388*—Woodrow Wilson, *Congressional Government* (Boston: Houghton Mifflin, 1885), p. 11. *p. 389*—Richard Bolling, *Power in the House: A History of the Leadership in the House of Representatives* (New York: E. P. Dutton, 1968), p. 29. *p. 390*—Clem Miller, *Member of the House* (New York: Charles Scribner's Sons, 1962), p. 110. *p. 396 top*—John Stuart Mill, *Representative Government* (London: Longmans, 1878), p. 42; *bottom*—*New York Times*, August 18, 1976, p. 22. *p. 397*—George A. Peek, Jr., ed., *The Political Writings of John Adams* (Indianapolis, Ind.: Bobbs-Merrill, 1954), p. 86. *p. 403*—Hubert H. Humphrey, "To Move Congress Out of Its Ruts," *New York Times Magazine*, April 7, 1963, p. 39. *p. 404*—Charles Clapp, *The Congressman: His Work As He Sees It* (Washington, D.C.: The Brookings Institution, 1963), p. 330. *p. 409*—David Broder, *The Party's Over: The Failure of Politics in America* (New York: Harper & Row, 1972), p. 169. *p. 414*—*U.S. News & World Report*, July 21, 1976, p. 18. *p. 415*—Television and Radio Interview, December 17, 1962, *Public Papers of the President: John F. Kennedy (1962)* (Washington, D.C.: U.S. Government Printing Office, 1962), p. 893. *p. 421*—*Washington Post*, March 24, 1976, p. A14.

CHAPTER 12: *p. 431 top*—*Newsweek*, January 10, 1977, p. 42; *middle*—Ibid.; *bottom*—Ibid. *p. 438*—George A. Peek, Jr., ed., *The Political Writings of John Adams* (Indianapolis, Ind.: Bobbs-Merrill, 1954), p. 90. *p. 439*—*United States* v. *Butler* (1936). *p. 441*—*Newsweek*, January 10, 1977, p. 43. *p. 442*—Ibid., pp. 42, 47. *p. 443 top*—Learned Hand, *The Bill of Rights* (Cambridge, Mass.: Harvard University Press, 1958), p. 73; *bottom*—*Washington Post*, September 5, 1976, p. A11. *p. 444*—Robert Dahl, *Who Governs?* (New Haven, Conn.: Yale University Press, 1961), p. 247. *p. 450*—*Washington Post*, August 20, 1976, p. A10. *p. 451*—*New York Times*, May 2, 1976, p. 54. *p. 454 top*—*U.S. News & World Report*, March 31, 1975, p. 32; *bottom*—*Newsweek*, January 10, 1977, p. 46. *p. 458*—Martin M. Shapiro, *The Supreme Court and the Administrative Agencies* (New York: The Free Press, 1968), p. 58. *p. 459*—*Newsweek*, June 13, 1977, p. 101. *p. 460*—Charles Warren, *The Supreme Court in United States History* (Boston: Little, Brown, 1922), I, vi.

EPILOGUE: *p. 468*—Henry Steele Commager, "200 Plus 1," *Parade*, July 3, 1977, pp. 1, 6. *p. 471*—*Time*, September 27, 1975, p. 35. *p. 472*—*Washington Post*, April 29, 1976. p. A16. *p. 473*—*Los Angeles Times*, December 14, 1976, Sec. 2, p. 7. *p. 474*—*Christian Science Monitor*, June 3, 1976, p. 17. *p. 475*—[Newark] *Star-Ledger*, May 29, 1977, Sec. 3, p. 3. *p. 475*—Ibid. *p. 475*—Ibid. *p. 476*—*National Observer*, January 10, 1976, p. 11. *p. 479*—Jimmy Carter, Inaugural Address, in the [Newark] *Star-Ledger*, January 21, 1977, p. 16.

Glossary

Glossary

Administrative law: rules and guidelines made and carried out by the various federal agencies and commissions.

Admiralty and maritime law: the law of the sea and shipping.

Adversary process: a system of justice based on two sides opposing each other.

Amicus curiae brief: additional brief presented by special interest organizations or individuals not parties to the case but seeking to influence the court in reaching a decision.

Appellate jurisdiction: authority to review case decided by a lower court.

Backgrounder: news story supplied by the government on condition that the source not be revealed.

Bail: money "posted" as a guarantee that a person will appear in court at the proper time.

Bicameral: a type of legislature consisting of two houses.

Bill of attainder: a legislative act punishing an individual without a trial.

Bipartisanship: cooperation between Democrats and Republicans.

Block grants: federal grants that the recipient government may use for a variety of purposes falling under a general heading.

Bureaucracy: any administrative system, but particularly a governmental agency, that daily implements policy pursuant to law, that follows standardized procedures, and that allocates specialized duties to employees.

Cabinet: a body of advisers composed of the principal departments of the executive branch whose heads (secretaries) are nominated by the president, subject to senatorial confirmation.

Categorical grants: see *conditional grants.*

Caucus: a closed meeting of party leaders to choose party candidates.

Civil law: law pertaining to relationships between individuals or organizations.

Civil servants: employees in the civil service.

Civil service: refers to governmental employees hired and promoted on the basis of merit; first adopted in the United States with the Pendleton Act of 1883.

Clean bill: a bill written by a congressional committee; when reported out of committee it receives a new number.

Clientelism: the special relationship between industries and the federal agencies or commissions that regulate them.

Closed rule: A rule preventing amendments in the House; also known as a "gag" rule.

Cloture: the closing of debate on a bill.

Common law: law made by judges, using similar cases as precedents.

Concurrent powers: powers that can be exercised by both the states and the national government, such as the power to levy taxes.

Concurrent resolution: resolution without the force of law that requires action by both the House and the Senate.

Concurring opinion: an opinion of one or more judges that supports the conclusions of a majority of the court but offers different reasons for reaching that conclusion.

Conditional grants: (also called *categorical grants* and *matching grants*): national grants, earmarked for a specific purpose, requiring state recipients to match with their own funds a specified portion of the federal money.

Confederation: an alliance among constituent governments operating from delegated and quite limited authority.

Conservatives: those who believe that political, economic, and social changes should occur gradually and within existing institutions of government and society.

Constitutional law: law based on a constitution and on court decisions interpreting and applying it.

Convention: a meeting of party delegates at the national, state, or local levels to decide on party policy and to nominate candidates for office.

Cooperative federalism: a relatively modern view of the federal system in which the federal government and state and local governments function cooperatively as related divisions of a single system.

Countervailing forces: checks on interest groups, such as opposing influence of other interest groups and governmental action.

Cozy triangle: self-interest relationship among interest group, bureaucratic agency, and congressional committee that helps to secure favorable action on what the interest group wants.

Criminal law: law dealing with crimes against the state or society.

Delegate: a member of Congress whose major goal in voting is to reflect constituents' desires.

Democracy: a form of government in which power is exercised by the people.

Direct democracy: a form of government in which political decisions are made by the people directly rather than by their elected representatives; also known as *pure democracy.*

Dissenting opinion: an opinion of one or more judges that disagrees with the decision reached by the majority of the court.

Division of power: governmental power divided between national and state governments.

Double jeopardy: being tried twice for the same offense.

Dual federalism: a traditional view of the federal system in which the federal government and state and local governments are responsible for performing various functions within specific areas in which each is autonomous.

Elitism: a theory of government which holds that the control or making of political, economic, and social decisions is in the hands of those persons of greater wealth, higher social status, or intellectual superiority.

Ex post facto law: a law punishing an individual for an act that was not a crime when committed.

Exclusionary rule: bars use in criminal trials of evidence obtained in violation of constitutional prohibition against unreasonable searches and seizures.

Executive agreement: an agreement with a foreign country having the legal status of a treaty but not requiring Senate approval.

Executive privilege: doctrine based on constitutional separation of powers whereby a president withholds information from the other two branches of government.

Express powers: powers specifically enumerated by the Constitution.

Extradition: the return for trial of an alleged criminal to the state having jurisdiction.

Fairness doctrine: principle established by the FCC that electronic media should report all sides of community issues fairly.

Federal: a system of government in which powers are divided among a central government and various local governments.

Federalism: division of power between the national and state governments.

Filibuster: unlimited debate on a bill intended to delay or prevent its passage.

Franking privilege: legislators' privilege to send official mail free.

Grandfather clause: voting requirement that granted the franchise to persons whose ancestors had voted prior to 1867.

Habeas corpus: a court order directing an official who has a person in custody to bring the prisoner to court and to show cause for that person's detention.

Impeachment: the calling to account by the House of Representatives of a public official upon a charge of wrongdoing while in office; a two-thirds vote of the Senate is necessary to convict.

Implied powers: powers, not specifically enumerated by the Constitution, which may be logically inferred from the express powers.

Impoundment: power of the president to refuse to spend appropriated funds.

Indirect democracy: a form of government in which political decisions are made by the elected representatives of the people; also known as *republican government* or *representative democracy.*

Inherent powers: powers that a national government has in foreign affairs by virtue of its existence as a government.

Interest group: an organized group, representing a special segment of society, that seeks to influence governmental policies directly affecting its members. (Also called *lobbies* or *pressure groups.*)

Interposition: an act whereby a state could impede a federal law by interposing its own authority.

Interstate compact: an agreement through which two or more states with a common interest or problem establish a legally binding relationship aimed at a common solution.

Joint committee: committee having members from both the House and the Senate.

Joint resolution: resolution passed by both houses of Congress that has the force of law.

Judicial activism: the philosophy that the Supreme Court should play a vigorous role in bringing about social justice.

Judicial notice: the act of a judge in recognizing the existence of certain facts without making one side in a lawsuit place them in evidence.

Judicial restraint: the philosophy that the Supreme Court should refuse to rule on cases involving political questions.

Judicial review: the power to review laws or executive actions and declare them unconstitutional.

Junketing: traveling for pleasure at government expense.

Jurisdiction: the limits or the territory within the authority of a governmental agency or a court.

Jus sanguinis: principle conferring citizenship by parental citizenship.

Jus soli: principle conferring citizenship by place of birth.

Justiciable issue: an issue that may be decided by legal methods (an issue not involving domestic politics or foreign policy).

Lame duck: a president who cannot succeed himself in office.

Liberals: those who believe that political, economic, and social change should occur at a faster rate of speed (than conservatives would allow) and outside existing institutions of society and government, if necessary, to enhance individual development and well-being.

Lobbyist: a person who represents an interest group.

Majority opinion: an opinion of a majority of the judges supporting the decision of the court.

Majority party: presently the Democratic party in the American two-party system; that party which has the largest number of people identifying with it.

Majority rule: a fundamental democratic principle which holds that the larger number of citizens should select officials and determine policies.

Matching grants: see *conditional grants*.

Maverick: legislator with unorthodox views or positions.

Merit system: the hiring of governmental employees on the basis of ability rather than political allegiance.

Minority opinion: see *dissenting opinion*.

Minority party: presently the Republican party in the American two-party system; that party which has the second largest number of people identifying with it.

Minority rights: a fundamental democratic principle which holds that the minority, notwithstanding the majority's right to govern, has rights that the majority cannot abolish, such as the right to compete to win majority support.

Modified closed rule: a rule allowing amendments from the House floor on some but not on other portions of a bill.

Multimember district: a district in which more than one candidate is elected.

Multiple access points: availability to citizens of many levels of state and local government plus the three branches of the national government, allowing for redress of grievance or opportunity to influence government.

National preemption: doctrine whereby action by the national government takes precedence over state action in cases involving concurrent powers.

Nepotism: the placing of relatives on the payroll.

Nullification: a doctrine whereby a state declares null and void a federal law within its boundaries.

Ombudsman: official charged with investigating citizen complaints about the bureaucracy.

Open rule: a House rule permitting amendments to a bill from the floor.

Original jurisdiction: authority to try cases for the first time.

Parkinson's law: a theory that work expands to fit the amount of time available.

Patronage system: the practice of allowing elected political officials to hire and fire employees at will.

Per curiam decision: a Supreme Court decision without a written opinion that upholds the decision of a lower court.

Peter Principle: persons tend to rise to the level of their own incompetence so that in time, every position tends to be occupied by an employee who is incompetent to carry out its duties.

Pigeonholing: a method of killing legislation whereby a committee chairman acting on his own refrains from scheduling committee work on a bill.

Platform: the policy positions on which a party or candidate runs for office.

Plea bargaining: the plaintiff (or prosecutor), the defendant, their attorneys, and the judge agree that the defendant will plead guilty to a less serious charge in exchange for a reduced sentence.

Pluralism: a theory of government which holds that diverse groups and organizations compete to determine public policy on political, economic, and social issues.

Pocket veto: an automatic veto if Congress adjourns within ten days after passing a bill and the president has not signed it.

Political party: organization with diverse membership that seeks to control government by winning elections and placing members in office.

Politico: member of Congress who votes as a delegate on some issues and as a trustee on others.

Polls: surveys designed to measure public opinion.

Pork-barrel projects: local projects, not of overriding importance, to be financed by federal money.

Presumed constitutionality: a law is presumed to be constitutional as long as there is a constitutional interpretation by which it can be declared valid.

Prior restraint: a form of censorship that forbids in advance the publication or the showing of a movie or play.

Private bill: bill involving the private interests of an individual or corporation.

Procedural due process: the principle that laws must be administered in a fair manner.

Project grants: federal grants that bypass state governments and are distributed directly to state or local agencies or to private groups or individuals that prepare applications for funds.

Propaganda: the deliberate selection and manipulation of information with the purpose of helping or harming a cause.

Public bill: bill dealing with matters of concern to the whole population.

Public opinion: expressed views and attitudes of citizens about government, politics, or public issues.

Reserved powers: powers belonging to the states alone.

Revenue sharing: federal money returned to state and local governments with few specifications for its use.

Safe seat: seat in Congress for which there is little or no competition.

Sample: in polling, a portion of a larger group being examined.

Secession: withdrawal from the Union.

Select committee: special committee created to explore subjects of extraordinary interest.

Self-incrimination: the Fifth Amendment provision that individuals do not have to testify against themselves in criminal prosecutions.

Senatorial courtesy: a custom whereby senators of the president's party exercise a veto power over presidential appointments in their states.

Seniority system: the method of selecting chairmen for congressional committees by which the chairmanships go to those of the majority party with the longest service on the committee.

Separation of powers: the division of constitutional authority among the legislative, executive, and judicial branches of the national government.

Shared powers: constitutional provisions for interaction and sharing of functions among the three branches of the national government.

Simple resolution: resolution that requires the action of only one house of Congress and does not have the force of law.

Single-member district: a district in which only one candidate is elected.

Special publics: special groups of citizens having views on particular issues, especially those affecting them directly.

Standing committee: committee that is permanent, continuing its work from one session to the next.

Stare decisis: a principle literally saying "to stand by things already decided." A previous decision by a court applies as a precedent in similar cases.

States' rights: a term expressing opposition to increasing the national government's power at the expense of the states.

Statutory law: law enacted by Congress or other legislative bodies.

Substantive due process: the principle that laws must be reasonable and fair.

Sunset law: reform proposal providing for automatic abortion of a governmental agency after a specified time period unless the legislature reestablishes it.

Third party: a party that runs candidates for office but seldom, if ever, wins elections. (Also called *minor party.*)

Totalitarianism: a form of government in which the government controls almost all aspects of the individual's life.

Trustee: a member of Congress who tries to vote according to his or her own judgment, experience, and information, rather than mirroring constitutent desires.

Unicameral: a type of legislature consisting of one house.

Unitary: a system of government in which all power is vested in the central government.

Universe: in polling, a specific group whose opinions are to be measured and analyzed.

Veto: the president's refusal to sign a bill that subsequently can become law only by a two-thirds vote of the Congress.

Vote of no confidence: device used in parliamentary systems when parliament votes "no confidence" in the executive branch, i.e., the prime minister and his party; election follows. This differs from impeachment in that the chief executive can run for office again.

Writ of certiorari: a court order to a lower court to send the record of a case for review.

Writ of habeas corpus: a judicial document directing an officer holding a suspect to show adequate grounds for holding that person.

Zero budgeting: type of budgeting requiring governmental agencies to justify all of their budget, not just their proposed increase.

Name Index

Name Index

Subject Index

Subject Index

and, 168–170
poor news coverage by, 163–164
symbiotic relationship of journalists with government, 171–172
Nigeria-Biafra civil war, 363
Nixon, Richard M., 7, 8, 12, 27, 59, 110, 164, 178, 231, 262, 279, 314
appointments by rebuffed, 331
China trip of 1972, 168, 305, 468
congressional power as check on, 415
financial support for in 1972 campaign, 271–274
Ford nominated as vice-president by, 328
governmental changes proposed by, 51
impoundment of funds by, 327, 332
on legality of presidential actions, 318
1960 election campaign of, 288, 294
1968 election campaign of, 183, 270–271, 287
presidential power and, 333–334, 336, 338, 339
prospective electoral judgment recognized by, 292
public opinion about, 264
relationship of with Congress, 331
resignation of, 328, 342
Supreme Court appointments by, 456, 457
Supreme Court criticized by, 439
as vice-president, 311–312
Vietnam War policies of, 218, 307, 343
Watergate affair and, 156, 157, 169–170, 176, 325, 326–327, 472
North Atlantic Treaty Organization, 318
North Carolina, 290
Northwest Territory, 39
Northwestern Industries, 197
Nuclear Regulatory Commission, 360
corporate influence in, 203–204
Nullification of federal law, 88

Obscenity issue, Supreme Court interpretations and, 117–118
Occidental Petroleum company, 197
Office of Economic Advisers, 350
Office of Economic Opportunity, 280, 363
Office of Education, 193
Office of Emergency Preparedness, 314
Office of Management and Budget, 341, 350, 353, 365, 372

function of, 315, 327
Ohio, 200, 251, 290
Oil crisis, 469
Oil depletion allowance, 207n
Oil lobby as influence group, 202
Ombudsman
congressional function of, 388–389
reform proposal for, 379
Open rule, congressional, 403
Oregon, 91, 200

Parkinson's Law, 356
Parochial schools, aid to, 115
Participatory democracy, federalism and, 99
Patronage system, 350
Pendleton Act of 1883, 349
Pennsylvania, 234
Pennsylvania v. *Nelson* (1956), 87
Pentagon, news coverage of, 168
See also Defense Department
Pentagon Papers case, 133, 173
Peoria Journal-Star, 163
Per curiam decision, 437
"Peter Principle," 366
Philippines, 67
Planning, Programming, Budgeting System (PPBS), 377
Playboy magazine, 288
Plea bargaining, judicial problem of, 449–450
Plessy v. *Ferguson* (1896), 111n
Pluralism, as equilibrium of group interaction, 25–26
Police
improvements in training of, 460
inequitable behavior of, 448
Policy choices
"civilizational malaise" and, 469–470
consumer cost problem and, 474
"crisis-mongering" and, 470
definition of, 468
democratic decline and, 471–472
despair or hope regarding, 468–472
economic policy-making models
capitalist model, 475–476
communist model, 476
fascist model, 476
mixed economy model, 476
socialist model, 476
environmental issues and, 473
foreign policy issues and, 475
future of for America, 468–472
limits to growth and, 472–473
nature of in the U.S., 477–479
complexity, 478

dynamism, 478
impermanence, 478
incrementalism, 477
multiplicity, 477
outside influence, 478
symbol and substance, 478
rationing problem, 473
social equality issue, 474
social welfare issue, 474
success in alleviation of poverty and, 471
Political organizations, freedom of, 24
Political parties
Constitution silent on issue of, 58
definition of, 225
determination of party identification, 225–226
as different from interest groups, 226
functions of, 226
historical summary of, 226–228
Democratic party, 227–228
Democratic-Republican party, 226–227
Federalist party, 226–227
Republican party, 227–228
Whigs, 227
influenced by voting, 291
interest group regulation and, 207
irrelevance of two-party system, argued, 229–235
"congressional" and "presidential" division of parties, 233
discipline and organization lacking, 231–232
growth in number of independent voters, 229, 231
as harmful holdover, 235
lack of differences between parties on basic issues, 230–231
loose coalitions of state parties make up national parties, 232
multi-member district system, 234
national convention problems, 235
"safe" candidates preferred, 233
single-member district system, 234
third-party movements discouraged, 233–235
party identification of voters becoming more rational, 282
political platforms of, 245
president's role as leader of, 310–311
primary elections and, 268

118–119
on limits to congressional inquiries, 409
Lincoln's actions declared unconstitutional by, 111
national preemption rule and, 87–88
nationalist interpretations aided by, 72–73, 75
number of cases presented to, 451
obscenity issue and, 117–118
"one person, one vote" ruling, 112–113, 119
precise limits of not defined by Constitution, 59
procedures of, 436–438
  concurring opinions, 437
  dissenting opinions, 437
  majority opinions, 437
  per curiam decisions, 437
public policy making by, 442–443
public school funding and, 218
reapportionment ordered by, 25
rights of cities and states recognized by, 73
school busing issue and, 442–443
school desegregation and, 111, 127, 442
on searches and seizures, 140
on student rights, 107
Tenth Amendment interpreted by, 72
Warren Court philosophy, 409
on wartime restrictions of liberties, 129
See also Judicial system
Survey Research Center, 259
Switzerland, 67
"Symmetry" of states with national government, 79

Taft-Hartley Act, 81, 239
Tax Court, federal, 372, 433
Taxation, as issue in Constitutional Convention, 41
Television
  commercialism of, 162–163
  commercialism of not manipulative, 176
  entertainment function of, 178
  freedom of the press and, 134
  government manipulation of news and, 168–170
  manipulation of political opinion of public by, 264
  monopoly control of
    benefits of, 176–177

problem of, 161
news analysis bias in, 167
news coverage rated highly, 178
Nixon's use of, 275
public trust in, 169
symbiotic relationship of journalists with government, 171–172
See also Mass media
Tennessee Valley Authority, 292, 377
Texaco company, 196
Texas, 218, 290
Textile industry, 81
Third parties and minor parties
  assimilation of by major parties, 293
  contributions of, 249
  discouragement of in two-party system, 233–235
  See also Political parties
Tidelands Oil bill of 1953, 414
Totalitarianism, definition of, 18
Train v. *City of New York* (1975), 332
Treasury Department, 313
Trilateral Commission, 197
Truman, Harry S., 59, 82, 109, 125, 164, 196, 251, 332, 359
  as commander in chief, 306
  Korean War and, 324
  on the presidency, 303, 334–335
  presidential power of, 333, 337, 339
Truman Doctrine, 318
Trustee role of representation, 413–414
Turner Joy (naval vessel), 169

Unitary form of government, defintion of, 67
United Auto Workers, 192
United States Catholic Conference, 211
U.S. Conference of Mayors, 193
United States Postal Corporation, 375
United States v. *Curtiss-Wright Export Corporation* (1936), 89–90
United States v. *Darby* (1941), 72
United States v. *Nixon* (1974), 326–327
United States v. *Pink* (1942), 90
Universe, in polling, 152
University of Michigan, 18
Upper class
  interests of protected by Constitution, 45, 47
  role of in Constitutional Convention, 44–45
Urban residents, unfair representation of, 5

Value determination, role of intellectuals in, 14–16, 24
Vantage Point, The (Johnson), 318
Veterans' Administration, 350, 369
Vice-president
  proposal for election of in case of vacancy of office, 329
  role of, 311–312
Vietnam, North (Democratic Republic), 30
Vietnam War, 157, 209, 324, 388, 415, 475
  agitation against by interest groups, 218
  mass media coverage of, 165–167, 168
  public awareness about, 181
  Tonkin Gulf affair and, 169, 173–174
Village Voice, The (periodical), 132
Virginia House of Burgesses, 56
Virginia Plan for the Constitution, 40–41
Virginia Resolution (1798), 88
Voting
  futility of voting affirmed, 259–279
    corrupt financial practices, 271–275
    difficulties and obstacles to voting, 267–268
    downward trend of voting, 268–269, 277
    electoral college anachronism, 277–279
    financial support for candidates, 270–275
    futility and frustration of public with elections, 277
    ignorance of the public, 259–260
    irrational and contradictory decisions by the public, 261–262
    long ballot problem, 267–268
    manipulation of public opinion, 264
    nonvoters characterized, 264–266
    opinion polls, 275
    primary election problems, 268
    reform of campaign financing ineffective, 275–276
    registration process obstacle, 267
  futility of voting denied, 279–294
    advertising techniques not effective, 282
    assimilation of minor parties as beneficial, 293
    effectiveness of voting, 291–293
    election campaigns as valuable,

1 2 3 4 5 6 7 8 9 10-RRD-85 84 83 82 81 80 79 78 77